HALIFAX

AT THE FOREIGN OFFICE

HALIFAX

The Life of Lord Halifax

BY

THE EARL OF BIRKENHEAD

ILLUSTRATED

HAMISH HAMILTON
LONDON

First published in Great Britain, 1965
by Hamish Hamilton Ltd.
90 Great Russell Street, London, W.C.1

Copyright © 1965 by the Earl of Birkenhead

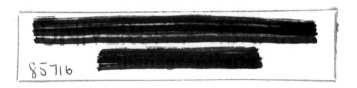

85716

Printed in Great Britain
by Ebenezer Baylis and Son, Limited
The Trinity Press, Worcester, and London

To
Dorothy, Lady Halifax
*In gratitude for her encouragement
and understanding*

LIST OF CONTENTS

PART FOUR

WASHINGTON

PART FIVE

THE LAST YEARS

LIST OF ILLUSTRATIONS

ACKNOWLEDGEMENTS

I MUST first thank the Dowager Countess of Halifax for the unfailing help she has given me during the writing of this book, and her great patience in spite of the considerable time required for its completion. I am also under a profound debt to her for the freedom she has permitted me in interpreting the subject, and her generous understanding of all the difficulties inherent in such a work. Members of her family, and in particular the Earl of Halifax, the Countess of Feversham, and the Rt. Hon. Richard Wood, have also given me invaluable help for which I am deeply grateful.

I would also like to record my thanks to Mr. Tom Ingram, whose careful arrangement and intimate knowledge of the Hickleton Papers greatly facilitated my research.

I am particularly indebted to Mr. Robert Blake of Christ Church, Oxford, for reading the book in manuscript, and giving me the benefit of his great experience. He made many suggestions how it might be improved which were all thankfully accepted.

To Mr. Ralph Warde-Aldam, a brother officer of Lord Halifax in the First World War, I must express my gratitude for the pains he took to provide me with information about Lord Halifax's service in that war.

I have had a generous response to requests for advice on the religious life of Lord Halifax and his father. I am deeply indebted to His Grace the Archbishop of Canterbury, Dr. Michael Ramsey, who kindly found time among his great preoccupations to write to me on this question. I must also acknowledge with gratitude advice from Dr. Alan Don, Canon F. Hood, Dr. Eric Abbott, Canon F. Hurst, the Reverend F. E. P. S. Langton and the late Bishop Hamilton.

For the chapters dealing with Lord Halifax's period at the Foreign Office I acknowledge with gratitude the help given to me by Sir Alexander Cadogan, Lord Strang, Sir Harold Caccia, Sir John Wheeler-Bennett, and Mr. R. W. Mason and Miss Margaret Lambert of the Foreign Office Library.

For the Indian chapters I must acknowledge with particular thanks the help given me by Lord Hailey, the late Sir Cecil Griffin, Major-General Sir Charles Harvey and the late Sir George Cunningham, all of whom read the manuscript and made most helpful suggestions and corrections. I am also indebted to the Secretary of State for Commonwealth Relations for permission to quote from the letters addressed by the Viceroy to the King-Emperor.

I received most generous help in the part of the book which deals with Lord Halifax's period as Minister of Agriculture from his Private Secretary Mr. C. T. Houghton, and in that dealing with his Presidency of the Board of Education from Miss P. M. Downie of the Department of Education and Science.

I have received invaluable advice from Lady Alexandra Metcalfe, for many years an intimate friend of Lord and Lady Halifax, and the letters in the chapter on Lord Halifax's Ambassadorship in Washington indicated in the footnotes as 'Private Correspondence' were written by Lord Halifax to her.

Lady Peake, widow of Lord Halifax's old friend Sir Charles Peake, has also given me the greatest assistance, providing me not only with a large number of letters, but also with the vivid diary her husband kept in Washington which helped to re-create the atmosphere of those wartime days.

I must also offer grateful thanks to my wife who read the manuscript with great care and made many helpful suggestions, and to my secretary Miss Otto who typed and retyped it and gave me constant assistance during the writing of the book.

So many people have helped me in the preparation of this book that I am sure they will forgive me if I thank them collectively. May I therefore express sincere gratitude to:

Mr. Dean Acheson, Mrs. May Amory, Lieutenant-Colonel A. G. S. Alexander, Mr. Joseph Allsop, Mr. C. Atkin, the Earl of Avon.

Sir John Balfour, Mr. James Barker, Mr. Chester Barksdale, Mr. J. W. Beattie, Sir Isaiah Berlin, Mr. John Betjeman, the Hon. Mrs. Betjeman, the late Lady Bingley, Mrs. Robert Bliss, the late Mrs. Violet Borwick, Mr. Eric C. Bousfield, Major-General W. P. A. Bradshaw, the late Lord Brand, the Reverend Canon G. W. Broomfield, Lieutenant-Colonel D. P. Bryce, Mr. R. A. Butler.

Sir Ronald Campbell, Mrs. Joan Hyde Cater, Lord David Cecil, Viscount Chandos, Mr. Godfrey Childe, the late Captain John Christie, the late Professor John Coatman, Mr. Ian Colvin, Mr. Charles Cook, Miss Alice Corry, Dr. Reginald Cox.

Mr. Evan T. Davis, Mr. C. S. A. Dobson (Librarian of the House of Lords), Mr. and Mrs. Lewis Douglas, Mr. Tom Driberg, the Reverend A. J. Dubois.

Sir Claude Elliott, Rear-Admiral Hugh T. England, Mr. L. E. Eyres.

Mr. A. H. Faulkner, Sir Keith Feiling, the Hon. Nathaniel Fiennes, Mr. Neville Ford, Air Vice-Marshal Macneece Foster, the late Mr. Justice Frankfurter, Senator J. W. Fulbright.

Mr. G. C. Garratt-Holden, Mrs. Geoffrey McNair Gates, Major Albert Ginsberg, Mr. J. B. N. Goldsmith, Sir Archibald Gordon, the late Earl Grey, the late Sir James Grigg.

The late Sir Robert Hadow, Mr. Max Hageman, Mr. H. E. Hansen,

Mr. H. Hanser, the Dowager Lady Harlech, Mr. Averell Harriman, Mr. Charles Harrison, Harvard University, Cambridge, Massachusetts, Lord Harvey of Tasburgh, Sir William Hayter, Mr. Clarence Hellewell, Mr. Christian Herter, Colonel J. Hills, Mrs. H. V. Hodson, the late Sir Maurice Holmes, Miss Veronica Hudd, Miss D. M. Hudson, Mr. Fielden Hughes, Sir Francis Humphrys, Sir Arthur Hutchinson.

Lord Inchyra, Mr. Winthrop Kean, Mr. Thomas Keep, Mr. Ian Kokhanek, Mr. Arthur Krock.

Mr. T. S. Lamont, Mrs. Enid Lane Fox, Sir Alan Lascelles, Mr. Valentine Lawford, Sir Reginald Leeper, Miss Violet Lincoln, Mr. Walter Lippmann, the Earl of Longford, Mr. Robert Lovett, Mr. Anthony Low, Pamela, Countess of Lytton, Mr. Angus Malcolm, Mr. Arthur Mann, Sir Arthur Massey, Sir John Masterman, Lady Dorothy Meynell, Lady Sybil Middleton, the late Viscount Monckton, Senator Michael Monroney.

Mr. John McCloy, the Reverend Norman McCurry, Colonel the Hon. Angus McDonnell, Major J. P. McKeone, Mr. Harold Macmillan, the late Sir Philip Nichols, Mr. J. L. O'Donovan, Sir Berkeley Ormerod.

Air Commodore W. W. Palmer, Major B. L. Pavey, the Earl of Pembroke, Lord William Percy, Brigadier Anthony Pepys, Sir Charles Petrie, Sir Charles Ponsonby, Mr. David Potter, Dr. H. K. Prescot, Professor Carroll Quigley.

Shri C. R. Rajagopalachari, Mr. Paul Scott Rankin, Mr. James Reston, Mr. Cecil Roberts, Mr. H. F. N. Robinson, the Franklin D. Roosevelt Library, Hyde Park, New York, the Earl of Rosebery, Judge Samuel I. Rosenman, Dr. George Rossdale, Mr. John W. Russell, Mr. Vincent Ryder.

The Marquess of Salisbury, Mr. H. Salkeld, Lord Salter, Senator L. Saltonstall, the Earl of Scarbrough, Sir George Schuster, Mr. Robert Sencourt, Lord Sherfield, Mr. I. Simmonds, Mr. H. H. Smith, Mr. M. A. Smith, Viscount Soulbury, Mr. John Sparrow, the Earl of Stamford, Mr. Ian Stephens, Viscount Stuart of Findhorn, the Hon. Mrs. Mary Sutton, Mr. S. C. Sutton (Librarian of the India Office), Mrs. Sushama Sen, the Earl of Swinton.

Lieutenant-Colonel S. E. Tidy, the Reverend J. C. Waters, Lady Watson, Mrs. E. M. Watson, Ava, Viscountess Waverley, the late Earl Winterton, Sir Llewellyn Woodward, and the late Alexandra, Lady Worsley.

Part One

EARLY YEARS

CHAPTER I

THE BACKGROUND

A T peace in the heart of Sussex after many wanderings Rudyard Kipling had written of the land where at last he had taken root:

> *God gave all men all earth to love*
> *But since our hearts are small,*
> *Ordained for each one spot should prove*
> *Beloved over all.*

To Edward Wood that place was Yorkshire, and when in maturity he allowed his mind to dwell on the distant memories of childhood he found that every detail of this *temps perdu* was as distinct as though the intervening years had never been, memories of tranquil houses and rolling parkland, of dogs and horses, and a country peace broken only by bereavements accepted as the will of God. When he thus looked back into the past it was upon a world of great possessions and a wealth that seemed inexhaustible. Already it is beginning to appear as remote as the chronicle of some bygone age, but to him the recollection of those days remained persistently sharp, to be awakened in an instant by a sound or a scent, by church bells at Evensong, or the whiff of gunpowder in the September mustard.

Such musings were not embellished in retrospect by some rosy afterglow of memory. The scenes of the distant past remained fresh because he had absorbed in childhood in a grey stone house in the West Riding an abiding love of the Yorkshire countryside which made him long for it in separation, and the soil of which contained for him a mystique which grew ever more engrossing with the passage of time. We feel that there is an affinity between the soil of Yorkshire and that unshakeable religious faith he learnt upon it from his father and from the instructions of the village priest, and that these were twin sources of strength which were to provide him with a means of escape from public life, which in the end led not, as in the case of many, to the tedium of retirement, but back to the land he loved and all its interests which he would have been content never to have left. When oppressed by political anxiety he would return for visits, however brief, to the invigorating air of Garrowby and the wolds above it, and the breath of the country would pass over him like a cleansing wind.

This vast county seems to possess an existence independent of the rest of

3

England, and to constitute a separate world of its own. It is a world of varied and entrancing beauty with waterfalls in the green heart of its windy and leafy solitudes, and vistas so awe-inspiring that Daniel Defoe almost retreated when he saw them. Across it lies the whale-back of the Pennines and, separated from them by the Vale of York, the chalky wolds, to Edward the very essence of Yorkshire, where a man could ride sixty miles across the great crescent of chalk hills from Flamborough to the Humber, and look down on the villages lying in their folds, on the flowers in cottage gardens, and on churches among the dark firs by the streams.

And who bred in Yorkshire could forget her moors, so much a part of the Yorkshire scene? The thought of them reminds us of that of Wuthering Heights of Haworth, where there could be a touch of melancholy beauty in summer when the heather was purple and the 'moor luxuriated in the sun like an animal', but in winter it was unspeakably lonely, its wastes often deep in snow and its silence broken by the curlew's cry, a moor scarred by black quarries and rocks brown with wind-withered grasses.

It is the endless variety of scenery that lends Yorkshire such enchantment. The broad valleys run eastward from the Pennines, holding their little stone villages and busy streams, the Yorkshire dales that inspired Wordsworth, where the dalesmen still go to bed by candlelight and 'the rivers flow down from the dales like the fingers of a man's hand—Tees and Swale, Wharfe and Aire, Calder, Derwent and Don, flowing stronger and faster, rushing on to the Ouse and the superb estuary of the Humber'.[1] And there, for those who seek them among their wild scenery are those waterfalls of Yorkshire, their names as melodious as the sound of their waters, Yarles Cave, the Whitescar Caverns, Hardrow Force, and Gardale Scar before whose majesty Turner stood awestruck, plunging sheer for a hundred feet, and exploding in a shower of sun-caught drops.

It was not only this multitudinous beauty of Yorkshire which left its stamp upon Edward Wood. For centuries the Ridings, through their staple trade wool, and later through coal, steel and engineering, have bred a sturdy race, gifted in commerce, rugged in a deal and devoid of sentiment in their business relations, and the spirit of the North is still one of the most vital elements of industrial England. The coalmines of Yorkshire have sustained an enormous output: 'Its ironworks have sent great bridges across the earth. Its quarries have paved the streets of our towns and cities and given West-minster Abbey its flying buttresses. Its steel is one of the enduring pillars of the modern world. Its mills make the finest cloth. It has the third great port in the country, and the biggest wool market.'[2]

There was a part of Edward Wood's character which derived its strength from this second and harder part of the Yorkshire scene, and it is perhaps not fanciful to imagine that there was a practical side of that character that

[1] Arthur Mee, *Yorkshire.*   [2] Ibid.

was akin to the pulsing life of the Colne valley with its forest of chimneys and clattering machinery, its mills and reservoirs lit up and roaring through the night—to Rotherham with its ironworks, Barnsley with its linen and paper mills, to Huddersfield, Halifax and Morley.

His legacy from this integral part of Yorkshire was a grasp of business and an inflexibility in negotiation which would not have disgraced one of their own ironmasters. Those who found incongruous this mingling of practical expediency with the spiritual principles by which his life was guided ignored the fact that Edward Wood was a Yorkshireman, and that therefore, rich as he might be, prodigality and incompetence in money matters were abhorrent to him, and he shared to the full his countrymen's dislike of being worsted in a deal or shown up as a simpleton.

* * *

Edward Wood, like his father, had a quiet but deep pride in his ancestry, and it pleased him to think that his roots lay deep in the soil of Yorkshire history. It was a matter of satisfaction to him that he came from an ancient Yorkshire family with branches in different parts of the county. In the West Riding alone there were Woods of Hollin Hall and Woods of Conynham Hall and of Hickleton, and that at some remote time they had a common ancestor is suggested by the appearance in various forms, on their crest or their arms, of a savage woodman, or wild man of the woods.

The Woods of Hickleton from whom Edward was descended sprang from a Robert Wood or de Bosco, and another member of the family looms a dim but tragic figure from the Tudor past, the Prior of Bridlington, Robert Wood, who was attainted for high treason and executed in 1537, the year of the bloody suppression of the Pilgrimage of Grace.

It was well written that 'it is only fitting that Edward Wood with his High Churchmanship, his love of Anglo-Catholic ritual, and his father with his lifelong devotion to the cause of union with Rome . . . can both claim descent from one who carried the banners of Robert Aske in the last and greatest challenge to English Reformation. It is hard not to believe that Edward and his father would have answered the call precisely as the Prior of Bridlington did, not simply to defend the Priory but to assure the continuity of the Catholic tradition which had impressed itself so deeply into the life and faith of the Northern shires.'[1]

It was an isolated act of resistance, and the Wood family, like others who had challenged the King's supremacy to their cost, achieved a *modus vivendi* with the Reformation, for one of the direct ancestors of the Hickleton Woods was George of Monk Bretton near Barnsley whose son became a collector of revenue of the dissolved monastery of Bretton. He succeeded on his father's death in 1589 to the lease of the Smithies, then a place of some consequence

[1] Alan Campbell Johnson, *Lord Halifax*, p. 17.

with ironworks,[1] and in due course was a joint Lord of the Manor of Bretton and bought the Smithies outright from the Crown, becoming a landed proprietor. When he died in 1638 he left the Smithies to his second son John, of whom little is known, apparently disinheriting the eldest son Robert who died at Royston in 1676. Direct descent was through Henry Wood of Barnsley, a son of Robert, and Francis of Barnsley, a justice of the peace, to Charles Wood, the third son of Francis. He was born in 1731, and it is from him that the Wood family of Hickleton and Garrowby is descended.

Those distant Woods are shadowy figures against an obscure background, and the imagination can but feebly penetrate to them. They are names on a list, and not yet living men. We cannot see them, or imagine them speaking, and it is hard to put flesh upon their bones. With Charles Wood the figure comes sharply into focus. Here was a naval officer of exceptional courage and professional ability, serving throughout the Seven Years War, until the Peace of Fontainebleau. In the Hickleton Papers we read of him on convoy duty for the Low Countries and North Germany; watching the Western Approaches and detecting sea movement by the French from Cherbourg to Quiberon, and with the frigate *Juno* on the expedition to Canada. We follow him into the blue waters of the Caribbean when he took part in the *Lizard* on the expedition to Martinique under Rodney, and in the assaults on St. Vincent and on Grenada, that lovely pearl in the string of the Windward Islands, with the red houses of Georgetown clustering round its volcanic harbour.

It was a life of watch and ward, of tedious endurance broken by violent actions. He commanded H.M. Bomb-ship *Terror* in 1779, and as Captain of the *Hero*, a 74 of Sir Edward Hughes's squadron, was in the thick of the fighting between Hughes and Suffren in the East Indies, and in 1781 was in action off Trincomalee in command of the *Worcester* which was 'furiously attacked' by two of the enemy. The last shot fired in the engagement wounded him horribly in both legs, tearing away one kneecap. Taken to Madras he was handed over to the agonizing surgery of the day and died on 9 October, an ancestor of flesh and blood out of the past whom Edward Wood could envisage as though his exploits had been those of his own day.

The Captain's second brother, Francis Wood of Barnsley, was created a baronet in 1784, with remainder to the issue male of his father. Thus on Francis's death the baronetcy devolved upon the eldest son of Captain Charles, Francis Lindley Wood, who bought the estate of Garrowby in the East Riding in 1803, and it is with his son Charles that the Woods first emerge from the position of an old Yorkshire family into national eminence.

* * *

[1] J. Wilkinson, *Worthies of Barnsley*, pp. 2–3.

This Charles Wood was born in 1800, destined for greatness. At Eton he was 'the most prominent man in every respect that they have had for some time'. At Oriel College, Oxford, he took a brilliant Double First in the Schools, and then set out on a lordly Grand Tour through Germany, Switzerland and Italy, from where he wrote home describing himself as an arresting figure on the mountains with 'straw hat, a face burned to the colour of a polished wainscot, a beard fit for a Bernese peasant, a black neckcloth twisted round my neck and the end tucked under a string on my shoulder which supported my coat rolled up on my back à la knapsack and fastened to the other shoulder by my handkerchief; waistcoat open, white trousers rolled up into short large breeches, dirty splashed stockings and large shoes, with a six foot pole with an iron spike. Me voici!'[1] At Verona he saw Marie Louise, a sad neglected ghost, 'plain, middle-aged and pale, and very uninteresting in manner and appearance', and on his return to England became a Whig Member of Parliament for Grimsby by the simple method of the day, his father disbursing £4,000, at the moment when the Whigs were at last emerging from their long seclusion.

Three years later, in 1829, marriage gave another happy twist to the fortunes of this young man. His wife was Mary Grey, daughter of the Whig leader Lord Grey, a self-effacing woman who left little mark on her times, but lingered on until 1884 when Edward remembered her as a 'frail but very particular old lady who had beautiful white hands and always wore gloves in the house', for whom money was washed before the butler handed it to her, who took her sheets with her when travelling, and when she visited the chiropodist summoned a four-wheeler rather than her own carriage for reasons of delicacy.

It was a love match that was also full of political advantage. The Greys were a great Northumbrian clan, one of those northern families close to the springs of power. Charles Wood was a north countryman too, and one of the most prominent of the younger Whigs. Lord Grey, like his great-grandson Edward Wood, was an aristocrat who embraced politics less from ambition than from a sense of duty. Like Edward he left his home, Howick on the gaunt wind-lashed Northumbrian coast, with reluctance, and returned to it with delight, the same delight with which Edward left London for the clean air of the Garrowby wolds. When Parliament was not sitting Charles and Mary Wood lived at Hickleton, a property some six miles from Doncaster, bought by Sir Francis Wood in 1829 from the Wentworth family, and it was in this grey house, built between 1730 and 1750, that the years of Edward Wood's childhood were largely to be spent.

It is a curious reflection that Grey and such followers as Charles Wood regarded reform as a restoration rather than as the act of emancipation envisaged by Charles James Fox. 'They looked back,' wrote J. G. Lockhart,

[1] J. G. Lockhart, *Viscount Halifax*, Vol. 1, p. 11.

the biographer of Edward's father, 'to a Golden Age, and, apart from a common hatred of Tories, had little in common with the Radicals who looked forward to a Utopia.' Charles Wood was a Whig to the fingertips; he was not one to yearn for radical measures of reform, nor to be stirred by the miseries of chimney-boys or child labour. In the second Peel administration his opposition to change was only by painful degrees broken. He was not converted to the repeal of the Corn Laws until 1844, and admitted that he detested Lord Ashley's Factory Acts.

Indeed he combined all the virtues and failings of his party to an extreme degree, reverence for property, oligarchic principles, independence, narrowness of vision and sense of obligation. To him the Reform Bill was an 'efficient, substantial, anti-democratic, pro-property measure', and it was in this spirit that he entered the arena of Reform, like the shadow of Lord Grey, for one of the great struggles of history, which, arising from time to time, convulse public life, snapping old friendships and estranging families, a time when men could feel the vast subterranean stirrings of the Industrial Revolution, a time of bitterness and movement.

There are certain resemblances in the careers and characters of Charles Wood and his grandson Edward. Like his grandson, Charles's early Parliamentary progress was a steady rather than an exciting advance through minor office. After losing his seat at Grimsby and Wareham he represented Halifax for thirty-two years. Like his grandson, he could not rely on oratory, but he was a far worse speaker whose utterances were so strange that they might have been outpourings in some foreign language. From Greville, prostrated by boredom, he once wrung the complaint: 'Charles Wood's speech of five hours was the dullest that ever was heard. The Speaker told Charles Villiers that it was the very worst speech he had ever heard since he had sat in the House.'[1]

But Charles was also shrewd and worldly-wise and skilled in administration. His judgment of men and events was sure, and he was, as Disraeli, who did not like him, told Greville, the ablest man in the Whig Cabinet— 'extremely quick, though somewhat unscrupulous, but endowed with tact, and knowledge how to manage men'.[2]

In 1846 Lord John Russell appointed him Chancellor of the Exchequer, but he took office at an unpropitious moment. The barricades of revolution were out in the great cities of Europe; the Irish peasants were starving in the potato famine, and at home trade and revenue alike were in alarming decline. In 1848 there were three supplementary Budgets, and Disraeli, in one of his wonderful moments of insolence, jibed at the harassed Chancellor, comparing him with 'a conjurer pulling yards of red tape out of his mouth'.

[1] *The Greville Diary* (edited by P. W. Wilson), Vol. II, p. 416.
[2] *Leaves from the Diary of Henry Greville* (edited by the Countess of Strafford), Fourth Series, p. 270.

Wood pursued his dogged and unpopular way. Too conservative to consider new taxes and expenditure, and determined to avoid any further dislocation of his Budgets, he ignored the protests of the humanitarians, and would produce no remedy for the starving Irish except that the surplus population should adjust itself by natural means. On the other hand, he sponsored a Select Committee on financial distress, and a £5,000,000 railways loan to Canada, and repealed the window tax. 'Lord Lignum de Budget', as the Opposition derisively called him, was still fighting his unpopular cause when the Government went out in 1852, at least leaving an Exchequer in a healthier condition than had appeared likely in the year of European revolution.

But it was to Indian administration that Charles Wood, like his grandson, made his most enduring contribution. His periods of office spanned the Indian Mutiny, and it fell to him in part to heal some of the wounds left by that deep gash in the body of India. Between 1852 and 1854 he was one of the last Presidents of the Board of Control (India), and after a period as Palmerston's First Lord of the Admiralty while the Crimean War was ending, became Secretary of State for India in 1859. In this office he was to build upon the new foundations which had been laid by the previous Government and were to replace the rickety dominion of the East India Company.

His Charter Act as President of the old Board was one of the most notable Indian measures ever passed by Parliament. By it the system of Government in London, in Calcutta and in the provinces was improved and modernized. It removed nepotism, established a separate legislative council for India, and gave provincial governments direct representation at the centre. His education policy in India was the beginning of a great process of change, and his historic despatch of 1854, which revealed a mind at once sympathetic and imaginative, was the logical sequence to Macaulay's Minute, and made possible for Indians that education which was the key to their future independence. As Secretary of State he passed Acts regulating the proportion of European troops to be used in India, thus recasting the whole Indian army in a new form, extended the railway system, dealt firmly with the finances, balanced the Budgets, reduced expenditure and liquidated the Indian debt.

He improved the conditions of the Civil Service and regulated the Legislative Council and High Court. In this Indian Councils Act of 1861, which gave Indian opinion a voice, faint to be sure, in the Supreme Council of India, there lies the germ of that future constitutional development which, through Morley and Minto, Montagu and Chelmsford, and the viceroyalty of Edward Wood, led ultimately to the independence of India. Thus it was by no mere figure of speech that Edward Wood was to appeal to the people of India by recalling his grandfather's achievements, for he had shown himself to be prescient when bloodshed and chaos in India might have prompted repressive measures which would not have been considered harsh by his contemporaries. His place among the creators of modern India is secure.

When he resigned from the Secretaryship of State in 1866 Charles Wood was raised to the peerage and chose the title of Viscount Halifax of Monk Bretton, and, in the annals of the Wood family, he is described as 'the first Viscount'. He had also come to be regarded with affection by Queen Victoria. Like Palmerston and Gladstone, and others of strong character, he had early discovered the penalties of collision with that imperious but narrow intellect. Granville had noticed that Charles Wood was an 'object of great indignation' to the Queen and the Prince. These were passing clouds, for the Victoria who could feel love and hate with an equal intensity was stirred by his work for India, and moved by the serious hunting accident which caused him to resign from his office. A flash of sunshine illuminated the Queen's own despair in the words she addressed to him on his sickbed: 'Alone, crushed, isolated, deprived of the help and advice of her beloved husband, the Queen clings strongly to all her old and true friends and advisers, and amongst them she has ever had cause to include Sir Charles Wood.'

She hoped that he would remain in her Cabinet, but in some office that would not tax his strength, and her wish was fulfilled when in 1870 Lord Halifax became Lord Privy Seal, and she could consult him to her heart's content. When he died in 1884 she wrote in her diary: 'Dear Lord Halifax died three days ago. I truly grieve at his loss. He has always been a true and loyal friend and servant of mine, and in 1859, when Lord Russell and Lord Palmerston did, and wanted to do still more, mischief, he was a great and real help.'

It has been necessary to dwell in some little detail upon the career of the first Viscount Halifax because it was his achievement which lifted the Woods from the position of Yorkshire gentry little known outside the Ridings, into one of the great houses of the North. When considering Charles Wood and his grandson Edward it is possible to trace a further resemblance between these two men. The nineteenth-century Whig who worshipped property and the *status quo* and hailed the Reform Bill as an 'anti-democratic' measure, had groped his way by degrees so imperceptible that he himself was not aware of them to the rôle of liberal statesman who planted in India the first tender seedlings of emancipation. The young Edward Wood, who was to enter Parliament some fifty years later, was to reveal himself as convinced a Tory as his grandfather had been a Whig, to hold similar views on the sanctity of landed property and to accept as a right his aristocratic inheritance. Yet he too, in spite of these instincts and this background, was to carry his grandfather's work to its logical conclusion and to stimulate Indian reforms far more sweeping and revolutionary than those of 1861.

*   *   *

Charles Wood, first Viscount Halifax, died at the age of eighty-five, leaving his family of four sons and three daughters one of the most eminent in York-shire. Edward Wood's father, the second Viscount, was born in 1839, and he survived until Edward himself was fifty-three and had returned from his vice-royalty of India.

This strange man, whose life is described in copious detail in J. G. Lock-hart's classical biography, exercised an immense influence over his son. So profoundly religious that he sometimes believed his true vocation to be the priesthood, his Anglo-Catholic devotions were the central theme of his existence, and their principles his guiding star.

A product of Eton and Christ Church, Oxford, he had been caught up in the Oxford Movement in its second phase after the first Tracts had been written, and absorbed from Pusey that conception of *Ecclesia Anglicana* as being less the Church of England than the Church in England. At Oxford he was familiar with that squat figure hurrying from his house to the Cathedral, deep in thought; he had listened to his sermons, and acknowledged him as his first master, as he was to salute Liddon, Pusey's pupil, as his second.

In a long letter to Lord Wolmer in which he set forth the nature of his beliefs he made plain that he shared to the full Pusey's conviction that the Church of England had not forfeited her Catholic heritage, but 'he never suffered from "Roman fever", that disease mounting at times to an epidemic, as prevalent among Anglo-Catholics as measles, and much more frequently fatal'.[1]

In one notable respect he differed from Pusey. He was a young aristocrat with a lively appreciation of the pleasures of life, reared in a great house with all the delights of the countryside at hand, and all the distracting resources of birth and riches. It was improbable that such a youth should be afflicted by that dark consciousness of sin and unexpiated guilt under which Pusey's sturdy shoulders were bowed, and which had tormented Newman for years. We cannot imagine him listening with sympathy to the despairing cry of Hurrell Froude:

> *Lord, I have fasted, I have prayed,*
> *and sackcloth has my girdle been,*
> *To purge my soul I have essayed*
> *with hunger blank and vigil keen.*
> *O God of mercies! Why am I*
> *still haunted by the self I fly?*

At first it appeared likely that Halifax would follow his father into politics, and he made a step in this direction when he became a Groom of the Bed-chamber to the Prince of Wales, a friend from boyhood, who was devoted to him and found him a delightful companion on his journeys abroad. But

[1] Lockhart. Op. cit., p. 15.

Halifax was aware of a deep inner consciousness that his life would be devoted to higher causes than those of politics and must be spent as a Catholic layman. Even as a boy at Eton he had felt a revulsion from the Puritans and Roundheads—'All my sympathies were with Charles I and Archbishop Laud,' he said, 'and I remember calling myself an Arminian, not that I knew in the least what an Arminian was, but because it was a reproach which was brought against Charles I.'

It was these convictions that caused him, in the London cholera epidemic of 1866, to work with priests and nurses in an attempt to quell this horrible disease. At one period he was tempted by the thought of becoming a lay-brother of a religious order. He had visited Rome and studied the hierarchy of the Vatican and the different orders. But he was no more tempted towards Rome than his son Edward, to whom he bequeathed his own religious beliefs and over whom his early influence was profound. He was never deflected from the High Church arguments against Roman Catholicism which were propounded in the seventeenth century by such divines as Laud and Andrewes, and in a more modern day by Keble and Pusey, and by Newman until, with tormenting doubts and taking with him, in Gladstone's words, 'a third of the stars of heaven', he turned to Rome.

When we consider the part religion played in the lives of Halifax and his son Edward we can only envy that unshakeable faith which so transcended all earthly griefs that it made the spiritual world the only true one in their eyes, and enabled them to accept all suffering on the earthly plane with a resignation denied to ordinary men. It was a faith which demanded kindness to others, and perfection of manners, and the father's counsels, not invariably heeded in his own case, again fell upon fruitful ground. It was a source of deep satisfaction to Halifax that his son proved such a faithful disciple. Indeed, far harder-headed than his father, and his feet more firmly planted on the ground, Edward was to discard gently much that was visionary and unattainable in the father's doctrines, while retaining the unquestioning faith and ritual he had accepted from him in his childhood.

Nowhere was Edward more truly the son of his father than in religion and churchmanship. Charles Wood was throughout the greater part of a long life the acknowledged lay leader of a movement in the Church which had the ardent support of many clergy and laity. The disciple of Pusey and friend of Liddon, he devoted himself to the cause known in its successive phases as Tractarian and Anglo-Catholic. The father believed, and passed the belief to his son, that the Church of England was a true part of the Holy Catholic Church, adhering to the faith of the undivided Church of the Creeds and the Councils. He emphasized the sacramental life and teaching which he believed the Church of England, rightly understood, to share with the Church of Rome and the Orthodox Church of the East, especially the doctrines of the Real Presence and the Eucharistic Sacrifice. He rejected the exclusive claims of the Papacy, and looked forward to a reunion in which Rome would acknowledge the Church of England to be a true part of the Church and the Church of England in turn would be in communion with Rome, retaining its own liturgy and customs but acknowledging the Pope to be a *primus inter pares* among the Bishops of Christendom.

Father and son thus believed in the Church of England as the Catholic Church in this country. Their care was for the true character, often forgotten, of her doctrine, structure and traditions. They disagreed with Rome not only as regards her claim to be the one true Church, but also in certain theological matters. They held that the main dogmas of the Christian Faith were defined by the General Councils, beginning with Nicaea, and that through *consensus fidelium*, the Holy Spirit was in every age leading the Church into truth, as its teaching became more articulate. It was held that the rupture in the Christian Church in 1054 was partly caused by the claims of the See of Rome, and that later Rome added as *de fide* doctrines without scriptural foundation, namely the Immaculate Conception in 1854 and Papal Infallibility in 1870. Charles Halifax taught his son that no doctrine was to be held as necessary to Salvation which was not taught in the Undivided Church. He reposed his faith firmly in the Vincentian Canon *Quod ubique, quod semper, quod ab omnibus creditum est* [What was believed everywhere, always, by everyone].

High Churchmen, in common with Rome, believed in a visible Church and in the Apostolic succession of bishops, priests and deacons. No religious body could corporately be a part of the true Church if it denied any article of the Creeds or had lost the succession. The Real Presence in the Eucharist was only found when a priest was the celebrant. Rome had accepted the validity of Eastern Orthodox Orders, though their Church was regarded as schismatic, and Charles Halifax devoted years of prayer, zeal and energy to an attempt to obtain a similar recognition of Anglican Orders, a demand which was refused by Pope Leo XIII in 1896 after pressure had been brought to bear by the Roman Catholic hierarchy in England. In spite of this rejection, by which he was bitterly hurt, Halifax never wavered in the Catholic conception of the priesthood, distinct though it was from the Evangelical outlook held by many Anglicans. The influence of Charles Wood, however, penetrated to a world wider than that of ecclesiastical politics. His deep personal piety extended that influence within the English Church, and he always felt an affinity with evangelical Churchmen whose devotion to the person of Christ he shared. Nowhere did his example strike more deeply than in his own family.

The difference between Charles Halifax and his son lay in the fact that Edward never followed his father in the rôle of a leader of a party or movement in the Church, or became conspicuous in ecclesiastical affairs in themselves. Rather was he to carry his religion with him into a life devoted to his country. In a way therefore his religion was more hidden than that of his father, and perhaps also it was more liberal in outlook towards other forms of Christian doctrine and experience although its deep roots were the same.

At the heart of the teaching handed down by Halifax to his son was the firm belief in the Blessed Sacrament of the Altar, to which, he wrote: 'I owe everything. I cannot imagine my life without it. It has helped me in all my temptations; it has kept me, so far as I have been kept, straight, as nothing else could.'[1]

Indeed it could be said of Halifax, and of Edward after him, that in their sublime fulfilment in the Eucharist, they shared in full measure the inward peace experienced by Pusey:

'He is insisting on a constant nearness to the Blessed Sacrament. . . . He is surrounding it with incessant attention, with the routine of order and regular service, with accurate rules of preparation, with formal methods of intimacy. He is himself felt to be living, year by year, and day by day, in unfailing and familiar intercourse with Its Grace.

'It is to him necessary and near as his daily food. It has all the common and unquestioned frequency of air and earth and sky. Yet ever his awe and wonder grow.'

*   *   *

But there was nothing austere and forbidding in Edward's father; a small man of intense vitality, with a beard which became grey in age, the words used by Churchill of Bernard Shaw come irresistibly to mind—'This bright, nimble, fierce, and comprehending being, Jack Frost dancing bespangled in the sunshine', a man of extremes, a fierce clinging to the old ways, physical toughness, family love, bursts of anger like tropical squalls, an impish humour, and underlying it all a deep and pathetic humility.

Feudal in his conception of the world and bubbling with vivacity, he loved to entertain in his great houses, to hunt and to shoot, and to give a not always flawless example of what he believed to be the Whig ideal of the country gentleman devoted to the pursuits of the countryside, with the affairs of his estate at his fingertips. But to a degree rare today he lived for and by his religion, attempting always to regulate his conduct by it, and finding in its mysteries an immeasurable solace for the personal blows which were soon to be dealt to him by fate.

All these qualities of religious belief he transmitted to his son and so inculcated them in him that those who were to become close to Edward, and be influenced by him, discovered a new meaning and purpose in life and a serenity they had never known before. Yet it was a virtue of both father and son that their religion was never intrusive, and that neither their goodness nor their influence was forced upon others.

[1] Halifax to Lord Wolmer, 1919.

No atmosphere of intensity surrounded them; indeed to Edward, although so devout, religion soon became a gay and delightful thing, and part of the background of family life. There are those who remember later days in the chapel at Garrowby, with his wife Dorothy playing the harmonium, and Edward in the dreadful old clothes he loved, always a bar ahead of her, and Dorothy saying: 'I do wish Edward would keep in time.' When they saw him in this chapel, sometimes in a pair of ancient riding breeches, and his sons in shooting clothes, they realized how much religion was part of their daily life. And was not Edward himself afterwards fond of recalling in a manner that testifies to the homeliness of his faith, the remark of an old parishioner unversed in ritual: 'When his Lordship jinks, we all jink too'?

Certain distinct human failings also deprived the father's churchmanship of arrogance. There was something wanting, as he was dimly aware, in the position he had built up in his mind of himself as the ideal country gentleman, and it will appear that this small bearded man, who could walk the strongest off their feet on the moors, included elements in his character not always in accord with his religious principles. He had an impish streak in his nature which sometimes led him to be unkind, and even cruel, in the unwitting manner of children. Upon Edward his influence was almost entirely benevolent. It was one that never diminished, for Edward to the end of his days regarded with profound gratitude a father who had not only guided his footsteps into the way of Faith but had also provided the earthly paradise in which his arcadian youth was passed.

It seemed to him, when he mused long afterwards on the reasons for his father's influence upon him, that it 'owed its power to a force which gave his own being an intense vitality and to which in turn he gave constant and unflinching loyalty. His whole life was based upon devotion to the Catholic Church, divinely commissioned to preach the gospel and entrusted with the guardianship of the revealed mysteries of the faith. How great then was the tragedy of the differences and diversions among Christian people, that made such wounds upon the body of Christ! And what work could be more close to Our Lord's heart than that of trying to overcome those differences and realize his own prayer for unity?

'So from this master thought of devotion to Christ's Church he moved naturally to conclusions which were decisive on the pattern of his life. If the Church was indeed of divine origin and commission, it was impossible for it to be subordinated as to its spiritual rights and duties to the State. Again, if the Church of England had been wonderfully guided through the years of reformation to preserve its own Catholic character, this seemed to carry a double consequence. In the first place the Church of England must have the right to enjoy the full privileges in faith and practice of the great Catholic Church of the West, which her own formularies did not expressly reject; and in the second a loyalty was due to *Ecclesia Anglicana* in regard to matters which might rightly be held within the sphere of local order and regulation.

'Such were the foundations of my father's life, and it was these that we gradually came to apprehend and respect. . . . But with all this grew steadily the recognition of some quite other quality in him that seemed to have a claim to our obedience not to be denied. It carried a real reluctance to say or do anything that he would not like. And this not at all for fear of punishment, but for fear of falling short of what he expected from us. Learning little by little what were his standards and values, we began to feel that we must try to make them ours, as we grew up in the atmosphere of his work and pre-occupations.'[1]

It was from his father's teachings, also, that Edward was to discover in the dual aspect of Communion and Sacrifice in the Service of Holy Communion, and the Real Presence of Christ in that service, that near-ecstasy of direct kinship unapprehended by ordinary people, the privilege he called 'the attempt to assist in humility and faith at these Divine Mysteries in union with all the company of heaven'. It was that intensity of feeling which in years to come was to lead Father Langton[2] to say of Edward that 'one could almost feel him praying'. We see it in the words in which he describes the privilege of Communion 'ever becoming more immeasurable, as it brought us fuller apprehension of this intimate relationship with our Redeemer. And to this daily meeting with Our Lord it would come to be the greatest reassurance and relief to bring the hopes, anxieties, sorrows, joys, doubts, failures of one's life or of the lives of others, and there leave them in the safeguard of perfect sympathy and understanding. In some such fashion I think my father trained us to feel about what to him was the very rock and foundation of his faith. My debt to him is beyond telling.'[3]

*   *   *

The course of the father's life was set in 1868 when at the age of twenty-nine he accepted the Presidency of the English Church Union which had become the watch-dog of these principles established by Keble, Pusey and Newman in the Oxford Movement, and assumed the duty of defending those people, lay or clerical, who could not defend themselves against injustice and interference in their spiritual affairs. All thoughts of a political career were abandoned; his life lay henceforth in the Church. Through the E.C.U., of which he was President for fifty-one consecutive years, he defended the Catholic Church against the various attacks made on ritualism at the time of Disraeli's Act for the Regulation of Public Worship, and undertook the interminable spadework for his long-sought union of the Christian world

---

[1] Halifax, *Fulness of Days*, p. 18.   [2] Vicar of St. Mary's, Bourne Street.
[3] Halifax. Op. cit., p. 24.

which was to lead to a tentative *rapprochement* between the Roman and English Churches.

Such a programme left neither time nor inclination for politics. He told his father that 'at a time when the idea of what the Christian Church is has well nigh faded out of their minds, Parliament does not seem the battlefield'. He thought that the Liberal Party was anti-clerical, and that if Mr. Gladstone had failed to convert it to sound churchmanship, it was unlikely that he would succeed.

'As a Liberal in Parliament,' he said, 'I should be in a false position. As a Conservative I should be false to all my traditions.' In spite of these protestations, it was to the Conservatives that he ultimately turned as a step in the best interests of the Church, and in doing so he made a final severance with the political principles of his Whig forebears, and created a new allegiance for his son. But he would always remain independent of parties. The Church must come first, and he would reserve the right to differ, in its interests, from the Party, or, if necessary, to defy it. His final decision to abandon his office in the household of the Prince of Wales was symbolized in the changing of the motto of his house from 'Perseverando' to 'I like my choice'.

Sometimes Halifax felt a twinge of uneasiness in his rôle of the ideal country gentleman living on his estates, loved by his dependents, devoted to field sports and all the activities of the countryside, and with it all the embodiment of High Church principles. The rich part in which he saw himself required an effort to sustain, and even Edward, most loyal and devoted of sons, realized that there was an element of farce in the attempt:

'The lawn meet was very typical on one side,' he said. 'There was a great deal in his make-up of the traditional country gentleman, who naturally supported the local pack of hounds, and enjoyed following them in the company of his neighbours. With my father, however, the ideal often supplanted and in its imaginary existence did duty for the actual which might lag behind. . . . But in fact his actual following of hounds was deliberate and unhurried; and he knew little about the shape a hound ought to be, or about the finer points of its behaviour in the field.

'In the same way his Whig ancestry made it natural for him to like the picture of the landowner living on his estate, among farm and cottage tenants, with something of a feudal air surviving. . . . I suspect this went with a dash of wistful regret that it was now considered quite proper for a farmer, if he so desired, to vote differently from his landlord. Again, I doubt whether he was ever completely happy about tenants being allowed to shoot hares and rabbits. Yet very often, in spite of the theory of intimacy and dependence, when I have been riding with him and we would see some figure in the distance, he would diverge in order to avoid meeting a possible tenant who might make some request to which he would not know the answer.'[1]

[1] Halifax. Op. cit., pp. 16–17.

Halifax was, in short, a Romantic, but although he venerated old houses and churches, he had little taste and knew nothing of art. This lack could be seen in the pictures he had bought for Hickleton, which were all copies, and in its sombre decoration. He was an insatiable reader of history and the Romantic authors, and of abstruse books on theological subjects, but he also enjoyed reading trash, and there were great gaps in his literary knowledge, as in that of his son afterwards.

The love of ghosts and the macabre also grew upon him when he was married and had a young family to amuse, and he was to subject his children to trials of terror which might seem to many today to be of some psychological danger. It is perhaps not surprising that although Edward as a child loved his father, and treasured the recollection of him, his love was mingled with fear.[1]

It was in April 1869 that Halifax married Lady Agnes Courtenay, daughter of Lord Devon of Powderham Castle in Devonshire, of whom he confided to his mother that she was 'just the nicest person I know, so good, so clever, so up to a lark. We had some of the pleasantest and most scrambling rides I have ever had in my life while I was there',[2] and it is a face full of character that confronts one from the canvas of Richardson. Like his father's, this was a love match, and it had the result of raising the distinction of the Wood family to an even greater height than had that of the first Viscount to the daughter of Lord Grey, for the lineage of the Courtenays was so ancient and so historic as to cause Gibbon to write that: 'The purple of three Emperors who have reigned at Constantinople will authorize or excuse a digression on the origins and singular fortunes of the House of Courtenay.'

The first known bearer of the name was Atho, a French knight with a castle at Courtenay fifty-six miles from Paris. His grandson Joscelin took part in the first Crusade, and became Count of Edessa, a precarious territory straddling the Euphrates. He died in battle against the Turks, and his son died in captivity in Aleppo. Another grandson of Atho, Reginald, had a daughter, Elizabeth, who inherited the Courtenay estates and married Peter, a younger son of Louis the Fat, who, such was the distinction of the Courtenays, assumed the name and arms of his wife. Their eldest son Peter, through marriage with the sister of the Count of Flanders, was crowned Emperor at Constantinople, but he did not live to reach his capital. His two sons Robert and Baldwin next succeeded to the Empire, being finally dispossessed by the first of the Palaelogi.

The Devonshire members of this ancient family, which was now to be united with that of Wood, claimed their descent from Reginald, grandson of Atho and father-in-law of Peter of France, who is said to have migrated to England, where Henry II, in gratitude for his services, provided him with an heiress 'with wide estates in the West Country'. Edward I created their

---

[1] Lady Harlech to author.   [2] Lockhart. Op. cit., Vol. I, p. 157.

descendant Hugh Earl of Devon. By diligent service and prudent marriage the Courtenays became one of the greatest families in feudal England, throwing everything into the Lancastrian cause in the Wars of the Roses, sharing their intermittent successes, and suffering attainder and execution during their eclipse, Courtenay after Courtenay falling upon the field of battle or under the headsman's axe.

Nor did their fortunes find relief during the Tudor dictatorship, for by marriage they carried in their veins the terrible inheritance of Plantagenet blood. The last of the original Earls of Devon, who had at one time been regarded as a possible husband for the Princess Elizabeth, died unmarried at Padua, some thought of poison. The earldom, which then fell into abeyance, was revived in 1831 in favour of a younger line of Courtenays who had been living 'inconspicuously and irreproachably' at Powderham Castle in Devonshire.

Lady Agnes's father was the second Earl of the revival and the eleventh in titular succession. His modest and prosaic life was a far cry from the Emperors of Constantinople and the savage battles of the Wars of the Roses. A Member of Parliament for South Devon for eight years as a Commoner, a President of the Poor Law Board and a Chancellor of the Duchy of Lancaster, it was a life creditable rather than dramatic.

His ambitions were limited, according to his son-in-law, to reading the Holy office and attending the Board of Guardians, and Halifax assured him that if no such Board existed in heaven celestial paupers would be created for him to relieve; a man perhaps of limited intellect but of a sweetness of disposition that made him beloved by his fellow Devonians, and caused a man proposing his health at a local dinner to remark: 'I don't know what Lord Devon du, but all I du know is if more people would du as Lord Devon du du, there wouldn't be as many as would du as they du du.'

The religious atmosphere at Hickleton was not likely to be lightened by the entry of Agnes Courtenay into the house. One of her friends indeed looked to her to stiffen even her husband's faith. Sarah, Lady Lyttelton told her granddaughters: 'I must not delay telling you (I hope I am the first with the news) of a charming, excellent, promising, virtuous match. Charley Wood and Agnes Courtenay! Both so good and in every respect so perfectly suited. She will be of immense use to him, in *keeping* him for our Church. He is not so safe as some people are. Manning the Archbishop says: "I give him six months—after that period he will be ours!" But the good sense and excellence of Lady Agnes will do for him what Keble's wife did—save him—without I hope being on her deathbed for a time, as Mrs. Keble was.'[1]

* * *

When the children came, Agnes was to prove as singleminded as her

[1] Hickleton Papers, 5 March 1869.

husband in fostering their spiritual life. But she was destined throughout her marriage to play the ungrateful rôle of disciplinarian, and for this reason was less successful than her husband in winning their love. They were a little frightened of her, and did not appreciate her properly until they were grown up. Halifax came to mean to them the spirit of adventure and escape, of furtive sorties from the schoolroom to ride, or listen to a ghost story, or later to play in the fascinating secret room at Garrowby.

'It was to him,' said Edward, 'rather than to my mother to whom we mainly looked for amusement and fun. He it was who would pull us out of the schoolroom for a ride or an expedition, or on a wet day for a romp in the stable loft, and read us exciting ghost stories before we went to bed.' Their father would speak very seriously to Edward when he did something wrong, but he never used a stick on him or had a long memory for bad behaviour. He would say exactly what he thought of him but would conclude: 'Come now, that is forgotten. Give me a kiss.'[1] From his father he learned that good must always be put before everything. Kindness to others and perfect manners were emphasized by both father and mother as strongly as religious instruction itself.

The marriage, although enriched by mutual interests and a shared religion, cannot in every respect have been easy for Agnes. From the beginning she submerged her own strong personality in that of her husband, and she had much to support in those puckish tricks, which he would no doubt have been astonished to hear were cruel and which he frequently practised on her, tricks which suggest the mischief of a child, but also indicate a strange lack of insight into the feelings of others. It amused him to take her for back-breaking walks and climbs, and to make her swim in dangerous waters in which she was once nearly drowned.

Even his biographer Lockhart, who has little critical to say of him, acknowledges the distaste felt by Agnes for one of his pleasantries when: 'While out walking with the children, he picked a loathsome toadstool. When he got home he settled himself on the sofa, put the toadstool in his mouth and covered up his face. Then he sent the children to tell their mother that he was not feeling at all well and did not like the look of his tongue. The poor lady arrived in haste and there was a moment of agitation and horror before she discovered the deception.'

Much of his eccentricity can be explained by the fact that he belonged to a generation that should have been that of Edward's grandparents, as Edward was the youngest of six children and his parents were both over thirty when they married. His forebears, the Greys and Woods, were held by him in almost excessive veneration, and Edward's bride was to find later that her father-in-law had a sort of 'culte' for the family, perhaps not unusual in his own generation but surprising in hers. He was extraordinarily quick and

[1] Mrs. Sutton (Mary Wood) to author.

intelligent, and there was a foreign air about him as though he might have been a French diplomat. His great physical energy was observed by all: 'Among the hills at La Croix,' said Cosmo Lang years later, 'there was something almost cat-like in the swiftness and stealth with which he led the way through the intricate paths.'

Such a joke as that of the toadstool indicates a mind slightly retarded in its author, and perhaps it was consciousness of the irresponsible side of her husband's character that lent vigour to Agnes's own discipline. She was not a clever woman, though shrewd and efficient, and was wanting in that blessed touch of frivolity that would have brought her closer to her children. There was about her a suggestion of repression which intimidated strangers, and it would be difficult to imagine anyone except her husband behaving in a boisterous way in front of her.

There might have been more balance, if less harmony, in the household if she had not allowed Charles to become such an unquestioned autocrat. Even Lockhart admits that he 'teased and bullied her dreadfully', and we only have his word for it that 'she thoroughly enjoyed the treatment'.

Both Lord and Lady Halifax were completely ignorant about illness. Blessed with marvellous constitutions they treated their children with insensitive negligence. This indifference was not even cured by the staggering blow of losing their three eldest sons in swift succession, and one of Edward's Oxford friends was afterwards to tell his wife that he was so disturbed about Edward's health when he was working hard for his Schools, that he had ventured to speak to his father about it. The response had been to beg the friend not to do anything to stop Edward working as Lord Halifax was most anxious for him to take a First. The mother was equally unmoved. Yet we are struck by her courage and unselfishness and the way in which she would fall in with Halifax's most outrageous wishes, even when contrary to her own. She had a good sense of humour and maintained perfect calm when her husband became excitable. The children were fond, but in awe, of her, except Edward, who in her eyes could do no wrong.

It is probable that in their formative years Agnes's six children were more deeply influenced in their attitude to life and religion and the ethics of human conduct by the patient and continuous instruction of their mother with its instant correction of thoughtless or unkind behaviour, than by the more stimulating but erratic behaviour of their father. It is also clear that while they respected the former, they loved the latter.

Edward was the last born of this family of six: Charles Reginald Lindley Wood was born in 1870, Mary in 1871, Francis in 1873, Agnes in 1877, Henry Paul in 1879 and Edward on 16 April 1881. At the time of his birth, therefore, his chances of succeeding appeared remote. The children were a constant pleasure and interest to their father, and the most delightful aspects of his character were aroused by parenthood, his letters to them sparkling with tenderness, humour and mischief. The inability to mature fully himself, that Peter Pan element in his nature, made it easy for him to enter the strange world of children with no sense of intrusion. When he built secret passages and rooms into his house at Garrowby, he did so as much for his own excitement as theirs, and when he played with them and devised ghostly effects in the dark, it was as a contemporary rather than an adult.

CHAPTER II

CHILDHOOD

THE last child, Edward Frederick Lindley Wood, was born at Powderham, 'the finest child you ever saw', thought his father, 'quite enormous'. But this child was cursed with a serious congenital defect. He was born with an atrophied left arm, without a hand. Such blemishes have in the past often produced baleful psychological effects upon their bearers, but Edward was saved from such unhappiness by the strength and balance of his character. When he reached an age to feel the real impact of this affliction he was extremely sensitive about it, but he was too strong, too simple-minded and too uncomplicated in his mental processes to be seriously affected.

No stronger evidence can be found of the serenity and balance of his character than that from childhood onwards, through schooldays and throughout his public life, he carried this burden so lightly that it was scarcely noticeable, and, when it was, merely enhanced his dignity, and that he did not allow it to prevent in any way his enjoyment of country life, becoming a fine shot and a beautiful horseman. He was later to tell his wife that the only action he found awkward was trying to drink a cup of coffee or tea standing up and smoking a cigarette at the same time.

If his parents gave the impression of bringing up their children with a certain ruthlessness and accepting their deaths with an almost unnatural fatalism, they showed the greatest delicacy in their understanding of the boy's misfortune. They thought it wiser to make few references to it, but Halifax, perhaps longing to make clear his sympathy once for all, and then have done with it, was later to write to Edward a letter which conveys with extra-ordinary intensity the father's love for the son, and his complete freedom from all the usual constraints of embarrassment and reserve.

'I remember as if it were yesterday the day you were born; my joy, and my grief too, for my darling, I knew about the trouble of your hand, and I felt I would have given anything in the world if I could have borne it for you. I prayed then with all my heart since we must all bear our cross that this might be yours and that others might be spared you. I do think that God has given you other good things, a temper and disposition and a desire to love Him that are better far than what you have not. But my dear son, I will not talk of this; only I want to tell you that I do love you with all my whole heart, that I pray God to keep you and bless you in all your ways, and keep you safe and faithful to Him. And if it should so please Him, to do something great for His Church before you die.'[1]

In 1884 Edward's grandfather the first Viscount died, and the year after his wife followed him. Edward's father thus succeeded to the title and the great estates at the age of forty-six when Edward was four years old. The weather appeared to be set fair for Halifax and his wife. They were aristocrats at a time when there was still a perceptible distinction between 'professionals' and country gentlemen. He was rich, and was now the lord of great possessions. Taxation was negligible, and the Pax Britannica prevailed over the world. He enjoyed a happy marriage with a woman who shared his own interests and beliefs, but was content that he should be the dominant and she the recessive. He was happy to be the champion of the Catholic Church in England, its 'Chevalier Bayard' as he was sometimes called, and to have freed himself from the dust of the political world. He 'liked his choice'.

Although his mind was inclined to be a flea-market of ideas, he was seldom vexed by comfortless reflections. In Lockhart's words, he had thus far 'been fortunate in his home, his upbringing, his marriage, his work, his children and, above all, his religion. "Slow glide the hours for thee, late be the change," William Johnson had sung of him long years ago at Eton; and change, when it came, dealt gently with him. Death, so frequent a visitor to the large Victorian families, had only lightly touched the circle at Hickleton; and deeply as Halifax had loved his parents, he had lost them in the fulness of their years. There was bereavement, but no sense of untimeliness'.

Halifax was also happy in the company of his brothers and sisters. Francis the sailor had died in 1873. Henry the third brother had served with the 10th Hussars in Ireland and been A.D.C. to Lord Mayo in India. In 1897 he married Laura Montagu, a widow, and went to live with her and the children of her first marriage at Melton Park, the home of the Montagus. Frederick the youngest brother lived with his sister Emily and helped her to manage the estates at Temple Newsam and Hoar Cross, and in 1878 married Lady Mary Lindsay, daughter of the Earl of Crawford. Alice Wood, another sister, married John Dundas, grandson of the first Earl of Zetland, and Edith the youngest married Henry Lowry-Corry, son of the third Earl of Belmore.

*   *   *

Sometimes, in the affairs of men, at a time when all runs smoothly and the idea of change seems unthinkable, there come sudden bereavements like a cyclone in some placid lagoon. Such were to come now to Halifax, in shocking succession, out of the blue skies of wealth and contentment, and between the years 1884 and 1890 they were to provide a grim test of the efficacy of his religious beliefs.

[1] Hickleton Papers, 16 April 1902.

Events which might have disrupted an ordinary family were endured through his invincible belief in the Will of God. They left him with his faith intact and his fortitude unshaken. Even in the extremities of grief he could derive a melancholy solace from the reflection that his sufferings 'brought him closer to the foot of the Cross', and however inwardly scarred, he was to emerge from this ordeal blazing with the light of redemption. For during these years he was to lose all his sons except Edward, the youngest, leaving him the sole surviving direct male heir to the accumulated inheritance of the Viscounts Halifax of Monk Bretton.

In 1885 Halifax, on investigating his financial affairs, found that, owing to his father's heavy recent expenditure, even his ample estate was for the moment a trifle embarrassed, and that it was necessary to economize. He therefore closed Hickleton for a while to ease the strain, and went first to Garrowby, and then to his Grey uncle and aunt at Howick, whom he found in wretched health, and thence to The Moult, the house near Salcombe which Lord Devon had lent him for use in the hot summer months.

Ten years later he was left another small house in Devonshire at Bovey Tracey by Lady Halifax's uncle Canon Courtenay, the vicar, and a Canon of Windsor, 'a man greatly beloved', who prepared Edward for confirmation before he was taken to Lincoln and confirmed by the celebrated Bishop King. To this peaceful hermitage, Bovey Tracey, the family were to return at Whitsuntide when the rest of their Devonshire life had ended. From Bovey Tracey they made long expeditions on Dartmoor, through the woods along the valley of the Teign, and to Becky Falls where the stream runs fast and dark over boulders, with the light and shade of the wood flickering and playing over it, to the falls, plunging over dark rocks in separate gushes of water. There was dark woodland all round and a profound hush and stillness that was filled by the sound of the falls.

From these expeditions they would return to Bovey Tracey and to Ashburton scones and Devonshire cream. This house, St. Mary's, had none of the medieval excitement of Powderham for the children, or the sea-enchantment of The Moult, but it was in a countryside they loved, and was a link with their Devonshire past, a solid unattractive house in local stone, standing at the end of a straggling village on the edge of the moor, with a fine view behind it from its Gothic windows towards Hay Tor. Inside was that curious wood smell of Victorian houses in which pitch-pine predominated, which must have struck Edward's nostrils instantly, and perhaps, when caught long after, may have brought back the days at St. Mary's.

At first much of their summertime was spent either at Powderham or at The Moult. This little house, a paradise to the children, lying in leafy seclusion, provided exhilarating walks along the cliffs, west to Bolt Tail or east to Start Point. Sometimes they would move to another cottage of Lord Devon's at Beckley on the edge of Dartmoor, where they would stay the

night, and in the cool of the early morning drive down to Bovey Tracey for
Mass and breakfast with Canon Courtenay at the vicarage; then driving
back, bathe on the way at a pool below Beckley. From The Moult they would
walk or ride over the Moor, taking turns on the pony. To the children those
bygone Devonshire days, seen in retrospect, were the best they had ever
known, when the kindly Lord Devon presided at Powderham, and Canon
Courtenay welcomed them to the simple pleasures of Bovey Tracey, when
each hot summer day seemed a year, and life was lived on the open moor and
by the sea, in places where the past lived for Edward more than anywhere
in the world.

In May 1886 the first blight fell upon this ill-omened family. Halifax had
taken the children to see the Birthday Parade from the Admiralty stand.
Henry Paul, the third son and the nearest to Edward in age, caught a chill
while waiting for the ceremony to begin. Three days later the child was in
a raving delirium with congestion of the lungs, and kept repeating his
prayers with desperate intensity, and in a lucid moment became distressed
because he had wanted to see an Ascension Day procession and had sent
flowers to decorate the nursery. On 6 June he died, aged seven.

*   *   *

It was the first of the bereavements, and, armoured in his faith, the father
accepted it with the humility and resignation he was to accord to future
deprivations. He had loved this child, who had always appeared to him to be
destined for some special vocation; who, thought a friend, had something
about his face that reminded her of the Holy Child in Raphael's pictures. He
had often said that he wished to be a priest, and such had also been his
father's desire. As it was, Halifax could take comfort in the reflection 'that it
was a happy time, the Sunday in the Octave of the Ascension, to leave this
world, and I think he will do more good for us where he is than he could
have done in any other way. I do pray that I may learn the lesson which I
know I needed of living more in the unseen world and caring less for the
vanities of this.'

It was in one or other of these houses, Hickleton, Garrowby, Powderham,
St. Mary's and The Moult, that the greater part of Edward Wood's childhood
was spent. Hickleton village is nearly midway between Doncaster and Barnsley, near the crest of the limestone ridge that rises above the valley of the
Dearne. The house is a solid eighteenth-century building of grey stone, built
in the manner of the Yorkshire countryside, with long rows of stables for the
hunters and carriage horses that once filled every loosebox, and kennels for
the dogs which used to roam about it. Fires once blazed in all the great
rooms that now seem cold and a trifle forbidding. In Edward's early memories, a low wing containing a chapel and dining-room had been added to the
central block. The short drive ran through a grass field which after haymaking

was sometimes fenced with sheep hurdles, and he was to feel a nostalgic regret when his father made the field into a formal entrance with enclosing walls and outer lawns, so that the field outside the front door disappeared, and the cry of the corncrake was no longer heard by the children at their lessons, and the games in the hay were a thing of the past.

Now Hickleton in winter is sad and a little gloomy, and the once unblemished country darkened by nearby collieries. But it would be a dull man who, knowing its history, did not feel that it was the centre of the story of a great Yorkshire family, and that its walls had once echoed to the happiness of large Christmas gatherings and the tumult of children. In this house the old Secretary for India composed his despatches, and it was here that his son established himself for fifty years and with unflagging industry wrote his innumerable letters, and transacted Church affairs. To Edward Wood Hickleton was to hold many memories of childhood.

But it was Garrowby in the East Riding, the family's other Yorkshire house, that was to make the strongest claim on his affections. In the days of the first Viscount it lodged only three or four people, and was surrounded by a few thousand acres of wood, arable and grassland.

Edward's father began enlarging this lodge in 1892, until in the end it became a considerable house. He transformed it, according to his fancy and employing no architect, into a house lying round three sides of a cobbled courtyard with french windows opening into the garden falling in terraces to a ha-ha beyond which stretched the park. It stands raised a little above the plain of York. The air is clean and invigorating, and the placid agricultural country still remote from the blight of industry or the speculative builder. Above it the wolds pile themselves up towards the sky.

Halifax's love of mystery and medievalism prompted him to build there an extraordinary secret room with a priest's hole and a chest with a false bottom through which a man could reach a secret passage and reappear in a different part of the house. The room also contained further freaks of his imagination, hiding places cunningly concealed, and doors which opened by the pressure of a spring, and spy holes from hollow recesses in the walls, commanding views of some of the rooms. 'For me and my family,' Edward was to write, 'Garrowby had always a place peculiarly its own,' remembering perhaps as he wrote the gallops on his pony down the dales by Thixendale, and turning his head for home over Brown Moor, the only place on the estate where heather grew, those rides which had seemed to him 'the height of human happiness'.

Garrowby is a house which gives the visitor the impression of having long been inhabited by happy people. There is no large town near it except York, fifteen miles away, and the country that surrounds it is agricultural and has remained almost unchanged through the centuries. At all hours of the day there is a profound silence in the park and gardens, a hush rare in the modern world, broken only by the sounds of the country, and on the wold and in the rich plain beneath it is a sense of remoteness lost for ever in the South.

Edward's love of Garrowby, his true home, was nourished by early memories—of a nurse who dislocated her jaw yawning, and was taken to the doctor in a dog-cart with a horse shod with frost nails slithering down the road to Stamford Bridge whence Harold had made his forced march south to meet William at Hastings Hill; and the beginning of the building additions in 1892, with his father and the agent talking on a patch of grass that used to be outside the front door, and himself trying to throw empty cartridges over a high wall with a stick, and how years afterwards the smell of gunpowder in a cartridge case would bring back the whole scene vividly before him.

The alterations gave the house a southern aspect and a gabled roof, and added a large sitting-room on the ground floor, a hall, and the panelled chapel where the family worshipped, with figures on the reredos brought back by Halifax from Oberammergau and set in position by the house carpenter. Here in the small gallery their mother struggled with the harmonium at the Sung Eucharist, and a volunteer choir supported her efforts. Outside a sunken terrace garden with low walls and yew hedges was constructed by a landscape architect, Frank Thomas. He was known as the 'archangel' on account of his awareness of his good looks, and Edward noticed that some thought that he gave himself airs. Worse still, he was an agnostic, a terrible thought in that house, and Edward wondered why one so wicked was not struck down by some sudden retribution.

Halifax's whimsical fancy next led him to stock the park with exotic animals, and the local farmers watched their arrival with astonishment, fallow, red and Japanese deer, yaks, emus and kangaroos. Sometimes on shooting days could be heard the beaters' cry of 'Kangaroo forward!' The strange creatures must have been a sore trial to the head keeper of those days, George Smith, another early memory of Edward's, a keeper of the old style, 'wearing a traditional green Melton coat with short tails, loading his own cartridges with black powder, keeping an old-fashioned, curly-coated black retriever, from time to time catching trout from the beck in a net for our breakfast, and exciting envy and admiration by the skill with which he could attract rabbits by the imitation of their cry'. He was the companion and friend under whose teaching Edward learnt much of his shooting and woodcraft, ferreting rabbits and beating out the hedgerows with a dog on glorious days of sunshine and frost.

*   *   *

Temple Newsam was another haunt of his youth, a superb Elizabethan house a few miles from Leeds, where his Aunt Emily, Mrs. Meynell Ingram, an awe-inspiring figure of his childhood, held sway. She was Halifax's eldest sister, and had been much spoiled by her father who had employed her for a time as his secretary. When twenty-three she had married Hugo Meynell Ingram who owned large estates at Hoar Cross, Staffordshire, as well as Temple Newsam, and was Master of the Meynell Hounds. He was forty-two when he married the twenty-three-year-old Emily whose life and temper were to be greatly affected by a riding accident which both prevented her from indulging a passion for hunting and made it impossible for her to bear children.

She was a clever and pretty woman with a determined chin, a great aptitude for managing her properties and a strong sense of her importance in the world. She carried to excessive lengths that aristocratic assurance, that conviction that she was not quite as others, characteristic of some of the great families of the North. Indeed, she was even grander than her brothers, and she left an abiding impression on Edward's mind as a châtelaine of formidable distinction, whose husband had died in 1871 after only eight years of marriage, leaving her at thirty-one to carry alone the responsibility of her great possessions.

An atmosphere of feudal servility surrounded her: 'Her entry,' said Edward, 'gracious, deliberate and stately, into the long gallery at Temple Newsam, where we were all assembled for luncheon was quite an event. Preceded by a footman carrying newspapers, or an eyeshade, or an air cushion, she would move forward with assurance leaning on the arm of her lady companion or whoever had been talking to her, with a Maltese poodle making up the party. Everyone stood respectfully still, conversation being frozen, as the little procession approached, when greetings were exchanged, and we presently sat down to luncheon. And it was not only we children who were insensibly impressed by the tacit assertion of personality and dignity.'[1]

And so as a haunt of childhood there was added to Hickleton, Garrowby and Powderham, Temple Newsam more magnificent than any of them, that 'Hampton Court of the North', with its Reynolds, Titians and Van Dycks, its tapestries and precious furniture, and, to Halifax's joy, its ghost. And Aunt Emily's love for Edward was such that when she died in 1904 she bequeathed Temple Newsam to him, although his father Halifax was to have the use of it for life.

The ancient house with its whisperings and crepitations had an atmosphere propitious to ghosts. 'We went there as children,' Edward remembered, 'and were always brought up to believe that the house was haunted. There were stories of doors that no one could keep shut at night; many people had been frightened hearing what they thought were screams; and there were said to be unearthly knockings in a certain room that portended an approaching death in the house. I know we used to have a lot of what I can only describe as "daren't-look-over-your-shoulder" feeling as we went up to bed through

[1] Halifax. Op. cit., pp. 26–27.

long corridors with dark panelling and only dimly lit.' In 1922 Edward was
to sell this great house whose walls and gardens had long become begrimed
by the smoke of Leeds. It was bought by that city and became a museum,
and today strangers wander through the rooms where Mrs. Meynell Ingram
once passed in majesty.

*   *   *

To Edward and his two sisters, Mary and Agnes, the recollections of
Powderham were the best, and a sound or a scent could bring back to them
in an instant the unblemished happiness of those summers of childhood. As
rich in memories as Temple Newsam was this West Country castle where
their mother had kept house for Lord Devon after his wife died, lying on the
estuary of the River Exe in a park lush with Devonshire green: 'As I look
back, I seem to see a succession of long summer days in the garden, picnics
in the heather at Haldon, paddling and bathing and building castles in the
sand at Dawlish and the Warren, fishing from a boat with Scott, our boatman,
and Mrs. Croome, the housekeeper, who had begun by being my mother's
maid, always ready to give us delicious preserved cherries with fingers of
sponge-cake, and her husband who was the butler, standing in the stable
yard smoking a strong-smelling cigar, with his black poodle Sambo.'
     Edward and his sister Agnes were both born at Powderham, and Agnes
remembered how they went three or four miles to the Warren to bathe, how
they always had their ponies and how they played in the great park and
gardens and went tree-climbing and birdsnesting in 'that delicious place'.
There was a sense of remoteness about Powderham; there was all the charm
of country silence over the woods and meadows that surrounded it, and yet
a tang of the sea from the estuary visible between the trees of the park to
which the garden descended in terraces with grey stone look-out posts
facing the water.
     Strange sub-tropical flowers grew in profusion in that gentle climate. It
was in this park that Edward learned to ride on a donkey, and the memory
lingered in his mind to his last days of how one of his sisters put a thistle
under its tail in the hope that it would kick him off. Not far from the park
was the Warren where he was taken to bathe, a sand-bar jutting out into the
estuary, a place of sandy dells covered with withered gorse bushes, enclosing
a lagoon since swallowed by the sea, and a sandy beach on one side where
the shallow water was warm as milk in summer.
     They loved The Moult as much as Powderham. There they were taken
down 'Lord Courtenay's Walk' along the cliffs above the sea leading down
by what they called 'the dangerous steps' to the rocks, and to a little beach
where they could bathe in warm clear water as long as their parents or
governesses would allow. The Moult at Salcombe lay on the cliffs up a steep
hill from North Sands, a little guarded bay with a ruined watch-tower on

one of its horns, a house with stucco painted a faded pink and built in the early nineteenth century, with a Gothic archway and slate roof, its gabled windows commanding the sea.

In the garden, which stretched to the edge of the cliffs, was an old loggia of grey stone with an ancient wistaria and an evergreen oak, and beyond the terrace cypresses, and a cactus that bloomed only once in twenty-five years, sending up a spear with a yellow flower thirty feet into the air. On the far side the garden looked down on to another little cove, South Sands, the haunt of a few fishermen, its beach inviting to the bather. 'The dangerous steps' led from the garden down the cliff-face to the rocks below where the sea seethed and boiled in a storm, dangerous indeed, but a fearful challenge to Edward.

This place with its hanging gardens and sea enchantment was as abiding in his memories of childhood as Lord Courtenay's Walk which lay between Bolt Head and Bolt Tail, overlooking South Sands harbour on one side and North Sands on the other. The way lay through a tunnel of green, past sycamore and oak and holly trees, where the sunlight filtered through the laced branches, and on days of sunshine the sea glittered with a million diamonds far below. One emerged from the green aqueous light where the walk continued in the open, through fern and bracken along the cliff, with grey crags above, amid the incessant shrieking of the seabirds. As he walked, he could see on the other side of the bay the rounded green hills and woods of Devonshire, and winding along the cliffs, the other walk he sometimes took to Start Point.

Each day the father would write to one or other of his children letters packed with fantasies. As from the hospital would come news of Edward's favourite doll, Jack Tar, who had broken an arm or leg, describing his progress towards recovery, and at last a letter with the news that Jack Tar was leaving hospital, and would be landing by sea at 'the dangerous steps' next day, and when the children kept the tryst, there he was, bobbing in a boat offshore. Whatever Halifax's eccentricities and failings, he understood the minds of children, and it was at this early period that he wrote to Edward preparing him for the gift of a pony on his birthday:

'I shall think of you a great deal tomorrow. I wonder whether you will be seeing another *Silver Tail* tomorrow. I think it is very likely for a little bird told me—he *did* see a Silver Tail with a new cart galloping to Hickleton who said he wanted to belong to Master Edward Frederick Wood and that he hoped this Mr. Edward would be kind enough to take him into his stables and give him plenty of corn and not beat him a great deal. I shall be so curious to know if this Silver Tail gets to Hickleton. If he does pat him for me. Good-bye my own darling. I love you with all my heart.'

'Powderham,' wrote Edward later, 'with its association of happy years with my mother and Lord Devon; Howick with the enchantment of his mother's devotion to it, and the romance of the Northumbrian coast; these places never lost their hold on my father's affections. When he was altering Garrowby it was natural that he should lay out a flagged terrace in front of the windows, enclosed by a chapel at one end, for so it had been at Powderham. From Howick came the practice of playing four-handed cribbage which was for as long as I could remember the unbroken after-dinner practice at Hickleton. Deep contempt was felt for the sorry shadow of the real thing, as expressed in the two-handed game, and for the debased expedient of marking the score with pegs instead of mother-of-pearl counters.'

From Howick too came the practice of eating an edible seaweed called laver which they gathered from the rocks and sand. This was no dish for strangers, and needed careful preparation, but the family acquired a taste for it mixed with salt and lemon, and carrying a strong tang of the sea. They liked both its taste and its tradition, and as Edward said significantly: 'In all these things tradition counted for much.' It counted also in the fact that although Halifax liked to read Sir Walter Scott's novels to the children, he was a trifle repelled by those of Dickens. The stark realism of those novels which sought to change the inhuman conditions of the day shook Halifax's ivory tower at its foundations, that fragile edifice of the imagination he had constructed as a retreat from reality. To Edward it seemed that the reason why his father so greatly preferred Scott to Dickens was that the latter's characters 'are all, or nearly all, vulgarians; there is no history in the programme; and all nice things that would have appealed to him in Scott—chivalry, legend, patriotism, religion—are not in evidence in Dickens at all, or very little. So to his taste one would have been very attractive, the other almost distasteful'.

*   *   *

Early in the New Year of 1888 the family paid a last and melancholy visit to The Moult. It had only been lent to them by Lord Devon, and their two houses in Yorkshire had greater claims upon them. There were rumours too that Lord Devon's financial affairs were in bad order. So for the last time the parents packed their luggage, and walked the old paths they had trodden on their honeymoon, and Lady Halifax fell into a rough sea from a boat, and Lord Devon caught a chill. By November he was dead, and Powderham, that second home, passed from the Woods' life for ever.

It was a little sad at Hickleton that Christmas, and even the children were subdued by the gaps that had opened in the old circle. But there were still the waits on Christmas morning, and cribbage with Edward's great aunt Georgiana Grey in the evenings. His two older brothers, Charlie and Francis, went back to Eton, and there was anxiety about Francis who had shown signs of heart trouble the previous spring. From Eton soon came the telegram that announced his promotion to the Fifth Form, but in February, when Halifax was entertaining his Aunt Georgiana at Hickleton on her eighty-eighth birthday, came the news that Francis was ill again.

Halifax at once became 'in a fidget', and decided to go to Eton where he found the boy seriously ill with congestion of the lungs. On 17 March, when he was staying with the Courtenays in the Cloisters at Windsor, he was woken by his son Charlie to tell him that Francis was worse, and although he dressed quickly and hurried to the sick room, he arrived too late. Someone met him in the passage outside and told him that it was all over, and two days later a second son was taken to the churchyard at Hickleton to lie beside Henry Paul, and Halifax wrote to Edward, and told him how much he was in his thoughts, and that they must think of Francis and Henry who were together in Paradise.

Charlie, the eldest son, was now nearly nineteen and beginning his last half at Eton. He was a charming but somewhat indolent boy who had sauntered amiably through school life, easy-going, attractive, no glutton for work, as his housemaster Walter Durnford admitted, but of an equable temper doing good to himself and others, and more and more of a companion to his father. In October 1889 he went up to Christ Church, Oxford, but within a fortnight he was ill with pleurisy, sending his father almost into distraction as he hurried down to Oxford, 'nearly dead with anxiety thinking of when I had gone to Francis'. After a crisis of several weeks, the boy was found to have a tubercular infection in the lungs so that there was no question of remaining at Oxford, and he was ordered to spend the winter abroad, preferably in Madeira.

It was an indication of the solidarity of the Wood family that Halifax, as a matter of course, took them all on this journey. They sailed from Dartmouth in the *Drummond Castle* just before Christmas which was spent on board, the vessel seething at night in a gale past Ushant, and on arrival Edward saw the island rising purple and mysterious from the sea to its mighty volcanic peaks the moment before dawn broke, and the lights still twinkling on the mountains.

They lodged at the Santa Clara Hotel, and Edward, running down the hill on which it was perched, broke one of his front teeth, 'necessitating much disagreeable contact with an American dentist'. Then they moved into a villa, the Quinta Bianchi, with a view over the sea and a pleasant garden at two levels on one side of a dry river bed, and a little garden house to which his sister Mary was sent when it was thought that she might have smallpox.

The Madeira of 1889 was like some lotus island where time stood still. The sun shone on the tropical flowers that rioted in the gardens of the pink and white villas or leaned over the walls, bougainvillaea, poinsettias, hibiscus and pink and white camellias, and the only sounds were the bells of the bullock carts, and the noise of their runners on the cobbled streets, and the shouts of the muleteers with their barrels of wine. Green lizards darted from the crevices and lay basking on the sun-baked walls. Edward and his sisters rode about this magical island on ponies, and galloped down the 'new road', then the only soft-soil road, and slithered down the cobbles on toboggans from the Terreiro da Luta and watched the glorious play of light at sunset and sunrise on the Deserted Islands.

Halifax did not enjoy his stay in Madeira. He felt separated from his work and his Yorkshire friends. His wife was far from well, and his daughter Mary gave them a great scare when she appeared to have contracted smallpox. Even worse, poor Charlie, to add to his other troubles, developed jaundice. Halifax, to distract himself, bought a parrot and tried to teach it to talk, and its raucous shrieks were a sore trial to the others. Nor was the mild and relaxing atmosphere conducive to intellectual exercise, and the invalids dozing in the sun were unlikely to provide him with foils for those discussions on sub-tractarian theology so dear to his heart. It was therefore with delight that he made a new friend on the island, the Abbé Portal, a member of the Society of St. Vincent de Paul, whose company now lent meaning to his rambles. The spiritless entries in his diary acquired a sudden vivacity. 'Walked by the sea with the Abbé Portal, a very pleasant walk—beautiful afternoon—much theological conversation.'

                    *   *   *

In March 1890 they mourned the death of Halifax's uncle, Francis Grey, and in May Charlie had a further attack of pleurisy. The family sailed for England in June, and took the boy to Hickleton, and thence to Aunt Emily's yacht *Ariadne*, in a last futile effort to save his life. Perhaps he knew that he was about to die, for he spoke much about his health, and how he had neglected it, and, as Halifax said, 'it almost broke my heart'. After returning to Hickleton on 6 September 'he slipped out of life without the least pain, "the sweetest and dearest of characters" as A. C. Benson called him, without the least touch of the hardness which often accompanies high principles among boys'.[1]

From the funeral of his son Halifax went to stand at the graveside of his greatest friend, Liddon, who had guided his footsteps, and from whom he had absorbed his own conception of the Catholic Church. It was to Liddon that he would have most naturally turned after his son's death for understanding and comfort. But no human suffering could deter Halifax from his religious duties, and we scarcely know whether to admire or be chilled by the detachment which enabled him to attend the Church Congress at Hull sixteen days later, and read a promised paper on Ritual.

During these years the blows dealt to this blameless couple might well have caused less deeply devoted people to falter in their belief in divine dispensation. Halifax's aunt, Caroline Grey, was the next to go in this numbing

[1] Lockhart. Op. cit., Vol. II, p. 14.

series of bereavements, and in January 1891 Edward's Uncle Baldwin, who had succeeded his father Lord Devon only in 1888, died of a stroke, and was followed, four days later, by Halifax's greatest friend after Liddon, Lord Beauchamp.

This succession of tragedies was softened and rendered bearable by his religious beliefs, and his serene confidence in an after-life, and he retreated into an inner world of his own. Thus Edward enjoyed an early familiarity with grief, and was given visual evidence of the efficacy of spiritual solace: 'The kind of influence,' he said, 'to which we were subject as children, must have been driven deep into our minds by the fact that for the six or seven years following 1885 there was never a year that did not mark some close family loss. My grandparents, two uncles, and three brothers all died between the time that I was four and nine, and thus we were early brought close to the solemn realities of life.'[1]

Another solemn reality was the fact that he was now the only remaining male child in his family. He had become the sole repository of his father's devouring affection, and all his leaping ambitions for the future. In his letters to Edward we shall see this love in its almost frightening intensity focused upon the child as though through a burning glass.

After these disastrous years haunted by sickness and death, the family life as if to recapture its old tranquillity, fell into a contented routine. Hickleton now became its headquarters, with Garrowby as an alternative, and the family's two ruling passions of religion and sport are indicated by the fact that Edward remembered their year being regulated to a great extent by the Church seasons and the racing calendar. Christmas and the early months of the New Year were always spent at Hickleton, where the structural alterations Halifax made to the house were an absorbing interest to his restless mind.

Even more thought and time were given to the restoration of the Church of St. Wilfrid which lay a hundred yards from it. So effective was his zeal and that of the new incumbent, Mr. Dalton, that Halifax was soon able to report: 'Mr. Dalton is converting not only the parish but the neighbourhood—the Church is filled to overflowing; the little brats of children come to Church on weekdays through the snow at 7.30, and the question of Purgatory is discussed in the Public House.'[2]

Strangely, for one so feudally inclined, he abolished the old family pew, which had really been a room to itself with a fire in the bitter Yorkshire winter which was always poked at the end of the Litany.

There were occasional visits to London for the family, when Halifax descended from Yorkshire to preside over the Council of the English Church Union, or attend debates in the House of Lords. There were visits to pay to Aunt Emily at Temple Newsam or Hoar Cross, and regular journeys abroad

[1] Halifax. Op. cit., p. 22. [2] J. G. Lockhart. Op. cit., p. 293.

to Mont Dore, Mentone and Biarritz, for Lady Halifax had fallen gravely ill
with typhoid fever after Charlie's death and had not fully recovered. At
Whitsuntide there was a joyful exodus to Bovey Tracey with its riding and
bathing and excursions on the moors. July usually marked the end of their
time in London, a bad period for the children in formal clothes and on their
best behaviour, and at the beck and call of a murderous dentist. Here the
Wood family lived at their house 79 Eaton Square in a grandeur equal to that
of their houses in Yorkshire.

Then the racing calendar beckoned to Hickleton and to Doncaster Races,
when Halifax, although his heart was not in racing, presided over a large
house-party. His conduct in doing so scandalized some of his puritanical
neighbours, who wrote to him expressing their pain that a man professing his
religious principles should encourage gambling and horse-racing.

But Halifax, like his son Edward, was not given to analysing the contradictions of his own character. In fact, he would willingly have avoided the
necessity of attending the races, for the whole affair bored him, and he did
not understand its finer points, finding it so tedious that he once left his party
and walked back to Hickleton in his top hat, meeting two ragged boys on the
road whose conversation so pleased him that he took them on a conducted
tour of the house. But the races could not be avoided; those house-parties for
the St. Leger were an essential part of the character he had subconsciously
built up for himself, leader of the Church, great landowner, ardent sportsman.

In that happy moment when the races were over and the last carriages had
clattered out of the gates of Hickleton, Halifax could contemplate with relief
his next move. The time of year had now come to leave this atmosphere,
which had already begun to be a little murky from new-found coal, and go
to the clean air of Garrowby, and to arrive before Michaelmas so that he
could eat one of the stubble-fed geese bred there which he swore were the
finest in the world.

*   *   *

Hickleton became the pivot of the children's life after Powderham was
lost to them, and it is of this house that Edward, as a man, was to retain the
most vivid memories. They were memories of happiness clouded only by
death, of devotions in the village church, of long days in the open air, of
ponies and innumerable dogs, of hunting and shooting. There is in them that
pastoral mystique which, exerting its spell in childhood, never deserted him,
and which found its symbol in the wolds which rose above his home at
Garrowby. There was enchantment for him in the smell of stables, in the
jingle of harness being cleaned, and in those dark summer dawns when he
went cub-hunting, and the ponies were saddled by candlelight. It was a
childhood so happy that its sorrows stood out in sharp perspective, the deaths
of his brothers, the anger of Miss Hilder, the governess, and a rap across the

knuckles with a ruler, and the visits to the terrible dentist, so dreaded yet so stoically endured.

Over his domain at Hickleton the father presided with a despotism unchecked by the slightest opposition. To any intrusion upon his privileges he reacted with the hauteur of a medieval baron whose supremacy had been disputed by one of his own serfs. When the local council proposed to alter the road through Hickleton he was splendid in anger. It appeared monstrous to him that these jacks-in-office should consider touching what he called 'my village'. They would do so at their own peril. He would dig a trench across their road, and if they filled it in he would dig it again, 'and', he concluded aggressively, 'I shall win'. Later he was to take the 1914 war as a personal insult, and return an angry refusal to the suggestions that he should set an example by ceasing to brew his own beer at Hickleton.[1]

Yet there remained something spurious, even to the devoted son, about the 'great country gentleman', notwithstanding the ardour of his feeling for 'my village', and Edward did not fail to notice that: 'He cared little for the practical details of estate management; partly because he was too ready to believe that things like drains and roofs, when once in position, took on an imperishable character and never required renewing. Nor, he felt, were these considerations of very much importance in a world which "is all going to be burnt up". But the implications of democracy were always offensive to him. Projects of a classless society or of economic equality would have seemed to him nonsense; in fact blasphemous nonsense, since Almighty God had placed people in certain stations of life and clearly intended them to remain in them.'

To excuse the contradictions in his quick, if somewhat excitable mind, he explained triumphantly to his protesting chaplain: 'I have no moral sense, and that is my strength.' To his servants he was a genial despot, although more deeply concerned with their spiritual than their physical needs. 'All the servants made their Communions except P.,' he wrote in his diary on a morning clearly darkened by P.'s abstention. He was truly disconsolate when a servant died—'a most dreadful grief,' he recorded of one of them, 'he had been with the family since 1859—a most faithful friend and servant.'

In sickness or trouble he tended them and prayed for them. In moments of exasperation he would shout: 'If you do that again, I shall beat you,' threats which were received with tolerant amusement. To a butler suspected of heavy private recourse to the cellar he said: 'If you don't answer, I shall shake you.' When the butler observed: 'I knew I had drunk some, my Lord, but I didn't think I had drunk as much,' Halifax was so pleased by this reply that his affection for the man became unassailable.

The life at Hickleton was so grand, so perfectly ordered and everything seemed so set in its place that the thought of change would have appeared

[1] J. G. Lockhart. Op. cit., Vol. II, p. 95.

like some monstrous reversal of nature. The terrors of insecurity, the expectation of fearful upheavals in the world outside, had no place in that tranquil
daily round nor disturbed the harmony of the great house, where the master
sat in his study composing papers on ritual, or writing letters defending those
of the faithful who believed that they had suffered hardship or persecution.
Perhaps we may see in Hickleton a microcosm of England herself at the turn
of the century. No speck on the horizon appeared to threaten her prosperity.
She was at the height of her Imperial grandeur, and her navy preserved the
peace of the world, so that not even the most clairvoyant could discern an
end to the golden age. To such families as the Woods there must have seemed
to stretch before them years of fruitfulness and ease.

In that house everything was pervaded by a strong aroma of the past. We
feel it in the host's courtly manners and exalted ideas of entertainment, in his
exaggerated care that every hour of the guest's visit must be filled with some
form of planned amusement. It is there also in his insistence on old customs
and proprieties, and in his obstinate lingering in a century which had already
passed. The new age seemed to him to exhibit already a deplorable social
declension.

'He detested the sloppiness which invaded English society in the twentieth
century, the rapid and promiscuous use of christian names, which he thought
vulgar, and the abandonment of those minor courtesies which, in his opinion,
made life gracious. "But times change, Charlie," Lady Grey said to him once
when he had been inveighing against modern tendencies. "But I like the old
things." "Yes, Charlie, but they change." They did, but he did not.'[1]

Certainly no concession to new-fangled ideas is evident in the Christmas
parties that assembled year after year at Hickleton. Patriarchal and welcoming, Halifax gathered in all the far-flung members of his family within an
encircling arm. There, from her grace and favour rooms at Hampton Court
where she held the officials in awed subjection, came Aunt Georgiana Grey
who lived to be ninety years old, and died deploring her failure in falling short
of the hundred, a memorable figure to children and adults alike. There too,
until his death, came the gentle and good Lord Devon, and any other aunts
and uncles and cousins who had no home to visit for Christmas.

The children would go into the kitchen and watch the joints turning on
spits before a huge fire, basted with the dripping fat by one of the kitchen-
maids. After tea the gardeners came into the house their arms full of hot-house
flowers for the dinner table, in the colour of which they sought to match the
silver and silver gilt, for at Christmas the whole content of the plate chest was
brought out for those immense eight-course dinners which were the tedious
custom of the day, soup, fish, entrée, joint, game, sweet, savoury, dessert.
The silver plates were carried on heavy hot-water containers from the distant
pantry up two flights of stairs and down a long passage to the dining-room,

[1] J. G. Lockhart. Op. cit., Vol. II, p. 103.

and some of Halifax's many retainers were brought from village, stables and gardens to help in the carrying. They were refreshed after their labours by a tremendous spread in the servants' hall, at which quantities of the bitter and invigorating Hickleton ale were consumed.

*   *   *

When Edward looked back years after on those ample days of his childhood, it occurred even to his mind, which was not one to concern itself with domestic problems, that the labour involved must have been considerable: 'All this dining-room work; no bathrooms, and every guest therefore having cans of hot and cold water carried up to their bedrooms for a hip bath in front of a coal fire, and the bath emptied with slop pails; lamps for the sitting-rooms and passages when it got dark, taken away by the footmen when the bell was rung to signal that everybody was going to bed, which they did taking one of the silver hand candlesticks, to be trimmed and cleaned next morning; no wonder it had to be a pretty considerable household to cope with it all.'

On Christmas Eve the children came down for dessert, a treasured privilege, and their elders traditionally were served champagne, toasted cheese and spiced beer. The estate carpenter performed the ritual of the Yule log which was paraded round every bedroom in the house. In each of these there blazed a coal fire, and to the housemaids' many other duties was thus added that of cleaning out forty or fifty grates. At five o'clock in the morning the waits would assemble to sing round the house on Christmas Day, and Edward and his sister Agnes would creep from their warm beds into the icy cold of dawn, and hold a light of thanks and encouragement at the window.

Two hours later, at seven o'clock, they would go to church, and sometimes again at eight, returning to a breakfast at which there was much giving and unwrapping of presents, and consumption of a sweet porridge called fermity, which Edward hated, eating it standing up as Yorkshire custom demanded. At ten o'clock they were in church again, for sung Matins with the Athanasian Creed, before sung Celebration. His mother played the organ, supported by three villagers on violin, 'cello and flute. It was a long service, and indeed a long morning before the Christmas tree was decorated for its formal showing to the children after schoolroom tea.

There is the flavour of a vanished world in the words in which Edward later recalled this part of Christmas at Hickleton: 'Tea had to be finished by the time the schoolchildren from the village were ready for the tree, illuminated meanwhile by the elders. To this the house servants came and were given their presents; the humbler maids in their lace caps all got a length of print for a cotton frock.'

Christmas also gave excellent opportunities for the exercise of Halifax's perverted sense of humour. He would hobble into the room hideously disguised as a witch, and it would be put about that this was Gagool from

King Solomon's Mines which he had been reading to the children. He made an alarming apparition. No trouble was too great to gratify this strange and macabre sense of fun. Uninhibited by psychological anxiety, he believed that children derived a delicious excitement from fear. He encouraged his coachman to rope in some friends and pretend to be a raiding party of gypsies who had been on the road that day. This bizarre tableau was acted with such realism that it made an indelible impression on Edward's mind.

'I remember it as if it was yesterday—a great banging at the front door, my father telling James, the butler, to go and see what it was, and James going to the door and coming back—an awful silence having overtaken the company inside the hall—to say that there were a lot of rough gypsies, who as far as he could make out said that they wanted a little boy and were coming to fetch him; and on his heels came in four or five of the biggest ruffians you ever saw, who were William and some of the gardeners, and William shouting rather bolshie sentiments about rich and poor, and how they wanted a fat little boy they had seen and had brought a sack to take him away in. My father furious, "I won't have people like you talking to me in that way—get out, at once." "We must take the little boy with us," from the gypsies—and absolute panic among the children: some fleeing upstairs, others screaming and hiding behind grown-ups, until order had been restored by the gypsy withdrawal, induced by the usual proceeding of crackers and carols, after which the schoolchildren filed out past my mother who gave them a present, and an orange and a bag of sweets.'[1]

Ghosts played an important part in this vanished scene with its long periods of devotion, its glittering Christmas tree, its battles in the snow in hard weather, with the children divided into sides and defending opposing forts on the croquet lawns, its skates ringing on the frozen pond, its hunting in open weather, with a lawn meet sometimes at Hickleton, and port and sloe gin for the horsemen, Edward feeling gauche and ill-dressed among the other boys. Sometimes the father read ghost stories to the children in the time after tea. At others they would play a game with Uncle Henry Wood, whom they called 'Friar', which involved crossing the floor without being caught and included the two bearskins in the hall, and caused much shouting and excitement. But the ghost stories were the best, as are all experiences which play upon the fundamental human emotions.

Halifax had collected ghost stories all his life and had compiled a library on the subject, and a large book in which he recorded the psychic experiences of his friends. This interest was partly, no doubt, yet another example of the youthfulness of his character, but it had an underlying seriousness. The unseen world to Halifax and Edward was not a mere matter of conventional acceptance, but a conviction so deep that it pervaded their thought on all things. Although he condemned spiritualism 'since the Church in her

[1] Halifax. Op. cit., p. 32.

motherly wisdom had placed a barrier across the road to Endor', Halifax believed ghost-hunting to be permissible.

There might be evil spirits to be exorcized, or unquiet spirits to be appeased, and Halifax had not a shadow of doubt that they were as real as flesh and blood. He longed to see one, and the phantom housekeeper who had hanged herself and was said to wander disconsolate down the corridors of Hickleton had always eluded him, but he was solaced by a glimpse of the Blue Lady at Temple Newsam entering the Damask Dressing-room where his sister Alice was sleeping. To him 'the seen was so trivial, the unseen so tremendous. . . . He would have agreed with Dr. Johnson that occurrences of a supernatural kind are sometimes permitted in order to keep us in a more vivid notion of an invisible world'.[1]

Halifax, like M. R. James, the ghost-loving Provost of Eton, had no use for benevolent phantoms. His stories, told in a darkened room with tremendous artistry, produced in the children a sense of fearful suspense and a strong reluctance to face dark corridors on the way to bed. They would look over their shoulders as they ran up the back stairs, and by long custom the green baize door of the hall became the signal to them of whether they were safe from ghostly pursuit, and a magic protection against it. As they passed the door they would throw it wide open crying—'Catch me if you can, devil, ghost or man', and then run up the stairs as though the Devil was indeed on their heels. If they reached the top of the first flight before the door swung to, they were safe.

This test of immunity produced a delicious spice of excitement, and made the ghostly evenings an experience alarming but strangely desirable. Sometimes after dinner tne big leather ghost book was produced, from which many of the stories were later published in *Lord Halifax's Ghost Book*, and Halifax would read aloud. There was a frequent visitor, Augustus Hare, and Edward remembered how he chilled their blood with his story of the vampire at Croglin Grange, 'which he could only tell when he wore a very much ribbed shirt so that, picking his shirt with his nail, he could represent the vampire picking the mortar from the window pane to get in. We used to be terrified when we went up to bed'.

*   *   *

In his passion for the macabre it never occurred to Halifax that the sinister buffoonery which gave him so much pleasure might have had a pernicious effect upon more delicate nerves. He acquired a supply of skulls from a medical friend in London, and these and a collection of hideous masks, disturbing even in daytime, he would hang about the attics in positions where anyone might suddenly come upon them. Sometimes, too, he would don one of these masks, and jump out upon the children in the dark with a maniac

[1] J. G. Lockhart. Op. cit., Vol. II, p. 107.

scream. Agnes Wood never forgot the lengths to which this strange man went in order to purge the children's emotions with fear. The skulls and masks were shrouded in black coverings. These were whisked off when the game began, and Halifax always wore felt shoes and moved in silence, creating an atmosphere of stealthy terror. The children believed that their only hope of safety lay in reaching their bedrooms and locking themselves in. Knowing this, Halifax used to get there first and leap upon them when they thought they had reached sanctuary.[1]

It is a tribute to their hard fibre that Edward and his sisters managed not only to survive but to relish these experiences. In fact, they had little effect upon them, and Edward's casual recollection of them was: 'I don't think it did us any harm, and my father always said it was very good for our imaginations.' As a father himself he kept up the practice, and when he read a gruesome book aloud would pause and say: 'Now I am coming to a really horrible bit.' The truth is that, in spite of the great houses and the privileges of wealth, their childhood was spartan. There was little ease in the hard schoolroom discipline, the indifference to illness and the constant religious exercise. Rather was it a life calculated to breed tough Yorkshire children, and it left no trace of the neurotic in Edward.

Their life was, in his own words, 'sedate, unhurried and traditional'. Speed had not yet succeeded in establishing its unsettling tyranny. There were no short cuts to amusement. After the deaths of his three elder brothers, Edward, the youngest of the family, was brought close to his two sisters, Mary and Agnes. Both adored him, and both, in old age, looked back upon him in childhood with an unalloyed affection. Mary, who was ten years his senior, remembered how, as a child, he had been loved by all the poor people who lived near the houses of the Wood family, for his kindness and friendship with them, and the delight he found in playing with their children. She did not think that he was always a good boy, being mischievous and given to tricks, like tying his cousin's hair to the back of a chair, and disobeying his governess, Miss Hilder, who would make him put his pinafore over his head in penance.

Edward and Mary gave much time and thought to devising tortures they would like to apply to this woman, such as putting her in a cask with spikes in it and rolling her downhill. Mary remembered that it was characteristic of Edward that when he became bigger he made a point of playing with little children and that even at that age he was always doing kind things for other people. 'Tom and I are going to play all the way,' he said before leaving for Devon with a small friend. He was extremely solicitous about his sisters' safety, and, when they went for a walk at Garrowby and Mary returned home through a different field, arriving late, he hung round her neck, sobbing with relief, thinking he had lost her.[2]

[1] Lady Bingley (Agnes Wood) to author.   [2] Mrs. Sutton (Mary Wood) to author.

In 1890, after their eldest brother had died and their mother fallen gravely ill with typhoid fever, Edward and his sisters were sent to the seaside at Filey. Mary made him learn Latin jingles, and she and her sister were afterwards disturbed by the fact that at the age of twelve he had hardly read a book. Indeed he read little as a child and seemed to feel no need for the books which normally stir the imaginations of children. It was surprising to Mary that those their father and mother read to them should not have stimulated him with the desire to read himself. Surely the adventures of the Swiss Family Robinson and Masterman Ready, and Captain Starlight in *Robbery Under Arms* with his horse Rainbow, should have set his senses more swiftly aflame? He did not like poetry then or afterwards, and could not see it even in the green valleys with their steep sides, or in the wolds or the windy Yorkshire sky.

He was even closer to his younger sister Agnes. These two were intimates and did everything together until the day he went to school. He showed an even greater care for Agnes than for Mary, and when they became separated on a ride when she and her pony went the wrong way home, and she did not return until dark, Edward was acutely anxious about her safety and, when at last she arrived, sat with her hands clasped in his throughout tea. He was not a shy child, but completely natural. He and Agnes arranged every amusement together and they had a memorable race over jumps at Hickleton on Shetland ponies, the fences arranged side by side at Bella Wood, higher for Agnes than for Edward because she was older.[1]

Agnes put her finger on the truth about her brother's character when she said that as a child, 'he was the simplest and most natural person with no complications whatever'. Still fresh in her mind at the age of eighty was the sunny friendliness of his character in childhood, and how he played cricket with the village boys, and loved ratting and ferreting with the keepers, and he had already an unusual sympathy with the point of view of others.

Miss Hilder, the governess so highly regarded by the parents, loomed in the memory of the children as a figure of awe and retribution. She was a governess of the old school, like a character out of some Victorian novel, and this grim and unsympathetic mistress with her Yorkshire terrier, Tiny, was one of the few discordant elements in that tranquil scene. To Edward she 'was a typical product of the old school; limited in intellectual range; knowing what she did know with great precision; a devoted admirer of my father; convinced that accuracy, application, discipline and good manners were by far the most important ingredients in education. For the inculcation of these qualities she was a great believer in the value of physical reminder'.

Agnes remembered with hatred after seventy years how Miss Hilder stood over her when she was practising scales, with a black ebony ruler, and when she struck a false note would bring it down on arm or fingers, causing

[1] Lady Bingley (Agnes Wood) to author.

agonizing pain in that cold schoolroom, and turning her arm black and blue. They would retire in tears to seek that sympathy and indignation which at Hickleton they knew would always be forthcoming from Sam the coachman, or at Garrowby from Mrs. Wordsworth the housekeeper with her gingernuts and cowslip wine.

When Miss Hilder made them stand outside the schoolroom as a punishment, there was always a rush to get back into it before the parents noticed that they had offended. They were well aware of the severity of Miss Hilder's régime and approved of it, leaving the children without qualms for months alone with her. In spite of their preoccupation with them, there was thus a strange insensitiveness in their behaviour which was to continue when Edward went to school, his parents seldom visiting him during that first unhappy absence from home. The atmosphere in which they were brought up was strict and sometimes harsh, and the principle that children should be seen and not heard closely observed. They were not allowed to relax in an armchair, and jam was allowed at tea only on Thursdays and Sundays. When grown-ups entered the room they must immediately stand up, as both parents properly held that good manners were next only to godliness.

Perhaps they gained by having to find their own amusements. 'Before the days of motor cars, gramophones or wireless, the boundaries of daily life were not wide and simple enjoyments had full value. So we quickly forgot the pains of lessons in the satisfaction of doing something amusing with my father, and in his reading aloud to us in the evenings when the lesson books had been put away. And periodically there was the excitement of seeing the beer brewed. This happened twice a year, in March and October, in the old brew-house adjoining the stable yard and was the quasi-hereditary duty of one of the oldest families in the village. It was fascinating to watch the mixture bubbling and boiling in the big witches' cauldron, giving off scented fumes and presided over by mysterious figures dimly discernible through the steam.'

*   *   *

As time went on Agnes's affection for Edward grew steadily more deep, and her nature emerges in the hundreds of letters with which she bombarded him. A strong character in her own right, she was sharp and intelligent, and full of her father's restless energy. She regarded these letters to her brother as a secret channel of communication conveying her inmost thoughts, and she was inclined to be censorious, particularly in religious matters, a fault she was not slow to condemn in others.

Edward's attention would sometimes wander in church on a hot day, but Agnes would sit bolt upright in rigid attention. To her Radicals and Nonconformists were synonymous with heathens, and many members of the Church of England were included in that category in her mind. Sometimes when worshipping away from Hickleton where the ritual was strongly influenced by Halifax, she would condemn the service as 'glorified Matins', and yearn for home. Nor did the service at Bovey Tracey please her, and she deplored there the atmosphere of the 'holy widows', as she called a regular group of devoted worshippers.

Three times on Sunday the Wood family went to church. Early Service, Matins and Evensong were accepted as a matter of course, with family prayers every day of the week in the chapel before breakfast, except when there were visitors. Frequent visits to church were also made during the week. The whole household attended family prayers and the cook and all the housemaids wore lace caps.

The various chaplains and priests who frequented Hickleton incurred Agnes's severe censure. Halifax would appoint chaplains in sudden enthusiasm, of whom he quickly tired, and their alien and irritating presence in the house and at every meal was the cause of many petulant letters to Edward from father and daughter. Only Mr. Dalton, the parish priest who lived in the vicarage in Hickleton village, maintained a precarious hold upon their favour.

This man, perhaps even more than his father, was responsible for the moulding of Edward's spiritual life. This 'devoted evangelist and lover of souls', who taught Edward and Agnes their catechism each day with the children in the village, came from a poor parish outside Rotherham. He was not a man of scholarship or theological learning but he had the supreme gift of being able to interpret the story of the New Testament and, above all, the Passion in a homely yet vivid manner which left a profound impression on the mind of a small boy, and which, once heard, was never forgotten.

'To hear him preach the Three Hours Devotion on Good Friday,' said Edward, 'was always for me a deep religious experience. If I had been older and more critical, I suppose that, like my father and mother, I might have been shocked by the intimate way the tragedy of Our Lord's agony was told in language the most ignorant could understand. As it was, my feeling was that of the people from the country round who thronged into the church and sat on the floor, on hassocks or wherever they could, so only they could hear what to them was the Word of Life.' Dalton knew exactly how to treat children, and Agnes believed that he had more influence over Edward than anyone else.[1]

---

[1] Lady Bingley (Agnes Wood) to author.

CHAPTER III

A VICTORIAN EDUCATION

ON 20 September 1892, at the age of eleven, Edward left home for the first time for his preparatory school, St. David's at Reigate. He was leaving much behind that was dear to him, those sharp days of frost when the rabbits bolted well and there was no need for the spade, Uncle Henry with his cavalryman's swagger and his sharp reminders, and Mama fussing over her dogs, Missie, Di and Pixie, and Jessie the Shetland pony he rode out hunting, and Robin who drew the chair, and the big hunters, Straddlebug and Lady-bird, clinking their bits and stamping in the stable; memories too, of Hickle-ton, of Papa picking primroses for the church at Easter, and looking for the first violets under the west garden wall.

St. David's was said to be one of the 'sensible and respectable' private schools of that period, containing eighty or ninety boys and staffed by well-educated masters presided over by a martinet in Holy Orders, the Reverend W. H. Churchill, whose strict régime was offset by a charming wife. This lady, before marriage, had been Constance Hilliard, and her mother was a sister of Ruskin's devoted friend Lady Trevelyan. Ruskin had taken Con-stance and her mother on several journeys abroad, and as a girl she had stayed at Brantwood with her brother Laurence who at an early age became Ruskin's secretary.

Work, play and discipline were the order of the day, recalled one of the old alumni of this school, and when play was impossible, a long walk on the hill above Reigate.[1] St. David's had the sinister reputation of turning out 'good specimens in brain and brawn with a high sense of duty'. The school must have appeared a pleasant enough place to Edward as he passed the old cedar tree in front of the house and entered the Gothic arch of its front door which was exactly like that of a church with great iron hinges and was an augury of the religious atmosphere of the place in which a chapel, also with Gothic windows, spanned two parts of the building like the Bridge of Sighs. It was a house of grey rugged stone and stucco with a red-tiled roof with two turrets rising from it, a house set in pastoral seclusion in a valley with a playing field and a pretty white wooden pavilion with slender pillars where Edward was to spend many listless hours keeping the score. The high ridge of the Reigate hills stood above the school, trees stark on the skyline in winter, its height suggesting a barrier against the world outside. Round the

---

[1] Sir Charles Ponsonby to author.

school was a garden with beds of roses shaded by fine trees and broken by bushes of yew and evergreen hedges. A tranquil secluded place it must have seemed at first sight to Edward, but inside it were the locker rooms redolent of damp football boots, the smell of carbolic soap, and the alien atmosphere of school which was soon to make him long for home with an intensity he had never felt before.

Lady Beauchamp of Madresfield Court was one of Lady Halifax's dearest friends, and Edward had spent many happy holiday hours there with her children. It was from this delightful childhood retreat that he left for his first school. His father accompanied Edward on this most harrowing occasion of a boy's life, his first separation from home, but neither father nor mother was to visit him more than once during his whole period at St. David's, and we are forced again to remark that although they idolized the boy, they were strangely insensitive in matters of ordinary human concern. In spite of this aloofness, Edward was now almost obsessively in his father's thoughts, but Halifax was lacking in the imagination to envisage the fears and unhappiness of a small boy away from home, and in contact for the first time with the cold reality of institutional life. On Edward's first day at school he wrote to him:

21 Sept. 1892.

'My own dearest Edward,
I was very unhappy at wishing you good-bye yesterday—but it would have been much worse if everything had not seemed so bright and you had not been looking forward to all that is before you. I shall be often thinking of you, indeed I believe you will never be out of my mind. And now that I have seen the place I shall be imagining you in your room—in the school room and at play in the garden. May God bless you now and always my very dearest child. You are more precious in my eyes than I can properly express, and I think it would break my heart if anything but good were ever to befall you. Good-bye my darling.'[1]

*   *   *

Even the most expensive private schools at the end of the nineteenth century were no bed of roses, and Edward detested every moment of his life at St. David's. He found it merely an extension of the methods he had grown to hate under Miss Hilder. The Headmaster was a firm believer in the moral and educational value of flogging, and applied it on many occasions and sometimes on the slenderest pretexts. Edward was beaten three times before breakfast with the heavy cane which was always kept at hand for such faults as having a bootlace undone, or not eating a piece of dry bread provided before early school. His physical handicap deprived him of one avenue of escape from the miseries, proficiency at games, and in spite of his father's buoyancy,

[1] Hickleton Papers.

he was to hate this school, and to dread his return to it, and 'the relentless approach of the day for going back was like a dark cloud, throwing everything into deeper and deeper gloom'.

The unhappy terms made him long for the holidays and appreciate freedom as never before, those days with the old gamekeeper, Hellewell, who told him stories of affrays with poachers, which made Edward think him the bravest man he had ever known. And there was waiting for him at home his uncle, Henry Wood, who had given him his first lessons in shooting and encouraged him to overcome his disability and to handle a gun safely. Edward long remembered the severity with which this lesson was driven home, and the bitter humiliation he felt when this stern but wise tutor made him hand over his gun in front of others and return home after some exhibition of carelessness.

Sometimes he would spend part of his holidays with Aunt Emily at Hoar Cross, and here there was much shooting with his aunt's brother, Uncle Freddie, who helped to manage her estates, and his son Fra, one of Edward's dearest friends. Uncle Henry, the ex-cavalryman, also naturally gave much attention to Edward's horsemanship, teaching him to dominate his pony rather than be controlled by it. He was a hard taskmaster, slamming a gate when the boy dawdled through it, and hitting his toes with a hunting crop when they were too far turned out. Edward felt gratitude rather than resentment for these frequent corrections, and they were broken by 'wonderful games of galloping hide and seek in a huge wood now felled and converted into farm land'. Thus Henry Wood planted in his nephew that passion for horsemanship in all its forms which never deserted him and was to remain one of the greatest pleasures of his life.

Back at St. David's Edward gave no hint to his parents or sisters, to all of whom he wrote regularly every week, of homesickness or depression. However miserable he may have been, he kept it to himself and made no attempt to enlist the sympathies of others. He gave no indication that his father's frightening expectations had rendered his inheritance oppressive, or that his hand was in any way a cause of the cruel mockery that might have been expected among small boys.

The headmaster clearly had this danger in mind when he wrote in October 1892 giving a shrewd preliminary assessment of Edward's character. He had, indeed, with great kindness, tried to anticipate any such trouble. John Christie of Glyndebourne, who was then a pupil at St. David's, remembered this effort: 'I remember very clearly Churchill telling us one general assembly day—"We have a boy coming next term who has only one hand, and you've got to treat him decently." I don't remember any mention of it afterwards, so presumably it worked.'[1]

'You will like a line about your boy,' wrote Churchill. 'He is getting on

[1] John Christie to author.

capitally in every way—both in work and generally. He knows all sorts of out of the way facts and is intelligent. Of course it is a little early for me to give you a decided opinion as to his intellectual capacity but I believe him to be quite above the average; in fact I believe he is a really clever boy only I am afraid to say much for fear of having to retreat. He is quite happy about his hand and no one takes any notice of it.'[1]

These encouraging words were eagerly read by Halifax who lost no time in telling Edward:

'Mr. Churchill gave me such a good account of you which was so entirely confirmed by your Mama that I have been quite happy since it reached me. My dearest child it is delightful, most delightful to hear you are doing well, and I hope and pray it may be always the same. I long for you to do your best in your games, and the best in your lessons, and that you may turn out the pride and happiness of our life. We have all had so much sorrow in the past that now everything seems to centre in you. May God bless you now and always, and above all other things make and keep you good. To be good is the one thing that really matters; to love God with all your heart, to be truthful, obedient and unselfish will make all your happiness here and here-after.'[2]

*　　　*　　　*

All his stability of character was required to withstand the devouring affection of his father. In letter after letter he was reminded of this burning love; that he was the last of the male Wood children, and that he was destined to succeed where his grandfather had succeeded before him, and his father had failed. It was an almost intolerable load to place on such young shoulders. The father poured out his adoration with none of the shyness or constraint common to English fathers writing to their sons. Grand schemes for the future are mingled with tender protestations of love. He is to graduate brilliantly and become a Fellow of All Souls:

'You know when you are big you are to get a First Class in History at Oxford and to do all sorts of grand things. Oh my darling may God bless and preserve you, and keep you to be the happiness and joy of my life.'[3]

Sometimes some contact, some episode, would bring back to Halifax a sharp and agonizing reminder of the sons he had lost, and after torturing reflections he would realize again the intensity of his love for the remaining child:

'It is very sad for me going down to Eton. My thoughts were full of dearest Charlie and Francis, and what a shadow had fallen on all our lives since they have gone. It is almost more than I could bear for indeed the thought of them fills all my days. My own darling child you will try to be

[1] Hickleton Papers, September 1892.　　[2] Ibid., 22 October 1892.
[3] Ibid., 20 October 1892.

good will you not? Nothing else in this world signifies except being good. Everything else comes to an end but goodness abides for ever. I think if any mischief happened to you, my only one son left, it would quite break my heart.'[1]

He was unable to leave this disturbing theme alone and returned to it in April 1893:

'You do not know how precious you are in my eyes my own dearest child, my only little son left now that God has taken my other three to Himself. All my hopes and joys are bound up in you, and I pray to God to keep and bless you—now—and all the days of your life. What should I do without you?'

His mother's letters to Edward at Reigate were also numerous, but they lacked the volatility and emotional excitement present in every line her husband wrote. The strange insensitiveness which accompanied her love for the children, and the spartan character of their upbringing are brought vividly home to us in these letters. Edward suffered all his life from his teeth, a family weakness, all of them enduring agonies at the hands of their dentist Mr. Rathbone. One is amazed at the callous jocularity with which she described to Edward her daughter Mary's sufferings at the hands of this terrible man:

'Fancy poor Mary having to go three days running to Mr. Rathbone, for endless stoppings. He hurt her a good deal too, for he thought the tooth was dead, and hammered at it, and it wasn't! The maid was had in to hammer, which seems so funny, as Mr. R. wanted both his hands, one to hold Mary's head, and the other the instrument on which the maid *tapped*.'

In spite of this and similar gruesome experiences by all members of the family, their confidence in Mr. Rathbone remained unabated.

*   *   *

Edward's father and grandfather had been Etonians, and it was natural that such a traditionalist as Halifax should send him there too, and on 28 September 1894 Edward went to Eton to the house of Walter Durnford, nephew of 'Judy' Durnford, one of the immortal spirits of the place. The Housemaster beginning a letter in a manner which might have irritated a more conventional parent, 'Dear Halifax', informed him that his son had taken Remove,[2] and was well placed, and that his cousin and intimate friend Fra Wood was in the same house and would keep a protective eye upon him.

At first Edward found the great school with its freedom to wander at will over the countryside a wonderful change from the irksome discipline of St. David's. He wrote to his father: 'It is ever so much nicer here than it was

[1] Hickleton Papers, 7 February 1893.
[2] The highest position a boy can attain on entering Eton without a scholarship.

AS A BOY ON JESSIE

at Reigate. . . . I have just been down town with Fra and invested in a pair of candlesticks. I think I shall enjoy myself very much here: you can do so much more what you like.'

Eton between 1894 and 1899 lived in the past, and the world outside it appeared to have come to an uneasy pause. The telegraph had not long been introduced, and the few panting motor-cars were regarded, as were the railways fifty years before, as merely a source of potential danger.

Little change, too, had taken place in the school by 1894. There were still the old rabbit warrens of the boarding-houses, the black walls of their twisting passages carved with the names of generations of Eton boys, houses that would have blazed like matchwood in a fire. Every day in the dining-room at Durnford's at luncheon and supper the boys were given as much beer as they wanted, with the choice of a glass of port or sherry on Sunday, solemnly handed round to all boys, large or small, by the fat old butler.

The senior masters, compared with those of the coming generation, seemed also to belong to the past. Yet these old men were of a breed never to be seen again, and had the heedless boys but known it, they were offered a rare privilege in being brought into contact with such men as Ainger, Luxmoore, Broadbent, Arthur Benson, Austen Leigh, Tarver, Daman, Arthur James, Bunny Hare, R. A. H. Mitchell and Edward's housemaster Walter Durnford. Miss Evans, last of the 'dames' who had first kept boarding-houses for the poor scholars, still presided over a whitewashed house in Keate's Lane, famous for the House Colours of scarlet with skull and crossbones, triumphant on many a field.

Over the whole scene towered the immense figure of the Headmaster, Edmond Warre, producing a veneration combined with awe in the boys, including Edward, which has never been approached by any other Headmaster in the history of Eton. Edward was deeply aware of this spell, of the tremendous power of Warre's words, of the nobility of his appearance, and his devastating anger. Edward did not pause, any more than the others, to consider whether the influence of this great man on Eton was a good one, that the Classics and rowing should be so exalted, and that 'Pop' the Eton Society, founded for political debate, should have become a paddock for prospective Blues. He was content to observe him as did one of his contemporaries:

'I can see him only in the full noon of his tremendous power. . . . When he came down in wrath, it very seldom happened, but when he did come down in wrath the earth shook, and his great voice was a trumpet, shattering the air. I have seen no one so grand in anger as Warre could be. I still behold him as he leans over the big raised desk at the end of Upper School, while we crowd in, hundreds of us, by the doors at the other end; we surge in, thronging the long room, packing closer and closer; and he leans motionless, and gazes very solemnly before him, and at last, when we are settled, the doors

3

are shut and silence falls—a dead silence—solemn with expectation, awaiting his voice.'[1]

Edward, perhaps fortunately for himself, was seldom brought into contact with this demi-god, whom he could observe from a respectful distance, or, with the swish of a silken cassock, entering a classroom fallen suddenly still as death. His daily business was with his tutor Walter Durnford, an able, cynical man, whose initial love of boys and zest for teaching had, on his own admission, become somewhat eroded after twenty-five years' experience of both. He also was one of the characters of the old Eton. 'There too,' said a contemporary, 'is heard the voice of Walter Durnford, planting its stroke in the dispute; you see him sitting in the circle, erect and compact, with asperity in the beak of his nose, in the uncompromising knock-you-down of his state-ment—with rich geniality in his rosy and festal good humour'—the very person to call the noble father of one of his pupils by his unadorned surname, and a man to whom a pleasing touch of comedy is given by periodic attacks of gout.

*   *   *

It was soon evident to him that Edward would never become a good classical scholar. Like many others, similarly handicapped, he found the classics intolerably wearisome, and his apparently cheerful application to them masked a hideous boredom. Had he been allowed to read them in translation, he might have found much to appeal to him in the tremendous epics of *Odyssey* and *Aeneid*, in the love songs of Catullus, or the worldly charm of Horace, but they were mummified in the classical curriculum. As one whose tastes already inclined towards history he would certainly have been captivated by Thucydides, and that unforgettable description of the Syracusan Expedition, so vivid as to give the reader the impression of having been present at the disaster.

As it was, he spent listless hours deciphering the dead languages for which he had no aptitude at the time, and in which he was to show little interest in the future. 'I managed to move along,' he said, 'in the normal stream of school promotion, with no great effort and no particular distinction.' It is not surprising that Walter Durnford, who through daily contact was the best person to judge his character at this period, should not suppose that he had a young genius on his hands.

Eton College,
Windsor.
17 Dec. 1896.

'My dear Halifax,

I sent you some reports about Edward. Broadbent his Division master is a difficult man to satisfy, and Edward comes as near it as most. Personally I

[1] Percy Lubbock, *Shades of Eton*, p. 11.

am very well pleased with him. He seems to me to do his work cheerfully and with a considerable amount of success. I do not think he is really clever, but he is steady, diligent and sound-headed. He is a most pleasant lad to deal with, friendly and good in every way: and one of the most argumentative I ever came across, besides being devoured with an insatiable curiosity.'[1]

A year later Durnford told Halifax that Edward would shortly be in First Hundred,[2] and that he would then find a wider field of study, and would be under Luxmoore, one of the most stimulating of tutors, and an excellent master for 'a cleverish boy who is none the worse for the spur'. But, he thought, 'he will never be a flyer in any one of his school subjects, but will always, I think, do respectably, and as he has plenty of general intelligence I hope when he goes up to Oxford in due course that he may do well in some such school as History or Law. His thirst for information on all kinds of irrelevant subjects, and his delight in argument continue unabated'.

Thus, although he duly reached First Hundred, and was bracketed first in the Prince Consort's French Prize with another boy, the greater part of his time was devoted to that long and futile period each day on the treadmill of the classics: 'The routine was boring, and I never learnt to appreciate the appeal of the classics through which we rather wearily ploughed. Arthur Benson was the only master who at that time ever made Homer come alive for me, by disposing quite quickly of the thirty lines set for the official lesson and then racing through as much more as time allowed, so that for half an hour we really caught a little of the romance and poetry of the Greek. . . . On Tuesdays the weekly copy of Latin verses was for me a burden without redeeming virtue. The labour of composition never grew less; the quality of the result never advanced.'[3]

The great heart of Eton beat even more strongly in her athletics than in her humanism. The rafts above Windsor Bridge were alive with racing craft in the summer Half, whiffs and eights and slender riggers, moving like beetles on the surface of the stream for the wet bobs to paddle off to race or practise, and heavier craft to take upstream, lingering in the gurgle of the lock, to Queens Eyot where the boys lay in the shade and drank beer, and the willows trailed their green tendrils in the water.

Cricket was played every half-holiday under the leafy elms on Upper Club. In the winter Eton Football, a game peculiar to the school, was pursued with equal devotion. Edward could hunt with the beagles and play fives and tennis, and in summer bathe in places with seductive names, Cuckoo Weir, Ward's Mead and Boveney Weir; and this last was a paradise as enchanting as any at Powderham or Bovey Tracey, where, as an old bather remembered, 'there was the sound of water pouring the sluices which is one

---

[1] Hickleton Papers, 17 December 1896.
[2] A loose term applied to the upper part of the school.   [3] Halifax. Op. cit., p. 48.

of the fullest sounds of high summer; there was the sunlight on the bubbles
racing down from the fall, and the sunlight on the short grass of the bank;
there were the shadows of alder leaves and poplar leaves flickering over the
level spaces . . . and all through the wind and air about the place was the
smell of water and weeds and wet earth, which is the true smell of the Thames
that blows from weirs'.

Owing to his handicap, he was allowed a bicycle, and in his rides about
Eton he acquired a close knowledge of every corner of the place, the flat
country across the Jordan which runs into Mesopotamia, full of hares for the
beagles, the winding lane beyond Upper Club, dusty in summer and girt
with cow parsley, the byways of Windsor Park, and all the holes and corners
that cast so strong a spell on those who have known them. Sometimes on his
expeditions he would catch a glimpse of Queen Victoria driving from Windsor to Eton, squat in a landau drawn by two grey horses, and on Sundays
ride to the Cloisters for tea with his uncle Canon Charles Courtenay and his
Aunt Car.

He was fortunate in that first year when the Great Floods engulfed Eton
on 15 November 1894, and were followed by an equally great freeze which
turned the Thames Valley into a vast skating rink, and froze the river so
deeply that a coach and four could drive on it, and oxen be roasted whole on
the ice. In the floods Eton became practically an island, and water lay a foot
deep in some of the pupil-rooms. The rising waters played a delightful havoc
with school hours and discipline. A desperate boat service was organized to
get the boys to school, and a common excuse for lateness was: 'Sir, I missed
the punt.' On 17 November the school was dispersed.

Eighteen ninety-nine was Edward's last year at Eton. Throughout his
blameless but uneventful sojourn there his mother had been little more
assiduous than Halifax in visiting him. There was an almost complete insula-
tion between his school and home life, bridged only by letters from Hickleton,
Garrowby or Mont Dore bringing news of home, of his sisters, of the health
of favourite ponies or the deaths of much loved dogs.

There was little more personal contact than at St. David's. Lady Halifax
constantly wrote saying she would come that day week or fortnight, 'or on
your next half holiday', but, as with her mercurial husband, something
always seemed to intervene. On 2 March 1899 she wrote: 'I am *so* sorry and
horribly disappointed but somehow things have cropped up so that I *cannot*
come down.' It was in his last half that Edward was allowed a bicycle, that
magic carpet that opened to him the charms of the surrounding countryside,
and it was his mother who suggested long rides for him, and procured for
him permission to ride in Windsor Great Park.

On 27 May she wrote to Edward about the preparation for a visit on the
Fourth of June. The party would be fourteen for dinner at the White Hart.
Would Edward arrange for the table and order dinner? 'Would they give us

strawberry messes or strawberry ice? Mind you order dinner *well*!' These preparations were frustrated by a twist of Halifax's unpredictable fancy. At this inopportune moment there came over him a most uncharacteristic desire to economize. Edward's spirits must have been daunted by the nature of his mother's next letter. Sadly but with firm conjugal obedience she told him: 'About the White Hart dinner, don't go and run us into any great expense, for it is not worth it. If it is a table d'hôte at 7/6 a head, of course we take what comes and that would be best—but Papa says in no case had you better let them give us strawberries, as they would be very dear and anything extra would be probably charged very high.'[1]

When the time came to go, Edward left Eton with little more regret than he had left St. David's. The twin cults of the classics and athletics had produced in him a dead sense of *ennui*. His five years there had been agreeable but a trifle monotonous. He could not but look on the wildly distorted value placed upon games with a certain contempt, and feel a longing for the woods and pastures of Garrowby and for horse and gun.

He had got into no trouble; he had worshipped regularly either in the chapels at Eton, or at St. John's Church in Windsor whose services he preferred. He had been placed in First Hundred and had won the Headmaster's Lower Boy French Prize. His progress had been respectable but not gaudy. He had done all that was asked of him in his work with the same adequacy with which he boiled or scrambled the eggs of his fag-masters, Charlie Helmsley, Roland Baring and Castlereagh, receiving from them in return an occasional lordly reject, the end of a pot of cream, or a sausage for Sunday breakfast. Eton had done little more to satisfy his needs than St. David's, and it was clear that no form of school life could have given him fulfilment. It was not the place for him, but he had not to wait long to discover where that place was.

*   *   *

It had been decided that as Edward had followed his father at Eton, so now he must tread in his footsteps at Oxford. He arrived at his father's old college Christ Church on 13 October 1899, and succumbed at once to the ancient blandishments of the University. One of his first actions was to write to his mother:

'Dearest Mama,

I got down here alright this morning and have got very well settled in. I have got a little gem of a scout who gets me everything and puts me up to all sorts of tips. It is a delightful place and I have quite fallen in love with it already.'

It was his good fortune that his first taste of the *douceur de vivre* occurred in an Oxford as yet unviolated, and for a few precarious years still a haven of

[1] Hickleton Papers, 8 May 1899.

cloistral peace. There were already signs of those changes which have since reduced her to an industrial shambles, but they were small and scarcely noticed. 'It was one of those boundary periods, the meaning of which is missed at the time, but is plain in retrospect. The place was still monastic, but the clamour of the outer world was at its gates.'

These gates were still barred, and behind them Oxford lay in the hush of the Middle Ages. Only a few horse-drawn vehicles were to be seen where the sweep of the High disclosed its successive beauties. Even the ugly Victorian houses to the north, with forsythia, lilac and syringa in their gardens, seemed part of the peace of the University. The other entries to the city were almost unblemished, and it could be seen from afar by the traveller like some beckoning oasis in the desert. This was an Oxford still redolent of the past, whose tranquillity proclaimed the purpose of her founders, a place dedicated to study and meditation. A man who was born at a time when he could drink deep of this cup before it became contaminated was granted a rich experience never to return.

Edward was not one able to describe the beauties of a town or a country-side in memorable words, but he was moved by those of Oxford, although he could not have recorded the first emotions she stirred in him in language comparable to that of one of his contemporaries, John Buchan, writing of his own first day there: 'It was bitter winter weather. The Oxford streets, when I arrived late from the North, were deep in snow. I wrote my examination papers in Christ Church Hall, that noblest of Tudor creations. I felt as though I had slipped through some chink in the veil of the past and become a medieval student. Most vividly I recollect walking in the late afternoon in Merton Street and Holywell and looking at snow-laden gables which had scarcely altered since the Middle Ages. In that hour Oxford claimed me, and her bonds have never been loosed.'

Edward was spellbound but inarticulate. He was conscious of enchantment in his strolls down Addison's Walk when the crocuses were out in the spring, or in the flat Christ Church Meadow where paths led down to the river and the painted barges; and in the Parks where the undergraduates lay in the long grass under the elms and watched the cricket on a hot day. It grew upon him when pleasure took him to the lovely country outside Oxford, to the little valleys of Windrush and Evenlode, where 'the names of the streams are in themselves a melody and the valleys wind into the recesses of the hills so softly that they combine upland austerity with lowland graces', that magical Evenlode of which Belloc wrote:

> '*A lovely river all alone,*
> *She lingers in the hills and holds*
> *A hundred little towns of stone*
> *Forgotten in the western wolds.*'

At Oxford too he would discover a new and invigorating relationship, that of don and undergraduate, so stimulating and so different from the watchful association of master and boy. A new world was disclosed by the possibility of such friendships, when the older and the younger men could be intimates, sometimes calling each other by their christian names, and the undergraduate could, with one step, enter an adult civilized world.

Edward was also fortunate to find at Christ Church a group of senior undergraduates of influence in the college and congenial to himself, who welcomed him into their midst. There he found Charles Helmsley, for whom he had made scrambled eggs in that cluttered Eton room, and whose son was afterwards to marry Edward's daughter Anne. He was delighted to meet 'Walter Buchanan Riddell, also an Etonian from Miss Evans's, and reared in the wide spaces of Northumberland; Edward Talbot, a Wykehamist, son of Dr. Talbot, successively Vicar of Leeds, Bishop of Rochester and finally of Winchester, himself to be for many years Superior of the Community of the Resurrection at Mirfield; and Charles Fisher of Westminster School, and younger brother of the Admiral and of Herbert Fisher'. George Baskerville was another brilliant contemporary and friend.

Edward realized his good fortune in finding such people already in residence. He understood that it would not have been possible to discover men more likely to exert the sort of influence he was prepared to accept: 'Talbot and Riddell were Churchmen,' he said, 'secure in their intellectual grasp of the faith, regular in their practical observance of its obligations, on both counts providing an example searching, stimulating and reassuring. Charles Fisher, differing from them, would treat Christianity with an appearance of tolerant and half-amused indifference, hardly compatible with the inquisitive reaction that Christianity seemed constantly to be exciting in his mind. But all three had much in common. They were all accustomed to reach their judgments, unaffected by popular convention or fashion, and well content to find their own way to interest and enjoyment under standards which they had tested and approved, and on an equal footing of independence. They were all working hard and able to fit this into as much social life as they desired.'[1]

These friends were all Edward's seniors, but there was another group a year junior, of which the chief were Ludovic Heathcoat Amory, Louis Egerton and Lord William Percy. With 'Ludy' Amory he would sometimes spend a week at his home Knightshayes in Devonshire, where he was offered a day's foxhunting, a day's staghunting, a day's harehunting and a day's shooting. Amory was perhaps the dearest of these younger friends, and after his death in the war, Edward was to write to his widow: 'I think there was no friend who was so close to me as Ludy, and none to whom I felt more close. We had done so much together, Oxford, round the world, Knightshayes,

[1] Halifax. Op. cit., p. 51.

Chevithorne, that it is pulling one's life in pieces to feel that one has wished him good-bye.' He would often be invited by William Percy to shooting parties at Alnwick and Kielder, and at no time of life, even in boyhood, did Edward find the slightest difficulty in reconciling his religious principles with his love of blood sports. His mind was not one given to introspection; it was simple and direct, and prone to accept anything as a matter of course that had continued for a long time and which he enjoyed.

At this last moment before the peaceful turn of the century it appeared to this happy band of brothers that their friendship was not only precious but permanent. The thought of change never occurred to them in that world of which the foundations seemed so secure, that closing phase of Victoria's reign, just before the sharp disillusionment of the South African War. 'Peace,' said one of them, 'brooded over the land, and we should not have believed a prophet had he told us that most of our group would fall in battle.' But a hideous swathe was to be cut through Edward's generation. Helmsley, Egerton and Amory were to be killed on the Western Front when the dream broke, and Charles Fisher at Jutland.

Of all these intimate friends Edward Talbot perhaps exercised the greatest influence over him. Their fathers had been lifelong friends, and one of the last actions of old Edward Talbot in 1934, when in his ninetieth year, was to attend the funeral of Edward's father. He had been the first Warden of Keble College, and it was there that Ted Talbot was born, and christened Edward Keble. He and Edward Wood had grown up together, and were to share digs at Oxford. Their friendship was to ripen from their Oxford days, and they spent many of their holidays together, at Oxford and at Hickleton, and later at Garrowby.

When the First War came, Talbot had been ordained, and served with great distinction as a chaplain, gaining the Military Cross and bar. Surviving the war, he became Superior of the Mirfield Community in Yorkshire, and he was often in those years at Garrowby, accepted almost as a member of the family, his visits only interrupted during the years when Edward was Viceroy of India. There were few secrets between these two men through the long unbroken years of friendship, and few griefs in which they could not solace one another. Both shared the religious beliefs of their fathers, but they shared also an intense zest for living. There was no crushing solemnity in their religious observances, no frigid disapproval of others. They enjoyed gaiety and sport and parties, and the badinage of old friends, so that it was a delight to be in their company.

*   *   *

All who met Ted Talbot succumbed to that irresistible spell. Tolerant, human and broadminded, yet level-headed and shrewd, he was a counsellor whom men sought for guidance and turned to instinctively in moments of sorrow. 'He was a vivacious, living man,' said a relation who had good cause to know him, 'whose religion was one of gaiety, happiness and laughter,' and a brilliant mimic who could hold dinner tables in thrall. He would check incipient heaviness in Edward with friendly malice, saying: 'Edward leaves too much to the Almighty,'[1] and to both these men their religion was a private and never an intrusive matter, by which they tried to regulate their conduct, but which they never sought to thrust upon others.

Edward spent his first two years in college, afterwards sharing digs at 15 Oriel Street with Talbot, Riddell, Egerton, Fisher and Baskerville. Paget was Dean, and Thomas Strong the tutor who taught Edward Aristotle's Politics. After his preliminary examination, Pass Mods, he decided to read for Honours in Modern History in which his tutor was Arthur Hassall of Christ Church. From this moment he planned his life with a method rare among young men, and adhered to his own rules with inflexible self-discipline. He had no intention of finding himself in the position so often occupied by undergraduates of entering his last year with no work accomplished, and being obliged to fight a desperate losing battle against time.

Lord William Percy noticed with envy that he never wasted his time, and that although he hunted and shot, and ran with the beagles, he always worked systematically. He was fond of brown sherry and introduced Percy to it, but after a glass or two would say, in a manner polite but dismissive: 'Now I am going to work.'[2]

He had already reached the stage, thought William Percy, when he liked everything to be exactly as he wanted it. He was astonishingly unselfconscious about his hand, but suffered from another affliction which soon yielded to treatment, telling his mother casually that he had been to his 'stammering mistress at Earls Court'. Wise beyond his years he led a well-ordered life. He enjoyed the pleasant lassitude of the summer term when he could play tennis and swim and explore new reaches of the river, but the turn of the season brought only an extension of his pleasure, for in winter there were shooting, beagling, and hunting which took him with the Bicester Hounds into the heart of the English Midlands, and with the Heythrop to the bleak stone-wall country round Stow-on-the-Wold and the heavy Gawcombe Vale. As always in the Wood family, there was a procession of animals through his Oxford life, the hunters Electra and James Pig, and Lord Lieutenant, the first horse he ever bought, and a dog Judy, brought to solace his evenings, who was sent home after being sick under the piano.

In February 1900 he described to his father, who was torn between pride and sickening anxiety, how he had ridden in his first steeplechase, the Christ Church Grind:

'My first experience of that form of amusement. I rode a horse for an old House man in the Old Members Race. It was rather a stiff course, one drop

---

[1] Lady Harlech to author.   [2] Lord William Percy to author.

of six foot, post and rails, wall, fifteen foot brook, wattles and all sorts of things. I rode a pretty good horse, but she was supposed to be going to refuse a good deal. She only refused twice over seventeen fences and did not come down over anything. The last fence was a brute with a very heavy take off. Helmsley came down head over heels at the six feet drop but he was fortunately none the worse. I got in third with a great race up the last field.'

In one compartment of his Oxford life he was thus a member of the hunting set at Christ Church. It was natural that he should also join the clubs to which the hunting men belonged, the Bullingdon, and the Christ Church club Loders, although he was a different kind of member from some other eldest sons cracking hunting whips and breaking windows in Peckwater Quad. It was no surprise to those who were aware of Edward's natural gaiety that he was by no means out of his element in these two famous hard-drinking clubs, and displayed no priggish disapproval of the wild habits of the others. Indeed he was not above participating in them himself, but with characteristic prudence. On Mafeking night each member of Loders drank a bottle of vintage port at the end of dinner to celebrate the Relief. All the members of the club became completely drunk, but Edward, with innate caution, went outside and tickled his throat to make himself sick, and thus avoided the worst effects of the evening.[1]

The Bullingdon, Loders, and Vincents, the athletes' club, to which he also belonged, were expensive luxuries, and on an allowance of £400 he found himself considerably in debt. He was mortified in having to apply for relief to his father to whom he wrote: 'I find I am worse than I thought I was and I should like to tell you exactly how it is.' He gave chapter and verse for all his expenditure, and begged his father to settle: 'I feel a perfect brute in being like this, and I shall quite deserve for you to be well annoyed with me.'

He was in fact not always staid in his amusements, and some of them caused anxiety to his father who had been terrified of his riding in the Grind and, after one misadventure, wrote in alarm: 'Your adventures on the Abingdon Road frighten me to death. My dearest child be careful and don't ride horses which run away against traction engines, and make you laugh so much. It would make me cry.'

Edward's main intellectual interest at Oxford was his study of history, and he did not take part in the debates at the Oxford Union. He had neither a background of historical study nor the habit of reading. As his work progressed, he found that the more he read, the more he realized how many questions there were of which he was 'absolutely and completely in ignorance'. The realization in no way depressed him. Calmly, methodically, and with no suggestion of panic he proceeded to remedy the defect. It is possible

[1] Lord William Percy to author.

that he took the opportunity which the study of history gave him to give particular attention to the history of the Church, and to consider the nature of his father's religious beliefs in the light of historical method. The Oxford Movement had quarried into history and emerged with a new religious interpretation of the Middle Ages. The theory of Anglican orders which his father had taught him, was based upon historical justification, and his study of the past may have enabled Edward's more stable mind to achieve a reconciliation of the conflicting demands of politics and religion with a far greater realism than was ever possible for his father.

Even as a boy he had kept his finger on the pulse of the Anglican movement, and, in spite of the excitement of his new life, it was never far from his thoughts at Oxford. He shared his father's indignation at the various assaults that were made upon it. In the nineties John Kensit was one of its most virulent opponents until a well-aimed brick ensured his martyrdom. It was his policy to send organized gangs to break up the services at ritualistic churches, and express their opinion of Anglo-Catholicism in violent and often obscene terms. Halifax, rightly anticipating an attack on his own church at Hickleton, wrote to Edward telling him how he was preparing for battle:

'Mr. Dalton and I have surveyed the ground and arranged a plan. I think it is a very good one. Mr. D. will be in the Tower where he *can't* be seen. The men, behind the walls of the wood-yard, where they *can* see the Tower and not be seen either. If the enemy attack the Crucifix the sign will be given and they will be caught and dealt with as they deserve. The question is whether we leave the Church open or not. If we do we have a splendid plan by which we should *lock* the enemy up *in* the Church. Salkeld and I as churchwardens by ourselves too. This is not yet *all* arranged. Mind you are back!'

Edward duly returned and the Kensitites appeared at Hickleton village in March 1900. They arrived in style in wagonettes, but their speeches were drowned by the banging of old coal scuttles and the blowing of horns by the villagers, inspired by fierce feudal loyalty. 'Whole thing most ridiculous,' commented Halifax, 'Edward and Agnes, and indeed all of us, burning for a fight.'

Halifax also kept his son in touch with the tribulations caused by the resident chaplain whose company he was forced to endure, and whose character he commented on with no trace of Christian forbearance: 'Mr. Golding Bird comes back today. He is a complete wreck. He is going away next week for a complete change. I think I never saw anyone so little able to see the proportion of things or who had got a more provoking little touch of spite and tiresomeness in his head. It seems to me he has got in him just that which certain idiots and almost mad people develop into a sort of perverse and childish spitefulness.'

Edward, a dutiful letter-writer as he was a son, kept his father informed of his progress:

'I have got started now on the 18th century, and think that I shall get interested in it when I know a little more about it. How very true Green's remarks seem to me to be, about the essential importance of grasping the "personality" of your people. The only way of getting hold of it. That is why to my mind all the tiresome Henry VIII history gets its interest from the *personal* characters of men like Cranmer and Thomas More etc.'

*   *   *

Edward was soon a young man of standing in the University. His manner had now become more mature and self-confident, but he still gave an absolute deference to the wishes of his father, however unreasonable they might be. He showed this respect in ways often tiresome and inconvenient for himself. Many young men would have resented the manner in which Halifax, in spite of his adoration, could not grasp the fact that Edward was now a man whose life was his own to arrange as he saw fit. When his father expressed pain at Edward accepting a shooting invitation during term, he at once abandoned it without protest. It was a little hard on him for his parents had just given him a pair of Purdey guns, but both were gratified by his submission:

'I am sorry, very sorry you had to resign or felt you ought to resign the joy of going after you had got leave,' wrote his mother, 'but I am sure you were quite right, and your Father was *so* pleased.'[1]

Even Edward's exemplary application to his work was not immune from occasional shafts of petulance from home. Remote as ever from true contact with Edward's world, they failed to realize how unusual he was among undergraduates in his steady and regular reading. When Lady Halifax told her husband what books Edward was now engaged on, Halifax had answered testily: 'Well of course that is much better than nothing only I don't call it much, and of course when people go up to the University they ought to try to improve their minds, and get all the knowledge they can, not merely just to pass exams.' She had protested that the summer term was not the best term for working, but Halifax replied: 'No, but then the hunting term isn't either.' 'I tell you this dearest,' concluded Edward's mother, 'not in any way to find fault, but just that if you can put in an extra hour regularly for reading history perhaps, how pleased he and I shall be, and how you will find the good of it.'[2]

After the loss of their first three sons it was natural that Halifax and his wife should watch Edward's health with a little more than their usual vague attention. He showed no signs of pulmonary weakness even in the dank air of the Thames Valley, and his illnesses were those which come to normal young men. He had, however, grown extremely tall. A few months before his

[1] Hickleton Papers, 20 November 1900.   [2] Ibid., 22 May 1900.

coming of age in April 1902, which was later celebrated with customary splendour, Halifax had written to his sister Emily: 'Edward is taller than ever, and though I say it who shouldn't, nicer and more delightful than ever. Coming out of Church this morning I said to old Mrs. Clark of Barmbro' who is always there: "Well, Mrs. Clark, he [Edward] don't grow any smaller!" "Nay, that he don't. He puts you quite in the shade. But never mind—there's good stuff in small parcels." Aren't our Yorkshire people delightful?'

By the spring of April 1903 Edward was working long regular hours for his Finals. It was a period of acute worry and frequent doubts about his own ability, but he was better balanced than most to endure it. He suffered from moments of depression which disturbed the expectant parents, and on 14 May his mother sent him an understanding note of encouragement:

'I was thinking from your last letter, that you seemed rather tired and out of heart. Well I suppose that just is natural enough at this stage of the work, and as for being out of heart—well you know, my darling, the value of the work is not to be judged by the results, but by the having *worked* and having done one's best—and that at all events you will have done, and that is what matters. I suppose no one ever got close to an exam without feeling like you!'

On 27 May Edward went to stay at Cuddesdon with the Bishop of Oxford. Four days later his mother wrote her 'positively last letter' to him before his ordeal. We can imagine those two adoring parents putting their heads together at Paraggi and deciding what they could best say at this grim moment, of sympathy and encouragement.

'My dearest Edward,
    This is positively the last letter I shall write you—now, because I shan't want to be breaking in upon your work, and disturbing you—only how we shall be thinking about you, and I shall be praying that it may not be very hot for your sake and the work . . . and now, my darling, all success and prosperity to you. Be sure you eat and sleep enough, and don't let yourself get run down.'

By 9 June Lady Halifax had come to the conclusion that she must reassure her son in his hour of need and convince him that even a poor showing in the Schools would make no difference to her confidence in him. It is almost as though she realized what an intolerable burden his father's dizzy hopes for Edward had placed upon the young man, and wished to spare him a too bitter self-reproach in the case of failure:

Paraggi,
9 June 1903.

'My own dearest Edward,
    We are, at least I know *I* am, constantly thinking of you! By the time you

get this your troubles will be mostly over, and whatever the result, will not make the slightest difference in our feeling. If you fail, we shall love you all the more for your disappointment! If the other thing—well we shall feel that success or non-success, you have worked your best, and there we leave it.'

When Edward arrived home in July he found that his sister Agnes had become engaged to George Lane Fox. It was a match which could not fail to fill Halifax and his wife with joy. George was the elder son of James Lane Fox of Bramham Park, Boston Spa, Yorkshire. James was a younger son who came into his father's estates as a result of his elder brother George, Halifax's intimate of Oxford days, being disinherited by his father on embracing the Roman Catholic faith. The brothers had arrived at a *modus vivendi*, George receiving an annual income from the estate and bearing no apparent ill-will.

It was a marriage of eminent suitability in Halifax's eyes. The Lane Foxes were an old-established county family of high standing in Yorkshire, devout, and living in a great house with gardens of legendary beauty, their superb beach avenues leading to enchanting vistas, and to temples sited with a master's eye.

George Lane Fox was thirty-three; Agnes, twenty-six, now fully recovered from a desultory love affair with Walter Riddell, and an unrequited yearning for Louis Egerton. George was indeed the personification of Halifax's ideal of an English country gentleman. Well born and high-principled, he was heir to an historic house and a great estate, Master of Fox-Hounds, Justice of the Peace, and an officer in the Yeomanry. He was a graduate of New College, Oxford, and had been called to the Bar. Indeed she could not have chosen a husband more acceptable as a son-in-law to her parents, and he quickly won their lasting affection and respect.

He and Edward were also to become as close as brothers. Edward was eleven years younger than George, but it is certain that he was not only deeply attached to him, but also valued his opinion on all the problems of life, politics, horses and hounds. George supplied several drafts from the Bramham Moor kennel for Edward's pack of harriers, looked out for and tried heavyweight hunters for him when he was abroad, and kept him *au fait* with local politics and Selection Committees. It was he who later advised Edward to put his name forward at Ripon, and the election of 1910 was to bring the brothers-in-law even more closely together, and Edward's frequent references in his family letters to 'the beloved George' bear witness to the sincerity of his affection.

Halifax and Lady Halifax were at Bovey Tracey when they got Agnes's letter saying how '*it*' had taken place at Mary's house, and there was great jubilation in the Wood household, the Halifaxes going to stay at Bramham with the Lane Foxes, of whom Lady Halifax reported: 'They were all more than kind, and 'tho the arrival and first evening was shy and alarming, now we are all quite at home.'

*   *   *

It must have seemed the beginning of the fulfilment of all Halifax's ambitions when Edward told him that he had taken a First Class in Modern History. It was also a success which tells us a great deal about Edward himself. The Headmaster of his preparatory school had never faltered in his belief in the boy's ability. At Eton Walter Durnford had, to be sure, qualified his praise by saying that Edward was 'not really clever', but he was thinking mainly of the Classics and recognized that his true abilities might well reveal themselves at Oxford when applied to History or Law. This had now happened, and Edward had accomplished a notable feat.

A First Class in a Final Honours School is above all else a real test of mental grasp. It was all the more remarkable an achievement in Edward's case in that he was not, in the true sense, a scholar and was not cast in the academic mould. The fact that he was not, as the word is now understood, an intellectual, his mind devoted exclusively to reading or to other aspects of learning, merely emphasizes its strong natural capacity. The details of his achievement are also of interest and show that his tutor and many of his friends regarded his First as a foregone conclusion. His tutor Arthur Hassall wrote to him on 1 August 1903:

'I expect you knew after your Viva Voce that you had got your 1st Class. *It was one of the best firsts* and you outdistanced the rest by yards! You have worked so steadily and continuously that I felt sure you would be rewarded. I once foretold to Lord Halifax what has now occurred; I feel inclined to make another prophecy, and to say that Walter Riddell and G. Baskerville will not be the only pupils of mine who hold dignities in other colleges. But this I fear will only come off after additional work on your part.'

'One of the best firsts too,' wrote Ted Talbot, 'that I'm told authoritatively,' and Thomas Strong had assured Louis Egerton that Edward was 'the best in'. The last sentence of Hassall's letter suggests that Edward might be applying for a Fellowship of some other college, and in fact he had been encouraged to storm the formidable ramparts of All Souls, thus making the supreme academic assault. His career was now approaching one of its decisive phases, and his father at this point had wise and generous advice to offer, showing that in the wider issues of life he was often a man of bold vision:

'I have also been thinking a good deal of you and your plans. It seems to me you have been working hard for some time and that a good rest and change would be a good thing for you. After this next Examination whether you get the Fellowship or not, you will be free, and it is a freedom that will not occur again in so complete a way. Would it not be a good thing to use it—

it might be more difficult to do so afterwards. County Councils, Yeomanry etc., all are impediments to getting away. It might perhaps be a good thing not to get entangled with all these till after you have corrected and supplemented the knowledge got from books by the knowledge which comes from *seeing* men and things.

'How would it be for you to go abroad for a year, to visit South Africa, Australia, and perhaps America with Japan thrown in? But I only throw that out as a suggestion for your consideration. I have no doubt I could get you introductions to other leading people both in our Colonies and America —in Paris, Rome, St. Petersburg etc. A great deal could be seen in a year or a little longer, and then with all this experience you might come home and energize on the London County Council, prepare to come into Parliament, and begin the course which, if you so please is to enable you to do great things for Him, the Catholic Church, England and the world generally.'[1]

It was a vision of great foresight, a suggestion for a Grand Tour of eighteenth-century amplitude. Everything that wealth and love can provide is to be enlisted to render this young man's way smooth. He does not have to ask for favours; they are pressed upon him:

'Then I should make Garrowby over to you as soon as you come back, and meanwhile your mother and I would economize for your benefit.' Not without reason Halifax adds: 'Seriously this is all at least worth thinking about.'

The parents were sent into transports of joy by the news that Edward had been elected a Fellow of All Souls in November 1903. The elation which Edward felt at this splendid achievement was no doubt great, but mainly for the joy he knew it would give his parents. We cannot doubt his sincerity when he assured his mother:

'You cannot possibly imagine what it means to me to have been able by God's help to do something to please you and Papa. It simply makes me as happy, and happier than I could have hoped to be.'

There was wild rejoicing at Garrowby, and Halifax wrote in ecstasy of the reactions of family, servants and friends, and uncovered his heart with pathetic humility in adoration of this wonderful son who had now realized the beginning of all his dreams: 'It was just a feeling of pure joy. I am indeed happy, happier than I deserve, for I never gave my father this pleasure. He was to his father what you are to me, a source of pride and delight, and I like to think that you are making up for my deficiencies and giving him too the pleasure which he would have been so pleased and happy if he could have had it at my hands, but of which I never gave him one drop.'

His mother was also stirred out of her habitual calm, and almost incoherent with emotion: 'Glorious news! Oh it is too delightful to speak of! I have never seen your father so pleased about anything, and as for me, well it is

[1] Hickleton Papers, 15 October 1903.

more than I can think of! We are indeed proud of you. . . . Oh I can think of nothing but *you* and *it*!'

She had every reason for pride. By winning, on his own merits, this blue riband of Oxford scholarship Edward had, as was truly said, 'gained admittance to one of the most privileged and select communities in the intellectual life of the nation. Here was a testimonial that would carry him through the preliminaries of any career he might care to take up'.[1]

[1] Campbell Johnson. Op. cit., p. 54.

CHAPTER IV

A VOYAGE OF DISCOVERY

EDWARD'S success at All Souls established beyond doubt his intellectual position. Questions as to whether Wood was merely an intensely religious young man with an average conventional mind could now be answered with finality: 'He took a First in History and won an All Souls Fellowship.' There are now no undergraduates at All Souls, called in its charter 'the college of all the Souls of the Faithful Departed', and the fellowships are filled up by elections from other colleges. By the statute of May 1882 provision was made for fifty fellowships of which several are tenable only in connection with University professorships or other offices. It was delightful for him to feel that he belonged now to this historic place which was to become a second home to him for fifty years, and which had been founded five hundred years ago as a memorial to Henry V and the men of Agincourt. He soon became intimate with every corner of it, the library, that noble panelled room with its exquisite ceiling glowing with angel corbels and heraldic panels carved by the hands of Elizabethan craftsmen; the Chapel with its superb hammer-beam roof, long muffled under plaster, and the succession of rooms in which the different wines were ceremoniously consumed after dinner.

Edward had been elected to All Souls together with a Northumbrian, Herbert Craster, who afterwards became Librarian of the Bodleian. Dougal Malcolm, who had been Captain of Walter Durnford's house when Edward first went to Eton, was one of their examiners. Sir William Anson, with Dicey the greatest of Oxford jurists, was Warden. It was inevitable that All Souls should perfectly suit Edward; that civilized atmosphere, the arguments erudite yet often frivolous, the sense of permanence, of companionship, of belonging. It was a smaller society than that of today, and fewer of its fellows were directly connected with the University in teaching or research. For most of them, however, the College was a rallying point at which they would often gather at week-ends, or for the more formal meetings at Whitsuntide or round All Saints' Day. It was a further source of pleasure to Edward that no distinction whatever was made for age or position, and that everyone met on terms of perfect equality.

Anson presided over 'these family parties, large and small, where good company, good talk, and good fare very soon combined to put even a nervous junior Fellow at his ease'. Even the College meetings had their lighter side. A long argument to decide between the alternatives of using a legacy to endow Research Fellowships or install a new electric light system, was ended by Raymond Asquith[1] who, drawing his gown about him, said he had put the matter to a simple test—which would he rather have in his room at night, a research Fellow or an electric light?

Edward, as Junior Fellow, found that it was his duty to make the mayonnaise sauce for dinner on Sunday nights, and decant the vintage port in Common Room, which was pulled round the table in a silver boat. Whatever his future plans were, he was expected to reside in college his first year:

'I accordingly did that, and dined most nights in the Common Room with the two or three elderly resident Fellows and Professors, waited upon by the faithful guardian of our Common Room comfort and a great character, Henry. This admirable institution, for such he was, frail in outward appearance, belonged to a school that I fear is almost extinct, and was entirely devoted to the College and its service.' Edward's companions on these occasions were usually the Domestic Bursar, Grant Robertson, Raleigh 'who had been legal member of Curzon's Council in India and who, except for W. P. Ker, had a greater gift for taciturnity than anybody I have ever known', Goudy, the Regius Professor of Civil Law, and Edgeworth, the Professor of Political Economy.

The conversation at these meals was desultory, but occasionally pierced by shafts of donnish levity. Edward remembered dining there after attending a young party at the amusements at Earls Court. He described how he had looped the loop on one of the machines, and how an old countrywoman had become so fascinated by the sensation that she had continued to repeat it until her money ran out. The Professor of Civil Law was somewhat disturbed by this story, and said: 'But, Wood, was it not embarrassing for all those who might be near that a lady should be seen in so unconventional a position?' To which Edgeworth, before the words were out of his mouth, replied: 'Come, come, Goudy, you mistake the situation; you do not detect any impropriety in the fact that Mrs. Seddon [wife of the New Zealand Prime Minister] is at present walking upside down in New Zealand.'

Edward found such talk and such an atmosphere highly congenial on these quiet week-day evenings. On Saturday nights there would often be a larger gathering. Fellows of the College, like Leo Amery, now busy and successful politicians, found a charm in this friendly place as compelling as Edward himself was to discover as the years passed. At a dinner table much fuller than usual, Amery would take the lead in the popular College pastime of trying to extract a definite opinion from Edgeworth on any subject. Some of the finest brains in England probed his defences remorselessly but in vain. 'He was proof against every approach; frontal attack, persuasion, guile, all were alike ineffective and the game therefore never ended.'

Edward, however, presents a somewhat strange figure in this academic

[1] Son of the Liberal Prime Minister Herbert Asquith.

setting. Perhaps he was dimly aware of a certain incongruity, when he wrote to his friend Ludy Amory in the breezy manner he reserved for his intimates:

'I am paying for my hunting expenses now by taking three pupils!! Pretty good flats they must be, but what of that? My colleagues among the professors, I think, regard me as a lazy, horsy, swashbuckling ruffian. Last night I was narrating the story of the fox on the roof and saying that I thought he had probably known his way about the farmyard for some time when one of them nips me with: "You would infer then, Wood, that he had been accustomed to browse on Chanticleer?" For the rest of dinner I was powerless.'

One of the many institutions of All Souls was the College walk on Sunday in the country, usually led by W. P. Ker. Sometimes under his guidance they would visit the haunts of the Scholar Gypsy, still brooding in pastoral seclusion, and 'cross the stripling Thames at Bab-lockhithe', or go by dusty lanes to Stanton Harcourt and that lovely reach of the river at Nuneham, lunching well at the inns and slaking their thirst on draught beer before returning in the late afternoon, tired and ready for Common Room tea and a drowsy Evensong in Chapel. Edward hunted regularly twice a week, sometimes setting out for the meet with his tutor Hassall, or with Arthur Johnson the College Chaplain, who, like himself, preserved an easy harmony between the Church and the chase.

It was in order to finance his hunting that he took the pupils he had described to Amory, teaching them history with a certain trepidation: 'With the more sensitive conscience which comes with years I wonder at my own presumption. . . . One of them I remember was Neil Primrose,[1] who used to come once or twice from New College, and not infrequently lapsed into dreamless slumber while I discoursed.' During these sessions he sometimes 'felt like an uneasy swimmer trying to tread water and wondering how soon he is going to drown'.

In January 1904 he was provided with a much needed experience of the seamy side of life by accompanying a judge on circuit in North Wales as marshal, an excursion which must have considerably broadened his mind. He was irked, however, by the company of the judge's wife and daughter, writing to Ludy Amory: 'Lady P. and Grace P. are on circuit with us. The latter is a decided trial, and I feel suspicious that she is designed for matrimonial purposes, but that is not the kind of bait for this fish. Here we have got some rather interesting cases, wounding, rape, arson etc. My judge has already done one very good thing—given a night poacher three years. Good job.'

*   *   *

While we notice the humility in Edward's character, and how deeply his life was enriched by religion, we cannot fail to observe also the manner in

[1] Son of Lord Rosebery.

which great possessions fell successively, and without the slightest exertion on his part, into his hands. The doting father had already bequeathed Garrowby to him. Temple Newsam had been bestowed on him by Aunt Emily, and fortune was to lavish another warm caress on this golden youth, when her large London house 88 Eaton Square was assured to him after his father's death. Halifax wrote from Marseilles on 13 March in the following year:

'We have had an offer of 15,000 for 88 [Eaton Square]. There seems great difficulty in getting rid of 79, but I have made a calculation. I think if we can get an extension of the lease of 88 from the Duke of Westminster for 60 years, paying £5,000 down and a rent of 200 or 300 a year it would be worth while. This would represent a rent of about 400 or 500 a year less than the 200 we pay for 79 and secure you an excellent house in London for the rest of your life.

'You see you will be 80 in 60 years and then probably the question of a house which you will want in the meantime when you are in the Cabinet and Prime Minister, will not signify. I am quite determined that you *are* to be Prime Minister and reunite England to the Holy See, and many other things besides. So 88 and the opportunity it will give you for entertaining will be a step in that direction. Dearest Edward what a joy and comfort you are! The apple of our eyes and the happiness of our life.'[1]

The young man who had completed his University career was well aware of how much he owed to Oxford. Hitherto his education had been a period of joyless restraint. There had been unhappiness at that school at Reigate, and in Eton, bored by the cult of athletics and longing for the freedom of his Yorkshire home with its dogs and horses, he had found scant inspiration. There had been something a little desiccated in him that craved refreshment, and had found it in the leisured ease and mellow wisdom of Oxford with the past all about her. There was already apparent in his manner the effulgence of a devastating natural charm. We should mark well this charm, for it remained with him through life. Later he became conscious of it, and took pleasure in its exercise, and it became so strong a factor in him that it resembled great beauty in a woman. When a man possesses it he can come to feel that he has only to see a person and talk to him to bring him to his point of view, and thus experience a false sense of having gained his point, and to some in the years ahead it would seem that this seductive gift had done much to shape his character. He was exceptionally tall, and the face in repose was inclined to a gravity which would suddenly be transfigured by a smile of extraordinary sweetness. There was already about him, in spite of diffidence, an impression not of arrogance but of patrician detachment, as of one sheltered in aristocratic seclusion from the common world. No trace of *angst*, that scourge of a later age, disturbed the serenity of his nature.

*   *   *

[1] Hickleton Papers, 13 March 1905.

In 1904, when his probationary year at All Souls was over, he set out on the Grand Tour with his friend Ludy Amory. By the generosity of his father he found himself almost in the position of one of the young milords of the eighteenth century making his leisurely progress through Europe by coach to absorb the sophistication of the European capitals, and an artistic knowledge and manners more suave than could be acquired at home. Edward, however, was not concerned, as they were, with the picture galleries of Italy or the temples of Greece, or the political turmoil of Europe. With Queen Victoria but recently dead, and the shrill trumpet of Kipling proclaiming the white man's burden, he had gone to study the problems of Empire at a crucial moment of organic change, and it was his fortune as a young inquirer with no knowledge of Imperial politics, to witness what was in fact the genesis of the British Commonwealth.

Great constitutional experiments had their beginnings at this moment of history. Edward went first to South Africa where he joined his mother and father who were staying with his sister Mary, now married to Captain Sutton who had an appointment in Cape Town. Halifax had enjoyed his journey to the Cape in the *Galeka*. His Italian servant had chased the cook round the table with a carving knife, and he himself had asked the Captain to put an over-amorous couple in irons one on each side of the ship. Edward and his parents travelled a little together in wagons drawn by plodding oxen, but they were soon disturbed by the news of Aunt Emily's death, which caused Edward, as heir to Temple Newsam, to break his tour and return to England.

In February 1905 he rejoined Ludy Amory at Port Said and they continued together their journey to India where they stayed with Lord Curzon in Calcutta. Here he made the rounds of the places with which he was later to become so familiar, Delhi, Agra, Benares, Cawnpore, Rawalpindi, Peshawar, the Khyber. They returned to Bombay to take ship for Ceylon, Australia and New Zealand: 'After a few weeks in Australia, gaining first impressions of Melbourne, Sydney and North Queensland, recapturing the mental picture of *Robbery Under Arms* . . . we moved on through the beauties of Tasmania to an unpleasant sea-passage to New Zealand.'[1] Here they began their month's visit to Lyttelton in South Island, and ended it at Auckland in the North.

At Auckland he lost his travelling companion. Ludy Amory departed for England by San Francisco, while Edward decided to turn in his tracks and make another visit to Australia, and thence home passing again through South Africa. At Sydney he was introduced to the leading political figures by the Governor-General, Lord Northcote. He met Deakin, Reid, and the Labour leader, Watson. The arguments of these men, so forthright, so different from any he had heard before, made a strong impression on him, and lent breadth to the tentative views he had already formed in England of

[1] Halifax. Op. cit., p. 60.

Imperial questions. He became aware that there was another point of view, and men who could express it in positive terms:

'From them I had my earliest lessons in the several shades of thought concerning the relations between Great Britain and what it was not yet improper to call the Colonies in other parts of the world. The relationship now seems a very obvious instrument for the reconciliation of independence and unity, so obvious in fact as to leave it a matter for perpetual surprise that we should only have been able to recognize it as such after an unnecessary revolution.'

It was as Northcote's guest at Government House that Edward's innocent eyes first fell with instinctive repulsion upon the spectacle of a woman smoking, and then only in private:

'It was a Sunday afternoon, and Lady Northcote asked me to come and talk to her in the sitting room. And when we got there and had made ourselves comfortable, she asked if I would be shocked if she lit a cigarette. I, of course, said "no": but none the less was greatly shocked, and found my opinion of my most kind and delightful hostess for the moment sadly lowered.'

Leaving Australia Edward again forgathered with his parents at the Suttons' house at Cape Town. He was taken on an expedition into Basutoland on which the wretched Lady Halifax was driven into agonizing activities by her husband who informed his daughter Agnes: 'Your Mama rode twenty or thirty miles a day, up and down precipices and across rivers, over, down and up dongas, and galloped for miles across the illimitable veldt in a way that was truly astonishing.'[1]

They travelled in a primitive motor-car to Kimberley where they descended in a cage the shaft of a diamond mine, and from Kimberley by train to Bulawayo, and on to the Victoria Falls, whose majesty rendered Halifax almost speechless with ecstasy, but did not prevent him bathing there in defiance of warnings of the crocodiles which lay like logs of wood in the green water.

They visited Rhodes's grave in the great hush of the Matopos. They explored Ladysmith and the battlefields of the war. Edward, to his regret, was left in Ladysmith, to return to England and missed the great excitement of his parents' journey, the trek across the Transkei by ox-wagon and Cape carts to that paradise Pondoland. This exquisite place moved Halifax as the first glimpse of the old Tahiti must have moved the visitor from another world:

'A most lovely country. Imagine all the wolds magnified a hundredfold, all grass, no enclosures anywhere, wood, forests, rivers, beautiful mountains in the distance, interesting valleys—a glorified Thixendale and Givendale, but glorified beyond conception and with the opportunity of riding for ever and ever, in all directions and wherever you like. . . . The garden full of red

[1] Lockhart. Op. cit., Vol. II, p. 172.

Natal lilies, daturas, sweet verbena, sweet geranium, passion flowers and white lilies, with below in a sort of marsh acres of arums.'[1]

*   *   *

In this tour, as Halifax had wisely foreseen, Edward was able to combine the pleasure of travel with valuable political experience. In Australia he saw the fruits of the great Act of Federation which on 1 January 1901 had united in a Federal Commonwealth the peoples of New South Wales, Victoria, South Australia, Queensland, Tasmania and Eastern Australia. In India he had seen the incessant labours of a Viceroy who symbolized an age that still believed that England could hold the gorgeous East in fee, and who restored to the Indian people the beauty of their desecrated monuments.

Above all, in South Africa he had watched that great work of reconstruction which affected the whole country and was mainly the task of Milner and the dedicated young men he had brought with him from England. Halifax had lunched with Milner shortly before his long-suffering wife was 'hauled and dragged' by him to the top of Table Mountain. He left Milner's presence completely under the spell. That Edward was more cautious in approach is suggested by the fact that although he must have shared their ideals in many respects, he did not attach himself to the young disciples who were helping Milner to bring order and tranquillity to the land, but we shall see his career taking a course which brought him to a certain extent under their influence.

Milner had cast his net wide. The doyen of the 'Kindergarten' was Patrick Duncan, the first South African ever to hold the office of Governor-General in the Dominion of his birth. Milner and his staff lived in a red-brick villa in the suburbs of Johannesburg, and among his secretaries was Geoffrey Dawson whose conduct as Editor of *The Times* in the locust years between the two wars was to be, after his death, the subject of a blistering analysis by the staff of his own newspaper. There was also a group with special duties assigned to them, in which were included Lionel Curtis, destined for great influence in constitutional changes to come, Robert Brand with his brilliant financial gifts, and Philip Kerr who was to become Lord Lothian and Ambassador in Washington. Dougal Malcolm, Edward's examiner at All Souls, John Buchan and Edward Grigg were also members of the group.

It was an impressive company and its loyalty to Milner was a hard cement that endured long after the South African period was over in the form of a côterie who created the *Round Table* in England. All of them in the early days in South Africa seemed so inevitably destined for greatness that it would have been a bold man who had declared then that it was their careers that would fall into comparative seclusion, and that their visitor, the quiet and unobtrusive Edward Wood, driven by no discernible ambition, would win the power and glory.

[1] Lockhart. Op. cit., Vol. II. p. 172.

He rounded off his Imperial experience by a visit to Canada in 1907 with Louis Egerton, who in September sent Lady Halifax a gay account of their adventures from Winnipeg:

'Just a line to tell you what I expect Edward has not told you; he is a perfect companion, as always; but as a traveller, he has no equal; he never loses his tickets; never loses his temper with the railway people who are exceedingly impertinent and inattentive; and, above all, he never loses an opportunity of gaining information, or an opportunity of getting introduced to a lady. Even last night, listening in the hotel here to a band, the hotel proprietor came up and asked him to come and be introduced to some beautiful young ladies. Of course he promptly accepted, and the next thing I saw was Edward surrounded by a bevy of entrancing females, giving them all his card.

'I dare say he told you of our dinner with the Lieut.-Governor Sir D. McMillan the first night of our arrival; his [Edward's] luggage had not arrived so he had to borrow his evening clothes from the *hotel proprietor*!! The evening coat, the latter declared, was of the latest cut from New York, and had a grey waistcoat and a sham bow tie "ensuite". It was a perfect coat, viz:—padded shoulders, square tails, and a cross breasted front; the trousers were up to his knees; and my shoes to finish with, held on by rubber rings. I think the Government House authorities thought we were a circus troupe, the funny clown and me the circus ring master . . . Edward has also had a great success with an actress from Toronto. . . .'[1]

The fastidious young man had often to live rough on this trip, sharing a bed with Louis Egerton in a room eight feet square in a village in the Rockies, and anointing himself with flea powder. Worse befell him on a ranch in Calgary: 'I never was so uncomfortable in my life only keep this to your-selves—FILTHY—and raw meat to eat. How can people be content, being men, to live like pigs?'[2]

He attended a duck shoot which might have ended in tragedy, but which gave him an opportunity of drawing a comparison between 'half-breeds' and white men at moments of crisis unfavourable to the former:

'It all came out right but it might have been a great nuisance if it hadn't. I swamped with my guide in a canoe in the dark in a storm, and we might have had to stay out all night, paddling aimlessly, I suppose, to keep our-selves from freezing. He was very pessimistic—explaining to me that there were only two alternatives. Frozen or drowned. I suggested a third, but he had no use for it! How funny it is that these half-breeds, however experienced they are and however much they have roughed it and knocked about, never have the self-control etc. that we have. Louis's man was simply chattering with fright and almost useless.'[3]

[1] Hickleton Papers, 9 September 1907.   [2] Ibid., 5 October 1907.
[3] Ibid., 15 October 1907.

Like many travellers, his most abiding memory of this first visit to Canada was looking down on the St. Lawrence River from the ramparts of the old citadel, beholding in imagination Wolfe's men landing and the place where the little band climbed up to the Heights of Abraham, and as he stood on that decisive field of battle and contemplated the scene of Wolfe's death, he felt a consciousness of the past which no other experience of his travels had yielded.

The Governor-General, Lord Grey, grandson of the Grey of the Reform Bill, was related to Lord Durham, author of the report that bears his name and which determined the future of Canada. It was the Governor-General's tremendous vitality, his incessant chatter on every conceivable subject that arose, that left the most durable memories of Canada on Edward's mind, and he felt gratitude to him for presenting him to the Canadian Prime Minister, Sir Wilfred Laurier, whose image lingered in the young man's mind, dignified and graceful, 'instinct as it seemed to be in the setting of Quebec, with the glamour and romance of eighteenth-century France. . . . I have never forgotten my short meeting with Sir Wilfred Laurier, and though I have been to Canada and Quebec several times since, the first sight of it remains as sharply cut in my memory as it was clear to bodily sight on that August evening in 1907'.[1]

[1] Halifax. Op. cit., p. 61.

CHAPTER V

POLITICS AND MARRIAGE

WHEN Edward had returned from the Grand Tour in 1905 and examined the political scene, he found little that tempted him to enter it. He saw in the Conservatives a party which had long outstayed its welcome and become an object of deadly tedium to the people. He could also see that they were struggling against a formidable combination of slogans. Four main issues, the catchphrase of 'dear food' which was the Liberal counterblast to Tariff Reform, the teetotallers' hatred of the licensed trade and the unpopular Education Act—all these, with other bitter draughts for the Tories, were drawn from the same contaminated well; then there was the Chinese slavery[1] fiction, which was not likely to impress a level-headed young man who had just made a dispassionate examination of conditions in South Africa. Fresh from this calm survey, the partisanship he found at home and the wild distortions of party strife must have seemed to him meaningless and even repulsive.

He was not one of the bold spirits who saw in the troubled political scene and the distress of his party the opportunity for a sudden personal triumph. Nor was he one of those men who were uplifted by a shouting crowd at the hustings and who caught fire from their insults. Indeed he only entered these grimy lists with reluctance. There was also in his character a strong vein of prudence. He had seen the fate of his brother-in-law George Lane Fox, for whom he had spoken at silent village meetings in the Barkston Ash division. George had been beaten in a by-election in 1904 before being returned at the General Election of 1906. Apart from these dictates of caution, he probably felt a sense of duty to his College All Souls, and to the opportunities it afforded him for further study.

For the next two years, therefore, he kept away from politics, and devoted himself to academic work on historical and religious subjects. In April 1907 he made a visit with his father to La Croix, and on the channel steamer fell in with Dr. Paget, the Bishop of Oxford. Halifax and the Bishop eyed each other with suspicion, and Edward, aware of his father's impulsive nature, thought that an indecorous quarrel might break out between the holy men on deck. He described to his mother how 'he and Papa, after a preliminary reconnoitring of each other from a distance, settled down and had a real good

[1] Unskilled labourers were imported from China to work in the South African mines in conditions which were represented by the Liberal Party in 1906 as being barely distinguishable from slavery.

talk. Exactly like two dogs who are not sure whether they will fight or not and so walk round each other making up their minds on the subject, until they finally settle it is less trouble to be amicable'.

At La Croix, a little village lying between Hyères and Fréjus, they found a small hotel which adjoined a Franciscan Missionary Rest House, where each morning they went to Mass at six o'clock. This friendly place brought memories of an earlier visit when he was reading for his Finals when the curé at the little village church had admonished his parishioners: 'Monsieur l'Evêque would be coming on Thursday. . . . Les jeunes filles de la paroisse would walk in the procession. . . . On ne doit pas demander trop aux petits garçons. Ainsi je demande seulement qu'ils soient un peu moins sales qu'à l'ordinaire.'

For the moment two preoccupations filled his mind. The first was his only attempt at historical authorship, when he agreed to write a short biography of John Keble. This book was designed as one of the series 'Leaders of the Modern Church', published by A. R. Mowbray between 1905 and 1909. They were under the general editorial supervision of G. W. E. Russell who contributed volumes on Pusey and Liddon. The editor had rightly concluded that ecclesiastical biography had but a limited popular appeal, and that general interest in the subject was likely to be submerged in the arcana of theological and ritualistic controversy. The publishers felt that this form of biography 'is apt to lose in attractiveness and interest by reason of the technical and professional spirit in which it is generally handled'. They held the sanguine belief that by entrusting the new series of short biographies exclusively to laymen the lives of these bygone churchmen might be invested with a more popular appeal.

Lord Halifax's lifelong High Church interests, as well as his own, made Edward Wood an understandable choice for this task, and his Fellowship of All Souls gave him the necessary leisure and distinction to carry it out. The choice of author, however, did little to fulfil Russell's hope that the subject would stand out more clearly as a human being by the subordination of the theological disputes that surrounded him, for Edward did not write this book in the manner of a layman. Nothing is more striking in it than his complete grasp of the complicated religious issues that were obsessing the Tractarians at the end of the nineteenth century, which suggests that during his reading for the Schools he had made a particular study of the question.

The book is written in adequate but uninspiring prose, and although it shows evidence of great labour, must be considered a disappointment. Well versed as he was in the issues at stake, the author was lacking in the technical equipment to bring alive these dead controversies which had generated such passions in their own day. To read this book now is like wandering in some old museum, but out of the cracks and crannies of its dusty walls pushes here and there a lonely flower, fragrant and enduring. There was much in Keble's story to appeal to Edward, and many aspects of his life for which he must have felt particular sympathy. He found charming Keble's love for his country vicarage, his rides from it to Oxford on horseback, his joy in country life, and his pleasure in the dogs and horses which were also so much a part of Hickleton and Garrowby. Placed as he was himself, hesitant after the Grand Tour to enter politics too quickly, he could understand the reluctance with which Keble left his rural peace for Oxford to take part in the no less bitter controversy provoked by the Oxford Movement. He had another affinity with Keble, too, which he was lacking with Newman and Pusey, that they were both brought up from childhood in a Catholic tradition. They could both, unlike Newman, contemplate changes of which they did not approve, in the belief that it was their duty to remain in the position where God had placed them, as long as they were free to maintain their own faith and enjoy the right of protest, and not to abandon it as Newman did by going over to Rome.

But these bygone issues are never brought to life in Edward's somewhat laborious prose. The ashes are still cold when he has finished stirring them. Keble emerges most clearly from the great triumvirate; his humour, his humility, his love of children and desire for country repose were all qualities that Edward could appreciate. It was not to be expected that he would understand Newman. The poetry, the mysticism, the torturing self-doubts were all a closed book to that happy and uncomplicated young man whose future lay rosy before his eyes.

Some of his own early character may be discovered in this book. We see it in the caution with which he picks his way through dangerous shoal waters. He is so objective that we are left in some doubt as to what his own opinion is. His whole method of presentation seems designed to avoid unpleasantness. There is also a certain lack of lucidity in his discussion of the Oxford Movement, so that a reader ignorant of the period would find it difficult to grasp both what the Movement stood for, and what were the 'liberal' threats to the Church which had called it into being, and would close the book with only a blurred outline in his mind of what it contained; yet the caution, the hatred of sudden instinctive action, which Edward shared with Keble, emerges significantly from its pages:

'To Keble hasty action was the height of folly. As he once wrote to Moberley, "Hurry is essentially a cruel thing." There are few things more dangerous than the constant anxiety for doing something definite. Many diseases may only be handled with gentleness and caution; violent treatment, the determination to force an issue at all costs, will result in nothing but catastrophe.

'The advocates of heroic measures should also recollect that although principles may be ignored or slighted, or even for the moment apparently destroyed, nothing can really affect them as long as their holders retain their faith in these principles and in themselves. Nor is it always possible to do anything but defend in face of attack. The only people who seemed to do anything definite in those years were Newman and Manning, and those who followed them to Rome. That Keble refused to be coerced into this kind of action, but was content to possess his soul in patience, and to appear in the eyes of the great majority of the undiscerning to do nothing, is the best tribute to his memory.'[1]

*   *   *

The continuity of his work on Keble was sometimes disturbed by a characteristic rival, the raising and hunting of a new pack of harriers at Garrowby. As life at Hickleton was regulated by the Church seasons and the racing calendar, so were the labours on Keble to be solaced by hunting. These hounds, which Edward hunted himself, were started in 1906 and survived for twenty years. His great-grandfather, Sir Francis Wood, had hunted his own pack of harriers in his day at Hickleton, and now Edward's father welcomed their revival.

Lord Middleton, the local Master of Foxhounds, also gave the scheme his blessing, and Edward was given odd hounds and drafts from other packs by his friends until he had assembled about sixteen or seventeen couple. Everything proceeded smoothly with summer exercise and preparations for the opening meet, which was planned for the end of harvest so that the farmers could take part, a lawn meet with cakes and sloe gin handed round in the orchard. The kennel huntsman and whipper-in was Atkin, one of the frankest and most affectionate of the Wood retainers, with a wonderful voice and holloa, but the hounds were a motley crew and on this first public occasion, with the eyes of the world upon them, they proved uncontrollable.

It was Edward's intention to draw a place called the Preserve, and he told Atkin: 'We'll draw those fields there.' Atkin had replied: 'You'll draw wherever they go when they get through that gate,' and when the unruly pack broke into the Preserve they found many hares and rabbits and other animals which they chased indiscriminately. Edward and Atkin got half the pack back to kennels, and eventually had all of them coupled. It had been a disastrous beginning.

'As soon as the temptation in the shape of a rabbit offered as we were moving to our objective, the whole party was off like a bomb, scattering in every direction and ignoring every attempt by authority to reassert itself. The wider the disorder spread, the more there was to hunt . . . hares, rabbits, cock pheasants, other dogs, an occasional sheep; little was lacking to make my humiliation bitter and complete . . . and we were eventually reduced to tying hounds up one by one to trees until we had collected a small party, which we then took back by hand to the kennels.'

[1] Edward Wood, *John Keble*, p. 236.

Edward took ruthless measures against the offenders. Five couple, the ringleaders, were destroyed by the vet, and he began breeding his own hounds from a Devonshire strain. They were the old West Country 'English' harrier, nearly white with a few patches. Edward became deeply engrossed in this new possession, and he put Atkin in charge of the stable with four men under him. He would summon Edward on hunting mornings by throwing pebbles at the windows of his room. They would hunt two days a week, always keeping behind the foxhounds in their meets, over a stretch of country twenty miles by twelve. Edward loved to take the harriers out himself, or with an Oxford friend, in the park for exercise, and would sometimes call to Atkin to bring on the horn to him when hounds were chasing hares.[1]

Keble and Pusey were insubstantial phantoms that day when they met at Wetwang, and six hounds jumped out of the truck squeezing through the cover, until at last Edward and Atkin caught them in time for the meet. The pack improved as they gradually weeded out the bad hounds, and Edward would take them far afield, sometimes to Hickleton or Temple Newsam. The delight he experienced in these harriers was partly the pride of personal ownership of a private pack which he could handle as he wished, and partly due to that profound love of hunting and horses which was not to him a mere relaxation but an integral part of his life. Nothing short of his appointment as Viceroy of India could induce him to part with these hounds, which were then dispersed among other packs.

The other great preoccupation led to the wisest decision of his life. It not only ensured a perfect domestic happiness, but was also of an importance to his career impossible to exaggerate. He became engaged to be married. His parents had long been awaiting such an event, only doubting the existence of a paragon worthy of their son. His mother particularly had watched the engagements of Edward's friends with mounting irritation. It was intolerable that her wonderful son should be condemned by his own diffidence to be so often outstripped in the race. She had thought it an opportunity prodigally wasted when Fra Wood became engaged to Lady Dorothy Legge in 1907:

'I cannot—oh—I cannot have you always cut out by someone else—and losing the pearls. My darling boy, I must pour out my heart to you. You *must* make haste and give us such a daughter-in-law as we can take to our hearts and love. We would love to cherish your choice indeed, but there are some pearls greater than others.'[2]

A few days later an encounter with this radiant couple, Fra and Dorothy, reminded her painfully of Edward's laggardly conduct:

'Fra and Dossie have just been here, and I am afraid both your father and I felt as though we could twist your neck! There! She did look so engaging and nice!'[3]

Halifax also regarded this marriage with a twinge of regret for Edward's

[1] C. Atkin to author.   [2] Hickleton Papers, 1907.   [3] Ibid., 10 June 1907.

sake, although his dynastic feelings were satisfied by the bride's irreproach-able lineage: 'Such a charming daughter to have in the home. All they could most wish—a good stock on both sides—all the Legges are good excellent people. Without a scrap of vulgarity which is not always the case.'

He made it plain to Edward that he expected a great deal of the lady of his eventual choice, but that he, too, had been disappointed by squandered opportunities:

'I only hope that when the time comes you may marry someone I may like as much in all ways, but I am afraid there are not many such. I believe I am old fashioned in my ideas but there are some marriages for you I could not condone and which would make everything else in the world a matter of indifference. I *won't* have you cut out by others and always come off second best.'[1]

Most of the thoughts that the parents could spare from their devotions were now concentrated upon Edward, on his private happiness and the triumphs to come. When so much that was selfish had been submerged in this consuming love it was natural that Halifax should await the next vital step in his son's life with acute anxiety. Having placed him upon such an exalted plane, having made him the repository of such a devouring affection, and regarded him as symbolical of every hope, he needs must demand in his mate qualities almost beyond human attainment. She must be devout and beautiful, gifted in mind, tender yet strong, of enduring fidelity. She must bubble with the vivacity and wit he loved, and be suffused with a delightful warmth:

'You are an absolute angel and that is why I want this angel to find another angel equally angelic. I dare say you are quite right and intend to believe it and indeed do believe it. But I do see that every angel which is snapped up leaves fewer possible angels and I don't want to come down to mere mortals —No. I must have a real archangel and then I shall adore it to my heart's content and shall feel I have nothing left to wish you except a nest-full of little angels.'

*   *   *

Even the Halifax parents could scarcely have hoped that Edward would in fact make a choice which would prove so delightful to them. Nineteen hundred and nine was a memorable year for Edward, for in it the life of Keble was published, and towards its end he married Lady Dorothy Onslow. It was in the autumn of 1908 that his friend Dougal Malcolm introduced Edward to her in the refreshment room at Berwick-on-Tweed station where they met by chance when changing trains on their way to stay for a ball at Kelso, and Edward remembered having tea with her in those grimy and improbable surroundings.

[1] Hickleton Papers, 14 June 1907.

AT OXFORD

IN LORD
LIEUTENANT,
1904

Dorothy's father, the fourth Earl of Onslow, held office four times[1] between 1887 and 1911, and had been Governor-General of New Zealand. At the time of his daughter's engagement he was Chairman of Committees in the House of Lords in the Liberal administration. Edward was to find him sympathetic in every way as a father-in-law, and always ready to offer him advice on his political life. This advice was sometimes stultifying in application, as when Lord Onslow begged Edward to choose some subject and make himself a specialist in it. He might, for example, master the detailed figures of the several items that make up the cost of running motor buses. 'Thus I should be able to put my finger, and the finger of Parliament on the cost of fares and correct anything that might be wrong. But I am afraid I did not adhere to this line very long, and Lord Onslow was very tolerant of my defection.'

There was no diffidence or hesitation in this proposal of marriage, and Edward was so excited that he burst into his father's bedroom at 2 a.m. on a July morning, and woke him with the news. Halifax gave his version of it in a letter to his daughter Mary:

'It happened last night at Lady Esther Smith's. Before it happened she, Lady Dorothy, and Edward were talking together, and she said, among other things, that she had been to a fortune-teller with some others, and she was sorry she had as it gave her a shock. After the event, Edward having said he did not approve of fortune-tellers, asked her what the shock was; she said the fortune-teller had seen *his* name in her hand. There's for you! What do you say to that? Edward is, I believe, going to bring the young lady to see us today. Everyone says she is delightful.'

It has been remarked that Edward's choice of Dorothy Onslow was the happiest decision of his life, and it is certain that in the wives of the great men of the past whose characters and actions could make or mar their husbands' careers, it is impossible to find one who more closely approached perfection. About almost all human beings there remains in the estimate of their friends, however favourable, a certain measure of reserve. About Dorothy there is none.

With astonishing unanimity they believe that of the two partners, and in spite of Edward's many virtues, it was she who had the greater share of the noblest human qualities. As her husband's career advances we shall see at his side a woman who, although endowed with an admirable brain and incomparable charm, deliberately subordinated all this to the solace of his private, and the advancement of his public life. It was particularly noticeable to those who were close to these two people that Dorothy practised an habitual self-effacement in her relations with Edward which at times he took for granted but, when reminded, was contrite. Sometimes, thought one friend who loved

---

[1] He had been Under-Secretary of State for the Colonies, Parliamentary Secretary to the Board of Trade, Under-Secretary of State for India, and President of the Board of Agriculture.

him, he was monstrously selfish, but she doubted whether any man married to Dorothy could have avoided such a condition.

By laughing off in him any tendency to undue earnestness, she was able to steer Edward into a far more human course than he might otherwise have followed, and the atmosphere which she created round her, gay, happy and informal, did much to dispel her husband's natural aloofness. She was one of those who could experience periods of immense grandeur without the slightest alteration in the basic simplicity of their character. She did not care a jot for privilege or position, yet when the occasion demanded could be a hostess of enchanting grace and an organizer of the highest efficiency.

It was natural to her character to treat those who worked under her, however humble, in precisely the same manner she would adopt with an ambassador or a Head of State, and she created for these subordinates an atmosphere of a family party at which everyone said and did what they wished. It is not strange that they became her slaves for life.

'I was struck,' said Dorothy, speaking of her early impressions of Edward, 'by his expression, which seemed to make one realize his personality and strength of character.' She also noticed that he was a tremendous worker and had a horror of wasting time, which she attributed to the early discipline which had made him conscientious and thorough, and serious in his view of life, and to the fact that he had early inherited a large property from his Aunt Emily and assumed heavy responsibilities. The fear of 'wasting time' was then almost an obsession, and was to continue until he learnt the art of delegation.

She noticed at once both his humility and his caution: 'He rarely acted on impulse or gave hasty answers, and usually, if asked his advice or opinion about something even quite unimportant, he would pause before he answered, but it did not take him long to make decisions, when he had carefully weighed the problem before him.

'When I first knew him he was very diffident about himself, and to the day of his death he remained one of the humblest persons I have ever known, but increasing responsibility gave him confidence and assurance.' She noticed also his great moral and physical courage, how he would never shirk a disagreeable duty, and would always choose an interview at which to discharge it, rather than the easier way of writing a letter.[1]

They were married on 21 September 1909 at Clandon, the family home of the Onslows, and spent a short honeymoon at Garrowby before Edward began his election campaign, for he had decided that the time had come for him to stand for Parliament. His father had already warmly accepted Dorothy into the family circle. He had written to say that he hoped he would get another glimpse of her in 'that gay going away gown', and after the couple had again visited Hickleton he added: 'We have all done nothing but sing her

[1] Lady Halifax to author.

praises. We began to love her for your sake, now we are going, indeed we are a long way on the road to love her a great deal more for her own. This is not flummery but the truth.'

*　　　*　　　*

There were great rejoicings at Garrowby Hall, and it seemed that the whole countryside joined in the festivities. Acrobats, conjurers, jugglers and ventriloquists performed on the lawns, and a cricket match was played. At five o'clock tea was served in the courtyard which was covered in by a large marquee, and as darkness fell the drive from the fish pond to the house was illuminated by Chinese lanterns and fairy lights. The bride and bridegroom arrived at York at 9 p.m. and changed from their motor-car into a carriage, and at the entrance to the avenue Dorothy was presented with a bouquet of Malmaison roses by the housekeeper Mrs. Wordsworth. The horses were unyoked, and with the band playing 'Here the conquering hero comes', the carriage was dragged by nearly a hundred stalwart men the rest of the way to the house, and into the marquee itself. Here a cup of solid gold nearly two feet high, which had been subscribed for by the tenants of the estate and the tradesmen and labourers of the district, was presented by the oldest yeoman farmer on the estate. And after this had been done, and they had shaken innumerable hands, they stood upon the lawn and watched a firework display of which the principal feature was an enormous set piece wishing 'long life and happiness to the Hon. E. F. L. Wood and Lady Dorothy'.

It was a typical Yorkshire scene and similar welcomes were given to them at Hickleton, and at Temple Newsam to which they passed through a series of triumphal arches bearing messages of friendship and welcome. At many of these crowds had collected to wish the pair happiness, and confetti was thrown. On the road to Halton their car was stopped several times so that aged people might approach them and convey their good wishes with characteristic Yorkshire fervour. The bells of the ancient church at Whitkirk were ringing for them as their car approached. Here they were joined by a dozen traps belonging to tenants on the estate, and there was quite a procession to the Hall. Venetian masts were erected along the avenue and high up on the walls of the ancient house were the words in gold letters: 'Edward' and 'Dorothy' and 'Health' and 'Happiness'. Hundreds of people were assembled in the courtyard, and five hundred were entertained in a banqueting tent.

Edward had been chosen as prospective Conservative candidate for Ripon in 1907, partly as a result of his electioneering efforts on behalf of his brother-in-law, George Lane Fox, in the Barkston Ash division. Ripon had been represented for many years by John Lloyd Wharton who, like so many other Conservatives confident in their seats, had been swept away in the landslide of 1906.

'So in due course,' he said, 'I appeared before the Selection Committee in

Harrogate and made my confession of faith, answering such questions as they might think well to ask. I had been warned . . . that one of their most teasing questions would concern the claims of Parliament to restore order in the Church by means of legislation. There was a good deal of chatter going on at the time about ritualism and so-called illegal practices, and in the argument my father was one of the protagonists. He was not very helpful, regarding the Protestant attitude and temper as utterly unreasonable and taking the view that the more often and the more plainly those concerned were told so the better. To me it did not seem quite so simple, and I used to lie in my bath at Garrowby thinking up answers to embarrassing questions.'[1]

Although there were certain rough corners, the constituency was predominantly Conservative. Lord Faber was President of the Association, and Andrew Lawson, well liked in Ripon and Boroughbridge, Chairman. The agent 'was a little man called Ainley, who had been there for a long time, and had never, I should think, varied his methods or his pace of action'. He used to delight Edward with stories of his election adventures with his predecessor Johnny Wharton; their drives to meetings in a two-horse brougham on pitch-dark nights along country lanes, 'with horses jibbing on a steep hill, and a perilous return journey to face after the driver had been regaling himself at the local inn while his passengers were occupied with their meeting'.

Edward had his adventures, too, in his night drives to those outlying villages, but they were in a primitive motor-car rather than a two-horse brougham. This rudimentary vehicle was driven by his chauffeur Harry Salkeld, who had entered his service in 1905. He was just six months younger than Edward and was the son of the carpenter at Hickleton who had been there for forty-seven years and had carried out the work on the chapel.

Edward had an old Beeston Humber with no self-starter, a folding canvas roof, acetylene lamps, side-curtains which flapped ineffectually in rain and snow, and a rear light that was constantly going out. In those days the car was kept in a shed at the foot of the long drive near the lodge. 'You had to walk the whole way to the house,' said Salkeld, 'as there was no road, only a track of old chalk and sticky lime.' Edward insisted on sleeping, whenever possible, in his own bed, and would drive home at any hour in the morning to reach it, trudging up the long track at the end of an exhausting day. One of his meetings on Blubberhouses Moor, where Lord Walsingham once shot five hundred brace of grouse to his own gun in one day, lasted until 1 a.m., with Edward answering questions up to the end. Then a fifty-mile drive home at twenty miles an hour, and the long walk to the house.

There were stormy meetings at Starbeck near Harrogate, and disturbances at Pateley Bridge when Edward held his first meeting in this Radical strong-hold. He had arranged to dine and sleep with the local squire, Mr. Yorke of Bewerley. Mr. Yorke took the chair at a crowded meeting, and was loudly

[1] Halifax. Op. cit., p. 63.

booed by the great majority of the audience. When it came to Edward's turn it was soon obvious that he was not going to be allowed to speak:

'Catcalls, boos, irreverent jokes followed by boisterous laughter and every known form of interruption made any attempt at a speech completely impossible. I can see now the principal interrupter, volleying the most unanswerable questions at my head, and a kind of running commentary in admiration of his intelligence from all parts of the hall: " 'E's a regular wonder"—"Aye, 'e's t'wonder o't valley"—"Coom on, lad; tha's spun 'im up this toime"—not bad tempered, but quite determined to allow no Tory heresy to be expounded within the Radical preserves. Mr. Yorke, as Chairman and local squire, was humiliated and outraged. He apologized for the manners of the disturbers of the peace, and said that we had better close the meeting and get away from the *canaille*.' Edward was reluctant to leave the stricken field without a further effort, and although he agreed to close the meeting, decided to go down among the audience and make less formal contact with them. 'So that is what happened, and Dorothy and I got off the platform and went straight across to "t' wonder o't valley" with his red tie, and immediately we all sat down to an argument! The argument of course got us nowhere, but we established friendly relations, talked, till eleven o'clock, and never had any more trouble at Pateley Bridge.'

* * *

It was the motor journeys late at night in the savage Yorkshire winter in that leaking rattletrap that made this election such an arduous experience. Wrapped deep in a fur coat, Edward would sit patiently hour after hour while Salkeld coaxed the decrepit car along frosty roads. Miraculously, they never had an accident. The car carried a stepney wheel which used to fly off, and was lost in a turnip field, and Edward was once forced to put a fur rug under a wheel on an icy road to obtain traction, ruining the rug but getting the car moving. In those days the highways were dust roads with sharp flints on them, and 25 m.p.h. was the maximum legal speed. Salkeld was fined at Normans Cross for driving at thirty-two miles an hour because an old farmer was frightened that his cattle would be run over, but was given a lift from court in his pony cart by the obliging magistrate. After the Humber Edward bought a Wolseley-Siddeley touring car which was as draughty as the other, fog and rain filtering through its ill-fitting side-curtains. A journey of six miles to Stamford Bridge was seldom made without a breakdown. 'You had to study the rules of the road,' said Salkeld, 'so we did not talk much on our journeys.'

Edward had no serious difficulty in being returned for Ripon in January 1910 with a majority of 1,244. After the poll was declared the horses were taken from his carriage, supporters harnessed themselves to it, and a triumphant procession into the city began. The ancient city had never seen scenes of such excitement, and there was a great audience in the square which Edward addressed from the old Unicorn Inn, and which greeted him with wild outbursts of cheering when he appeared at the window. His father wrote on 23 January that 'the servants had champagne and danced in your honour last night. When the news arrived here, Susan, because she could do nothing else, rang *all* the bells in the house. The men played, some on concertinas, some on horns. They say there was no such noise in this world before. In short a universal hubbub and universal rejoicing'.

In spite of his victory, Edward disliked electioneering and constituency work. The shouts and jeers flying to and fro across the smoky halls, the hecklers, rough as lumps of their own Yorkshire coal, found him out of his element. Nor could he yet bring himself to enter with much conviction into the forced heartiness, the handshaking and backslapping which are required on these occasions, and which some can counterfeit with such conviction. He was too shy and reserved to find it easy to unbend, and there was at times something incongruous at village meetings in this tall figure expounding serious arguments which often soared above the heads of his audience.

After the election Edward and Dorothy went for a short holiday to Bordighera. It was while they were there that Halifax wrote to his son one of those letters which are a pathetic indication of his feeling of personal inadequacy, that belief that sometimes pierced him that the great gifts of his family had withered for a generation in his person. These disclosures of his inmost weaknesses cause the readers of his letters a sense of both admiration and pity. After making a speech of fierce protest about the constitutional dangers that faced the House of Lords, he wrote:

'I did not look at a single paper yesterday morning to forget all about it. My speech was an abysmal failure, an opportunity thrown away, and I have HATED myself every time I have thought about it ever since. I have tried to do so as little as possible. The fact is my vanity is excessive, and I *hate* having it brought home to me of how little use I am. One realizes when it is too late how different the past might have been and ought to have been and that it is all one's own fault one is so little good in the present. It is a comfort to think that this is a reproach you will never have to make yourself. "Si jeunesse savait, si vieillesse pouvait"—that is my life. The worst is I might have known and should have known if I had not been a conceited donkey.'[1]

It is a letter that gives a curious glimpse into their relationship, and few fathers can ever have so abased themselves before their sons without the slightest fear of ridicule or contempt.

*   *   *

The election had taken place in January 1910, and the new House met on 15 February. It is sometimes supposed that in those last four years of the old

[1] Hickleton Papers, 29 March 1910.

world which was soon to vanish for ever, with peace accepted as a natural state, and the glory of the British Empire at its zenith, the debates in the House of Commons were leisurely and civilized compared with those of today, and the life of a Member of Parliament agreeable and easy. In fact this period, 1910 to 1914, Edward's introduction to Parliamentary life, was one of the most tempestuous in the annals of the House of Commons. In it an issue was fought out which was to determine the future structure of the constitution; whether the House of Lords should continue to reject Liberal measures of reform, or whether it should be deprived of that power. It saw the attempt to pass a Home Rule Bill for Ireland which would include a fiercely resisting Ulster, incited by two of the greatest advocates in the country, with the full approval of the Leader of the Opposition, to defy the sovereign will of Parliament to the point of civil war.

As in the eighteenth century, at moments of particular hatred, the ladies of opposite political parties coldly ignored one another at the opera; the House of Commons was suspended after the Prime Minister, Asquith, had been howled down for thirty minutes in an organized demonstration never since surpassed in venom. By the end of the troubled period Ulster, urged on by the Conservative Party, was preparing to resist Home Rule by force of arms, so that it appeared to many that civil war had been averted only by the greater tragedy of 1914.

Edward Wood's novitiate was thus served in a House of Commons under continuous strain which erupted into sudden rages more suited to the Chamber of Deputies and repugnant to his dispassionate outlook on affairs. He was already convinced that the way of sanity in politics lay in the calm examination of difficult problems, and the choice of the most equitable solutions. To one who believed that the indulgence of raw emotion precluded clear thinking, the great issues which convulsed this angry House of Commons from 1910 onwards offered little scope. It was rather an arena made for guerrilla warfare, for the condottieri of politics, the men like Lloyd George and F. E. Smith who loved a fight.

If the causes that were fought for were of a fundamental character, the leading actors were in every way worthy of them. It was an era of great statesmen brought together by some chance, at the same moment of history, and their stature invests the whole period with a fascination that seldom lingers round spent issues. There was the Liberal Prime Minister, Asquith, with his towering intellect and wonderful dexterity in debate, the essence of Oxford humanism, who was to show equal nerve and skill in these four years of struggle. To his opponents it sometimes appeared that Asquith, with all his supreme gifts, was yet lacking in a sense of reality, so that in the later words of one of them, L. S. Amery:

'The supreme power of the state has fallen into the hands of a man who combines unrivalled gifts of parliamentary leadership with a complete incapacity to face facts or to come to any decision on them. Again and again in the last few months Mr. Asquith has averted a breakdown by the exercise of his amazing skill in debate, but he has never shown the slightest trace of understanding of the forces at work outside. . . . It would be futile to attempt to strip off the outer integument of debating points in order to get at the real Asquith underneath. There is no such person. For twenty years he has held a season ticket on the line of least resistance, and gone wherever the train of events has carried him, lucidly justifying his position at whatever point he has happened to find himself.'

There, too, was Balfour, the Conservative Leader, who had given the finest intellect of his age to politics, elegant, aloof and learned, a philosopher who seemed strangely detached from mundane affairs, yet capable of administering a rebuke languid and annihilating; a pampered member of 'the Souls', who in Parliamentary speeches would sometimes dreamily improvise upon a theme, soaring into regions of abstract thought, or probe a political issue with the clinical detachment of a surgeon, a practice often exasperating to his followers. Winston Churchill and Lloyd George were two other memorable figures in this House of Commons, and although the worst enemies of the former could not deny his untutored genius, he was already saddled with a reputation for recklessness and ill judgment. Lloyd George, under whom Edward Wood was later briefly to serve, had just introduced the notorious People's Budget in 1909 in which he made a naked appeal to class hatred, and had defended it at Limehouse and elsewhere in speeches of inspired scurrility.

The events that followed are well known. Acting with questionable constitutionality and unquestionable folly the Lords threw out the Budget. It was at the ensuing General Election in January 1910 that Edward Wood first entered the House. The Liberals suffered heavy losses but in some respects the new situation was more dangerous for the Conservatives than it had been in the days of the arrogant Mountain of 1906. For the Irish party now held the balance of power and their price was Home Rule.

In the midst of the crisis King Edward became dangerously ill, and he died in May. The news brought back to Halifax many sad memories of his former master. He requested of Lord Knollys the privilege of an old servant and friend, to see him in death, and described this experience in a letter to Edward:

'I saw Francis Knollys for a moment at St. James's Palace and asked him if I could see the King. The result was that I got a message from the Palace in the afternoon to say that I could come, and I was taken up to his room. He was not the least altered and had that look on his face that death so often brings. He was lying on a little bed screened off from the rest of the room, just under the picture of Prince Eddie and his mother. He looked just as one would have wished.

'After I had been there a little while and had left the room the Queen sent for me and she took me again into the room and looked for a time, uncovering his face and said: "Does he not look beautiful?" And then how she had felt that she must get home, with a sense that she could not delay, and that something would be amiss. She was most brave and touching, calm but breaking down now and again. I thought all the time of how I had seen her come down the stairs as a bride in all her beauty, to attend the Reception she and the Prince had in St. James's, life beginning for her in all its brightness, and here it was finished and the chapter closed, her life, so to speak ended and she standing a widow all in black beside her dead husband.

'In the midst of life we are indeed in death, and how completely God's Providence sets at naught all human anticipations. I was much touched by her taking up a prayer book on a table by the side of the bed, and saying, "That is the prayer book you gave him; he always had it with him." It was the one, the Treasury of Devotion, I had had bound and sent to him at his Coronation. She said he had not suffered beyond the discomfort of the difficulty of breathing and the panting for breath.'[1]

It was soon found that the King's death had done nothing to assuage party hatreds. On the contrary the bitterness between them seemed to have increased: 'Malicious stories were invented and believed about eminent people; old friendships were sundered; men and women declined to meet one another on neutral ground; the common basis on which party politics had gone forward seemed suddenly to have disappeared. Eminent men on both sides were talking of going to all lengths at all costs and "damning the consequences". Everything seemed laid out for an exciting and dangerous conflict with an eager public and excited Press denouncing moderation and weakness. Women were as excited as men and went about their business of winning the vote with a determination to shock and scandalize.'[2]

All attempts at a compromise failed, but before his death King Edward had insisted on a second General Election to secure the country's verdict on the House of Lords. This took place in December and left the numerical balance in the House practically unchanged. Edward faced a stronger opponent than on the first occasion, Norman Rae, and his majority fell from 1,244 to 874. In future he was to be spared these formalities. No one was to stand against him again at Ripon, and at the elections of 1918, 1922, 1923 and 1924 he was to be returned unopposed.

Tempers grimly deteriorated during that steaming summer of 1911 which seemed charged with menace, when day followed day of brazen skies, when rooms were shuttered against the sun and the water-carts laid the dust in the streets, and even those accustomed to the tropics were oppressed and longed for a change and the refreshment of rain. Asquith considered that he had a

---

[1] Hickleton Papers, 8 May 1910.
[2] J. A. Spender, *Great Britain, Empire and Commonwealth 1886–1935*, p. 380.

4*

clear mandate to cut down the powers of the Upper House, and in August
1911 after scenes of unparalleled fury during that summer of blazing heat the
Parliament Act, abolishing the Lords' veto on Money Bills and reducing it on
others to a suspensory one of two years only, was carried by the threat to
create enough peers to swamp the Conservative majority in the House of
Lords.

The way now lay open for an Irish Home Rule Bill which the Lords would
merely delay, not kill. The Bill, however, made no separate provision for
Protestant Ulster which deeply resented the idea of being governed by a
Dublin Parliament with a Roman Catholic majority. A new bitterness was
infused into politics. The Conservatives were deeply committed to the Ulster
cause and it was symbolic, though accidental, that Balfour should have been
replaced in the autumn of 1911 by Bonar Law who was of Ulster extraction
and felt more passionately on this issue than on anything else in public life.
'I can imagine no lengths of resistance to which Ulster will go in which I shall
not be ready to support them,' he declared in a startling speech at Blenheim
Palace.

Asquith introduced a Bill in April to give effect to a measure of Home
Rule, and in spite of a stream of congratulations from the self-governing
Dominions, the Conservatives declared that they would resist it at all lengths
and at all costs. The House of Commons was in continuous session until the
end of January 1913. Passions rose to white heat as the Bill was contested at
all its stages. The House became a shambles in which speeches were drowned
in screams of 'traitors' and 'rats', and the First Lord of the Admiralty was
wounded in the face by the Speaker's copy of Standing Orders, seized and
hurled at him by an enraged member of the Opposition. The Bill passed its
third reading in January, only to meet its fate and be rejected by the House
of Lords by a majority of 257.

*   *   *

We cannot doubt that such exhibitions of naked emotion were repellent
to Edward Wood. All his instincts were to reduce a high temperature rather
than to bring it to the boil. When others caught fire, he remained cold, and
his attitude to the crisis was almost irritatingly objective. He believed that
the British character, like his own, recoiled from extreme courses: 'When the
Home Rule issue was joined,' he said, 'most people thought the Ulster attitude exaggerated, and the Conservative support of civil war at least mistaken,
and probably indefensible.' He was also still to some extent under his father's
political influence, and the sympathy he might have felt for Ulster in her
predicament may have been chilled by Halifax's assertion that 'The Orange-
men are the most senseless and bigoted faction on the face of this earth, and
the sooner the Conservative and Unionist Party can get rid of them the better
for that party'.

The course of events also produced in Halifax a deep momentary disgust with politics. Like Mercutio, he wished a plague on both their houses, and from his despair of the Irish situation his volatile mind sought refuge in that panacaea for all ills, the macabre. In September, while the Ulster leaders were forming their Volunteer Force and civil war seemed to be approaching with terrifying bounds, he sat in a train speeding north from Peterborough to York, and wrote to Edward, gleefully relating an extraordinary story he had just heard from the Eton master Luxmoore:

'When George IV opened the vault in St. George's Chapel in which Henry VIII and Charles I were buried, Sir Henry Halford and the Doctor took out of Charles's coffin the bit of the vertebrae which had been separated by the axe, and cut off a piece of the King's Imperial. These were kept in a glass table in Sir Henry Halford's house in London. Later they were given to King Edward when Prince of Wales, who desired to restore them to where they had been taken from. The Queen heard of it and absolutely forbade the graves to be again opened. She was eventually persuaded to relent, but only on condition that when nobody was about and none would know of it.

'Accordingly one night the Prince of Wales and the Dean of Windsor (the present Archbishop of Canterbury) went to the Chapel and the vault was opened. The Prince would allow no one to touch the box with the relics except himself, but though they saw the coffin at the bottom, the vault was too deep to allow the Prince to place the box upon it, although he lay on the floor of the Chapel on his stomach and stretched down as far as he was able.

'The difficulty was only surmounted by their all tying their pocket handkerchiefs together and letting the box carefully down till it was deposited in its proper place. Later on the Dean was so impressed by the scandal which might develop if the story came to be known of a small box having been buried secretly at night by the Prince of Wales himself in St. George's Chapel, that he persuaded the Queen to allow the fact of the restoration of the relics to be announced in the papers.

'The bones of Henry VIII were all lying about the floor of the vault. The body (he was a man of gross habit) having burst the lead coffin. Later the Dean had them collected and put into a new coffin. It was remarkable, he said, how big the bones were, the shoulder blades especially showing what a big man the King must have been. Did I tell you that Edward VII's own body burst its lead coffin and after its burial at Windsor had to be put into a new one? This Mr. Nutt told me the other day, and that they had to put a pipe up to the roof of the Chapel to let all the fumes out. How horrid all the details of dying are and how true the expression is "the body of our humiliation".'[1]

There is no need to trace in detail the way in which the Irish impasse

[1] Hickleton Papers, 1 September 1913.

continued to dominate English politics until the outbreak of war in 1914. Looking back now in tranquillity upon this troubled scene, it appears strange that the Liberal Party failed to understand that the coercion of Ulster, a small people, predominantly of a different religion and national origin, and passionately determined to remain a part of Britain, into accepting an alien rule was a direct contradiction of their Liberal ideals of the rights of small peoples. When preparing their Bill they had indeed given much thought to excluding from it the Six Counties of Ulster, but they knew that the Irish Nationalists were pledged to the principle of an undivided Ireland, and would refuse a Bill introduced in this form. And they did not think it likely that the Conservative opposition to Home Rule for the rest of Ireland would be overcome by the exclusion of Ulster.

Both sides, for different reasons, were nervous and inclined to shrink from the responsibilities they had assumed, and there were in late 1913 tantalizing and abortive movements towards a settlement, so that we are aware of the quiet rustle of olive branches amid the din of battle. There were meetings between Asquith and Bonar Law and Carson which revealed an eagerness for peace that would have surprised the outside world. But Carson would consent to nothing short of the exclusion of Ulster, 'the clean cut', as he called it, so that these efforts came to nothing, and when war broke out in 1914 the Irish problem was postponed but not solved.

It will be clear from this succession of events that these first four years in Parliament had not been an easy period for Edward Wood, or any other young Conservative of moderate views. The struggle with the Lords had been brief, but it had left a corrosive bitterness in its wake. Even more enduring was the rancour left behind them by Lloyd George's Budgets. There had also been an indecorous wrangle over the National Insurance Bill, but all these issues had been overshadowed by the Irish struggle. Feeling had never run higher in the House of Commons, and perhaps never would, than during this period, and 'there was no want of dramatic irony in the fact that the leaders in this masque of anarchy were also the leaders of that party which was pre-eminently devoted to the maintenance of law and order'.[1] It was an atmosphere distasteful to Edward, so cool and circumspect, and aloof from the crasser forms of party fanaticism. What place, indeed, he may well have thought, could there be in this mêlée for one so objective as he?

He was also unfortunate in the circumstances of his maiden speech, a milestone in the life of every Member of Parliament, and an adventure to be long meditated in advance. The maiden speaker always enjoys by convention the right to choose his own moment for intervening, normally on some subject to which he has given special study. Such a consideration is intended to soften a great Parliamentary ordeal, but in the case of Edward's maiden speech it was withheld through the fault of his own whips, and he was to find himself

[1] Stuart Hodgson, *Lord Halifax*, p. 31.

in the position of being given an hour's notice to prepare the speech, and that on a subject not of his own choosing and of which he was completely ignorant.

It was 13 June 1910, and a foreign affairs debate was taking place, with particular reference to Egypt, where the Prime Minister, Boutras Pasha, had recently been murdered, and where Theodore Roosevelt had advised the British Government either to 'govern or get out'. In 1910, in the midst of that long period of peace and Imperial greatness, foreign affairs did not command the same general interest as today. When all was quiet and there appeared no threat to the safety of the island, diplomacy was regarded as the domain of the professional, and there was little general knowledge of what passed behind the walls of the Foreign Office.

There was, therefore, a small attendance at this debate. Edward was there because he wished to learn something about a subject that was strange to him. His friend George Lloyd had already spoken, and the Foreign Secretary, Grey, sat patiently on the Treasury Bench making notes for his reply. While Edward was listening to the debate one of the Opposition whips approached him and asked: 'Are you going to speak?' Disconcerted, Edward replied: 'Good gracious no—I know nothing about Egypt. I'm only listening.' The whip was clearly more conscious of his own duties than the young Member's feelings when he answered, to Edward's consternation: 'Well, I'm afraid we must ask you to speak. The debate had been timed to finish before dinner, but the chief [Balfour] can't get back to speak till after dinner, and so we've got to carry it on, and there are very few of our people here.'

Thus this young man who had not yet addressed the House was ordered to do so virtually impromptu as a matter of party convenience on a subject of which he knew nothing. It was a cruel and unimaginative request by a whip who merely wanted to keep a house in the dinner hour, and it is greatly to Edward's credit that he was sufficiently self-possessed to rise to the occasion.

Perhaps he remembered Balfour's advice to him, so cynical, so characteristic: 'Speak as often and as long as you can, and you will rapidly acquire that contempt for your audience every bore always has.' After making protests which were curtly brushed aside, he was left to collect his thoughts, make a few notes, and have a hurried conference with George Lloyd in the Library before making his way back to the Chamber. Here to his relief he found an audience confined to the Deputy Speaker, the Serjeant-at-Arms, the Foreign Secretary, who was there because he had to answer the debate, and one Liberal Member who was only present because he wanted to speak himself.

We can agree with Edward who, when reading his maiden speech forty years later, was surprised 'that it was not worse than it was'. The issues which it attempted to discuss are now dead and cold, but it has a pleasant period flavour, and we may derive from it some impression of his ideas at the time on the position of subject peoples.

He showed a curious mixture of condescension and prescience. No doubt he was reflecting the temper of his day in its belief in the tutelary duty of the mother country towards those races to whom Kipling referred in *The White Man's Burden* as 'half devil and half child'. But there is a strong whiff of superiority, and a sound that rings strangely in modern ears in his assumption that the Egyptians are 'a black people', and in his frequent comparisons between 'superior' and 'subordinate' races. Certainly it would be unwise to make too much of this apparent arrogance or to relate it to a modern viewpoint. His speech represented the opinions of an intelligent and observant young man who had travelled widely among these peoples, and had not failed to observe their rudimentary stage of development, and to realize that an indefinite period must elapse before they could govern themselves without tragic consequences. But he also foreshadowed that this would come to pass at some time in the future. We must retreat through the years and imagine ourselves in the atmosphere of 1910 to appreciate the force of Wood's arguments on this occasion, and consider them in a manner free from retrospective wisdom.

'One often hears,' he said, 'that when a white nation is dealing with a black nation it is practically government by force. . . . Anybody who has lived or has passed his time among those conditions among black people must recognize that government in that case is also government by consent—by which I mean that the black people are prepared to be governed by the white people —or your government is not worth a day's purchase. If that is true, and I think it is, surely the argument that under all conditions and at all times all men are equal is one of the most flimsy and one of the most academic that could possibly be brought forward . . . and while we on our side most emphatically disclaim any attempt permanently to hold down the black races, we do at the same time insist that if our position in those countries is to be maintained, it can only be as it is at the present moment, by maintaining the position and fulfilling the functions of a superior race.'[1]

Having made it plain that the present was not a moment for weakness, Edward uttered some sentences significant for the future:

'I think in the minds of some hon. Members there is the idea when the word [prestige] is used, that it means right or wrong—the white man will be upheld and supported and the black man will be downtrodden. That is not my meaning when I use the word "prestige". My meaning is that the subordinate race should by all means be fairly treated, and that there should be no sense of injustice. But given that condition, surely you are in a position to insist that the black race must and can only be treated as subordinate to the race charged with the government of their country for the time being. . . .

[1] *Hansard*, House of Commons, Vol. XVI, Cols. 1134–6, 13 June 1910.

'The time may come,' he added, 'and I hope it will come, when those races with whose government we are now charged may be in a position to assume control of their own fortunes and may be able to work out their own destiny. When that time is reached, I am sure that all parties in this country will be prepared to assist them when they make the attempt.' It would be a disaster if this attempt were made prematurely when, in Edward's words, those races were 'in the condition of political children', and it would bring 'into most serious jeopardy the white races wherever they are in contact with the black races'.

Although it bore little relation to the subject of debate, this maiden speech was a gallant effort, and Edward was afterwards to do himself an injustice when he said that he had no cause either then or later to congratulate himself on the event. Sir Edward Grey, in replying to the debate, gave the House the assurance that he had no intention of discontinuing the occupation of Egypt, and that Egyptian agitation against it would be met by more 'assertion of our authority'.

Grey also performed a characteristic act of personal courtesy to Edward. When winding up the debate he had picked up a number of points raised by other speakers, but had not noticed his speech. Next morning Edward found a note on his breakfast table from the Foreign Secretary regretting that in the haste of his reply he had overlooked his most interesting speech, adding that he had been so pleased to see him taking part in the debate, and hoping that he would often speak in the future.

*   *   *

Edward was delighted by the birth of his first child Anne in July 1910, but the pleasure of his first two years in Parliament was diminished by his father-in-law's drawn-out illness and death. The condition of his own heart had also caused anxiety, and in July 1910 his mother wrote to him from Hickleton:

'I do wish, darling, that you would not kneel so long at a time. Everyone knows it is *the* most trying attitude for the heart—and especially so when with such a long back as yours the poor heart has to travel such a distance to do its work. So do curtail the *kneeling* prayers.'

Edward and his wife were also much distressed by an accident which had befallen her younger brother Huia, a gifted young man who had derived his strange name from the fact that he was born in New Zealand when his father was Governor-General. He had struck his head on a rock when diving in a mountain lake in Switzerland, and become paralysed from the waist downwards.

He adapted his life to these new conditions with great courage, and began what was to develop into a distinguished scientific career at Cambridge in biology and genetics which included a brilliant investigation into the causes of the beautiful iridescent colour on the wings of butterflies and insects. He was wheeled every day into the laboratory when he was well enough, and thus 'spent his time, absorbed, interested, and forgetful of his own cruel disabilities'. Lord Onslow died in 1911, having been for the last year of his life an invalid. He had always been fond of his son-in-law who remembered that 'on his good days nothing gave him greater pleasure than to hear any political news or gossip that any of us might be able to contribute'.

Apart from his maiden speech, Edward's only contribution worth recording to the brief 1910 Parliament was in the debate on the Accession Declaration Bill. This was a measure close to Halifax's heart, and concerned the Declaration each sovereign was required to make on his accession of his intention to uphold Protestantism. It was a law with its roots deep in history which had been passed in an atmosphere of hysterical anti-Catholicism at the time of the Popish Plot. It contained phrases about such doctrines as Transubstantiation which were not only anomalous but deeply offensive to Roman Catholics and High Anglicans alike. The Prime Minister, Asquith, and the Archbishop of Canterbury had drafted this measure with the object of redressing an ancient grievance.

It was agreed by all people not blinded by religious bigotry that it was a civilized and necessary measure, and only the automatic muttering of a few Ulstermen about the Scarlet Woman and the Mass in the shadow of the back benches disturbed the general harmony. The debate which took place in the House of Commons on 27 July was unlikely to stimulate brilliant exchanges, but Edward, that dutiful son, faithfully reflected his father's views on a point which seemed to some to verge on the academic. He followed closely Halifax's lead on the Declaration, and it was inevitable that he should also follow him in protesting against the definition of the Church which was included in the Bill. He declared himself satisfied that the Protestant succession was strongly secured by the Act of Settlement and the Bill of Rights, and also by the fact that the King took Holy Communion according to the rites of the Church of England. Like his father he found it difficult to stomach the description in the Bill of Rights of the Church of England as 'the Protestant and Reformed Church'.

'There is a sense,' he said, 'in which the Church of England is Protestant and Reformed, but we do not regard that as the true constitutional or historical description of the Church to which we belong.'[1] He had, however, even at that early stage of his career, and in spite of his principles, already recognized, as he was to state nearly forty years later, that in politics what is ideally right cannot always be reconciled with what is practically possible, and he endorsed the Declaration with no further twinges of conscience.

It was in Edward's second parliament elected in December 1910 that the battle over the House of Lords was joined in earnest. The Tories divided into

[1] *Hansard*, House of Commons, Vol. XIX, Col. 2176, 27 July 1910.

two groups—the 'ditchers' who were willing to defy Asquith's threat to create enough peers to carry the Bill and were ready to die in the last ditch, contrasted with the 'hedgers' who believed that it was better to abstain and let the Bill go through than suffer the indignity of being swamped by four hundred new peers. Halifax, who for a moment had been startled by Asquith's threat into saying that he 'preferred the Bill by itself to the Bill plus the Peers', allied himself with the 'ditchers'.

Edward, who was bound by every imaginable tie of blood and relationship to the House of Lords, and who was himself the heir to a peerage, might have been expected to take an equally positive line in the face of this threat to wrench the constitution apart. Restrained by that native caution, and recognizing perhaps in his objective mind that there was much substance in the Liberal claim that an unrepresentative chamber was wrecking progressive legislation, he picked his steps carefully.

He supported the two Conservative amendments in the Committee stage of the Parliament Bill. The first of these was intended to provide a slight alteration in the case of money Bills, of the provision by which the Lords were compelled to pass such a Bill without amending it within a month, failing which it became law. The amendment Edward supported proposed that where the Lords refused unamended passage of a money Bill there should be a further debate in the House of Commons before the Royal Assent was given. It is difficult to see why the sponsors of this amendment entertained any hope of its acceptance, and it was duly opposed by Asquith on the grounds that it involved a fourth reading of the Bill, which was 'an entirely novel proposition and one which goes beyond the constitutional powers of this House'. Edward made an ingenious argument in support of a case which he must have realized was hopeless:

'All this amendment would do,' he suggested, 'would be to transfer some of the power and a portion of the position which are at present held by the second House to this House. . . . There might well be a discussion in the House of Lords . . . which might turn upon quite different points to those which had been raised in this House, and the points which emerged there might be quite different from those which emerged from the discussions here. If you had an obstinate Government who was conscious of a weak case it might well be that they might snap their fingers at what had been found to be the most effective criticism in another place, and would hold that having run the gauntlet of criticism in this House they should withdraw their Bill from discussion at once and pass their Act in the way contemplated by this Bill.'

His second intervention was in support of an amendment which attempted to weaken the provision of the Parliament Bill which ensured that if the House of Lords rejected a non-money bill in three successive sessions it should become law. The clause represented the hard core of the Parliament

Bill, and was essential to force through such legislation as the Home Rule Bill. The Conservatives now proposed, on 26 April, that when a Bill had been rejected three times a referendum should be held. Again it can hardly have been with any hope of its acceptance that Edward supported this sanguine amendment, which was rejected by Herbert Samuel on the unquestionable grounds that it would bring chaos to Liberal legislation, and would be applied to every measure, except money Bills, which were thrown out by the House of Lords.

Edward was undoubtedly sincere in his support of this proposal, and in the belief that with the mutilation of the Lords the balance of the constitution would be dangerously altered, and he was speaking from the heart when he said:

'We know that the real objection to the referendum is that the Government and their supporters wish to make the House of Commons today not only supreme as between the two Houses, but sovereign over any Parliament and over any possible wish of the people outside. . . . We have hitherto had the power of insisting at certain times that the House of Commons shall be brought into touch and into line with public opinion, and the check or guarantee we have had up to this time being removed, we are bound to insist upon another.'[1]

In October 1912 his second child and eldest son was born, and given the names of Charles Ingram Courtenay, an event which did much to rouse him from the slight depression caused by what had so far been a somewhat desultory Parliamentary career, and by the general malaise of Conservative politics. It required an ecclesiastical cause to bring him to life again, and he found it in the proposal to disestablish the Welsh Church. The spearheads of the assault on this Bill were Lord Robert Cecil and his brother Lord Hugh, and they were men whom Edward could follow without reserve: 'Lord Robert, tall, fairly broad, with a permanent stoop caused by an injury when young, gave one the impression when he was denouncing the Bill of a benevolent hawk, if there be such a bird, anxious to swoop upon the Liberal Party to remove it from its evil environment of Radicalism and Nonconformity and secure it body and soul for the Church.

'Lord Hugh, on the other hand, tall, pale and very thin, behaved and looked like an English Savanarola, whose mission it was to scarify the impiety of the Government and frighten them into repentance.'[2] But Edward himself was also an arresting figure with his towering height and the intense earnestness of his arguments as he bent over his neighbours, bringing into the dull wrangles a gleam of sincerity and vision. Edward and his father had been stirred by this dreary and complicated measure to an extent difficult to comprehend today. Both opposed it vigorously in Parliament and

---

[1] *Hansard*, House of Commons, Vol. XXIV, Col. 1838–39, 26 April 1911.
[2] Winterton. Orders of the Day, p. 64.

believed, rightly or wrongly, that the Conservative leaders were prepared to sacrifice the Welsh Church in a Parliamentary deal for the benefit of Ulster. Not for the last time in his life Edward found himself turning a sympathetic eye upon the Labour Party, and using words which must have fallen strangely upon the ears of his more orthodox colleagues:

'What we need to learn is that every citizen is individually responsible for any other citizen, and that there is a real social membership of the State. I am quite sure that the Labour Party will agree with that, and I submit that you can only establish that upon a moral basis.'[1]

In these early years in the House of Commons when he was still a private Member with few ties, he so organized his life that the demands of the House did not unduly interfere with hunting. He would hunt in Yorkshire on Mondays and catch the evening train, so that he could be, if needed, available in the Division Lobby, and return to Yorkshire on Thursday night to hunt on Friday and Saturday. Always a countryman, he looked forward with joy to these escapes from the sometimes intolerable atmosphere of the House. Hunting was a perfect antidote to those long hours in the stale air of the debating chamber. When hounds were running he was conscious of an exhilaration which abolished every anxiety of life, and a quickening of the pulses when all cares were blown to the winds and nothing existed but the present, the same liberation of the spirit that Tolstoy knew when he hunted wolves at Nikoloskoe.

In August 1914 the strife that had long poisoned political life abruptly ceased. The old bitter rivalries could never be the same again, and there occurred an instinctive change in the temper of the people and their leaders. The battles in Parliament that had been fought with such intensity were forgotten; the civil war, whose approach had filled all men with dread, receded and grew dim, and the hatred between the parties passed like an April shower. Men realized that the greatest menace of all was now upon them; that all others paled in comparison, and they were drawn into instant cohesion, for 'the lights were going out all over Europe', and the end of an era had come.

[1] *Hansard*, House of Commons, Vol. XXXVIII, Col. 1063, 14 May 1912.

CHAPTER VI

A WORLD AT WAR

EDWARD'S own position at the outbreak of war was largely determined for him. He held the rank of Captain in the Queen's Own Yorkshire Dragoons, the Yeomanry Regiment which was recruited in South Yorkshire round his home at Hickleton, and was immediately embodied at the outbreak of war. The squadron marched from their headquarters at Sheffield to join the rest of the regiment at York, and from there to Driffield. On their way they passed Garrowby and watered their horses in the park and ate their haversack rations. Then they moved on to Londesborough Park and began their training in fine harvest weather on the wold.

Edward next found himself sent to the east coast of Yorkshire where his regiment formed part of the defence system. They remained throughout the following winter in this bleak and inhospitable place, manning the Castle dykes at Scarborough against the improbable event of a German invasion, and watching the grey dawn break each morning over the wastes of the North Sea.

The obligations of the Territorial Army in 1914 were strictly limited, and the contract of those in it did not include the obligation to serve overseas unless they specifically accepted this duty. Although his heart was suspect, Edward can have had little doubt as to his proper course of action, but in this, as in most other questions, he consulted his father, whose answer left him free to follow his conscience:

'My dearest Edward, my own very dearest son,

What can I say about this? There are very good reasons, both ways, undeniable reasons, why you should volunteer to go and why you should not. I think it is very likely you might really be more useful at home than fighting abroad, but there are other things, things which one may mistake, but things which appeal to something higher than reason, and which, if a man feels them he must needs obey. No one can decide for another what such things involve, so I can only say that whatever your decision may be, and whatever the consequences it may involve, I shall feel from my heart you have made the right decision. Your mother—we have talked much together, bids me say I am speaking for her as well as for myself. One thing only I know, whether you go or whether you stay, we shall all be equally in God's hands. I cannot write about other things today.'[1]

[1] Hickleton Papers, 18 August 1914.

If Edward had felt any hesitations about volunteering for foreign service they were shared by his brother-in-law George Lane Fox who found himself in a similar position:

'The question of foreign service has caused me, like you, a great deal of hard thinking. And after I had decided what in my mind was right I went over to Bramham to meet Agnes, mainly, though she did not know it, for that reason. She was in this, as in all things, the greatest help to me. We tried to look straight into the future for a few minutes and she agreed that it was right that I should volunteer to go, and that being so, that she wished it. I am no fire-eater and I don't deny that I came to the decision with rather a heavy heart. As to yourself, I fear the option will probably not come, but if it does your position is rather different to mine—your father and mother; your far greater value to the community. I can think of many reasons that absolutely justify your not volunteering. And honestly I doubt whether you are really strong enough to bear the awful fatigue of a campaign.'[1]

There was truth in the last sentence of this letter. Edward was wiry, but some of his strength had been absorbed in his great height, and his heart, although organically sound, was a questionable asset which would certainly not have escaped a strict medical examination. He was arriving at his decision in his own reflective way. He came to the conclusion that if his Commanding Officer, Lieutenant-Colonel William MacKenzie Smith, gave him command of 'B' Squadron, it was his duty to stay with the regiment. On 24 February 1915 he wrote to his wife:

'I had a long talk to Billy[2] last night, round and round, the upshot of which is that he has tonight transferred me to command B! I shall now have my work cut out for me—getting hold. It is too soon to say if I'm pleased or not. I am doubtful of how I shall do it. It will be awkward starting.'

In spite of any doubts he may have felt about the future, he was in good spirits, and proved to be an excellent companion to others. Roger Lumley[3] remembered him in these Scarborough days, waiting for embarkation orders. Like others before him, Lumley was struck by Edward's easy camaraderie in a hard-drinking crowd not particular in its language. He noticed with admiration that although abstemious, and clearly religious, he was completely free from priggishness and cant, and one of the best mixers in the sometimes wild regimental parties. It appeared to Lumley that Edward's faith was a matter personal to himself; that he had already learned to be tolerant of the feelings of others, and he came strongly under his influence.[4]

In the early summer of 1915 the three squadrons of the regiment were attached to three separate Divisions to form the Divisional Cavalry. 'B' Squadron was posted to the 37th Division, commanded by Count Edward Gleichen, and it was in this rôle that later in the summer they went to France.

---

[1] Hickleton Papers, 19 August 1914.   [2] Lieut.-Colonel MacKenzie Smith.
[3] Afterwards the Earl of Scarbrough.   [4] The Earl of Scarbrough to author.

It was reassuring for him to know that in his absence Dorothy would be fully and most usefully occupied with war work both at Hickleton and at Temple Newsam which became a military hospital. The family solicitor, Mr. Clegg, had visited her at Hickleton, and had told Halifax how impressed he had been with her business capacities and that he thought he had never seen anyone more capable of managing business and affairs than she seemed to be. 'That is a delightful thing,' Halifax told Edward, 'to have said of one's wife or daughter. It is what I have long thought myself.'

                    *   *   *

Edward and his brother officers had volunteered for service in the expectation of a mobile war in which the cavalry would have ample scope for the offensive, a galloping war in which they would charge the enemy and make breaches in his line. They were not alone in this pathetic illusion. Like many others better placed to judge, they had entirely misconceived the nature of the war to come, and it was not in their power to foresee the devastating effect of machine-gun fire, or the impenetrable obstacle of barbed wire on a front petrified from Switzerland to the North Sea by trench warfare.

Their Division was not destined to take part in the battle of Loos, or to see any action during the summer of 1915, or the following winter. The Yorkshire Dragoons were used instead, first as Divisional and later as Corps Cavalry, and assigned a series of necessary but soul-destroying tasks, police work, road repairing, clearing battlefields, providing prisoners' escorts, engineering trenches, helping in casualty clearing stations, burying the dead, and many weeks in the winter were spent in the woods of Famechon preparing 'fascines' to repair muddy roads. While performing these duties, and for the duration of the war, they maintained their full establishment of horses, and a large part of Edward's time was spent in keeping them fit and healthy, often in appalling conditions. One of his chargers, High Sheriff, grew so fond of him that it followed him about like a dog.

Edward had already begun to worry about his constituency, and the fact that in his absence it was virtually disfranchised. He wondered whether it was his duty to resign his membership for the duration of the war, writing to his wife: 'As to the House of Commons, I doubt if one is ever likely to feel it one's duty to come home for it. I do feel though that it would be a tactful act to offer to resign. I don't think for a moment they would accept it, but it would put me very much on the right side and serve to remind my constituents of my military existence.' We hear no more of this suggestion.

They had joined the Third Army south of Arras, and after a first sight of trench warfare it dawned on Edward that it was unlikely that there would be any active use for mobile troops like his in any foreseeable situation. Indeed, five days later, their work was permanently allotted as Divisional Headquarters Guards. It was from this time that his hour of trial began, although

there were to be moments under fire exhilarating in contrast to the normal
duty which now settled upon him like some heavy cloud. The dreary months
in the mud behind the line dragged by, a period of appalling monotony. His
hours were spent in a series of tedious occupations, duties so bleak that even
the rehearsal of a pierrot troupe for the concert appeared a welcome diversion. It was a testing time to the soul, and calculated to induce melancholia
in unphilosophic minds.

Edward supported it with admirable composure. His character, patient
and simple, and not given to introspection, endured this prostitution of the
cavalry with regret, but not despair. There was a strain of fatalism in him
which prompted him to accept situations as they were, and to deal with
events to the best of his ability as they arose. It was, of course, for him, as
for others, a period of intense frustration, which he was able to support more
easily than they. What in some were prolonged bouts of depression were in
Edward passing moods of exasperation. He could not, however, fail to be
aware of the prodigal waste of his ability in those pack-horse duties, and to
realize that he could make a far greater contribution to the war at home.

From various sources came suggestions that it was ridiculous for a man
of his age and ability to be frittering away his energy on such menial tasks.
His brother-in-law, Hugh Sutton, Mary's husband, now commanding a
corps, wrote to him saying that he had always thought that Edward would
be of more use at home, particularly if recruiting was to be accelerated and
some form of compulsory service introduced. Edward was not ready to
depart, although he was prepared to ask for a longer period of leave than
usual: 'I'm not certain if there are going to be important doings in Parliament about National Service that one might not chip in there with some
advantage. The House of Commons is not my "forte" as you know, and I
count for nothing there, but I should rather like to lift my voice in the
cause.'

By May 1916 even his monumental patience had begun to wear thin: 'Yes,
I see Winston has come home. I am a good deal tempted. Nobody can
possibly be more bored with this job than I am although I think I conceal it
better than some!' In this month they had again moved farther north, posted
to II Corps under Lieutenant-General Sir Claud Jacob, and stationed near
Hazebrouck. But Edward soon found that the rearrangement of their duties
involved little change in them.

Before the Battle of the Somme they were addressed by the Corps Commander who told them that 16 Division would attack with Bapaume as its
objective. Jacob assured them that when the gap was made in the enemy
front they would be the first to be sent through it after the regular cavalry.
Edward was no longer beguiled by these siren voices. Those desolating
chores behind the line still had to be performed, and it was more economical
to use the territorial cavalry than to deplete the infantry. In letters to

Dorothy he would assure her that he was no fire-eater and would put up with monotony as long as it was his job, in preference to extreme danger.

In spite of this oft-vaunted preference for safety, Edward seized every opportunity of being in the front line and under fire. A man of exceptional physical courage, he was perhaps secretly mortified at not being more often in the trenches. When his men were sent on dirty missions to the line he invariably visited them. Probably, in spite of his pessimism, he was, deep within him, sustained by the thought that perhaps, after all, the 'Gap' might be opened and the galloping war begin.

When the regiment was moved to Senlis in July 1916 Edward lived close to his squadron horse-line, in a bell tent by summer and by winter in a shack built of wooden shell-boxes. Whenever possible, training was continued so that the regiment should be fit to take advantage of any opportunity for cavalry that might occur.

In the squadron lines there was constant anxiety for the horses. They were the background to his service—horses clattering and slipping on the pavé while the troopers cursed; horses up to their bellies in mud; screams of horses kicking in agony from shell splinters; and with it all the incessant drumming of rain on the tin roof of his hut in winter, and the sun turning the bell tent into an oven in summer, and the paper work piling up on the table, nominal rolls, punishment sheets, farriers' reports.

He grappled wearily with this mass of detail, sitting in the tent which looked down the horse-lines to a farm and a pond where the frogs croaked their raucous music at night to herald rain. Certain memories lingered sharply in his mind, horses plodding between the poplars on a Flanders road, heads lowered to the rain, and once a cornfield on a summer evening golden in the sun which reminded him of Garrowby and made him resolve passionately never to leave home again, and the untuneful voices of his men singing nostalgically 'The Long Long Trail' and 'Roses of Picardy' at concerts.

Edward was now seriously thinking whether he could not be more useful at home, although his views on what he might do there were as yet too indefinite to justify making a break. Sometimes he talked vaguely about helping recruiting; at others he felt that he could play some part in setting the post-war scene. Perhaps his thoughts were influenced by the birth of his second son Peter in October 1916, but a hard offer of useful employment had not yet been made to him, and the coming of 1917 saw him still in France.

*   *   *

In January his long devotion to duty was rewarded when he was mentioned in Despatches. He immediately sought to deprecate the honour like a subaltern fresh from his public school. Writing to Dorothy, he said:

'You may have been amused, surprised (and shocked) if you noticed it, to see that I am mentioned in Despatches today, in *The Times* of Jan. 4.

Heaven knows what for! Also George with a good deal more reason. I cannot help being a good deal ashamed of this sort of thing when one knows how other fellows who have deserved a good deal get nothing. However it will please the constituents if they get to know!'

After the German retreat from the Somme battlefield, II Corps moved north to prepare for the coming offensive in the Ypres sector, and Edward found himself immediately in rear of the battle area. When the offensive opened on 31 July the first attack failed, as on the Somme, to pierce the German trench system, and again no opportunity for the use of cavalry was created.

The doubts that still vexed Edward about leaving France were diminished when he heard that it had been decided while he was on leave that he was to relinquish 'B.' Squadron and become second-in-command of the regiment. He had acquired for his squadron an almost paternal affection. He knew the names of all his men and where they lived in Yorkshire, and the size of their families. He had helped them in their difficulties, solaced their grief, and punished their delinquencies. The idea of leaving them was suddenly unbearable to him:

'I think I never hated anything quite so much as giving up the squadron,' he said. 'It had got well round one's life.'

He had not been an easy-going officer. In the words of one who served with him in the Yorkshire Dragoons: 'As a soldier he was a strict disciplinarian with a keen eye for detail. At a kit inspection nothing escaped his notice. After a march troop leaders came to dread the little chit they would receive with a list of articles of equipment which their men had lost on the march and which Edward's policemen had collected in the rear of the squadron. But nobody resented this, and the yeomen were quick to realize and to remark that strictness made everything go better and that the lot of the trooper was happier so than under loose control and slacker discipline. He was beloved, respected, and efficient as a squadron leader.'

He was further saddened by the deaths in the war of some of his dearest friends. Charles Fisher had been killed at Jutland; Louis Egerton had gone too, and Helmsley and Hugh Dawnay. Of Egerton he wrote: 'Nothing except Hugh Dawnay has come more closely home to me. Somehow I never thought Louis would not get through this war. I doubt whether we will have the heart to hold our Christ Church dinner again, for about six of our twelve are gone.' He mourned too over Charlie Helmsley, his old fagmaster in that smoky room at Eton: 'No individual loss,' he said, 'has shocked me more in the whole war.'

In August came the definite news that the Yorkshire Dragoons were to continue in their present rôle, keeping their horses, and that the Yorkshire Hussars were to be dismounted and become fighting troops. This decision condemning him to the old routine helped to overcome his scruples about leaving France. In September he received a letter containing a definite suggestion to which he could at last pay serious heed, and which he described as the 'valley of decision'. It was an invitation on behalf of Auckland Geddes to become Deputy Director of the Labour Supply Department of the Ministry of National Service.

Edward was much attracted by the prospect of turning his mind at last to work more worthy of it. He had been in France for two and a half years, and had never raised a finger to extricate himself or make use of Parliamentary privilege to leave the army. He had found little to do as second-in-command of the regiment, and thought that the moment had come when he might legitimately accept the offer of useful employment at home. Yet he was reluctant to leave his Commanding Officer, and even more concerned at the thought that it might be felt that he was shirking his duty. It was a difficult decision, and he did not make up his mind without considerable heart-searchings. Major Albert Ginsberg remembers that Edward's squadron of the Yorkshire Dragoons was next to him and the II Corps Mounted Troops in 1917:

'He received a request from England to take up an appointment, and he was greatly troubled to know what to do. His father wished him to take up the appointment, but his conscience told him that he should stay in France with the fighting troops. We were at Senlis at the time, and for two or three days he discussed the matter with me—a battle of whether what his conscience led him to believe, or whether his other call to duty, namely going home to England, was right. I think it was I who persuaded him to take up his Government appointment.'[1]

He was consoled by the thought that it was now almost certain that the regiment would never be used in a combatant rôle:

'It is far easier,' he told Dorothy, 'to think clearly about a definite job than about the vague problem of vague usefulness in the House of Commons. Well, there it is. It is, as you will believe, hateful saying good-bye to what has been one's life for three years, but I should feel it much more if I was still with the Squadron, and if our general future was not so apparently unsatisfactory. There seems to be a good deal less to stay for.'

He gave a farewell dinner for the regiment, the first time they had all been assembled since Scarborough days. Trooper Engels, the 'B' Squadron mess cook, and in private life chef on a Cunard liner, 'produced a dinner that would not have disgraced the Ritz', and Trooper Robinson brought the house down with his rendering of 'If You Were the Only Girl in the World'. There were speeches and singing to the piano until 2 a.m., the sound pouring out into the sleeping farmyard, sentimental as such occasions are, but at once hilarious and moving for the host.

'One of the best evenings I have spent since Oxford days! Made me feel

[1] Major Ginsberg to author.

ten years younger, and oblivious of the war. Now today comes the reaction, and I am feeling as full of humps as it is possible to be. One seems to have definitely turned over a page and to have no great interest in beginning a new one.' With a heavy heart Edward went to apologize to the lady of the farm for disturbing her sleep with the din of the night before, but she smiled charmingly and told him that she was happy to hear any merriment 'pendant la guerre'.

The natural consequences of the war for serving Members of Parliament had been to limit their contacts with the House of Commons to attendance on special leave at moments of crisis. Edward was not in England during the days of manœuvre and intrigue when Asquith was replaced by Lloyd George, but he had already taken the opportunity of speaking in the House when on leave. Early in 1916 he had put the case for a smaller War Cabinet, being convinced that a large Cabinet, 'even if it were a Cabinet of Archangels was not the ideal body for administering a great war',[1] or to be effective at a time of emergency when instant decisions must be taken.

He believed that there should be men 'at liberty to think without being immersed in departmental work', and asked the Prime Minister so to reconstruct the Government that 'we may have a real small War Council, with supreme responsibility and supreme powers, who will not be fettered by departmental work, but who will be at liberty to think out the great problems, and to put the results of that thinking into execution'.[2] Asquith did not follow his advice, and it was left to Lloyd George to form a smaller Cabinet, which showed a constant tendency to increase in numbers, indicating that while a small Cabinet may be theoretically the ideal instrument in wartime, it is not an easy one to achieve.

Nor did the second point which he made in this debate meet with approval. Sir John Simon, who had preceded him, had declared himself an inflexible opponent of compulsory military service. It was a matter on which the Member for Ripon had pondered much in France and on which he held strong views. Perhaps he had been affected by the complaints of the French, who had for years enforced conscription and looked with anger and incomprehension upon the English failure to do so. He urged its immediate introduction. 'I think,' he said, 'that in after years it will be thought a somewhat extraordinary thing that in the twentieth month of the war we should still have been having one delay after another, that we should still up to the last moment have been making frenzied efforts in the cause of straightforward voluntary recruiting, and that we should have been having one recruiting statement after another.'[3] It is probable that this speech from a young Conservative straight from the front influenced the decision to apply conscription.

[1] *Hansard*, House of Commons, Vol. LXXXI, Col. 2638, 2 May 1916.
[2] Ibid.   [3] Ibid.

In Edward Wood's conviction that the war must be prosecuted to the bitter end, and in the thoughts, inflexible, almost revengeful, about Germany which sometimes occupied his mind is revealed the hard core which lay at the heart of his character. At such moments there was no trace of that weak forbearance so often mistakenly attributed to him. To those who observed how much he relied upon Divine aid it sometimes came as a shock to discover that he was also capable of ruthless action. None of his less devout colleagues was more determined than he to fight the enemy to a standstill. He was ready to split the Coalition in 1916 to do so, and to give his support to any Government, even that of the Labour Party, which was 'prepared to carry on the war, as I conceive, with more vigour'.

In the war to come much tender scrutiny would be made of the pangs of those who put forward objections of conscience. Edward, in 1917, made no such nice moral distinctions. He regarded such people with unmitigated contempt: 'I have absolutely no sympathy,' he said in the House of Commons, 'with the real conscientious objector. I am told that in the United States they do not waste time over passing special laws and legislation over conscientious objectors, but if they are quite sure they have the right people they compel them to wear scarlet uniform and walk the street.'[1]

There could be no clearer indication that in another compartment of his mind to that of the devout churchman lay the power, once that mind was decided, of forceful and even harsh decision, arrived at with no difficulty and followed by no misgiving. It was the same characteristic which was later, in India, to enable him to confirm a death sentence when convinced of its necessity, and immediately dismiss the matter from his mind.

                          *   *   *

While on leave at the end of 1916 Edward made a speech which was listened to with the great respect which the House of Commons always shows to a speaker who is taking his courage in his hands. The subject was Ireland. There was no need, he said, to emphasize the importance of Ireland as a war problem. In their most optimistic moments there was always the recollection of this skeleton at the feast. They had witnessed the Easter Rebellion, and now they had the spectacle in which a large section of Ireland was resolutely standing aloof from the effort the rest of the Empire was making. He rejected both the idea of England applying compulsion, or washing her hands of Ireland entirely and winning the war without her. Both were admissions of failure:

'What was the part the Government and the House ought to take?' he asked. 'He and many of his friends had come to the conclusion that the only course to adopt with regard to that country, which promised any satisfactory results, was to make a bold and generous departure on new lines, and give

[1] Ibid, Col. 2639.

Ireland the self-government she demanded. So he appealed to Ulster to make her sacrifice and fall into line with the rest of Ireland, and he appealed to the new Government to seize its great opportunity and find a settlement the urgency of which he could not properly exaggerate.'[1]

It is significant that in this speech Edward demanded a great act of faith from Ulster the difficulty of whose position he had never properly grasped.

It was in this spirit that he was later to accompany his father in May 1918 to Downing Street and, lunching with the Prime Minister, Lloyd George, to support an idea which had occurred to Halifax's fertile mind. The political world was at that moment much exercised over the proposal to apply conscription to Ireland. Halifax had been outraged by the danger and stupidity of this suggestion. He raised the subject with Edward at breakfast one morning, saying that the Government must be mad to contemplate such a measure when it was touch and go with the war.

How could they expect the Irish to see the force of reason? They never had and they never would. But a plan had entered his ingenious mind: 'What the Government ought to do was to get the King to go over to Ireland at very short notice, convening a gathering of all the notables to meet him in Dublin. The King would speak to them and say that he had come over personally because he was not satisfied with the proposals of his Government about conscription. There was a great shortage of men in France, and he did not believe that once they understood the need, his Irish subjects would allow his English and Scottish subjects to be unsupported. That was why he wished to speak to them himself—to tell them of the need, and to appeal to them to use all their influence to get the young men of Ireland to come forward. If, as he confidently expected, they told him of their readiness to do this, he would go straight back to London and tell his Ministers to drop their conscription proposals.'

Perhaps Halifax realized that this bold idea would appeal to the Prime Minister, and Edward soon found himself and his father lunching with a man with whom their only previous contact had been violent disagreement over education and Welsh Disestablishment. Over a decanter of excellent white port Lloyd George expressed interest in the plan but doubt as to the King's part in it, and Edward found himself suggesting that the Prince of Wales should be substituted for him and hurried over to Ireland in a destroyer with the mud of Flanders still on his boots. The Prime Minister's Celtic imagination was fired by this suggestion, but he was concerned at the thought that if the Irish response was negative, he would have been responsible for launching the Prince of Wales on his career with an initial failure. He therefore ruled the suggestion out for this and other reasons, with genuine regret that such an original course could not be pursued.

Edward returned to England in October 1917, and in the following month

[1] *The Daily Telegraph*, 22 December 1916.

was confronted by an important decision. The Lansdowne Letter, written by the fifth Marquis of Lansdowne, appeared in the *Daily Telegraph* in November 1917. In it Lord Lansdowne advocated an immediate end of the war with Germany on terms of compromise. With the Germans again confident of victory, Lloyd George and the advocates of the knock-out blow in power in England, and Clemenceau and the 'jusqu'au-boutistes' in control of France, there was little chance of the leaders on either side weakening at this moment, but Lord Henry Bentinck supported Lansdowne, and asked Edward Wood to write to *The Times* in similar terms.

The famous letter had already produced a disturbing effect on certain sections of opinion. Some who were sickened by the war and doubtful of ultimate victory, felt a quickening of the heart at the thought that an end might be put to the slaughter, but Edward Wood was not among them. Rather did he believe that however long the war might last, and whatever mortgages the English might draw on the vitality of their race it must be continued until some deep humiliation had been inflicted on the German people, and some indelible scar on their hubris. This was undoubtedly his basic attitude towards the prosecution of the war, and a year later in October 1918, when Germany was almost on her knees, he was to write to his father: 'I am dreadfully afraid of events turning out in a sense to let the Germans off, and it goes much against the grain not to burn some of their towns etc. But the great thing—in spite of Wilson—is to humiliate the German power beyond possibility of misunderstanding.'

But the circumlocution of the letter in which he declined to support Lansdowne suggests that another side of his character, which was afterwards to dominate it, was already forming. He was by nature, and on his own admission, to become a pacifier and an adjuster in public life. He made no denial of the fact that the strong tendency of his mind was to see both sides of a question with equal clarity, and whether this characteristic proved a weakness or a strength depended entirely on the circumstances in which he found himself. This pacific strain owed nothing to timidity, for Edward was without nerves, and would face a riot or war with equal courage, but was due to an abhorrence of force as a substitute for reason. The future would show that the willingness to understand the springs of action of such a man as Gandhi and to make concessions to him with no sense of weakness or submission was a source of strength, and that the patience required to woo and convince an America deeply suspicious of his motives and those of his country was, in the circumstances, a desirable quality. But the same inner need for the dispassionate appraisal of a problem, and the discovery of a means of its smooth adjustment could also prove a source of weakness when confronted by a dictator whose depravity he found difficult to understand, when moderation in thought seemed inappropriate and almost inhuman, and righteous indignation the proper moral reaction in the face of disgusting evil.

When confronted by an obstacle he already preferred to go round by the wings, and at this moment was reluctant to give an immediate refusal on the question of the Lansdowne Letter, choosing to examine every argument and every aspect of the matter, leaving himself several avenues of withdrawal, before refusing his support. Thus he gave a foretaste of possessing that negotiating type of mind, always ready for accommodation, which afterwards proved so valuable in India. It was therefore natural to him not to be positive when answering Bentinck but to seek a longer path which made a détour round the swamp.

'The general impressions of Lord Lansdowne's letter seem to be three.

1. Those who think he is a pacifist in disguise and take the *Daily Mail* line;
2. The pacifists who are genuinely pleased and think it a great asset;
3. Ordinary people who, except for phrasing, don't quarrel with the substance but think its moment singularly ill-judged.

I am one of the last party, I think.

'I can hardly imagine it possible *at this juncture* to do anything but talk about going on to the end and laying your plans accordingly. Russia, Italy, the conscription struggle in Canada, Australia etc. At the same time I am more and more convinced that, sooner or later, the ordinary man in the street like oneself will wish—and be bound—to make an estimate of the facts. And his decision as to whether he expresses his doubts publicly will be made, it seems to me, by the extent to which he thinks facts substantiate his doubts.

'At the present moment with the undefined asset of America on our side, I doubt whether people of my way of thinking could feel justified in giving open expression to doubts and in so doing help to tilt the scale against the chances of success. But that time may come, and that it will bring the necessity for a decision *on an estimate of probabilities*, I am convinced.

'A Secret Session may be demanded, and granted. But it is improbable. The House of Commons is too stupid an assembly.

'I personally should like to see a strong small and thoroughly trustworthy House of Commons and House of Lords Committee to whom the Government could make a full statement of all the data at their disposal.

'It would, I think, reassure people a good deal to know that thoroughly good and fresh people were tackling it, instead of feeling that all our judgments are permanently in commission to a body of which L.G. is the leading member.

'Really it comes, doesn't it, to this. We all profess to be fighting to make future wars impossible, or as impossible as can be. How are we to do this?

'Not by relying as in the past on Treaties, Frontiers, Armaments and Balance of Powers. Rather, as has been said, must we have some sort of international coercive "Pact" machinery.

'But this can only be effective as and in so far as it is inspired by a genuine determination for peace on the part of human beings who compose the various nations of the world. And this determination depends on the extent to which they have learned the lesson that has been before them since 1914. The real point of difference, therefore, is that, if war stopped *now*, Germany would forget much in the perspective into which the military party could undoubtedly throw the picture.

'And there is this, which one must weigh well. Don't you think that the U.S.A. has got to learn the lesson too? So that the British Empire and the U.S.A. may be bound together in the common learning; and stand together for the cause of peace by the strength of what they have learned in common?

'Summed up, my mind is that as things are we have no option. We must, if we think American help likely to be as substantial as we are told, hang on, and give it time to tell. But—if the situation alters—we must keep our minds as clear as we can—to review it.

'As against all this there is the line of thought of Page's letter to *The Times* of last Monday—that *nothing* matters except a continuance of the attempt to make Right completely victorious. I wonder.'[1]

*   *   *

Edward Wood remained at the Ministry of National Service from November 1917 until the end of 1918, and the importance of the work fully justified his return from France. He was able to throw himself into it with conviction. Since the beginning of the war he had been disgusted by the failure to apply conscription, and in 1915 he had written to his father of the Coalition Government: 'I look to it to do what no Party Government would dare to do—namely really label every physically fit man for the job in which he is most use. And isn't that the purpose of its creation?'

It was for this reason that a department of Government had at last been set up with the power to conscript labour without which, in Edward's opinion, they had previously been trifling with the issue. A system of conscription for military service had been only slowly achieved. The question of industrial compulsion bristled with far greater difficulties, of which the Prime Minister, Lloyd George, was painfully aware. 'Patriotism,' he said, 'has eccentric and incalculable limitations in different countries. It is often the result of some ancient conflict which has left traditional resistance in a nation's mind, just as in deep ploughing you come across boulders deposited in the soil during the glacial period.' The task of supreme difficulty for the

[1] Hickleton Papers, November 1917.

WITH WALTER B. RIDDELL (*left*) AND L. H. AMORY (*right*) IN FRANCE

Government was to provide that every man should be used in a position where he would be of the greatest value, but it was a task that was never fully carried out, owing to the endless prejudices, traditions and jealousies which conspired against it.

Much of the suspicion of the representatives of labour was caused by the belief that the proprietors of works engaged on Government contracts were profiteers. The idea of conscripting them for industry appeared to workers equivalent to forcing them by law to work for the benefit of private capitalists. Much of this work was as essential to the continued waging of war as the maintenance of the armed forces. Yet, although for these the Government could lay their hands on men almost at will, for the Home Front they were forced to rely on the voluntary system. It was for these reasons, among others, that the first Ministry of National Service under Neville Chamberlain largely failed in its task of controlling and distributing the whole manpower of the country in the most economical manner. The Cabinet had, however, agreed in principle that if voluntary enrolment failed, the introduction of compulsory universal national service should follow. By the time Sir Auckland Geddes had succeeded Neville Chamberlain, and Edward had joined him, the new Ministry was smoothly functioning, and as the war proceeded its tasks increased in difficulty and importance as the dual problem of securing drafts for the army and yet maintaining the labour supply of the country were rendered even more harassing by labour unrest.

CHAPTER VII

POLITICS IN PEACETIME

WHEN the war was over Lloyd George and Bonar Law decided that the Coalition should continue, and that a General Election should be held with the least possible delay. The existing Parliament had been elected nearly eight years previously on issues now dead and forgotten, and in the meantime a new Franchise Act had been passed abolishing property qualifications and giving the right to vote to 8,000,000 women. It was natural that such a far-reaching measure should be followed by an election, and it was also plausibly argued that Ministers should be supported by a mandate from the new voters before their departure for the Peace Conference in Paris.

The situation was entirely in the hands of Lloyd George and Bonar Law, and in order to meet the demands of the latter that the Conservative strength in Parliament must be increased from its minority of more than a hundred, Lloyd George did not hesitate to eliminate a sufficient number of Liberals to achieve this purpose, thus sentencing to political death a large number of the members of his own party which never recovered from the blow. The Government would have been certain of a large majority in this Coupon Election[1] on whatever line they had appealed to the country, but Lloyd George had surrendered to the prevailing mood of chauvinism, and before the election was over had committed himself to trying the Kaiser, punishing war criminals and exacting vast indemnities from the conquered enemy. These were the days when men spoke of 'squeezing Germany until you can hear the pips squeak', and the economist Maynard Keynes was to describe the Government supporters in the new Parliament as consisting mainly of 'hard-faced men who looked as if they had done very well out of the war'.

After the Coupon Election the independent Liberals led by Asquith were reduced to a pathetic 33 and Labour mustered only 63 against a Coalition block of 526, and since the 80 Irish Sinn Feiners did not attend, the Coalition was left with a working majority of 430. Lloyd George had been looking for docile and reliable men who would support him through thick and thin for the full period of the Parliament, and for the moment his desire seemed to be gratified.

He certainly needed all the support he could summon to deal with the enormous confusion awaiting him at the beginning of 1919. His Government

---

[1] Candidates certified as desirable by the Government were given letters of recommendation described by Asquith as 'coupons'.

was at once faced by a number of intractable problems, labour trouble of every kind, a civil war in Ireland, the threat of insurrection in India and Egypt, expeditions against the young Soviet State, unemployment and depression, and friction between the Allied delegates at Versailles. At home a vast army had to be demobilized, industry reconverted from a war to a peace footing, and expenditure drastically reduced to meet the appalling financial situation which showed a deficit of £326,202,000. When the new Parliament was opened on 4 February 1919 it was evident that great changes had taken place. The places of those who had departed had been filled by an influx of businessmen, most of them wholly ignorant of politics, who 'considered it their main duty to support the Government in carrying out the unsparing mandate of the Victory election'.[1]

In spite of such newcomers, there was more in this assembly to appeal to Edward Wood than in those turbulent Parliaments before the war, which seemed now like some distant memory of the past when the violence of naked emotions had jarred upon him, and reason had been so often usurped by passion.

He did not think that that was the spirit in which important issues should be decided, and he was happy to find the new House of Commons as placid as a lagoon in comparison with its predecessor. No major issue divided the parties; the Labour and Liberal opposition was small and innocuous, and the Government, with the Prime Minister at the pinnacle of his dazzling career, appeared to be in an impregnable position. The great phalanx of the Coalition was bathed in the afterglow of victory, and the other stars had paled before the Prime Minister's rising. In this new atmosphere Government legislation relating to India, health, transport and housing was placed with little discord upon the Statute Book.

Who would have believed that behind this stately façade which seemed so mighty and enduring there would soon begin the erosion which was to eat so deeply into its fabric that in the end it powdered away at a touch? The old balance of the parties had been destroyed, and one of them had emerged predominant in influence. The natural result of this enormous strength was a relaxation by the whips of party discipline. Their position at this moment appeared so secure that they saw no danger in incipient revolts and little need to nip them in the bud. The moment was ripe for a group of active young men to emerge and to attempt to ensure that the Government's advantage was not dissipated in complacency and in clinging to outmoded policies. Such a political position gave Edward Wood an opportunity denied to him before the war.

'It was not long before complaints of both Government policy and performance began to make themselves heard from the ranks of Government supporters. When the Government majority was, as it plainly was, secure,

[1] J. A. Spender. Op. cit., p. 601.

118

HALIFAX

minor excursions into opposition on the part of some of the Government's supporters offered considerable attraction. To sit day after day in silence until the regular Opposition party had exhausted itself and the question could be put, was very dull and earned no recognition from constituents.'

To avoid such obscurity, a small number of Conservative Members of Parliament formed a group with the objects of consulting together, criticizing and keeping a vigilant eye on the Government, and generally establishing a right to be heard. The original members were Edward Wood, Lord Wolmer, Samuel Hoare, Walter Guinness, William Ormsby-Gore, Sir John Hills, Philip Lloyd-Graeme, Walter Elliot, Sir John Davidson, George Lane Fox and Lord Winterton. The last, always happiest in rebellion and later uneasy in office, believed that Prime Ministers were naturally prone to give heed to those supporters who offered them the least trouble, and held that it was the duty of the group to oppose this tendency, and to render service to their party by sweeping away the cobwebs, ridiculing the toadies, and 'giving to their side a sense of youthful vitality and enterprise'.

There were some who, excluded from the group, referred to it derisively as a mutual admiration society playing into each other's hands, and designed to achieve office by drawing attention to themselves, but office was certainly not the main object of Edward Wood. He was beginning, perhaps for the first time, to find mild enjoyment in the House of Commons and the easy fellowship to which the group had given a new purpose. He and his able friends, all but one of whom became Ministers, grew to be a force in the House. In a humbler way and with far less audacity and genius, they repeated the tactics of Lord Randolph Churchill's Fourth Party.

They gradually developed an effective technique for mutual support. At a preliminary meeting to discuss the week's business they settled the questions to be put to the Government and how they should be pursued, and the part each member of the group should take in the debates. Their plans depended upon the manner in which they supported each other, and 'if a Minister tried to fob one of our number off with an evasive reply, another of the group would immediately be on his feet protesting against such cavalier treatment of a serious suggestion of my honourable friend'.

In the Government's housing policy, in particular, they found an ample field for comment, and the maladroit efforts of Dr. Addison to provide the 'homes for heroes', which Lloyd George had promised in the sunlit hours of victory, provided them with many happy moments. Edward began to feel that he was now an actor in the drama of which he had too often before been a depressed spectator. 'Day after day,' he said, 'in one form or another the hunt was on. It was great fun and I have no doubt was slightly irritating to the Front Bench and to the Whips' Office.' His attitude to politics resembled that of the eighteenth century. He was now content in Parliament as a member of this group, and was regarded as an effective House of Commons man, but he was not one to relish the rough and tumble of debate. The arguments in his speeches were invariably traced back to first principles, and he believed himself far better at dealing with general reflections than with concrete details. His speeches were therefore leisurely, contemplative, and inclined to be diffuse, but his judgment was sound, and he had already grasped the fact that politics was the art of what was practically possible. Never a man who could see only black and white he was far more prone to compromise than his fellow Anglicans the Cecils, who stood like rocks on matters of principle, and rigidly followed their conscience.

*   *   *

Apart from keeping the Government alert Edward was also watching the gathering storm in Ireland. Here both sides in the tragic dispute were confronting each other across an abyss of principle which it appeared impossible to bridge. To the Irish leaders with their long memories of the heavy hand of England through the centuries, and their consciousness of a burning sense of nationhood, the daily ambushing of soldiers and police appeared only as the passionless shooting down of an alien army of occupation. They believed that the time had now come for the English to realize plainly that Ireland, in spite of centuries of British rule, had never been a colony of England; that they were a different race who intended to have their independence now, even if it meant murdering and dying for it.

The English, on the other hand, were still too close to the issue, and too filled with indignation to appreciate its true proportions. They could see only that the Irish Nationalist leaders had rejected every effort to appease Ireland, and that they had given orders for a cowardly and clandestine policy of murder and stealthy terror. The muttered word and the snick of a rifle bolt at the moonlit crossroad, the pitiless ambushes plotted in secret in cellar and drink shop by men on the run, the mutilating of cattle, the burning of farms —these were the methods used to win freedom, and men in England read of them and longed to give some expression to their fury. In those savage days, as in all civil conflicts, the worst aspect was the ferocious desire for revenge which followed each murder, releasing one of the strongest and most atavistic instincts of man. The Black and Tans were sent out to Ireland ostensibly to buttress the forces of law and order, but soon their reprisals, as violent as the outrages which prompted them, further increased the hatred.

All these circumstances conspired against cool reflection on this issue. Nor did the Government appear to have any remedy for the evils in Ireland except the application of further force, and it was with general approval that the Prime Minister spoke of having 'murder by the throat'. The qualities which Edward Wood was to show with such abundance in India are already apparent in his attitude towards this melancholy problem. While most men allowed their judgment to be warped by emotional excitement, his remained ice-cold.

There were many who welcomed the assurances of further repression before they were driven by harsh experience to realize that the programme of compulsion had not succeeded, and could only lead to more bloodshed and unlimited reprisals. The time was soon coming when the Prime Minister and his colleagues would be driven by the realities of office to the conclusion that it was no longer practical politics to pursue the will-o'-the-wisp of coercion into the bogs of Ireland; that negotiation with the 'murder gang' was now the sole remaining hope of peace, and that they must nerve themselves to stretch out their hands and gather this tart fruit.

Edward Wood contemplated the problem in his own dispassionate way. Sooner than most, he realized that in dealing with Sinn Fein there were only two possible courses, to suppress it or to treat with it. He saw more clearly than most of his angry contemporaries that Sinn Fein was a living force in Ireland, and that it was nourished by the long memories of the Irish leaders who believed that they were coming at last to the end of their bitter road. Nor did he fail to understand how great would be the odium which would attach to those who sought accommodation with men whose hands were so stained with English blood. He realized that it would strike many with all the shock of a monstrous betrayal in which recent solemn pledges would be promissory notes which had become rubbish upon the market. It would be a terrible decision for a party, largely Conservative, both in the face of past history and the daily toll of outrage and death.

When the Government sent the Black and Tans to Ireland to reinforce the hard-pressed Irish Constabulary, Edward was not disturbed that they would be enforcing order with a heavy hand. The Lord Chancellor Lord Birkenhead had observed that 'you could not cure the mischief in Ireland by uttering the sublime admonitions of the Sermon on the Mount', and the Black and Tans were admitted by their own side to be 'a rough lot'. Edward's shrewd eye soon detected that their reprisals were part of a deliberate policy, but he was not in the least shocked by that. He merely believed that such measures seldom achieved success, and in the years ahead in India he was to be convinced again of the ultimate limitations of force.

On this occasion he would not have protested if the Government had declared their intention to carry out a policy of reprisals, although he might have doubted its wisdom. He was, however, repelled by the explanations given because he believed them to be hypocritical and false.

'They denied,' he said, 'in the most positive terms that there was ever any idea of reprisal; when the acts of reprisal took place, they were due to the overwrought feelings of those who had seen their comrades mutilated or shot, and as such certainly ought not to be harshly judged.'

Day after day the Canadian Chief Secretary for Ireland, Sir Hamer

Greenwood, sang this discordant lullaby to his anxious followers. To Edward it seemed that 'those who would not have been disturbed by a policy, however ruthless, courageously and honestly declared, were increasingly resentful of what they soon came to feel was sheer mendacity'. He was indeed so disgusted by what he considered transparent dishonesty that his belief in the Coalition and its leader was from that moment impaired, and the conviction formed that no further good could flow from such a tainted source.

It was Edward who made the first attack on the Black and Tans from the Conservative benches, and he lifted the subject far above the stale air of the debate, expressing a feeling on those benches which had long been reluctantly suppressed. He was by now a familiar figure in the House of Commons, although he was little known yet in the country outside Yorkshire. When the tall figure rose and he began to speak with such evident sincerity and such careful thought, he was always given attention. T. P. O'Connor, who had watched so many come and go, and described them with a gifted pen, wrote of him: 'He had no great fluency. He never made a brilliant phrase nor attempted an epigram. Yet he was always listened to.'

He had no illusions about his own powers of speech. He believed himself to be pedestrian and dull, and contrasted himself ruefully with such spellbinders as Lloyd George and F. E. Smith, underrating, with genuine humility, that power of matchless conviction which was later to alter so often the temper of the House of Lords and swing it to his side.

Edward Wood's attitude towards Ireland was clearly expressed in an article published on 10 August 1920:

'If the position,' he wrote, 'were not one of such overwhelming tragedy, there would be much of the ridiculous in the notion that is entertained in some quarters of creating an armed camp and calling it peace, and ignoring the fact that without consent you can neither hope to check disorder nor apprehend assassins.

'If this be true, it would seem that instead . . . of deluding public opinion with a notion that a sufficient application of force will provide a remedy, a wiser course would be to set about taking such steps as may be the means of recovering that consent without which society in Ireland cannot exist.

'Let us recognize that just as in the war the purely military effort was just a percentage of the whole national task, so in Ireland the matter is in by far the larger proportion a question of political amelioration rather than of firm administration.

'As such evil never will, and never can, be cured by drastic administration, it demands the making of a political offer to the Irish nation, conceived on the most generous lines consistent with Imperial security, and with guarantees of the same liberty for Ulster as is claimed by the rest of Ireland; on

lines which would at once arrest the imagination of Ireland, and give proof
to all concerned of the sincerity of Great Britain.

'The Prime Minister's position apparently is that he can make no such
offer unless assured of its acceptance. Those who might be in a position to
accept it are not likely to make any forward step unless they are assured that
the offer will be firmly made. Let us face the facts and be at once more
generous and more wise, and, converting hypothetical statements by the
Prime Minister into a firm offer, backed by the resolution of the House of
Commons, say frankly how far we are prepared to go.

'Having done this, let us invite, say, Lord Grey of Fallodon, a statesman
of international reputation and proved sincerity, to proceed to Ireland as the
head of a mission on behalf of the British Government, with plenipotentiary
powers for establishing the certainty of whether or not any settlement with
the leaders of Sinn Fein is possible.

'All history shows that in our dealings with Ireland we have always been
just behind our market. There is just a chance that we may retrieve this
failure if we act quickly. Of course it's a gamble. What isn't? . . . Even if we
were to make this offer to Ireland and it were refused, we would be no worse
off than we are today. Certain it is that only by making it is there any chance
of again creating a position in which whatever moderate Irish opinion may
still survive will once again dare to be articulate.'[1]

*   *   *

Apart from housing and the trouble in Ireland, agriculture was the subject
on which he felt most strongly and of which he had already much practical
experience. When speaking on this subject it was natural that he should
approach it from the point of view of the producer, and in February 1918,
in a debate on food supplies, he had already suggested that the price of food
to the consumer should be based on the cost of production, and that if the
ensuing price was too high, temporary subsidies should be given so that food
could be marketed without making it impossible for the producer to grow it
at a profit.

On 4 June he startled the House of Commons by setting out and moving
a motion which was carried on a free vote by 187 to 34, that 'the time has
come for the creation of subordinate legislatures within the United Kingdom'. This must have appeared a strange, even academic, measure to bring
forward in a Parliament so harassed by the problems of peace, which had
been obscured in the minds of all by the relief which followed victory, but
Edward cherished few illusions as to the chaos which would follow the defeat
of Germany. While still in the army he had foreseen the jobbery and oppor-
tunism to come, and declared the necessity for some lucid statement of

[1] *Evening Standard*, 10 August 1920.

Conservative policy which would concern itself with the welfare of the people rather than the advantage of individuals.

Towards the end of the war he had joined with his friend George Lloyd in writing a little book, *The Great Opportunity*, a pamphlet of 25,000 words, which attempted to lay down such a policy, and contained the explanation for his motion in the House. George Lloyd was an intimate friend, although he was not one of the 'group', and the friendship survived many disagreements, even a fundamental cleavage on the future of India. There was something in it of the attraction of opposites, Lloyd full of movement and vitality, of instant decisions and sudden passions, his striking face burned deep by eastern suns, his nature impatient and autocratic, his true bent administration and the exercise of power; and Edward, reflective and sober, a stranger to impulse, preferring a reconnaissance in force of each problem, and slow to kindle at his friend's flame. They were as fire and water, a strange alignment of authorship.

Edward had already decided that the House of Commons was no fit place for his impetuous colleague. Lloyd, like T. E. Lawrence, had soon become sickened with an England which, as it seemed to them, had already defaulted on their assurances to the Arabs and tainted the shining image of her which they had presented. Lloyd, with his mind fixed entirely on the larger issues of Imperial and foreign policy, must have yearned for the administrator's desk from which would go forth a stream of edicts unchecked by irritating contradiction.

George Lloyd had, in fact, little to do with the writing of the pamphlet. The hand of Edward Wood lies upon it, heavy and unmistakable. We feel it in the consciousness of class structure, in the interest in agriculture, and most strongly in the insistence on the Christian society. We look in vain for the staccato sentences of Lloyd who had already departed to govern Bombay before the book was published, and may conjecture that it was present discontent with post-war England and affection for Edward which caused him to be associated with a work which set forth a coherent but academic policy for his party.

The writing of party literature is a thankless task, but *The Great Opportunity*, although somewhat ponderous in style, is one of the best examples of it that has been preserved. The pamphlet was written before the end of the war, when the minds of most were fixed upon the fighting, but in spite of the general belief in a golden age, it anticipated difficult problems and suggested high-minded solutions. When published, its sincerity shone like a beacon through the squalor and self-seeking of many of the new members of the Tory Party. It made an extraordinary appeal to the young and idealistic, who, impatient with the sorry mess they believed their elders had made of the world, looked forward to a new millennium. Sir Charles Petrie, then an undergraduate at Oxford, remembered that: 'Edward Wood had a great

5*

following in Oxford in those days, chiefly on account of the book *The Great Opportunity* which he and George Lloyd had recently published. It was a bible to many of the young men of the immediate post-war era.'[1]

The motion for devolution is explained in the pamphlet. The authors remark that as soon as the war was over the pressure upon the time of Parliament would be enormous. Already its continuous session reacted unfavourably on the work of all immediately concerned. Ministers were forced to spend too much of their time answering questions when they should be directing their departments; Members, compelled to spend all their time in London, had lost touch with their constituents. The result had been an excessive strain upon the whole machine of Government and a deterioration in administration.

'The difficulty that confronts any Government and most of all a Government staggering under the responsibility of a world war, is that the country generally is not conscious of the cause of the evils we have referred to, but only of the evils themselves'. Concentrating entirely on victory, men would be irritated by talk of constitutional reform until victory was won. 'None the less,' wrote the authors, 'we believe that it is the duty of Government to deal with this question.'

They suggested that certain powers now vested in the United Kingdom Parliament should be devolved to England, Scotland, Wales and Ireland. These powers would be purely local, and such matters as justice, defence, foreign affairs and economic policy would remain in the hands of the United Kingdom Parliament. The object of this federal devolution was to free the hands of Ministers and others for more important work, and give the local assemblies experience in conducting their own affairs. This was the proposal which the authors developed at length and regarded as *The Great Opportunity*.

They also devoted their arguments to the protection of landlords from unfair criticism—and here the authorship cannot be doubted—to economic policy, the position of the House of Lords, the Civil Service, the trades unions, the League of Nations, housing, drink, education and agriculture. It was a painstaking blueprint of a better world, redolent of spiritual rectitude. A number of propositions were made *ex cathedra* which were to be sadly belied by events. On the subject of agriculture they wrote: 'The nation must be convinced, and led to act on the conviction, that its interest in agriculture is more immediate than that of any other industry, and that it is shortsighted folly to neglect it.'

Throughout their argument the authors repeatedly emphasize that the success of the course they advocate depends upon a religious revival and that all progress must be permeated by its intangible influence:

'Religion brings a new value to humanity and human beings, and those for whom the great sacrifice was made on Calvary and lives for which so great

[1] Sir Charles Petrie to author.

a Person once saw fit to pay so dear can never again be counted cheap. . . . Even from its own point of view the state should strive to afford all material and moral support to religious forces, of whatever kind, operating within its borders. They, on their side, must act in season and out of season as sharp goads to the conscience of the nation, and fearlessly draw attention to matters that belie the nation's Christian profession.'

The Great Opportunity was thus an expression of that idealism characteristic of one of its authors. Perhaps they were right to include so strong an element of optimism in their book, but it did not correspond with the harsh reality of what was to come:

'Neither of them was any economist,' wrote a critic, 'and neither had much knowledge of industry. They did not apparently foresee the vital facts which actually governed and controlled the national life during the miserable post-war years, and made it a mockery to talk of them as offering any "opportunity", great or small. They saw nothing, for instance, of the catastrophic collapse of the export trades, and the strangling of international trade by economic nationalism; nor of the over-production, in trades like steel and shipping and coal-mining, the result of the enormous development of their plant and output during the war, which was one prime cause of the ghastly post-war Unemployment . . . nor of the weary war debt squabbles and the evils that followed in their train.'[1]

                              *   *   *

The year 1919 was notable as a period of disillusionment, of cynicism and of self-deception. The appalling slaughter of youth on the Western Front had left a deep scar on the English people. The holocausts of the Somme and Passchendaele, which had so much impoverished the nation, had caused a deep repulsion from the mere thought of war. It was natural that many were prepared to surrender their safeguards for the future with dangerous impulsiveness to a new instrument dedicated to banishing the dread of war for ever from the minds of men.

In this mood of the day it was unthinkable that such horrors could ever be repeated, and an untried system, the League of Nations, based on no empirical experience, and which assumed a fundamental change in the human character, was eagerly grasped in a state of emotion rather than of reason, and exalted to a position so sacrosanct that to question it was heresy. In such a condition it was difficult for men to give to the League of Nations the dispassionate scrutiny which might have convinced them that while it could perform valuable work in its minor spheres, the larger claims made on its behalf were void of realism.

Edward Wood had made a number of public references to the League of Nations after the war. At this time he was one of those who succumbed too

[1] Hodgson. Op. cit., pp. 46–47.

readily to this seductive vision. In several speeches he dwelt warmly on the future of the League, which he regarded as the one solid gain to be derived from the sufferings of the last four years. On this matter he showed an eagerness to embrace the new faith, and a neglect to examine the true springs of human action: 'As I understand it,' he said, 'the ultimate ideal of the League demands at least three things: it demands universal disarmament, it demands economic freedom, and it demands arbitration.' It was with eyes less starry but more piercing that Balfour regarded the future when he rejected Edward's 'noble and interesting idealism', observing that 'Nations that do not want to keep the peace will not be bound by these treaties of arbitration'.

Edward was not alone in this misunderstanding of the Old Adam, and in the belief that man would behave better in the future than he had in the past, but there is a confusion of thought in his advocacy of universal disarmament for he had by no means altogether renounced war.

'It is right to remember,' he told a deputation at Harrogate, 'that there are things more detestable than war, for which it may be, in the present state of human development, that war is, in fact, the only remedy. . . . And therefore I believe that the best way of preventing war is to make it plain to the world that though the very name of war is hateful to us, yet we are ready and able and unafraid in the last resort to have recourse to it.'

*   *   *

In April 1919 Halifax and Agnes celebrated their golden wedding. It was considered too early in the season for festivities for tenants on the estates. They were postponed until later in the summer, and were never to be held. Lady Halifax was already ailing on the day of the golden wedding. Her heart was weak, and she had undergone an operation in February, but the people from the village did not know this and said that they had never seen her look so well, in the blue velvet dress she had worn at her daughter Agnes's wedding in 1903. They stayed at Hickleton until 21 May, and to Halifax it seemed that his wife was growing stronger every day, and they took long walks with the dogs through woods full of bluebells. Then he took her to Devonshire, hoping that at Bovey Tracey they could live again in the atmosphere of the past:

'We spent the most delightful month,' he wrote to a friend, 'almost the happiest month of our lives. Edward, Dorothy, and their children Charles and Anne came down to us; each day was finer than the last. We made an expedition to The Moult at Salcombe, the house where we had spent so many happy days during Lord Devon's life, with the children. We landed at Boat Steps, which Agnes managed without difficulty, though the landing was not easy and the steps appallingly steep. We went all over the garden; Agnes scrambled over a fence and down a wall where the gate on to the beach was locked.'

They looked again for the pink sea shells as they had done when they were a young married couple, and Halifax took Edward and Dorothy along Courtenay's Walk, through the leafy tunnel above the sea, and looked down on the old bathing place where Edward as a child was tied to an air-cushion and left floating in the sun. Their drives on the moor and down the narrow lanes were to Halifax redolent of the past. 'One I remember along the Terrace Drive down to Becky where Agnes drove the pony down such a road —the old disused Manaton Road, as nobody but she would have looked at as possible.' In their last two days in Devonshire, when they were alone, Halifax was conscious of deep contentment:

'She could not have been better than she was, or we both happier together than on that day. God had granted all my prayers. She seemed to have completely recovered. We had been at Hickleton again leading our old life; we had walked together, done everything together; there had been the pleasure of the dogs and the puppy Laddie she was so fond of, and which was so fond of her. We had kept our golden wedding; everyone had been so good to us; all was so prosperous; in fact there was not a wish unfulfilled.'

This serenity was soon broken. When they returned to London the doctors were forced to perform a second operation on Agnes for the removal of a swelling, and soon there appeared local complications which refused to yield to treatment, and after a long and agonizing wait the doctors came to tell Halifax that his wife was dying:

'I said I would go up and tell her myself. We had not talked much during the day. Her voice was weak and I could not hear very well. I said: "My dearest, you remember when you were so ill at Garrowby in 1890 after Charlie's death that we then said that it would be you and the three children within the veil, and I and the three others here. The doctors have just told me that it will be like that now; that there is no hope and that it won't be long. We have to be brave."

'She just cried a little, and then said, would it be painful? I said I believed not, but that she might ask the nurse. The nurse confirmed what I had said. She then put her arms round my neck and kissed me two or three times, and then said she should like to be alone for a little. I left her, and when I came back we spoke to one another, and then I said: "You would like to see some of the servants." She said, "No, I would like to see them all after I have seen Mr. Whitby."[1]

'We again spoke a little, and then Mr. Whitby came. The servants, meanwhile, had all come up and were outside. She saw Mr. Whitby alone and made her confession. Then all the servants came in. She was given Communion and anointed, and prayers for the dying were said, and then she wished all the servants good-bye, shaking them each by the hand. "Good-bye, James," she said to my servant who had been with us for a long time, and

[1] The vicar of St. Mary's, Bourne Street.

to her maid she whispered: "You will be kind to the dogs." (Her maid used to take them out and feed them at night.) She saw and spoke to all the children, including George Fox, told them to take care of me; said something that I should know what she wished, that she would like her little religious books given to the children (the grandchildren) and then she spoke again to me.

'She began to doze. The last prayers were said, and when death came he came so gently (she had always been afraid of the act of dying) that it was difficult to say whether it was death or only a deeper sleep. She had been conscious and herself almost to the end. The nurse said they had "seen many people leave this world, but none quite like Lady Halifax". It was the transfiguration of death, everything seeming unreal except the things invisible within the Veil.'[1]

Edward, after this harrowing scene, had the strange impression that he had not known his mother completely until he looked down upon her in death.

'For myself,' he said, 'as perhaps by natural law must be the normal case, her passing was something that in the old phrase had, and could have, no fellow. A mother's death is bound to remain in the strictest sense, unique. As I stand in memory once again in the first days of that loss, I seem to have been conscious of a double and curiously disconnected train of thought. One side of it was completely egocentric, in the sense that I felt myself rather startlingly pushed forward into a much more exposed situation as regards life and death than I had been aware of before. . . .

'The other train of thought concerned my mother herself, and gave me an impression of her that I instinctively felt to be more representative than anything I had known prior to her death. The explanation is I suppose that so long as a person is alive the picture of any particular moment is dominant. . . . The perfect balance of qualities which makes up the personality is by that much, therefore, the more difficult to catch. I certainly, after death had, as it were, for human eyes finally fixed the mould, felt myself to have a very much better understanding of her than I ever had before.'[2]

For his father it seemed, Edward thought, as if the immediate anguish of her death must destroy both the power and the will to live. Under the first impact of this dereliction it seemed that even religion had failed to provide the mysterious anodyne that had consoled him in the loss of his sons. In a mood of listless despair, unable to attend to business, and with the memories of the past and his idyllic marriage heavy upon him, he turned to his remaining son for succour and for guidance. To Edward he wrote on 14 July 1919:

'Dearest Edward,

I cannot tell you what you have been to me all these days—such a prop, such a help, such a comfort and consolation as, I think, no father ever had

[1] Hickleton Papers.   [2] Halifax. Op. cit., p. 93.

before. May God bless you, and make your sons to you what you have been to me.

You and Dorothy, Mary, Agnes and George, with your dear children, are now all I have to look to. You will have to manage and settle everything. It is all beyond me.'

Slowly and almost imperceptibly Halifax began to recuperate, and, in a state of gentle convalescence, to gather together the threads of his emotional life. Some member of his family was always at hand to keep him company at Hickleton where he found the church an unfailing source of interest and comfort. He began to return to Devonshire at Whitsuntide, and soon the memory of his life with Agnes at St. Mary's brought him solace rather than affliction. 'I do so like being here,' he told Edward; 'I am so fond of this little house and all that is in it. We did it all together, and the past lives again almost more than it does anywhere else.'

He had already resigned the Presidency of the English Church Union in February 1919. 'I have grown deaf,' he said, 'my sight is failing, my memory is not what it was.' He had cast round in vain to find a successor to this tiresome legacy. He was convinced that Edward was the only man with the tact and charm to reconcile the discordant elements in the Union. An appointment demanding so much time was now impossible for Edward to accept, even at his father's urgent invitation, for his ministerial career was about to begin when in April 1921 he was invited by the Prime Minister to become Under-Secretary of State for the Colonies.

CHAPTER VIII

A TOUR IN THE SUN

AT the time of this appointment Edward was forty, but he would probably have attained office earlier had it not been for the interruption of his war service. During the year 1920, in the October of which his third son, Richard, was born, he had come to be regarded in the House of Commons as a thoughtful and moderate man given to the objective rather than the party attitude of mind.

It was not the first proposal he had received of Government employment. In May 1920 he had been offered, and had accepted, the Governor-Generalship of the Union of South Africa. Lord Milner, the Colonial Secretary, had already written to say how happy he was at Edward's acceptance, but on further inquiry was forced to withdraw the offer:

'I am sorry to say that the South African Government refuses to fall in with my ideas about the Governor-Generalship. I always knew there was a chance of this, but I hoped that any objection on their part might be avoided, or that, at worst, it would not be seriously pressed.

'Now, however, they are raising a point of principle, basing themselves on the "increased status of the Union", and want either a "man of Cabinet rank or a member of the Royal Family".

'I think this quite wrong. To limit the area of selection in this way would constantly preclude the selection of the fittest man. It does so, in my opinion, in this case.

'All the same, I think we must humour them at this critical juncture, especially as, unless we do, we shall certainly be met by the demand for the appointment of a S. African. To that we could not agree, and there would thus be a very dangerous situation at once.

'It is *their* loss and *my* disappointment. I hope it may not also be a serious annoyance to you.'[1]

When Edward was appointed Under-Secretary of State, the Colonial Office was the all-embracing controller of the whole British Empire outside India, and it was not until some four years later that the Dominions Office was created in 1925. The new field in front of him was therefore immense. Winston Churchill was Secretary of State. Edward first read of his own appointment in the press on 1 April 1921 without receiving any intimation from the Prime Minister, Lloyd George, of this important turn in his affairs.

---

[1] Hickleton Papers, May 1920.

He remembered spending the next twenty-four or forty-eight hours wondering whether it was a hoax. At last, thinking that if it was a genuine appointment it would appear ungraceful if he did not take it up, he approached the Colonial Office cautiously, and explained to the doorman that he was the new Minister. He found that Winston Churchill was away at the Cairo Conference on business connected with the new British mandates in Iraq and Palestine.

Edward awaited his return with uneasiness. His brilliant superior was only seven years his senior, but already he had fought in Cuba and in India, in Egypt and South Africa. He had been President of the Board of Trade, Home Secretary, First Lord of the Admiralty and Minister of Munitions. He was an orator of the first order, and, in addition to his achievements in politics and on the battlefield, he was recognized as an author who had already imposed his own stamp upon the English language, and had composed the finest filial biography that had yet been written.

In a Government containing some of the greatest statesmen of the modern age he had been recognized as one of the most forceful, if unpredictable, members. He was, and continued to be for the next twenty years, the most mistrusted and unpopular politician in England. To many there was then something alarming in the almost obsessive purpose and ambition which drove him down the path of his own glory. The legend had been widely accepted that his judgment was so wild that his employment in high office was a positive menace to the state, and that his self-absorption verged on mania.

At this moment it was rumoured that Churchill was suffering from a double sense of injury: annoyance at not having been made Chancellor of the Exchequer, a post which had been given to Sir Robert Horne, and resentment at having been palmed off with Wood as his Under-Secretary when he had asked for someone else. 'I did not know him at that time,' said Edward, 'and felt slightly apprehensive of how closer acquaintance might work. For some weeks it did not work at all, as in spite of constant efforts on my part to make my number with my chief, he steadily refused to see me.'

The tried social dexterity of Churchill's Private Secretary, Edward Marsh, was tested to the utmost in a series of desperate little rearguard actions until even he ran short of plausible excuses to segregate the Minister from his colleague. It should be noted that Edward did not meet this impasse in any mood of saintly resignation. In the end he forced his way into the Presence and told the Secretary of State with indignation that he had no more wished to be his Under-Secretary than Churchill had desired his appointment, but that since he was there he claimed the right to be treated like a gentleman.

This outburst in no way disturbed Churchill who had not intended to be discourteous, but whose one-track mind had been focused upon the Middle East to the exclusion of all other considerations. It was, indeed, one of the habits that had made him so unpopular. Edward, by his outburst, had now brought himself to Churchill's full attention, and this situation once established, he would never be neglected again. His affection for Churchill, accompanied by many reservations about his judgment, was formed at this moment:

'From that day on no one could have been kinder than Churchill was to me. He constantly sent for me to his room in the afternoon to have a glass of vermouth, and would talk about what was happening in politics, making entrancing comments on his colleagues, or ask my opinion on some speech he was going to make, and I look back to the months with him at the Colonial Office as having been the start of a much valued friendship.'

With the ice broken, and perhaps dimly realizing that he had offended his Under-Secretary, Churchill concentrated upon him the full batteries of his impish charm and incomparable humour. He was also free with advice from his own experience, and perhaps Edward, when in July he formally moved the Ministry's Vote of Supply, bore in mind his master's sage advice about the use of notes when speaking:

'Never try to pretend to your audience that you're not using them. If you do that, you get them into a kind of competitive game of hide-and-seek with you, in which you're bound to lose. But if you are perfectly open about it, you can keep them waiting as long as you like while you find your place in your notes and put on your glasses to read them, and they won't mind at all.'

*   *   *

In that same month of July 1921 it was announced that the Under-Secretary was to pay an official visit to the West Indies, and it is certain that when he left he carried with him another piece of advice from the same source, based on personal experience as a young officer under tropical suns, of how to inspect a guard of honour. 'There is only one thing that's important to remember,' Churchill told him. 'Look every man straight in the face as you pass him. The sergeant-major has had them all standing on parade in a hot sun for at least two regimental officers to see them one after another before you come on the scene, and if you go by talking to whoever it is with you and looking the other way, it's pretty flat for the men.' This advice undoubtedly contributed to the good impression he made on all ranks in the army in the West Indies, and was later to be remembered by him with gratitude in India.

Accompanied by W. G. Ormsby-Gore, M.P. and R. A. Wiseman of the Colonial Office who were associated with his inquiry, Edward sailed from England in November 1921, and reached Kingston, Jamaica, on the afternoon of 13 December. The importance of his tour lay in the fact that it was the first of its kind in the history of the West Indies, and the occasion was therefore regarded as a new departure by the Colonial Office, designed to promote closer relations between those in England who administrated the colonies and their inhabitants.

In Jamaica he was given a foretaste of the rigorous programme which was to be repeated at every island he visited. From 13 to 26 December he was taken on an exhaustive tour of the island, interviewing members of the Executive and Legislative Councils, Parochial Boards, and representatives of local organisations, visiting sugar plantations, and being taken to Chapelton, Montego Bay, Gayle and Spanish Town, and the Government Stud where he did not like the look of the stallion. This pattern of inspection was to be followed at all the other places visited on the tour, and from those islands he was unable to visit, Montserrat, Tobago and the Virgin Islands, he received deputations. He was prevented from inspecting British Honduras by two reported cases of yellow fever, but the Colonial Secretary presented himself to Edward at Spanish Town, and, while courteously received, was dismissed by him as 'an indifferent fellow'.

On 22 December the warship H.M.S. *Valerian*, Captain T. H. England,[1] had arrived at Kingston from Bermuda to take Edward and his party to the Leeward and Windward Islands, Barbados and Trinidad. Edward now embarked on a triumphant progress, in which every day his self-confidence increased, and his touch became more sure. No royal tour provoked greater scenes of mass enthusiasm or more moving demonstrations of loyalty. The Commander of the *Valerian* thought that it was impossible to exaggerate the effect of the tour, and of Edward's charm and accessibility, and that it was greatly heightened by the fact that he was conveyed in a man-of-war. He was touched by the almost pathetic eagerness with which he was everywhere greeted. Flags and decorations of every kind were paraded even in the poorest communities, and he was to write in his report of the islands:

'Diverse as they are in almost every other respect, there is no difference in the matter of loyalty to the Throne and to the person of His Majesty The King. It is the feature of our tour which stands out in boldest outline and which I recall with the greatest satisfaction. . . . The effect of it is constantly to direct the gaze of the West Indian communities towards Britain and towards the visible symbol of unity that the person of the Sovereign affords.'

In spite of the tight schedule on which he was working, and by which almost every hour of the day was apportioned, he found time to keep a private diary which differed in a notable manner from his official report. From it we learn his candid opinion of many of the people he met, and we find too that he was by no means oblivious of the enchantments of these islands, arched like a sickle over the waters of the Caribbean, each one appearing an earthly paradise to the traveller. He became thrillingly aware of the water, so clear that an anchor could be seen biting the white sand ten fathom down, and of so pale and translucent a blue that to gaze into it was like looking into the

[1] Afterwards Rear-Admiral Hugh T. England, C.B., D.S.O.

heart of an aquamarine, and when the wind stirred the surface the changing hues of blue, dragon-green and indigo. Through glass-bottomed boats was revealed another world where fish brilliantly striped and pied threaded their way through fantastic coral gardens. Tropical flowers rioted like weeds in all the islands, hibiscus, poinsettias, flamboyants and bougainvillaea, and the immortelles flamed against the dark green creepers of the forest.

They came first to St. Kitts, to the blinding glare from the pavements at Basseterre; to green acres of sugar cane, and Brimstone Hill, that Gibraltar of the West Indies, its ramparts rising 700 feet sheer from the sea. Then to Antigua with its rolling hills dotted to the horizon with the old sugar mill towers, almost as much a little England as Barbados, and here he felt the past heavy on the old brooding dockyard at English Harbour, and the house where Nelson lived. His pleasure in the island was spoiled by a tragedy which took place there on the *Valerian*:

'Afternoon. Motored for tea to Clarence House—English Harbour—the old dockyard for the W.I. and the last dry ground on which Nelson trod before setting off for Trafalgar. A wonderful place and complete in every detail, landlocked harbour, equipment of dockyard etc. Only spoiled by mosquitoes which attacked us furiously. The general atmosphere rather clouded by the shooting incident on the *Valerian*, one seaman shooting another accidentally and then committing suicide. No. 1 died on Jan. 4 and owing to having to wait for the funeral, we had to skip Montserrat which we had proposed to visit.'

Instead they went to Dominica where a general holiday was declared in Roseau, and here he was afforded a striking example of the diversity of the islands. In St. Kitts and Antigua he had found the green smoothness of an English county, with few of the shrill primary colours of the tropics, and a sense of demure conformity. Their wildness tamed, they had become domesticated like fireside cats. But Dominica more resembled a tiger. The wildest of the islands, it had defied the attempts of man to subjugate it and had never been completely explored, a place of dizzy heights and vertiginous landscapes, and tropical forest that grew almost visibly, a tangle of bamboo, mahogany, cedar, mango and palm leading to the green heart of the interior which could be reached only on horseback.

Here were the finest limes in the West Indies, and he looked over the lime farm and factory at Sylvania, and drove down the valley with the sound of the Layou and Pagoua waterfalls in his ears through groves of cocoa and limes to a planter's house for luncheon. 'He is coloured,' observed Edward, 'but they all say as near a white man as can be except for his skin. Across a footswing bridge and a stiff walking climb to his house.' Here he confronted a huge West Indian meal of Hors d'œuvre, Soup, Frogs, Curry, Roast Chicken, Sucking Pig, Asparagus, Sweet and Cheese, followed by potent liqueurs.

From Dominica they sailed to St. Lucia and a French Catholic atmosphere, with a tendency to look down on its neighbour St. Vincent, which lay next ahead of Edward, as an island of Puritans and heretics, for St. Lucia had changed hands many times between English and French, and pride in French culture was strong. Here again he saw abundant signs of the inexhaustible beauties of the Lesser Antilles, another mountainous landscape pierced by deep valleys glowing with hibiscus, oleander, flamboyants, wild orchids, roses and lilies, and, towering over all, the twin peaks of the Pitons, once the haunt of the deadly *fer de lance*.

At St. Vincent he met another warm gesture of loyalty and welcome. After he had addressed the crowd in the square and assured the cheering people with a certain optimism that England had not forgotten St. Vincent, 'we were met by more crowds of natives, addresses, triumphal arches, rifle salutes. I made speeches from the car and told them how greatly I was struck by their loyalty and should hope to tell H.M. so.' He found it wonderful and moving beyond words that such fervour could survive in the degrading slums and shanty towns that disfigured the islands like disgusting sores upon a beautiful body.

'The archdeacon told me that in the poorest native shack you nearly always see some sort of picture of Queen Victoria, King Edward, King George and the Prince of Wales. Lobb the Administrator told me that one old woman had had two sons killed and in due course received the customary condolences from the King. She wrote back to say that her double loss must not be thought to affect her loyalty and to beg Lobb to waive the rules about 3rd sons, and to call up her 3rd boy.'

*   *   *

The proud ruling classes of that home from home Barbados, which he next visited, who enjoyed exceptional power and privilege in the Caribbean, were happily unaware of the impression they had produced on their courteous and smiling visitor. In his official Report he was to remark cautiously: 'Barbados has enjoyed, since the seventeenth century, an uninterrupted and unchanged constitution of which the inhabitants are extremely proud based upon a House of Assembly entirely elected by a small electorate with high franchise qualifications. . . . It is in the House of Assembly that political power lies, since without their consent the Governor is powerless to carry either votes of money or legislation.'[1]

By the end of his visit to Barbados Edward's equable temper had been sharply roused, and in the heat of the moment he wrote of it in his private diary in terms very different from those which he employed in the Report.

'Barbados itself makes you rub your eyes. It is England of the mid-eighteenth century. Governed by a narrow oligarchy, which in great measure

[1] Cmd. 1679, p. 31.

rests upon the most exclusive social distinctions of "old" families and which has finally satisfied itself that their own prosperity is synonymous with the prosperity of the island, it presents a complete contrast to all the other islands we have visited. Along with this, and interacting with it, goes a very strict social colour line, operating not only in the matter of society, but not at all infrequently prejudicing the white governing class against the most obvious measures for the advancement of the Negro. Lady O'Brien (Governor's wife) has had no end of trouble over her efforts to organize baby-saving schemes. Why save babies of Niggers!

'The franchise and qualifications for membership are high, and in an island of large estates as opposed to small settlers effectively debar many of the black population from obtaining votes. Those who have votes are said to be subjected to not inconsiderable economic pressure if they betray signs of independence. The white "Plantocracy" and mercantile community seem for the most part deficient in social sense of responsibility—and in the instinct of "Noblesse oblige"; and to be primarily concerned with their own pockets. It surely can't go on like this indefinitely.'

At Barbados they were joined by Dorothy, Lady Beatrice Ormsby-Gore and Lord Salisbury, who had come from England to accompany them on the last stages of the tour which next took them to that jewel of the Caribbean, Grenada the spice island of the west, and her capital Georgetown with its deep volcanic harbour where the greatest vessels could lie, its blue locked lagoon, its gabled houses, terra cotta, pink and blue, clustered about the harbour, and the aromatic scent of spices in the air, the loveliest little city in the West Indies. By 23 January his voyage was almost over. They were making the passage between Grenada and Port of Spain in Trinidad, passing through the Bocas into the Gulf of Paria—'a regular tide-race running in the narrow channel—Venezuela quite close on the right, and the sea for miles out on the Bocas, muddy coloured with the water from the Orinoco'.

Edward had by now become a popular figure on board the sloop, and the Captain had noticed the invariable politeness and consideration which he had shown to the humblest members of the crew. He loved to be liked and it was with genuine pleasure that he noted in his diary the details of a little ceremony that was performed on this passage:

'Just before tea, all the ship's company was formed up on the Quarter Deck, and after one or two introductory words by England, the Leading Signaller (Purnell) made a little speech of farewell to us, and said very nice things upon how much they had all enjoyed having us on board. Then Petty Officer Goddard on behalf of the ship's company presented me with a wood box for cigarettes and cigars, that had been made on board with my initials on the lid, and a photograph of H.M.S. *Valerian* inside. Really rather touching as they were all very simple and had been I think genuinely interested in all they had seen of a side of things probably new to them. I thanked them and told them what was quite true that I could not measure the extent to which they had all helped to make me at home by the difference of feeling with which we stepped on board *Valerian* and today.'

Edward had by then only Trinidad and British Guiana to visit. On 31 January 1922 he left on the S.S. *Magar* for British Guiana, and on 2 February set sail for home on the *Oranje Nassau*.

The conclusions of the tour were published in a Report to the Secretary of State (Cmd. 1679) which became a best-seller and was recognized at once as a notable State Paper. It was his first duty to examine the growing demand for a measure of elective representation, which would mean including in the legislatures of the islands a number of persons chosen by direct election. It was a principle which had already been approved by Lord Milner in the case of Grenada, and this concession had naturally brought similar demands from the other islands.

When Edward examined the methods by which each island was governed he found some disparity in their constitutions. Barbados was virtually independent of the Governor; in Jamaica the constitution centred round the vote of a minority in the Council called 'the Power of the Nine', which had become a sufficient thorn in the Governor's flesh for Edward to recommend its abolition. Apart from these two exceptional cases, he found that the islands were administered under a system of Crown Colony Government by a legislature composed of an official majority, controlled by the Governor, and an unofficial element nominated by him.

The problem, therefore, that faced him was whether other islands should admit elected members to their legislatures as had been done in Grenada, and, if so, to what extent. As in Ireland in the past and in India in days to come, it was his nature to look with sympathy on those striving for political advancement, and not to cling to forms that were already becoming outmoded. Therefore, although he believed that the demand for elective representation had been greatly exaggerated and inflated by agitation among an ignorant people, it would in the long run prove irresistible, and that 'it would be an act of grave unwisdom to allow this consideration to lead to the refusal of the privileges now claimed'.

He made it clear that neither in Jamaica nor elsewhere was there any demand for responsible self-government as it was understood in England, and that such a demand could not be conceded within measurable distance of time.

'For all this mosaic of humanity the Crown, through the Secretary of State, is in the position of responsible trustee, a responsibility of which it cannot morally divest itself until it is satisfied that it can delegate the charge to hands of not less certain impartiality or integrity than its own. Coloured and black well-wishers of their own kind will tell you that that time is not yet.'[1]

[1] Cmd. 1679, p. 7.

He assumed, therefore, that the control of the Secretary of State must continue in effective form, but that the movements towards elective representation must be met. He suggested that the first stage in this evolution should be on the basis of that already agreed for Grenada; an adjustment of numbers which, while leaving the official 'bloc' in a clear majority, would give place to 'elected members' by reducing the numbers of nominated officials. He envisaged the next stage as a further adjustment of numbers which would transfer the majority of the official bloc to the hands of elected and nominated elements conjointly. Under such a redistribution the nominated unofficial members would retain their complete liberty of voting as they wished. He thought it reasonably probable that the responsible element represented by the nominated members would be found in support of the Government even if the elected members were unanimous against it.

On these lines it was possible to take the first steps in associating the people directly with the task of their own government. It was admitted that the conditions in Jamaica were exceptional, and that proposals to meet them might not be suitable for general application. These suggestions for advance, although unsensational, were perfectly suited to the circumstances, and over them was suspended an ultimate safeguard, the control of the Secretary of State. Edward and his advisers examined and rejected the solutions offered by Dyarchy[1] and Federation. In the West Indian colonies the field of government was too restricted and the communities too small to derive any advantage from the division of government into reserved and transferred services as in India. In fact a form of dyarchy already existed in the reservation of weightier matters of policy to the Secretary of State, and there were other considerations which made such a policy out of the question.

*   *   *

Edward's views on the Federation of the West Indies are of interest in view of its subsequent trial and collapse. Unlike Ormsby-Gore, he had no preconceived views on the subject, and he certainly never committed himself to a federal solution, although he was prepared to admit that the comparative ineffectiveness of the West Indies in the affairs of the Empire was due to the lack of a single organization to speak on their behalf. Approaching the subject with an open mind, he found that the idea of federation was almost universally unpopular in the islands, and that the obstacles to it appeared insuperable.

The first and greatest of these was physical. The political theorists in London who advocated federation and peered at the West Indies on small-scale maps had no idea of the vast distances involved or the almost complete lack of communications. Jamaica was separated from the Windward and Leeward Islands by a journey longer in time than that from England to Jamaica. Steamship services between the islands were deplorable, and a

[1] A system by which certain key Departments were 'reserved' for Government control.

visitor from one to another might have to wait a fortnight before being able to travel home. The Commanding Officer of the troops in Jamaica told Edward that it had taken him five and a half months to receive an answer to a letter addressed by him to Trinidad. Indeed, the postal authorities in Jamaica sent mails for Trinidad and Barbados via England, New York and Halifax. Edward could not possibly have carried out his own tour unless he had been conveyed in a warship.

The second difficulty in federating an archipelago was political. He found that the sea tended to divide rather than to unite, and that sentiment and development did not flow naturally over it from one island to another. He found too that 'an astonishing diversity of physical feature, climate, language, religion and historical tradition' caused the centrifugal tendency to be deep rooted. The familiarity of the West Indians with the Governor of an island and his accessibility to them were a personal contact that could not be replaced by a High Commissioner.

In the Leeward Islands, where there was already a measure of federation, he found the inhabitants clamouring for 'defederation'. Where distances were so great the smaller islands thought that in a federation they were paying too much and receiving too little, and that the views of the local Government familiar with their own conditions were overruled by a non-resident Governor. Mainly for financial reasons, Edward was not in favour of changing the system, but he made a number of constructive suggestions as to how its working might be rendered more popular.

The Report also made detailed recommendations on economic, medical, educational and other subjects. In doing so, Edward had to remind himself constantly that he was operating on a shoe-string, and that he had been warned that there was little money available for these purposes. He was even compelled to speak in deprecating language of the 'altogether fictitious idea of the ability of the Government to help financially', and had to admit that the colonies were disappointed that there were no loans or grants-in-aid available. But his proposals were valuable because they pointed the way for the more generously endowed schemes of the future. As an educational reform he supported the temporary employment of an Educational Adviser and an Intelligence Officer for the West Indies generally, to accelerate the introduction into them of modern educational methods from England.

In the field of public health and sanitation he found a lamentable picture. Although yellow fever had been banished from the islands, malaria, dysentery, typhoid, tuberculosis, hook-worm, venereal diseases and other scourges were rife, and incubated happily in the filthy hovels of the shanty towns.

The infant mortality rate was alarming. Edward felt that there was a temptation to place too much reliance on the medical staff and the Government, and too little on personal initiative. He had observed how rudimentary was the knowledge of most West Indians on the subject of hygiene, and believed that the surest way to improve conditions was to educate the community from childhood in the need of acquiring sanitary habits. He invited some odium by remarking: 'There is no use in providing a well and then finding that the persons using it are allowing it to be contaminated with sewage.'

In the course of his economic survey he became aware that sugar was by far the most important and universal of the crops grown in the West Indies, and that the industry was at the time passing through an acute period of depression. This morbid condition was analysed with great care and patience in the Report, and a recommendation made which gave deep satisfaction to the planters that the Government should undertake to maintain for ten years a minimum preference of £3 15s. 0d. per ton on sugar.

Edward could make no claim that his visit would lead to any noticeable improvement. The passing prosperity of the war years had been followed by a severe recession. Sugar prices were low, and the general standard of life was depressed. The pressure of population was unrelenting: 'There was little that any of the respective governments could do but cut their coat according to their cloth, and I am afraid that over all that field there was not much that our mission, or any mission, could suggest by way of immediate help.'[1]

Although Edward's tour could not bring immediate relief to the West Indians, it marked a great increase in his own political stature. It had brought him from seclusion into the full glare of public acclaim. He had been the central figure throughout it and had been given an almost royal welcome. To those simple people he was the Representative of the King, who had been sent by that remote deity to listen to their appeals and to redress their hurts.

There was something pathetic in the fervour with which they had hailed him, almost as a deliverer, and the mystique with which they had invested his official position. As the tour proceeded his political flair sharpened. By constant daily practice he became ready in graceful impromptu speech. His tact was unflagging, and his extraordinary charm of manner, at once shy and forthcoming, achieved a personal conquest no less dazzling than that of the Prince of Wales. Behind this charm and accessibility was an eye observant and sometimes censorious, which registered impressions like a photographic plate. He had seized a wonderful opportunity, when all were eager to help him, of studying the machinery of colonial government, and no experience could have been a better preparation for the future.

[1] Halifax. Op. cit., p. 98.

CHAPTER IX

THE END OF THE COALITION

WHEN Edward returned from his tour he found that the Coalition behind a still imposing façade was slowly disintegrating from within, and before long portentous cracks were to appear in its structure. Its leaders, Lloyd George, Churchill, Austen Chamberlain and Birkenhead, who formed the inner council of Government, were largely out of contact with their followers and had neither the means nor the desire to analyse the anatomy of their discontent. They were indifferent to what their subordinates thought, provided that they did what they were told.

It is a fact that, as one rebellious Under-Secretary recorded at this time, 'there is an inherent tendency in all coalitions to coalesce more closely at the top than lower down in the scale of party organization. Cabinet business gets despatched more expeditiously and more amicably if the issues dividing the parties are kept out of the discussions. Tacitly sidestepped they presently come to be regarded as of secondary importance, or even as a rather tiresome element to be postponed, or, if possible, eliminated by some compromise.'[1]

It appeared to many of the rank and file that by putting forward from the first anti-socialism and the defence of the constitution as a policy and continually emphasizing them, the Coalition leaders had proved themselves bereft of any other, and negative in their attitude towards unemployment, wage reductions, and the other unsolved economic problems.

The great shadow of Ireland still lay across the future of the Coalition, and the Irish issue was to prove one of the main causes of its downfall. Its leaders had made the Irish Treaty and they prided themselves on its accomplishment, but in their state of detachment from the opinions of others they failed to realize that few of the Conservative supporters of the Government welcomed the Treaty, while many abhorred it. The Treaty itself provided, indeed, much of the explosive which was to blow Lloyd George's Government to pieces, but there were other corrosive agencies at work on the fabric, and many wondered how the Coalition had survived so long.

When Lloyd George considered his position he found much to recommend an early election, in which internal discontents would be met by the promise of distracting remedies. An election seemed imminent at the beginning of 1922, but these plans had been frustrated by Sir George Younger, the Chairman of the Party organization, who denounced the scheme as a betrayal

[1] L. S. Amery, *My Political Life*, Vol. II, p. 224.

of the Conservative Party. Had their leaders known it, the Conservatives, far from approving a Coalition election, were coming to the conclusion that Lloyd George and his Liberal followers were no longer an asset, but a liability that was now becoming intolerably heavy upon their shoulders.

The Irish Treaty was, in the end, fatal to the Coalition. If it had brought immediate peace to Southern Ireland, the Conservatives might have swallowed this sour gruel. But now there was open civil war in Dublin where an insurgent Republican force was holding the Four Courts against the Free State troops. Bonar Law expressed the real Conservative view when he said that in spite of the endorsement of the Irish Treaty by a general election in Southern Ireland, they would never have voted for it if they had had any inkling of its outcome. The Government now tottering, but apparently serenely unconscious of it, was dealt another heavy blow by the murder of Sir Henry Wilson on his own doorstep.

Gradually all these fears, discontents and hatreds had come to be concentrated squarely on the Prime Minister, Lloyd George. While the political world crumbled about him, he continued to live sustained by the memory of his past glories. The great man, the war winner, still the outstanding figure in Europe, it must have appeared inconceivable to him that he had anything to fear from his puny courtiers. Careless of warnings, he pursued his way, usurping the functions of his Foreign Secretary and blatantly selling Honours to the highest bidder for his personal political fund.

From the first he had gone little to the House, leaving the details of daily business to Bonar Law, and now it was to cost him dear. His methods of administration appeared to many disorderly and opportunist, and the scandal over Honours further imperilled his position. They had been traded cold-bloodedly across the counter as a grocer dispenses figs, and this cynical commerce had done more than any other grievance to alienate honourable men like Edward and his friend Leo Amery, who believed that apart from the little inner circle of deluded intimates at the summit, the whole Conservative Party was now in a state of simmering revolt.

The final breach was to come upon a foreign issue. Mr. Lloyd George was not the first or the last Prime Minister to become intoxicated by his own skill in foreign affairs, or to persuade himself that he was better equipped to deal with them than those whose business it was to do so at the Foreign Office. One of the ablest observers of diplomacy in our time wrote of the repercussion of these events on the declining fortunes of the Coalition:

'It was not, however, on a domestic issue,' wrote Sir Harold Nicolson, 'but as a result of errors or misfortunes in foreign policy, that during the course of 1922 the fissure within the Lloyd George Coalition widened into a final breach. The Prime Minister had become increasingly enamoured of international negotiation. Finding that his dexterity was hampered by the phlegmatic caution of the Foreign Office, he had surrounded himself with a small, gifted and obedient cohort of extraneous advisers. Lord Curzon, the Foreign Secretary, was obliged to accept these intrusions upon the responsibility of his office: but he did not do so light-heartedly, or without many a groan of warning, without many deep sighs of discontent. His friends in the Conservative Party were well aware that the Foreign Secretary viewed with grave misgiving some of the more imaginative of the Prime Minister's excursions. The blame for the checks, the disappointments and the calamities that followed was thus increasingly, but not always quite fairly, attributed to Mr. Lloyd George alone. . . .

'The final rupture of the Lloyd George Coalition was occasioned by the Chanak crisis of September. The armies of Mustapha Kemal, having driven the Greeks into the sea, advanced in jubilation to the neutral zone, which, under the conditions of the armistice, was occupied by allied forces on both sides of the Dardanelles.

'The French and Italians recalled their own detachments to the safety of the European shores. The slender British forces stood their ground in Asia, while the Turkish soldiers spat and gibbered at them across the barbed wire at Chanak. On the afternoon of 17 September Mr. Churchill, in the temporary absence of Lord Curzon, issued a communiqué inviting the dominions and our allies to assist in resisting the Kemalist aggression by force of arms. The British public realized, with sudden dismay, that they were on the verge of a new and totally unwanted war.'[1]

It was due entirely to the firmness, moderation and negotiating skill of General Harington at Chanak, with a handful of British soldiers behind him, that war with the Turks was avoided and a convention signed at Mudana on 11 October to regulate the evacuation of the Straits and of Constantinople by the British force. But the 'coup de Chanak' was the last blow to the Prime Minister, providing the Conservative opposition with a heaven-sent opportunity of stigmatizing him as an enemy of the peace, and a menace to the safety of the state. The sudden approach of war had profoundly shocked them. It had convinced them that by his intrusion into foreign affairs Lloyd George could wreak an even greater havoc than he could within the country. The way lay clear to the Carlton Club and to the fall of the Coalition.

*   *   *

Edward found himself in a certain quandary during these events. His confidence in the Prime Minister and the Coalition had long since disappeared. Lloyd George's character, its charm only matched by its ruthlessness, was not likely to appeal to one who liked to cling to logical processes and calm decisions and to subject them to the scrutiny of religion. If there was much in the Prime Minister's character that was displeasing to him, he had also lost all confidence in his judgment.

[1] Sir Harold Nicolson, *King George V. His Life and Reign*, pp. 367–8.

On the other hand, he was not yet prepared, as were some of the other junior Ministers to engineer his destruction. He believed that some gratitude was due to the Prime Minister for the moral courage he had shown at the darkest moments of the war. Nor could he forget that Lloyd George was the leader under whom victory in that war had been won. It seemed to him also, although it escaped attention in the case of others, that he owed his present appointment and his rosy prospects largely to the Prime Minister, and that it was a matter of common decency to remember that fact when determining his line of conduct.

A memorandum on the situation which he wrote in the early summer of 1922, shows, like his answer to the Lansdowne letter and his article on Ireland, the extraordinary objectivity with which he could examine questions which were so strongly agitating others. After an analysis of the position, he wrote:

'As far as I know, the possible courses are limited to three.

'1. To throw over the Coalition now—by Members of Parliament going definitely into opposition, and by the organization in the constituencies being encouraged forthwith to adopt candidates in opposition to sitting candidates.

'2. To dissolve the Coalition at or before the Election, in order that the Conservative Party may stand alone, as a party, and appeal for support on the ground that it has resumed entire independence of action.

'3. To encourage the Prime Minister to resign; to remodel the Government under a Conservative Prime Minister and with a stronger Conservative element.

'It is worth examining briefly each of these alternatives.

'1. Is only possible on the assumption that those so acting
   (a) are in irreconcilable disagreement with present policy;
   (b) are prepared with an alternative policy in the event of their opposition meeting with success.

Neither (a) nor (b) condition is today present as far as the bulk of the Conservative Party is concerned.

'2. Logically this also postulates a difference of policy whenever the dissolution of partnership is effected. At present no such difference exists, and it is difficult to see, while this is the case, in what way Unionist leaders can justify the abandonment of those with whom they have collaborated for the past six years. So long as Conservatives are unable to point to definite divergence of policy, it would seem disingenuous to seek to escape their share of the responsibility for the actions—and mistakes—of the past years, which is theirs not less than that of their Liberal colleagues.

'3. The last consideration is particularly germane to the third alternative—that of getting rid of the Prime Minister. Leaving aside the question of whether he would be likely to accede willingly or the reverse to the suggestion, if made, the attempt to recover popularity over the dead body of a leader whom a very short time ago Conservatives were thankful to follow savours of the ungenerous. At the lowest he is presumably not worse, as an individual or as a politician, than he was two or three years ago when I joined his Government; he has not unnaturally been made the principal target for all attacks on the Government as responsible for all the ills of mankind; but I think we should with some cause lay ourselves open to a charge of shabby dealing if we were to seek to make him the scapegoat for all our sins, imaginary or real.

'Certainly, I myself, if I only considered my own comfort and ease of mind, should vastly prefer to occupy an independent position in the House of Commons, free to criticize as I liked, free to vote on any occasion against the Government. But I am not less certain now than I was when I was invited to join the Government eighteen months ago, that to forego a share of common responsibility out of regard for the sweets of independence was to give less to the country than it had a right to demand, as long as its state was so anxious and disturbed.

'It is not otherwise with the great party to which we all owe allegiance. Were we to consult only our own natural sympathies, we should certainly seek to revert at once to a course of independent political action, and in so doing we should doubtless propitiate many lions that at present beset our party path. But I think that history would say that in the attempt to be mindful of the claims of party loyalty, we had been too little mindful of the wider obligations of national service.'[1]

* * *

By October 1922 Edward's attitude towards the Prime Minister had hardened. He had now reached the conclusion that he could give no further support to Lloyd George, and that the only honourable and straightforward course was to state his position without ambiguity to one of the leaders of the Coalition. He chose Austen Chamberlain. The junior Ministers had already appeared before three of the leaders, Balfour, Chamberlain and Birkenhead, and had been stung by a hectoring address by the Lord Chancellor, rebuking them for insubordination.

'The conclusion,' Edward wrote to Chamberlain, 'that was derived from those present at our meeting from the general tenor of the remarks made by the Lord Chancellor, Lord Balfour and yourself was that in your judgment it was the duty of the Conservative Party to go to the election as one section of an existing composite Government, appealing for continued support as a Government under its responsible leader, the Prime Minister. . . . If this be the case, I cannot conceal from you that I shall find great difficulty in following such a course.

'It is, I think, evident that any member of the Conservative Party who goes

[1] Hickleton Papers, 1922.

to election on that platform, most of all any member of the Government, is pledging himself, in default of any sharp divergence of policy, to give a vote of confidence to Mr. Lloyd George as Prime Minister for another Parliament.

'I would be the last to suggest that any of those who have supported the present Government in this Parliament are entitled to shirk any of the responsibility for the general policy that has been pursued, or for the mistakes—if such there have been—which the Government has made. Nor, as you know, have I much sympathy for the so-called 'Die-hard' element among our friends, and I fully recognize the probable necessity in the next Parliament of some coalition between parties.

'But I am increasingly doubtful as to whether Mr. Lloyd George, with all his great qualities, is the person best qualified to guide the country at this juncture. . . .

'It might be said that such a conclusion was inconsistent with the fact of having agreed hitherto to continue to serve him in office, and that until some actual difference of policy arose there was no justification for such a change of view. To this I can only say that the measure of confidence one may, or may not, feel in a particular individual is not wholly, or even it may be mainly, a question of particular policy.

'At the conclusion of the present Parliament I conceive that it is open to any of us who accepted the Prime Minister's leadership in 1918, for the post-war Parliament, to take different action without exposing ourselves to the charge of lack of frankness, or disloyalty. If, on the other hand, support accorded to the Prime Minister at the forthcoming election was subsequently withdrawn, he might not unreasonably feel that he had received disloyalty when he might have expected different treatment. Apart from the question of political expediency, which I venture to think is not so clear as the Lord Chancellor would have us believe, I cannot therefore feel that the course sometimes suggested of concentrating on the immediate necessity of getting over the next election, and relegating any political readjustment to a later date, is justifiable.

'For these reasons I have come to the conclusion that, if you decide to ask the Conservative Party at the election that is imminent again to fight under the leadership of Mr. Lloyd George, and, in the event of victory, again to follow him as Prime Minister, I must ask leave to revert to a position of Parliamentary independence.

'It is not without the greatest regret that I have reached this decision for every reason, and not least the recollection of the personal kindness I have experienced both from yourself and also from the Prime Minister.'[1]

Edward had brilliantly seized his opportunity in the West Indies, and he was marked out for advancement. While refusing to hound the dying Coalition, he had not forfeited the respect of those who had. He was exactly the

[1] Hickleton Papers, October 1922.

Photo Sport & General

WITH THE GARROWBY HARRIERS, 1924

man to appeal to one dark horse who had emerged as a national figure overnight after the Carlton Club meeting[1] and was soon to become Prime
Minister. Stanley Baldwin had warned that meeting that Lloyd George was
a dynamic force, but a force that had already destroyed the Liberal Party,
and that he was fearful that it might destroy the Conservative as well.

But his hatred of the Coalition was more personal than political. He
believed Lloyd George to be almost the Devil Incarnate. His puritan soul
shrank from his private reputation which led him into the habit of referring
to the Prime Minister as 'The Goat'.

Baldwin had had ample opportunity of observing Edward Wood in those
long afternoons in the House when, a prey to *ennui*, he would beguile the
leaden hours by studying and analysing the character of its members. In him
he saw a spirit kindred to himself, stable, placid and morally inflexible. It was
the beginning of a long friendship between them which both believed to rest
upon an identity of moral purpose. It was also at this time that Edward
formed another association momentous for the future, for it was in Neville
Chamberlain's early days in Parliament that the friendships of that ill-starred
leader were formed, particularly with Edward Wood and Samuel Hoare.[2]

*   *   *

Edward's way to the Cabinet was now clear. Lloyd George, Churchill and
their Liberal colleagues had gone, and the ablest Conservatives in the
Coalition, Chamberlain, Balfour, Birkenhead and Horne, had loyally followed their leader into exile. The election in November gave the Conservatives 344 seats in a House of 651 Members, and thus a majority of 73
over all other parties. Bonar Law, in forming the new Ministry, fell back
largely on those who had been Under-Secretaries in the late Government.
After a glance at the list, Birkenhead dismissed it as terrifying in its sheer intellectual mediocrity, but it could at least boast one brilliant newcomer,
Douglas Hogg, and three Fellows of All Souls, Curzon, Amery, and Edward
Wood who now entered the Cabinet as President of the Board of Education.

He occupied this post twice; first from October 1922 to January 1924,
and secondly as Lord Irwin and Lord Halifax from July 1932 to June 1935.
It was unfortunate for him that on both occasions he took office shortly after
a financial crisis, when economies of almost hysterical severity were being
pursued in every department of government. In 1921 the Geddes Axe had
fallen heavily on the spending departments in Whitehall, depressing Ministers
and paralysing initiative, and in October the Geddes Committee announced
stringent economies in education which were introduced in Circular 1190.

However anxious he might have been for reform, it was, therefore, impossible for Edward to do more than to refrigerate the proposals in the

[1] At the historic meeting at the Carlton Club on 19 October 1922 it was decided that the Conservative Party should leave the Coalition, and go to the country on its own.
[2] Iain Macleod, *Neville Chamberlain*, p. 82.

Education Act of his great predecessor, H. A. L. Fisher, until easier times allowed their implementation. Fisher's Act of 1918 contained the seeds of reform which lay dormant for years, only recently beginning to germinate. Among many other far-seeing suggestions, it empowered the Local Education Authorities to raise the upper age limit of compulsory full-time school attendance to fifteen, and recommended 'continuation schools' without fees for boys and girls up to the age of sixteen after leaving school, where they would spend part of their time in industry, and part in extended education, thus providing an invaluable link between school and industry.

By the time Edward arrived at the Board these provisions had already become inoperative. It was now suggested that grants to education should be reduced by about a third; the raising of the school-leaving age had been indefinitely postponed; the building programme drastically curtailed, and teachers made to suffer by having their salaries reduced and their pension scheme put on a contributory basis. These were the results of the Geddes Axe, which, in the opinion of one education expert, 'led to a meticulous examination of local expenditure, and the unnecessary holding-up of the programmes of Local Authorities; to absurd economies on buildings and staff and to the indefinite postponement of continuation schools', and a glance at the Board's Circular 1190 of 11 January 1921 to Local Education Authorities shows how bleak was the prospect for years to come of realizing the high hopes embodied in the 1918 Act.

In these circumstances it is doubtful whether the most zealous educationist or reformer could have made any noticeable impact on the education of the country. Edward was neither, but more vigour, less *laissez-faire*, and a more obstinate resolve to triumph over circumstances might have been shown in this thankless office. His Socialist successor Charles Trevelyan, confronted by the same conditions, was much concerned lest this vital subject should languish, and he showed the ardour of the true reformer in his efforts to renovate or replace 'black-listed' elementary schools, to reduce the numbers in the enormous classes which were the despair of teachers, and to expand secondary education.

The truth is that Edward's imagination was not stirred by the subject of public education; that his heart was never in it, and this lack of interest can be measured by the fact that he makes no reference in his autobiography to either of his periods of office at the Board. He had little, if any, interest in educational problems, past or present. Nor did he betray curiosity about the history of English education. He was ignorant of the painful steps by which men had struggled up this ladder, and of the names of the pioneers who had led the way, Kay Shuttleworth, Forster, Maurice, Morant, and a host of others. His Assistant Secretary, Maurice Holmes,[1] suggested that the young men in his office should draft some of his speeches, and he agreed, but said

[1] Afterwards Sir Maurice Holmes and Permanent Secretary of the Board of Education.

that he did not want anything too philosophical: 'I want to be able to say: "All this would have been impossible, had it not beeen for——"'; he paused, groping in vain for the name of a single educationist, and concluded lamely, 'Tompkins!'

Sometimes he would begin a conversation with his civil servants with a display of interest in some aspect of education, but it would quickly evaporate. The fascination of the subject eluded him, and his mind was remote from the work in hand, dwelling, perhaps, more on when he could decently escape to the two days' hunting he allowed himself each week, and the dogs and horses at Garrowby. It was inevitable in the circumstances that Edward, like others before him, would regard the office as a mere stepping stone to more delectable places. He had some excuse for this attitude for, however brilliant the schemes for reform that might have entered his mind, it would have been impossible to give effect to them.

*　　　*　　　*

It has been said that Edward, although humble to a fault about his personal abilities, was less modest about his worldly position, and sometimes unintentionally conveyed to others an impression of aristocratic assurance that seemed to place him apart from lesser men. The Board of Education was perhaps the only office he held in public life where he failed to captivate all the civil servants by the charm of his manner. Here they were a little deterred by an air, unconsciously given, of patrician remoteness. 'I regarded him,' said one of them, 'as something from a different world.'

Two of his Secretaries, who afterwards became Sir Maurice Holmes and Sir Griffith Williams, were conscious of a certain aloofness in their Minister. To his fellow Anglo-Catholic, Griffith Williams, it seemed that this aloofness increased, and that although he went round the office during his first period there, in the second he scarcely saw his civil servants at all, and, when he did, alarmed them. Personally he liked and respected him, although he found him a trifle inscrutable at first, and did not fail to notice that Edward had an acute sense of irony rather than of humour, and a boyish love of amusement and fun not apparent until one knew him intimately.[1]

But there were occasions when his subordinates were a trifle daunted by the loftiness of his manner. It was thought desirable, in those early days of broadcasting, that the King and Queen should broadcast to the schools, and that the young men in the office should draft their speeches which usually contained some reference to religion. It was of one of these drafts that the Permanent Secretary remarked to Edward that he thought the religious allusions somewhat obscure, to be crushed by the ponderous answer: 'I should be reluctant to believe that my Sovereign did not understand what must be a cardinal tenet of the Christian Faith.'

[1] Sir Griffith Williams to author.

Some of his civil servants also looked askance on his habit of using them for functions which were sometimes menial, and had little connection with their duty. Maurice Holmes did not relish being asked by Edward to telephone the barber to arrange for his hair to be cut, a practice much resented by Holmes's wife, who thought, with reason, that the office messenger was the proper channel for such an order.

It was noticed too, at the Board of Education, that in small ways Edward was extremely careful about money, and that he disliked spending an unnecessary penny.

Holmes first became aware of this quirk on the part of a wealthy man when the question arose of increasing by £50 the salary of a Second Secretary out of a fund for helping civil servants. Edward at once asked what the man's salary was, and on being told that it was £550 gave a drawn-out 'whew' of amazement at such an already ample sum. The explanation of Edward's extreme carefulness over money, which struck many of his friends, was that he had been brought up by Lord Halifax on a small allowance for which he was held strictly to account, and, on the rare occasions when he exceeded it, made to feel his father's strong displeasure. Apart from this he was, by nature, exceptionally shrewd and gifted in all financial transactions, and felt a horror of waste and extravagance. A further cause of prudence was that for years he had been forced to observe his father's hopeless prodigality with money, and his deplorable procrastination in paying his bills which sometimes resulted in the accounts of local tradesmen being unsettled for months on end. All this had left a deep impression on Edward, and led directly to his own extreme caution in all matters related to money.

Although there were but meagre opportunities for the President of the Board of Education to distinguish himself in either administration or legislation, he made good use of the few that came his way, and again displayed the quickness of mind which gave him an immediate grasp of a complicated subject in which he was not fundamentally interested. He was forced to sing the same dirge of economy and retrenchment as were many of his colleagues in other offices. Sir John Simon raised the subject on the adjournment on 29 March 1923, claiming that the Fisher Act had been involved in the common ruin brought about by the financial panic that followed the war, and that the Board of Education had been almost as assiduous as the Treasury itself in assisting the sweep of the Geddes Axe. Edward could only plead that the reforms had not been abandoned but merely postponed:

'As I conceive the duty of the Board of Education in these days, it is to endeavour to pursue economy having regard to the general exigencies of the public service in such a way that the system of public education is not impaired, and that when times become easier, the original position can at once be resumed. . . . However much we may deplore it, it is not primarily damaging the efficiency of the system if we preserve for ourselves and the country the power and capacity to jump off again as soon as the opportunity comes.'

*　　*　　*

We may pause here to note one of Edward's earliest excursions into the field of foreign affairs in which he found himself in a difficult and unfamiliar position. In April 1923, while the Foreign Secretary Lord Curzon was occupied at the Second Lausanne Conference, Edward was sent to Geneva to represent Great Britain at a meeting of the Council of the League of Nations. The British delegate presided over this meeting at which nineteen States were represented and at which the question of the Saar was raised. Under the Treaty of Versailles France was enabled to exploit the coal mines in the Saar Valley in compensation for the French mines destroyed by the Germans during the war, but she had no territorial possession. The League appointed a Governing Commission which in 1923 consisted of a French President, a representative of the Saar citizens, a Belgian, a Dane and a Canadian. As a result of a strike of miners in January 1923 the Commission, on 7 March, with the Canadian member dissenting, decreed heavy penalties for publicly casting discredit on the Treaty of Versailles, insulting or traducing the League of Nations and the Governing Commission of the Saar. Meetings, processions or demonstrations could be prohibited by the decree if thought likely to lead to such offences.

When the Council met in April Anglo-French relations were under great strain, and the British Government, while deploring the decree, were anxious not to exacerbate tension between Britain and France. Edward, as Chairman, was thus placed in a delicate position. Branting, the Swedish representative, expressed strong disapproval, with which Edward agreed, of the decree that had been passed. The President of the Governing Commission then explained that the strike had been caused by political agitation soon after the French occupation of the Ruhr and that the French could not exploit the mines without some such regulations as those contained in the decree. Edward dissented, but the meeting concluded without any member having formally proposed the cancellation of the decree, although the Council set up a Committee to make inquiries.

On his return home Edward had to face a hostile Parliament. British opinion resented France's unilateral action in occupying the Ruhr, and the Liberal and Socialist Opposition felt no inhibitions in venting their anger about the Saar decree. On the reduction of the Foreign Office Vote on 10 May Sir John Simon maintained that the decree had been put into operation illegally, and asked what instructions the British spokesman had received before going to Geneva. The League Council could at any time revoke the appointment of any member of the Governing Commission of the Saar. In view of undertakings to Germany that the Saar people should live under a resident government with no occupation and no interest except their welfare, there was a strong obligation on the British Government to see that steps were taken to put a stop to what would otherwise expose the League to contempt and derision.

In this unpromising situation Edward gave one of his best performances in the House of Commons. He said that he had been given discretion to raise the matter before the Council; as acting Chairman he had thought it courteous to allow Branting to go forward with his motion. He had been advised that the decree was within the legal powers of the Commission, although in reply to Asquith he had to admit that he had not consulted the law officers of the Crown. It had not been necessary to bring the decree before the Council for approval.

Even Branting had not called for cancellation of the decree. He had agreed with Branting and had stated unequivocally in Council that it had created a bad impression in his country. But the President of the Saar Commission was the responsible instrument of government chosen by the League, and they had had to consider whether it was wise to reject his advice. The Government had decided that the whole question of the administration of the Saar should be the subject of an impartial inquiry, and he had therefore been reluctant to make an issue of this relatively smaller matter when more fundamental questions would soon present themselves for solution.

There was a great deal of criticism in this debate but it was not directed personally at the British spokesman who, it was thought, had acquitted himself, if without distinction, at least with moderation and honour in the somewhat unrewarding rôle that had been thrust upon him. Indeed it could be regarded as a tribute to the confidence which his superiors felt in his powers of conciliation that, in the absence of a Foreign Office representative, they had chosen him to undertake such a delicate and thankless assignment.[1]

*   *   *

Edward had no easy task in presenting the Estimates for his Department for 1923–24, but he gave an enviable Parliamentary performance, using his threadbare material with such dexterity as to bring a tribute from H. A. L. Fisher himself. The Estimates were £3,300,000 smaller than in the previous year, and £9,000,000 less than those for 1921–22, but Edward argued stolidly:

'It is quite true that the vision of 1918 may be still unfulfilled, but the framework of the 1919 Act stands on the Statute Book unimpaired, ready to carry the Bill as soon as building operations can be resumed.' While presenting his depressing balance sheet, he persuasively emphasized its few assets:

'This year for the first time the Estimates provide for the retention of children at school up to the end of the term in which they reach fourteen. . . . the pupils are entering these secondary schools earlier and staying

[1] Campbell Johnson. Op.cit.

longer. It is also a fact that these schools contain a larger number proceeding from elementary schools, and there is also a larger number paying no fees.'

He even managed to find something favourable to say about the policy of retrenchment itself which had brought the machine to a standstill, claiming that it was a blessing in disguise which in a few years would enable Local Authorities to build far cheaper schools. He promised that more would be done for special schools for the blind, the deaf and the mentally defective. Edward deserved greater credit for this speech than many a more silver-tongued Minister with a story of achievement to unfold, and he received it from the man who had made the closest study of the subject in the House of Commons, and had produced a Bill which was a landmark in English education. Later in the evening H. A. L. Fisher said:

'The Committee is greatly indebted to the President of the Board of Education not only for the skill and lucidity with which he has unfolded his story, but also for the fine spirit which clearly informs him in relation to the great responsibilities of his office.'

In July 1923 Edward introduced one further measure during this first period at the Board, the Universities Bill, which provided two bodies of Commissioners for Oxford and Cambridge Universities to make Statutes and determine any emoluments or endowments required by the findings of the Royal Commission as to grants. His own love of Oxford and his deep gratitude to her were apparent in his speech on the Second Reading, in which he concluded:

'It is because I know that at the present time Universities are handicapped by the lack of material resources in the conduct of their work, and it is because as a son of Oxford I am so sensible of the advantage of what Oxford gave to me, and because I regard this Bill as the essential preliminary to enable the Universities to continue and develop their work, that I confidently invite the House to give this Bill a Second Reading.' There was a sly irony in his reply when it was suggested by a Tory Member that as one of the proposed Commissioners was a Socialist he should not be appointed by a Conservative Government:

'It never occurred to me to inquire what the politics of any of them was, and I think it is a new suggestion that in appointing academic bodies of this kind, it is necessary to have such a careful regard for the niceties of political representation and balance.'

His first period at the Board was ended by the fall of Baldwin's Government in January 1924. It had been rendered sterile by conditions over which he had no control, but he was not yet finished with the Board of Education to which he was to return as to some quiet backwater in 1932 after his labours in India. He was to be as much frustrated by economy as a revenant as on the first occasion, but we shall see that in spite of this, his opportunities were to be a little greater and his achievement less negative.

CHAPTER X

A DISASTROUS ELECTION

AFTER the 1922 Election the Government had soon found itself facing an unemployment figure of 1,300,000, which showed every sign of increasing. Hunger marchers tramped from the industrial north to London, precursors of those despairing processions which were to become so familiar in their misery in the next decade. By the autumn of 1923 it was clear that a winter of even greater discontent was at hand. The moment had come, it was felt, for drastic action, and the eyes of all were turned on the enigmatic figure of the man who was now Prime Minister, Stanley Baldwin. It was difficult to plumb the thoughts that were revolving in that inscrutable mind. Perhaps, thought one of his colleagues, there were none: 'Thinking with him,' said Leo Amery, 'was not a definite process, but rather the gradual self-conscious maturing of vague impressions towards some sudden instinctive conclusion; a development which might itself be precipitated or thwarted by some wholly inconsistent, unthought-out action.'[1]

At this moment there had been forming in the Prime Minister's mind the belief that only Protection could arrest the progress of unemployment and bring the Conservative Party together again. A large proportion of that Party, including Baldwin himself, believed that the solution lay in tariffs, and the Prime Minister gave a number of public hints as to the direction his mind was taking. But in doing so he was, from the beginning, in a position of great danger. In an effort to obtain Free Trade votes Bonar Law had pledged himself at the General Election of 1922 to make no radical change in the financial policy of the country in the subsequent Parliament. For the new Prime Minister to talk of turning to Protection before that Parliament had lasted even a year left him poised between repudiating a solemn undertaking and ending the life of the Parliament. He proceeded to kill the Government in a few sentences of a speech at Plymouth.

The Cabinet had been justifiably uneasy about such a course, and tried to persuade the Prime Minister to confine himself to a personal statement without committing any of his colleagues. At Plymouth on 23 October 1923 he declared that his own opinion was that the only way of conquering unemployment was by protecting the home market. The reactions which followed this dramatic declaration of a change of policy caused Lord Salisbury to summon his colleagues Devonshire, Robert Cecil and Edward

[1] L. S. Amery. Op. cit., Vol. II, p. 279.

154

Wood to meet and consider their attitude, and it is a remarkable proof of the respect in which Edward was already held by these men that it was he who was delegated to convey their conclusions to the Prime Minister. He did so on 8 November in a letter in which anxiety is plainly visible beneath its polished surface:

'I think that it is vital that we should give Parliament, and through Parliament the country, an adequate opportunity of examining the question on which they are to be asked to pronounce.

'If this is not consistent with a December election, I think we should be acting both unwisely and wrongly, and should aggravate the difficulties of some of our number, if we were to attempt to snatch a verdict, and that, if this is so, the appeal should be deferred.

'All this in great deference, recognizing that fixing these matters is your special perquisite.'

At the Cabinet on 9 November Baldwin, in spite of this strong appeal still refused to show his hand, and we are told by one of his biographers: 'The impression left on the minds of his colleagues was that he had made up his mind to dissolve: and his announcement on Tuesday, 13 November made certain what for some days they had been expecting. The same group met at luncheon with Salisbury to consider their action. Some of them believed that Baldwin was deliberately forcing them out to make room for Austen Chamberlain and Birkenhead. That evening Wood asked him point-blank whether that was his intention: if it was not, he must see Salisbury, explain his position and make it as easy as possible for the Free Traders to stay. Then followed all the comings and goings, the conversations and letters customary on such occasions— . . . Salisbury has had a friendly interview with Baldwin; Wood has got assurances; and Robert Cecil has prepared a draft.'

The draft was delivered on the afternoon of the 14th, and handed back annotated and initialled by Baldwin the following morning. His interpretations being found satisfactory, the group decided to stay, and Birkenhead and Austen Chamberlain were informed that, though their support on the platform would be appreciated their services were not otherwise required. . . .

The policy on which the reunited Cabinet were to go to the country was absolute freedom in all fiscal measures, with the reservation that no further taxes should be placed on essential foods; protection for particular industries; assistance to agriculture; and 'a sound foreign policy based on the principles of the League of Nations'.[1]

It was characteristic of its author that this dangerous solution was partly a personal ruse of party politics, such an expedient as a woman might use to forestall a rival in society. We have seen Baldwin's strong moral revulsion from Lloyd George. It had, moreover, come to his attention that Lloyd

[1] G. M. Young, *Stanley Baldwin*, p. 67.

6*

George was returning from a visit to America with the conception of a bold Empire policy with Imperial Preference in his mind, and was preparing to spring this box of tricks on the nation.

It was not in Baldwin's nature to welcome his *bête noire* as a convert to his own opinions. Rather did he see in the manœuvre the strengthening of that sinister hold upon Birkenhead and Austen Chamberlain and the other Coalition malcontents, and the reassertion of Lloyd George's own regrettable influence over the Tory Party. The statement which Baldwin later made to Dr. Tom Jones in 1935 to explain his conduct on this occasion gives a curious glimpse of those intuitive flashes by which his mind was liable to proceed:

'On political grounds the tariff issue had been dead for years, and I felt it was the one issue that would pull the party together, including the Lloyd George malcontents.

'The Goat was in America. He was on the water when I made the speech and the Liberals did not know what to say. I had information that he was going Protectionist and I had to get in quick. . . .

'Dished the Goat, as otherwise he would have got the Party with Austen and F.E. and there would have been an end to the Tory Party as we know it.'[1]

In its main object of discomfiting Lloyd George the ruse was brilliantly successful. Lloyd George's course of wisdom, being thus anticipated, would no doubt have been to acclaim the Prime Minister's policy, and in so doing to acquire over it a gradual and insidious control. But the issues between them were too bitter. He would not deign to give the appearance of support to this obscure man who had accomplished his ruin at the Carlton Club, even if the reward was his enemy's downfall. He would have done it, he said, if it had been one of the men who had stood by him in his hour of need. 'But Baldwin knifed me, and I shall knife Baldwin'—and when the election came it might have been the old savage days at Limehouse again. His terrible vindictiveness thus aroused, Lloyd George was to regurgitate the half-forgotten scurrilities of his anti-tariff reform days, lashing wildly about him, indifferent to logic or truth in his desire to wound, alienating friend and enemy impartially.

*   *   *

If Baldwin dished 'The Goat', he also dished his own party and shattered their nerve by the reckless folly of this election. Although he claimed 'to have got the Cabinet in line with his views', this was in fact a far from accurate description of his colleagues' attitude when he decided to go to the country, which itself had but the cloudiest ideas of the issues involved and had not been properly informed upon them. There was still a strong party of dissent in the Cabinet, and on 12 November Curzon wrote to a friend: 'We

[1] L. S. Amery. Op. cit., Vol. II, p. 280.

are being involved, and I think quite unnecessarily and unwisely, in a conflict which can only be solved by an Election.' A fugitive and unnatural alliance between Asquith and Lloyd George enabled the Liberals to fight the election with a precarious common front. Resentment at the action of a Government with an adequate majority inflicting a General Election upon the country within a year of its formation almost equalled the dislike of a tariff. It was not remarkable that the Government suffered heavy losses, the figures being: Conservative 254, Labour 192, Liberal 149.

The Conservatives were still the strongest party in the House. Neither of the opposing parties could hold office except by permission of the other. The Baldwin Government remained in office until Parliament met early in 1924, when they were defeated, and resigned. When the first Socialist Government was formed under Ramsay MacDonald it was soon evident to Edward and his friends that their exile would not be long. All the disunity of the new Government, that disharmony between moderate and extreme elements, was emphasized by its dependence upon Liberal support to sustain it in office. The disintegration of the Liberal Party had already begun. It was, thought Austen Chamberlain, 'visibly bursting up'.

During the brief period of Labour government Edward put his time in opposition to quiet but useful purpose. He spoke often in the House on many subjects, including agriculture on which he was now becoming recognized as a practical expert. It was a subject to which he could devote himself with unfeigned enthusiasm. Here there was no need, as in education, to flog a listless interest. He was a countryman bred upon the soil of Yorkshire, and a great landowner who managed his own estates. He knew the moods of the seasons and the ills of crops and animals without having to learn them from the study of Blue Books. Particularly he knew the men who lived upon the land and worked it, and regarded them with paternal affection.

There were few debates in Parliament on agriculture that did not include a contribution from Edward Wood, and his obvious knowledge of the subject drew the attention of Baldwin who liked to play a rich rustic part himself, although his efforts in this direction were of a somewhat spurious character. The authentic ring in Edward's speeches may well have convinced him that here, when the time came, was his Minister of Agriculture.

Edward again showed himself free from party pettiness, welcoming any Socialist legislation which seemed to him in the interests of agriculture. He supported their decision to carry out research into animal diseases, and on a Supply Day drew attention to 'a most astonishing disparity' between the numbers of Co-operative creameries in Denmark and Great Britain, and to the low consumption and quality of the milk produced by the latter.[1] He demanded more Co-operative milling and slaughtering. He deplored the steady shrinking of the area of cultivated land in England, and declared the

[1] Campbell Johnson. Op. cit., p. 119.

cardinal problem to be 'to reverse or retard the great movement of economic forces by which agriculture is already threatened'.

At the same time he had begun to acquire the reputation of being one of the more progressive and less ossified members of his party. He supported a Labour motion calling for State pensions for the proper upbringing and maintenance of children for all widows with children, or mothers whose wage-earners had become incapacitated. He believed strongly that it was the duty of the State to provide for the casualties of modern industrial life:

'I have often thought it a rather astonishing thing that the State should have made a move in other directions, such as old age, sickness, and so on, before attending to the matter. . . . We do not offer any opposition to a proposal that makes its appeal to our hearts no less than to the hearts of hon. Members opposite.'[1] For equally praiseworthy reasons he supported the scheme for the continuation of teachers' pensions. Unless this was done, 'they must be the victims of ordinary day to day anxiety. That anxiety breeds dissatisfaction and unrest, and a person in whose mind these influences are operating is not the right person to mould the character of the younger generation'.[2]

*   *   *

In April 1924, during the Easter Recess, Edward was summoned by his father to a visit which was concerned with wider issues. We left Lord Halifax in a state of prostration after the death of his wife. Confused memories of the past haunted his period of despair, yielding to a painful awareness of the present. 'The death of his wife,' wrote his biographer Lockhart, 'his resignation of the Presidency of the English Church Union, and his increasing infirmities, seemed part of a process of liquidation. There would be a respite in which he might arrange his papers and "make his soul"; then his summons would reach him to leave a world with which he found himself yearly at greater variance, and to join the company of those who had been dearest to him.'

He was eighty-two. Neither he nor his friends would have credited that there was shortly now to begin for him the period of his intensest spiritual activity, a vivid autumnal lighting up of the scene before darkness fell. He was now to embark on that series of religious conferences which are known to theological history as the 'Malines Conversations'. Thirty-four years had passed since he had discussed matters of the Faith with the Abbé Portal in the Madeira sunshine. Together they had succeeded in bringing into the realm of practical politics the question of reunion between Rome and Canterbury. 'For a while,' said Edward, 'the prospect of progress was not unhopeful; Pope Leo XIII was friendly, and my father, whose natural reaction was to under-

[1] *Hansard*, House of Commons, Vol. 169, Col. 1895–6, 20 February 1924.
[2] Ibid., Vol. 172, Col. 1031, 14 April 1924.

rate the difficulties of any scheme to which his energies were pledged, was disposed to be sanguine of success.'

These hopes had been disappointed by the unfavourable report of the Commission appointed by the Roman authorities to examine the question of the validity of Anglican orders, and by the Papal Bull, Apostolicae Curae, in 1896, which condemned them. In 1921 Portal suggested to Halifax that they should travel together over some of the French battlefields, and combine with this journey a visit to Cardinal Mercier, who had lately been declaring himself much concerned with the possibility of reunion.

It seemed at first to the old man that in the Belgian Cardinal he had found a priest on whom he could lavish almost the same devotion as on Liddon. Mercier had emerged from the war high in the world's esteem. 'He had met the military repressions of General von Bissing with pastorals so outspoken that men feared for his liberty and even his life. The Germans could not silence, but dared not imprison him; and for four years to the outside world and to his own people he had appeared an incarnation of Belgium, bloody but unbowed.'[1]

The Abbé Portal's impetus towards a further effort at reunion came from a decision of the Bishops of the Anglican Communion assembled at Lambeth in 1920, which acknowledged the share of Anglicanism in the guilt of the schism, and asked for a new vision of a united Catholic Church. Here, it was thought, 'in addition to other complications, appeared the glimmering of a way round the lowered horns and massive resistance of Apostolicae Curae which had blocked the road for so many years'.[2] Now that the Anglicans were prepared to consider the revision of their ordination, it appeared that the great barrier might be surmounted. The prospect that he might at last be approaching this spiritual fusion of which he had for so long been the tireless postulant, rejuvenated Halifax like an elixir of life and suffused his aged body with an unearthly vigour.

As companions in this pilgrimage he chose the learned Dr. Frere, Superior of the Community of the Resurrection at Mirfield, and Dr. Armitage Robinson, the Dean of Wells. The unofficial blessing of the Archbishop of Canterbury, Dr. Randall Davidson, accompanied the little party. Halifax kept Edward informed of their progress in letters glowing with optimism, his spirit chafing at the delays inevitable in such a delicate matter.

During the lull Davidson found misgivings among his episcopal brethren about the Malines Conversations, and this uneasiness was reflected in Rome where there was a significant bestirring of the Jesuit Society, and a movement in the Vatican to influence the Pope against them. The Archbishop, delicately poised in this matter between the different elements in his Church, insisted that the delegation should be strengthened at the next meeting by the inclusion of Bishop Gore and Dr. Kidd, the Warden of Keble, for the Anglicans,

[1] Lockhart. Op. cit., Vol. II, p. 268.   [2] Ibid.

and by Battifol and Hemmer for the Roman Catholics, and that the fundamental dogma of the Supremacy of the Holy See must be given priority in the
next conversations.

The third session in November 1923 encountered many obstructions from
both Rome and England, and had it not been for Halifax's fanatical will, the
Malines Conversations might well have foundered. It is impossible to doubt
that his faith alone kept alive their fitful flame. Even so, no further meeting
had been decided by April 1924, and it was during this enforced lull that he
arranged a private and unofficial visit to Malines at the end of April.

With him he took the Abbé Portal, Lord Hugh Cecil and Edward. Halifax
explained his reasons for this visit to Cardinal Mercier. He was old, and he
could scarcely hope to make many more journeys to Malines; but it was his
wish that Lord Hugh, and his son, who he hoped would succeed to his task
when he was gone, should meet the Cardinal.

In spite of his many virtues, Mercier scarcely recognized the existence of
the Church of England. Warm with apostolic charity, he had moved through
the negotiations as one blinded by the tremendous and exclusive glare of
Rome. The reunion he so ardently desired was rationalized in his mind on
the grounds of scholastic logic. The abyss in understanding between him and
Halifax was disclosed in this visit by the suggestion that the latter should
make his personal submission to Rome. Perhaps a shrug of Gallic despair
accompanied the Abbé's comment on this *bêtise*: 'Au fond il ne comprend
pas votre position.'

But if religious understanding was impossible between them there was
abounding love. When the Cardinal lay dying, after having received Extreme
Unction, in the house where the Duchess of Richmond gave the Waterloo
Ball, Mercier told Halifax that he wished him to have his gold episcopal ring
with its great amethyst, and when he protested, Portal had said: 'Yes, yes,
for you and for Edward.' The day would come when Edward would set it in
the base of a chalice and give it to York Minster for use at Mass on the
anniversaries of the deaths of his father and the Cardinal, an emblem of that
dying hope of reunion which Mercier expressed to the Archbishop of Canterbury before the shadows fell: 'Ut unum sint; it is the supreme wish of Christ,
the wish of the Sovereign Pontiff; it is mine, it is yours. May it be realized in
all its fulness.'

CHAPTER XI

MINISTER OF AGRICULTURE

MEANWHILE, in London the Labour Government had succeeded in antagonizing Liberals as well as Conservatives by concluding a loan to the Bolshevik régime, and withdrawing the proceedings against J. R. Campbell, editor of the *Workers Weekly*, on a charge of inciting the army and navy to refuse to fight in a military or class war. They had sung the Red Flag instead of the National Anthem at the Albert Hall before the last election, and there was a deep symbolism in that melancholy dirge.

Already they were locked in their fatal embrace with the forces of subversion in Russia, which appeared to them a comradely bond with men who had broken tyranny, and which was to remain, clinging and tainted, long after the true nature of those forces had been revealed. Edward's own uncomplicated opinion was that 'People were disgusted with the sloppy internationalism of the party which idolized Russia and demanded the extinction not only of one's patriotism but also of one's personality in favour of a vague idea which might be regarded as the L.C.M. of all the nations. The English people objected to being asked to sink all their feelings and ideas as Englishmen, and putting themselves on a level, say, with the blacks of Haiti'.

Edward's adroitness as a politician was shown by his intervention in the Campbell affair when, by opposing the Conservative Shadow Cabinet's intention of moving a vote of censure against the Labour Government and pressing for another meeting, he obtained the support of the Liberals when the Government refused an inquiry, and was brought down. A Liberal motion for a Select Committee was carried by a large majority on 8 October, and the following day Ramsay MacDonald announced that he would appeal to the country. The affair of the Zinoviev Letter, which was written by the President of the Presidium of the Third Bolshevik International and which urged the creation of Communist cells in the British army and navy and munition factories, resulted in the Conservative Party's greatest victory at the election which followed. They won 415 seats, thereby obtaining a majority over the other two parties combined. Two wandering lambs, Birkenhead and Austen Chamberlain, were welcomed back into the fold with varying degrees of enthusiasm. Balfour returned as Lord President of the Council, and Winston Churchill was the recipient of one of Baldwin's most singular appointments as Chancellor of the Exchequer. Edward was offered the Ministry of Agriculture, and although this office was the most appropriate that could have been given to him, his efforts, as in his previous two ministries, were stultified from the outset.

'In that administration,' he was to write many years later, 'I served as Minister of Agriculture, a post at that time of almost complete futility and frustration. There was little to be done outside routine administration, except to decide on a scheme for tithe redemption. . . . For the rest, it was dispiriting to know that given the political atmosphere prevailing in both parties, the soundest advice to give to any farmer was to get out of his head all fancy ideas of high production, to lay his land down to grass, reduce his labour bill, and run his farm with the traditional stick and dog.'

In spite of this sour memory, there was much at the time to cause Edward happiness in his new office. If all aspects of his native countryside, the wolds and the moors, the villages with melodious place-names, and the wide expanse of the Plain of York were in his blood, he also wished to convey this deep contentment to others. In his mind was a vision of the pastoral education of which he had written in *The Great Opportunity*, by which country children would absorb 'something of the infinite variety of interest by which their lives are constantly surrounded, so that the countryside would cease to be a dull grey place in unpleasing contrast to the gas lamps and cinema shows of the towns'.

It was true that the activities of the Ministry during his period of office did not produce spectacular results, and did something to justify his own gloomy retrospect, for it was an unpropitious time for Ministers of Agriculture. The industry was in an unhealthy condition owing to the fall in prices since the war, and the repeal of the Corn Production Acts which had guaranteed the price of wheat, barley and oats. There was no lack of goodwill towards agriculture, and the air was thick with suggestions of how it might be helped. To these suggestions the farmers turned increasingly exasperated ears.

The only immediate remedies involved either some form of fiscal protection, but the Conservative Party had pledged itself at the 1924 election not to increase the price of food by introducing it, or some form of subsidy, but subsidies were excluded as being too costly and precarious in the economic circumstances. The only exception to this rule was a subsidy for sugar beet, a measure agreed to by both Conservative and Labour Parties as being designed to establish an infant industry, and optimistically regarded as temporary.

*   *   *

Edward began his task with an energy and enthusiasm which was quickly tempered by events. One of his first actions was the announcement of his intention to call a conference representing all the agricultural interests—

landowners, farmers and workers—with the object of framing an agreed policy to ensure continuity on a change of Government, and to avoid a repetition of the disastrous experience of the Corn Production Acts.

He soon became aware of how wayward were the elements he was seeking to fuse into one. The Farmers' Union was the first to show itself fertile in unhelpful objections. The workers' unions refused to participate. They were joined in this abstention by the agricultural workers as a body, and the Great Council of the Soil which Edward had envisaged could not even be constituted. He was disappointed by a rebuff so early in his administration, telling the farmers that they had 'lost a great opportunity', but at least he was reminded by this reverse that farming was not a homogeneous industry, but a collection of different trades in almost random association, some of but slight mutual benefit, others actually inimical to one another.

He was a Minister of great patience, and he persevered doggedly, announcing next that he proposed to interview the various organizations separately. The outcome of these consultations was not announced before he ceased to be Minister of Agriculture in November 1925, but while they did not produce the 'security' he held to be vital in agricultural life, the farmers were at least encouraged by the interest shown by the Government in their affairs.

Although the results were not known before his departure from the Ministry, a White Paper was issued at the beginning of February 1926 giving particulars of the Government's agricultural policy. There is little doubt that Edward had agreed to the substance of this document, and probably to its actual terms. The White Paper had a thoroughly bad reception at the hands of the Farmers' Representatives. Bored to distraction by woolly admonitions and conditional clauses, and statements in general terms which seemed to bear no relation to the urgency of events, they demanded quick and spectacular remedies for their grievances.

One of the leaders of the National Farmers' Union, in a speech to the Statutory Council of Agriculture, was driven to remark: 'The Government's White Paper reminds me of a fussy housewife who is always sweepin' and dustin', but there's never any smell of cookin' about the house.' It was a form of ribaldry to which Edward had become accustomed in his own East Riding, where he had attempted to explain with courteous gravity to a meeting of farmers that the Government's policy was calculated on a long and not a short-term basis. This academic exercise was ill-received by a hard-headed audience who demanded quick results. Edward persisted: 'You are practical farmers—you put the rams to your ewes in November, but you don't expect to see a flock of lambs next day.' To this a lonely figure replied in broadest dialect: 'Nay, but we do expect to see some satisfied faces.'

If the angry farmers had examined the White Paper with a more discerning eye, they might have seen the seed of some sound and useful crops in the measures which Edward Wood initiated. The White Paper promised an extension of the provision of Small Holdings; a continuance of the Sugar Beet subsidy; a scheme for the provision of agricultural credit; increased grants for land drainage; and a development of the comprehensive scheme of agricultural research, education, and advisory service.

Perhaps the Small Holdings 'seed' fell upon somewhat stony ground. A Small Holdings Bill was passed soon afterwards, but mechanization has now left little place for such holdings, and opinion has become more generally in favour of the amalgamation of small farms into larger units. But the sugar beet subsidy, although not temporary as had been hoped, introduced a valuable cash crop into the arable rotation which has not only benefited the growers, but enabled them to produce all the sugar used for domestic purposes during the Second World War. Edward had been aware of the danger of this experiment, and the temptation to the farmers to accept the money, and give little in return, and had tried to bring it home to them. He begged them to take a 'national' view and not to exploit the situation for their own ends. 'Clearly he realized that some farmers were taking anything but a national view of an experiment which they treated simply as a grant in aid of a distressed industry.'[1]

The agricultural credit 'seed' blossomed in less than two years into the Agricultural Credits Act 1928, which established the Agricultural Mortgage Corporation. This corporation has loaned millions of pounds to farmers for the purchase or improvement of their farms and is a substantial and permanent part of the agricultural credit structure. With statutory and financial aid drainage has been carried out on a large scale since 1926, producing a definite improvement in the condition of the land.

When the White Paper was issued, the Ministry's Marketing Division was busily engaged in an investigation of marketing methods in this and other countries, and the results of these efforts can be seen today in the farmers' marketing boards which have been of immense value to the industry. Finally, the scheme of Agricultural Research and Education and Advisory Service has produced the most valuable returns of all: improved materials and techniques discovered by research, and knowledge of how to use them conveyed to farmers by education and advice.

Thus Edward's period at the Ministry of Agriculture, although frustrated, was not altogether sterile. It was the long-term policy that had so irked the impatient farmers, a seed time in which the fruits were of slow germination, a policy designed to bring a gradual, but not spectacular, improvement to the industry. His Ministry, like all other departments in the Government, was under constant attack for complacency and inertia, but his personal position was unshaken.

*   *   *

[1] Hodgson. Op. cit., p. 56.

The two Bills that Edward steered through the House of Commons were the Agricultural Returns Bill and the Tithe Bill, and in his handling of the former, and in his speeches on it can be clearly seen his deep attachment to the soil. This measure made it compulsory for farmers to fill in annual returns showing their acreage under different crops and the number of their livestock. In the debates on this Bill, Edward's speeches showed how deeply embedded were his roots, and how unquestioning his conception of the hierarchy of the countryside. There is a strong flavour of the past in his vision of a squirearchy holding sway with happy paternalism. There is much in it of his father, that lover of the old ways; much, too, of his own distaste for the organization of the soil, a living thing, into a cold factory efficiency. 'Is your object,' he asked the House of Commons, 'a system by which you can produce what you want to get out of the land as efficiently and cheaply as you can? If that be your object you will go in for all sorts of machinery and for the development of labour-saving devices. The more you develop towards that ideal, the more you will find the population of the land going down. It is not my ideal. My ideal is a form of agriculture which, while well carried on, will strike a balance, with the balance slightly tilted, or a good deal tilted, in favour of keeping on the land the maximum population that the land will support.'

If this belief seems archaic, it should be remembered that in 1925 there was much unemployment in urban areas. Nor could Edward have foreseen that subsidies (now generously given), and mechanization, stimulated by war and by improvement in the internal combustion engine, would bring about an agricultural revolution which would increase total output and raise the standard of life of all those working on the land, while reducing their hours of work, their burdens of physical labour and their numbers.

Edward gave expression to the vision of the squire on his estates in a conversation with his Private Secretary, C. T. Houghton. He had been musing on the nature of industrial unrest. He thought that 'one reason why the country squire was liked much more than the industrial employer was not that the squire was a much better fellow but that he was on the spot and all the poor people could go to him in case of need. If some of their tiles were blown off, for instance, and the rain was coming through the roof, instead of cursing landlordism, they would have no hesitation in going to the squire and telling him of their trouble with some reasonable hope that he would put matters right. In industry we must to some extent follow the example of officers with their men during the war. Officers did not appear merely on the battlefield and then go away and leave their men when they were out of the line; they were always with them and shared their experiences. They took a personal interest in the affairs of their men, even to the extent of knowing how many children they had and the state of their teeth! That was his idea of unity'.[1]

[1] C. T. Houghton to author.

The belief in the healing magic of the soil appeared to some to suggest that Edward was living in a bygone age. It was again apparent in his support, in March 1925, of a Private Member's Allotment Bill. 'The Allotment movement,' he said, 'is, and always has been, to my mind a kind of meeting point where town meets country, and country meets town, and on which they may both meet and shake hands, and understand one another better. . . . In all this you are dealing with one of the primitive instincts of mankind. It is the call of the soil from which we spring, and to which we are, therefore, so to speak, enchained in our instincts. I have known men willing to go three, four and five miles out of town to their allotments, so strong was the call of the soil to the town-dweller.'[1]

During the summer of 1925 Edward was occupied in mastering the intricacies of the Tithe Bill. Before this Bill became operative the amount of tithe payable by the tithe payer in any year was based on the average price of corn in the previous seven years. Owing to the fall in prices after the war, this basis was considered unfair to tithe payers; they were already suffering generally from the low prices, and they had to pay tithe on a calculated price of corn that was considerably above the current price.

The 1925 Bill abolished the septennial average, and substituted a fixed annual payment on the basis of £105 for every £100 of tithe rent-charge. Out of this £105 a sum of £4 10s. was to be paid into the Sinking Fund for the redemption of the rent-charge in eighty-five years. The rest of the money, after deduction of a sum on account of rates, charges and cost of collection, was to be paid to the incumbent of the benefice on account of which the rent-charge was held. This Bill for the Commutation of Tithes was a measure of great complexity, and the easy manner in which Edward mastered its details and steered it through all its stages in the House of Commons is ample proof of the mental grasp which he had shown in the Schools at Oxford.

After the Tithe Bill came his final Supply Day for his department, on which he gave an account of his stewardship, which he told the House, 'deals with fish and fertilizers, sugar and sheepscab, rats and reclamation, and if I may add, without any offence to anyone, it deals with pigs and also with parsons'. He made a painstaking survey of his record, but he could point to no Protection and to no subsidy, and for the rest of the summer was forced to submit to a stream of hostile memoranda from the National Farmers' Union condemning the Government in general and his department in particular. It was only the beginning of the tribulations of that Ministry, and Edward was but one of a succession of Ministers of Agriculture who were restrained from giving specific assurances because they knew that they would be unable to honour them.

He left office with the resolution of the Party Conference at Brighton of October 1925 ringing in his ears, now with a note of positive exasperation,

[1] *Hansard*, House of Commons, Vol. 181, Col. 2661-3, 20 March 1925.

demanding that the Government should make a definite statement without delay on their agricultural policy, and to carry such policy into effect.

Although conscious as before, in that uneasy period, of frustration, Edward Wood made a definite personal contribution to the formation of long-term agricultural policy. In this Ministry he was a changed man from the indifferent President of the Board of Education who kept such short hours, and whose mind so frequently wandered to the meets of the Middleton Hounds and the peace of the Garrowby wolds.

In the Ministry of Agriculture his secretaries were impressed by the hours he worked and the concentration he put into them. He began to write his own speeches, making the notes himself on narrow slips of paper with a broad margin in which to write answers to the points picked up in debate.

Sometimes, when he was going to Yorkshire for the week-end, he would have his lunch brought into the room, and ask his Private Secretary to sit with him while he ate it. He would talk about his next important speech, and tell Houghton the general lines of it, and what information he required. His relations with his subordinates were now easy and agreeable, and that loftiness of manner, which had sometimes been interpreted as condescension at the Board of Education, was no longer noticed.

He was a Minister who had shown steady capacity in three departments, but the future seemed to offer no obvious advancement. No one was less prepared than Edward for the next tremendous turn in his affairs. Houghton was one of the first to hear of the event which was to lift his Minister out of the party politics he disliked, far above the level of minor Conservative Ministers into an eminence of which he had never dreamed.

'Another thrilling memory stands out very vividly. One morning he rang the bell and on my entering the room he said simply: "Houghton, I'm to be made Viceroy of India." Later in the morning his daughter Anne called to see him. This time he said to me: "Houghton, Anne won't believe that I'm to be Viceroy of India. Will you confirm that it is true?" '[1]

---

[1] C. T. Houghton to author.

Part Two

INDIA

CHAPTER XII

THE LIFE

THE invitation to become Viceroy of India had been made to Edward in October 1925 by the Secretary of State Lord Birkenhead, and had he known that the suggestion had originated with King George V his answer might not have been an unqualified refusal. It had not been easy to find a worthy successor to Lord Reading whose viceroyalty was now ending in such distinction. The King had first suggested the name of Lord Haig, but it had been pointed out to him that a civilian would be better adapted to the situation. He had then suggested Edward Wood, and the suggestion had met with the immediate approval of the Cabinet.

Edward was reluctant to leave England for five years. His father, one of the two lynch-pins of his life, was eighty-six. He had suffered much and was now a frail old man, and it was difficult to believe that he would survive until his son's return. Edward felt that if he accepted the post he would be parting from his father for ever, and the ties between them were so strong and their mutual devotion so profound that this alone would have made his acceptance a tremendous decision. But he had also to consider his children. His three sons were either at school or about to go there, and he felt that he should not be separated from them during the formative years.

All these doubts he confided to Birkenhead, but he added that should circumstances arise in which it was his plain duty to go, he would feel bound to reconsider the whole question. But he knew that there were other names under review besides his own. He thought the matter closed, and had dismissed it from his mind, when he was summoned with Dorothy to Chequers on 22 October by the Prime Minister, Stanley Baldwin, to discuss the proposal which he thought had been definitely withdrawn. The Prime Minister was an old friend, and the master, when he chose to exert them, of great powers of blandishment, and, a week later, after much heart-searching and self-scrutiny, Edward called upon him again and accepted the appointment.

Whatever Edward's doubts might be, he received no encouragement in them from his father. To one who had watched his career from boyhood with adoring eyes the attainment of this glorious position seemed to the old man to be the crowning of all his hopes. There could be no doubt of the advice that he would offer, and it was with joy that he had read the letter in which Edward had told him of his acceptance:

'I've just seen the P.M. and you will have got my telegram. I think the decision is right. I can't tell you what I feel about it, though we know what we each feel, I think. It was a joy and a help seeing you and I could not have reached the point of decision without knowing all that you said and feeling all that you left unsaid. Thank you so much, dearest Papa, for all and everything you are to us all.'

Both men knew how slight were their chances of seeing one another again, but any regrets that might have lingered in the son's mind—any fear that his father might have dreaded or resented that severance, were dispelled for ever by his reply, so warm, so typical, so comprehending:

'I think you have decided right. Something inside, higher than reason, tells me so, and whatever the future may have in store for us both, I shall be glad you have decided as you have, and be sure that to have decided otherwise was not what it was intended should be done. This being so I shall see nothing but the bright side of the matter—all its interest, and all its high thoughts, great possibilities and happy anticipations of good work achieved, and, in addition to this, though these are more personal matters, the special pleasure it must be to my Father, the glory to the family, the pleasure of all your friends—and the pride and glow I shall be always feeling in having such a son. My dearest, dearest Edward, you have been all your life, and now more than ever, the pride and joy of my life. Think how pleased your Mama would be, and of all dear Lord Devon would be saying. . . .'[1]

The appointment was announced in November. Thus was fulfilled the prophecy of the Hindu astrologer of which Sir John Lawrence had written to Edward's ancestor Charles Halifax in 1868, that a member of the Wood family, yet unborn, would succeed him one day as Governor-General of India. 'If ever he comes, however, this descendant of yours,' old Lawrence had written, 'he will have a quicker voyage to England than mine was; for I hear that hare-brained scheme of Mr. Lesseps for digging a canal from Suez to the Mediterranean is actually taking place.'

Edward relinquished his seat in the House of Commons and was created Baron Irwin of Kirby Underdale, the parish in the East Riding of Yorkshire in which Garrowby lies. There was a connection here between the name Irwin and Temple Newsam, for an Ingram had been raised to the peerage after the Restoration and assumed the Scottish title of Lord Irvine.

*   *   *

When the last official toast had been drunk and the last farewells made, the new Viceroy and his family left Victoria Station on the first part of their journey on 17 March. They took with them their Military Secretary C. O. Harvey, that able and devoted man who was only once to leave the Viceroy's side in the five years of his rule, and their friends Jack and Mary Herbert whose vivacity and lightheartedness were sometimes alone to

[1] Hickleton Papers. October 1925.

sustain them during the moments of intolerable pomp when a jest was like a benediction. They had decided to take with them their younger sons, Peter and Richard, to supervise their early education, and Lady Irwin had also invited a friend, Lady Worsley, who had intended to stay for three months but who found the life so delightful that she stayed for twelve, and later returned to India each subsequent winter until the end of their vice-royalty.

Lord Irwin, had he been less preoccupied, might have recognized in the throng on the platform a foretaste of the almost daily ordeals that awaited him in India. His office already held him in its grasp, and from that moment he had forfeited almost all the blessed anonymity of private life. His great appointment was the cause of this gathering which was a cross-section of everything that was most potent in English life. The King had sent a representative; the Prime Minister and the Archbishop of Canterbury were there too, so that Church and State might be associated at this departure and the blessing of the latter bestowed upon it.

Birkenhead was there of course, and he had had much to do both with the choice of Viceroy and with the setting of this scene, and Winston Churchill, his mind as yet unclouded by any apprehensions about the Imperial glories of India. Old Lord Halifax could not have borne to miss this spectacle, this hour of glory for his wonderful son. He had made the long journey down from the North, and now he too was on the platform with his white beard and animated gestures, leaning on his walking-stick with the silver band, and braced for a parting of poignant significance.

Irwin had not yet had time to become acclimatized to political grandeur. That would soon come, but at the moment he seemed a trifle overawed by the circumstances of his departure. His short speech was diffident, and in it he took care to emphasize his understanding that this brave send-off was a tribute to his office and not to himself.

But he would have been inhuman if he had not felt an intense excitement at the thought of becoming Viceroy of India. Perhaps only Dorothy had realized how thrilled he had been when the proposal was first made. He was only forty-four. It was a dazzling prospect even for one whose ambitions were as sluggish as his; they were now definitely stirred. Habitually modest, he told his wife 'that he did not think he was up to the job'. There even appeared to him something faintly ridiculous in the fact that it had been offered to him, and he came home from discussing it with a friend and said to her: 'It's absurd. I can't do this.' But the real obstacle to acceptance was the thought that in all probability he would never see his father again, and it was perhaps Halifax's declared intention of visiting him in India which removed his last hesitations.

They joined the *Mooltan*, on which they were to sail to India, on 19 March at Marseilles. Wherever Edward and Dorothy were, there were always dogs

to be found; a much loved elkhound, Musti, was included in the suite, and
Dorothy noted with regret that he did not behave as well on ship-board as
the Herberts' dog Midge. It is unlikely that a less typical Vicereine ever left
the shores of England. Exalted positions, palaces and endless retinues of
servants—all the pomp of viceregal power meant nothing to her, and we shall
see that her happiest days in India were those when she would escape from
this constraint and find freedom in simple things and wild places.

They paused for a while on 24 March at Port Said where they met their
old friend Lord Lloyd, the High Commissioner of Egypt and late Governor
of Bombay, and his wife; the men discussed the Bombay Reclamation Scheme
which was threatened with ruin, and Lady Lloyd gave Dorothy a dispiriting
lecture about the awful work ahead of Edward and the probability of Musti
catching rabies.

On 1 April they set foot on Indian soil, landing at the Gateway of India in
Bombay, a great archway of grey stone at the head of a flight of steps leading
up from the water, and had their first glimpse of the city which seems half
drowned in the sea, and lies flat against the dark promontory of the Malabar
Hills.

The men in full-dress white groaned at the tightness of their uniforms in
the heat, and Colonel Harvey's braces snapped in the launch and were
hastily secured by the Vicereine with a safety pin. They were conducted to
two thrones at one end of the archway where they received an Address, and
the Viceroy replied to it.

At Government House they were received by Lord and Lady Reading,
who were soon to return to England, and met the Commander-in-Chief Sir
William Birdwood. Dorothy noticed Lady Reading's pallor, and her depression at the thought of departure. Everything that was to appear irksome
to Dorothy had been the breath of life to her, and she had openly admitted
her delight in being a queen.

Now it was hard to bear the thought that those glorious days were over for
ever. This reflection was a strange one to the new Vicereine who was so
complete a stranger to the *folie de grandeur*. 'I felt very sorry for them,' she
said, 'but I wondered whether it could be possible, if and when the day came
for E and me to leave, that we should not be skipping down the steps trying
to hide our obvious delight.'

It was long believed that the Viceroy had landed in India on Good Friday,
and ignoring his official welcome, had gone straight to church, and thus at the
outset planted in the minds of the Indians an indelible memory of his religious
devotion, but this was a legend, for he had landed on Thursday in Holy
Week and taken his full part in the elaborate ceremony of welcome.

They had a strange feeling at the swearing-in ceremony at Convocation
Hall, and to Dorothy it seemed that it was just like getting married again, for
the Hall reminded her of a church, but that this time she had to wait for him,

and when they left the building they were again conscious of a feeling of constraint, as after a wedding, and of doubt as to whether they should bow and smile to friends as they walked back down the aisle. She who could always find diversion in the most improbable surroundings found much to amuse her in those three days in Bombay. They 'were really very funny. There seemed to be a good deal of confusion about who was what, and everyone called everyone else "Your Excellency", until it gave me a *fou-rire*'.

They left Bombay for Delhi after dinner on Easter Sunday in the gleaming white viceregal train, with the Viceroy's coat-of-arms on every coach, the magic carpet that was to waft them to every part of India from the forests and marismas of the South to the snows of Simla, softening their unending labours by its wonderful comfort. Edward and Dorothy each had a large bedroom, sitting-room and bathroom, and the train stopped for meals and baths. Great boilers for the hot water were kept on the simmer at local stations where the Viceroy's arrival was timed to a minute by a schedule kept with military precision. The line was guarded the whole way down the Viceroy's route by men standing at twenty-yard intervals. At night they carried torches whose flickering light could be seen for miles, so that the line resembled an endless golden snake stretched out before the engine.

They came to Delhi on one of those lovely mornings when the swift mysterious dawn of the East had just broken. The hot weather had not yet come and the atmosphere was deliciously cool and clear and free of dust as they drove through the streets past the Red Fort of Shah Jehan to Viceregal Lodge. They were accompanied by an escort of cavalry and Royal Horse Artillery which jingled ahead of them, and by the Viceroy's bodyguard, a hundred and fifty magnificent men drawn from the martial races of India, each over six feet high, formidable in their red and blue uniform.

The cavalcade trotted along the winding red paths into the gardens of Viceregal Lodge. The Viceroy inspected the Guard of Honour which had given him a Royal Salute. Then they stood in a tent, Edward in a grey frock coat and white topee, and shook hands with all the people who had come to welcome them, until at last the ceremony was over and they could explore their new home.

They saw a long, low white building on one floor in a fine Moghul garden, with a high white-pillared porch, and a colonnade of rounded arches which would make a cool refuge when the hot weather came. Although a large building, it was in no sense a grand one. Walking through it they found that their private rooms were in the centre of the house and had their own side entrance. There was little in them of viceregal pomp. They wandered into a Council room that was modest, and even mean, and next door to it a larger, gloomy wooden-lined room with a gallery, which they were told was the dining-room, where there hung a picture of old Charles Wood, and to which the food had to make a long journey from the kitchens. A vast ballroom, which had recently been added and was out of all proportion to the other rooms, seemed to give sinister promise of the scale of entertainment to come.

Although the house was elegant and shapely, it seemed too simple and unsophisticated for the grand purpose for which it was used. It was clear that it would be insupportably hot in summer months, for there was little shade round it and the sun would beat upon it as through a burning glass. But at that moment the weather was perfect, like an English May day. There was something strangely English too, Dorothy thought, in her first Indian garden with its water-courses which the Moghuls from beyond the mountains had made to provide an illusion of coolness in the debilitating heat of the Delhi plain, for side by side with exotic tropical blossoms were the flowers of high summer in England, hollyhocks, phlox, petunias and verbena.

You passed down the drive through a street of tents in which lived the members of the staff, and there was a delightful pavilion in the garden built for the visit of the Prince of Wales, which they contemplated taking for their own. All round the house in those days was open country, and there was no building in sight. They were to find that they could ride for miles along the Canal bank, and by the Ridge which had been the scene of bloody events in the Indian Mutiny, that spine of rock on which British soldiers had lain under the terrible sun that beat upon the scrub and rose-pink quartz, and looked down through a shimmering heat haze upon the old town of Delhi and the Red Fort of Shah Jehan.

They found viceregal life at first a trifle depressing, and Dorothy was the greater sufferer. The formality which had so delighted her predecessor rasped upon her nerves before she became accustomed to it, and at first produced a slight and uncharacteristic malaise of spirit:

'I feel very depressed,' she wrote in her diary soon after arrival. 'It is dreadful to be the only two examples male and female, with your own pens, and a feeling that when you leave them you make everybody uncomfortable because they have to get up and be on ceremony. I emerged for luncheon the first day and found that I ought not to have done so until fetched by an A.D.C.!

'It also gets on my nerves to be called "Your Excellency", which I am sure is overdone by the ex-Reading staff. One hardly ever calls the Q and K "Your Majesty"; it seems to me rather vulgar.' Her fingers itched, as did those of Jack Herbert, to rearrange the furniture in the drawing-room, but when discovered doing so by the Comptroller, Colonel Muir, the Vicereine felt 'like a child caught doing something naughty'. This brief depression soon lifted when she became involved in the new life with its infinite variety and interest. Those hordes of servants, at first so oppressive, melted into the background and became a familiar and accepted part of the scene.

Lord Irwin was well aware that the fortunes of every Viceroy were largely made or marred by his personal staff, and realized how fortunate he was in this respect from the beginning to the end of his viceroyalty. His Military Secretary, Colonel C. O. Harvey of the Central India Horse, added to a thorough knowledge of India a remarkable power of organization, great discretion and an ability to take decisions, and he was bound to the Viceroy by deep personal loyalty and affection.

Sir Geoffrey de Montmorency, Private Secretary to Reading, who remained with Irwin for the first few months, was clearly a man of great ability with a sardonic humour, and a character that seemed to Dorothy both attractive and enigmatic. He was a difficult man to replace, but the Viceroy was particularly fortunate in his successor, George Cunningham, who remained with him throughout his term. Once an international Rugby player he was to become Governor of the North West Frontier Province both under British administration and, after her withdrawal, under Pakistan, and of him Irwin was to say truthfully later that 'few names have been held in more respect along that wild strip of Asia that lies between India and Afghanistan'.

*   *   *

The Viceroy soon found that his life in India would follow a regular pattern. He would spend the early part of the year in Delhi, and when the heat became oppressive in the plain by the middle of April would go to Simla into the crisp air of the Himalayas, staying at the Circuit House at the little town of Dehra Dun on the way. In December he would go to Calcutta for Christmas, for since 1911 when the capital had been moved to Delhi, it had become the custom for the Viceroy to spend some weeks in Calcutta during the winter months, to keep his finger on the pulse of non-official opinion and to obtain more intimate impressions of it than could be gleaned from an official file.

A few miles to the south, away from the babel of the Old City, a new town was about to be born in the great open spaces of the Delhi plain, and the new Viceroy's palace, designed by Sir Edwin Lutyens, was rising slowly from the dusty earth. It is strange irony indeed that the minds that gave birth to this tremendous plan had little conception that the days of British rule were numbered.

New Delhi seemed rather designed for its perpetuation. The broad leafy boulevards, the green open spaces, the gardens with their water-courses and lawns and formal ponds, laid out with a prodigality greater than that of any Moghul Emperor, the great palace itself, all was conceived with the grandeur of a new Versailles, and for an equally mighty succession of rulers, and seemed to bear the signature of the dominant race. As yet the town of New Delhi had hardly begun to rise round the palace, of which only the second storey had been built, and all round it stretched the great plain and the tombs of dead kings, and only the voice of the jackal was heard at night by its unfinished walls.

The Irwins were not to move into the house until December 1929, but during the whole of their time in India they were both deeply and personally concerned with its progress. For three years they watched the immense structure rising, and at the end Dorothy and Lady Worsley had put months of hard work into the furnishing and decoration of the house with Sir Edwin Lutyens and the Chief Engineer, Sir Alexander Rouse.

But all this was in the future. It was already becoming hot in Delhi in April, and it was time to leave for Dehra Dun, that tranquil halting-place on the way to the Hills, where the plain is suddenly broken by the great water-shed of the Himalayas, a haven of rest in a mountain valley where they would always stay for a while to give time to the household to settle into its new quarters, and to the Government of India to transfer its machinery to Simla.

You approach it from Delhi across the sun-drenched plain, with its tawny earth stretching for hour after hour with no feature on the landscape. But at last the outline of mountains appears on the horizon, and as you draw near them you leave behind the monotonous fields of sugar cane, the huddled villages and the clay hovels.

The road winds upwards suddenly, thickly wooded through the Siwalik jungle where tigers and panthers roam; there are wild elephants not far away at Kansaro, and the forest is green and inviting after the torrid plain; there is a promise of refreshment in the air as you ascend, and drop into the sun-blighted little town. There the grass is burned grey in the great open space where boys play football and the townspeople saunter. The temples are decaying and the bells ring hollow on the ear. The stucco is peeling from the medallions on the Roman Catholic church, and the bazaar reeks with the age-old squalor of the East.

But the Viceroy would not linger in the town. He would turn off the main street and leave behind the tin shanties and the herds of black and white goats, and enter a leafy area with white houses in their green gardens, and a hint of coolness in the air. Then to the Circuit House where they were to stay, and they lost their hearts to it at first sight, an old thatched bungalow in an enchanting garden that lay in profound silence beneath the foothills of the Himalayas.

They knew at once that here was a true place of repose. The garden was quiet after the clatter of the town—a great sweep of turf watered deep green, and shade everywhere from mango and teak trees, and all about it weeping cypresses and jacaranda and Indian plum, and the smell of lemon-scented eucalyptus.

Dorothy saw with delight that again, as at Delhi, among the palms and bamboo and bougainvillaea were the English flowers she loved, and which made Edward think of the garden at Garrowby, lupins, eschscholtzias and marigolds. There was an Indian grave in the corner of the garden, and at night from her window she could see the mourners showing little lights of

Photo Massers', Malton

AS VICEROY, IN PROCESSION
The trainbearers are Richard Wood and
the son of the Maharajah of Bharatpur

homage to the dead. Peter and Richard were there to greet them, already beginning to talk Hindi, and with tall stories about riding elephants in the jungle.

The Viceroy had intended to go to Lahore that April, but the visit was cancelled when he went down with fever, and he stayed for ten days at Dehra Dun instead. There was little official business as the offices were on the move, and he was convalescent, so there was 'plenty of time to read in the garden, a friendly visit to the Military Academy and the Army College, and Forestry Institute . . . and as much time in the jungle as tiger reports might suggest'.

When he was stronger he made an expedition to Sikhala forest, to Mohand where they rode elephants in the jungle and sat up in a machan watching the game. The flowering shrubs were out and the air was full of chirrupings and spring odours, and little spotted deer grazed beneath his tree. The silence and stealth of the jungle cast an instant spell upon the Viceroy. It was so quiet that he could hear the sound of every animal for miles, and it was strange to hear the scream of wild peacocks which reminded him of Hickleton on a summer evening.

It was exciting to think that tigers lived within reach of his house, and they beat for them at Mohand in the middle of the day when the sun was at its full power, and the tigers lay drowsing in the shade of the thickets. The excitement of the moment for Edward was never dulled, even by constant repetition. He did not believe that there was an experience on earth more thrilling than this waiting for the tiger, while the shouts and the tom-toms of the beaters grew closer, and the fantastic creature showed its muzzle through the undergrowth.

It was with reluctance and a certain foreboding that they prepared to leave this tranquil refuge and begin their official duties at Simla. 'We are packing up and leaving for Simla tonight,' Dorothy wrote in her diary, 'feeling very sad, for this place is perfect and such a holiday, and now we have to begin the job in real earnest, and the more I hear of Simla the less attractive it sounds.'

Nor did she find inviting the journey to the summer capital which clings to the mountains like a swallow's nest amid fir-clad peaks. They left the vice-regal train at Kalka where the broad gauge ends, and changed into the rail-motor, a sort of open railway carriage run by petrol in which, they had been warned, many people were made sick as it twisted and turned. Tightly wedged as in a bus, they rode upwards in this contrivance for five hours with a stop for breakfast at Barog.

The weather was thick and menacing, and the splendid vistas of the Himalayas were blanketed in mist. All they could see were the endless barren hills in front of them which reminded Dorothy of some Italian landscape with patches of cultivation struggling up the mountain side. It was arctically cold. Sir Geoffrey de Montmorency beguiled the time with sardonic reflections on the horrors of the Simla social life to come which he detested.

'I am terribly afraid we shall all hate it,' said Dorothy, 'but I have never expected anything else as far as I am concerned, as I loathe living in mountains and this is the most concentrated mountain one could possibly imagine! It is like living on the edge of a knife.'

They walked up a steep path from the station, and got into a carriage, and with the bodyguard clattering in front of them drove to Viceregal Lodge. The way lay up through a precipitous drive with hairpin corners. It was dark in the shadow of the trees that almost met overhead, but they could see the crimson blossoms of the tree rhododendrons and brown monkeys leaping about its walls.

The house was set on one of the highest spurs of this mountainous region, and on all sides commanded awe-inspiring views of Himalayan peaks. It was so vast and so hideous that it took the breath away. Made of huge slabs of yellow-grey sandstone, it bristled with every gruesome feature that architecture could assume at the hands of a lunatic; two huge baronial porches; tiers of galleries; an erection like some minaret gone mad, and another the shape of a parish church tower in yellow sandstone. A red-tiled roof that might have graced some Spanish *posada* added the last touch of incongruity to the appalling building. Over the main porch was a lion and unicorn, and an inscription which announced that this monstrous edifice was erected in the viceroyalty of Lord Dufferin.

The first sight of it produced a numbing effect. It seemed to resemble the country houses of those immensely rich but tasteless German industrialists— the Krupp mansion at Essen, or the pencil magnate's house near Nuremberg. To Dorothy it was a monstrosity only appropriate to some depressing institutional purpose, a lunatic asylum, or an inebriates' home, while to Edward it suggested a hydro in some English watering place. Her heart sank at the prospect of having to spend six months in this place, but she found solace in the delightful garden behind the house where there were lawns sloping down to the tennis courts, and clumps of bamboo, and banksia roses that would soon be in their full glory, and pleasant houses for the staff, black-and-white-beamed.

In the dim interior of the house, oppressive with its dark rooms and pseudo-baronial hall, they found the silver howdah that Lord Curzon had used for the Durbar. There was an immense picture of the bearded Maharaja of Patiala on the staircase. On the green walls Warren Hastings, with his 'mouth of inflexible decision', and all the old Governor-Generals and Viceroys of India looked down from innumerable prints. In the great dining-room there was a mahogany table and red leather chairs, and, in some of the rooms above, old-fashioned brass bedsteads and muslin curtains.

About all this there was a flavour of the Victorian and Edwardian past as appropriate as the smell of cheroots in an abandoned smoking-room, but unhappily it was not all. Lady Reading had had a weakness for the colours mauve and grey and in certain rooms had applied them with no sparing hand. Dorothy set to work at once with the help of Jack Herbert to rearrange her sitting-room, and when the mauve carpet had been dipped and the cretonne of mauve tulips changed, it was easier to live in, although the windows had wire netting as well as glass to keep out the thieving monkeys, and too much had been done by the Readings to justify any major alterations.

Her forebodings about the life at Simla seemed to be fulfilled. There were a hundred servants in the house and she found it irksome to be surrounded by them at every moment of the day, rising suddenly with deep salaams, and anticipating her most trifling needs. Her unhappiness increased when she discovered that she was not supposed to leave the grounds of Viceregal Lodge without an escort. If she stayed out late at night the rickshaw men had to wait outside, whatever the hour, until she emerged, and everyone in the house sat up in rows along the walls to await her return and see her to bed. 'How different,' she reflected, 'from a taxi and a latchkey.' Edward and Dorothy made it a rule always to breakfast alone with one another every day and to dine by themselves once a week, and without such quiet moments the strain of official and social life would have been unendurable.

Neither she nor the Viceroy liked their official duties at Simla. There was something petty and depressing about it, and these periods spent in Vice-regal Lodge were for the Vicereine one of the least enjoyable aspects of her Indian life. Lodged on the mountain side there was sometimes a feeling of claustrophobia in the place, and the provincial character of the society added to its limitations. Although there were always guests in the house they were both much in the company of officials, and in their appearances at gym-khanas and private theatricals they were always on duty and there was little opportunity for the informality they so greatly preferred.

In fact the entertainment at Simla was so incessant that there had to be a rule that the Viceroy did not dine out except with the Governor of the Punjab, the Commander-in-Chief, Members of Council and his own staff. In 1926 the Punjab was still ruled by Sir Malcolm Hailey, whom Dorothy at once recognized as 'a charmer', and who was to become the Viceroy's most brilliant and influential adviser in the days of conflict ahead.

There was scarcely a moment of privacy. Streams of visitors came and went, Indian Princes, politicians, friends and relations. Often as many as eighty people sat down to the Viceroy's table and then it was seen in what magnificence he lived. He never forgot that he was the representative of the King-Emperor, but there was a side of his own character, too, that appreciated grandeur.

There was gold plate on the table, and crimson rhododendrons or gladioli, and all the flowers of India in their season, and the khidmutgars made a brave show in their scarlet and gold, standing behind the chairs, one to every two guests, putting both hands to their foreheads and bowing as the guests entered the dining-room. Whatever they felt, the Viceroy and Vicereine were hosts of incomparable skill. The charm which both of them possessed in such full measure was never relaxed, but, without the slightest loss of dignity, their attitude was, from the first, friendly and informal, instead of regal and forbidding. The stiff protocol was humanized, and after dinner, before the men came in, the Vicereine would walk round talking to the ladies instead of having them brought up to her as the custom had been before.

Yet in spite of her triumphs as the presiding goddess, she could not like Simla. She hated the claustrophobia of the place, and the monsoon bringing its weeping skies from the end of June to September. But she thought that the first fortnight of September was heavenly, the weather like warm days in Scotland, and cool at night, the whole dusty country washed clean by the monsoon, and a fresh and delicious smell from the woods.

The Viceroy loved this season as much as she: 'The wonder of the first weeks following the end of the monsoon in Simla had to be experienced to be believed,' he wrote: 'a clean atmosphere in which every line and shadow stood out sharp and unmistakable; the smell of vegetation reviving and refreshed; a sun perpetually shining out of a cloudless sky; and in the great distances the ridges of snow mountains catching all the changing lights until these faded into darkness with the last rose-coloured rays of the setting sun.'[1]

Dorothy soon grew to hate the road to Annandale where most of the outdoor social activity took place, although it was a beautiful place, a great artificial terrace scooped out of the mountains in a valley below the Ridge and surrounded by deodar trees. There were cricket and polo grounds, with the woods all round them, and here Simla society forgathered to watch and take part in polo and the weekly gymkhanas. The place was always alive with people, schooling ponies, practising their polo shots, shooting at the range, or cantering round for the sake of their livers. She felt like one attending compulsory games at school when she drove down to Annandale to watch polo or the football matches for the Durand Cup in which the Indians played without boots.

There were two escapes from Simla for the Viceroy and Dorothy which provided their refuge from the uneasy house, and an assurance of peace and solitude. One was a hill cottage near Mashobra called The Retreat, which was perched like an eagle's eyrie on the summit of fir-clad mountains. This hermitage was about eight miles from Simla, and they would snatch at every opportunity to visit it, riding or driving over after early church on Sunday with a sense of wonderful buoyancy and relief, and sometimes spending a night or two there in blissful recuperation.

They would turn off from the little village of Mashobra into a wood where

[1] Halifax. Op. cit., p. 135.

there were bear and panther, and the brown monkeys chattered in the trees, and the path wound steeply upwards covered by ferns, iris and mountain geranium. The Retreat stood on the summit of eight thousand feet, small, yellow and with a double red roof, a balcony on the first floor and gabled windows, a place of refreshing simplicity after Viceregal Lodge. Below it, and descending in almost vertical tiers were orchards of apple trees, and of cherries which the Viceroy loved to pick and eat hot from the sun when he wandered there from the garden full of English flowers.

To sit in that garden in the absolute hush of the mountains and the woods where no birds sang, and where there was a feeling of elemental solitude, was to believe that you were on the very roof of the world. All round you was a landscape of white peaks, suffused with rose at sunset, more staggering even than that seen from Viceregal Lodge. The deep silence and solitude of Mashobra were a balm to jangled nerves, and the peace of the mountains seemed to pass over the place like a healing wind.

There was a wonderful aroma of peaceful days inside the little house. It was full of Victorian furniture of bamboo and wicker; there were muslins and faded rose chintzes left there by Lady Minto, and little staircases leading haphazard to the rooms above. The whole place with its scent and the aura which hung about it was redolent of the past, and of the dead Viceroys who had loved Mashobra's peace, so that entering it was like dropping back into another age. Edward and Dorothy took long walks in the woods to the consternation of the staff who had never known a Viceroy walk alone with his wife. There Edward strode along with his great ambling stride, with Dorothy trying to keep up. 'There was a tremendous dog life,' said one who visited them at Mashobra, and it was here that C. O. Harvey's black and white terrier Chops was taken by a panther.

Even dearer to them as a refuge was the standing camp at Naldera, a few miles beyond Mashobra, pitched on a plateau in a wood of magnificent deodars. Here again was a silence and peace which made them feel a hundred miles from the nearest human habitation. The tents or shamianas were permanently set up, and each was the size of a large room with Persian carpets laid on the floor, and outside the tent a lean-to, also with rugs on the ground, where they could sit out in the shade or eat their breakfast. There were bathrooms, beds, dressing tables and washing stands in every shamiana, so that they lived in the camp in the height of comfort.

In the middle of the clearing on the plateau was an immense tree with five trunks, 'Lord Curzon's Deodar', in the shade of which that Viceroy was said to have pitched his own tent, and they would often have their dinner under its branches and sit talking late in the moonlight. The camp looked down on a little golf course cleverly laid out on the only possible ground and meandering round a green temple built of wood, from which they could look down on the Sutlej river flowing five thousand feet below, where Dorothy would sometimes fish for mahseer in the stream. Only the Viceroy, the Governor of the Punjab and the Commander-in-Chief were allowed their own motor-cars in Simla, and there was then no road to the camp, only a precipitous track just wide enough for a small car. The others approached Naldera in rickshaws or on horseback in a long cavalcade down the dusty path.

*   *   *

Towards the end of May the Princes would gather in Simla for their Council, and the Viceroy became acquainted with these picturesque figures whose characters were as various as the size of their domains and the efficiency with which they were administered. He was much taken with the panache of these rulers, saying of one of them that he was 'the greatest gentleman he had ever met', but he noted their backslidings with a shrewd eye.

One of the first to pay his respects was the deplorable Maharaja of Alwar, who claimed to be descended from the Sun God and whose continued presence on his throne was thought by many to be an affront to public decency and a reproach to the Government of India. Here was a strong and baleful personality; a tall man of reptilian beauty and remarkable accomplishments, a philosopher, a scholar and a fine orator even in a day rich in the power of speech. Clearly a victim of schizophrenia, he was known to be a sadist and a pervert, and he had developed towards the English a manner at once insolent and correct that was difficult to endure. He was commonly supposed to have murdered more than one person who had crossed his path, and was said to have tethered a recalcitrant polo pony to the side of a hill in the hot weather, and made daily visits to watch it dying of thirst. Indeed, he was later to have a goat tied outside the Vicereine's window in his palace at Alwar so that it might be killed in the small hours of the morning by a tame panther and terrify her by its dying screams, but she was fortunately able to forestall these hospitable preparations by releasing the goat.

Like some Sultan in the seraglio on the Golden Horn he went in constant terror of assassination, and yet was so brave that, disdaining the safety of a machan, he would hunt panther on foot with a spear and follow wounded tigers into the jungle without a qualm. He was a man who could literally produce a shiver in those who encountered him.

Part of Alwar's insolence consisted in having all dogs removed from his sight, however distinguished their owners. Their proximity, he said, made him feel sick, and it speaks volumes for the man's personality that he was able to enforce this intolerable rule on the Secretary of State, Birkenhead, and the Viceroy, two men in whose lives dogs played a large part.

He was also given to a cynical pretence, in order to cause inconvenience, that as his religion forbade him to touch leather he could not ride in an ordinary saddle, a claim that was never made by other Hindu princes, or hold ordinary reins. A buckskin saddle had to be found for him to use on the ride to Annandale, and brown silk gloves prevented contamination by the bridle. The rule of this evil man, who seemed to belong to some other age, was eventually ended by an uprising of his subjects, and he was to die miserably in Paris.

A welcome relief after Alwar was Hari Singh, the Maharaja of Kashmir, a fat and good-natured young man whose *bonhomie* had to some extent been impaired by his experiences as Mr. A. in the English courts, and the Maharaja of Patiala, who had a house near Simla at Chail, a burly Sikh with his beard done up in a net. This friendly prince had endeared himself to Dorothy by possessing eighty-three dogs, and by breeding elkhounds, one of which he presented to her and was christened Dehra Dun. But their favourite prince was the Maharana of Dholpur who had a summer house at Khandeghat, eighteen miles from Chail, and was a distant cousin of Patiala, and he, too, became devoted to the Irwins, and, when they visited India after the war, flew down to Colombo, where Edward was in a nursing home, to see them.

Of all the Indian States Edward best liked to visit Dholpur, where he had once rolled over a galloping tiger like a rabbit at a hundred yards with a rifle shot, but even better than driving tigers, he said, 'was going round one of the lakes with the Maharana in a motor launch and seeing his tigers in a sanctuary he kept there, lying on the bank in the sun, asleep or licking themselves like the great cats that they are, and taking not the slightest notice of the inquisitive gallery on the launch. He was a great lover of his animals, and we often used to laugh at him for giving the tigers in a special area near his jungle palace bowls of chilled milk and frozen cheeses in the hot weather.'[1]

They were also fond of the ten-year-old Maharaja of Gwalior and his sister of twelve, 'George and Mary' as they had been named after the King and Queen, and of the Maharaja of Jaipur, 'a nice fat boy of fifteen', who had been married at the age of thirteen to a woman of thirty, and of 'poor little Indore', a boy of seventeen who came to stay with his tutor, and was delighted when Edward said that he could go to Oxford.

Less enthusiasm was felt about the Nizam of Hyderabad, the maladministration of whose State was the subject of constant censure by the India Office and of embarrassment to the Viceroy. One of the richest men in the world, yet one of pathological meanness, he had a treasure of jewels in the vaults of his palace too great even to be valued, but refused to spend an unnecessary rupee on his people or the improvement of his State, and continuous pressure had to be maintained by the British authorities to secure a decent level of administration.

His children lived in terror of this old man who was said to keep them on a semi-starvation diet, and his two sons Azam and Muazzam told the

[1] Halifax. Op. cit., p. 142.

horrified Viceroy how, when a dentist had recommended that their father should have two or three of his teeth crowned with gold, he had ordered that his sons should have it done to them first to find out whether or not it hurt. The two boys had then had all their perfect teeth ground to the gums and capped with gold, and when the Nizam had heard that it was a hideously painful process he had refused to allow the dentist to touch him. At home the Nizam, who seldom washed, wore a dirty fez, ancient flannel trousers and a pair of the cheapest yellow boots, but when he came to Delhi he brought with him five hundred servants, two hundred soldiers and an astonishing number of wives.

More interesting to the Viceroy and Dorothy than this deplorable old skinflint was the Maharaja of Bikanir, suave, Europeanized, and a man who had exalted snobbery to the realm of genius. One would not have taken him at first sight for an Indian prince. He might have been a European diplomat of some distinction who spoke English and French perfectly and was clearly on easy terms with the great in London and Paris, as one could tell by his casual references to their christian names. At dinner he was effusive to Dorothy about Edward and herself, but less amiable about those who had gone before them. He told her how nice it had been that Lady Reading had enjoyed India so much. She had positively radiated happiness, but it was perhaps a pity that she had eaten cheese on her knife.

He had to confess that when he went to Viceregal Lodge in Chelmsford's day he always prayed that there would be someone there of higher rank than himself so that he would be spared the necessity of sitting next to Lady Chelmsford. Dorothy began to wonder what he would say later about the Irwins. It was curious how few of the princes seemed to have liked Reading, who was not only an outstanding Viceroy but also a man of unusual charm.

When Alwar had given a birthday party in London after Edward's appointment, at which Reading had been present, and had made a caddish speech full of innuendoes against him, saying pointedly at the end, '*Now* we have a real gentleman as Viceroy', with great emphasis on the 'Now' and looking hard at Reading, Dholpur and Patiala, although shocked by his manners, clearly found little to dispute·in his sentiments. Many other Princes came to Delhi and Simla, and the Viceroy was to visit the States of all those of sufficient importance, but among them all he found but one with a kindred sense of humour, the immortal 'Ranji', the Maharaja of Nawanagar, known as the Jam Sahib.

By July the monsoon would come to Simla, and the sunsets become lovelier each evening, turning the stones of the buildings pink, so that even Viceregal Lodge looked like a magic castle, and then the afterglow when the sunken sun became a deep clear orange, and above it a flush of violet. The period of the monsoon when the rain beat down with tropical intensity and persistence was maddening to the nerves. The Viceroy could no longer ride or play tennis, but he knew that he must not succumb to the weather and every day went for long walks in the rain with Harvey or one of his A.D.C.s.

He enjoyed most of all his experiences in India the journeys he made from Simla into the hill countries, trekking in the Himalayas on hill ponies, or back to Dehra Dun, long days in the open in the invigorating mountain air, through woods aromatic with the smell of pine, when they would walk or ride as the mood took them, pitching their camp at night:

'Morning to night in the open air, blissfully winding our way through lovely Himalayan scenery on foot or on sure-footed ponies taught to amble along at a comfortable pace, and apparently insensitive to precipices. As evening fell we would reach our camp, pitched by our *avant-garde* in some delicious spot, and we would sink pleasantly into deck chairs, to be served with welcome iced drinks. The locals would draw near with salaams, bringing their "Dalis", great trays of vegetables and fruit, and deposit both these and themselves at our feet. Perhaps at night after we had dined, village dancers would come and dance for us round the bonfire by the light of the moon and the stars.'[1]

He tried to give his father some conception of these treasured moments in the wilds, how they moved each day from place to place, sleeping in little forest bungalows, shooting and fishing, completely cut off from the world: 'I cannot tell you how we enjoyed ourselves—lovely country, snowcapped hills seen quite clearly, magnificent trees and masses of wild flowers. The whole ground was strewn with the most lovely dark blue forget-me-nots and wild Michaelmas daisies. I only wished that we had all been doing it together.'

Never given to introspection or worry, he lived entirely for the day. He was not called upon to make even the most trivial arrangement for they were always preceded by an army of servants, and the tents would be pitched by the time they arrived at the night's resting place. It was right that the Viceroy should have these days to atone for the deadly tedium of so much of his life, and to enable him to return to his work in Delhi refreshed in body and spirit.

*   *   *

His routine at Delhi was different from that at Simla where he seldom went out before breakfast. He started work at 9.30 a.m. after an early ride, or twice a week a hunt with the Delhi Hounds. He would work and give interviews all morning, and there were usually guests for lunch. After this he would play a short game of tennis or ride, and then work until dinner time. He was known sometimes to ride down to the polo ground so that the A.D.C. on duty should not miss the chance of a chukka, for he was always considerate to subordinates. After dinner he might play a rubber of bad

[1] Halifax. Op. cit., p. 136.

bridge or the 'Murder Game', which amused him, and he was generally asleep by midnight. Throughout his working life in India his Private Secretary, George Cunningham, was constantly at his side and was in a better position than any to form a true estimate of his executive capacity.

'Not everyone,' he said, 'could be aware of the great ability with which he controlled the ordinary detailed work of the Departments of Government. I doubt if there ever had been a Governor-General before him, except Curzon, who had shown greater ability simply as an administrator. I formed the opinion after perhaps two years of his office that he could with ease have taken over any of the six portfolios—even Finance—which the Civil Members of his Council administered. He could master a file or memorandum quicker than most people. He had a remarkable facility for reading quickly. I often placed before him a minute or report which I had had time to study carefully beforehand. As he read it for the first time, while I looked over his shoulder, he was always turning the page before I was ready, and he had the whole essence of it in his mind.'

The A.D.C.s found that to live at Viceregal Lodge was like being a member of a large family party presided over by indulgent parents who loved young people and had the gift of making them say whatever was in their minds, and a genius for creating an atmosphere of happiness. When the Viceroy and Dorothy were alone with their staff there was a refreshing absence of formality, and one of the A.D.C.s remembered that it 'was just like Garrowby', and that there was constant laughter in the house.

Indeed, such a family atmosphere was created that it was sometimes difficult to remember that Edward was a Viceroy and that they were all in India. The Viceroy loved parties and at the closing stages of dances was sometimes to be found joining in Follow-My-Leader and blowing a hunting horn. All formality was absent from the permanent and delightful house-party at Viceregal Lodge, and a lady who attempted to curtsey to the Vicereine in her dressing-gown on the way to the bath was an object of much ridicule.

The old incorrigible curiosity still possessed the Viceroy. He could not bear the thought that he was missing anything amusing, and if he heard sounds of laughter when working in his study would leave his desk and hurry to the drawing-room to find out what was happening. He was skilled in ensuring that quarrels never started between members of his household. 'You felt,' said Harvey, 'that you could not be nasty to each other. He would not like it,' in the same way that people felt that they must go to church at Garrowby, whether they wanted to or not, because it was so much part of his life.

The A.D.C.s adored him. They were impressed by the incredible calm with which Irwin confronted every situation, however critical. He seemed so completely balanced that it was almost unnatural, and he was only once seen to lose his temper in five years in India, when he lost a disreputable old Homburg hat, and was upset for several days.

He was fond of clearing his mind on a difficult subject by talking aloud to his subordinates, and he once stopped his car and asked one of his A.D.C.s, Captain Alexander, to sit with him on a hillside. 'It was an awkward political moment, and Irwin just sat there talking quietly using me as a reception. I did not have to say anything.' Edward was fond of driving or riding with the A.D.C.s, and when a long way from home with Captain Pepys, his horse had fallen like a stone, and the young man had found himself with an unconscious and apparently dead Viceroy on his hands, and remembered how agitated he was and how calm the Viceroy when he came to.

His physical courage and indifference to danger were constantly in evidence, and coming back from a place where serious rioting was in progress he said to Alexander: 'I hate all this police business,' and got out of the car and walked. 'The police,' said Alexander, 'were terrified, but he went among the people and let them do as they liked. There was an enormous cheering crowd, and he was practically chaired to the station.' He did not like to use force to quell riots, and thought it was an admission of failure.

It seemed to some of those at Viceregal Lodge that this closeness to him gave them, after a time, a clearer insight into his character. This had often appeared to those who did not know him well aloof, and even sanctimonious. But these men who saw him every day and in all circumstances came to realize that his true nature was not represented by this impression, and was, on the contrary, simple and affectionate. The youthful curiosity, the love of sport and anything that carried a spice of danger, the preference for simple places and amusements, the kindness to youth, the ignorance of so many aspects of life, all these were true indices of this nature and pointed to a side of it that was unsophisticated and charming.

In spite of the simplicity of his own life, his character was one that appreciated grandeur on state occasions, and he understood its effect on the oriental mind. Like Lord Valentia he might have said: 'I want India to be ruled from a palace, not from a counting house; with the ideas of a Prince, not with those of a retail dealer in muslin and indigo.' His investitures were as magnificent as those of Curzon and caused Bishop Gore to say: 'When I get home I shall suggest that Edward Irwin be impeached for exceeding the King in grandeur.'

But the affection of some of his subordinates did not blind them to the fact that, like everyone else, he was not perfect. His wealth and standing had given him an apparently unquestioning confidence in his position in the world, and he would often assume an attitude that was almost feudal in its obsolescence. He really believed that privilege was a good thing, and that men in his position and of his world had the background that warranted their being in positions of authority.

They noticed, too, that beneath a modest manner lay a strong belief in his own judgment. He was not easily dissuaded from a course of action. He took a long time to reach a decision but, once made, he never pondered it afterwards and was seldom deflected from its course. He was receptive to advice but indifferent to criticism. They could see no trace of the humbug he was sometimes said to be, but they realized that in some respects his simplicity was deceptive; that he was a politician and had been through the mill. But his great virtues outweighed any faults. Those who had come close to him and under his influence felt that they had discovered a new purpose and meaning in life; even a serenity which had before been wanting. His rock-like faith was so impressive that even to the sceptical it gave a feeling of refuge and strength. Although in many ways out of date in his attitude to life and modern standards, he could project himself into the problems of others, and his desire to help and comfort those he loved made him, in the words of one, 'a unique friend who would never, never fail or let one down'.

It seemed to those round him that he was seldom bored, and he gave them the flattering impression that he wanted to listen and learn rather than to instruct. He was indeed a wonderful listener; he never laid down the law and was fundamentally humble about his abilities, saying that he had never had an original idea in his life. He envied those who could speak brilliantly, for his own speeches were to him pedestrian and boring, but he did not believe that oratory was a good way of influencing people's opinions. To him there was something unfair in using its magic for this purpose, and he preferred to persuade others by quiet discussion.

His friends found that human contact was essential to him. He made no barriers of age and was as happy talking to children as to adults; he showed a tireless interest in their thoughts and everyday lives, and although he was a little remote from the minds of modern children, he loved to listen to them, and he was one of those rare spirits in whose presence they could be natural and at ease. His friends felt that they could not have confessed something discreditable to him, and that the seamy side of life was to him a closed book. They found, too, that in spite of his ability he had an uncomplicated and in some ways almost naïve mind and approach to life, and that one of his most attractive qualities was his simplicity and lack of introspection. It was noticed that the Viceroy had no ulterior motives himself and that he found it difficult to recognize them in others.

In December the move to Calcutta began. Their daughter Anne arrived from England in October, and their eldest son Charles, home from Eton, joined them in Calcutta with Edward's sister Agnes. Their way took them through Cawnpore. It was a city of ghosts and evil memories of the Mutiny, and it was well for Edward's peace of mind that he could not foretell that events would soon take place there as bloody as any that had defiled the name of Nana Sahib.

The Viceroy spent a fortnight in Calcutta at Christmas, and the Governor of Bengal became a cypher during his presence there. It was a situation that might have been awkward with less tactful visitors, but the Governor, Lord Lytton, and his wife were old friends and behaved with the utmost correctness, although they did not like it, and Edward and Dorothy were at great pains to avoid giving any cause of offence. The Viceroy had already made up his mind to sever the Calcutta link gently when the Viceroy's House at New Delhi was finished.

They were received in state by Lord and Lady Lytton at Government House, that great palace built on the model of Kedleston Hall in Derbyshire, its magnificence designed to win the respect of the Eastern mind, the central pile with curving corridors radiating from its four angles to detached pavilions, each a house in itself, perfectly adapted to a climate where every breath of wind from whatever quarter must be seized, and where a perpetual *courant d'air* relieved most of the petty vexations of life.

From there they drove to Belvedere, yet another palace, where they were to stay, although Edward in his grand way called it an 'unpretentious house'. The reeking squalor of Calcutta was seen in greater contrast against the peace of this white house set in cool gardens in the shade of mahogany trees. The way to it lay past the Maidan, the vast open space in the centre of the city on the east bank of the Hooghly river, past the racecourse and across a stream where black and white buffaloes wallowed in the tepid water. Hard by Belvedere were the Zoological Gardens, and from his house the Viceroy could hear the roaring of the animals at night.

Belvedere had been the home of the Governors of Bengal before it became a rest house for the Viceroy, and as they came to the front door they could see over it the symbolical figure of a Bengal Tiger, and a long white house with pillars in the centre and arches spreading on either side of them, plaster work above them, and a balustrade running the length of the roof. Like all his houses in India, it was designed for entertainment, and the banqueting table sometimes used in the immense ballroom of this 'unpretentious' house was 114 feet long. Again they were fortunate in the garden with its beds of cannas in full bloom, its pools covered with lotus and water-lilies, and the trees that shaded it from the Bengal sun, banyan, almond and mahogany.

Even in December they found it hot and sticky in Calcutta, like living in a vapour bath. They missed the country background of Delhi and Simla. Although there was much riding at Calcutta and people mounted their horses at the door of the Governor's House, there was little pleasure in it, for they could ride only on the Maidan or the racecourse and the horses got stones in their feet. Edward's own recollections of Calcutta were a medley of loosely connected impressions; of how much India owed to Curzon for the preservation of her historical treasures, as expressed in the Victoria Memorial, of an unceasing pressure of political and social engagements, of making contact with the European business community, and of meeting Rabindranath Tagore at his country home where they found the poet sitting in a grove of mango trees, surrounded by adoring pupils.

He made friends with the head of the Anglican Order at Behala, Father Douglas, and it was probably this remarkable priest who encouraged Edward to visit the slums of Calcutta, perhaps the only Viceroy ever to do so, and his knowledge of the city was, therefore, not only that of the places that former Viceroys knew, the green turf of the racecourse, the Maidan and the shade of the trees at Belvedere.

He wished to study the worst that India had to offer at first hand, and with 'the fearless and incomparable Chief of Police', Sir Charles Tegart, as his companion he would explore such festering rabbit warrens as the market area of Sealdah. There was a squalor depressing to the soul in these stinking alleys; shops of corrugated iron where the owners sat cross-legged on a ledge in front, butchers' shops where the meat was festooned with flies, and a sickening smell of fat from the food shops; an open drain with pie dogs eating from it, and open latrines against the walls.

Crows would pick at the dusty heaps of offal and hop away too gorged to fly; and sacred cows wandered forlorn down the lanes, picking their way over brown recumbent figures, whether dead or sleeping it was hard to tell, and the incurious passers-by did not seem to care. Empty rickshaws rattled by, and over all there was an indescribable babel and clatter of life, the sound of a temple bell, and sometimes a whiff of an unforgettable scent compounded of spices and wood smoke, of jessamine and dust and cow-dung smoke, the smell of India.

They took him to the slums inhabited by Anglo-Indians, an area of straw huts with corrugated roofs where the residents were dark-skinned men and women, but with Irish and Scots names, Riordan, McGregor, Macpherson, Rorke, who spoke no English but a form of Hindi. In each hovel were coloured prints of King Edward VII and Queen Alexandra, the Union Jack draped over them. The Viceroy was profoundly moved, as once before in the shanty towns of the West Indies, by the passionate loyalty of these poor people to the Throne, and the intensity with which they clung to their British connection[1].

It was terrible that districts like this should extend to the furthest suburbs of Calcutta starting almost immediately after one had left the formal part of the city; terrible to reflect, as one drove out of it, that millions of lives were lived in such a way. The Governor of Bengal's summer house at Barrackpore, fifteen miles out of Calcutta on the Hooghly river, with its tropical Garden of Eden, provided a heavenly refuge from these horrors for a tired man.

[1] H. E. Hanson, former Deputy Commissioner to the Special Branch of the Calcutta Police, to author.

When the Viceroy visited Lytton there it was not necessary to drive through those dreadful suburbs. They went chugging peacefully up the river in the Governor's steam launch, avoiding the débris of the Calcutta slums, to the landing stage in front of the house. He could feel on this journey the same peace and contentment as that experienced by Curzon when he sat in a deck chair in the twilight of a Saturday evening or the radiance of a Monday morning and watched the changing panorama of the river banks as they flew by, crumbling Hindu shrines, or the towers of some pagoda against the sky, and walked up the gravel path at Barrackpore with the handborne lanterns twinkling in the darkness.

Of all the gardens they had seen in India Barrackpore was perhaps the loveliest with its lawns stretching down to the river. Lady Canning had opened out the gigantic banyan tree that dominated the garden and somehow seemed to be the centre of life at Barrackpore. It served as a leafy sitting-room and dining-room, cool in the heat and open to the stars at night, adorned with the creepers and orchids that hung in festoons from its many trunks. To Lady Ripon was due the bamboo avenue which converted the path from landing stage to house into a green tunnel of shade, inside which the scorching walk to the house could be made in cool green darkness with the bamboos meeting overhead and shutting out the sun.

There was a great park at Barrackpore which reminded the Viceroy of England, and the house was white and friendly with green shutters. In the garden was a marble basin and fountain, which some thought had been brought from Agra, and had once adorned the palace of the Great Moghul, and the 'pathetic grave' of Lady Canning who had loved Barrackpore so deeply and been laid to rest by the Viceroy beside the quietly flowing river. The magic garden, where roses flourished like weeds in the rich soil and which was full of cannas and morning glory, looked down the river to the fantastic pinnacles of Tittaghur and across the water to the white houses of the old Danish Settlement at Serampore. It was a delight to Edward to visit this friendly house with its flowered chintzes and mahogany furniture, and to rest in the shade of the huge banyan.

The first Christmas weeks at Calcutta made heavy demands on them all. Edward described them as 'a combination of a miniature General Election, the social obligations of an Ascot Week, and Cabinet meetings and interviews to fill up the spare time'.

In every part of India, in towns and remote districts, the English were preparing for Christmas: 'There was Christmas Camp, too, with partridges and jungle-fowl and hopes of a tiger in his royal winter coat, with wonderful picnics of cold turkey and chestnut stuffing, cold game pies and cold brandy butter with the pudding. Still mornings there were too in the cold forests before dawn, every leaf, every blade of grass cold with dew, the air sharp with the fragrance of bruised leaves and of dust wet with dew, the deer hooting in voices shrill with sudden fear, the jungle cocks crowing as darkness grew thin to the east. And there was the mixed soupy smell of elephant and driver, the breathless scramble into the tree above the tiger's kill, the sharpness of dusk when you counted the birds and went into the tents for tea and Christmas cake.'[1]

This was the sort of Christmas Edward would have loved, but his own was boisterous and happy. At Belvedere there was a dinner of sixty on Christmas Day, consisting of the Viceroy's party and the Lyttons and other friends, when the dining-room was decorated with garlands and strings of coloured lanterns and balloons. How characteristic it was of the Irwins that this large gathering was just like a dinner party at Garrowby with Edward's presence merely encouraging the young, and 'Harry Stavordale leaping over chairs on all fours like a horse', and the Viceroy blowing his hunting horn. 'It was indeed difficult to believe that we were at Belvedere,' observed Lady Lytton. 'Thoughts of the Reading régime helped, I think, to increase the general enjoyment.'

In that first New Year they visited the Raja of Benares after leaving Calcutta, and were taken in the State barge, painted with lilies and with two carved horses at the prow, to his palace at Ramnagar. They were entranced by the beauty of Benares seen from the river. There was a luminous quality in the light early in the morning, as in a painting by Canaletto. It played on the palaces built by the Rajas above the Ganges for occasions of religious festival, on the minarets of the mosque of the Moghul Emperor Aurangzeb and the Nepalese Temple of Love. The holy river ran by, murky and sluggish. The pilgrims had come there from all parts of India to immerse themselves in the water believing that by doing so they would wash away sin.

On a feast day, or at a solar or lunar eclipse, they come to the bathing ghats in thousands. They wade into the filthy water, swallowing, spitting and rinsing. Sometimes a black porpoise leaps in the river; yellow flowers lie on its scummy surface where the pilgrims have left their garlands, and white water-birds with long necks pick their way delicately among the bathers.

They watched the busy scene with fascination. They saw the priests in long draperies sitting on each ghat under umbrellas made of plaited bamboo to bless the pilgrims after the bathe, and the laundry people, often children, washing clothes, vigorously slapping them on stones; they saw the streaks of sect on the wrapt faces, the strident colours, purple, yellow and orange, and heard the twang of strange instruments of music. On a projecting pier sat a group of old men like decaying sea-birds.

The Raja's barge passed down the river from the bathing to the burning ghats, and they saw the ultimate rites of Hindu life. The bereaved must perform this last duty themselves, with their heads shaven to connote grief.

[1] Philip Woodruff, *The Men Who Ruled India*, Vol. II, p. 285.

They placed the corpses on the faggots, and laid more wood upon them, so that the body was sandwiched with sometimes the feet projecting like a sleeper with too short bedclothes. The mourners fed and poked the fires at intervals, for all must be consumed.

They were back in Delhi on 8 January 1927, and they were to repeat this circuit with minor variations in each of their five Indian years. It was the same day that Sir Samuel and Lady Hoare arrived by air, having accomplished their famous flight taking the mails from Croydon to Delhi in eleven days. The novelty of this momentous journey caused tremendous excitement in Delhi where the Secretary of State for Air was hailed as a modern Columbus. He invited the Vicereine to name the aircraft 'The City of Delhi', and after the ceremony the whole party, including Richard, were taken up for a flight.

Sir Samuel Hoare's courageous journey was a forerunner of the whole future development of aviation in India, and of her strategic position in the chain of Imperial communications. The distance between Great Britain and India began to shrink from that moment. The regular Air Mail Service between England and India was inaugurated in 1929, and the first air mail arrived on 6 April, having come from Croydon in under fifty-four hours' flying time. After a few months the service was thrown open to regular passenger traffic, and it was clear that for busy men the long sea journey would soon become a thing of the past. Inside India herself the Indian State Air Service was begun in 1929, which was to make it possible to traverse her own vast internal distances with unprecedented speed.

When Horse Show Week came to Delhi in February the house was always full, and the Viceroy's party entered as many horses and riders as they could, and there was polo and a duck shoot, and daily entertainments of an exhausting character which culminated in a State Ball at Viceregal Lodge. The Princes wandered through it in the splendour of their full regalia, Patiala with the great Sans Souci diamond, and on his arm a flat emerald an inch and a half across, and Dholpur in his gold coat studded with pearls and his hat with the diamond of Akbar set in its peak. There was something Curzonian in the splendour of these occasions, thought one who had attended them, and the onlooker was dazzled by 'waistcoats of silver lace and aiguillettes of gold, by the more delicate finery of the women, by the brocades and jewels of the Princes. To the eye there was not much difference between the guests who had attended Lord Curzon's Ball and those who now wandered among the fountains of the Moghul Garden'.[1]

In his time in India there was one task that was particularly dear to the Viceroy's heart. On 23 February 1927 he laid the foundation stone of the Anglican church in New Delhi. When he had first arrived in India there was already a project to build a church in the new capital. The congregation,

[1] Philip Woodruff. Op. cit.

which was almost entirely official, composed of Government servants who would spend at most three or four years in New Delhi, had succeeded in raising £10,000. He realized that such a sum was insufficient to build a worthy witness to the Christian Faith which would not be lacking in dignity beside the Government buildings designed by Sir Herbert Baker. The Viceroy, therefore, wrote to Lady Pembroke, and through her and Lady Titchfield and other friends in England another £30,000 was raised. Mr. H. A. N. Medd was commissioned to design it, and the Church of the Redemption was consecrated in February 1931 shortly before Edward sailed for England at the end of the viceroyalty.

The Viceroy was pleased with this church and thought that its spacious chancel and transepts and its height gave it a dignity which was without any impression of coldness or austerity. The Silver Cross was the gift of King George V; the candlesticks were presented by the Ladies of Yorkshire, and the altar, altar rails, pulpit and the figures above the reredos 'were the generous contributions of York Minster, as part of its own celebration in 1927 of thirteen centuries of Christianity from the time of the baptism there of King Edwin of Northumbria'.[1] Edward had first suggested the title of the Church of 'God the Father' in his correspondence with the Bishop of Calcutta, but the Bishop could find no precedent for such a title in the Western Church, and it was consecrated under the other name exactly four years after the Viceroy had laid its foundation stone.

*   *   *

Sport was in Edward Wood's blood and there were unlimited opportunities for it in India. New Delhi was still only the skeleton of a town, and the plain and the country round the old Viceregal Lodge were wide and empty. The Delhi Hounds hunted jackal over this open country, among the Moslem tombs on the great dusty plain dotted with sugar plantations. The jackals would dart in and out of these and there was rough riding over boulders and up and down nullahs. The only new building on this vast expanse was the aerodrome which had just been built there, and the horses were sometimes startled by the noise of the machines. The hounds met at five in the morning in the dark, partly to avoid the heat, and partly because there was a day's work ahead in the office, and they began to hunt in the shrill Indian dawn to an orange and purple sunrise with the dew heavy on the ground.

The sport which the Viceroy enjoyed in the Indian States did much to lighten his burden; clouds of sandgrouse floating over the guns at Bikanir, tiger in Gwalior, Alwar and Dholpur, duckshoots in Bharatpur, Kashmir and Bahawalpur, when the duck rose from the lake in their thousands with a sudden explosion of wings at the first shot. He was introduced to hawking

[1] Halifax. Op. cit., p. 145.

by a Punjab nobleman. With an extraordinary absence of logic he found it cruel, as the partridge had little chance to escape the hawk, and he wrote to his father: 'I am afraid the truth is that all sport is really cruel, and it surely shows how deeply rooted we are in the elemental instinct that steeplechasing and clay pigeon shooting, in which the fact of killing is absent, does not make nearly such an appeal to us as hunting something for its life.'

When the Viceroy went on tour it was like a Royal Progress and he was accompanied by a grand entourage. In addition to members of the family and a few friends, he would be attended by the Private Secretary to the Viceroy, the Military Secretary, a surgeon, three A.D.C.s, a clerical establishment of a dozen or more, a household establishment of valets and ladies' maids and about eighty Indian servants. The tours were planned with military precision and split-second timing by C. O. Harvey.

But these tours were not confined to shooting and fishing and sightseeing expeditions. They were a constant and demanding service; formal receptions, visits to hospitals and schools, opening canals, laying foundation stones, inspecting irrigation schemes and all kinds of public works. For the Viceroy, who carried his office with him wherever he went, besides his endless paper-work there were continual interviews, for it was his habit to be easy of access. The Vicereine worked tirelessly for the All-India Women's Education League, and for the health and education of all classes; she was particularly concerned with the emancipation of Indian women and the improvement of their status.

In their five years in India they visited all the major Native States and Provinces, but a few of them lingered particularly in their minds: Nagpur in the Central Provinces where they were given scented silk handkerchiefs, and rode upon an elephant dyed green from the tip of his tongue to his waist, with two stags painted on his face whose eyes were his eyes; and after that Poona in the Bombay Presidency where they stayed with the Governor, Sir Leslie Wilson at Ganeshkind, and Edward hunted with the Poona Hounds, and attended a review on the racecourse in a dark frock-coat and overalls on a horse that was, for once, big enough for him. From there they went to Bikanir, a city of pink sandstone, and the Lallargh Palace built like some temple round a courtyard with arched cloisters. Here the Maharaja was suave and sophisticated, and his 'shooting-box' was a series of carved sandstone palaces in the desert at Gajner, where the light was exquisite in the early morning, and when it changed at sunset you felt, as Kipling had, that you were standing at the heart of a king-opal. It had been even more lovely in Kashmir where the Maharaja met them four miles outside Srinagar, dressed in blue and silver brocade, and they were rowed up the river to Srinagar in painted barges, and walked in the moonlit garden of Shalimar, and saw the Kashmir mountains with their tiara of everlasting snow.

It was pleasant, too, for the Viceroy to visit Mysore, for it was the best-governed State in India, and to drive in a carriage with four horses and postillions, escorted by a crack bodyguard on dark brown horses, and to be flanked by infantry running beside him carrying long spears engraved with silver and gold; pleasant, too, to see the clean town with its well-kept parks and trim gardens and wide boulevards. It was here that they were shown a Keddah and initiated into the mysteries of catching and taming wild elephants. From Mysore they had driven through the jungle to Ootacamund, the summer house of the Governor of Madras, Lord Goschen, where they hunted and fished in a country of rolling downland, fragrant with mimosa and blue gum-trees.

The Princes with whom they stayed admired the reckless zest with which the Viceroy threw himself into the most dangerous sports. He had already experimented with pigsticking at Delhi, and he was again attracted by it when staying with the Maharaja of Jodhpur. He could not, of course, owing to his handicap, take part in it himself, but he would join the riders and was much exhilarated by the speed, so much faster, he said, than hunting pace. It was a strange sight to see the Viceroy at full gallop over rough ground which might have sent his horse flying at any moment and broken his neck, but he was thrilled by the experience, and the Maharaja mounted him on 'a perfect Pegasus', a surefooted horse that went like the wind, and he said that he had never galloped so fast in his life.

And who could forget the first day at Udaipur, the City of the Dawn, superbly poised among hills and lakes, with palaces at the water's edge and on the islands? That of the ruler rose sheer from the water, a mass of white stone, and he himself was a figure much to the Viceroy's taste, at once courteous and saintly, ruthless and despotic, His Highness the Maharana of Udaipur, the Sun of all the Hindus, the Chief Minister of God, the highest in rank and dignity of the Rajput Princes. His nobles were not allowed to drive into the palace precincts, but were required to approach humbly on foot. The flavour of the past in this place was so strong that it was like slipping back through the centuries to the Middle Ages, and the Maharana's retainers who lined the roads or manned the ramparts might have stepped out of some Indian frieze. Udaipur seemed to them almost as beautiful as Agra, to which they were also fond of taking their guests, where the Taj Mahal rose like a white lily from the cypresses and water-courses of its Moghul Garden.

Certain scenes and places stood out in the Viceroy's mind like crystals in a rock. He could never forget the caves at Ajanta and Ellora in the dominions of the Nizam of Hyderabad: 'The Ajanta caves,' he said, 'are an amazing relic of the religious life of the early Buddhist monks. They chose a great wall of rock running round the hillside in a semi-circle with a river in the valley below, and there proceeded to hew out their monasteries and chapels.

... In many of the caves the walls and ceilings are decorated with frescoes ... the carving wonderful, instinct with life and grace. The Ellora caves are more varied than Ajanta ... the main temple, the Khilassa, is of dignity and beauty quite unique; carved out of a complete block of rock itself cut out of the mountain, standing in solitary grandeur with endless carvings from the foundation to the top. Surely the world can hold no more precious legacies from earlier civilizations.'[1]

In 1928 Lady Irwin, taking Richard with her, returned to England to bring out her daughter Anne during the London Season, and to spend the summer school holidays with the children, and in her absence the Viceroy made a tour of Orissa and Bihar. Orissa is a low-lying strip of land between the hills and the States behind, a natural delta for the outlet of inland waters. At Walthair in Bihar he was amused to see placards in the street with such slogans as 'Dominion Status India's minimum demand' side by side with 'India demands equality of status with the Colonies', and he reflected that it was unlikely that one in a thousand of the population could have given an intelligible explanation of what the mottoes demanded. And then on through the Central Provinces where he was once again the guest of Sir Montagu Butler, and from there to Indore, and to Jaipur where he was met with a bejewelled chair and carried through the streets in honour between rows of brilliantly clad Sardars and Durbars, and of which his most vivid recollection was that of peacocks screaming on the palace walks.

When Dorothy had returned from England they toured Burma and the Shan States, and here again everything was as they had expected, all vivid colour and the women with their hair piled on the top of the head so that it looked like a shiny black hat, with a trail of flowers or jewels over one ear. Edward thought the women charming; oncoming too, and perhaps that was the greatest contrast with India—how much women were to the fore; that and how green the land seemed after the parched, thirsty earth to which his eyes were accustomed:

They went up to Taung-Yi in the Shan States where there was a Durbar of Chiefs at which Dorothy and Anne were nearly overcome by the translation of Edward's speech into Shan, which sounded like 'Po, ta, fi, lo, chi, tum', pronounced in a high key. They ended this tour at Mandalay in a Government House with a huge carved roof and a gold spire looking up to Mandalay Hill, clustered with pagodas, and the misty Shan Hills beyond. And here their memories were of endless pagodas, vivid colours, trees and water, of sailing up the Irrawaddy and visiting the ruby mines at Mogok.

*   *   *

Edward's home leave became due in the summer of 1929, and when he returned to India in October of that year the new Viceroy's House was at

[1] Halifax. Op. cit., pp. 133-4.

last ready for occupation. The occasion of the official entry into New Delhi was marred by an unsuccessful bomb attack on the Viceroy's train as it approached the city, and by the fact that the opening ceremony took place in a thick mist. After years of watching the building and the gardens growing; of hard work by Dorothy and Lady Worsley on the furnishing and decoration of the three hundred rooms with Lutyens and the Chief Engineer, Rouse, on plans sent up to them at Simla, they moved at last into the great palace. 'For the ceremonial entry a year later,' wrote the Viceroy, 'an elaborate programme was planned, and great numbers of people gathered, and we had a houseful of guests. Representatives from the Dominions, Lord Hardinge, who had been responsible for the first planning, and of course the two architects, Sir Edwin Lutyens and Sir Herbert Baker. Less than twenty years later the last British Viceroy had left India.'[1]

Meanwhile they began to settle into the new house. Their working rooms and offices were in its centre, and their bedrooms to the left, facing the garden. The guests slept on the right side of the house with the same beautiful view, and the A.D.C.s occupied a separate wing on the left of the main entrance. The servants' quarters were in a separate walled-in enclosure near the stables. Sir Edwin Lutyens was not a master of domestic architecture and he put no central heating in the house, and the bedrooms left something to be desired, with too many doors leading into them and the bathrooms across the passage, but the entertaining rooms and Durbar Room were magnificent. The garden was finished before the house and was ready for them, and it was pleasant on warm nights to dine out on the paving stones of the terrace. The Viceroy's imagination had from the first been fired by the heroic grandeur of Lutyens's conception of this new Versailles, and his emotions are well expressed in his own words:

'New Delhi was a remarkable conception, and buildings, layout of tanks and fountains, the broad sweep of Kingsway, and the Indian War Memorial, were fully worthy. There were no doubt mistakes and failures, but these were lost in the beauty of the whole. The Viceroy's House, with its grandeur and simplicity of detail, was always to my mind the most satisfying of all. The great entertaining rooms were good, though they would have been better had it not been necessary on ground of cost to cut down the size of Sir Edwin Lutyens's original design. The large Durbar Hall, with its crimson hangings; the ballroom decorated with black looking-glass on the walls; the great open loggias, overlooking the garden; the State dining-room with its long tables to seat a hundred and twenty, a blaze of colour with the scarlet and gold of the khidmutgars, the portraits of Viceroys, and the gold plate presented by the Goldsmiths' Company set out at the end of the room against a rich red velvet; and everything lit by lovely glass chandeliers; the general effect of all this could not have been better.

[1] Halifax. Op. cit., pp. 144–5.

'In spite of its size, it was essentially a liveable-in house; admiration and affection for it steadily grew together, and every day that we lived there we came to love it the more. There could have been no better setting for it than the Moghul Garden, with the combination of its oriental design of water and lawns and formal trees with the riot of colour from the best of Western flowers. Only when we returned to India many years later were we able to appreciate the full glory of the creepers and the trees, but even in its first beginnings it was a paradise of which the enjoyment never waned. In the centre of the main approach from the Imperial Secretariat buildings designed by Sir Herbert Baker to the Viceroy's House was set the Jaipur Column. Together Sir Edwin Lutyens and I gave it its inscription, based on an earlier draft of his own. It has been often quoted, but will perhaps bear quoting again:

> *In thought faith*
> *In word wisdom*
> *In deed courage*
> *In life service*
> *So may India be great.*'[1]

After he had moved to the Viceroy's House one of his great pleasures was to ride in the early morning across the Delhi plain to the Moslem Tombs with his daughter Anne and Penelope Chetwode, the daughter of General Chetwode who succeeded Sir William Birdwood as Commander-in-Chief in 1930. There were only a few white bungalows as yet in New Delhi, each with its own garden and stables, and tan tracks running between them. The Chetwodes' house, now the Prime Minister's, was in the only shopping area. Beyond and round this vestigial town there was nothing but the great plain burned tawny in the sun, and one dusty road that led to the Kutb Minar. The plain stretched on either side of it, and the only buildings on its immense surface were the tombs of dead kings.

In November the mimosa trees were in flower and the tamarind, and they would start at six-thirty in the morning and return to breakfast after an hour or two of riding. The Viceroy's party would meet Penelope Chetwode at the Commander-in-Chief's house, which was bordered by a nullah across which they rode straight on to the open plain. They were always accompanied by an Indian A.D.C. When crops were growing on the plain they would canter down the many dirt tracks which were bridle paths, past the patient bullocks walking in a circle to pull the stone wheel for grinding lime, and the haughty camels bringing in the crops. In the spring there was corn, bright and green, and they rode past fields full of turquoise-blue linseed glistening with dew. In autumn they could ride straight across the plain.

The would go to the Kutb Minar, which commemorated the coming

[1] Halifax. Op. cit., pp. 143–4.

of Islam to India, that soaring tower of victory which dominates the horizon, and from which the conquerors looked down in triumph on the vanquished plain; or to Tughlaqabad, the largest of all the ruined cities of Delhi, a fortress palace of the first Tughlaq king, a vast ruin with Cyclopean walls and battlements, and there they would sometimes picnic among the fallen masonry, and watch the brown monkeys in the banyan trees on the shady road beside them.

Their favourite ride was to Haus Khas where the Emperor Firoz Tughlaq had built a university six hundred years ago. It was surrounded by a great tank of seventy acres, and steps led down from the college cloisters to the water. Now the tank was dry, and thin cattle grazed where the lake had been, but there were still the rows of narrow rooms which were once the cells of scholars opening upon the water, rooms that had been cool in summer, and, facing east, warm and sunny in winter, and cloisters and pavilions that had once been classrooms. When Edward and the two girls rode there the old university was silent and deserted, and green parakeets flew in and out of the cloisters. Low dusty tuka trees grew about the tombs, and jungle plum and camel thorn, and the past brooded over the place.

Penelope Chetwode remembered laying a trail for a paperchase to Haus Khas, and the Viceroy and the Commander-in-Chief trotting behind, deep in affairs of State, refusing to follow it; and how they sometimes breakfasted among the tombs; and she remembered vividly riding with Edward and Anne to Khirki Masjid, a superb mosque in a village on the left side of the plain, and the Viceroy standing among the little black domes on the roof.

Macaulay, in a passage that revealed his own love of India, wrote of Burke: 'India and its inhabitants were not to him, as to most Englishmen, mere names and abstractions, but a real country and a real people. The burning sun, the strange vegetation of the palm and cocoa-tree, the ricefield, the tank, the huge trees, older than the Moghul empire, under which the village crowds assemble, the thatched roof of the peasant's hut, the rich tracery of the mosque where the imaum prays with his face to Mecca, the drums, and banners, and gaudy idols, the devotee swinging in the air, the graceful maiden, with the pitcher on her head, descending the steps to the river-side, the black faces, the long beards, the yellow streaks of sect, the turbans and the flowing robes, the spears and the silver maces, the elephants with their canopies of state, the gorgeous palankin of the prince, and the close litter of the noble lady, all those things were to him as the objects amidst which his own life had been passed. . . .'

Lord Irwin had acquired a knowledge almost equally deep, and a sympathy fully as wide. By the time he left her shores he had travelled the length and breadth of India; he had received the homage of her glittering princes; he had argued on equal terms with Indian politicians of every shade of opinion; he had formed an abiding affection for the many humble Indians who had served him; he had penetrated into the stews of the big cities, and understood how the poor lived in India—and died. He had seen India flexing muscles which were suddenly becoming mature, and the knowledge and love of the country he had thus gained were a positive source of strength in the troubles which, after his first year in India, were to press upon him with ever-increasing severity.

CHAPTER XIII

THE PROBLEM

THE Viceroy had begun his period of office with a mind free from apprehension, and although he regarded his great position with humility and even felt astonishment that he was occupying it, he was conscious of no feeling of morbid self-mistrust. He had been told by his predecessor Lord Reading, and by the Secretary of State Lord Birkenhead, that things would at first be easy, but afterwards he must look for squalls. He had certainly no inkling that his viceroyalty would coincide with a climacteric in the affairs of the sub-continent; that during his period of office a fundamental change would transform relations between India and England, and that by the time he left she would have gone far in undermining her condition of subjection, and have advanced already half-way to the control of her own future.

It was not a process that could be achieved without birth pangs. The five years of his rule were a time of constant turbulence, while at home he was to be assaulted by a powerful faction led by Winston Churchill, which accused him of weakness in administration and, virtually of abdication of duty. None of these strains made the slightest impression upon his habitual serenity or caused him to depart by an inch from the policy he had adopted.

He had not arrived in India ready to apply some preconceived balm to her troubles, and he had evolved no theory of her future development. According to the demands of his own temperament he preferred to begin with a mind as open to impressions as a piece of wax, to allow his own judgments to form gradually, as he proceeded, and to permit no intrusion upon them of anger or disappointment.

The mighty changes which Irwin wrought in the relations between England and India were symbolized in the Round Table Conference for which he was directly responsible, and at which Indians and British Members of Parliament were to meet on terms of complete equality. The long years of British rule which had contributed so much to the material well-being of India had at the same time sharpened the leaders' sense of inferiority, and blunted that of responsibility. At the Round Table Conference they found themselves suddenly deprived of the grievance that they were treated by the English like clever children who were given from time to time political toys to play with like the Montagu-Chelmsford Reforms, but toys where the swords never had sharp points, and the little guns no dangerous ammunition.

At the Round Table Conference they found themselves in a position which they both desired and feared. Treated suddenly as adults, they were given the opportunity of solving their own problems, and themselves shaping the future they would ultimately control. To build the great edifice of Federation, to bring into harmony after centuries Hindu and Moslem, these were indeed different matters from irresponsible chatter, and obstruction of a Government for which they bore no personal responsibility.

The opportunity of the Conference, and the Viceroy's statement that Dominion Status must be regarded as the natural goal of Indian development marked an immense stride forward from the Government of India Act of 1919 by which it was ordained that India should advance by successive stages, the time and the extent of which could be determined only by Parliament, and which had kept the whole question of Indian political advance within firm Parliamentary control.

The new Viceroy had also been cautious in absorbing the immense implications of the problem confronting him before formulating a policy. 'At first faintly,' wrote one who lived through these events, 'and in part only, Lord Irwin saw the true character and trend of events in which he found himself. As his knowledge grew, his ideas expanded and his policy clarified and strengthened, until during the last years of his viceroyalty, the turbulent, never-resting, continually changing whirl of Indian politics eddies round him, and the story of his doings and the development of his policy become largely the whole story of Indian affairs. . . . He could not control the development of those years any more than the Captain of a ship can control the elements. But he could, and did, know the port to which he wanted to go, and he laid his course and handled his vessel accordingly.'[1]

He did not come quickly to his estimate of this tremendous problem, and it was only after some years of personal contact with it, and after exasperating experiences at the hands of Indian politicians, that he discerned the true and irrepressible strength of Indian Nationalism. As in Ireland before, now again in India he became conscious of a dynamic force that could be checked but not arrested. Remembering the trail of murder and hatred that had preceded the Irish settlement, he was to see the only wisdom in taking time by the forelock, and thus curtailing an Indian repetition of a tragedy that could have been avoided.

In Lord Birkenhead, the first Secretary of State with whom he served as Viceroy, he found a man of temperament almost exactly the opposite of his own, and in his approach to Indian affairs as unbending as the Viceroy was flexible. By the time of Irwin's appointment Birkenhead had already come to form for the Indian Congress Party a complete and withering intellectual contempt. It was constantly in his mind that these men were in no sense representative of the vast illiterate mass of the Indian people whose welfare

[1] J. Coatman, *Years of Destiny*, p. 18.

he regarded as his main responsibility and whose interests he sincerely cherished, and that their motives were too often those of self-advancement and the pursuit of power. Remote in the India Office from contact with the Indian scene, it was far more difficult to feel the feverishly rising pulse of Indian nationalism than it was for the Viceroy at the heart of the battle in Delhi, who held himself accessible to one and all, and whose door was open to a continuous stream of visitors.

In his outlook on the question of Indian constitutional advance Birkenhead held views which, although appearing reactionary today, were then shared by many others who felt that in view of the warring creeds, the diversity of language and dialect, and the inability of India to defend herself, the demand for self-government was the wildest of fantasies. Birkenhead indeed was far from happy about the advance that had already taken place. Two years earlier he had written to Reading:

'I think you know that alone in the Cabinet I distrusted and indeed to some extent opposed the Montagu-Chelmsford Report. To me it is frankly inconceivable that India will ever be fit for Dominion self-government. My present view is that we ought rigidly to adhere to the date proposed in the Act for a re-examination of the situation, and that it is not likely, unless matters greatly change in the interval that such a re-examination will suggest the slightest extension.'[1]

These views were strongly held, and a year later, in January 1925, he had again expressed his conviction that the Indian fabric could not cohere without the cement of British rule:

'In the ultimate analysis the strength of the British position is that we are in India for the good of India. The most striking illustration of the truth of the position is supplied by the infinite variation of nationality, sect and religion in the sub-continent. The more it is made obvious that these antagonisms are profound, and affect immense and irreconcilable sections of the population, the more conspicuously is the fact illustrated that we, and we alone, can play the part of composers.'[2]

The Secretary of State and the Viceroy were certainly a strange couple to be thus thrown together by fate, and their association was surprisingly harmonious, for by the time Birkenhead had resigned Irwin had not yet embarked upon the policies which so greatly angered his former colleague.

The characters of the two men emerge with fascinating clarity from their despatches. The commanding intellect of the Secretary of State sought relaxation from weighty affairs in extracting humour from every subject, from delinquent Maharajas, from the odd behaviour of the retinue of the King of Afghanistan, and from the habit of Sir John Simon of spending a full half hour looking for each lost golf ball.

[1] Charlton archives, *Private Letters from Lord Birkenhead to Lord Reading*, 4 December 1924.
[2] Ibid., 22 January 1925.

Irwin, who appreciated levity and liked to have amusing stories to retail to his friends, enjoyed the unconventional side of their exchanges, and his own despatches were rich in that ironical understatement which was the essence of his own humour. While these two men were together the Viceroy knew that he could rely on his Secretary of State for undeviating support, and although some of Birkenhead's uncompromising speeches undoubtedly made Irwin's task in India more difficult, he loyally refrained from complaint.[1] It would not have been easy, reading these letters, to anticipate the painful and complete political breach that occurred between them.

Although the Viceroy brought no specific remedy for the Indian fevers which had been raging under his predecessor, he was a historian and could not fail to be aware in general terms of the situation that would confront him. He knew that the political development of the self-governing Dominions had come to be regarded by the intelligentsia in India with envy and with aspiration; that they saw in it the same principle that caused the American Colonies to free themselves, and had elevated other colonies to the same status as Great Britain herself. It was inevitable that when the world contracted with the swift increase of communications only education was required to suggest to them as members of the British Empire their own right to a similar place in the sun, and to fill the minds of ambitious men with new and disturbing thoughts. That education was forthcoming; it had been supplied by the British.

When Irwin saw Indian students in England hurrying to Inns of Court and University, avid for the knowledge that they hoped would lead them to distinction in their own land, he could reflect with particular pride that their opportunity was due in part to his ancestor Sir Charles Wood, who had seized upon Macaulay's Education Minute and carried out its provisions with brilliant imagination. The decision taken in 1835 has been described as one of the turning points of Indian history. 'It opened the floodgates of European thought and literature, and subjected the best brains of India, from their childhood onwards, to the powerful influence of English liberal and scientific thought.'[2]

Once this vital step was taken, it was inevitable that there would arise a politically articulate class of Indians, an intelligentsia trained in Western thought, whose reading of history disclosed new vistas for India, and whose knowledge gave them, a tiny minority, an immeasurable advantage over the great mass of their fellow countrymen and a position of importance out of all proportion to their numbers.

By imperceptible degrees the Viceroy was to realize that something of

[1] There is no trace in Irwin's Indian papers of the uneasiness which he later claimed to have felt at the policy of the Secretary of State. He was, however, to write to a friend during his ambassadorship in Washington: 'I remember so well how b——y it was serving under F.E.'
[2] Percival Griffiths, *Modern India*, p. 55.

tremendous import for India was ripening and becoming mature, held in check, but not subdued, by Reading's firm hand, and which now awaited his decision either to foster or repress. This was no less than that rich commotion of the blood, that restlessness of spirit, that fierce rejection of the present, that indicate that a country is passing out of adolescence and fretting under tutelage.

All these discontents found their focus in the Indian National Congress founded by an English civil servant in the viceroyalty of Lord Dufferin in an attempt to stimulate Indian political thought, and which was for years regarded as a harmless debating society with a large admixture of cranks, who discussed theoretical resolutions with the tireless fluency of their race. Irwin was to find that in the intervening years it had grown into a different and far more formidable body. In this way Indian nationalism had been cross-fertilized by the British themselves.

It was Lord Ripon who had carried his liberal principles so far as to attempt in the Ilbert Bill to allow Indian magistrates to try European offenders, a measure which was fiercely opposed by Europeans but which had a momentous result: 'Out of the clash of hostile opinions and angry passions roused by this attempt, a new light appeared—as when two dead worlds meet in space and a mighty incandescence tells astronomers that a new star is born. . . . It was the idea, hitherto foreign to the oriental mind, that it is the duty of a citizen to stand up for his rights, an idea the justice of which no Englishman, least of all men, can deny . . . the principle that every man is entitled to his own opinion and that it is right and lawful for him to give expression to it, provided that in so doing he keeps within the limits of the law of the land and does not seek to destroy the rights of any of his fellows.'[1]

In spite of such events, the Nationalist movement could not for many years become a threat to the ruling power. Curzon indeed, in the pride of his great achievement, believed that Congress was 'tottering to its fall', and relished the thought of its demise, but such feelings were soon to be submerged in the Liberal triumph of 1906.

It was a mordant irony of fate that immediately after Curzon, by incredible labour, had renovated the whole structure of Indian administration, a party should succeed to power dedicated to freedom rather than to discipline, and autonomy rather than efficiency. A strong and earlier 'wind of change' was also blowing through the British Empire. The Transvaal and the Orange Free State achieved responsible self-government in 1907, and the Union of South Africa was created, and these events were closely followed by the Morley-Minto Reforms in India.

It is significant that those Reforms, which gave wider influence to popular representatives on the Central and Provincial Councils, and provided for

[1] J. Coatman. Op. cit., pp. 46–47.

the first time for an Indian member of the Viceroy's Council, while preserving the control of Parliament intact, completely failed to satisfy the National Congress Party which had hoped that the whole of India would be divided into large popular constituencies. The Morley-Minto Constitution was never more than a half-way house, but even this meagre grant of reform was sufficient to whet the appetite for more, and to stimulate political Indians in their hostility to the Government, while the military success of another Asiatic country, Japan, increased Indian discontent and led to a demand by an extreme section of opinion for direct action producing revolutionary crime.

The departure of England from India would undoubtedly have been followed by anarchy and massacre on an appalling scale, but this did not alter the fact that there were existing in the country circumstances that were helping her to grope towards a form of unity. Chief among these were the growing communications which were bringing Indians into close contact with foreign countries, and enabling them to draw some comparison between the relative positions of the men they saw abroad and their own, and the education which gave them the key to the literature of the world, the English language, the lingua franca in which they could read how other nations had won their independence. Hence came that consciousness, so passionately held by intellectual Indians, of the dignity of their status, and the inviolability of their rights, which Irwin was to respect, and to study with sympathy and delicate insight.

The two sides approached this question of India's constitutional progress from opposite angles, but by the time of Irwin's viceroyalty the English were already heavily committed in that direction. The progress had been deliberately tentative and surrounded by many safeguards. India had not kept pace with the great self-governing Dominions, and for a good reason of which the new Viceroy was well aware. Her case was entirely different from theirs, and the task of her English overlords had been, in the arresting phrase of Macaulay, nothing less than 'the stupendous process of the reconstruction of a decomposed society'.

The English, therefore, conscious of the great obstacles still to be overcome, knew that their task in India was not yet accomplished, and that their trust could not safely be abandoned. Although propelled by Liberal trends in England and in the rest of Europe, they advanced slowly, holding that the moment of India's emancipation was for them alone to determine, as were the steps by which she approached it. Educated Indians, on the other hand, having drunk deep for the first time of the cup of knowledge, demanded in accents growing rapidly shriller that self-government which they now regarded as their right from birth, brushing aside as trifles the enormous obstacles in its path. These two rival attitudes confronted one another at the beginning of Lord Irwin's viceroyalty.

*   *   *

The immediate act of preparation for the events which took place from 1926 onwards was the Government of India Act of 1919, the famous Montagu-Chelmsford Reforms. On 20 August 1917 Edwin Montagu, the Secretary of State, made the most momentous announcement on British policy in India since the sub-continent had first passed under the control of the Crown. He laid down four principles for future guidance, the first of which was 'the increasing association of Indians in every branch of the administration'. The second principle proclaimed 'the gradual development of self-governing institutions with a view to the progressive realization of responsible government in India as an integral part of the British Empire'.

Thus was laid down for the first time in the dominion of the British in India in the clearest terms a positive goal on which the Indian Nationalist movement would in future focus its demands. It was from this moment that the Indian parties began to clarify their ideas and to form their allegiances, and that of Congress, in particular, to sharpen and perfect a new technique of agitation.

The third principle laid down—that old English reservation, 'that progress in this policy can only be achieved by successive stages', but this was a precaution that could only produce contempt among Indian leaders whose excited eyes were now fixed only on the green light of the second principle.

Lastly it was provided that the Home Government together with the Government of India, 'on whom the responsibility lies for the welfare and advancement of the Indian people, must be judges of the time and measure of each advance'. The tendency of advanced Nationalists henceforth would be to disregard all the prudential aspects of these proposals, to deny the right of England to fashion the destiny of India, and to demand immediate realization of the second principle, that of responsible self-government.

After this announcement the Secretary of State visited India to consult with the Viceroy, Lord Chelmsford, who had succeeded Lord Hardinge in 1916, finding on his accession a state of violent unrest in India with the Hindu firebrand Tilak preaching the doctrine of Swaraj or Home Rule in company with one of those singular Englishwomen on whom the tropics sometimes produce so strange an effect, the theosophist Mrs. Annie Besant. It did not appear to be a propitious atmosphere in which to introduce new reforms when the extremists gained the upper hand in the Lucknow Congress of 1916.

On Montagu's return a Report was published containing proposals for reform which the Viceroy and Secretary of State recommended to the Imperial Government for adoption. The most important of these was that in the Provincial Governments the departments should be divided into two sections, the 'reserved' and the 'transferred'. Such important subjects as Law and Order were to be 'reserved' subjects.

The object of this system, which was called dyarchy and caused much

above THE VICEROY AT SIMLA HORSE SHOW, 1927

below WITH VITHALBHAI PATEL

criticism, was that the 'reserved' subjects would continue to be managed by an executive responsible to the British Secretary of State for India, and that the 'transferred' subjects would be handed over to Indian Ministers responsible to enlarged legislative councils elected by a franchise as wide as should be found practically possible. It was contemplated by the authors of the scheme that as time passed the distinction between 'reserved' and 'transferred' subjects would, like the Marxist state 'wither away', and that all departments should be ultimately under the control of Indian Ministers responsible to Indian electorates.

It was envisaged that if the new system proved successful in these Provincial experiments it would ultimately be extended to the Supreme Government at the centre, which was at present to be responsible only to the Secretary of State and to Parliament. It was also recommended that there should be created a bicameral Legislature consisting of a Council of State of fifty members with an official majority, and an Indian Legislative Assembly, two-thirds of which were to be elected members. Among other proposals it was suggested that Parliament should appoint periodic Commissions at intervals of perhaps twelve years, to consider when the next steps in advance, or, if necessary, in retraction, should be made.

Although Indian control was not conceded at the centre, and the Viceroy was left with a limitless power to 'certify' legislation which the legislatures had failed to pass,[1] and force it through by Ordinance, a great breach had been made, characteristically by themselves, in the wall of British supremacy in India. Previous reforms had made but little impact on her. Now it was as though a great rock had been thrown into a lake, tranquil for centuries, causing ever widening ripples. It had been felt that after the magnificent fidelity of the Indian peoples in the war a gesture of gratitude and an act of faith must be made; Montagu had intended his reforms to 'disturb the pathetic contentment of the Indian masses', and in this desire he was successful beyond his wildest expectations.

There were many British officials in India who received the proposals in a pessimistic spirit, claiming in the words of one, that the dyarchy of the double executive was open to almost every theoretical objection that the armoury of political philosophy could supply. It was objected, too, that the soil for the sowing of new seed was in any case not yet favourable for reforms so drastic in their nature.

Even those who feared the outcome could not, however, honestly deny that the whole trend of her policy in India since 1858 committed England, at least by implication, to some such promise in advance. Henceforth the thought of any step backwards from the new policy was inconceivable. 'To reverse it,' said Sir Valentine Chirol, 'would be regarded, and reasonably regarded, in India as a breach of faith which would do more to shake the

---

[1] To 'certify' legislation the Viceroy issued an Ordinance to compel its passage.

foundations of British rule than the worst consequences which its gloomiest critics see from persistence in it.'[1]

Looking from a distance on these reforms so full of significance for India, it is now easy to see that their most vital provision was the definition of a goal, and the clarification of the desires of Indian Nationalists. Once that goal was defined as Responsible Self-government it should have been clear to anyone who knew the speed of their minds and the extent of their ambitions that such a half-way house would soon be deserted in their breathless haste for advance, and that a demand for Dominion Status would inevitably replace it.

All the influences, all the changes, that had come over her, some almost imperceptibly, ensured that articulate India would henceforth refuse to be regarded as a special case whose inherent difficulties set her apart from the Dominions that had achieved self-government; that from now on, and often by questionable methods, her little band of spokesmen, in no way representing India herself, would yet advocate her cause with passionate intensity. We can see, too, that when Lord Irwin later created such a storm by his declaration that Dominion Status was the ultimate goal for India, he was merely drawing a natural inference from a fact that had long been implicit in the Act of 1919.

Between 1919 and 1921, when the Act came into force, India had passed through one of her most grievous periods of disturbance. There had been trouble in Delhi, in the Bombay Presidency, and in the Punjab, the recruiting ground of the great majority of the Indian Army. General Dyer's appalling lapse had provided the martyrology, and the scars of Amritsar were so enduring that even today the bullet-holes in the walls of the compound of Jallianwala Bagh are enshrined and hallowed behind glass. The shadow of this tragedy lay ominous over India. It endured into Irwin's administration and was reflected in the 'non-co-operation' movement which had bedevilled that of his predecessor Lord Reading.

The author of this movement was Mohandas Karamchand Gandhi, fresh from his labours in South Africa on behalf of expatriate Indians. The Mahatma had claimed, whether truthfully or not, that he had been outraged by the callous indifference of British public opinion to such tragedies as Amritsar, that henceforth he must regard their Government as 'satanic', and devote all his future energies to the destruction of British overlordship and its replacement by 'Swaraj' or Home Rule.

It was with this object that Gandhi began his campaign of 'non-violent non-co-operation' in August 1920. It was a matter of importance that he succeeded in associating with him in this gesture of defiance the Indian National Congress which was now the most powerful and highly organized party in the country. Only a handful of moderate Congress members, who

[1] Sir Valentine Chirol, *Quarterly Review*, October 1918.

were content to abide by the time and method of advance laid down by the British Government, broke away at this point and formed the Liberal Party, and 'this', wrote S. Gopal, 'in personal eminence and collective futility formed a striking parallel to its namesake in England at this time'.[1]

'Non-co-operation', although designed to accomplish the overthrow of British rule, sought this end in a manner which made a subtle appeal to the mysticism of the Indian character. This movement, in Gopal's words: 'despite its negative prefix, was a positive concept; not cowardice, or supine passivity, but a dynamic force of the spirit. By non-violent non-co-operation Gandhi meant an insistence on truth, an impatience of evil, and a willingness, even an anxiety, to suffer an opponent's anger till the latter sickened of it. He would appeal from the British system to the British conscience; it would be a fight to the finish, but its aim was not the defeat, but the conversion of the foe'.[2]

When this pallid conception produced no noticeable results Gandhi took a far more serious step in the following year, 1921, when in association with some of the Moslem leaders, who had been affronted by the treatment given to defeated Turkey, he inaugurated Civil Disobedience, or, as he called it Satyagraha, which he regarded as the 'truth and love force, the vindication of truth not by the infliction of suffering on the opponent but on oneself'.

Civil Disobedience was in fact a dangerous movement for the British. It was non-co-operation in its most aggressive and intransigent form, and it involved constant and serious breaches of the law, and incitement to non-payment of taxes. It was to be the main weapon in the struggle between the Congress Party and Lord Irwin. To Gandhi it was 'civil' because it was neither criminal nor violent, but he failed then or later to understand that in its naked appeal to the passions of millions of Indians it was in itself a producer of violence and the direct cause of a long series of lamentable crimes. The nature of these were soon made clear when at Chauri Chaura in the United Provinces a mob inflamed by Gandhi's message of peaceful resistance burned twenty-two constables to death in the village police station.

Gandhi realized that this horrible crime was something of a setback to his policy of non-violence, but although the Civil Disobedience movement was suspended for the moment, and put into cold storage, he still obstinately failed to link cause and effect. When the moment came for his declaration of war on Lord Irwin the weapon still lay ready at hand, and he did not hesitate to use it.

In the meantime, as Gopal wrote, there had already been certain tangible results of its brief operation. 'It converted the Congress from a mere debating association of intellectuals into a party with roots among the people, roused a widespread spirit of resistance, transformed arrest from a stigma

[1] S. Gopal, *The Viceroyalty of Lord Irwin*, p. 6.   [2] Ibid., p. 4.

into a privilege.'[1] Such it had been for Gandhi who had been imprisoned in 1922 and on his own admission enjoyed the easy restraint always imposed on him in English jails.

On his release in 1924 he had attempted to revive the fugitive alliance between Hindu and Moslem which had existed during the non-co-operation movement and Khilafat agitation.[2] In an attempt to stop the communal riots, which Gandhi realized were destructive of the hopes of Swaraj, five Moslem Presidents of Congress were appointed in ten years. The Moslems, however, pursued a realistic policy of entrenching themselves as strongly as possible in the event of a British departure from India, of consolidating their separate electorates[3] in which their rights as a community were protected, and of staking their claim to power in certain Provinces in which they were predominant.

Gandhi at this period lived in retirement. He realized that conditions in India were so turbulent that for the moment he could make no further impression on events. By propagation of the doctrine of 'Khaddar', or homespun cotton, as opposed to foreign materials, and by insistence on its symbol the spinning wheel, he sought to encourage the cottage industries of India and to impress on the Indian masses the need for unity and understanding, and the love of simple things.

Khaddar was to become an obsession with him. In order to emphasize his devotion to it, he discarded his flowing dhoti and his cap, and adopted the loincloth as his 'mendicant's' garb, carrying in a homespun bag his writing paper and the nuts or dates that served him as a diet. During this period of retirement his remarkable mind, the convolutions of which so often maddened those accustomed to Western processes of thought, but cast so strong a spell upon the East, was occupied continuously with the transformation to come and the attainment of Swaraj.

The weapons he was to use were already being forged, and they were those most calculated to discomfort his English opponents. Ahimsa, the doctrine of harmlessness and innocence, and hartals, the days of abstention from work, were elevated in his intention to a perpetual and shaming reproach. His own integrity, windswept as it was by inconsistency and sudden baffling changes of direction, was to suffer from his association with the Congress Party which had already adopted a cynical propaganda of battle that rejected the truth in which he professed to believe, as irrelevant to its purpose.

Remote from politics, he surveyed the violence and anarchy with which Lord Reading's Government was attempting to grapple. The load on this exceptionally gifted and determined Viceroy was almost intolerable. The

[1] S. Gopal. Op. cit., p. 6.

[2] The Khilafat agitation was the result of Indian Moslem concern at the state of Islam outside India.

[3] Communal representation was the separation of religious communities for electoral purposes, in order to safeguard the position of minorities.

Hindu-Moslem *entente* had collapsed in 1922. The creed of non-co-operation prevented the Congress Party from entering the Central and Provincial Legislatures which were open to them under the new Act, and the abstention of the most powerful party did much to invalidate and discredit the Reforms.

'It was as though a motor lorry should have to drag a heavy load up a hill with one of its cylinders out of action. . . . And, worse, the Reforms of 1919, instead of functioning steadily and broadening from precedent to precedent which was the vision of the best minds in Britain and India, developed into something perilously like a battlefield, with the Government on the one side and Congress and allied groups on the other.'[1]

*   *   *

Such, in brief outline, were the conditions which prevailed when Lord Irwin began his viceroyalty in April 1926. It opened, as Lord Reading had predicted, with a period of deceptive calm, broken by the violent communal agitation which was to continue, hideous and inexorable, and defying all efforts at solution, a heartbreaking background to all the other events of his administration.

Lord Irwin had been only a short time in India before his attention was to be harshly drawn to this state of affairs by the Calcutta riots. It did not take him long to discover that it had been possible for Hindu and Moslem to live side by side for centuries in perfect harmony, but that the antagonism between the two creeds could be whipped up at any moment by agitation for political ends leading to senseless and ghastly slaughter.

The Moslems had all but forgotten their days as the overlords of India under the Moghul Empire, and it was difficult for foreigners to understand why the ancient feud could not be composed. Unfortunately, in India collision between the two faiths was sharply accentuated by religious practices. To the Hindu the cow was sacred, while the ceremonial sacrifice of cows was a feature of the Moslem festival of Bakr'Id. Hindu music played through the streets as an idol passed or a marriage was held, too often coincided with Moslem worship at a nearby mosque.

But there were other causes which were fostering the hostility. The Moslems had been far later than the Hindus in availing themselves of the education offered by the English, but disturbed by Hindu ascendancy in business and the public services, they had made up for lost time and were now in vigorous competition with their rivals in a market where supply already exceeded demand.

Secondly, the Moslems in India, always acutely sensitive to outside events affecting their co-religionists, had detected in the Turkish war with Italy, in the Balkan wars and in the triumph of Ataturk in rebuilding Turkey thrilling manifestations of the revival of Islam. In the circumstances Irwin

[1] J. Coatman. Op. cit., p. 81.

could have expected no better legacy than that bequeathed to him by Reading. He had handed over to his successor an administration in full working
order, but he had been driven to continuous resort to emergency powers
and Ordinances to achieve this end. The fact remained, as the new Viceroy
would soon discover, that strong government had barely contained, and in no
way daunted those forces which had so swiftly developed and were demanding further radical changes in the relations between India and Great Britain.

It was clear to all who knew the character of the new Viceroy that as soon
as he became sufficiently familiar with the Indian scene and the new possibilities in it he would play a direct personal part in the constitutional
struggle that lay ahead, and would never consent to become an agent, however exalted, of the British Government, and transmit the orders of the
India Office without placing his own interpretation upon them. There was a
further reason why Irwin was destined to play a particular part in these
developments. The 1919 Act directed that after an interval of ten years the
British Government should appoint a Commission to investigate the political
condition of India, and consider when and how the next step in advance
should be taken.

Five years of those ten had elapsed before Irwin left England, and the
Commission was anxiously awaited by many representatives of political
opinion outside the Congress Party. There was general eagerness that the
arrival of the Commission should be accelerated, and an excitement and
unrest throughout political India which was reflected in the 'National
Demand' which was moved by the Congress Party and passed in the Indian
Legislative Assembly.

This resolution, which was opposed by the Government, called for the
immediate drafting by a representative Round Table Conference, and enactment by the Imperial Parliament of a constitution which conferred full
Dominion Status on India. The hands of the root and branch opponents of
the Government were strengthened by the General Election of 1926 which
gave the Congress Party and their sympathizers substantial gains both in the
Central and Provincial Legislatures.

All the storm signals now gave warning that another assault on the Government of India was in the course of preparation, and the most violent and
irresponsible vernacular Press in the world was pouring out shrill insults and
incessant criticism of British rule. Nor was it difficult to imagine what the
casus belli would be. It was lying ready to the hand of Congress in the
approaching appointment of the Statutory Commission, the preparations for
which had begun soon after the Viceroy's arrival in India, and whose Report,
it was believed, would be momentous in the shaping of India's destiny.

The Montagu-Chelmsford Reforms had included one element of caution
in their general prodigality. The Commission were empowered, if necessary,
to recommend retreat rather than advance, but the mere thought of it was

derisory in the present temper of the Indian leaders. Advance there would have to be, and many responsible Indians were not averse to receiving it through constitutional channels, while the extreme wing of Congress denied the English the slightest justification for the claim to determine their political future.

The trouble that faced the Viceroy was therefore the result of a combination of circumstances beyond human control. There was no position that was in a sense more lonely than that of Viceroy of India. He had a Council of able advisers, but the responsibility for whatever happened was exclusively his own. The Executive Council was not composed entirely of members of the Civil Service. Since 1919 there had always been one non-official Indian Member of Council, and from 1924 onwards there were normally two such members. There was no cabinet to share that responsibility, and the Viceroy himself was the true ruler of India. It was he who laid down the policy which would be carried out both at the centre in Delhi and in all the Provinces of his vast domain. A wide range of Ordinances with the force of law were his alone to issue in time of emergency; he had the power to certify legislation which had been rejected by the Assembly. The Viceroy was responsible to the Secretary of State for India. He could and did exercise powerful influence on the Government at home, but in the last resort, on a question of high policy, he would either have to bow to their decision or resign.

Lord Irwin found that the Government of India in 1926 was organized in seven departments, each with its own Member of Council, and that it was the custom for the Viceroy to retain the Foreign and Political departments under his personal control. Below the Members came the Secretaries to Government in the various departments who were senior members of the Indian Civil Service. It was a constitutional obligation on the Secretaries of Departments to report to the Governor-General any case where there was a difference of views between two Members of Council in regard to action to be taken by them in the conduct of their departments. This was intended to ensure that the Governor-General could, if he desired, insist that any such difference could be discussed in Council before action was taken on it.

It was customary for the Viceroy to receive the Secretary of each department once in a week and it was the duty of the Secretary to see that the matters which were submitted to the Viceroy for decision were proper and desirable, and the Secretary would usually inform his Member of the submissions he was making to the Viceroy. Irwin also learned that an important part of his duties was to have a weekly interview with each Member on the work of his department. The Council met once a week with the Viceroy in the Chair, and important questions arising out of departmental or Provincial proposals would be discussed, and action taken. The Viceroy had the right, in certain exceptional circumstances, of overriding the majority vote, although it was obligatory for him in such a case to report the fact to the Secretary of State for India.

He found that under this system very considerable demands were made of the Members of Council, for in addition to their ordinary duties they were expected to sit in the Indian Parliament and answer for Government in the debates in either of the two Houses. This, he thought, was not easy, for there was only a handful of official members, heavily outnumbered by unofficial members. In opposition to the little band of Government representatives, who had been appointed rather than elected, was a large Swaraj (Home Rule) block which was Hindu, a Moslem block, and some Europeans and independent representatives.

'Moreover,' he said, 'the official members had had no training in the arts and devices of democratic chambers, and it was asking a good deal of them to pick up such popular tricks late in their careers. . . . Many of them, like Sir Basil Blackett, Sir Alexander Muddiman, Sir Charles Innes, or Sir George Schuster, would have been at home in any chamber, but owing to the composition of the Assembly, situations not infrequently arose in which the Viceroy found himself compelled to use his special powers for or against particular legislative action, or in order to secure the necessary financial provision for the carrying on of Government.'[1]

Above all, the Viceroy observed the character of the Government of India itself. He saw that it was in fact a branch of the Civil Service whose members kept themselves strictly within their own ring fence. He saw how completely aloof they were from popular opinion and popular support. Appointed, and not elected by popular vote, the members of the Government did not depend for their places on the support of the public, and had few means of keeping in touch with the movements of opinion in India.

Lord Irwin had behind him a background of ministerial experience in two departments, neither of major importance, in both of which he had been frustrated by economic stringency, and the rather detached and gentlemanly membership of an Under-Secretaries' revolution to unseat Lloyd George. Now, as Viceroy of India, and excluding his special relationship with the six hundred Native States and their 80,000,000 subjects, he presided over the destinies of 270,000,000 of her peoples. Of the nine Governors' Provinces, Burma was larger than France; Madras and Bombay larger than Italy. The United Provinces and Bengal had greater populations than Britain, France or Italy.

Over all these millions of human beings the Viceroy ruled, and they included a Moslem minority of 80,000,000. The Depressed Classes, the 'Untouchables', whose mere touch brought pollution to Caste Hindus, stood at the enormous figure of 75,000,000. Two hundred and twenty languages were spoken on the sub-continent.

Education had indeed provided India with the lingua franca of the English language, but it was spoken by only two and a half per cent of the population whom it invested with disproportionate power because it made them articu-

[1] Halifax. Op. cit., pp. 127–9.

late. Over ninety per cent of the people still lived in the half million villages of India in circumstances of medieval squalor, and practising the same primitive husbandry as their forebears had used under the Moghul Emperors. These simple ryots or peasants were still remote from any knowledge of politics or the great issues that now agitated the supple minds of those recently returned from London University and Lincoln's Inn. The Viceroy knew that he must be circumspect in quartering so vast a field, but he soon came to realize that the main problem that he had to solve was the reconciliation of the just position which the British held in India and all the immeasurable benefits it had conferred upon her, with the inevitable and ever-rising claims of Indian Nationalism.

The natural sympathy which Irwin had always felt for the political desires of others convinced him that there was justice in this movement, and that there had grown a passionate determination among the politically minded classes of all Indian races and religions to assert and uphold the claim of India to her due place in the world, and that it would be a profound mistake to allow geographical dimensions, or complexities of religion, caste, and language to obscure its significance.

The lull in the first year of his administration gave the Viceroy the opportunity of exploring the maze of Indian politics and studying the character of some of the men with whom he would have to deal and the parties they served. It soon became clear to him that the Congress Party was the most highly organized and powerful body in India. In spite of the austerity of Gandhi in his mendicant's garb and the appeal which he alone could make to millions of the poorest inhabitants of India, it relied largely for its ample finance on the rich owners of cotton mills and other industrialists in Bombay.

The eyes of its more extreme members were fixed upon the attainment of Home Rule, and the establishment of themselves as the new ruling class. They were an oligarchy remote for the most part in sympathy from the masses of the people, and seldom in personal contact with them. It was the great advantage of the Congress Party as a revolutionary unit that, like Sinn Fein in Ireland and the young Soviet in Russia, they knew exactly what they wanted, were restrained by no scruple in its pursuit, and were organized to exploit every opportunity of attaining it.

The Viceroy soon perceived that there was nothing whatever democratic in the organization of this party, and that although they used a demagogic propaganda frequently poisonous and deliberately mendacious, a great deal of power in their ranks was concentrated in men rich and privileged by birth, although there was also a large representation of lawyers who did not belong to the land-owning or industrial classes. He also became aware that although Congress was often riven by internal discontents leading to sudden fissures in its structure when the more moderate men would briefly recoil from wild measures, it was none the less the most potentially effective element of

8*

disruption in India because its leaders had learned at last that revolutions cannot be made by moralizing dilettantes.

It was unquestionable that these men had provided Lord Birkenhead with much justification for his contempt. It was also true that they had little, if any, contact with the dumb millions of India, the ryots with their wooden ploughs and patient oxen, and were in no sense their representatives or champions. None the less, it was soon borne in upon the Viceroy that with all their failings they were the most powerful articulate embodiment of the new Indian nationalism.

The Viceroy began to study the character of the political leaders, and the formation of the parties. Tilak, and C. R. Das, the remarkable Bengali lawyer who had forced Gandhi into retirement on the question of Congress participation in the new Legislatures, were gone, but the Viceroy soon came to know their successor, Pandit Motilal Nehru, father of the future Prime Minister of India, the most influential statesman to challenge the Government during Irwin's viceroyalty. He was to remember Motilal as a politician of infinite subtlety and resource, supposedly more reasonable than many, but as inflexible as Gandhi himself in the pursuit of Swaraj, and almost as intractable; a man who had turned away for this purpose from a former contact with the English and admiration for them; had abandoned his elegant European clothes and assumed for ever the flowing robes of white homespun which he seemed to some to wear with the majesty of a Roman senator.[1]

The Viceroy became convinced that the influence on Motilal of his son Jawaharlal Nehru was wholly detrimental. There was then little of the remote and condescending neutralist of later years in this handsome product of Harrow School. We shall see him throughout Lord Irwin's period of office a stormy petrel scouring the waters of discontent, although later a complete change came over him with power and responsibility. He had stationed himself to the left of even the most extreme wing of the Congress Party but he was still groping for a purpose. He admitted to a puckish delight in stimulating conflict. He could hardly at this time be described as a politician at all. He was a revolutionary. Whenever there appeared some tenuous hope of settlement, he was always at hand to urge extreme courses, and his efforts were reinforced by a beautiful appearance and a glowing eloquence. Worst of all, in those days he exercised a disastrous influence upon the Youth Movement of India, and in so doing gave great encouragement to another idol of Indian youth from Bengal, Subhas Chandra Bose, whose incitements led them to revolting revolutionary crimes, and who was to harness his peculiar gifts to the service of Hitler in the Second World War.

The Viceroy was also to come to know those who had broken away from the Congress Party to become 'Responsive Co-operators' in the new National

---

[1] The Vicereine, however, noticed that he clung a little to his former sartorial grace, and that his white 'Gandhi cap' was made by Scott of London.

Party formed to provide a measure of co-operation with the Government by participating in the new Legislatures provided for by the Montagu-Chelmsford Reforms, and attempting to make the experiment a success. These men were Mahratta Brahmins of a fierce fighting race, some of them members of the All-India Mahasabha, a body of delegates representing local Hindu organizations in all parts of India, whose attitude to any political issue was of considerable importance.

He was to meet the combative Dr. Moonje, and the aristocratic Pandit Malaviya, the purest fruit of the Brahmin tree. Coming from a modest Brahmin family and having graduated from a college in the United Provinces, his life was governed by the strictest orthodoxy of the Hindu religion, of which he was an accomplished interpreter. 'Clad invariably in spotless white, even in a London November, Pandit Malaviya, with his intellectual and aristocratic face, much fairer than that of most Southern Europeans, looks what he is, namely the quintessence of Hindu civilization.'[1]

It was among this body of politicians that the Viceroy was to find a man whose views and temperament most closely resembled his own, a man ready to compromise, eager for constitutional advance, and to whom the rigid party line of Congress and its brazen propaganda struck a note of discord, but whose very moderation was almost a guarantee of his ineffectiveness in the jungle of Indian nationalism. This was the admirable Jayakar from Bombay on whom the Viceroy was to place a reliance in the years to come which was always rewarded by loyalty and common sense.

The Indian Liberals, as the Viceroy came to realize, were equally hamstrung by the moderation of their aims and the leisurely tempo at which they were willing to achieve them, but it was inevitable that a liberal Viceroy would be strongly attracted to them although he might be sceptical of their prospects.

He was to be deeply grateful later in his administration for the wise counsel of Sir Tej Bahadur Sapru, an intellectual Liberal who detested mob politics, and a commanding figure on Committees. With all his qualities of mind there was a trace of the futility of Kerensky in this admirable man, as in his fellow Liberal Sastri, when their leisurely methods and civilized approach to politics were contrasted with the ruthless dynamic of Congress.

Another important group of whom the Viceroy soon became aware was the Justice Party, whose main power lay in the Madras Presidency, and whose members consisted of non-Brahmins. This Party, whose influence was also considerable in other parts of India, was led by Sir Annepu Patro and was founded to loosen the Brahmin stranglehold on every branch of political life at the end of the nineteenth century, and provide opportunities in public service for Hindus of other castes.

There was also a certain division in the Moslem ranks which the Viceroy could not fail to notice. He observed that the followers of Shaukat Ali

[1] J. Coatman. Op. cit., p. 98.

formed a small group with extreme views known as the Khilafat Committee which stood well to the left of the great majority of orthodox Muhammadan statesmen who in the main sought their ends by constitutional methods.

It became clear to him that between these two there existed another body which, like Congress, believed that only vigorous assertion and an uncompromising attitude towards the Government of India could ensure the iron guarantees for the security of their followers on which all elements in the Moslem world in India were inflexibly determined. This centre group was led by Muhammad Ali Jinnah, whose name was to come into great prominence in the later history of India. The Viceroy also became sickeningly aware of the problem of the 75,000,000 members of the Depressed Classes, and he came to appreciate the characters of their able leaders, M. C. Rajah of Madras and Dr. Ambedkar of Bombay.

It was evident that many responsible Indians outside the Congress Party were pinning great hopes upon the findings of the Statutory Commission, and asking that its arrival should be accelerated. The British Government had no objection to such a course. The Secretary of State had written to Lord Reading announcing his intention of antedating the Commission, and giving his own personal reasons for doing so:

'I always had it plainly in mind that we could not run the slightest risk that the nomination of the 1928 Commission should be in the hands of our successors. You can readily imagine what kind of Commission would have been appointed by Colonel Wedgwood and his friends. I have, therefore, throughout been of the opinion that it would be necessary for us, as a matter of elementary prudence, to appoint the Commission not later than the summer of 1927.'[1] From the point of view of the Viceroy the situation in India was at the moment far from propitious for the great inquest. During the first twelve months of his viceroyalty there were to be forty communal riots, the worst of which, those in Calcutta, took place shortly after his arrival in India and, raging for a month, caused a hundred and ten deaths. In this ominous atmosphere the Viceroy chose the subject of communal strife for his first great public announcement in India on 17 July 1926.

*   *   *

He chose for the scene of this vital début, by which as he well knew, he would be judged throughout India, the Chelmsford Club in Simla, named for the Viceroy of the Reforms. His speech would be the first public indication to millions of Indians of the sort of man their new Viceroy was, and it was significant that he chose the Chelmsford Club, which, unlike many others in India, was open to Indians as well as to Europeans.

The audience contained the leading representatives of all the communities in the Indian Empire. There sat the devious Vithalbhai Patel, whom we shall

[1] Charlton archives, *Lord Birkenhead's Private Letters to Lord Reading*, 10 December 1925.

see as President of the Legislative Assembly driving the Viceroy to the limits of his incredible patience; there was Pandit Madan Mohan Malaviya, the aloof and cultivated leader of the Hindu Mahasabha; and in strong contrast Sir Abdul Karim Ghuznavi sat at the banquet, a virile and acknowledged champion of the Moslem community. Representing the Liberals was Sir Tej Bahadur Sapru, whose intentions towards the Viceroy were to be as well-meaning as Patel's were obstructive.

The Viceroy was prepared to take full advantage of the occasion. Perhaps there were ringing in his ears the words of the Indian Member of the Legislative Assembly who had said that the Government of India had lost the moral leadership of the country. Speaking with that gravity which well became him, and with a sincerity which touched the hearts of the most sceptical of his audience, the Viceroy sought to regain it.

It was perhaps typical of Irwin's own character, its innate caution, its lack of Utopian dreams, that after his words had melted the audience at the Chelmsford Club, and placated even the Indian Press, he himself should have remained cool and doubtful of its effect. The speech was impressive and well phrased throughout, and the passages of deep sincerity in which the Viceroy made his appeal to the consciences of the two communities were listened to with rapt attention. There was something extraordinarily compelling in his deep voice and measured utterance. He urged the leaders of the two religious communities to accept the great responsibilities they each bore for communal tension, and to realize that there was a limit beyond which the Government could not contribute to peace:

'They can watch; they can advise; they can damp down ardour as it shows itself in different places; they can stamp out isolated outbreaks of fire; they can protect life and property to the best of their ability; but they can do little to change the combustible nature of the mass of the material or to eradicate its potentialities for generating destructive heat. . . . The cause of the disease lies deeper. We are faced with a situation where the minds of the people have been wrought up to such a point that the most absurd rumours find ready credence; and both sides, nervously apprehending attack, imagine their apprehensions realized in the most trifling incident. A false report, a petty squabble, is sufficient to start a general conflagration and to give rise to those savage and senseless outbreaks which are a disgrace to the name of religion, and a blot on the national life.'[1]

Religion—it was one of the causes of these horrible excesses, but to the Viceroy it was also their only effective cure, and it was in its name that he made his last appeal in this speech to a spellbound audience:

'In the name of Indian national life, in the name of religion, I appeal to all in each of the two communities who hold position, who represent them in the Press, who direct the education of the young, who possess influence,

[1] Government of India Press, *Speeches by Lord Irwin*, Vol. I, p. 29.

who command the esteem of their co-religionists, who lead them in politics or are honoured by them as divines. Let them begin each in their own community to work untiringly towards this end; boldly to repudiate feelings of hatred and intolerance, actively to condemn and suppress acts of violence and aggression, earnestly to strive to exorcise suspicions. . . .'

No one present was to forget the Viceroy's noble peroration in which he appeared to be invoking the light of belief against the powers of darkness:

'I appeal in the name of national life because communal tension is eating into it as a canker. It has suspended its activities. It has ranged its component parts into opposite and hostile camps.

'I appeal in the name of religion because I can appeal to nothing nobler, and because religion is the language of the soul, and it is a change of soul that India needs today. In all religion, I suppose, there must be present in the mind of the individual a sense of personal deficiency, a consciousness of failure to apprehend more than a fraction of life's mystery, which constantly impels him, with irresistible yearning, to reach out for higher and yet higher things.

'Whatever indeed be the creed men possess, such creed is the attempt men make to know the Forces that lie beyond human vision, and learn the secret of how human nature may be refined, and in doing so realize the ultimate purpose of their existence. Achievement is hard and can only come through much patience and humility, which will in turn beget a wider tolerance of the deficiencies of others. But the reward is great, and there surely can be no greater tragedy than that religion which should thus be the expression and support of man's highest instincts, should be prostituted by an alliance with actions through which those instincts are distorted and disgraced.

'Such a development, if it were unchecked, could only end in the infliction of a mortal wound upon human character, upon India, and upon the cause of that religion in whose guise it was allowed to masquerade.'[1]

The impact of the Viceroy's speech, and the burning sincerity that was evident in every word of it struck all the Indian leaders in the audience irrespective of creed, and even induced a mood of approval in the vernacular Press. The organ of Congress, the *Bombay Chronicle*, described the speech as 'in parts all that could be desired', an unusual if qualified departure from its normal policy of sustained abuse.

To many Indians it seemed as though the Viceroy, no longer detached and alien and surrounded by pomp and the threat of power, had descended from his eminence to walk among them as a friend, and to discuss the eternal verities common to them all. It was an attitude that produced an immediate response in Indians. 'This appeal,' said Gopal, 'by one who was obviously a deeply religious person sounded a note which had been unheard in viceregal statements since the days of Lord Ripon over forty years before, and struck a response in India. Motilal Nehru . . . sponsored the formation of an Indian

---

[1] *Speeches by Lord Irwin*, Vol. I pp. 32–3.

National Union, a non-political organization to combat communalism.'[1]

Irwin had, in fact, briefly regained the moral leadership of India which the English had been accused of losing, and for two months there was a blessed lull in communal strife. The Viceroy had no illusions that this would last. He was well aware that the effect of his speech, although deep, would also be transient, and in his inaugural address to the House of the Legislature he made it clear that his character was not wholly compounded of idealism and religious yearning, and that in the event of trouble he intended to keep order.

There was a ring of unmistakable authority in his voice when he told them: 'It cannot be too clearly emphasized that Government have no intention whatever of allowing any unjust or unreasonable claim, still less any violence or threat of violence, to deter them from their clear duty of maintaining the public peace and . . . the right of the individual citizen to pursue unhampered his lawful avocations.'[2]

By the end of 1926 a peculiar situation had developed in the working of the legislatures as amended by the Montagu-Chelmsford Reforms. We have seen how Congress boycotted the first elections to the reformed legislatures in 1920. In 1923 the group led by Motilal Nehru had abandoned the original policy of non-co-operation and entered the various legislatures with the object of paralysing the work of Government from within. Swarajists had taken part in the ordinary work of the Chamber, even sitting on Committees; only in two of the Provinces had their obstruction succeeded in making dyarchy unworkable.

On the whole their wrecking policy was a failure. The Swarajist leaders were distressed to observe the frailty of human nature in some of the weaker brethren prevailing over loyalty to party. Some of them had already accepted official positions, and the controversy was to cause one of the many splits in the mercurial ranks of the Congress Party.

At the annual Congress Session of 1925 acceptance was again sought of the 'National Demand', and in the event of its refusal the Swarajists proposed to leave the legislatures. This policy of non-co-operation was rejected by the influential group whose leaders were Mahratta Brahmins of influence and distinction who still preferred to seek similar ends by constitutional means. This group, led by such men as Jayakar, Moonje and Malaviya, had split off from the main body and formed the party of Responsive Co-operation which came to be known as the National Party. These men were not only prepared to enter the legislatures, but were also ready to accept any office of responsibility that was offered to them. On 8 March 1926 Motilal Nehru led his followers out of the Chamber, and this domestic rupture in Congress was regarded as a success for the Government, and yet another indication of the falsity of the claim of Congress to be an All-India organization.

*   *   *

[1] S. Gopal. Op. cit., p. 17.   [2] Ibid., Vol. I, p. 58.

We have seen that it was the custom of the Viceroy to go each year in December to Calcutta. Before leaving Simla on this first journey Lord Irwin decided to avail himself of the opportunity of gaining first-hand knowledge of conditions in the Punjab and the North West Frontier. In the city of Lahore, which had seen the unfolding of the young Kipling's genius, he was given a welcome by the crowds lining the streets for his drive to Government House that warmed his heart, and seemed a proof of the esteem in which he was already held.

There was a Durbar at the Old Fort, Kipling's 'Fort Amara', in the audience chamber of the Emperor Akbar, and a walk in the dusk in the magical Shalimar Gardens. At the Durbar he spoke to them of their future, and reminded them of their martial past: 'You of the Punjab have always been a race of soldiers. Fate has placed your lands on the high road from the hungry uplands of the North to the rich plains of Hindustan, and your five rivers have often run red with the blood of your ancestors and of the invaders they struggled to repel.'[1]

It was a happy inspiration also that caused the Viceroy to make an extended tour of the North West Frontier at this early period of his administration. He had looked forward with youthful zest and a sense of adventure to visiting these fabled regions, for so long the vulnerable point of India, but at that moment in a state of precarious peace. It was his intention to make a thorough inspection of this turbulent province which lies between the Hindu Kush in the north and Baluchistan in the south, and between Kashmir and the Punjab in the east. To the west the Durand Line marked the boundary between tribal territory and Afghanistan. The 'Administrative Border' was an invisible line running south for hundreds of miles through the desolate Suleiman Mountains from Peshawar to Baluchistan, and marking the frontier of five regularly Administered Districts populated by two and a quarter million people, overwhelmingly Muhammadan.

To the west of the border lay tribal territory, a bleak and terrible country of savage forays and implacable vendettas, where the Pathan tribesmen held sway in their various regions in a state of permanent mutual mistrust, Afridis, Wazirs, Mahsuds, Mohmands, and others of similar character. This grim country was known to its neighbours over the border in the Administered Districts as 'Yaghistan', the 'land of unrest'.

Between Afghanistan and the Indus stretches one of the most formidable mountain systems in the world, and this frontier had been for centuries a cause of unending vigilance by the rulers of India, and a local problem of enormous complexity. It was over the passes that pierce these mighty ranges like narrow sword-cuts that the invaders from Central Asia had made their way towards the rich plains of India. It was in their deep and tortuous valleys that were found those bodies of fanatical tribesmen who could scarcely wring

[1] S. Gopal. Vol. I, p. 69.

a livelihood from their stony soil, and were therefore always avid for spoil, for the capture of a caravan, or for a bloody raid on the settled districts beneath them.

These tribes were acknowledged as being within India's sphere of influence, but the Government of India had no desire to interfere in their lives, still less to undertake further wars of conquest in the heart of their grisly territory. Rather was its policy, as far as possible, to bring to them some meaning of the civilization outside through those great arteries of the modern world, roads and railways.

'For centuries,' wrote J. Coatman in 1932, 'the North West Frontier had been her heel of Achilles, a region of dread and menace. But from now onwards it would begin to see the light of day, be drawn by the invisible bonds of benefit and enlightenment into the orbit of India's life, and become her buckler instead of her naked side.' In the meantime the tribesmen continued to do what was right in their own eyes, living inside their fortified farmsteads, following their primitive methods of cultivation, and maintaining a constant state of feud with their neighbours, and knowing that if they killed them the crime was unlikely to be brought home to them by the British courts.

The Viceroy, on his travels, was to notice one curious aspect of Frontier life. Whatever the danger lurking in those harsh mountains and ravines, the road was sacred. On that which ran through the Khyber from Peshawar to the Afghan border through a landscape of lunar bleakness, he could see the khassadar or guard, recruited by the tribesmen, a tall figure standing at intervals, etched against the skyline on some crag along the road, an assurance to the caravans plodding with their loaded camels from Samarkand or Bokhara that they might pass with safety on their way to the markets of Jamrud and Peshawar.

Lord Irwin gained an exceptional insight into the North West Frontier Province by his free use of the still primitive aeroplane, inspecting the whole length of it from Malakand in the north to its southmost boundaries. It was by this same instrument that the evacuation of British and other nationals would be accomplished two years later from Kabul during the Afghan rebellion, when five hundred and eighty-six men, women and children were flown to Peshawar by one Handley Page Hinaidi and seven Vickers Victorias in the first operation of its kind ever to be carried out, and one believed at the time to be unique in the history of the world. His route took him to the head of the Khyber. Here the Political Officer told him that there were two sections of a tribe who were discontented with Government and proposed making themselves a nuisance to the Viceroy.

The Officer had suggested to each section that the day of his visit might be a convenient opportunity to put into effect the attack it had contemplated on the other. This was done, and Irwin was delighted with the manœuvre and thought it a classical example of the principle 'Divide and Rule'. He went to Razmak in Waziristan, where he made a State entry, the first Viceroy ever to enter the country. Razmak was purely a garrison town where a large number of troops were maintained to safeguard peace in Waziristan and the neighbouring tribal areas. Here, as elsewhere, he received jirgas, or delegations of the people who presented loyal addresses, and, behind a grave countenance, he was secretly diverted by these fierce, hawk-faced men, so evidently on their best behaviour.

By these encounters he was not only extending his own knowledge of India, but was also giving the wildest of his subjects the experience of meeting the Viceroy face to face. These Pathans of the hills did not wear their hearts upon their sleeves, but when at last he departed it was said of him that 'the frontier has met Lord Irwin and accepted him'.

While the excitement of his tour was still fresh in his mind, he sent his father a vivid account of it. His visit to these gaunt but invigorating hills had been a wonderful tonic and refreshment amid the endless social duties which he so stoically endured:

'It is an extraordinary thing suddenly to find yourself in a region of forts, barbed wire entanglements, loopholes, raids, blood feuds and all the rest of it. . . . It is full of interest, and you really feel up there that you are dealing with things that matter. The people are real men, very primitive in their habits and not above shooting anybody to draw attention to their grievances. The whole road was picketed for us and we got through with no misadventure.

'Waziristan is really a very wonderful piece of work. Up to two years ago we had a lot of trouble there. . . . Since then we have been developing roads, and as a result it is very much more difficult for the tribesmen to raid down into the settled territory than it was, for they are always apprehensive of having their retreat cut off, whereas before the roads were there we could not get about. . . .

'I met all the various tribes who came to present primitive addresses to me, and who all looked as though butter would not melt in their mouths. The Political Officer told me that there were two men present yesterday at one of those meetings who had a bitter blood feud one against the other, and of whom it was quite certain one would kill the other before any great time had passed. And there they were on the lawn of the garden of the Political Officer's house, looking at each other out of one eye and no doubt relieved to find themselves for the moment on neutral territory.'[1]

After this visit Irwin became engrossed by the frontier problem, and the wild land of Afghanistan, and he would listen with fascination to stories about them from that legendary figure Sir Francis Humphrys, who was almost the spirit of the region. Humphrys told him that when he took up his post as British representative in Afghanistan, Curzon had said to him: 'You

[1] Hickleton Papers, *Correspondence with Viscount Halifax*, p. 48.

will never have a Russian in your Embassy, and when you call on the Afghans you will have six Bengal Lancers riding in front of you and six behind.'

Irwin would have hated such pomp though he would have liked to visit Kabul, but after the Third Afghan War, 'the war of independence', it would have been inadvisable. He learned from Humphrys the danger of Russian penetration into any part of Afghanistan, and how it had always been believed that if they crossed the border and reached the Hindu Kush it would be the knell of doom for India.

He liked to listen to stories of that savage background; of how King Amanullah, in concert with his mother, had murdered his father to win the throne; how when Humphrys had said that a certain bandit should be brought to book, an Afghan had gone out and killed him, and cut off his head; how he had brought it back to Humphrys to please him and, finding him asleep on his balcony and not wishing to disturb him, had rolled the head gently over to the bedside so that he would see it when he awoke.

Humphrys told him, too, of a Russian Ambassador to Kabul, too moderate for his superiors in Moscow who arranged for him to be murdered by the Afghans on his way home on leave as part of a deal convenient to the two Governments; and of another whose habit it was to bring beautiful women to Kabul for a two-year period, and had murdered one of these who had palled on him, and how Humphrys and his staff, who were aware of the facts, had to maintain an attitude of grief as mourners at the funeral. The Viceroy was later to see Amanullah himself dethroned for trying to modernize Afghanistan. He had begun by cutting the beards of his mullahs with a pair of scissors, like Peter the Great and his boyars but with less success.[1]

The Viceroy next turned his attention to his relations with the Indian States and their rulers which were regulated by a special portfolio administered by the Viceroy personally with the assistance of the Foreign Secretary and the Political Secretary, although the final responsibility here, as everywhere else, belonged to the Viceroy alone. Lord Irwin was by temperament attracted by the grandeur and the panache that surrounded the Indian Princes, but he was in no way dazzled by their glitter or unduly influenced by their protestations of loyalty. As an aristocrat himself and the representative of the King-Emperor, he was unlikely to be awed by feudal splendour, and his shrewd judgment of men soon enabled him to discern which of them were able administrators and which mere parasites upon their States.

When, therefore, he followed his tour of the North West Frontier by holding a session of the Council of Princes at Delhi on 22 November, it was with a clear idea of the ambitions which were secretly nourished by some, and of his attitude towards them. He lost no time in reminding his audience that in the light of the Reforms and the gradual shifting of power and responsibility in British India that was already in progress, the relations between the

[1] Sir Francis Humphrys to author.

Indian States and the Government of India had now become a matter of crucial importance. He therefore proposed that the Chamber should authorize the Standing Committee to hold important talks with him and his advisers whenever he considered it necessary.

By some happy instinct the Viceroy achieved a perfectly appropriate manner in his relations with the Indian Princes, at once courteous and superior, and discouraging the slightest familiarity. When the odious Maharaja of Alwar offered him a beautifully chased rifle as a gift, it was at once rejected. The Maharaja had on this occasion informed the Viceroy with astonishing insolence that Lord Reading had been less punctilious in this respect, and Irwin had coldly answered 'that each individual Viceroy must be the judge of his own conscience in such cases'.

When the Secretary of State had drawn his attention to the delinquency of a particular ruler, such as the Nizam of Hyderabad, the Viceroy never flinched from the most embarrassing and painful interviews. He disliked these necessities, but when they arose he regarded it as an inescapable part of his duties to issue polite but unmistakable warnings.

Nor was Lord Irwin likely to view with approval the tendentious opinions which were soon to be put forward by such Princes as the Maharaja of Bikanir on the subject of the excessive control exercised by the Paramount Power. On the contrary, he lost no time in circulating among the Princes a note on the principles which he desired to see applied to their administration,[1] a document which reads like an essay on Bagehot or Dicey and which, in its insistence on Responsible Government, the Rule of Law and the reduction of the Princes' personal expenditure, must have caused many a lifted eyebrow among its more cynical recipients.

The Viceroy was not sanguine about his efforts to induce a realistic approach to the question of the future relations between the Native States and British India. 'The truth, I think is,' he wrote to King George, 'that while the more far sighted of the Princes recognize that it is a problem which is likely to become increasingly important and are anxious to find a solution for it, the desire of the great majority is to be left alone. I think they scarcely have any appreciation of how closely public opinion in British India is bound to react within their States, and are consequently slow to see the inevitable necessity of making adjustments and improvements to meet it.'[2]

*   *   *

The pieces in the mosaic of India were beginning to fall into place in the Viceroy's mind. He had now gained some knowledge of the North West Frontier, and the problem of the Princes which hung like a great question

---

[1] S. Gopal. Op. cit., p. 126.
[2] India Office Library, MSS. EUR.C. 152/1, *Lord Irwin, Correspondence with H.M. The King-Emperor, 1926–1931*, p. 24.

mark over the future of India. The most intractable issue of all, the antagonism between Moslem and Hindu, was ever before him, and his consciousness
of it had been constantly renewed by a series of bloody communal riots,
senseless in their inception and sickening in their consequences.

His experience up to this time had made him aware that he had merely
touched the fringe of the India over which he was ruling, and he next turned
his attention to Finance and the India of big business as represented in
Calcutta. In this city, the second in size in the British Empire, economic
control was almost entirely vested in foreign hands. Bombay was an Indian
city, and there he would have encountered the great industrialists of India,
but in Calcutta he was brought into touch with the full strength of European
non-official opinion in one of the world's great cosmopolitan business centres.

He went there after addressing the Chamber of Princes, and after a pause
at Cawnpore, where he addressed the Associated Chambers of Commerce of
India and Ceylon, discussing general economic conditions, and reform in
currency and banking. The streets of Calcutta were hung with flags, and at
night the fireworks were gold and silver in the sky, and the coloured lanterns
twinkled in the darkness, but it was not the symbols of carnival, so often to be
repeated, that moved the Viceroy. It was the fervour of the welcome he
received from the crowds in the seething city who poured from their alleys
to line the streets down which he was to pass. Calcutta was a fertile breeding-
ground for riot and agitation, and on his arrival the Swarajists had organized
processions to mourn the imprisonment of that idol of revolutionary youth,
Subhas Chandra Bose, and the motto inscribed on their banners contrasted
strangely with the loyal bunting: 'Bengal's heart bleeds white while Subhas
lies in Mandalay gaol.'

Irwin was left in no doubt of the regard in which he was held, at least for
the moment, when this gesture of protest was completely submerged in the
triumph of his ceremonial entry into the city. It was characteristic of his
complete indifference to danger that he refused to take the short cut that was
suggested, but preferred to show himself to the people by driving through
the districts of North Calcutta where the riots which had greeted his arrival
in India had been most intense.

It was no accident that he chose the capital city of Bengal, still in every
real sense the capital of India, as the scene of an important message to India
and to the world. At the annual dinner of the European Association of India
it was customary for the Viceroy to address the powerful non-official English
element in the country, to make clear to them the lines on which his mind
was working and the policy he intended to pursue, and through them also
to reach a wider audience at home.

In this speech the Viceroy came quickly to the heart of the matter. Sensing
perhaps that among his audience were many hard-headed men of affairs who
contemplated with dismay the transference of further power to Indian hands

and deplored the advance towards it that had already been made, he reminded them that it was hardly possible that England would have acted differently, since throughout her history she had been the pioneer in the application of representative institutions to the science of politics. Irwin, who was in many ways as hard-headed as his audience, fully understood the danger of entrusting political power to those whose functions had been hitherto that of an opposition not liable to be called to the responsibilities of office. He could not predict how or when the moment of transference would come:

'Few would be so bold as to hazard any very assured prophecy as to when the British Parliament was likely to feel disposed to entrust full responsibility to India. . . . The answer to that question is likely to depend much more upon the foundations that India can lay for her own political development than on any preconceived notions of the British Parliament. As I have already said, the whole instinct of Parliament . . . must be to wish well to India in this matter. But if Parliament is a well-wisher, it is also a shrewd and competent judge, and Parliament will, I suspect, realize that at the root of the whole question lies the problem of what I may call the average political sense of a wider electorate. An educated electorate . . . is the only sure basis of democracy. Without it, politics are the possession of a small class of the intelligentsia, and the leaders of political thought, who must be pioneers of political development, would be the first to recognize that in those conditions the political system, instead of resting broadly based on intelligent popular judgment, is insecurely poised on an inverted apex.'[1]

By the end of 1926 the Viceroy had clearly arrived at certain provisional conclusions. He had shown an undeniable sympathy with the desire of political India for further responsibility, but as yet he was restrained from giving too marked an encouragement to this tendency by the policy of the Secretary of State, the impulsiveness of Indian politicians who could twist the mildest words into a hard promise, and the formidable obstacles which his clear mind perceived in its path. Among these the communal question must have appeared to him almost incapable of solution. He could look back upon a year strangely stagnant in political activity; Gandhi was still in seclusion in his ashram, preaching his creed of homespun and spinning wheel, not to emerge for two years, and the Indian political scene was impoverished by his absence.

And yet there was a movement beneath the surface. Flat and uneventful as the year seemed, it appeared to one who lived through it that 'it was a year that history will cite as marking the change-over from the old to a new conception of policy in regard to India's political future and the terms of her relationship with Great Britain and the rest of the British Commonwealth'.[2]

---

[1] Government of India Press, *Speeches by Lord Irwin*, Vol. I, pp. 165–6.
[2] J. Coatman. Op. cit., p. 138.

CHAPTER XIV

THE SIMON COMMISSION

THE consequence of this subterranean process was a quickening of the tempo of events in the coming year, so that there was a building up of emotion and a growing intensity in Indian politics until the Statutory Commission was appointed at the end of 1927 and the period of rebellion began.

There were certain evident reasons for this growing tension. The Congress, which for some time had been in discreditable seclusion, and appeared to some to have shot its bolt, was able to revive its fortunes by identifying itself with the attack on the Currency Commission and on the Finance Minister, Sir Basil Blackett. It would have seemed an impossible task to extract political propaganda for the masses from a measure of such complexity as the Rupee Stabilization Bill which was moved in the Indian Legislature in the autumn of 1927, and was designed to stabilize the gold value of the rupee, but this end was somehow accomplished.

It was a measure understood by only a handful of economic specialists, but the circumstances of the day made it possible for agitators, by wild misrepresentation, to interpret it as the doom of the peasants of India. The war had left economic dislocation behind it, and there was a wide gap between the prices of primary products and those of manufactured goods. In the general depression the millions of India's peasant proprietors suffered without understanding the cause of their suffering, and it was not difficult for the eager emissaries from Congress to attribute the blame to the tyranny of the Government of India and its satanic weapon, the Rupee Stabilization Bill, in a manner reminiscent of 'Madame Veto'. The efforts at subversion were assisted by the depression in the price of agricultural products, and this was particularly the case where the rural economy was that of landlord and tenant, and the latter paid cash rentals. A long period of internal peace and rising population had led to a notable increase in the pitch of money rentals; the depression had caused a similar fall in the price obtainable for agricultural produce, and it was this situation that was responsible for much rural unrest, and the consequent support given to Congress agitation.

Another fruitful cause of unrest and agitation was the status of Indians overseas, and in other parts of the British Empire, and the plight of these people, real or imaginary, was deftly seized by the vernacular Press and used as a persuasive argument for Home Rule, for to protect her oppressed brothers, it was claimed, India must herself be free.

All these circumstances were exploited by men who were pastmasters in the anatomy of discontent, and a change was wrought in the opinions and the temper of the people, largely impalpable, and perhaps fugitive, yet one that could not fail to convey its message to a sensitive ear. 'A movement of opinion or feeling,' wrote Coatman of this time, 'starts in some part or other of India, and sweeps across the country as the wind sweeps across a cornfield. When or how it starts is usually impossible to say, and even its effects are not, as a rule, very obvious. When the wind has passed, the field looks much the same as before. Only here some stalks are bent, and there, some have been laid low.'

The Viceroy was, of course, in no way to blame for the post-war conditions which were exercising so depressing an effect on the Indian economy, but he was aware that the rejection of the Rupee Stabilization Bill would produce the most serious crisis that had yet confronted him in India, and that if he forced through the Bill by his special power of certification, he must face the probability of the whole opposition leaving the Legislative Assembly, a disaster which would have paralysed the working of the new constitution.

In fact, it required heroic exertions on the part of Blackett, and the support of Sir Alexander Muddiman and the Indian Member of the Viceroy's Council, Mitra, to defeat an amendment, which sought to stabilize the gold rupee at 1s. 4d. instead of 1s. 6d., by the narrow majority of three votes. But the hostile propaganda which had been directed against the measure was not quickly forgotten, and sharpened the tempers of the parties to a level of discontent which was to abide until they were confronted by the Statutory Commission.

The aspect of this matter in which the Viceroy was particularly interested was the effect of the economic depression upon Indian agriculture. One of Lord Reading's last acts had been the appointment of a Commission under Lord Linlithgow to examine this problem, and this body was at that moment engaged in taking evidence. Irwin had already shown the interest of a great landowner and a practical farmer in the affairs of the Indian countryside. At the Lahore Durbar he had spoken of the lure of the soil, and how bountifully it repaid the efforts that man put into it. He had extolled modern methods of invigorating that parched land in words at once philosophical and utilitarian. Nor was his shrewd mind forgetful of the fact that the constitutional changes of the future would place a power hitherto unknown in the hands of the vast anonymous mass of country dwellers.

He began to wander incognito among the villages of India, and to study the lives of the humble ryots who formed the great bulk of the population of the country. He saw that the cultivators of the soil had no farmsteads but lived in the village near the strip of land they tilled. He watched them at work under the devouring Indian sun on maize or sugar cane; saw their wooden ploughs make the same ineffectual scratches in the earth that were once made by Primitive Man, and the patient buffaloes plodding round in their endless circles to grind the corn. He saw the peasants return to their village with its stifling houses of mud and its tin shanties.

While these straws were blowing hard in the wind, the unabated communal tension was always foremost in the Viceroy's mind. He could never escape the feeling that until this question was settled a further transfer of power to Indians would merely be to build on sand. He was given during the summer another sharp reminder of its existence. This time the agitation had been provoked by a scurrilous pamphlet about the founder of Islam, which had been published in Lahore and was called Rangila Rasul—'The Gay Prophet', and the blasphemy had been wafted up to and even beyond the North West Frontier into the domain of the Afridi where Hindu and Moslem had lived for centuries in perfect harmony.

Once again, and in new surroundings, the old synthetic hatred was fomented, and hundreds of Hindus were driven or fled in terror across the border into the land of British India they had never seen before, and their exit was a sinister portent for the future, for the sacred tradition of hospitality of the North West Frontier was not lightly broken. During that grim summer the Viceroy witnessed a disturbing repetition of such scenes. In a succession of riots a further hundred people were killed and a thousand injured, and probably only resolute action by police and military prevented that at Lahore becoming one of the most ghastly in the history of British India.

The Viceroy addressed himself once again to this melancholy topic when the Combined Legislatures met at Simla on 29 August 1927. No statesman in the world could have made a more convincing appeal to the consciences of his audience, enriched it with more persuasive arguments, or reinforced it with more compelling moral conviction. Few indeed of his audience as they sat in that assembly high in the Himalayas, could fail to have been moved by an appeal couched in such language, directed towards such exalted ends, and designed to arrest the contamination of the religious principle. It was the voice of sanity in a mad world, and it is some measure of the communal problem that his words could be but feebly translated into action. It was the question that still dwarfed all others in the life of India.

Another consideration, besides the ending of this incessant religious strife, was also occupying the Viceroy's mind. He had lately been giving much thought to the setting of the scene for the arrival of the Statutory Commission. There could be no worse atmosphere for their operation than one still clouded by communal tension, and this realization lent an added force to his words. He reminded the 'representatives of the people' that during the seventeen months he had been in India the whole landscape had been overshadowed by this dreadful issue.

'From April to July last year Calcutta seemed to be under the mastery of some evil spirit, which so gripped the minds of men that in their insanity they held themselves absolved from the most sacred restraints of human conduct. Honest citizens went abroad in peril of their lives from fanatical attack, and the paralysis that overtook the commercial life of a great metropolis was only less serious than the civic loss which flowed from a naked and unashamed violation of the law, which perforce had to be reasserted by methods drastic and severe. Since then we have seen the same sinister influences at work in Patna, Rawalpindi, and many other places, and have been forced to look upon that abyss of unchained human passions that lies too often beneath the surface of habit and of law.'[1]

He read out the appalling figures of those who had already been killed and mutilated in the name of religion, and he continued:

'Nor are the many houses of mourning the only measure of the damage which is being done to India. Is there not much in Indian social life that still cries out for remedy and reform and which enlightened India of today would fain mould otherwise? Nowhere perhaps is the task before the reformers more laborious; for in India civilization is agelong, immemorial; and all things are deep-rooted in the past. United must be the effort if it is to gain success; and on the successful issue of such work depends the building of the Indian nation. Yet the would-be builders must approach the task sorely handicapped and with heavy hearts, so long as the forces to which they would appeal are distracted and torn by present animosities. For nothing wholesome can flourish in unwholesome soil, and no one may hope to build a house to stand against the wind and the rain and the storm of life upon foundations that are rotten and unsound.'[2]

Again and again in this speech he sought to drive in on the Indian members of Parliament that their future lay in their own hands, that self-rule, with all that it implied, could not be tossed to a country which was still unable to control its fundamental passions, but was an organic thing that must grow and strengthen like the sinews in the human body, and without self-control would be merely an empty name concealing something perilously akin to civil war.

It was believed that the British Government would expedite the appointment of the Statutory Commission which was to inquire into the workings of the Montagu-Chelmsford Reforms. At the moment it seemed as though the political destiny of India now reposed in that body whose Report could determine the extent of the next constitutional advance, and already rumours, sinister in Indian ears, had been widely circulated.

Sir Tej Bahadur Sapru, the Liberal Leader, had returned from a visit to England in the summer of 1927 with the report that there were to be no Indian members on the Commission, and the reaction to this news in India was immediate and explosive. It was to be expected that the vernacular Press would excel itself in vituperation, and Congress leaders express their outrage

[1] Government of India Press, *Speeches by Lord Irwin*, Vol. I, p. 282.   [2] Ibid., p. 283.

and disgust in terms more violent than any hitherto used. The deliberate exclusion of Indians appeared to these hyper-sensitive men, with their sense of inferiority, their dread of patronage, and their illusions of persecution, to be a denial of that equality of status which meant so much to them, and a slight upon India herself.

It was extraordinary that the India Office should have been so startled by the storm it provoked. The touchy Nationalist leaders had already made plain their resentment that India should be made the subject of an inquest by the British Government by which their fitness for nationhood should be decided. It was a process which seemed to them to emphasize the gulf between governors and governed which they did not acknowledge, and when it became clear that the examining body was to be an exclusively British and Parliamentary Commission their cup of discontent was full. It was significant that this angry reception of the news was not confined to the Congress Party, and that the Liberals also joined in the initial protests and the subsequent boycott.

However much the Secretary of State and the Viceroy underrated the psychological dangers of their course, they had not decided upon a Parliamentary Commission without long and anxious thought, and their reasons for doing so were, in strict logic, unassailable. Birkenhead had, for some time, kept an open mind on the subject of the personnel of the Commission, and, unlike Irwin, had at first envisaged Indian participation in it. On 29 July 1926 he had written to the Viceroy: 'In the meantime I should be very glad to hear any suggestions you have in your mind as to the personnel on the Indian side. On ours I am not bothering particularly, for there are so many people who would be suitable that the only difficulty will prove to be one of selection.'[1]

The Viceroy was evidently a little disturbed by this allusion to Indians. His own advisers in India had been unanimous in thinking that a British Commission drawn from both Houses of Parliament would be the best method of gaining the sympathy of the Indian Liberals and causing them to exercise a moderating influence upon the more extreme policies of Congress. They also nourished the hope, sanguine as it proved in the event, that as the Moslems would in any case support the Commission, the fear of their thus gaining its sympathy would prevent any considerable attempt to boycott it by the Hindus, a miscalculation which was rightly described by Gopal as the first and greatest mistake of Lord Irwin's viceroyalty.[2]

The Viceroy replied to the Secretary of State on 19 August 1926 in a letter which clearly represented the point of view of his advisers at that moment, one of whom thought that a mixed Commission 'will engender such heat that its pistons will seize'.

'With regard to what you say in the first paragraph of your letter of

[1] Charlton archives, *Private Letters from Lord Birkenhead to Lord Irwin.*
[2] S. Gopal. Op. cit., p. 21.

29 July about the personnel of the Royal Commission, I gather from it that you contemplate a Commission including Indians. I have grave doubts about the wisdom of this course. Once you begin to select Indians, it will be almost impossible to avoid making your selection representative and extending it to include officials. Apart from the danger of making the Commission unwieldy, I think it pretty certain that a Commission so composed would end, as did the Sankey Commission, in producing at least two reports, one of which might have been written before the Commission began. Would it not be wiser to create the Commission as an outside impartial body, small in numbers, and representing the soundest balance and judgment that you can secure, and rely upon evidence to put them in possession of various Indian views?'[1]

The Viceroy was anxious to carry the Secretary of State with him in the view that a Commission chosen from both Houses of the British Parliament was the most suitable instrument for the task. He saw in such a Commission the best hope of neutralizing Indian hostility which he now recognized would be considerable.

What could be more natural than that Parliament, charged with this inquiry, would wish to inform itself through its own members? If the Commission included outsiders it would at once be attacked for not appointing Indians. The Viceroy realized that if the Government followed the course he suggested there remained the danger of disagreement on the Commission. He believed that this danger was inseparable from any Commission on which the Labour Party was represented but that this risk was small compared with the far greater danger of a Commission on which they felt that their point of view had not been fairly represented.

In March 1927 Birkenhead's mind was still open. He was not yet convinced of the wisdom of excluding Indians from the Commission. He had weighed the pros and cons of every conceivable combination without yet arriving at a decision. He had never desired that the Commission should recommend a great measure of advancement, for which he believed that India was entirely unprepared, and at this moment appeared to see some advantage in the representation on the Commission of both the great communities:

'I am well aware of the arguments in favour of the exclusion of natives, and my mind is absolutely open upon this, and indeed upon every other point; but you must remember that the arguments against the exclusion are a priori very strong. It will be said that the determination of this constitution, with all that it may mean for India, cannot be settled with the least appearance of authority by a Commission which contains no Indian Member. It will also be pointed out that there are Indians of considerable distinction who have never taken up an irreconcilable attitude in relation to the present constitution, and that to deny the chance of membership to all Indians is to

[1] India Office Library MSS. EUR.C. 152/2, Letters to the Secretary of State for India, p. 79.

make evident to all the world the "inferiority complex" with which we chose to brand the peoples of India. . . .

'Are you quite certain that the presence on the Commission, both of Hindu and Moslem representatives, that the controversy which would follow, that the probability of divergent Hindu and Moslem reports, might not be of great assistance to you and us if the Commission took the view that a very considerable advance was not to be recommended at the moment when they report?'[1]

In spite of this rather singular argument in favour of the inclusion of Indians, the case against it appeared formidable to both Viceroy and Secretary of State. If the Commission was to be a comparatively small body and at the same time to include Indians, the Indians would not be more than two or three in number, and these would have to be selected in some manner that would ensure that they were reasonably representative of all the cross-currents of Indian views, a condition that was plainly unattainable.

The alternative would be to fix the number of Indians at a figure which would enable all the various interests to have their own representative, and to transform the Commission into a body of considerable size. Even so, unless the representatives of Indian interests were duplicated or triplicated, any given interest would have ground for complaint that it was not represented in the membership of a particular sub-committee which was regarded as of primary importance. Even if such a large and all-embracing Indo-British Commission worked according to plan, the prospects of an agreed report, or anything approaching it, would be negligible. If, to avoid this difficulty, Indian representation were confined to two or three Indians, the Commission would hardly be more acceptable than if Indians were excluded altogether.

If Indians were to be excluded for these reasons, it is clear that officials and 'experts' must be excluded also, and the case for a Parliamentary Commission was greatly strengthened. By July 1927 the Viceroy was confirmed in his opinion that such a Commission, if likely to produce a unanimous report, would have advantages that would outweigh the opposition it would create. He knew now that it would be badly received in India, that its appointment would unite all Hindu opinion in opposition, and that its failure to produce an agreed report would have the most damaging results. Whether it did so or not, he believed, would depend upon the attitude of its Labour members. If such unanimity could not be achieved, he believed that a mixed Commission, although it would produce more than one report, would be far more favourably received, that it would diminish the probability of uniting all Indian opinion against the Commission and that its minority report would be less injurious than one proceeding from a Parliamentary Commission.[2]

[1] Charlton archives, *Private Letters from Lord Birkenhead to Lord Irwin*, 23 March 1927.
[2] Correspondence with the Secretary of State for India on the Statutory Commission, pp. 35-40.

If it was decided to appoint a Parliamentary Commission it was clearly necessary to find some method of associating Indians with the determining of their own future, and this question also had been thrashed out in the preceding months in letters and telegrams between Viceroy and Secretary of State before their decision was embodied in the Viceroy's announcement of the Simon Commission on 8 November 1927.

The Viceroy had originally suggested that before laying the report of the Statutory Commission before the English Parliament it should be submitted to a Select Committee of both Houses of the Indian Legislature. It would be unreasonable, he thought, to invite Parliament to waste time on a scheme that Indian opinion had rejected in advance. He suggested that a report of such an Indian Select Committee could be submitted to Parliament together with the Report of the Statutory Commission.[1]

This suggestion did not commend itself to the Secretary of State, who believed that its only result would be to produce a purely destructive criticism from the Indian Legislature, and that a deadlock would follow. He suggested that possible procedures might be an Indian Convention representative of all Provinces and interests to frame a new Indian constitution in advance of the arrival of the Commission, or a Round Table Conference of all interests before which the Report of the Commission might be laid.

When these and other suggestions had been considered and rejected for various reasons by the Viceroy and his advisers, the Secretary of State made another proposal which appeared to him to have advantages over both Convention and Round Table Conference. In a telegram of 12 July 1927 he suggested that when the Commission had reported and a Bill had been drafted to give effect to those of its recommendations on which the British Government had decided, a Select Committee of the Indian Legislative Assembly and the Council of State, representing all interests including official and European, should be sent home to discuss the draft Bill with the Joint Select Parliamentary Committee of both Houses of the English Parliament.

It appeared to him that although this method might make a less striking appeal to Indian sentiment than a Round Table Conference, it would give the only constitutional representatives of India an opportunity of arguing their case with an organ of Parliament in a calmer atmosphere than would prevail in their own country. He added that 'they would, of course, have no voice in the report of the Joint Parliamentary Committee'.[2]

The Viceroy was favourably impressed by this suggestion, but he feared that its advantages might be discounted by the fact that the Indian representatives would be brought in only after the Bill had been drafted, and presumably received a second reading. The Indians would regard this as yet another slight which would be sufficient to damn the proposal in their

[1] Correspondence on the Statutory Commission pp. 35-40.		[2] Ibid., p. 26.

eyes. The Secretary of State sent a reassuring reply, explaining that his intention was that the draft Bill should go to the Indian Committee and the Joint Select Parliamentary Committee before it was introduced into Parliament at all, so that it would not carry with it the general approval conferred by a second reading.

The Cabinet had decided, on 21 July, to appoint a Parliamentary Commission, to be set up in the following spring, of which Sir John Simon was to be Chairman. In a further unavailing attempt to meet Indian objections the Cabinet agreed to the appointment of Indian Assessors to help the Commission in taking evidence and to deliberate with it, but to take no part in framing its report.

It was also agreed that the opportunity should be given for a Select Committee of both Chambers of the Indian Legislature to deliberate either with the Commission before its report was finished, or with a Select Committee of Parliament, on a Bill prepared after the presentation of the Report.

The Viceroy and the Secretary of State had now burned their boats. On the eve of the announcement of the Simon Commission on 8 November, Birkenhead wrote to Irwin:

'I have, of course, no delusions as to the howl of rage with which our proposals will be received by the Indian Press. But no one can charge against us that we had not deeply applied our minds to the problem or that we had not examined every conceivable alternative scheme. Nothing remains but to face such criticism as we shall encounter with coolness and composure.'[1]

If they were so clearly aware of the consequences of appointing a Parliamentary Commission, why then did the Viceroy and the Secretary of State persist in this course? On the Viceroy's own admission, a mixed Commission containing three or four Indians would have been well received. It would have been charged against those Indians that they did not represent India, but the prejudice would have been racial rather than political.

They persisted because the case in favour of a Parliamentary Commission appeared to them overwhelming. We have noticed the arguments in favour of it of the Viceroy's advisers, men deeply versed in Indian affairs, and their wholly mistaken belief that the Hindus would not boycott such a Commission. But there was much in logic to support the appointment of a Parliamentary Commission. In law the British Parliament was still responsible for India's political future. The Montagu-Chelmsford Reforms had been in operation for eight years, and Parliament had both a right and a duty to demand clear guidance on the action that it should take after the ten-year period of trial, laid down in the 1919 Act, had expired. It appeared perfectly reasonable, therefore, that Parliament, having those responsibilities, should send to India delegation of her own Members, belonging to all the

[1] Charlton archives, *Letters from Lord Birkenhead to Lord Irwin*, 3 November 1927.

three parties, to make their inquiries in the country and report their conclusions to her.

Those who advised Lord Irwin also had in mind the state of communal tension. To them it was undesirable that this question, with all its bitterness, should be forced upon the Commission by the inclusion of Hindu and Moslem members. It also appeared obvious that the appointment of moderate men would be violently challenged by extremists, and that the inclusion of extremists themselves, who had been confronting one another in communal strife, would have brought the proceedings of the Commission to a standstill.

Another danger of a mixed Commission which had occurred to the Secretary of State was that an unreal alliance might be created between the Indian and British Labour representatives. The result, in the Viceroy's opinion, might have been 'that proposals, which when critically analysed with knowledge would seem to be patently ill-judged, would be presented to a not-too-well informed public as the considered recommendations of a clear majority on the Commission'.

It was futile to deny that strong arguments could have been brought forward in favour of a mixed Commission. Thus, however logically right, the decision proved to be a disastrous psychological misjudgment. The Viceroy and the India Office were aware that their decision would not be popular, but they had not realized how tender were the susceptibilities on which they had so heavily pressed.

The intense desire of the Indians to convince themselves that they were the equals of the English, and their almost pathetic *amour-propre* were deeply affronted by this further implication of their unworthiness. They chose to regard their exclusion as a suggestion that there were not to be found in India statesmen of sufficient calibre to sit in conference with men of experience. 'The Commission came to be looked upon in India as an inquisition by foreigners into India's fitness for self-government.' Its composition[1] was announced by the Viceroy on 8 November 1927, and Lord Irwin was left to face the music.

He soon became aware how mistaken his advisers had been in assuming that because the Moslems co-operated with the Commission the Hindus would not dare to boycott it, and that the Liberals would be on the side of constitutional progress. Instead a movement sprang up throughout India to deny all help to the Simon Commission in its inquiries.

It was a painful moment for the Viceroy when Sir Tej Bahadur Sapru, the Liberal leader and constitutional lawyer and a former Member of the Viceroy's Council, with the Liberal Federation decided to boycott the Commission. It was an instance of rare agreement with Congress which was sitting

[1] Sir John Simon (Chairman), Lib.; Viscount Burnham, Unionist; Lord Strathcona, Con.; Mr. C. Attlee, Soc.; Mr. E. C. G. Cadogan, Con.; Mr. V. Hartshorn, Soc.; Colonel George Lane Fox, Con.

in Madras at the same time and passed a similar resolution. The Hindu Mahasabha wavered for a moment before following the lead of Malaviya into the boycott camp. The Moslem League was riven by the crisis. The majority followed Sir Muhammad Shafi and a policy of co-operation; the remainder, under Jinnah, allied themselves to the boycott movement.

Jawaharlal Nehru was in his element in this sudden excitement. The young fisher in troubled waters was one of those who found tedium in the orderly process of events. He was at this time an agitator who thrived on tumultuous meetings where motions subversive of British rule were passed amid wild excitement. He was one of the foremost agents of the new 'propaganda of war' which, indifferent to truth, organized hatred with ice-cold logic.

At this Madras Congress he succeeded in passing a resolution which declared that complete independence was the goal to which India must strive. He thought that 'Dominion Status' smacked too much of peaceful evolutionary progress. What they needed was a sudden and complete break with the past.[1] It was characteristic of the manner in which Congress conducted their affairs that this motion was not taken seriously, and was passed mainly in order to humour Jawaharlal, and that another motion was carried proposing an All-Parties Conference to draft a constitution on the basis of Dominion Status.[2]

Thus by the end of 1927 the political apathy which had prevailed at the beginning of the year was over for ever, and the leaders of some of the most influential parties in India, including the Liberals, were united in their intention to boycott the Simon Commission. Irwin had made his announcement, and aware of the strained situation, he had pondered its terms deeply. He explained to the Indian people with perfect fairness the reasons which had led to the appointment of a purely Parliamentary Commission. In an effort to influence those whose opinions were still in the balance he denied that the Commission was merely a judicial inquiry ordered by the Imperial Government over the passive body of the Indian people.

On the contrary, it was essential that Indians should be closely associated with this historic investigation, and he hoped that a Committee from both Houses of the Indian Legislature would be invited to give its views to the Commission. In addition to this, he explained the machinery which had been devised for members of the Indian Legislature to confer with the Joint Committee of Parliament in London on the finished draft Report.

A week after making the announcement the Viceroy wrote to the Secretary of State explaining the position and saying that in spite of the chatter and abuse he would not have handled the affair differently. It was still his belief that a Parliamentary Commission was less dangerous than a mixed Commission.

[1] S. Gopal. Op. cit., p. 22.   [2] Ibid.

It was soon to be seen with what sudden tropical swiftness political India had matured during the working of the Montagu-Chelmsford Reforms. During the seven years of their operation many Indians had worked the machinery of government themselves, and their education had taken a mighty leap forward, so that when the Commission was appointed they were ready, after this period of hot-house development, with a philosophy of action which now openly repudiated the right of the English to determine their future.

The Viceroy was already aware of the transformation of opinion, but it did not affect his belief in a Parliamentary Commission. In a letter to the Secretary of State on 16 November he said:

'If we had had a mixed Commission I still think that with the commitments of the past it would have been almost certain that unless you had had tame Indians which would have been quite useless from a political point of view here, those Indians whom you had appointed would have sought refuge, as is their way, in signing together a report containing general aspirations. . . .

'They would not have been out to ascertain facts, but rather to press their case. If to such a nebulous report they had managed to attach one or two of the British members, we should have had to contemplate either of two undesirable prospects. The first would have been that British opinion, even if unwilling to accept such advice, would have found itself gravely embarrassed in resisting it; and the second would have been that even if it had been a minority report which the British opinion had decided to reject, the fact of its doing so would have been hailed as conclusive proof that we were impervious to argument and had decided the case in our own minds before the investigation began.

'I am afraid I feel that at some point or other a clash between what even moderate Indian political leaders feel bound to demand and what the majority of British opinion would feel able to give is inevitable, and I am not sure that it is not better to have it at this stage than later.'[1]

But the Viceroy was aware that although the clamour was directed against the exclusion of two or three Indians from the Commission, the real point at issue was fundamental.

'I think that political India of nearly all shades of thought is more and more tending under extremist pressure to revolt against the claim of the British people to judge the rate of Indian progress. Their conception of how matters ought to proceed is that India has an inherent and indefeasible right to self-government, and that, this being so, the precise method should be decided by consultation between equals. We all know the answer to this, which I believe more and more to be the truth, but we must not expect that

---

[1] India Office Library, MSS. EUR.C. 152/3, *Lord, Irwin. Letters to the Secretary of State for India*, pp. 224–5.

hat it will ever win acceptance in the outward acts or words of any substantial section of the political intelligentsia.'[1]

The answer was that at the present moment it was impossible for the Viceroy and the British Government to regard the political and articulate classes as representative of the dumb masses of India or to forget their responsibility to these millions of people. 'We have,' he told his father, 'a responsibility to these last, however unpopular it may be to say so, we cannot rightly share with Indians who will not for some time take the same view of their responsibilities to them as we do. I think too we are bound to have a clash with Indian opinion at some point, inasmuch as what they are bound by past professions to demand is very much in advance of what I can imagine any British opinion at present willing to give.'[2]

*   *   *

The Viceroy had now come to the arduous part of his journey. The smooth road had broken at his feet into a boulder-strewn track winding up into ever rougher and more unfriendly regions. He was reassured by the knowledge that however violently he was assaulted, he would be buttressed in every unpopular decision by the robust authority of Birkenhead who, although his speeches on India sometimes caused embarrassment to Irwin, gave him powerful and continuous support as long as their policies coincided.

But in the present circumstances, as was truly said, 'Were the Secretary of State never so strong or well-informed, he could not command the Viceroy's conduct any more than the Secretary of State for War can control the decisions of his Commander in Chief in the field when the battle is fairly joined, and the ranks of the fighting men sway to and fro, and the issue, with all its dread import, hangs in the balance.' Such a man may have able subordinates, but the responsibility is his alone. So it was with Lord Irwin the moment that India was on the move, and the ultimate decision to parley with the leader of the rebels was his, and not that of his advisers.

Before publishing his announcement of the appointment of the Simon Commission the Viceroy decided to invest the occasion with as much importance as possible by inviting the chief All-India leaders of every party to a private and personal meeting in Delhi at which he explained the terms of the announcement and invited comments from his guests, and it was at this meeting that he met Gandhi for the first time.

Gandhi had made the long journey from Mangalore in the South of India, and the Viceroy's treatment of him at this first meeting has been seriously misrepresented. It was stated by one of Gandhi's biographers, Louis Fischer, that Irwin merely handed Gandhi the document and dismissed him with a

[1] Ibid.
[2] Hickleton Papers, *Correspondence with Viscount Halifax*, April 1926–April 1931, p. 136.

few curt words, thus missing a priceless opportunity of discussing the issues that lay between them.[1]

Gopal observed that 'The cursory nature of the interview was disappointing to Gandhi and Indian opinion; they did not appreciate that the Viceroy was regarded by many as having gone alarmingly far in seeing Gandhi at all.'[2]

In fact, Gandhi and Irwin had a long conversation at this first meeting at which they listened to one another with exemplary patience and courtesy. Gandhi was in good humour and made several cumbrous efforts at badinage, promising to convert the Viceroy to Khaddar. He listened to Irwin attentively, and, after he had finished, developed his own general political philosophy at length. He saw no need for British tutelage. He was prepared to wait indefinitely rather than ask India to impair the self-respect she ought to have. Parliament, he said, should give India what India desired. Therefore he felt remote from all these things. Congress was trying to serve an idea—the idea of non-co-operation, which would ultimately impress itself upon the mind of Parliament. Communalism would pass; the communities had been trying to absorb India.[3]

It was Irwin's first experience of the Mahatma's incoherent political technique. He found him vague and discursive but without bitterness, and in conversation pleasantly reasonable. But there was little in his rambling discourse on which the Viceroy's practical mind could take hold. It was like grappling with a wrestler whose body had been greased and on whom no purchase could be gained. Only when Gandhi and the others said that they attached little importance to the procedure by which the representatives from the Indian Legislature would be invited to confer with the English Parliamentary Committee did Irwin seize the chance of telling them sharply that if they refrained from availing themselves of this opportunity, they would be committing a political blunder of the first magnitude and would hopelessly prejudice British opinion against their case.[4]

The Viceroy hastened to describe to his father his first impression of this baffling creature:

'I have broken the ice and met Gandhi. He really is an interesting personality. Of course his political position is that England and the English Parliament have no moral claim to be the judges of Indian progress, and inasmuch as they are constitutionally in the position of exercising legislative authority, what they ought to do is, as in the case of Ireland, to recognize that India should be accorded Dominion Status, and then to meet Indians and discuss the precise methods and the details by which and through which this could be accomplished.

[1] Louis Fischer, *Mahatma Gandhi*, pp. 273-4.
[3] S. Gopal. Op. cit., p. 20.
[2] Correspondence with the Secretary of State for India on the Statutory Commission, June 1926–April 1928, pp. 71-2.
[4] Ibid.

'This being his broad position, he was naturally, as he said, not greatly interested in any procedure that rested upon the totally different basis of Parliament having a moral obligation and responsibility itself for what should be done in the matter, and he struck me as singularly remote from practical politics. It was rather like talking to someone who had stepped off another planet on to this for a short visit of a fortnight and whose whole mental outlook was quite other to that which was regulating most of the affairs on the planet to which he had descended.'[1]

This first meeting with Gandhi then had in no way been a question of an ultimatum bluntly presented, and a curt dismissal. There had been friendly and wide-ranging conversations which, if they led to little, at least established that essential contact. The fact, also, that the mighty Viceroy of India had at last descended from Olympian seclusion and taken the Indian leaders into his confidence, and received them in his own palace was not lost upon the Indian people whose imagination was stirred, and who saw in this gesture a happy augury for the future.

We have seen that there was a sound convention in British India that the Viceroy should spend Christmas in surroundings where he could make personal contact with the non-official elements in the country and learn their opinions more realistically than was possible through the cold medium of official reports. After his announcement of the Commission he decided to visit Bombay and the West of India, passing on his way through districts badly damaged by floods two months earlier.

A great deal of importance was attached to the Viceroy's visit, and it was hoped that by his personal influence and tact he might do something to arrest the growing hostility of the great Indian city, as much a centre of commercial activity as Calcutta, but where power was concentrated in Indian rather than in European hands.

The great Bombay industrialists and leaders of high finance were, at the end of 1927, nourishing grievances against the Government of India based on complaints of currency legislation, which was said to have affected adversely the export of agricultural produce, one of the most important concerns of the city of Bombay.

The wealth of these industrialists and financiers was largely responsible for maintaining the Congress Party, and their contributions provided a solid basis for the Indian Nationalist movement. It was inevitable that these men, by virtue of their power, should be more directly concerned with politics than their counterparts elsewhere in India; and it was hoped that the Viceroy, by a mixture of charm and common sense, would do much to neutralize the present sourness of their disposition, and even to reconcile them to the Statutory Commission.

A second reason for the Viceroy's presence in Bombay was the visit to

[1] Hickleton Papers, *Correspondence with Viscount Halifax*, p. 137.

the city of King Amanullah of Afghanistan, the strategic position of whose country lent him a particular importance in the eyes of the Government of India, and whose arrival with a retinue of villainous appearance and dubious moral habits was now awaited. Lord Irwin was not invigorated at the prospect.

'I am afraid Bombay will be a tiresome week,' he told his father, 'very full of engagements and with this dreadful Afghan visit stuffed in on top of everything else. I would like, when it is over, to go to bed for a week.' This, unhappily, proved to be his destination, for after a few days in Bombay he was attacked by a violent bout of malaria which left him limp for weeks, and feeble as a child. It was an unfortunate development, for his accessibility to Indians, his extraordinary patience in listening to involved narrative and his quick mental grasp might well have caused the business community to offer a less bleak welcome when Sir John Simon and his colleagues disembarked in their city. As it was, he could only lie in bed in Government House at Bombay feeling 'like a chewed bit of string', and extracting what amusement he could from the reports of the Afghans' behaviour.

'The Afghan visit,' he informed Halifax, 'went off quite well. One or two were inclined to be tiresome at first and Sir Francis Humphrys had to speak very plainly to them. I believe when they heard that I was ill, and not going to meet them at Bombay, they decided it was not necessary for them to land in Full Dress, and accordingly packed all their Full Dress up in their Heavy Luggage which they were sending on shore when Sir Francis Humphrys went on board to pay his respects to the King. He protested and said they must at once get it all out again, and when they demurred, said to them: "If King George heard of this he would say you were a lot of barbarians who ought never to have come down from your trees in Kabul." I think the suggestion of trees is delicious. . . . According to Dorothy, their conversation at meals was very limited; it mainly turned upon inquiring how many children everybody had got and why they hadn't got more.'[1]

When the Viceroy had recovered from his fever and surveyed the scene at the beginning of 1928, it did not appear to him altogether gloomy. The greater portion of the minority communities had decided to co-operate with the Commission, as had also the majority of the Sikhs. He had reason to believe that other Provincial Legislatures would follow the lead soon to be given by the Punjab, Burma and Assam in appointing Committees to help the Commission in its investigation. He was also much encouraged by a prediction that there would be found even on the Councils of Bombay and Bengal a preponderance of members who wished to co-operate.

He was aware, however, that when the issue came to be decided in the Central Legislature, it would be a desperately close-run thing. Here where the vote counted so much in general significance, and where opposition to

[1] Ibid., pp. 142–3.

the Government would be most widely certified to the public understanding, the forces were evenly divided, with a section of the Moslems under Jinnah committed to the policy of boycott.

The Viceroy had made a strong but vain attempt to detach Jinnah from a course of action which he believed injurious to both the Moslem community and the interests of India as a whole. On 23 December he had informed the Secretary of State that: 'Present indications seem to show that the protagonists of the Bombay boycott party, i.e. Setalvad and Jinnah, would be willing to meet Simon on his arrival. I met the latter in Bombay a week ago and urged him to hold his hand until he had talked to Simon, and I have reason to believe from a third party that he was impressed by this exhortation.'[1]

There were ominous symptoms abroad which the Viceroy did not fail to observe. He could perceive a mood of arrogant assertion in such members of the Hindu Mahasabha as Moonje, which had caused the Moslem leader, Shaukat Ali, to say that they were aiming at a Hindu dictatorship, a new raj. Such Hindu leaders had made it plain that their great majority was in no way to be denied, and that whatever report the Commission made, they would not tolerate communal priorities with Moslems in charge of them.

The old communal spectre, far from withering away, was assuming a new and more malignant guise. Meanwhile, the Congress was carrying their propaganda of hatred and lies into the Indian villages and countryside, trying, like Montagu, but for less worthy reasons, to disturb 'the pathetic contentment of the Indian masses', to stir them out of their ancient torpor and to remove the wax of centuries from their ears. The emissaries of this resourceful and well-organized party were sent out over the length and breadth of rural India and subjected the peasants to a process of conversion equivalent in its mendacity to debauching the minds of children. Their efforts were rewarded by a slow and irrational surge of resentment against the Government of India and those who served it.

An agitation equally intense was carried out among the youth in the great cities of India, and here the results were entirely evil. Youth movements were formed and incited with appalling irresponsibility by Jawaharlal Nehru and Chandra Bose, the two *jeunes premiers* of this macabre drama. It was difficult to believe that the slick youths of the Indian cities, half-educated on Western lines, horribly excitable, and longing for violent methods, could belong to the same country as those humble ryots who had lived for centuries in the sunswept villages of India, remote for so long from the turmoil of the world, their interests confined to their strip of land and instruments of primitive husbandry. But they were both part of that same India over which

[1] Correspondence with the Secretary of State for India on the Statutory Commission, June 1926–April 1929, p. 113.

the Viceroy was ruling and for whose problems he must soon discover some kind of solution.

His next step was made on the day before the arrival of the Simon Commission in Bombay, and was a last-minute attempt to obtain co-operation with their efforts. On 2 February 1928 he addressed the Indian Legislature. The Chamber was set for a great occasion, and the leaders of all parties crowded the benches. There was Motilal Nehru, inscrutable in white homespun; there was Malaviya with his nationalists, and the Moslem leaders with faces as 'rugged as their own frontier hills'. There was a sense of expectancy in this Parliament where every inch of floor and gallery was occupied, which was noticed by a member of the Viceroy's staff in whose recollection the scene was enduring:

'From the scarlet, gold-embroidered throne on the President's dais Lord Irwin looked down on his audience, and as they looked up at the tall figure reading the measured words with grave emphasis, their eyes could not have missed a row of bright metal plaques on the panelling of the Chamber and on both sides of the throne.

'For those gifted with imagination there was a whole world of promise in those plaques which caught the hard, glaring sunlight of a brilliant February morning in Delhi and transmuted it into soft colours, sending blue and crimson and purple bars across the motes dancing in the shafts of sunlight. For these plaques were the heraldic devices of India and the other Dominions of the great Commonwealth of Nations. And below them Lord Irwin was pointing out to India's representatives the road for India to take to find herself an acceptable and accepted member, resting in that Commonwealth as her device rests among theirs on the walls of the Parliament Chamber.'[1]

The Viceroy tried in the most persuasive language to recover lost ground, and to persuade his audience of the generosity of the arrangement by which the association of Indians with the Commission had been provided, but he cannot have failed to observe many grim and unresponsive faces surmounting white Khaddar on the benches where sat Motilal Nehru and his Congress supporters. The Viceroy drew an almost cosy picture of the consultations that would take place between the Indian legislators and the English Parliamentarians in some Committee Room at Westminster, and he made an emphatic denial of the charge that by appointing a Parliamentary Commission the British Government had placed a deliberate affront upon the Indian people:

'In the present case British statesmen of all parties have stated in terms admitting of no misconception that the appointment of a Parliamentary Commission was in no way intended as an affront to India. Time and again this assertion has been repeated, and I would ask in all sincerity by what right do leaders of Indian opinion, who are as jealous as I am of their own good

[1] J. Coatman. Op. cit., pp. 183–4.

faith, and would resent as sharply as I any refusal to believe their word, impugn the good faith and disbelieve the plain word of others?'[1]

Lord Irwin's courtesy and compelling arguments, and the harder note that had entered his speech when he spoke of honour impugned, made their due impression on a large part of his audience, but could not move from their path those who had determined to wreck the Commission.

*   *   *

On the following day, 3 February, Sir John Simon and his colleagues landed at Bombay. Their arrival was saluted by crowds bearing banners with the hospitable inscription: 'Simon Go Back'. The more optimistic observed that the welcome was a mixed one and that many Indians carried garlands and flowers. The hartals and demonstrations that were to herald their arrival were damped physically and morally by the heavy rain that was falling and were, even to their most sanguine promoters, half-hearted affairs.

On arrival at Delhi Simon and the members of his Commission were taken to the Western Hostel where many members of the Indian Legislature were lodged when the Assembly was in session. Rosy visions had been entertained by the Government of India of Simon and his colleagues in easy social intercourse with members of Congress in its pleasant atmosphere, and thus breaking the ice at an early stage. This pathetic illusion was soon shattered when the Indian leaders and their party members cut the Commission dead and froze the smiles of friendship on their lips.

This remorseless attitude caused even the patience of the Viceroy to wear thin, and he showed his acute disappointment in a letter to the Secretary of State on 9 February which contained sharp references to the Indian leaders and described how Simon had believed that the situation could be restored by the issue of a statement inviting Indians to co-operate in his work.

It was Simon's belief that such immediate publication was desirable both from the point of view of his own task in India, and also having regard to the probable reaction of the English Labour Party to the hartal agitation in Bombay. He was emphatic that nothing in what he intended to say conflicted with the principle laid down by the Government.

'The grounds on which he reached this conclusion were principally the necessity of making his own position clear without delay, and of giving the Labour Party at home a good platform from which to repel any attacks of their own Left Wing. . . .

'The second reflection is that the Indian politician, to a greater extent even than I had thought possible, is lacking in moral courage. I haven't yet discovered the man who is prepared to stand up against the clamour of his friends or of newspapers. They just wilt. . . . Until they can acquire some

[1] Government of India Press, *Speeches by Lord Irwin*, Vol. I, p. 396.

quality which they at present lack, I fail to see how they can effectively gain the self-respect of which they are so jealous.'[1]

With the approval of the Secretary of State and the Viceroy, Sir John Simon then played his trump card. He proposed that the evidence that came before the Commission should not be examined merely by himself and his colleagues, but should come before a 'Joint Free Conference' over which he would preside, consisting of the seven British Commissioners and a corresponding body of representatives chosen from the Indian Legislature, 'just as we ourselves have been chosen by the British Parliament'.

The Joint Free Conference would sit and take evidence in regard to the central subjects, and a similar proceeding would be adopted in the Provinces. Simon was at pains, in the letter in which he put forward this proposal to the Viceroy, to emphasize the importance he attached to Indian co-operation. He made clear, as was indeed his duty, that the British Commissioners must report to Parliament which had set them up, just as the Indians, he presumed, would make their report to the Indian Legislature that had chosen them. But if they preferred it, he would make their report an annexe to his own document so that both might be presented to the King-Emperor and made public simultaneously.

No olive branch could have been more delicately proffered, but the part of the letter which dealt with the method of reporting gave the boycotting leaders the opportunity for rejection which they desired. They would no doubt have accepted a suggestion that the Indian members chosen should sit on the Commission on equal terms with the English members and sign a joint report, but it was precisely this kind of Commission that the British Government had already refused.

Sir John Simon's well-meaning proposals had once again stirred that sense of inferiority and deep suspicion. The Indians found implied insult where none existed, believing that once again they were being denied that equality of status to which they clung as their birthright. 'Indian leaders of opinion,' wrote Gopal, 'had no difficulty in rejecting the offer outright. So long as the Indian communities could not share the authority and duty of the Commission it was difficult to believe that they would enjoy equal status. No "Joint Free Conference" could take the place of the Commission which alone could report to Parliament and whose recommendations alone would carry weight.'[2]

Another passage in Sir John Simon's letter, equally reasonable and expressed with consummate tact, merely accentuated these suspicions. In it he had observed that it was obvious that both sides of the Joint Free Conference, British and Indian, would on occasion desire to meet on their own. Normally evidence would be given to the Conference as a whole, but:

[1] India Office Library, MSS. EUR.C. 152/4, *Lord Irwin. Letters to the Secretary of State for India*, pp. 117–18.
[2] S. Gopal. Op. cit.

'If a case arises when this general plan cannot be followed I should make no secret of it, and should ask my colleagues in the Joint Free Conference, when, as I hope, they learn to have faith in my sense of fairness, to accept from me such account of the matter as I can give them on behalf of the Commission, with due regard to the reason why the testimony has been separately received. I imagine that the Indian side may find occasions when they would think it well to act in the same way.'[1]

In this simple and friendly statement the boycotting parties found further Machiavellian undertones. They saw visions of Simon and his friends in sinister collusion with European businessmen, disloyal Indian witnesses, Government officials and other agencies venomous in their intentions towards the cause of Indian nationalism. This suggestion of separate sessions was afterwards withdrawn, too late to affect the boycott. This had been decided upon in mid-February, and its leaders wasted no time in their response to Simon's approach. A few hours after his letter had reached them their answer was published, and it was a declaration of war.

'We have most carefully considered the line of procedure indicated in the statement of Sir John Simon issued today. But our objections to the Commission as constituted, and the scheme as announced, are based on principles which remain unaffected by it. In the circumstances we must adhere to our decision that we cannot have anything to do with the Commission at any stage or in any form.'

It seemed to the Viceroy, when he considered this intransigent statement and contemplated the general behaviour of the boycotting parties, that the dominant motive in their minds was to use every means to escape being placed in a position that would involve the acceptance of a constructive obligation. The position of destructive critics on a mixed Commission would, he thought, have suited their desires 'much more nearly than any position such as we propose to allot to them, in which dissent from any scheme recommended by the Commission would have placed them under the necessity of countering it by a watertight effort of their own and where failure to do this would have laid them under discredit naked and unconcealed'.[2]

A week later the great debate on the Simon Commission took place in the Legislative Assembly on a resolution moved by a Hindu Nationalist Member from the Punjab that the Statutory Commission was not acceptable to Parliament which should dissociate itself entirely from its proceedings. The forces were so evenly divided that intensive lobbying took place on the eve of the debate, the weaker brethren reeling back and forth under the impact of the last advice they had received.

The Viceroy thought that the motion would be carried by a narrow margin

[1] *Correspondence with Sir John Simon on the Statutory Commission*, 6 February 1928.
[2] India Office Library, MSS. EUR.C. 152/4, *Lord Irwin. Letters to the Secretary of State for India*, p. 18.

and contemplated the possibility with his habitual calm. Once again the scene was set for high drama, and this time it was provided by an unforgettable speech by a leader of the Depressed Classes, Rao Bahadur M. C. Rajah. It required courage of a high order for this Untouchable to confront the disdainful ranks of the Brahmins and other Caste Hindus who sat before him, and to utter with such eloquence and passion his *cri de coeur* on behalf of his afflicted people.

It seemed to the onlookers that the debate was lifted in those moments above the stale air of ordinary politics. 'Behind Rao Bahadur M. C. Rajah,' said one of them, 'were thousands of years of such oppression and degradation as no European countries have ever known, not even in the days of slavery. The Rao Bahadur was breaking through mental and spiritual inhibitions forged and wielded by uncounted generations of depression and deprivation of many of the fundamental rights of humanity.'

Sir Basil Blackett, the Leader of the House, made a brilliant speech for the Government, but on 18 February, amid intense excitement, the motion was carried by six votes. An Indian reporter was so transported that he hurled a despatch case from the Press Gallery striking Sir Basil on the head, and the Minister's resilience was immortalized in a telegram which, by an error of encoding, informed the Secretary of State that Blackett had 'never entirely lost conscientiousness'.

It was an irrevocable step that was taken that day by the Hindus and a group of dissident Moslems, and one that could not be retraced, brutally widening the gulf that already yawned between the Hindus and the rest of India, a miserable caricature of statesmanship pregnant with future suffering. But it cannot be denied that this victory enhanced the stature of the Indian political leaders to an extent which even they, flushed with triumph, failed to appreciate.

That moment marked an invisible but momentous shifting in the relations between England and India, in which her leaders had immensely strengthened both their bargaining position and their claim to equal status with the ruling Power in a manner which bore no relation to their statutory inferiority. Juridically they were still entirely subject to the control of the British Parliament. In fact they had already advanced to the position of men who could discuss their future on almost equal terms with their English rulers.

Such a fundamental change was not easy to discern at the time it was taking place, and the Viceroy was not unduly concerned when he reported the result of the debate to the Secretary of State:

'The influences making for boycott are of course varied; with some the expectation that the Government or the Labour Party will change their policy in the matter; with others a curious conviction that everybody in England have made up their minds that India is to have no advance and that where nothing is at stake nothing is lost by standing on one side.

'I find this attitude of mind prevailing very much among men of the Liberal school, from whom, if from anywhere, one might expect a reconsideration of the course on which they have embarked. The general result may be that having got so far, they will stick to boycott. I still rather doubt it, but I am quite certain that the right course, now that they have been plainly told by you in England and by Simon and myself out here that the Commission must carry on its work, is to leave them quite alone and simply let the business go on, saying as little as possible about it. I think it is really very much like a child refusing to eat its supper. There comes a point when it is no good pleading or reproaching any longer and when, if its tempers are ignored, it may return to eat it on its own.'[1]

Instead he was to find that the boycotters held to their course, and even attempted to achieve some kind of unity among themselves, but the series of 'unity conferences' which were held in 1928 did not succeed in their object. They had rejected the offers of mediation made by the one man whose persuasive powers of conciliation and unique prestige could alone have drawn them together.

The Viceroy's known willingness to preside over meetings of both communities was ignored. The majority of Moslems refused to attend these unity conferences, and even the sacred bond of boycott itself could not confine the Hindus and Moslems who were applying it within a common purpose. In a manner typical of the whole hopeless dispute each busied themselves with intrigues to further the interests of their own community.

At this period the Viceroy had not yet turned to the bold expedient he was to recommend of a public statement that Dominion Status was the accepted goal of Indian progress. No such ideas had yet entered his head. On the contrary, he was conducting a straightforward policy in entire agreement with the Secretary of State of awaiting the Report of the Simon Commission, and in no way interfering with its activities. How far he was from any such step at that moment is evident from a letter written to the Secretary of State in May 1928:

'I see that Ramsay [MacDonald] has been spreading himself on the line of promising Dominion Status to India when a Labour Government is returned after the next election. I hope this means that he has no serious doubt about our Party coming back to power, and it has been generally so interpreted in the Indian Press, with the honourable exception, so far as I can gather, of Annie Besant. But it would sound an unprincipled statement for him to have made, because he knows too much about it all, I should have thought, seriously to believe his own statement.'[2]

*　　　*　　　*

[1] India Office Library, MSS. EUR.C. 152/4, *Lord Irwin. Letters to the Secretary of State for India*, p. 28.
[2] Ibid., p. 115.

While these abortive efforts at cohesion were petering out another and more comprehensive experiment was launched, also directed towards the achievement of Hindu-Moslem harmony, by hammering out an agreed constitution for India which would prove to the English that the two parties were not in fact irreconcilable, and would be both a rival to the proposals of the Simon Report and a grave embarrassment to its authors and to the Government which had appointed them.

A permanent body called the All-Parties Conference was set up in February 1928 by the President of the Congress to carry out this task. Their efforts had been much stimulated by a speech of Lord Birkenhead whose name was anathema to Indian nationalists, in which he had spoken of the inability of Indians to combine in a common purpose, and had appeared to challenge them to produce a constitution of their own.

It seemed that Birkenhead's analysis of the situation was correct when the All-Parties Conference almost immediately became a battlefield of communal dissension. The discussions were further darkened by the news that every Provincial Council in India but one had decided to co-operate with the Simon Commission, and they were forced to take refuge in that last resort of conferences, a sub-committee. This was appointed in May with Motilal Nehru and Sapru as its most prominent members, and it was mainly due to the resolution of these two men that a document, which was afterwards to become famous as the Nehru Report, was published in August 1928 and discussed at the All-Parties Conference at Lucknow on the 28th of that month.

This then was the answer to Birkenhead's challenge to the Indians to show creative rather than destructive powers. It represented an effort to reach the highest common measure of agreement on the political issue and link it with a solution of the communal problem.

The Nehru Report provided that India's status was not to be lower than that of the self-governing Dominions and that the India Office was to be abolished. 'Full Responsible Government', a phrase designed to cover both Dominion Status or Complete Independence, was to be transferred to the people of India. Separate electorates were to be discarded but there was to be reservation of seats for ten years to Moslems in Provinces where they formed a minority, and to non-Moslem minorities in the North West Frontier Province and Baluchistan. Sind was to become a separate Province with a Moslem majority.[1]

It was an ambitious performance, but it contained provisions that were utterly unacceptable to Moslems and were to range the entire Muhammadan community against it. For there was to be no reservation of seats except in Provinces where Moslems were in a minority, and this was a paralysing blow to their hopes of obtaining the majority of seats in the Bengal and Punjab Councils, and to their demands for the continuance of separate electorates.

[1] S. Gopal. Op. cit., pp. 28-29.

Birkenhead had been right in his belief that no constitution which enjoyed the unqualified agreement of both sides would emerge from India. Indeed, one result of the Nehru Report was so to sift the boycotting elements that the Moslems were to desert their ranks and join the majority of their co-religionists outside.

The Viceroy was not surprised by this trend of events which he had closely followed. He was irritated by the facile manner in which the Nehru Report skirted round such matters as defence, and by other formidable objections to the scheme which did not fit in with their political desires. Explaining the situation to the Secretary of State on 6 September, he wrote:

'The great majority of Muhammadans, who were not represented at the Lucknow Conference, are, through certain of their leaders, going to hold meetings at Simla this week-end with the idea of issuing an authoritative rejection of the so-called agreements reached at Lucknow. Meanwhile the leaders of the Hindu Mahasabha are significantly silent, and it is interesting that on Tuesday afternoon Pandit Motilal Nehru ordered certain members of his party, who wished to move a resolution about the Lucknow Conference and its decisions, to take no action of any sort. The reason seems to be that any resolution on this subject moved from the opposition benches would be defeated, for practically all Muhammadans in the Assembly are opposed to the Communal sections of the Nehru-Sapru constitution and a debate in the House would be likely to impair, if not altogether wreck, what is being described by certain newspapers as the Second Lucknow Pact.'[1]

Jawaharlal Nehru had been unable to stomach the moderation with which a Government 'in no event lower than that of any self-governing Dominion' had been demanded at Lucknow, and at the Calcutta session of Congress in December demanded unqualified independence, and a compromise had been reached that if the British Government did not accept the Nehru Report by the end of 1929, Congress would organize a campaign of non-violent non-co-operation. The Calcutta session also destroyed any lingering hope of a settlement with the Moslem politicians by granting reservation of seats in the Provinces for ten years only, and making no provision for separate Moslem representation in the Central Legislature. The Viceroy spoke with indignation to Patel about these proceedings in a manner which showed that he was still firmly behind the Statutory Commission:

'I directed his attention to the situation created by the recent meeting of Congress at Calcutta, and, in particular, the Resolution foreshadowing Civil Disobedience on 1 January 1930, if by that time Dominion Status had not been conferred on India. I told him that this action . . . had created an impossible situation from which, so far as I could see, there was no issue. I could not foresee it possible that the present Government in England, or any

[1] India Office Library, MSS. EUR.C. 152/4, *Lord Irwin. Letters to the Secretary of State for India*, p. 193.

Government that might succeed it as a result of the Elections, would be willing to tear up the Royal Warrant appointing the Commission and ignore the Report the Commission would make. . . .

'Any such action would be so complete a stultification of everything that Parliament had done that it was outside practical politics. . . . The moderate wing of Congress, Liberals and Parliament, each from their different point of view, were or would be outraged by this ultimatum and by the future that it envisaged. . . .

'In reply to this he said that he had seen Gandhi when he had returned through Delhi, and that Gandhi had said to him quite categorically that he was in favour of the British connection and that he would not make difficulty about an accommodation of the Dominion Status idea by which Foreign Affairs, Political and possibly Defence should be reserved in some manner to be defined. He added that he himself thought the time limit a mistake, though he said that without it an open split could not have been avoided.'[1]

Nineteen twenty-eight was thus a year of preparation, of alignment of forces, of manœuvring for position. Towards the end of it V. J. Patel, the President, had begun that course of obstruction in the Legislative Assembly which was to continue until his resignation and imprisonment. Lord Irwin's relations with this devious old man alternated between amusement at his antics and exasperation at the trouble they caused. The skirmishing had begun in the autumn session of 1928 on the initial stages of the Public Safety Bill, which was designed to empower the Government to deport non-Indians guilty of subversive activities, and thus to counteract the dangers that were now threatening India through the infiltration of Communist agents.

It was also falsely believed that the Government of India had instigated European journalists to question the fairness of Patel's rulings. Patel and his supporters, by encouraging such rumours, succeeded in creating the impression that the ageing President of the Assembly was a martyr riddled by arrows. He spent his ample leisure in studying precedents and devising traps, particularly for the Home Member, Sir James Crerar, who became the principal victim of his machinations. By such methods Patel soon became the darling of the Left Wing of Congress, and in the hothouse atmosphere of Indian politics the most absurd rumours and accusations were seldom weighed and examined.

They were accepted like a revealed religion with the President as its new deity, the scourge of the Government of India and all oppressors. Nor had these aspirants to 'complete independence' the least conception of how adversely this deplorable behaviour reflected on their own capacity as parliamentarians and their prospects for the future. Rather were they disposed

[1] India Office Library, MSS. EUR.C. 152/5, *Lord Irwin. Letters to the Secretary of State for India*, pp. 18–19.

to regard the whole business as an amusing game, recounting the latest discomfiture of Crerar and his colleagues to members of the Government as though they were participating in a huge joke, while Patel himself, discussing his functions as President and Speaker, observed that 'Sweet reasonableness to the British was no part of my duty as I understood it.'[1]

The Viceroy, although determined to remain aloof from these squalid altercations and to avoid any suggestion of partisanship, was occasionally forced into the *mêlée*, and some of his interviews with the President produced an entirely false impression of favouritism on the minds of a number of Government officials, and a feeling that the Viceroy had given inadequate support to his Home Member. The Viceroy did not, in fact, mince his words when dealing with Patel. He reported to the Secretary of State:

'A very uncomfortable situation had developed in the course of the last days in the Assembly. A great deal of irresponsible chatter has been going on, alleging partiality on the part of Patel, and suggesting that his rulings were put-up jobs with the Leader of the Opposition. This has found an echo in some messages of Press Correspondents, and the result has been to throw the Assembly into a great ferment of indignation, in which the wildest rumours of Government intrigue have obtained ready credence.

'The situation was rapidly becoming impossible and seemed to me capable of doing considerable harm. I accordingly sent for Patel on Sunday night and had a long talk to him. . . . I made it plain to him that the situation was largely of his own making, in that, if he had seen fit to impose the same measure of restraint on his external activities as was observed by the Speaker of the British House of Commons, the soil in which the gossip grew would never have been prepared, and that accordingly he had himself very much to thank for the discredit that the events brought both on the Assembly and on its principal officer.'[2]

It was depressing for the Viceroy to be compelled to witness the steady debasement of Indian public life, but he knew that it would be dangerous to take the normal constitutional step of removing Patel from the Chair. The President had established himself in the eyes of his supporters as the symbol of India at bay. Lord Irwin had little opinion of the man; he regarded his character as shifty and his brain slow and muddled, but he knew that his removal would be a fatal mistake. It would destroy, at a blow, the fragile edifice of confidence the Viceroy was building with the Indian leaders, and gravely weaken his hand in any future negotiations that might depend upon their goodwill.

Anxiety, at the end of 1928, was not confined to the Viceroy and his advisers. In the ranks of the Congress Party had begun one of those splits so

[1] S. Gopal. Op. cit., p. 40.
[2] India Office Library, MSS. EUR.C. 152/4, *Lord Irwin. Letters to the Secretary of State for India*, p. 210.

characteristic of Indian politics and their volatile practitioners. The leadership had now come to be disputed by Motilal Nehru and Srinivasa Iyengar, whose reliability for the position may be judged by the fact that when Lord Irwin confided in him in strict confidence the names of the Statutory Commission he had immediately revealed them to the Press. The issue between them lay partly in the alternative demands for India of Dominion Status or complete independence, Motilal believing that to persist in this extreme claim would split the Congress Party, and also detach the Liberals and Nationalists from their ranks.

The background to these events was a sudden and grim acceleration of those crimes of violence to which India is so prone in moments of political or religious excitement. Industry was paralysed by protracted and violent strikes, trains were wrecked, buildings burned, and men killed in the streets. A young policeman, Saunders, was brutally murdered in Lahore. It was a crime which, more than any other, brought home to the Government the full extent of the *dégringolade*. It impressed the older and more sober members of Congress with the fear that their politics had become touched by the fever of anarchy, and would, before long, drift into utter disruption, but to the younger element the murderer was an idealist who had struck in the cause of India, and, when the Viceroy later refused to reprieve him, a martyr who had died for her.

CHAPTER XV

THE VICEROY'S OFFER

As a result of these disturbing events Gandhi had been recalled to public life to exert the old magic of his influence upon the people. He alone of the Indian leaders had remained aloof from the politics of the last four years. The scene of his return was the Calcutta meeting of Congress, and the drafting of the Resolution too had been his work, a masterpiece of the reconciliation of conflicting opinions, and a revelation of how far Congress was prepared to go to present the appearance of a united front.

Gandhi had devoted the years since his release from jail to 'purifying India' and preaching the brotherhood of man to an uncaring world. The ghastly communal riots that poisoned these years would have daunted a less ardent spirit. He told the faithful disciples in his ashram that when India was purged she would be freed, and he devoted much thought in his seclusion to the Hindu-Moslem impasse and wrote about it at length in his paper *Young India*. His fellow Hindus did not escape the lash. He chided them bitterly for those two great disfigurements on the Hindu religion, child marriage and the Depressed Classes. He fasted in the house of a Moslem in a symbolic effort to provoke a spiritual response in the two communities and to move them towards harmony.

During this period he had not directed his teaching against the British power, and, except for one period as President of Congress, he sought by moral precept to elevate his countrymen from within. Certain barriers had still separated him in spirit from the educated Hindus in the Congress; he regarded them as intellectuals and professional politicians, and himself as a man of the people whose ear was tuned to the beating of their hearts. His greatest concern, he said, was the hardness of heart of the educated.

Slowly he had broken down the scepticism of these men about his campaign for wearing homespun. To Gandhi the spinning wheel was 'a gateway to my spiritual salvation', and to Jawaharlal Nehru, the rebel, these rough garments became 'the livery of our freedom'. In his journeys about India in 1925 Gandhi's identification with the people was finally achieved and the process of deification begun. 'At night his feet and shins were covered with scratches from people who had bowed low and touched him; his feet had to be rubbed with vaseline.'[1] But Gandhi disclaimed these efforts to thrust divinity upon him. When he was told in one place that a whole tribe was

[1] Louis Fischer. Op. cit., p. 249.

worshipping him, he repudiated the idolatry: 'I claim,' he said, 'to be a mere mortal, heir to all the weakness that human flesh betrays.'[1]

The Viceroy was aware that the return of this extraordinary man from his retreat presented him with a problem more subtle and impalpable than any he had yet encountered. He knew that ideas could not be confined behind prison bars, and that he would soon be at grips with his most formidable opponent whose weapons were those of the spirit, a most baffling enemy, generous, irrational and elusive, and as hard to pin down on a point of logic as a butterfly on the plains of his native Gujerat.

The Nehru Report had widened the gap between Hindu and Moslem, and Jinnah had carried this process a stage further at the All-Parties Conference which had met at Calcutta in December 1928 at the same time as Congress. He had now come to the conclusion that the relations between the two communities were approaching breaking point. He demanded for his followers a third of the elected seats in both Houses of the Indian Parliament, reservation of seats in the Punjab and Bengal, the vesting of residuary powers in the Provinces in a federal constitution, and the unconditional separation of Sind.

These terms were refused by the Hindu leaders at the All-Parties Conference, and Jinnah was said to have recognized in their decision the parting of the ways.[2] The issue between the two religions now seemed to him fundamental, and their reconciliation an insoluble problem. This attitude was later emphasized at a meeting at the beginning of 1929, presided over by the Aga Khan, which made demands even more inflexible than those of Jinnah and opened the way to the disruption of India and the creation of a separate Islamic State. 'So the end of the year saw the Congress preparing for struggle and losing the support of all sections of Moslem opinion outside its own ranks. Gandhi envisaged no severe campaign. The Constitutional Scheme embodied in the Nehru Report would be the war-cry, and boycott of foreign cloth and liquor, the programme of action.'[3]

The Viceroy also saw trouble ahead when he wrote to his father in January 1929:

'We have got a lot of tiresome shoals and storms around and ahead of us— Communists and people who are preaching Independence, and political agitators of all sorts, and particularly an obstreperous Press. And all this is a country where anti-Government agitation is apt to be taken at its face value and where there is little public opinion or judgment by which the extravagance of such things can be weighed. In short I look forward to a stormy year; and in the present temper of the Indian politician, I don't see any great prospect of easily getting things back into smooth waters at present.'[4]

He was right in this prediction. In the coming year, 1929, he was to become more and more involved in the tumult of Indian politics, first as an

---

[1] Louis Fischer. Op. cit., p. 249.   [2] S. Gopal. Op. cit., p. 87.   [3] Ibid.
[4] Hickleton Papers, Correspondence with Viscount Halifax, p. 22.

exponent of the Government's and, later, of his own personal policy. As time passed, the issue was to contract to a collision between two men, himself and Gandhi, each of whom had caught the imagination of the people in a manner astonishingly different. The patience, decency and integrity of the Viceroy were now widely recognized. He had made himself accessible to all with a freedom unknown in his predecessors, and men of different parties and conflicting religions left Lord Irwin's presence captivated by his charm.

Gandhi, even in the darkest moments to come, never faltered in his belief in the Viceroy's immaculate code of honour. Even Patel, although he believed him an enemy to the cause, was struck by his moral purpose and puzzled by how to deal with a character so foreign to his own.

There was, however, another aspect of the Viceroy which they soon learned to appreciate. They found that he was no starry-eyed idealist with misty visions of a better world. His mind had been trained in the Oxford Examination Schools and was a well-tempered instrument sharpened upon the academic grindstone, which cut without mercy through obscurantism and cant. In the place of an unworldly saint they often encountered a logician.

It was this radical dissimilarity which gives his relations with Gandhi in the struggle for the soul of India their peculiar fascination, and the Viceroy's strongest weapon was that patience which he opposed to all the twistings and contradictions of his evasive opponent. He offered to Gandhi the prospect of orderly and peaceful advance in agreement with the British Government, and he became an exemplar to all those elements in India which desired progress without chaos, and evolution without rebellion.

The Calcutta resolution of Congress had been a compromise in the cause of unity, and the Viceroy had kept a sharp eye on the situation that had developed from it. On 17 January 1929 he summarized it for the Secretary of State:

'The one thing that is clear is that everybody is dissatisfied with the Congress compromise Resolution. The Independence[1] people think that the pass has been sold, the Dominion[2] people see themselves being dragged into very dangerous quagmires, and the more moderate elements are, as always, inarticulate or not sufficiently organized to make their voice heard. There is quite clearly a strong movement to the left among advanced Hindu political opinion; there is equally clearly an increase of feeling and suspicion between Hindus and Moslems. The gulf between the Princes and British India is, as might be expected, being dug daily deeper by the extremism of British Indian politicians. . . . I propose to address the Assembly on the 28th and

[1] Those extremists who demanded complete independence from Britain rather than Dominion Status.

[2] Those who would have been content with the granting of Dominion status.

shall take the opportunity of pointing out, in language as little provocative as realities permit, what folly is enshrined in the Congress Resolution.'[1]

The Government of India had decided that the time had come to deal firmly with the terrorism and subversion of industry which had now gained an alarming strength, and at the January session of the Legislature they pressed on with the Public Safety Bill, and with the Trade Dispute Bill which made political strikes illegal.

Each measure was taken as a *casus belli* by the Opposition who developed the most violent attack on them that had been seen in the Assembly during Irwin's period of office. The vernacular Press maintained a shrill obligato of abuse; the President of the Assembly, Patel, did not even simulate the impartiality proper to his office, stretching the rules to the utmost in the interest of Opposition speakers. The Public Safety Bill was rejected by the Assembly, Patel using his casting vote against it. The endless wrangles were protracted into the savage heat of April in the plain of Delhi, and tempers grimly deteriorated. The whole of literate India hovered over the angry deliberations as relations between the Chair and the Government benches approached a crisis.

The ultimate disaster for the Viceroy and for India herself of the whole Opposition walking out of the Chamber for good, and leaving there only the Government and its supporters was averted largely by the personal influence of Lord Irwin. Those frequent journeys of Patel to Viceregal Lodge were not in vain. Irwin even discovered that he had a sort of affection for the incorrigible old fellow whose clumsy deceptions amused him, and, when Patel was constipated, gave him his own bottle of Petrolagar.

It was like playing chess, he thought, with someone who made no attempt to observe the rules that governed the game. Whatever the Viceroy thought of his difficult visitor, his temper was always serene, and his patience infinite. He knew, he told Patel, exactly what he was doing, but 'I will forget all your antics'. The Viceroy listened to the recitation of Patel's difficulties, and gave him encouragement and shrewd guidance. It was these frequent contacts that led to the murmurings of favouritism and weakness from official critics, but they were unfounded, for Irwin never forgot that he was speaking to an enemy, and was determined that the interests of the Government should not suffer.

It was not in his character to feel bitterness towards those who thought differently from himself, and during those difficult weeks he had constant visits from other members of Congress whom he treated with a similar courtesy, and it may well be that the confidence and admiration that his personality inspired at these meetings were a strong factor in preventing the Opposition from leaving the Assembly.

[1] India Office Library, MSS. EUR.C. 152/5, *Lord Irwin. Letters to the Secretary of State for India*, p. 15.

Irwin himself was now slowly arriving at the belief that the position in India had so deteriorated that it might require drastic treatment. 'I am impressed,' he wrote to the Secretary of State . . . 'with the possibility of the problem becoming even more intractable than it is at present, and assuming a shape that would not readily yield to the kind of treatment that the extreme wing of our Party might be disposed to recommend.'

A conversation with Chimanlal Setalvad a few days before lingered in his mind, and perhaps a seed had been dropped which, although he rejected it at the time, was afterwards to germinate. Setalvad had repeated several times that everything could be put right by some genuine gesture from the home Government:

'I pressed him as to what he meant, and the nearest that I could get to his mind was that at some stage the spokesmen of His Majesty's Government should make it plain that it was our object to lead India to Dominion Status, and that once this had been said the ways and means of doing so would be less intractable. I pointed out that it seemed illogical for any such statement to be made at this juncture, whatever its intrinsic merits or demerits might be, when for all he or I knew the Simon Report might be a unanimous recommendation in favour of going back instead of forward. . . . I give you this for what it is worth . . . because it is indicative of what I more and more come to believe is true, namely that in nearly all quarters except the most extreme there would be very genuine relief if some face-saving device which afforded an excuse for the introduction of saner counsels could be found.'[1]

The object of the Viceroy's meetings with hostile members of Congress had been both to understand the workings of their minds, and to plant in them a conviction of his own integrity. He could not forget that the Viceroy stood as intermediary between India and Great Britain, and that it was part of his duties to interpret the hopes and desires of Indians to the Government at home, and as he said in his speech at the beginning of this ill-omened session, 'to beg His Majesty's Government ever to place the most favourable construction upon all their proceedings'.

No such construction could be placed upon the events that were now unfolding themselves in the Legislative Assembly as the thermometer crept upwards, while the dry air bristled with accusations. Patel's arrogance appeared to increase with the intolerable heat. He began to claim the exercise of powers that had never existed, probing into English Parliamentary history of the distant past to find justification for them in the actions of bygone Speakers of the House of Commons. He now proposed to rule the Public Safety Bill out of order.

It became clear to the Viceroy that, in spite of all his efforts at conciliation,

[1] India Office Library, MSS. EUR.C. 152/5, *Lord Irwin. Letters to the Secretary of State for India*, p. 22.

Patel had failed to respond, and that his pretensions must be challenged. Lord Irwin had now to consider a step he had tried hard to avoid, the removal of Patel from the Chair, and he would undoubtedly have taken it had there not occurred an event in the Legislative Assembly which shook India to her foundations and echoed round the world. The Viceroy described his intentions at this moment in a letter to the Secretary of State:

'At that juncture there still seemed to be a fair chance of Patel reconsidering his position, but we knew that Motilal Nehru was doing all he could to stiffen him, and we had to lay our plans on the assumption of his ruling being adverse to us. Our intention was . . . to put down a motion affirming that the Chair did not possess the powers he claimed and—if he refused to let this motion come on—to move for his removal from the Chair. If, as we anticipated, Patel had given his ruling on Saturday, or even on Monday morning, this was the course we should have adopted. As you know, Patel postponed his ruling from Saturday to Monday, and on Monday as he was opening his mouth to say the fatal words the bombs were thrown from the gallery.'[1]

This outrage, which caused even extreme nationalists to recoil in horror, produced a shattering effect upon India. It showed how long was the arm of the murder clubs of the great cities that it could reach into the debating chamber itself, and was a shocking illustration of the evil that was brewing in those alleys and rabbit warrens. This desperate affray was the work of a terrorist organization, the Hindu Republican Association, formed in Allahabad, and one of the two men concerned in it was afterwards identified as the murderer of the policeman Saunders.

'Two men in the public gallery,' the Viceroy told his father, 'proceeded to throw two bombs at the Government benches. Luckily, partly owing to the bombs being bad and to a combination of fortuitous incidents, they did practically no damage, and everybody concerned had a most miraculous escape. Having discharged the bombs, one of the men proceeded to shoot with a revolver, which again luckily jammed after the first two shots had missed. There were the usual hairbreadth escapes of people who had moved a yard or so one way or the other, who must have been killed if they had stayed where they were. Anyhow the whole thing was a providential deliverance. The Assembly was immediately adjourned.'[2]

Sir John Simon had been in the Parliament building that day and learned, we may conjecture, with dismay of this latest manifestation of a country whose political advancement he was attempting to hasten. The Viceroy had thought that this event would have some influence upon the ruling Patel had been proposing to give, but nothing could overcome the determination of this

---

[1] India Office Library, MSS. EUR.C. 152/5, *Lord Irwin. Letters to the Secretary of State for India*, p. 83.
[2] Hickleton Papers, *Correspondence with Viscount Halifax*, p. 244.

obstinate old man to oppose the Public Safety Bill. On 11 April he ruled the Bill out of order after an elaborate explanation, claiming that he was entitled by his office to do so. Thus he assumed the power to deny both to the Government and to the House as a whole any opportunity of bringing forward or expressing its opinion upon legislation.

It was then seen with what vigour and firmness the Viceroy could move when he had exhausted the arts of persuasion. He was determined to secure the powers of the Public Safety Bill, the necessity for which had been so violently emphasized by the bombing, and the means by which he could protect the Legislature from such misuse of the President's power in the future. He decided that his proper course was to announce his intention of getting the rules amended, and of taking the powers of the Public Safety Bill by Ordinance. He would call both Houses to attend the following day to inform them of his intention.

Standing in the Assembly on that 12 April he explained to the silent benches his reasons for amending the law in language so positive and accents so full of authority as to be a powerful refutation of the charges that he was a weak Viceroy.

It was not difficult for him to justify his case for the Bill after the outrage of the day before. When he came to the misuse of the Presidential power there was a ring of steely determination in the words in which he announced his intentions:

'If therefore the interpretation of the rules by the President of either House gives rise to a situation in which Government for grave reasons is unable to acquiesce, the only effective remedy is that early measures should be taken to secure by due authority such amendment of the rules as may be necessary to prevent any recurrence in future of a similar interruption in the normal legislative procedure.

'That course we propose to follow without delay, and in order that there may be no misunderstanding, I will add that the broad purpose of the amendment of the rules which we propose to seek will be to secure that the progress of legislation, which is within the power of the Indian Legislature to pass, shall not be prevented by the President of either House, except in virtue of express powers to do so conferred upon him by the Rules and Standing Orders.'[1]

This decisive step, which put an end for good to the exorbitant claims of the President, indicates another form of courage in the Viceroy, for the ignominious defeat of Patel might in itself have proved fatal to the policy of conciliation he was pursuing. This policy might well have foundered if Patel, instead of licking his wounds, had resigned and led an agitation in the country against the Government. The fact that he refrained from this step is creditable to both men. The Viceroy's decision was vindicated, and the President acknowledged its justice.

[1] Government of India Press, *Speeches by Lord Irwin*, Vol. I, pp. 571-2.

The outrage in the Assembly, with its revelation in the broad light of day of those sinister forces which were now showing such insolent assurance, produced an atmosphere in India heavy with fear and expectation, and the official reaction to this heightened tension was to arm the executive with still more massive authority.

Already, in March 1929, a number of Trade Union leaders, some of them Communists, had been brought up for trial in what became known as the Meerut Conspiracy case. It is interesting to observe that Gandhi felt little sympathy with these efforts to conquer terrorism and preserve the peace. 'The Government,' he said, 'is giving the usual periodical exhibition of its red claws which usually remain under cover.'[1]

By June 1929 the Viceroy had taken up his position, a position of strength. He had shown that he was prepared to govern and that terrorism would get short shrift at his hands, and he was later to sign death warrants without remorse and without losing a moment's sleep.

But tranquillity and order were not his only, nor even his main, objectives. Had he not repeated that it was easy to create a desert and call it peace? More exalted ideas were now filling the Viceroy's mind and it was his greatest desire, as he said afterwards, 'to bring to the body politic of India the touch that carries with it healing and health'. He had already told the people of India that he saw his duties in part as being the interpreter of their desires to the Parliament in England, and he was now planning his two memorable steps in that direction.

*   *   *

The time had come for the Viceroy to return home for the customary mid-term leave. By the time he left India on 27 June 1929 the Conservative Government of 1924 had at last departed; a minority Labour Government was in office in England, and Mr. Wedgwood Benn had become Secretary of State for India. It was a change welcome to the Indian leaders, except those of extreme views to whom any form of British Government was equally abhorrent. It was also welcome to the Viceroy, who wrote to his father on the eve of departure with joy in his heart at the prospect he had scarcely dared to indulge, of seeing him again:

'I am not much afraid of any policy they are likely to produce as long as the direction remains in the same hands as at present. I think Wedgwood Benn ought to be rather good for the India Office. He is a nice fellow, keen, with lots of ideas, and a gentleman, which is worth a good deal. He was always rather a friend of mine in the House of Commons, and I have no doubt I shall get on with him.'[2]

The Viceroy was now convinced that the moment was ripe for some

[1] B. R. Nanda, *Mahatma Gandhi*, p. 281.
[2] Hickleton Papers, *Correspondence with Viscount Halifax*, p. 256.

gesture such as Setalvad had asked for, which would stir the imagination of India, regain the contact that had been lost, and restore faith in British purpose. It cannot be denied that this decision was in direct contrast to the contemptuous words he had used about a similar proposal by Ramsay MacDonald, but he felt that the atmosphere had changed, and that an act of faith was now necessary. However inevitable, the exclusion of Indians from the Commission had inflicted a deep wound upon their pride. This grievance must now be effaced. Far from contact with events, many in England demanded a strong policy of repression, the proscribing of Congress, the arrest of Patel and the ruthless employment of police and army. The Viceroy knew that such a policy would destroy everything he had striven to achieve, confidence, goodwill, moderation in thought, and would leave an India a hundred times more sullen and intractable than before its application.

He was aware of the trend of the proposals which the Simon Commission would make, and knew that they would find little favour with Indian political opinion. He felt that it was for him to retrieve lost ground, and he assured Patel that 'You may rely on me to do my best to find a way of peace out of our present difficulties. I hope that you will use whatever influence you have . . . to get Congress leaders to meet it half-way'.[1]

He found the new Secretary of State as eager as himself to make some memorable gesture of friendship, to recapture confidence by an act of faith. He could rely upon the Socialist Prime Minister, Ramsay MacDonald, who had already, when out of office, looked forward to the day when India would become a Dominion. Ironically, the aristocratic Conservative Viceroy would soon find himself in warm alliance with Socialist Ministers and in pursuit of a policy deeply disturbing to the Conservative and Liberal Parties.

The Viceroy had in mind two steps of the greatest possible consequence. The first, by which it was hoped to erase by a stroke the *malaise* caused by the imagined slight on India in the Commission, was a calling together in conference of members of the British Parliament, and Indians representing all sections of opinion.

Secondly, he had convinced himself that it was necessary to give an assurance that Dominion Status, and no lesser status, was the accepted goal of Indian progress. He had already, in January 1929, repeated that the 1917 Declaration remained a solemn pledge of full national political stature for India, but this was too stale and too nebulous to satisfy impatient natures.

But the prospect of Dominion Status, he believed, would do so, for although to the English the term meant a settled constitutional position, to Indians it involved a promise of full rights to come. Irwin had discussed these two ideas with Geoffrey Dawson, the Editor of *The Times*, early in 1929 when they had 'talked reform' together.

The Viceroy's speech opening the Assembly had made a good impression

[1] B. R. Nanda. Op. cit., p. 256.

upon the more sensible non-co-operators who had approached him with apparent anxiety to make a move. Motilal Nehru had told Dawson that some positive gesture was needed, such as a statement that Dominion Status was the ultimate goal,[1] and the Viceroy had discussed with Dawson the best approach to the Government, and had prepared a draft statement containing a phrase about Dominion Status which he afterwards removed. They also considered the idea of a tripartite meeting between Parliament, British India and the Indian Princes, which Dawson had repeated verbally to Baldwin.

The Viceroy regarded these steps as essential for drawing Congress and its allied parties back into co-operation. He did not envisage the goal of Dominion Status as being quickly reached, and it was no part of his intention that the conference should act as a constituent assembly. Rather did he see it as a meeting of men of different creeds who would discuss, on equal terms with the English, the means of attaining the Dominion Status which he had brought before their eyes.

He believed that if the suggestion for a tripartite meeting of Parliament, British India and the Indian Princes was put forward by the Commission itself, it might anticipate a possible boycott of the Commission's Report and strengthen its chances of a fair reception in India, and that the Dominion Status announcement would prevent the drifting of Indian political opinion on to separatist lines.

Many charges were made at the time and afterwards that by his actions the Viceroy had cut the ground from under Simon's feet and rendered the tremendous labours of his Commission useless, and the question is worth a brief examination.

Irwin had arrived in London on leave on 13 July 1929, leaving Lord Goschen in charge as Viceroy and Acting Governor-General of India. He brought with him the drafts of an imaginary correspondence which he had prepared, between Sir John Simon and the Prime Minister Ramsay Mac-Donald in which Simon would initiate the Round Table proposal, and in his reply the Prime Minister, after agreeing with this suggestion, would give a definition of the policy of Dominion Status which, he would say, was considered by the Government to be implicit in the Declaration of 1917.

On 18 July Simon, after meeting Irwin and the Secretary of State, circulated a minute to his colleagues on the Statutory Commission. This was the draft letter from Sir John Simon to the Prime Minister containing the proposal for the conference. At this stage, therefore, the Commission did not see the Dominion Status Declaration which was contained in the Prime Minister's reply, but Simon was apparently not yet disturbed about it. A week later Irwin made a statement to the Cabinet which declared itself in favour of the exchange of letters between Simon and the Prime Minister containing a

[1] Evelyn Wrench, *Sir Geoffrey Dawson and Our Times*, p. 272.

Declaration of Dominion Status to be achieved by stages, and the announcement of a Round Table Conference.

Every effort was made to ensure that these actions should be made as
enticing as possible to the Indians. On the advice of Lord Goschen and
Sir Malcolm Hailey, Irwin suggested changes in the Prime Minister's letter.
The Declaration about Dominion Status was to be made more explicit and
'full-blooded', and the conference was to be made more 'free' by removing
the earlier suggestion that it should only consider draft proposals put before
it by the Government.

Under the new arrangement the conference would simply be for the purpose of exchanging views, and seeking agreement on the final proposals. The
completed draft correspondence was sent by the Prime Minister to Mr. Baldwin, the Leader of the Opposition, who was on holiday in France. He agreed
both to the Conference and to the Declaration announcement, 'provided that
the Commission accepted them'.

Simon next placed the draft letters before the Commission on 24 September. They accepted the proposal to hold a Round Table Conference but
objected to being concerned in correspondence in which the Prime Minister
was to make the announcement about Dominion Status, and this decision was
communicated orally to the Secretary of State the same day.

As a result of the Commission's objection, the statement about Dominion
Status was omitted altogether from the Prime Minister's reply in the exchange of correspondence, which confined itself to the setting up of the
conference and its procedure, and on 25 September the Cabinet agreed to
the general plan on the understanding that it was made clear that the initiative for the Round Table Conference came from the Statutory Commission.

It was, therefore, necessary to make the Dominion Status Declaration
independently of the Commission and the exchange of letters. Goschen had
advised Irwin that it would be well to defer the announcement in India until
his return. It was finally published, together with the Round Table Conference Announcement, on 31 October 1929 in a Gazette Extraordinary.

Sir John Simon was thus privy to all these proceedings, and Irwin was
much perplexed by his attitude. At first Simon had seen no objection to the
declaration about Dominion Status, but had been extremely sensitive about
the idea of a conference on the grounds that it was likely to affect the status
of the Commission's Report. After much discussion, however, he had agreed
to it, and had indeed gone a great deal further in accepting, however reluctantly, Wedgwood Benn's intention of a 'free' conference. But Irwin found it
difficult to understand the protest which Simon was later to make about the
announcement on Dominion Status, and he expressed his perplexity in a
letter to Lord Salisbury in December 1929:

'Certainly up to the time I left London, while I knew that Simon's Commission at the end did not like the Dominion Status declaration and felt

bound to dissociate themselves from it, I had never heard a word to suggest
that they thought it in any way trespassed upon their own position. . . . I
remember very well when he and I had luncheon with Reading that Simon
himself rather minimized the Dominion Status part of it on the lines of
saying that it was academic, and that if I thought it would do good he
personally did not feel very strongly.'[1]

The Viceroy had heard from others of complaints by Simon, but they had
not been pressed home directly to him. There were many who believed that
the new developments had made his Report a dead letter and that it was now
stillborn before it had even been considered. Simon had the further grievance
that he had only concurred in the scheme at all on the assurance of the
Viceroy that draft conclusions by the Government would form the agenda of
the Conference, and that now the Secretary of State had made it a 'free'
conference at which delegates could discuss any subject that they wished, and
in which his Report would be submerged.[2]

It cannot, however, be denied that Sir John Simon had ample opportunity
of protesting against infringements of his own position, and that he had
finally accepted, even with misgivings, the policy that was now carried out.
In this decision he was accompanied by the other members of the Commission: 'They shared my view,' he said, 'that if we were going to acquiesce
in this treatment, we should do it handsomely.'[3]

After the Viceroy had made his Announcement, he was left in no doubt
that, whatever anger it might provoke in England, it had transformed the
situation in India in an instant. A large gathering of Indian leaders was
assembled in Delhi when the Announcement was made, Gandhi and Ansari,
Mrs. Annie Besant, Motilal and Jawaharlal Nehru, Malaviya and Moonje,
Sastri and Sapru.

The leaders were in a state of unaffected excitement as though at last they
saw the prospect of advance. Indeed, it appeared likely at the beginning that
the Viceroy's offer would be accepted unconditionally. Jawaharlal Nehru,
impatient as always of accommodation, alone opposed any settlement by
negotiation. On the second day of this meeting a document known as the
Delhi Manifesto was issued accepting the invitation to the Round Table
Conference, but suggesting that steps should be taken to induce a 'calmer
atmosphere'; political prisoners should be released, and the Indian National
Congress should have the largest representation at the Conference; they
understood the Viceroy to have said that the purpose of the Conference was
not to determine whether or when Dominion Status would be introduced,
but rather to draft a constitution for the Dominion.

[1] India Office Library, MSS. EUR.C. 152/18, *Correspondence with Persons in England and
Abroad*, 1928–29, p. 368.
[2] India Office Library, MSS. EUR.C. 152/28, *Correspondence While in England*, June to October
1929.
[3] Sir John Simon, *Retrospect*, p. 153.

It was at least an advance that the moderate statesmen had persuaded the extremists to sign a document in which they promised co-operation, and to do so by making recommendations rather than laying down binding conditions. It was a tragedy that having come so close, the two sides were soon to drift apart, and that the distrust which Irwin had for the moment deflected, should take possession again of the Congress policy. Although its leaders sought an interview with the Viceroy for elucidation of his statement, they began to prepare themselves for the Civil Disobedience movement scheduled for 1930. Gandhi was reported to have said that he would not be sorry if the Conference fell through.[1]

But whatever the antics of Congress, the Viceroy's personal action had made a deep impression on the rest of articulate India which realized that he had imperilled his own position to get the waterlogged craft on the move again. 'He had accomplished,' wrote Coatman, 'a feat almost without precedent in the history of our dealings with India. At a stroke he had entirely transformed the political situation, replacing ill-will and mistrust by good-will, and the beginnings, at any rate, of a renewed confidence in British rule and its intentions towards India.'

The Viceroy had not reckoned with the explosion of anger in the British Parliament that followed the Announcement. The suggestion that he had done something of great danger to British policy and destructive of the Simon Report were to him incomprehensible. He told his father on 4 November:

'Our purpose has always been proclaimed to be that of Responsible Government; and for the last four years public men in England of all parties have constantly talked about the object of British policy being to bring India into partnership with the Dominions, and the same hope is formally expressed in my Instrument of Instructions from the King. Everybody has, of course, gone off at a tangent, confusing the ultimate purpose, which is one thing, and the present policy which at any stage is another.

'It is obvious, and I was very careful to say it, that in regard to the latter, e.g. present policy, everybody must await what Simon and Co. may have to say. But I don't begin to see how the definition of your final purpose can be held to queer the pitch of decision as to your immediate policy. F.E., of course, has always disliked and would like to go back on the 1917 Declaration ... but I am certain that the only solid asset, looking to the future, that we have in India, except bayonets, is that our word should be above suspicion, and that we should afford no ground for it being said that we are seeking to wriggle out of hastily given pledges.'[2]

Lord Reading, whose voice mattered much to Indians, for it was that of the great Liberal Party of Gladstone and Ripon whose principles they

[1] S. Gopal. Op. cit., p. 52.
[2] Hickleton Papers, *Correspondence with Viscount Halifax*, p. 258.

revered, and at whose hands they particularly looked for help, seemed to
them full of doom. His massive juridical onslaught on the Dominion Status
announcement in the House of Lords, coming from a former Viceroy,
carried great and, to them, ominous significance. Birkenhead, who had seen,
as he thought, all the precautions he had laboriously contrived swept away by
the Viceroy's single gesture, also made a savage onslaught on the new policy,
terrible invective that overwhelmed the hapless Government representatives,
Lord Parmoor and Lord Passfield, who could only plead that the conditions
and reservations of the 1917 Declaration were still in force, and that the
announcement had been made in advance of the Simon Report only to
provide a friendly atmosphere for its reception.

Birkenhead had advised the members of the Simon Commission 'to treat
that which the Government have instructed and authorized the Viceroy to
do as irrelevance'. His old sympathetic relations with Irwin were now at an
end. He wrote blistering articles in the Press saying that the Simon Report
had been wantonly short-circuited, and that the appetite of the Indians
would be merely whetted by the Declaration which would lead them to
further and more extravagant demands.

These and other speeches strongly critical of the Viceroy were like a cold
douche thrown in the face of the expectant Indians, and their effect was
increased by the debate that followed in the House of Commons. Baldwin,
who by then must have regretted his hasty personal acceptance of the
Viceroy's proposals, formally dissociated the Conservative Party from the
Declaration when he heard that the Simon Commission had rejected it, while
Lloyd George contributed an able and mischievous attack upon it. The
Government case was more forcefully defended in the Commons than in the
Lords, and Wedgwood Benn's resolute speech winding up the debate was
about the only crumb of comfort left for the angry Indian leaders.

How did the Viceroy himself feel at this unexpected challenge? On
3 December 1929 he wrote to his father:

'I don't think that anything that has been said in England has led me to
change my view that it was right to make this statement. It has undoubtedly
rallied all moderate opinion here and I feel very little doubt that they will
remain thus rallied for some time to come. The extremists are in a considerable quandary, and though, as I think I told you before, I shall not be
surprised if a good many of them run out, they are likely in the process to
forfeit a good deal of support and to find themselves compelled to fight on
bad tactical ground. So on the whole I am not dissatisfied with the way events
have gone.'[1]

The Viceroy awaited the next move from the other side. It came shortly
after the debate in the House of Commons when the leaders who had produced the Delhi Manifesto met again at Allahabad to discuss what their next

[1] Hickleton Papers, *Correspondence with Viscount Halifax*, p. 264.

steps should be after this revelation of the temper of the British Parliament. Some of the words used in the debate were cited by Jawaharlal Nehru with telling effect in an attempt to convince the meeting of the hypocrisy of English politicians in their dealings with India.

But Lord Irwin had done his work too well to be flouted completely even by this gathering. The less fanatical elements in it, who still retained some sense of human values, the Liberals and Hindu Mahasabha, and some other Congressmen, realized what the Viceroy had done; how he had defied the two great parties in England, including his own, in what he was convinced were the interests of India, because he believed that, living among them and sniffing the hot atmosphere of their politics, he was in a better position to judge what the situation demanded than those who criticized him eight thousand miles away.

The Delhi Manifesto was reissued. Gandhi appeared at this moment to be in one of his moods of indecision. His interest in the Round Table Conference seemed to have become tepid, and it was believed that he would insist on impossible conditions as his price of attending it. It was felt, however, that civilized behaviour demanded some recognition, however futile, of the Viceroy's sacrifice, and a last-minute effort was made, in which Patel and Sapru were the prime movers, to attempt a reconciliation between the Congress and the Government before the December session of Congress at Lahore. Motilal Nehru was openly pessimistic. 'I expect no results from our interview,' he said, 'but I have to redeem my promise. At present all roads lead to Lahore.'[1]

Sir Tej Bahadur Sapru, on the other hand, nourished a curious optimism about Gandhi's intentions. 'To the best of my belief,' he told the Viceroy, 'Mr. Gandhi will make no unreasonable demands . . . I feel persuaded that he honestly believes in your sincerity.'[2] The Viceroy himself was far from happy at the prospect of meeting Gandhi at this moment. More realistic than his Indian Liberal friend, he now had reason to believe that Gandhi would be content only if Ramsay MacDonald would telegraph the Viceroy a definite promise of Dominion Status at the Round Table Conference, and stake the political life of the Government upon it. In the absence of such a promise he knew that the Lahore Congress might declare for complete independence, and launch a campaign of Civil Disobedience.

'Though I am, as you know, a pacifist by nature,' Irwin told Wedgwood Benn, 'I am not disposed to go all lengths to meet people who seem to be behaving with utter unreason.' He was also apprehensive that he might be accused of making a deal on the other side with Congress if he took the initiative in this matter. In spite of these doubts, he felt that on balance it would be wrong to allow any opportunity, however meagre, to pass, and it

[1] B. R. Nanda. Op. cit., p. 284.
[2] Government of India archives. National Library of Calcutta.

was arranged that Gandhi should meet the Viceroy on 23 December on his way to the Congress session at Lahore.

*   *   *

Lord Irwin returned that day from Hyderabad to Delhi where he was to take up his residence for the first time in the new Viceroy's House. As his train was drawing near the city toward 8 a.m. in a dense fog on a high curved embankment at about forty miles an hour, there was a loud bomb explosion near the middle of the train under the communicating portion between two coaches. Terrorists had laid a fuse from the Purana Qila, the Old Fort, three hundred yards away, to the curved railway track, and had intended to touch the bomb off after the pilot engine had passed, and just before the engine drawing the viceregal train reached the spot. Owing to the fog, they mistimed their action, and the engine with four coaches, including the Viceroy's, had passed before the explosion occurred, and was able to pull the rest of the train across the gap. The bomb blew a hole four feet wide in one of the rails, and had the engine passed over it, being on a curve it would have been certain to overturn and plunge down the steep embankment dragging the train with it.

He bore this attack with his usual complete indifference to physical danger, and a sense of wonder that anyone could believe that the cause of self-government could be in any way advanced by such an action:

'I can't pretend that I personally was at any moment greatly disturbed by it,' he told his father. 'I heard the noise and said to myself "That must be a bomb", and fully expected to hear something further happen. I then smelt all the smoke that came down the train . . . but as nothing happened I went on reading Challoner till someone came along and told me it had been a bomb and I went to see the damage. . . .

'Apparently the author of it thought it would be a dramatic thing to do something to me on the day on which we entered New Delhi, which happened to be the seventeenth anniversary of the day on which Lord Hardinge was bombed when he declared the intention of building the New Delhi capital. It is really astonishing that there should be people who think that those kind of things can sincerely benefit them in the advancement of the policy they profess to desire. I anticipate that the result will be rather to harden general opinion in England, and, in India, to strengthen my own position for what that may be worth.'[1]

This was not the only occasion when the Viceroy narrowly escaped death. Many years later Colonel Harvey, his Military Secretary, travelled on the steamer from Dublin to Liverpool and fell into conversation with an Indian who revealed that he had been much involved in revolutionary activity during Irwin's viceroyalty. Harvey asked him if he had taken part in the attempt on

[1] Hickleton Papers, *Correspondence with Viscount Halifax*, p. 269.

the viceregal train which he denied, but admitted that he had been detailed to assassinate the Viceroy on a visit to Lucknow. He had been waiting in readiness on the platform, 'but,' he told Harvey, 'when the Viceroy got out and began shaking hands he gave such a delightful smile that I could not do it.'[1]

His nerve absolutely unshaken, the Viceroy received Gandhi, Motilal Nehru, Sapru, Jinnah and Vithalbhai Patel in the afternoon. After many protestations of concern about Irwin's narrow escape, they turned to the business in hand. The two Congressmen had not taken their colleagues into their confidence about the line they were going to adopt, but it was soon obvious to the Viceroy's sinking spirits that Gandhi was at his intolerable worst; that his mind had been closed long before the meeting to any argument, however reasonable and convincing.

He said that his point briefly was that not Parliament but India ought to frame India's future. India was capable of solving her own problems of defence, and unless Dominion Status could be presumed as an immediate result of the Conference, he could take no part in it.

Gandhi went further on this occasion than the now familiar rehash of Congress principles. He even said that he doubted the sincerity of English purpose, although he recognized that of individuals.[2] Motilal Nehru was equally intransigent, and there was nothing left for the Viceroy except to remark wearily that there was obviously no common ground between himself and Gandhi, and to dismiss his enraging guests.

'They really were impossible,' he wrote to the Secretary of State, 'and left me more than usually depressed about the lack of political sense that extremist politicians naturally betray. I can't help feeling that the main idea in their minds is that the Indian differences are too deep-seated either to be concealed or surmounted at any Conference, and that participation therefore in a Conference would leave them with their platform so badly riddled as to be incapable of reconstruction. It therefore seemed better to their minds to invent a reason for not taking part in it and thus maintaining themselves in the position of being able to say that the reluctance of Great Britain to give them all they wanted at once was again responsible for all the difficulties of Government and life in India.'[3]

He had also to face the disturbing prospect of the launching of Civil Disobedience. If this indeed came, he was in no mood to handle it with kid gloves. 'I propose to take an early opportunity,' he told his father, 'of making it plain that, if and when the extremists try any policy of what they call Civil Disobedience, we shall lose no time in jumping on their heads.'[4]

[1] Lady Sybil Middleton to author.

[2] Archives of the Government of India. Sir George Cunningham's Minutes of the Meeting.

[3] India Office Library, MSS. EUR.C. 152/5, *Lord Irwin. Letters to the Secretary of State for India*, Vol. IV, p. 185.

[4] Hickleton Papers, *Correspondence with Viscount Halifax*, p. 271.

The 23 December had indeed been a busy day for that saintly apostle of peace and reconciliation, Mahatma Gandhi. By one maladroit gesture he had struck aside the Viceroy's outstretched hand, and severed the Congress from the rest of political India. All Irwin's efforts in defiance of his own party, in defiance of bitter accusations of grovelling in the face of England's enemies had been in vain. The Congress that was now assembling at Lahore was meeting to declare revolt. There would be no more talk of 'the minimum national demand' embodied in the Nehru Report. Swaraj, now meant in the sense of complete independence, would henceforth be the goal.

It was also significant that Jawaharlal Nehru had been elected President of this meeting at the instigation of Gandhi, and that Chandra Bose would also be present. There had been grumbling by the young men a year ago at the Calcutta meeting of Congress that the party had fallen too much into the hands of old men of outworn beliefs, and that an infusion of vigorous youth was required in its counsels at this critical moment. Jawaharlal was only forty, and the breath of rebellion was in his nostrils.

It was perhaps appropriate that this critical session should take place in the unquiet city of Lahore. It was preceded by intense excitement as a town of tents rose like mushrooms from the parched earth on the banks of the Ravi river. Wild rumours were passed from mouth to mouth by chattering messengers; the Moslems were about to obliterate Congress by force of arms; three thousand Sikhs were marching on Lahore and the Viceroy was about to prohibit the meeting.

The excitement was worked up by the followers of Gandhi who indulged in ceremonies of extravagant worship, by the crowds surging about in ecstasy, white teeth gleaming in brown faces, by flags rattling like gun shots in the wind, by processions of horsemen and the parades of enraptured youth.

All this panache and din concealed a deep misgiving in the leaders of the party, and rifts which had opened between Gandhi and the two Nehrus on the one hand, and the members of the Hindu Mahasabha and other more sober-minded Congressmen. Against the back-curtain of parades and demonstrations a bitter argument was thrashed out in the Subjects Committee, the heart of the Congress Party.

And here, day after day, Gandhi gave an exhibition of the incredible mulishness of which he was capable when his policy was determined. The most eminent men in the movement, men whom he admired and liked, begged him not to give so dusty an answer to the Viceroy's friendly initiative. Malaviya and Kelkar, Mrs. Naidu whose poems were known all over the civilized world, and Ansari the Moslem and a former President of Congress, all exhausted themselves in entreaty, but their efforts splintered against Gandhi's defences. They found there, as others were to find later, an obstinacy undiluted by any sense of responsibility.

At midnight on 31 December 1929, at the first flush of the dawn which marked the coming of a new year, the Indian National Congress unfurled the flag of Independence on the banks of the Ravi river. The Congress called upon its members in the Central and Provincial Legislatures to resign their seats and authorized the All-India Congress Committee to launch Civil Disobedience.[1]

In this disastrous conference Gandhi allowed but one faint gesture of conciliation towards the Viceroy. He asked that a resolution should be passed condemning the attempt on Lord Irwin's life, and it was a clear indication of the temper of Congress at that moment that such a resolution condemning a would-be murderer was carried by a majority of only thirty-eight out of one thousand eight hundred and thirty-two votes cast.

When the Viceroy considered the situation in the light of these events it seemed to him that the control of Congress was now passing into the hands of younger and wilder men in a manner so obvious that the reasonable elements in the country were being stirred to resist it. It was encouraging to him that his Liberal friend, Sapru, had said that the enemies of India were to be found not in England, but at home, and that the war against them must now be one of extermination; encouraging, too, that the Liberal Federation which had been meeting in Madras had begun to take steps to prepare themselves for that struggle, and to support the Viceroy whose Declaration had given a new impetus and hope to Indian political life.

He believed that the action of Congress would leave deep scars on its own body; that the revival of the plan to boycott the Central and Provincial Councils would be widely resented, and that many who had hitherto financed Congress would now have second thoughts at the prospect of Jawaharlal's vision of an ideal future. Above all, moderate and liberal opinion was on the move, and the gap in the Moslem ranks was about to be closed. He therefore would have regarded it as the height of folly at this moment to follow the advice of the *Morning Post* to proclaim Congress as an illegal organization, and prosecute its leaders.

'I should be disposed to stick to our existing line of country as regards speech-making, that is to say, prosecute when the language or the circumstances of the speech seem in our view to constitute an incitement to violence; and at the same time to be ready to jump as quickly and as vigorously as we can upon any movement to civil disobedience. . . . If they do try it we shall not hesitate to hit it as hard as we can. . . .'[2]

'I do not think that I am over easily induced to see bogeys, but at the same time I do not think it is possible to dismiss the Lahore conclusions lightly as the mere academic statement of a remote objective, because there is no doubt

[1] B. R. Nanda. Op. cit., p. 288.
[2] India Office Library, MSS. EUR.C. 152/6, *Lord Irwin. Letters to the Secretary of State for India*, p. 2.

that, as now stated, it is not a remote objective and that it involves very mischievous and dangerous potentialities.'[1]

There were now a few storm signals which showed that Civil Disobedience could not be far away. There were ugly outbreaks of revolutionary crime all over India, and in the Bardoli area of Gandhi's birthplace Gujerat in the Bombay Presidency, where his influence was strong, an ancient movement for non-payment of land revenue by the peasants to the Government was revived. Once again the Patel family were to play a foremost part in agitation. This time it was Vallabhai Patel the brother of the President of the Assembly who was to urge extreme courses. He and Gandhi regarded the incitement of the peasants at Bardoli as a test case in the coming struggle with the Government, and they hoped that, if it was successful, the movement of non-payment of revenue would spread to the Provinces.

The Viceroy was not yet ready to come to grips. Regarding the Bardoli agitation as mere skirmishing, he refused to give Sir Frederick Sykes, the Governor of Bombay, special powers to deal with the emergency. A compromise was reached with Patel, and the Bombay Government agreed to a considerable reduction in land revenue rates. But it had been an event of some significance:

'The Bardoli no-tax campaign,' wrote Gopal, 'formed a landmark in the career of Patel, the history of Satyagraha and the viceroyalty of Irwin. . . . But the effort at Bardoli succeeded only because there was at the head of the Indian administration one who was not blinded to reason and equity.'[2]

That man was now about to reach the end of his patience, for Gandhi's Civil Disobedience movement was launched on 12 March. With his customary flair for finding the issue which would inflame the greatest number of people, he decided to begin by violating the Salt Law, and to march due south from his Sabarmati ashram at Ahmedabad to the Salt Pans at Dandi on the seashore. By choosing the Salt Laws for his first act of defiance he had made a gesture of genius. The incidence of the tax was minute, but Indians believed that such a tax on the salt which could be gathered from the sea and which was consumed by man and animal was symbolical of human oppression.

It was in the form of this trivial impost that British rule was most forcibly brought home to millions of Indians, and by exploiting it as oppressive, Gandhi could penetrate to those millions, inflame their anger, and incite them to break the law in every Province of British India. To many his appeal seemed almost to transcend the human element. 'By calling on the people to pick up salt from the earth or distil it from the sea he seemed to be rallying the forces of nature on his side'.[3]

[1] India Office Library, MSS. EUR.C. 152/6, p. 38.
[2] S. Gopal. Op. cit., p. 32–33.   [3] Ibid., p. 57.

On 12 March at six-thirty in the morning Gandhi left his ashram and began his two hundred and forty mile march to Dandi and the sea. Seventy-nine Satyagrahis followed him, old men and boys, untouchables and weavers, scholars and editors. Gandhi, carrying a lacquer bamboo staff, led them at a pace so brisk that the young men could hardly keep up with him down roads where the grey dust was strewn with green leaves.

Public interest in his progress was not as great as he had expected. 'Gandhi,' said the Governor of the Punjab, 'was dreadfully anxious to be arrested,' but the Viceroy refused to oblige him. He remembered that there were still many Hindu leaders between the Centre and the Left whose minds were not yet decided. To arrest Gandhi before he had committed any offence would have brought them down on the side of Congress and non-co-opera-tion.[1] He also had a lingering belief that the whole policy of Civil Disobedi-ence had been embarked upon with little confidence in its ultimate success, and that many of the Indian people had no sympathy for it. There was a hope, too, in his mind that the march, inauspiciously begun, would peter out in failure and ridicule, and he had no desire to martyrize Gandhi prematurely.

Here he was guilty, in the eyes of some, of undue optimism and an uni-maginative estimate of Gandhi's hold on the Indian masses. 'This belief that Gandhi could be ignored,' said Gopal, 'suggested a lack of imaginative understanding. For years he had been engaged in building the emotional integrity of India and now the sight of this old man marching along the dusty roads, without arms, and without allies, to do battle with the British Empire stirred the hearts of men not only in India, but throughout the world.'[2]

The Viceroy was not so naïve as this gifted Indian supposed. He had already thought deeply about Gandhi's character. He remembered that Sastri had told him that the Mahatma must be wooed like a capricious woman; that he was a 'philosophical anarch' who could not be caught and held by ordinary argument. If you told him, Sastri had said, that his actions would lead to chaos, he would reply that only by chaos would we get back to the natural society. His most dominant quality, thought Sastri, was vanity, unconscious, but not less real.[3]

But the Viceroy knew also how profoundly the religious and mystical character of Gandhi's movement appealed to the Indian mind, and recog-nized the great gulf by which in public estimation Gandhi was separated from every other leader in India. He had no intention of allowing a legend to grow up that Gandhi could not be arrested. He knew that it might soon have to be done, but he was anxious to defer it. He regarded the situation without sentimentality and there was a hint of that steely inner toughness in his words to the Secretary of State on 7 April:

'The will-power of the man must have been enormous to get him through

[1] J. Coatman. Op. cit., p. 279.   [2] S. Gopal. Op. cit., pp. 60–61.
[3] Hickleton Papers, *Correspondence with Viscount Halifax*, p. 284.

his march. . . . I was always told that his blood pressure is dangerous and his heart none too good, and I was also told a few days ago that his horoscope predicts that he will die this year, and that is the explanation of this desperate throw. It would be a very happy solution.'[1]

During this period of forbearance violent attacks were made upon the Viceroy in England. Unforgettable among these were a series of classical onslaughts by Winston Churchill, superb in eloquence, biting in scorn and containing charges of the Viceroy's weakness and irresolution, which indeed skirted the frontiers of his honour. Convinced of the wisdom of his actions, Irwin treated these attacks with icy disdain. Damaging as they were, and expressed in incomparable language, they disturbed him no more than the whining of an intrusive mosquito.

It was soon clear that in spite of Gandhi's many protestations of the non-violent nature of Satyagraha, and his own abhorrence of force which was said to stem from Jainist and Buddhist infusions in his Hinduism, its effects were completely beyond his control.

On 6 April Gandhi reached the sea. There he picked up some salt left by the waves, and by this simple gesture broke the law which made it a punishable offence to possess salt not obtained from the Government monopoly. The poetess, Mrs. Sarojini Naidu, who had tried to stay his hand at Lahore, now stood by the Mahatma's side and, as the symbolic gesture was made, cried 'Hail, Deliverer'.[2] We are forced to agree with Gandhi's biographer that 'to walk for twenty-four days and rivet the attention of all India, to trek across a countryside saying, "Watch, I am about to give a signal to the nation", and then pick up a pinch of salt in publicized defiance of the mighty Government and thus become a criminal—that required imagination and the sense of showmanship of a great artist.'[3]

The sort of appeal that he made was not long in disclosing itself in an ugly rash of revolutionary crime. On the night of 19 April a band organized by the Hindu branch of the Hindustan Republican Association raided the arsenals of Chittagong, and after murdering six people escaped into the jungle. It was the same murder gang whose members had killed Saunders and thrown the bombs into the Assembly. Gandhi expressed futile regrets at this outrage, but the news of it rang over India. The Viceroy wrote to the Secretary of State of these and other disturbances in a manner that showed he was fully alive to his responsibilities:

'They have exploded rather earlier than we expected the theory of non-violence. They have reminded us that an anti-Government campaign finds inevitable expression, when feeling is running high, in racial hatreds and

---

[1] India Office Library, MSS. EUR.C. 152/6, *Lord Irwin. Letters to the Secretary of State for India*, p. 73.
[2] Louis Fischer. Op. cit., pp. 293-4.
[3] Ibid.

assaults on Europeans, and that our countrymen and women will be the first victims if ever we lose grip on the situation.'[1]

The raid at Chittagong was followed by an even more disturbing *émeute* at Peshawar caused by the arrest of Gaffar Khan in the city on 23 April. He was a leader advocating reform in the North West Frontier Province, and the arrest was followed by violent outbursts in the city which was for a time handed over to mob rule. 'Peshawar city,' said Coatman, who knew it well, 'is the focus on which converge streams of humanity from the fighting tribes of the border, from warlike Afghanistan, and from Central Asia, and it holds, at any given moment, a mob potentially as turbulent and dangerous as any the world can show.' When the military were called in to quell the riots, two platoons of the 39th Garhwal Rifles, one of the finest units in the Indian Army, refused to reinforce the city, and a detachment of Gurkhas was called up instead, and took Peshawar on 4 May. This evidence that even the military might not be immune from the prevailing agitation disturbed the Viceroy, who told the King that 'the episode was a very uncomfortable one that inevitably sets one thinking . . . obviously the sort of thing on which the less press comment there is the better'.[2]

But the Viceroy's patience was now running out fast. He knew that the time was coming when he must arrest Gandhi. 'Before this letter reaches you,' he told the Secretary of State, 'it may have been necessary to take decisive action. Even so, the temporary immunity granted to him will be on the credit side of our account. His arrest will have followed and not preceded outbreaks of violence by those who profess to serve under his banner. . . . We shall have avoided the impetus to his movement which his arrest in the initial stages would have given.'[3]

That decisive action was taken on 4 May. Even in the interests of the Round Table Conference, at which he hoped to see the delegates from Congress taking their places, he could afford to delay no longer. Gandhi was in his camp at Karadi, lying peacefully asleep under an old mango tree when the policemen came to fetch him, and the ashramites sang hymns as they led him to Yeravda jail.

Shortly before his arrest Gandhi had intended to raid the Dharsana salt depots with his followers. In his stead went Mrs. Naidu with 2,500 volunteers who were instructed to advance on the depots in waves, and to offer no resistance to attacks by the police. No body of men had been more sorely tried than the Indian Police during the recent disturbances since the Royal Irish Constabulary during the Troubles, and there seems little doubt that they lost their tempers and handled the waves of Satyagrahis roughly, causing the United

[1] India Office Library, MSS. EUR.C. 152/6, *Lord Irwin. Letters to the Secretary of State for India*, p. 94.

[2] India Office Library, MSS. EUR.C. 152/1, *Lord Irwin. Correspondence with H.M. the King-Emperor, 1926–1931*, p. 117.

[3] India Office archives, *Lord Irwin. Letters to the Secretary of State for India*, Vol. V, p. 93.

Press Correspondent, Webb Miller, to write that 'In eighteen years of reporting in twenty-two countries I have never witnessed such harrowing scenes as
at Dharsana. From where I stood I heard the sickening whack of the clubs
on unprotected skulls'.

The Viceroy took a different view of this scene which he described in a
breezy letter to the King:

'Your Majesty can hardly fail to have read with amusement the accounts
of the several battles for the Salt Depot at Dharsana. The police for a long
time tried to refrain from action. After a time this became impossible,
and they eventually had to resort to sterner methods. A good many people
suffered minor injuries in consequence; but I believe those who suffered
injuries were as nothing compared to those who wished to sustain an honourable contusion or bruise, or who, to make the whole setting more dramatic,
lay on the ground as if laid out for dead without any injury at all. But of
course, as Your Majesty will appreciate, the whole business was propaganda
and, as such, served its purpose admirably well.'[1]

*   *   *

The Viceroy had waited for what some thought a dangerously long time
before using his emergency powers. With the country drifting into anarchy
he had no further choice. Once he had decided on action, he provided it, as
he had promised, with no sparing hand. Between April and December 1930
he issued ten Ordinances to meet the emergency, the greatest number that
any Viceroy had ever promulgated, the Bengal Criminal Law Amendment
Ordinance, the Sholapur Martial Law Ordinance, the Unlawful Instigations
Ordinance, and many others.

The military authorities had been disturbed by recent events on the North
West Frontier, and they were buttressed by the Peshawar Martial Law
Ordinance. Even Mr. Winston Churchill must have smiled with approval
when the Viceroy proceeded to arrest Jawaharlal Nehru, muzzle the vernacular Press by Ordinance, stamp on unlawful gatherings of people and fill
the jails of India to bursting point.

The Provincial Governments were encouraged by the Viceroy to proceed
without mercy against Civil Disobedience, and themselves decide the seriousness of a crisis, and the appropriate measures to be taken. In June he declared
the Working Committee of Congress to be an unlawful association and out-
lawed it, together with the All-India Congress Committee, and threw its
august President, Motilal Nehru, into jail.

Congress also stoked up its fires to the utmost and indulged in an effective
boycott of British goods, British-owned shops, businesses and banks. The
participants in Civil Disobedience were no longer confined to those who

---

[1] India Office Library, MSS. EUR.C. 152/1, *Lord Irwin. Correspondence with H.M. The King-
Emperor, 1926–1931*, p. 123.

believed in non-violence as an article of faith. 'All who accepted it, even as a matter of policy, be they Government officials, students or lawyers, were invited to join in on raids of salt depots, breaches of forest laws and refusal in chosen areas to pay taxes and revenues.'[1]

It was a struggle in which one side was attempting to bring the Government of India to a standstill, and the other to prevent this disaster at all costs. By July the Congress seemed everywhere in retreat, in Madras, Assam, Bihar, Orissa and the Punjab, but Civil Disobedience was far from dead, and the men in the field who were fighting for the Government felt that there was no room for complacency. The Viceroy also recognized that one of his fears was being realized, and that by his firm action he had alienated the Hindu Mahasabha, some of whom publicly withdrew their support of the Round Table Conference.

The date of that conference had now been fixed for October 1930. India could scarcely have been in a less happy condition for such a momentous step in her political life. The Civil Disobedience movement had produced a high commotion in the blood of the Indian people. Their Mahatma was languishing in Yeravda jail, delighted indeed with his leisure, but the object of pity and awe to millions. The police, stoned and battered, and on one occasion, having had burning coals thrown down upon them had sometimes lost their heads and brought an ugly note into the general discord.

It was hardly to be expected that the tribes from 'Yaghistan, the land of unrest' beyond the North West Frontier, would fail to take advantage of the tumult in India. As always before in history, when they thought that the grasp of the English on the rich lands below them had relaxed, they descended in search of loot. The Afridis prowled round the borders of Peshawar, and strong groups of tribesmen penetrated deep into the Peshawar district, and for a time held part of this borderline under their control, while at the same time the Government was distracted by a rebellion which had broken out in the forests of Burma.

To all these aggravations was now added the agitation caused by the publication of the Simon Report. The second volume of the Simon Commission's Report, which contained their recommendations for the future of India, was published on 24 June 1930. A brilliant first volume, one of the greatest State Papers of modern history, consisting of a survey of the Indian scene which it described in four hundred masterly pages, had preceded it on 10 June.

The Report, which bore in every line the lucid imprint of the Chairman of the Commission, had been, since the announcement of the Round Table Conference, reduced to one of the many items on the agenda which might be discussed at that meeting. The decision to make that Conference 'free' which

[1] S. Gopal. Op. cit., p. 71.

the Viceroy, advised by Hailey and Goschen, had urged upon the Government, had further reduced the scope of its importance. By that decision the delegates would be at liberty to raise almost any subject they wished, and it was improbable that they would waste much time over the Simon Report which had not even mentioned the words 'Dominion Status' in its recommendations for reform.

Events in India had now far outrun the modest proposals for reform contained in that document, and the minimum Indian demands had already been put forward in the Nehru Report. Unless Simon and his colleagues had been able to offer a plan almost equally far-reaching, in which Dominion Status was proclaimed as the goal of Indian progress, and proposals made for the means of arriving at it without the necessity for further inquests and Royal Commissions, his Report was doomed.

Nor was the atmosphere in any way receptive to such a carefully reasoned document. There was not the slightest intention on the part of the Hindu leaders to weigh its arguments with the care they deserved. They merely wished to know how much control the Report recommended should be transferred from English to Indian hands, while the sole concern of the Moslems and other minorities was the extent to which the rights of their communities were to be safeguarded.

Neither party was satisfied by the Report, of which the essential recommendations were the abolition of dyarchy, the institution of Provincial Autonomy and the separation of India and Burma. It did not propose the transfer of control to Indian hands, and it did not satisfy the communities that their safety was secured. Large reservations were placed on this suggested form of Provincial Autonomy by the emergency powers of the Governor.

Nor were the proposals for the Central Government likely to arouse much enthusiasm. The Viceroy was to remain 'the actual and active Head of the Government'. Although the Cabinets in the eight Provinces were to be responsible to their Legislatures, their measures could still be disallowed by the Governor acting under the authority of the Viceroy and Secretary of State. It was the hope of the authors of the Report that, while proposing autonomy in the Provinces combined with an executive at the Centre responsible only to Parliament, the scheme would enable each of the Provinces to develop the machinery of Government most suited to it, and give Indians an opportunity of judging in the Provinces how far the British system of government was suited to their needs. But it is improbable in the highest degree that such a system would have worked even if it had been accepted.

The Simon Report had in fact been outstripped by events. In its insistence on the old method of slowly ripening progress it now seemed to the Indians like a prehistoric monster moving in the wrong geological age. It was a great Report, and a panacea that would have been perfectly appropriate in more peaceful seasons, but now it was brushed aside with impatience. But in one matter it showed particular foresight. It was an exponent of a Federated India, containing both British India and the Indian States, which, if it had been accomplished, would have saved India from partition. The authors of the Montagu-Chelmsford Report had said: 'Granted the announcement of 20 August [1917], we cannot at the present time envisage its complete fulfilment in any form other than that of a congeries of self-governing provinces associated for certain purposes under a responsible government of India; with possibly what are now the Native States of India finally embodied in the same whole, in some relation which we will not now attempt to define.' Experience in India had convinced Simon and his colleagues that Indian nationalism was a phenonemon which could not be disregarded by the rulers of either British India or of the Indian States, and that it was only under a federal system that the sentiment underlying the movement could be given effective expression.

Lord Irwin, after a first hasty perusal of Volume II of the Report, put his finger at once on what he considered to be the weakest spot:

'The fundamental omission of all his Report as I read it,' he told the Secretary of State on 20 June, 'is his very obvious and deliberate refusal to take the bandage off his eyes and admit the existence of the "Dominion Status" claim in terms. The thing seems to me very much to lack imagination. Surely it would have been quite possible for him to say: "You want Dominion Status; we want you to have it; there are such and such difficulties; they can probably be discussed at the Conference: but our suggestions for overcoming them are so and so!" Instead of this not a word, and this will do harm.'[1]

He was also concerned about the lack of psychological insight which he discerned in the Report, and which reminded him, he told his father, of the difference between the views of a Harley Street specialist and those of the family doctor who knew all the foibles of the patient. He felt also that owing to the boycott of the Commission by Congress, it had failed to grasp the full strength of the Indian nationalist movement which had grown at a speed and gained a momentum which astonished even those learned in the affairs of India.

The central point of his reasoning was that the relations between England and India had radically altered in the last ten years. The old tutorial attitude of the British that they were a parent nation patiently educating an immature people into political responsibility was to him now a thing of the past. Too much had happened in the meantime, and the problem was no longer as simple as it had seemed to Montagu and Chelmsford. He was now convinced that the Simon Report could not be regarded as the last word at the Conference,[2] and suggestions from the political leaders of his own party in England that it should, filled him with impatience:

[1] India Office Library, MSS. EUR.C. 152/6, *Lord Irwin. Letters to the Secretary of State for India*, p. 175.
[2] Ibid., p. 187.

'It really makes me weep to think that in a matter of this kind Stanley Baldwin should submit his judgment to Austen,[1] whose contact with India is distant and whose mind is always that of a log of wood,' and two days later he again wrote to the Secretary of State about a telegram from Baldwin which roused the Viceroy's slow temper to an even greater degree of annoyance:

'I suppose the telegram represents the views of Austen Chamberlain, Peel, Birkenhead and Eddie Winterton. I cannot help feeling that Stanley Baldwin must have had a comparatively small hand in it. The suggestion that Simon's Report is to be treated as gospel, which it is profane to criticize, seems to me perfectly ludicrous, and as you say, to reduce the Conference to a perfect farce. Nor for the life of me can I understand why or how Provincial Governments or the Government of India can be debarred from the liberty of disagreeing if they so desire. . . . It really makes my blood boil that people with mentality like that, not knowing the A.B.C. of the problem as you and I have to deal with it, should have such capacities for making mischief.'[2]

So angry did Irwin become and so deeply were Indian problems now obsessing his mind that he even added to the Socialist Secretary of State:

'I must confess to you quite frankly that the reflection I made when I read Baldwin's telegram was that, if events so turned out that this clash of opinion ultimately and unhappily led to an Election and if I was at home at the time, I should quite definitely feel it impossible to wish to see the return to power of the mentality that the telegram represents!'[3]

Baldwin's telegram which had so irritated the Viceroy had again stressed the Conservative Party's objection to the phrase 'Dominion Status' as certain to be interpreted in India in a manner not intended by the Viceroy or the British Government, and while recognizing that the Round Table Conference must be 'free', urged that its freedom of discussion should be confined within the framework of the Commission's recommendations which made it plain that the ultimate goal could only be reached by slow degrees. This gradualness, Baldwin had reminded him, was fundamental to the whole scheme of the Simon Report, and was essential if all-party agreement in England was to be maintained.[4]

It was with some difficulty that Irwin restrained himself from an angry reply. Even so, he stated frankly that he would be unwilling to remain Viceroy of India if any ground were given for the impression that his Declaration on Dominion Status was to be withdrawn or modified. He told Baldwin that he realized that agreement among the British parties was important, but that he

---

[1] The Rt. Hon. Sir Austen Chamberlain.
[2] India Office Library, MSS. EUR.C. 152/6, *Lord Irwin. Letters to the Secretary of State for India*, p. 187.
[3] Ibid.
[4] India Office Library, MSS. EUR.C. 152/15, *Lord Irwin. Telegrams to and from the Secretary of State for India*, 4 July 1930.

hoped that opinion at home would not overlook the importance also of securing agreement from those in India who would have to work the constitution. He also told Baldwin that although he valued the support of the English parties, he would no longer do so if it involved an indefinite continuance of the repressive policy he was at present compelled to pursue, and he begged him to believe that most Europeans in India realized that a genuine attempt must sooner or later be made to reach agreement with reasonable opinion.[1]

The political leaders in England were not alone in viewing the prospects of the Simon Commission with apprehension. King George V through Lord Stamfordham had also expressed the hope that the Simon Report, after all the labours of its authors, would not be thrown to the wolves. We have seen Lord Irwin's opinion of the Report; how he deplored the absence of a reference to Dominion Status, and believed that Simon had left an impasse with an elected Assembly and an executive which was not responsible to it. Holding these views, he was less straightforward than usual in his effort to reassure the King:

'I am very sorry that anything I should have said about the Simon Report should have caused Your Majesty any uneasiness. I have never had any doubt that it would in fact be the principal basis of discussion at the Conference.'[2]

Even if this statement was not true, it cannot be charged against the Viceroy that it was his announcement of Dominion Status and the summoning of the Conference that wrecked the Simon Report. The reaction to it in India had been immediate and unambiguous. It was attacked by all Hindu opinion because it gave only the semblance of control in the Provinces and at the Centre, and by the Moslems who disliked its Provincial provisions, and said that their frequently expressed claims had been disregarded. The Sikhs objected to those parts of it which affected their own position in the Punjab. 'It was, however, not merely Indian opinion that was hostile. The Government of India, committed by the Viceroy to Dominion Status, still based their hopes on a Round Table Conference, and both the British and Indian Governments declared that such a conference would be a free one, and would in no way be bound or circumscribed by the Report. . . . The Report of the Statutory Commission, in fact, had been overtaken by events and was dead before it was born.'[3]

The Viceroy had done his best to provide a temperate climate for its reception by postponing the election due to be held at the end of 1929 because he knew that it would return an enormous majority in the Central and

[1] Ibid, 5 July 1930.
[2] India Office Library, MSS. EUR.C. 152/1, *Lord Irwin. Correspondence with H.M. The King-Emperor*, p. 129.
[3] S. Gopal. Op. cit., p. 91.

Provincial Legislatures pledged to boycott the Report. His sole object in doing so had been to give the Report a fair chance.

It is easy now to understand the state of mind both of the Viceroy and of his critics in London. Reading and Birkenhead objected to any alteration of the procedure laid down for the Statutory Commission. They believed that nothing but harm could come from a declaration of policy or any other interference before the Report had been presented to Parliament. The Viceroy, close to the fast-beating heart of India, believed that the situation was slipping out of his control, and that he must make an effort, however dangerous, to retrieve it. This had been the reason for his announcement; to give reassurance to the Indians when they were losing confidence in the intentions of the British Government, and he believed the gesture to be one of immense psychological importance.

So also did Sir Malcolm Hailey, greatest of Indian public servants during Lord Irwin's viceroyalty, who told the author:

'You ask whether opinion in India was by November 1929 or January 1930 moving so fast that it had already outstripped the proposals contained in the Simon Report. I think that the proposals embodied in the Nehru Report represented something that was not merely more advanced, but something that had secured a measure of popular support far greater than most of us realized. . . . One thing I think very clear. Matters had already arrived at a stage when the Viceroy was compelled to take any action open to him to seek a calmer atmosphere. And he was justified in going to some lengths to do so. But in the end it was his personality and the general belief in his sincerity which did more to win the confidence of responsible Indians than any declaration he could make regarding Dominion Status or the appointment of the Round Table Conference.'[1]

[1] Lord Hailey to author.

CHAPTER XVI

THE IRWIN–GANDHI PACT

THE First Round Table Conference was opened by the King-Emperor on 12 November 1930. Gandhi was still in jail and the Congress took no part in its deliberations. Some attempts had been made during the summer by Sapru and Jayakar to arrange a compromise between Congress and the Government, and enable Gandhi to get into personal touch with Irwin. In June, on the eve of his arrest, Motilal Nehru had said that negotiations were possible if the Government would support the demand for Full Responsible Government for India subject to agreement as to terms of transfer of power necessitated by India's special position, and which could be discussed at the Round Table Conference.[1]

With their customary optimism and goodwill, Sapru and Jayakar asked the Viceroy's permission, which was granted, to confer with the caged Mahatma in Yeravda jail in an effort to splice the severed bond and induce Congress to be represented at the Conference. They found the old man in obstinate mood, and took themselves to Naini Prison at Allahabad for another conference with the two Nehrus. Here their pacifying efforts were met by a flat rejection of anything short of Independence for India. Rebuffed but not defeated, Sapru now asked permission to hold a joint conference of the detainees, and the Viceroy, sceptical but co-operative, again agreed, and arranged for the Nehrus to be moved to Yeravda.

Here the Liberals met in melancholy conclave Gandhi, Motilal and Jawaharlal Nehru, now reinforced by Mrs. Naidu and Vallabhai Patel. Here the outraged Sapru was presented with an even more brutal ultimatum. The Nationalist leaders demanded the right to secede and the transfer of all powers, even economic and military, to a responsible Government in India. The Viceroy had placed little confidence in these meetings, but he must have been at one with the disgusted Sapru who said that he had 'never underestimated the difficulties, but had not anticipated encountering quite such a degree of obduracy'.[2] Thus yet another olive branch was rejected.

It is unnecessary to enter into details of the First Round Table Conference which was described to the Viceroy in India by Hailey in brilliant and often caustic despatches. Tasks of incredible scope and complexity lay

[1] S. Gopal. Op. cit., p. 92.
[2] Sir Tej Bahadur Sapru to Lord Irwin Archives of the Government of India. National Library of India.

before the delegates; to unite the peoples and communities of British India by arrangements acceptable to all and which protected the rights of the minorities, so that the whole of that great land could become one stable element in the greater scheme of All India; to establish workable relations between British India and the Native States, so that both might become harmonious parts of the greater whole; and to determine what position such an all-India Federation should occupy in the British Commonwealth of Nations. It was a task that involved the lives of one-fifth of the human race.

There was little encouragement in the attitude of the delegates at this first Conference. Men of all persuasions agreed that the future of India should be a federation of all India, composed of British India and the Native States, and the delegates, including the Princes, were united in the view that the character of such an arrangement should be responsible self-government, leading on at a future date to Dominion Status.

It was a conclusion that relieved the minds of the British leaders of the fear that the Conference would demand that it should immediately devise a constitution for the Dominion Status of India. But when the delegates separated they had made little progress towards these grandiose goals.

On the opening day of the Conference the Government of India had published their proposals for constitutional reform which went a little further than the Simon Report in an effort to placate the Indian Nationalists. It was unlikely to move them, for it proposed no surrender of control by the Central Government, but only that the members of the Viceroy's Executive Council, which was the Government of India, should be chosen from the elected members of the Indian Parliament. The old position that the Viceroy's Council was not responsible to that Parliament remained untouched because it was too vital to surrender. To the eyes of Indians this offered no progress in the evolution of self-government.

The absence of the Congress Party seemed to give the proceedings an air of unreality. 'The demand by all the delegates, including the Indian Princes, for responsible self-government both in the Provinces and at the Centre served only to show that the party that was the most vigorous spokesman of this demand could not be ignored. Worst of all, the Conference failed utterly to solve the old intractable problem of the minorities, and the sub-committee to which it had been entrusted had abandoned its task in despair.'[1]

It was thus in no buoyant mood that Sir Malcolm Hailey wrote to the Viceroy at the end of the Conference:

'Really this has, in some respects, hardly been a conference at all, except perhaps in so far as it has afforded a very valuable meeting ground for the discussion of Federation between the States and British India. Judged at all events from the somewhat prejudiced view of one who has taken a pride in the British connection with India, it has simply afforded a lamentable

[1] S. Gopal. Op. cit., p. 97.

spectacle of constant and one-sided attacks on the British rule. When there have been gross misstatements of fact, it has been no one's duty to answer them. The jackals have been left to scream perpetually, without a single bark from the watchdog. All this may minister to that curious pride in his tolerance and fair play with which the Englishman excuses what is often nothing but his own carelessness and incapacity for studying his own history.'[1]

In spite of these hard words, the Conference had not been fruitless. It had established the fact that responsible self-government on definite terms with a Federal Constitution for the whole of India was now the goal and that there could be no turning back from it. The minorities question was indeed unsettled, and many loose threads had been left behind, but the Viceroy felt that his initiative had achieved a partial break-through, and a new recognition of purpose which had been understood by millions of Indians and endorsed by Lord Reading, who, after doubtful beginnings, had ranged himself and his party behind Responsible Government with strict safeguards, and a Federation of All India.

When the Indian delegates returned home they were astonished to find a complete transformation in the political scene. They heard that the Viceroy was about to release Gandhi from prison, and that thousands who had trodden the road of Satyagraha with him were to be freed. The issue had now contracted to the personalities of the two men, Irwin and Gandhi. They were soon to come face to face in personal conversations, and to sign a pact which was to bring peace to strife-worn India for nearly a year. It would secure Congress representation at the next session of the Round Table Conference, and might have been the prelude to the settlement of immense troubles had not Congress, for its own ends, been bent on their perpetuation.

In early February the focus of attention was again in Delhi, that beautiful city which, seen from a height, looks like a great forest, in which white houses lie with cool green gardens and herbaceous flowers. The Viceroy himself had to obtain the co-operation of Congress in the new policy, and their representation at the next session of the Round Table Conference. He wanted to see peace in India and the abandonment of Civil Disobedience. He was aware that the omens were not good, and that while there was a Right Wing of Congress containing such men as Malaviya, there was also a Left Wing, represented by Jawaharlal Nehru who rejoiced in an atmosphere of disturbance and believed that a wide revolutionary upheaval would be good for the soul of India.

He knew that those who were working for peace were directing all their endeavours to influencing Gandhi, believing that he was the key of the position, and he was constantly revolving in his own mind what the possibilities of accommodation might be.

[1] India Office Library, MSS. EUR.E. 220, *Hailey. Letters from London, 1930–1933*, 12 January 1931.

He prepared the way with skill and tact in his speech to the Indian Legislature in Delhi on 17 January 1931:

'However mistaken any man may think him to be, and however deplorable may appear the results of the policy associated with his name, no one can fail to recognize the spiritual force which impels Mr. Gandhi to count no sacrifice too great in the cause, as he believes, of the India he loves. . . .

'Deeply as I crave to see the dawn of a happier day in India, I am bound, so long as a movement designed to undermine and sap the foundations of the Government holds the first place of the great Congress organization, to resist it to the uttermost of my strength. Is it not now possible, I would ask, for those responsible for this policy to try another course that in the light on the one hand of sinister events in India, and on the other of the encouragement offered to India by the progress of the Conference in England, would seem to be the more excellent way?'[1]

These generous words, spoken of an opponent in jail for sedition had never been used by a Viceroy before in the history of India, and could not fail to strike a note of sympathy, but they were shrewdly conceived, for the Viceroy's study of Gandhi's character had not been in vain. The 'other course' which he invited Gandhi to follow was disclosed in the speech made by Ramsay MacDonald two days later in winding up the Conference, in which he promised that, in addition to Provincial Autonomy, the Central Executive would be made responsible to a federal legislature with the necessary safeguards for a period of transition.

Even this striking concession failed to interest Motilal Nehru and his friends in Congress, and the Viceroy decided that he would make no further progress while Gandhi remained in prison. He was unconditionally released on 25 January, and the illegality of the Working Committee was revoked. This action was the Viceroy's personal decision and required a high degree of moral courage. In the eyes of Indians the British Government was already committed to a policy of dissolution, and no more graceful manner could have been found for forwarding such a policy than the release of Gandhi and the rendering lawful of a party that had been in open revolt.

But Irwin had to face intense hostility both in India and from the political leaders in England. He was reminded by the Provincial Governments that it was not the British Government but the Congress which was the defeated party, and that to pander to them now would involve an appalling loss of face. The Army, the Provincial officials and the local District Officers, in fact almost all those outside the inner circle of the Viceroy's advisers in his Council were against his gesture.

Even H. W. Emerson, the Home Secretary, and James Crerar, the Home Member, two of his most valued advisers, warned him of a stampede among

[1] Government of India Press, *Speeches by Lord Irwin*, Vol. II, p. 319.

his best supporters, the Moslems, the Services, the Army and Police, in the face of a gesture so fulsome to the party of sedition.[1]

To those in England who had already found contemptible the Viceroy's liberal tendencies in India, the release of Gandhi seemed a crowning act of pusillanimity. Irwin himself, once his mind was convinced of the wisdom of his action, was, as usual, sturdily indifferent to these warning voices. He believed that he would have the support of enlightened opinion in all parts of Europe, and had left Congress in the position of having to make the next move.

'I am hungering for peace,' Gandhi had said in Bombay, and many of his followers now shared this desire. After ten months of Civil Disobedience they had begun to feel that they had shot their bolt, and there appeared to be no limit to the resources of the Government or of its intention to continue using them in combating the movement. At the Congress meeting at Allahabad they had done no more than to pass a token resolution to continue the struggle, but this rang hollow even in their own ears for fresh campaigns were privately forbidden. Gandhi's position was further weakened by the death, on 6 February, of Motilal Nehru, which left a gap that none of his followers could fill.

Gandhi's first move was a tactical manœuvre of little credit to himself, by which he hoped to embarrass the Government while at the same time appearing to respond to their overtures. He demanded an inquiry into what he considered the excesses of the police during the troubles.

It was only one of many moments of exasperation which the Viceroy was to endure in his relations with Gandhi. 'I really have no patience,' he told his father, 'with a mentality which professes to be greatly shocked if and when a few policemen have done wrong, and remains quite unmoved when the forces that he has called into action all over the country have led to innumerable attacks on the police and continued persecution of law-abiding citizens.'[2] He returned to this impudent suggestion a flat and emphatic refusal, urging the Mahatma to forget the past and consider the future.

Sastri, Jayakar and Sapru were at Allahabad in touch with Gandhi who was now in a state of indecision, and it was through them that the stalemate was broken. On 14 February Gandhi wrote to the Viceroy—a strange letter from a released prisoner to the mighty ruler of India:

'Dear Friend,

As a rule I neither wait for outward prompting nor stand on ceremony, but straightway seek personal contact with officials whenever I feel such contact is needed in the interest of a cause. But somehow or other in the present case I have missed the guidance of the Inner Voice. But I have

[1] B. R. Nanda. Op. cit., p. 302.
[2] Hickleton Papers, *Correspondence with Viscount Halifax*, p. 342.

received suggestions from friends whose advice I value that I should seek an interview with you before coming to any decision. I can no longer resist this advice. I am aware of the responsibility resting on my shoulders. It is heightened by the death of Pandit Motilal Nehru. I feel without personal contact and heart to heart talk with you, the advice I may give my co-workers may not be right. The friends I have referred to read into the proceedings of the London Conference a meaning and a hope I would like to share. There are other difficulties to be overcome before I can advise suspension of the civil disobedience and co-operation in the remaining work of the Conference. It was felt that, before the Working Committee took any final decision, it might be better for me to meet you and discuss our difficulties with you. I therefore ask you, if you are willing, to send me an appointment as early as may be possible. I would like to meet not so much the Viceroy as the man in you.

Could I expect a reply by Monday next? In the absence of a reply I propose to leave Allahabad on Tuesday for Bombay where I expect to pass four days. My address in Bombay is Laburnum Road.

I am,

Your faithful friend,
(Sgd.) M. K. GANDHI.'[1]

Two days later, on 16 February, the Viceroy told the Secretary of State that he had accepted this suggestion and was taking the necessary steps to meet Gandhi.

'Things are moving rather fast here. I have telegraphed to Gandhi saying that I will see him tomorrow or Wednesday. All the information that I get suggests that it is really going to be a question of personal appeal and conviction, rather than of any argument. The cards I fancy are sympathy, understanding of his hopes, suspicions and disappointments; some play on what everybody says is characteristic, namely, vanity of power and personality; but above all, striving to convey to him, through what one says, a real echo of the sincerity that pervaded your doings in London. You may trust me to do my best, and one can't do more. Sastri . . . summed it up by saying: "He is like a woman; you have got to win him; therefore before you see him, perform all your ablutions, say all your prayers and put on your deepest spiritual robes!" He told me also that he had said to Gandhi: "If you see the Viceroy I guarantee you will come out a conquered man and you will be his man henceforth," to which Gandhi had replied: "I wish to be conquered." '[2]

*   *   *

[1] India Office Library, MSS. EUR.C. 152/6, *Lord Irwin. Letters to the Secretary of State for India*, p. 392.
[2] Ibid., p. 389.

Thus it came about that on 17 February 1931 the diminutive brown figure, with his bald head and toothless smile, walked between the two soldiers of the Viceroy's bodyguard, waiting mounted at the gate, to the lower side door of the palace, that great building, the fruit of Lutyens's genius, which rising out of the flat Delhi plain amid the mosques and tombs of Moghul Kings seemed to symbolize the enduring character of British rule. The Vicereine noticed that almost every servant in the house seemed to have found some urgent task near the entrance. It was the occasion for one of Mr. Churchill's most memorable diatribes. His mind alight with the glories of Britain's Imperial past, this acceptance of the rebel into the innermost sanctum of power struck him with a sense of outrage. He was revolted by 'the nauseating and humiliating spectacle of this one time Inner Temple lawyer, now seditious fakir, striding half-naked up the steps of the Viceroy's palace there to negotiate and parley on equal terms with the representative of the King-Emperor'. Perhaps he saw in that insignificant figure the doom of the long British dominion in India, but there were hundreds of others, typified by Lord Lloyd, equally indignant, who demanded angrily that this masochism should now cease. They, too, were sickened by the spectacle of the ruler of this great sub-continent, 'the brightest jewel in the Imperial Crown', meeting in friendship and equality the man whose declared object was to destroy that rule, and causing the Moslems who had been its friends to denounce this 'betrayal of the Loyal to the Disloyal'. He was aware that he was taking immense risks in accepting this meeting. 'I was fully alive to it,' he wrote to Hailey, 'but I could not feel after everything that had happened at the Conference and since, any other course was open to me when Gandhi himself asked to see me. And I have always thought that discussions about peace terms would in some form and at some time become inevitable.

'I never believed that when it came to the point it would be possible for Government to say: "We shall tell you nothing of our intentions by way of reciprocal action, till you have abandoned all Civil Disobedience and we are fully satisfied that you have attained to a change of heart." To think that things would work like that seemed to me to traffic in ideas that had little touch with reality. Nor do I believe it is, as George Lloyd would say, that we are lacking in fibre and morale, but only that we do seek faithfully to face facts which are, whether you like it or not, altering very fast.'[1]

He believed that if he had declined to confer with Gandhi on the grounds that it was improper for the Viceroy to meet the principal leader of a subversive movement, such action would have been almost universally misunderstood and condemned in India, and that the only ultimate means of killing the Civil Disobedience movement was to get public opinion opposed to it. From this point of view the effect of a refusal to see Gandhi was 'pretty

[1] India Office Library, MSS. EUR.C. 152/19, *Correspondence with Persons in England and Abroad*, p. 299.

conclusive'.[1] He had embarked on a policy which he believed could alone save India, and it was clear to him that it would not work if it was opposed by the enormous sections of Indian opinion represented by Congress.

*   *   *

There was an astonishing difference between the Viceroy and his visitor, between the six-foot-five English aristocrat, the product of Eton and Christ Church, and the little brown man naked except for a loin cloth and dhoti. There was something almost repellent to many European eyes in that strangely shaped bald head, those heavily magnifying glasses, and the naked grin, for Gandhi only inserted his teeth for the purpose of eating; something repellent, too, in the messes of dates and goat's milk which he produced from some recess of his garment.

One had been born near the mouth of the mighty Indus in the dark right-hand corner of a room eleven feet by nineteen; the other near the mouth of the quietly flowing Exe in the tranquil grandeur of Powderham Castle. One had been nourished upon the sermons of Pusey and Keble, the other on the Bhagvad Gita. The houses where the Viceroy took his ease were Garrowby and Hickleton with their great rooms and broad manors. To Gandhi home was the ashram or hermitage of Sabarmati, a few whitewashed huts in a grove of spreading trees, and below the compound the river where the women washed their laundry and the cows and buffaloes wallowed in the tepid water, huts where, in spite of his cleanliness, there was no sanitation and his rebellious sons emptied the chamber pots. He had long abjured fleshly pleasures, those 'shackles of lust' which had tormented him in youth like St. Augustine, and clouded his memories of his father's death with a degrading recollection of carnal desire. He was now devoted solely to 'Swaraj from within'.

Whatever thoughts passed through Irwin's mind as he awaited his strange guest, he knew that Gandhi alone among Congress leaders had achieved a mystical ascendancy over millions of the Indian people, and that bafflingly entwined with the sophistries of a lawyer and a maddening inconstancy of thought was the mystique of a holy man who had lifted politics above the level of common life, and shown that even the mighty Government of India could be shaken by an idea.

The Viceroy described to the King the curiosity with which he awaited Gandhi:

'I must confess to Your Majesty that I was, too, greatly interested in having the opportunity of discussion with this strange little man. I had met him of course before two or three times, but never in circumstances that permitted conversation to be entirely free. I think that most people meeting

[1] India Office Library, MSS. EUR.C. 152/1, *Lord Irwin. Correspondence with H.M. The King-Emperor, 1926–1931*, p. 152.

him would be conscious, as I was conscious, of a very powerful personality, and this, independent of physical endowment, which indeed is unfavourable. Small, wizened, rather emaciated, no front teeth, it is a personality very poorly adorned with this world's trimmings. And yet you cannot help feeling the force of character behind the sharp little eyes and immensely active and acutely working mind.'[1]

Mr. Churchill's distress would have increased could he have followed Gandhi into the viceregal presence, and observed the meeting of the 'two Mahatmas', as Mrs. Naidu described them. Sir Francis Humphrys, former British representative in Afghanistan, was present at one of these meetings and recalled: 'I remember Gandhi squatting on the floor and after a while a girl coming in with some filthy yellow stuff which he started eating without so much as by your leave.' Humphrys added that he would have liked to have seen this happening to Curzon.[2] The Viceroy's A.D.C.s did not like the Mahatma whom they considered to be a devious little lawyer who played up to the Indian servants in order to attract publicity. There were seven hundred of these in the establishment, and Gandhi thought that they were ordinary people who had assembled in order to welcome him.

Gandhi and Irwin met eight times during the four weeks that followed their first discussion on 17 February. They did not, however, as was reported, kneel down together in prayer, although when Sir Cecil Griffin asked him if Gandhi had been tiresome, Irwin had replied: 'Some people found Our Lord very tiresome.' The Viceroy knew that he was in for some fierce horse-trading, and was prepared to listen for hours to Gandhi's rambling monologues. He had the happy facility for dismissing the matter entirely from his mind the moment his visitor had left the room.

Their agreement was finally drawn up on the night of 4 March. These negotiations are a good example of the hard, practical side of Irwin's character. Apart from the immense prestige that Gandhi won among his followers in India by bearding the Viceroy in his lair, and to which Irwin was indifferent, the Viceroy drove a hard bargain, and the real advantages gained were almost entirely on his side.

Beneath all the charm and simplicity of manner, beneath the sweet reason and the desire to please that were the outward appearances of his character, that hard streak of Yorkshire ruthlessness and acumen, that shrewdness in a deal, and that inexhaustible patience, enabled the Viceroy to prevail over an opponent as unpredictable as a snipe in flight.

He knew that having taken such risks the price of failure would be heavy. He had therefore to watch Gandhi, as a cat watches a mouse, for any sudden move of flight, to keep his sympathy and interest constantly engaged, and the

[1] Ibid., p. 153.
[2] Sir Francis Humphrys to author. The lady was Miss Slade, the daughter of an English admiral and for many years a disciple of Gandhi.

conference itself in a state of continual movement. It was an ordeal that would have been excruciating to ordinary nerves, but the Viceroy's intimates never saw in him the slightest signs of depression or foreboding.

After Irwin had explained that any decision made must be based on the assumption that India's goal was an All-India Federation with a responsible federal government with safeguards, they discussed the Salt Laws, the conduct of the police, and the release of political prisoners, and Irwin wrote to the Secretary of State of the 'superhuman efforts that have been necessary to get Mr. Gandhi along'.

The Viceroy refused even to discuss the question of releasing men who had been convicted of crimes of violence during the troubles, but those who had been arrested for other offences were about to be discharged. He was also loyal to the much abused Indian Police, and resolutely refused to consider holding an inquiry into the excesses of which they had been accused. He knew that an intolerable strain had been placed on the police during Civil Disobedience, and that their conduct in general had been beyond praise. Always too few in numbers to cover all points of unrest, they had been derided and attacked and subjected to every form of humiliation. They had been pelted with stones and bricks; insults had been screamed at them, and their lives had been constantly in danger.

The Viceroy would not accept the suggestion that a few cases in which discipline had collapsed under stress justified an inquiry into their general behaviour any more than the excesses of a few soldiers in a large army in the heat of battle. It was on this point that the conference almost foundered. Sapru and Jayakar, who had been acting as peacemakers, called upon him and made the mistake of using menacing language on this subject. Their attitude produced one of Irwin's rare losses of temper.

'I rather lost my temper with them and told them that they had to choose on which side of the fight, if there was one, they intended to be. I added that if on a matter of comparatively minor importance they ranged themselves against those who were trying to do constructive work, in order to stand alongside those who had for twelve months been trying to wreck all efforts of a constructive kind, I should have frankly little opinion left of either their judgment or their character.'[1]

The subject of picketing also caused Irwin some anxious moments. Gandhi was anxious to keep this weapon of economic boycott in reserve, and pressed for the right of 'peaceful picketing' of shops and business premises. The Viceroy was equally firm in maintaining that there was no such thing in practice as 'peaceful picketing', and in demanding that the boycott, as a political weapon, should be abandoned.

The Irwin–Gandhi pact was announced on 5 March 1931, and no clearer

[1] India Office Library, MSS. EUR.C. 152/6, *Lord Irwin. Letters to the Secretary of State for India*, p. 397.

proof could be found of the masterly manner in which the Viceroy had negotiated than the anger of Jawaharlal Nehru at the extent of the concessions Gandhi had made.[1]

These were substantial. It was agreed that Civil Disobedience in all its forms should be stopped, and that Congress should be represented in future sessions of the Round Table Conference. It was agreed that this representation should be on the basis that Congress agreed that the subject of discussion should be the future of India in an All-India Federation, with responsibility for the federal Government subject to safeguards in the interests of India for such matters as defence, external affairs, the position of minorities, the financial credit of India and the discharge of obligations.

The Government reserved the right, if Congress did not honour its obligations, to act as it thought fit for the protection of the public and the maintenance of law and order. This concession by Gandhi did not attempt to define the safeguards or provide the right to secede. The Viceroy told Gandhi that he supposed the right of secession could be raised at the next session of the Conference, but that to do so would produce a lamentable impression on the English parties, and lead to inevitable shipwreck. Gandhi had assented.

Gandhi was anxious to keep the economic boycott as a rod in pickle for potential disagreements, and the Viceroy was equally determined that the financial well-being of India should not be manipulated by a particular party as a weapon in any future conflict with the Government. Irwin had also to consider the interests of the textile industry in Lancashire which were heavily involved, and he called in his Home Secretary, Emerson, a Punjab civilian, to reinforce his arguments. 'I should like to see Mr. Emerson very much,' said Gandhi. 'I have heard so much about Mr. Emerson. Such a hard man and so unkind to the poor people.' But Gandhi was soon won by the personality of this straightforward and friendly civilian, and the *rapport* between them was a powerful factor in solving the dispute about the right of boycott.

This boycott had been directed entirely against British goods, and was therefore a weapon of political warfare. It was agreed in the pact that there should be no compulsion on merchants who made their living by dealing in English goods, and that the cloth dealers should be free to deal as they liked. The Viceroy would have been glad to have been free of picketing for good, but judged it prudent in this case to make a mild concession in the interests of Indian industry by allowing propaganda on its behalf to include peaceful picketing. Irwin had no fear that this sop might prove dangerous: 'I have very little doubt,' he said, 'that if you can get rid of the political weapon-drive of it, and have it as a purely economic and social thing, it will be dead in three weeks.'

[1] Jawaharlal Nehru to author.

The Viceroy had thus been unbending on all the points to which he attached real importance, and had, miraculously, as it seemed to many, gained his ends. But if the balance of advantage lay with the Viceroy, Gandhi, from his own point of view, could also contemplate the result with lively satisfaction. He had secured the withdrawal of all Ordinances, after Civil Disobedience had been abandoned, that had been promulgated during the troubles, except those restraining terrorist activity. Notifications which during the disturbances had declared certain associations to be unlawful were to be withdrawn, as were prosecutions for offences committed during that time except those involving violence.

All prisoners who had been jailed during Civil Disobedience were to be released, except those convicted of violent offences or of inciting violence. Fines and securities were to be remitted. Moveable property not of an objectionable character such as arms and seditious literature, and not in illegal possession, which had been confiscated by the Government was to be returned. Local Governments were to remove, where possible, auxiliary police who had been assigned to the district at the expense of the inhabitants.

The Viceroy recognized that the question of salt, with its symbolism in the public mind with the beginning of Satyagraha, must be delicately handled, and he had no intention of allowing the negotiations to be wrecked on such a paltry reef. 'I fully recognize,' he said, 'the psychological objection to doing anything on a matter so publicly identified with the inauguration of the Civil Disobedience Campaign. A good deal will turn on how it can be done, but I do not believe that we ought to allow settlement to wreck on the abstract principle that salt is the inviolable ark on which no hand must be laid.' He could not condone breaches of the existing Salt Law, or in the prevailing conditions alter the Salt Act, but he was willing to allow the inhabitants of the seaside villages to collect and make salt for their own consumption provided that they did not sell it to people outside their area.

But Gandhi's greatest reward was in the blaze of glory that followed the signing of the instrument, when he was followed everywhere as in the great days of Satyagraha by worshipping crowds. He could claim glory, too, as Gopal has pointed out, in the very phraseology in which the document was couched. It was full of phrases like 'It has been agreed that', which seemed to accept the status of the rebel as almost equal to that of the Viceroy.

Even the clause which dealt with constitutional questions: 'The scope of future discussions is stated with the assent of His Majesty's Government,' might be interpreted as meaning that the British Government had merely been required to approve the terms which had been reached in consultation with Gandhi. Lastly, the Viceroy's action had suggested a belief that without the goodwill and co-operation of Congress there could be no real progress in the determining of India's constitutional future.

Official opinion in India on the Irwin–Gandhi pact was divided. To some it seemed that by picking up his floored opponent and dusting him down, the Viceroy was recklessly mortgaging the future and that Gandhi was merely holding him in suspense while he prepared for a fresh assault, but neither Emerson nor Haig was against the negotiation. There was in fact no opposition to it in the Government of India. On the contrary, they hailed it at the time, although later they were prepared to criticize it when things went wrong.[1]

The Viceroy's mood was one of quiet elation at the achievement of this *détente*, and he expressed his feeling to the Secretary of State on 9 March 1931:

'Looking on the whole thing, I do regard it as a very astonishing thing that Gandhi should have been so far persuaded to come into line. I had moments of hoping it might happen, but I never dared feel confident, and actually on Sunday the 1st I had made up my mind very clearly that we must break and that within a week or ten days we should be back in the old circle. . . .

'Although many people are giving me a share of the credit, I don't think very much is really due. I believe that the broad forces that were at work were working very hard in the direction of peace; and it may even be that we could have got something more stiff through. But I do not think that if we had tried too hard in this direction that we should have been as successful as I believe we were in carrying Gandhi on the sentimental side, in the sense of mobilizing all his energies with real goodwill to find the way of permanent agreement.'[2]

The Viceroy was not a man of intellectual subtlety, and although he won Gandhi's trust and respect, it was inevitable that he should be baffled by a mind so Eastern, so unpredictable in its working, and so oddly compounded of mystical and opportunist elements. His failure to probe this strange instrument is apparent in the words in which he tried to describe Gandhi to Lord Halifax:

'I kept on asking myself all the time "Was the man completely sincere", and I think as our conversation went on that I came to feel about this in rather double fashion. I came to have no doubt whatever that, if Mr. Gandhi gave me his word on any point, that word was absolutely secure, and that I could trust it implicitly. On the other hand, I found what had always been my impression being confirmed, namely, that though intentionally he was completely sincere, yet in some matters he was the victim of unconscious self-deception. The tendency to this showed itself in the importance he attached to different matters, and the weight that he seemed prepared to give to different kinds of evidence.'

Irwin was certain that everything now depended on how Gandhi was

[1] Sir Cecil Griffin to author.
[2] India Office Library, MSS. EUR.C. 152/6, *Lord Irwin. Letters to the Secretary of State for India*, Vol. V, pp. 415–16.

handled at the Conference discussions. 'Whoever does it must realize that it is no good appealing to his head unless you have first got entry into his heart.' Gandhi, on his side, must also be careful about his hosts' susceptibilities.

The Viceroy sent for him and begged him to have regard for British opinion on the subject of 'Purna Swaraj', which to the English meant 'complete Independence' which would suggest that his goal was the disruption of the British Empire. Gandhi was prepared to admit plenty of safeguards or adjustments, once the equality was secured—'If he could get this sort of relationship, he would say that he had got independence with partnership. And this he thought a higher conception than independence in isolation. If, however, he could not get his independence through partnership, he would have to go for it through isolation.'[1]

Although he felt a quiet pride and satisfaction, the Viceroy was not so naïve as to suppose that the pact would be a panacea for all the ills of India. He thought that 'We are perhaps in danger of investing it with too high a degree of permanent sanction', and he told his father: 'I am under no delusion as to the further difficulties that have to be surmounted, many of which may prove insurmountable. . . . It brings the Congress people definitely to the point of having to apply their minds to the practical facts instead of just vociferating about the rights of man.'[2]

Congress leaders were to represent the Delhi Pact as a Machiavellian device of the Government to induce Gandhi to call off a struggle he was winning, and to take part in the Round Table Conference where failure was certain, and would be attributed by the British to that fatal Indian disunity which bedevilled progress. The Viceroy had therefore had to work for the agreement against heavy odds. The Prime Minister MacDonald and even the Socialist Secretary of State, who had never wavered in his support, began to show signs of losing their nerve, and to suggest revisions in the text, but Irwin telegraphed back to say that agreement had already been reached, and that to reopen the issue would be merely to invite disaster.[3]

The Viceroy was aware that he was risking his own future, but he was indifferent to personal considerations. He only knew that every day it was borne in on him more harshly that repression led nowhere, and he acted in the hope, unduly optimistic, that Congress would be enticed into adopting constitutional methods at last, and that they would play their full part in founding the new constitution.

He believed, rightly, that Gandhi trusted his sincerity, and that he regarded the Delhi Pact as a new chapter in the relations between Congress and the British Government. Both sides, in their different ways, had done well out

[1] India Office Library, MSS. EUR.C. 152/6, Vol. V. pp. 415-16.
[2] Hickleton Papers, *Correspondence with Viscount Halifax*, p. 347.
[3] B. R. Nanda. Op. cit., p. 305.

of the Pact, and its conclusion brought peace which lasted for a year; and the Indians, so sensitive about their status, so vulnerable to slights, were warmed in their hearts by the incredible action of the Viceroy who was willing to take an arch-rebel from prison and parley with him if only peace could be secured by these means.

The scene now changed to Karachi, where at the end of March the Settlement was handed over for ratification to the tender mercies of Congress. Prominent among the delegates at this session were reckless young men eager to prevent that ratification, and the situation was seriously affected by the fact that the execution of Bhagat Singh, the murderer of Saunders, and the terrorist who threw the bomb into the Assembly, was arranged to take place at the time Congress was assembling at Karachi.

Gandhi and Malaviya entreated the Viceroy not to make the mistake of having the sentence carried out at that moment, but he had no hesitation in refusing a reprieve. In a speech at the Chelmsford Club on 26 March, he explained the reasons which had led him to decline a course which would have enabled him to leave India with the acclamation of a conquering hero:

'I from time to time, on the advice of my Council, concur in, or remit, death sentences that have been imposed. But I should regard it as wholly wrong to allow my judgment on these matters to be influenced or deflected by purely political considerations. I am well aware of the interest taken by large numbers of people in the fate of Bhagat Singh. But I could discover no argument by which commutation of that sentence could have been justified that would not have involved, if justice was to be equal, the commutation of all other sentences involving the death penalty. For I could imagine no case in which, under the law, the penalty had been more directly deserved.'[1]

So Gandhi had gone to Karachi in the worst circumstances to persuade Congress to ratify the Pact he had made with the Viceroy, and many who had once fawned upon him and called him Deliverer now screamed abuse and even threatened him with personal violence, although he believed that the Pact in no way forbade Congress to claim independence. But Congress ratified the Pact and agreed to send representatives to the Conference, although they did so in a resolution, ominous for the future, which reaffirmed their goal of Purna Swaraj, and their intention of gaining control over the Army, external affairs and economic policy. The Viceroy still persisted in his optimism, even in the face of this resolution:

'If I have accurately read the Resolution they propose to pass it is significant and adroit, for it begins by pitching the case at the highest, i.e. complete control of defence, finance, etc., and ends by saying that the representatives should have authority to accept less.'

But in fact it was now beginning to appear questionable whether Gandhi would go to London at all. Bhagat Singh had been executed on the night of

[1] Government of India Press, *Speeches by Lord Irwin*, Vol. II, p. 364.

23 March, and the death of this murderer who had killed for 'patriotism' sent an electric shock through India. Members normally loyal to the Government walked out of the Assembly in protest at what they thought a judicial crime, and in mourning for the dead. When the news spread to Cawnpore it was soon discovered that whatever pacts might be made between leaders, the Hindu-Moslem hatred continued to have an independent terrible existence. The Hindus proclaimed hartal, a pause in all business activities, and the Moslems revolted. Soon the town was aflame and the old horror began again—the blazing houses, the eruption of hideous irrational passions, the hacking to pieces of human beings.

'At about the same time as the terror was beginning in Cawnpore,' wrote Coatman, 'the President of the All-India National Congress was entering Karachi. Frenzied bands of youths met him with the news of Bhagat Singh's death, but the grimmer news of Cawnpore came later in the day, breaking harshly on ears that were only too loath to hear it. But it was true enough, and every day increased the tale of deaths, until, far away in Karachi, it looked as though half the Ganges valley must become aflame. Yet in spite of the presence of this dread two-handed engine at the door of the Congress *pandal*, the academic resolutions of independence were framed, and meaningless phrases about Indian unity were coined while the bitter gloss on them was being written in Cawnpore.'[1]

The troubles in this city were soon followed by disturbances in Kashmir, also caused by communal dissension, which had to be quelled by police and soldiers, an action which enabled Congress to accuse the Government of violating the Delhi Pact. But another event of tragic significance now contributed to the darkening scene in India on the eve of the Viceroy's departure, which seemed to show that a slow process of disintegration was about to begin. The Princes had begun to waver in their adherence to the principle of Federation.

The Maharaja of Patiala, a former Chancellor of the Chamber of Princes, supported by a number of others, had proposed an alternative scheme, and a lethal blow was thus delivered in advance of the coming Round Table Conference.

In this heartbreaking atmosphere the Viceroy left India for the last time on 18 April, but his own heart was not heavy for he knew that he had devoted himself to the reconciliation of hatreds and the guiding of the Indian people towards a destiny which could not now for long be withheld from them. For the last time he took up his pen to write to the Secretary of State who had shared the abuse that had been heaped upon him, and sturdily protected his flank:

'This will be the last letter I shall write to you before I leave. It is difficult to believe that one has really come to the end of one's Indian existence, and

[1] J. Coatman. Op. cit., pp. 343–4.

one has something of an impression of living in an atmosphere of dreams. I cannot possibly tell you how much I owe to you, Ramsay, and all your colleagues for your unfailing confidence and support that you have so generously given me during the last two years in which we have been working together. . . . Every day makes me feel more certain that what we are trying to do is right. We have no doubt made mistakes, but I don't think that this affects the broad perspective of the policy. Whether we shall succeed or not lies in other hands than ours, but I am quite sure that the general line His Majesty's Government has been taking has immensely strengthened our moral position both here and all over the world. It has been a great privilege to have some part in this great play.'[1]

It was now time to go, and in the crowded weeks before they left Delhi for the last time there were so many ceremonies of farewell that there was little time for feelings of sadness that this long, crowded chapter in their lives would soon be closed. If he had sometimes felt bitterly about the members of Congress he would have been touched had he known that one of the greatest of them, Rajagopalachari, would remember him thirty years after with admiration and affection:

'My colleagues and myself in the Indian National campaign,' he wrote to the author, 'have dealt with many Viceroys in India in our campaign for freedom lasting over many decades. I can testify to the general feeling among us all that Lord Irwin, as he was then called, was both as a man and as a Viceroy the most Christian and the most gentlemanly representative of Great Britain among them all. I can testify to the fact that Mahatma Gandhi certainly was of this opinion. Faith in a higher Power and sincere allegiance to moral principles bound Lord Irwin and Mahatma Gandhi together from the first time when they met and it lasted right through. They became friends in a common cause though they began as consecrated knights in opposing camps. The Gandhi–Irwin Pact over the Salt Satyagraha was a historic memorial of what two God-fearing men could achieve though history placed them in opposite camps.'[2]

The Viceroy, when he had a moment for reflection during these last weeks, was sometimes melancholy at the thought of all he was leaving behind him, the tremendous office, the new friends, and the vivid Indian scene he had loved and now knew so well, and Dorothy, although she had once spoken of the relief with which she would return home, was now heavy-hearted at the thought of departure.

Meanwhile there were endless functions to distract their minds, and speeches to be made. In February had been Inauguration Week in New Delhi when the Viceroy unveiled the Dominion Columns and the Indian

---

[1] India Office Library, MSS. EUR.C. 152/6, *Lord Irwin. Letters to the Secretary of State for India*, p. 445.
[2] Shri C. R. Rajagopalachari to author.

War Memorial, and held his last Investiture, and there was a garden party and a fête and a State Ball at the Viceroy's House. For the last time they endured Horse Show Week, and it had been amid the polo matches and the fireworks that he had begun his fateful talks with Gandhi.

He made innumerable speeches of farewell, and of these the most significant was that at the Chelmsford Club in which he briefly reviewed his viceroyalty and made a last earnest appeal for unity and tolerance, significant because he spoke again of that force that he had seen rising in India and whose challenge he believed must be met and acknowledged:

'There are those who see in the present movement and stirring of thought in India merely a movement engineered by a negligible minority, which ought never have been allowed to attain its present importance, in that much of it is frankly seditious, and with firm Government could readily be suppressed. Therefore, the conclusion is—let us only have firm Government and get back, as we rapidly shall, to the good old days of paternal administration, with populous markets reserved for British trade!

'That diagnosis I believe to be superficial, distorted and wholly divorced from reality. That there is sedition in India no one will deny; that the members who are politically-minded are a fractional minority of the whole is also true; but these things are not the whole, or the most important part, of the picture before which we stand.

'Great Britain will delude herself if she does not recognize that, beneath all the distinctions of community, class and social circumstance, there is a growing intellectual consciousness, or more truly self-consciousness, which is very closely akin to what we generally term nationalism. I know well that any general statement of this kind requires great modification if it is to fit the manifold diversities of the great continent of India, and this feeling of which I speak makes itself felt through a great variety of ways. But that it is a real thing of growing potential force, few who know modern India intimately will be concerned to deny.'[1]

Wherever he went he was met by demonstrations of affection. It was clear that he, more than any other Viceroy before him, had succeeded in reaching the heart of the Indian people, and this knowledge must have given him a glow of achievement. At a garden party for the Government of India Secretariat he received an ovation, altogether extraordinary in India, and his short speech of gratitude to the Government clerks was cheered without restraint. On 7 April they gave their farewell Ball at the Viceroy's House, and the following day the Citizens of Delhi entertained them at a garden party at Talkatora Gardens, and five days later the Viceroy had an informal meeting with the delegates to the First Round Table Conference to discuss arrangements for the Second. Gandhi attended this meeting as the prospective Congress delegate.

[1] Government of India Press, *Speeches by Lord Irwin*, Vol. II, p. 357.

Two days later, on 14 April, they made their personal farewells in the yellow drawing-room to everyone on the estate; then they ascended to the great Durbar Hall which had been the scene of so much glittering pageantry, where they had invited their friends to come, to avoid the ordeal of a station farewell. They shook hands with each one of them and then went out by the great door and down the steps, and drove away along a road lined on each side by the Viceroy's servants.

Next day they came to Bombay, and Edward had his last conversation on Indian soil with Gandhi who made a final concession, perhaps as a farewell gesture to the departing Viceroy, by giving an assurance that no discrimination would be practised against British goods. It was a gesture pleasing to the Bombay Chamber of Commerce which presented the Viceroy with a Farewell Address to which he made reply. There were only a few more duties left to perform—to receive the Moslem Committee and to speak to them of the fears of the minorities, and of the recent savage outbreaks at Cawnpore; to be entertained by the Byculla Club, and make his farewells to the Princes, who had come to Bombay to see him leave, and to his successor Lord Willingdon.

Then they drove through the city to the Gateway of India where they had landed five years before. Standing on the Apollo Bundar, the Viceroy received an Address from the Bombay Municipal Corporation, and in his reply, now deeply moved, he bade his last farewell to India. Then they entered their launch, and were carried away over the blue waters to the *Viceroy of India* which was waiting to take them on their long journey home.

*   *   *

When we look back on this viceroyalty it is its boldness that most impresses us. It was not apparent at the beginning when, under the watchful eye of Birkenhead, the Viceroy had followed the conventional road and attempted no sorties down its inviting by-ways. But the Secretary of State had resigned in 1928, his dazzling career brought into seclusion, and before long Lord Irwin had found himself serving a Socialist Government eager to use the prestige of their Tory Viceroy in pursuit of policies which they themselves with their limited authority would have found it difficult to undertake.

He had learned much during those two years; slowly, but with growing certainty, he had come to believe that those who clung to the doctrine of *force majeur* in India were the advocates of an Imperial philosophy whose vigour was already spent and which was no longer a solution for the problems of the day; that the old proprietary conception of Empire, that benevolent paternalism of Victorian days, had passed away for ever, to be replaced by the new Imperial ideal of partnership. And it seemed to him a ridiculous paradox that India alone should escape from a movement of political thought that was affecting every other part of the British Empire.

It was thus that Irwin was able to set his personal mark upon the period, and in that respect, as was well said, he was in the great line of Dalhousie, Wellesley and Curzon. But his task was more difficult than that of Curzon who had ruled India during a 'golden pause of history' when the creaking institutions demanded reform, and his word alone was law, and he could refashion her to his heart's desire and leave his indelible imprint upon her life and culture, a proconsul of executive genius, whose career was clouded only when the shadow of Kitchener fell upon it.

Irwin had none of the unshackled power which had permitted Curzon to transform the face of India, engrossing every detail of administration from the partition of Bengal to the architecture of a Hindu Temple, but he was no less determined to lay down policy himself, and this resolution grew with his own conviction of its wisdom and generosity. He might fitly have administered any of the departments of Government, but he was wise enough to refrain from the attempt. He had mastered the art of delegation and by exercising it found freedom for the supreme task, the fashioning of the political future of India.

He realized how fortunate he was that in the departments with which he was least familiar and which were both of vital importance to India, Finance and Defence, there were men of outstanding ability who would take the whole burden off his shoulders, and whose work he made no attempt to direct. Sir Basil Blackett and Sir George Schuster performed wonders in solving the intricate currency questions and in nourishing the finances of India in a series of prudent Budgets which enabled her to weather the depression of the 1930s.

In Defence he was happy to leave the reform of the Indian Army to Birdwood and afterwards to Chetwode, who with wide experience and deep understanding of the Indian soldier required no guidance from the Viceroy, only encouragement and support. The excellence of all these officers must be counted as one of the most fortunate aspects of the viceroyalty, and had their positions been held by inferior men lasting mutilations might have been made on the body of India.

In his main task of hastening constitutional reform and lubricating its wheels, the Viceroy stood almost entirely alone. His only was the attempt to plant in the suspicious minds of Indian leaders a new conviction of the sincerity of British purpose and to certify it to their conscience. The Viceroy's Council, able though its members might be, could at most advise and hope to influence him, but he did not hesitate to reject their advice when he saw fit. One man, Sir Malcolm Hailey, stood alone in his influence upon the Viceroy's mind. This great public servant, who, it was thought by some would himself have made a worthy Viceroy, had been a member of the Executive Council of the Governor-General, and was successively Governor of the Punjab and the United Provinces, and his brilliant mind and profound knowledge of

MOUNTING THE STATE ELEPHANT

India caused Irwin from the first to place a particular reliance on his judgment.

The greatest problem of all, communal strife, was not solved during his viceroyalty, but this was a task beyond the power of human mediation. He had left India issuing further appeals for tolerance and understanding between the creeds but his shrewd mind entertained little hope of their adoption. From the beginning he had seen his chief task as the solution of the problem of British India. At a moment when many in England were still clinging to the tutorial approach in their Indian thinking he became conscious of the breath of an earlier wind of change blowing hard through India, and bringing its unmistakable warning.

It was difficult for critics eight thousand miles away in England to realize that the distinguishing feature of the problem which confronted Lord Irwin was an exhibition of racial feeling which had no precedent in the history of the Indian Empire. Up to this moment India could still have been regarded from the British point of view as a collection of peoples with outstanding divergencies of ethnic origin, language, religion and social development, and the best justification for this outlook was to be seen in the attitude of India at large to Curzon's most contentious problem—the partition of Bengal. Acute as was the feeling to which this gave rise in that Province, elsewhere there had been little reaction among the Indian people. But the characteristic feeling of unsettlement caused by the First World War, and followed by the massacre at Amritsar had been exploited by Congress to extend an influence which had hitherto been confined to a small body of educated Indians. This began to regard itself as the natural successor to British rule, and in 1920 and 1921 interest in the course of political developments began to spread further. A wider section of the Indian population progressively acquired a marked anti-British bias, a development which received in addition an emotional impetus from Gandhi's campaign with its underlying aspect of Hindu revivalism. It was with the aftermath of this process that Lord Irwin had to deal.

It was his particular merit that he recognized clearly that the advance of the country was now a problem for immediate consideration, and that indefinite promises and vague undertakings could only lead to a dislocation of Indian life and a vista of continual repression. He saw more clearly than those who advocated such a course that, as in the case of Ireland, it was a policy of despair, and that in the end it would have been necessary to throw open the jails, and to come to terms with Indian leaders, but then in an atmosphere a hundred times more bitter, to decide the terms on which they and the English were to live.

Perhaps few would deny today that Lord Irwin's policy was abundantly justified, but they are now able to judge by the yardstick of history. At the time he had to face charges of weakness and grovelling at the hands of those who were unwilling to realize that the days of Imperial splendour were numbered. It is not difficult to sympathize with their attitude. Irwin was able to bear their onslaught with composure for he felt in his bones that he was right. He treated with contempt the accusation that his policy had favoured the enemy Hindu at the expense of the loyal Moslem, that he had abased himself before Gandhi, and 'taken tea with treason'.

For the Viceroy was blameless of the suspicion that he was shoring up a Hindu dictatorship. Rather was his desire to bring the parties together to decide on equal terms with the English how they were to live in peace and how the Dominion Status he had set before them as a definite goal could be achieved. He could not ignore the fact that the Hindus were in a great majority in India, and that Congress was her most powerful political party. Nor could he forget that the man whom Churchill derided as a seditious fakir was the repository of the hopes and dreams of millions of Indians by whom his name was held in mystical adoration.

When in 1931 the Viceroy approached the climax of his relations with Gandhi, and put everything to the hazard, he had already won his heart and left in it a warm memory of spiritual affinity. Above all, it was the simplicity of Irwin's character which made his place in the affection of Indians so extraordinary and so different from his predecessors, for here was no Curzonian might, no dreadful remoteness, no *terribilita*. To Rajagopalachari he was 'the most Christian and the most gentlemanly' Viceroy of them all. To Gopal, the gifted Indian who described his rule with such delicate insight, 'character was the keel of the viceroyalty. It was a character free of meretricious ornament; there was in it no element of the florid or the facile; it was formed not of colour and fire but of dignity, human warmth and the "plain good intent" which Burke rated above all other qualities in public life', and it could be said of Irwin as it was once said of Curzon that his name would shine like a silver lamp in the changeless mind of Asia.

CHAPTER XVII

THE RETURN

THEY sailed from Bombay on 18 April, two days after Edward's fiftieth birthday. It was noticed that he looked older and more fine-drawn, and that the physical and emotional strain of the last five years had left their mark upon him, but the sea voyage was a wonderful restorative. He could sleep long and deep, and breathe invigorating sea air, enjoy a blessed immunity from intrusive visitors and harassing decisions, and regard Cairo, Port Said and Malta where the ship called as places of interest rather than of duty. At Victoria Station he found an enormous reception party of friends among whom were Mr. Baldwin and his wife, and many leaders of religious opinion, and showed his usual indifference to a few unfriendly cries raised by those who appeared to think that he had betrayed the British Empire.

Old Lord Halifax was not present at this scene, for Edward had known that there would be too much noise and crowding at the station; that he would be involved in tiresome formalities, and a visit to the Secretary of State. He wanted this reunion, so precious to both of them, to take place in peaceful surroundings. 'I am quite sure,' he had written to his father in his last letter from India, 'that the ideal thing is that we should meet at Hickleton in the middle of everything you have been doing and that you will show me.'[1] Lord and Lady Irwin went on that day of arrival to luncheon with the King and Queen at Windsor Castle where the King invested Edward a Knight of the Garter. He had already received the two highest honours awarded for service in India, the Grand Cross of the Star of India and the Grand Cross of the Indian Empire. His friend, Stanley Baldwin, wrote to congratulate him on this last and greatest distinction:

'My dear Edward,
    This is but a line as I hope to see you tomorrow.
    My only regret about your Garter is a selfish one. I wish I could have had the great pleasure of recommending it to H.M.! I am thankful you are home again: I was not really happy till you were on the ship. We want you in England now.
    You have justified and more than justified all my hopes and expectations. Do you remember how you had to be almost kicked out of England?

[1] Hickleton Papers.

I am proud that I can call you my friend.
God bless you.

Yours ever,

S.B.'

When he came to Hickleton the villagers and tenants were out in force, and the young men from the estate stopped his car and pulled it up with ropes in triumph to the front door. His father was standing on the steps to welcome him. It was a moment of overpowering emotion for both of them. When Edward had waved good-bye to his father at Victoria as the train steamed out of the station and he set forth on his journey to a new world and a new life, he must have believed in his heart that it was farewell. 'I still remember,' said an eye-witness who was watching the old man, 'his grey hair, and the way he straightened his back as the great moment of welcome arrived, and his clear ringing voice as he said: "I think that with God's help, my son has been able to do a good work in India for his King and country, and for that other great country that has so many claims on his affection and interest." '[1] It was an occasion so passionately longed for by father and son as to invite bathos in its realization, but their meeting filled them with even greater happiness than they had imagined: 'You and Dorothy are wonders,' Halifax told them. 'I had been counting the days ever since you had gone five years ago till your return. Expecting *so much*—such expectations are apt to be disappointed, but in this instance they have been surpassed.'[2]

He was now an elder statesman, and he had reached the moment when honours began to fall on him like the leaves of autumn, civic welcomes and freedoms of cities, the acclaim of universities, honorary degrees, and an Hon. D.C.L. conferred by the Vice-Chancellor of Oxford on one he addressed as '*vir sagacissime*'. He had lost no time in returning to Garrowby which had so long been a distant dream in exile, and he was gratified, above all, by the honours showered upon him by his native Yorkshire.

Sheffield University gave him an honorary degree, Harrogate a civic welcome, and Doncaster the Freedom of its City. Here he spoke of the past and recalled the far-off days of boyhood when he had made his first public speech upon a Doncaster platform, and the generosity with which it had been received; how when a boy on holiday from school he had always asked for Doncaster butterscotch, and how he felt like a schoolboy on holiday again after an exacting term.[3] In his Yorkshire speeches he gave an account of his stewardship in India; and he did not forget to thank the *Yorkshire Post* for its steadfast support and to commend the restraint and sobriety with which it had commented on Indian affairs.

He had returned to his house at 88 Eaton Square, and his first public

---

[1] Campbell Johnson. Op. cit., p. 329.   [2] Hickleton Papers, 7 May 1931.
[3] Campbell Johnson. Op. cit., p. 328.

appearance in London was on 15 May 1931 at a luncheon given in his honour by the British Indian Union, a gathering of great distinction, over which Lord Reading presided, and which included most of the leading members of the Indian colony in London. He defended his actions in India in an important speech to which he devoted a great deal of thought. The main object of his policy, which he emphasized in almost every speech he made on India at this time, was to retain a prosperous, willing and contented India within the Empire. That could never be achieved by 'strong government' and compulsion alone, but must rest, if it was to endure, upon agreement. In a later passage of the speech he spoke of the Simon Commission in a manner which gave little indication of his true opinion of their Report or of the manner in which his own policies had contributed to its eclipse. Referring to the Commission and the Round Table Conference he deprecated the tendency he had noted in some quarters to belittle Sir John Simon's work, and to set it in antithesis to that accomplished by the Conference:

'They were complementary one to another. On Sir John Simon and his Commission was laid the onerous duty of presenting a lead to Parliament on the whole problem. They were careful, as I know well, when they were in India to make it plain that it was no part of their function to be final lawgivers from the Mount. Indeed the suggestion of the Round Table Conference was formally put forward by Sir John Simon. But that Conference, meeting in totally different circumstances from those which prevailed when Sir John Simon made the proposal, found themselves confronted by an entirely different problem.'

It was on this same day that Winston Churchill publicly declared the Delhi Pact to be 'a great disaster and a humiliation and negation to this country', but Irwin cared no more for this sort of language in England than he had in India, and insisted, whenever invited to speak on the subject, that the policy which he and the Government had pursued was right and wise. So convinced was he of this rectitude that he had no hesitation in meeting his critics in the Conservative Party in a Committee Room in the House of Commons, and to answering questions for three-quarters of an hour, mainly on the implications of the agreement with Gandhi. With Winston Churchill and Lord Lloyd foremost among the inquisitors it was something of an ordeal, but Irwin was almost always successful on such occasions. His mind, as George Cunningham had found in India, was swift and agile; he was far better seized of the facts than his questioners, and he was in no way intimidated by an attack in force. His gift of gentle irony enabled him to deflect the hammer-blows of Churchill whose views on India appeared to him to belong to some bygone period of the world's history.

In the autumn of 1931 the second session of the Round Table Conference took place in London, attended by Gandhi as the representative of Congress after many threats of non-appearance. It proved to be a miserable fiasco. The importance of Indian affairs at this moment was greatly diminished by the panic which had struck the Stock Exchanges of America, and the economic crisis in London which broke the Labour Government in August. In this atmosphere of fear and confusion the whole fabric of the country appeared on the point of dissolution, and it was borne in upon the Indian delegates that they would now be increasingly brought into contact with the Conservative point of view in the shaping of their future.

The new Government did not disown the work of its predecessor, but there was a fresh resonance in its language, a new impatience with bargaining, a new emphasis of the divisions that bedevilled India, and of the rights of minorities. Although Gandhi made frequent protestations of affection for Irwin and of loyalty to the Delhi Pact, he showed himself lacking in either the courage or the desire to defy the extreme elements among his followers and make a genuine attempt at constructive solutions. As a delegate he was worse than useless, his rambling discourses reducing everyone to despair, and in this intransigence he was fully matched by his Moslem opponents who opposed any advance until their claims to security against Hindu domination were granted.

These Moslem claims, startling in themselves, brought an atmosphere of increasing gloom into the Minorities Sub-Committee over which Gandhi ineptly presided. They would, if granted, have made the Moslems masters of North-Western India, and included demands for a clear majority of seats on the Councils of the Punjab and Bengal, the creation of a new Province in Sind, separated from Bombay, and the establishment of complete self-government in the North-West Frontier Province.

All the important business of the Conference was held up by this hopeless wrangle. It ended in a deadlock on the Minorities Sub-Committee whose task was to decide the allocation of seats in the new Council to the rival communities. Gandhi met the Moslem claims with a flat rejection, and he refused to grant separate representation to the Depressed Classes on the grounds that they were an integral part of the Hindu community. More ominous still was the fading belief in Federation that began to mark the Conference. The hearts of some of the Princes had already been faint before it opened, and the Congress itself was becoming uneasy about its own prospects in an All-India in which a combination of the Moslems and the Princes against them seemed to disclose alarming possibilities.

And so the Second Round Table Conference was a complete failure, but during its disastrous course Gandhi's affectionate regard for Irwin never faltered. It is even possible that his mind was haunted by a sense of guilt. The last great days with Irwin at Delhi had now become treasured memories. 'Dear Friend, I plunge into work tomorrow,' he had written to him on the eve of the Conference; 'In all I am and shall be doing, you and our talks are and will ever be with me.'[1] And as the Conference began to falter he had written: 'You will have seen with sorrow the failure of my first effort. It does not dismay me. I shall toil on. I repeat the promise given to you that I shall take no decisions on the important questions discussed by us without first seeking an interview with you and placing my difficulties before you.'[2]

It was as though he was conscious that the claims he now made for full control of the Indian Army, Finance, and Foreign policy were wholly inconsistent with the solemn pact he had made with the Viceroy, and that people were bewildered by his attitude, and believed that he was not genuinely seeking peace but merely awaiting an appropriate occasion to wreck the Conference. Even in his most difficult moods he was pathetically anxious to preserve Irwin's friendship and not to forfeit his esteem. He told him that he subjected all his actions to his 'Friend's' unspoken censure, and his affection for the man is apparent in every letter he wrote to him.

Faithful to his promise, Gandhi had several conversations at Eaton Square with Irwin who had remained in touch with the India Office, but in his detached position was unable to persuade Gandhi to be more flexible in his attitude or to inspire more confidence in his English colleagues, although on his own admission Gandhi was much taken with the new Secretary of State, Sir Samuel Hoare, and had many private conversations with him. The hopeless Conference broke up, and the Prime Minister, in dismissing it, could do little more than express the resolve of the Government to continue on the lines laid down at the first session in spite of the failure and chaos of the second.

Gandhi left England, and from Villeneuve wrote to his 'Friend' expressing futile hopes for the future: 'If the situation in India does not force a quarrel, co-operation might still be continued. Anyway, I can give you the assurance that I shall do nothing in haste or without first approaching the Viceroy.' And from Bombay he sent Irwin a last telegram:

'Pray believe me I tried my best but failed. Nevertheless I do not lose hope, and God willing I shall retain same spirit that you believed actuated me during that sacred week in Delhi. I shall not belie your certificate. Gandhi.'

But it was to a different Viceroy that Gandhi was now returning. Lord Willingdon had had experience of him as Governor of Bombay and did not share Irwin's belief in the Mahatma's spiritual elevation. He was to write later to Irwin of these events:

'It may be perfectly true that Gandhi was anxious to co-operate, but it was certainly equally true that all his leaders were opposed to him, and he never has had—and never would have—the courage to stand out for the co-operative side. You I know see something in him, but I have never been

[1] Hickleton Papers, 14 September 1931. [2] Ibid., 8 October 1931.

able to discover it, and to my mind it is his combination of qualities that makes him really dangerous. I have never been able to discover anything in him but a little *bania* who is the most astute and opportunist politician I have ever met.'[1]

These left-wing leaders of Congress were now in full control, and if Gandhi indeed desired co-operation he was singularly ineffectual in obtaining it. Sir James Crerar, the Home Member, analysed the situation at this moment for Lord Irwin:

'I do not think myself that Gandhi was for war. He came back, however, with all his old megalomania and apparently aspired to a position somewhat higher even than that of a co-ordinate power treating with the Government of India. He proposed, in fact, to raise himself above them both and to be an arbiter between them. We now know that the whole of the Working Committee were unanimous in clamouring for war, and, whatever Lord Willingdon had done, there was no prospect either of Gandhi being detached from Congress or the Congress itself being split.'[2]

The campaign of resistance and disobedience was started once again, but Lord Willingdon's patience was more quickly exhausted than his predecessor's. Much as he disliked it, he had no hesitation in returning to repression. Within three weeks of his arrival in India Gandhi was again in prison, and by April 34,000 political prisoners had joined him behind the bars. The movement of revolt, which had flared for a few months, went dead, and it seemed, although this was an illusion, that Congress had at last received the *coup de grâce*, and that the Government could carry out its Indian reforms in this comfortable belief.

*   *   *

Thousands of miles away in that strange Eastern land, and under the glare of unrelenting sun the Viceroy had often thought of Garrowby, and in the autumn of 1931, when the leaves were turning in the park and keen winds blowing over the wold, he had followed the advice of his father to 'spend a week riding through some part of the country that one had not seen, staying at local inns and thinking of nothing more serious than whether your pony was sound, or how the weather was likely to behave and how beautiful a place England can be'. Accompanied by his fellow Yorkshireman, Geoffrey Dawson and his wife, and his own children he made expeditions through the Yorkshire dales and the moors that divide them. One of these led them from Coxwold on a wide circle of exploration to the moors between Helmsley and Stokesley, another from Settle in north-west Yorkshire to Aysgarth, crossing Wharfedale at Kettlewell, and making a digression to the head of Nidderdale.

[1] Hickleton Papers, Lord Willingdon to Lord Irwin, 10 January 1932.
[2] Ibid., Sir James Crerar to Lord Irwin, 5 January, 1932.

He found in these riding tours something of the freedom and the absence of care of those heavenly days trekking in the Himalayas when he had seemed to be the inhabitant of a different world:

'It would be impossible to think of a more perfect way of spending a few days for anyone who loves the country and loves riding. I do not think I ever enjoyed myself more. In that sort of country particularly you reap the benefit of being out all day; for the lights and shadows on the large landscapes are changing constantly, and you miss none of them. You must take pains beforehand to have the way reconnoitred, so as to avoid roads, and bespeak accommodation for man and beast at night. . . . As a method of ensuring complete relaxation I can without any hesitation guarantee its value.'[1]

By the time the Second Round Table Conference broke up, there was a new Government elected to attempt to stem the drift to economic ruin which had been apparent since 1929. In August 1931 Ramsay MacDonald had resigned as Prime Minister of the Labour Government, but had re-accepted office as Prime Minister, and succeeded in forming a National Government in which Sir Samuel Hoare became Secretary of State for India.

Most of the Labour Party, unable to stomach this arrangement, went into opposition, leaving only a handful of Labour Members supporting the Government, and giving it a majority of fifty. In November MacDonald went to the country, and the National Government was returned with an unprecedented majority. These great events, and the fear of economic ruin that had prompted them had eclipsed the Second Round Table Conference, and India, which had long been one of the chief topics of interest in press and politics, was thrust into seclusion.

Edward was still free from any official contact with these events or from any formal obligations, when he was invited by Vincent Massey to visit Canada and to deliver the inaugural Massey Lecture at Toronto University. He was an old friend and it was pleasant to see him again and to revisit the haunts of his youth, and he recognized the importance of justifying his Indian policy on every occasion, although after five years' exile he now grudged every moment spent away from Garrowby.

The subject of the lecture was 'Some Aspects of the Indian Problem', and, after tracing the history of Indian civilization and the origins of Hindu-Moslem rivalry, he told his great audience how England had laboured throughout the nineteenth century to restore stability to India, and spoke of the profound influence on her of English education and through it the diffusion of Western thought. It was this education that had caused that longing for freedom which was now running like fire through the veins of the Indian nationalists. 'Above all,' he said, 'English literature is the literature of freedom, and India has drunk her fill from this life-giving source.'

'What are we trying to do in India?' he asked. 'We are trying within the

[1] Halifax. Op. cit., pp. 176–7.

British Empire to foster the creation of a united India, sufficiently at one with herself in respect of those fundamentals on which every nation state must rest, that we may devolve upon her people the power for the control of her own affairs, and the ordering of their own political life.'

He explained the baffling maze of communal and geographical complications which made up the Indian mosaic, and he ended his long speech by reaffirming with tremendous conviction his own heartfelt belief that, in spite of difficulties which at times seemed insurmountable, England must seek a solution of the constitutional problem on lines not dissimilar from the rest of the Empire, a democratic form of Government based on Indian consent. The alternatives were either for control to remain with Great Britain, or to devise some form of Indian autocracy or oligarchy. The first would be an admission of failure, and the second would find no acceptance in India or in England, and would be opposed alike to the spirit of the times and to the whole political history of India as England herself had made it.

This speech was his longest and most important pronouncement on India since his return. He wrote in his diary with habitual diffidence: 'I think it did pretty well. At least everybody seems to say so. I am glad to have it off my chest—and I only hope it won't make too much clatter in India.'[1]

He was home by 27 May, and later that summer we find him at a celebration at Newcastle to mark the centenary of the passage of the Reform Bill and to do honour to its principal sponsor Lord Grey. As members of the Grey family the Woods were invited to take part in the proceedings, and the indefatigable old Halifax, now ninety-three, found himself once again at his beloved Howick snug in its woods behind that rugged coastline now tranquil in summer. With Charlie and Mabel Grey they attended a dinner with the Lord Mayor before the meeting, and the audience rose to Lord Halifax as the old man entranced them with reminiscences of his grandfather Lord Grey and his dog Pincher at Howick, and of the politics of his childhood. He became so inspired by their applause and so transported by his own eloquence that he appeared to be in danger of overbalancing beyond the edge of the platform.

Though still delightfully free from the bonds of office, Edward was much in the thoughts of those at the head of affairs. When Ramsay Mac-Donald was forming the National Government in the autumn of 1931, he asked Baldwin, who was Lord President of the Council in that administration, to invite Irwin to be Foreign Secretary.

'I told Baldwin that I thought there were particular reasons why my appointment at that moment would be from his point of view ill-judged. I had just returned from India and was much like the proverbial red rag to many of the more right-wing Conservatives.' He also knew that the Foreign Secretary would have to attempt to carry the country in favour of some plan

[1] Hickleton Papers, Diary, 27 April 1932.

of disarmament, and he felt that he would be unfavourably handicapped for such a policy, particularly with his own party. Baldwin had agreed, and Edward returned with relief to Garrowby where he was happily occupied with his estate, and in picking up the threads of his old life.

We gain much insight into that happy period from his own recollections of it, and it is mainly, as we should expect, a record of great houses and noble families and spacious week-ends. It is rich in droll episodes in the leisure hours of his exalted friends; Lord Salisbury toying with Buchmanism at a 'Groupist' week-end at Hatfield, and Edward listening earnestly to their 'confessions'; Lord Hugh Cecil in the hunting field, always out of control and jammed in the gates, and the object of abuse of a kind to which he was not accustomed; William Temple, the Archbishop of York, imitating Charlie Chaplin with bowler and stick, supported by 'deep chuckles and boisterous gusts of his own laughter'. Irwin's world was that of the powerful landowners and aristocrats of the day, and he writes of them with such casual affection because he was one of them himself:

'The Duke and Duchess of Portland must have been nearly the last people to maintain the kind of life that up to the later years of the nineteenth century was common to most great houses. The large house with its many treasures, chapel, library, gardens, cricket ground, stables, park, with two herds of white fallow deer, a large estate, touching much of the old Sherwood Forest with its romance of Robin Hood, everything was beautiful and of the best, and all in perfect order.' When he describes how beloved the Duchess was for providing orthopædic treatment for the miners before the Welfare State was ever heard of, we see a reflection of his own unquestioned acceptance of the figure of the noble landowner whose position entailed obligations as well as privilege. Perhaps there was some inkling in his mind that these spacious days were passing away for ever when he wrote:

'Such contact in country houses as the changing habits of the day still offered were by far the best means that a society with some opportunity for leisure had to offer for the making of new acquaintances or for the renewing of old ones. The inevitable disappearance under pressure of taxation and staff difficulties of the well-assorted week-end party in pleasant surroundings, and with plenty of scope for easy conversation, is a real impoverishment of one side of our social life.'

Hatfield, Cliveden, Welbeck—these were a few of the great houses at which Edward was welcomed, but there were many visitors to Garrowby itself; Randall Davidson the Archbishop of Canterbury whom Edward took for long walks; Lang and Temple, successively Archbishops of York over difficult years; Ted Talbot on his summer holiday from Mirfield, or ministering in the chapel at Garrowby at Christmas and Easter; Walter Riddell, his old Oxford friend who had been the best man at his wedding. Lord Hugh Cecil was one of the most devoted members of the circle:

'When he came to Garrowby all ages revelled in whatever might be the topic or manner of talk; lively arguments on all subjects, casual instructions on history and theology, recollections of the House of Commons, and of the great figures of an earlier day, judgments of books and literature, all stimulating, and leaping from one point to the next as all good conversation should.'

The cricket week was another recurring fixture of the Garrowby August. This was organized by Edward's cricketing sons, Peter and Richard, and Dr. Prescot, an Eton Master to whom they were both devoted, who, collecting friends from Eton, made up the team with the required number of locals. They played regular matches in the neighbourhood, and a Sunday afternoon match against Hickleton which was an occasion of both rivalry and danger on account of the fierceness of the pitch. In the evenings Edward would hob-nob with Hugh Cecil or Ted Talbot in his study or read the stories of Saki aloud, and when the seniors had gone to bed the young men would gamble happily into the small hours of the morning.

They noticed their host's extraordinary curiosity, his terror of missing anything, and how he would constantly say: 'Why did you come in that way?' or 'Wait a minute. I did not hear'; and his unwordliness in a long discussion as to whether he should sit down at table with someone who had been divorced. For Edward belonged to that school of churchmen who believed that marriage, being a Sacrament, must remain indissoluble. In exceptional circumstances he might give a reluctant approval to separation, but divorce, followed by remarriage, carried for him almost the taint of bigamy. He was to cling to this orthodoxy for many years, and it was to provide some awkward moments in his relations with his friends. One of the visitors at these cricket weeks, Nathaniel Fiennes, remembered how kind Edward was to him, and indeed to all young men, asking him innumerable questions and later going to infinite trouble to help him at the beginning of his career. Edward was deeply stricken when six of this little group, including his own son Peter, lost their lives in the war, and erected a tablet in the chapel at Garrowby to their memory.

He had returned with delight to the hunting field, and in May 1932 took over the Mastership of the Middleton Hounds, thought by some to be one of the half dozen finest packs in England. The kennels were close to Garrowby at Birdsall, and Edward's old friend and neighbour Colonel Borwick of Aldby, who sometimes irreverently referred to him as 'Holy Joe', had been Master before him, succeeding Lord Middleton. The children of the two families were much of an age, and Borwick and his wife Violet had provided a second home for the Wood children during much of their parents' absence in India, imparting to them their own beautiful horsemanship. Edward had been closely associated with the Middleton ever since he had lived at Garrowby, and he was to remain Master until 1938 when his eldest son Charles succeeded him. On his return from Washington he resumed the Mastership, and remained Joint-Master with Charles until his death.

Edward's devotion to hunting, one of the great passions of his life, glows in every sentence that he wrote of those winter days with the Middleton as a young Member of Parliament twenty years before, when he thought nothing of hacking twenty miles to the meets, and the same distance back at night. The blood horses of the hunt were brought into the stables only as made hunters at five or six years old: 'There used to be between thirty or forty of them, all of a stamp, beautifully kept, standing in the rows of stalls. . . . One looks back wistfully to conditions that are long past; not much wire, no poultry claims, little grass-ley farming, so that you could ride very much where you liked.' When he now returned to the Middleton Hounds he had found certain changes. Perhaps the thoroughbred hunters in the stables were fewer, and the wire beginning to encroach, but they were still the finest pack in the North of England, and Edward felt for them that deep affection that comes from long association with intimate ties.

*   *   *

But it was not long before another opportunity presented itself to induce him to leave these country delights and to join the Government again. In the summer of 1932 the Liberal leader, Sir Donald Maclean, died suddenly, leaving vacant the office of President of the Board of Education, which the Prime Minister now offered to Irwin. He had, as we have seen, little real interest in the subject, and the rôle of revenant offered scant attraction, but with commendable public spirit Edward accepted the office. It is probable that the object of this appointment to what, for economic reasons, must prove a bleak and uninviting post, was to put Irwin's knowledge of the Indian problem at the disposal of the Cabinet and, in particular, of the Secretary of State Sir Samuel Hoare, and the offer is an indication of how quickly the agitation against his name in connection with India had died down in the intervening months. That he had no desire for this office is evident from a letter to his father on 15 July 1932:

'After taking a night to think it over with Dorothy I have come to the conclusion that, little as one wants to do it, it would not be right to refuse to take a hand if they think one can help. . . . I can hardly tell you with what distaste I surrender one's very pleasant liberty, but I feel the burden of affairs on those who have to carry them is so heavy that it would be wrong to shirk them if it is really thought that one can be of help.'[1]

The comparative indifference with which Irwin had regarded the Board of Education in 1922 had been partly due to the economic pressure which had prohibited any reforming legislation. Then it had been the Geddes Committee which had paralysed the work of the Departments. Now, ten years

[1] Hickleton Papers, 15 July 1932.

later, it was the May Committee that was appointed for a similar purpose as a result of the world crisis which again enforced a period of strict economy.

In 1926 the Hadow Committee, set up in 1924 to inquire into the education of the adolescent, had published its memorable Report which had been welcomed from all quarters. The essence of the plan was to make secondary education not a privilege restricted to ten per cent of the population, but the normal course for all children between eleven and fifteen, when the school-leaving age was raised. It was envisaged that there would henceforth be two parallel streams of secondary education: Academic (Grammar School) up to 16 plus which would be generally regarded as an approach to the University, and Practical (Modern School), a three-year course up to 15–16 plus. It was intended that the grammar schools should include all schools of the academic type, whether old foundations or new municipal or county secondary schools which had come into existence under the 1902 Act. The secondary modern schools would be analogous to the central schools started in London in 1911 and designed as 'higher elementary education', and provide an education different in kind but not in quality from the grammar school. At 13 plus selected pupils might, on examination, be drafted to Junior Technical Schools.

England was again in the grip of the world depression before the Hadow recommendations could be carried out. Even Sir Charles Trevelyan, President of the Board again in the Labour Government of 1929–31, and an ardent educationist who had been responsible for setting up the Hadow Committee, was unable to make the slightest headway. Three times he tried to bring in legislation to raise the school-leaving age to fifteen, but his efforts foundered on financial and religious rocks, the non-provided[1] schools being unable to pay for the necessary new building, and the local authorities refusing to give them financial assistance without exercising closer control. His first Bill was talked out and withdrawn because it contained no provisions for the denominational schools, and he made the mistake of asking the Churches to come to agreement among themselves instead of imposing it upon them. At the third attempt a Roman Catholic Socialist M.P., John Scurr, put down a celebrated amendment to the effect that the Bill should not come into operation until another Bill had been passed enabling building grants to be made to non-provided schools. The Government had accepted this amendment which effectively killed the Bill, and the school-leaving age was not raised until 1936. This failure had a most depressing effect upon all those concerned with public education.

Thus, in July 1932 when Lord Irwin returned to the Board the prospect was not rosy for any substantial progress, and it is difficult to point to any outstanding achievements in education. Between 1932 and 1935 he had to

[1] The 'Non-Provided' schools included Church schools, charitable foundations, private schools: i.e. all schools not supported by the rates.

face two critical debates in the House of Lords—the first on Circular 1421 which abolished free secondary education and substituted Special Places for Free Places, by which parents of adequate means had to pay higher fees, and which contained a form of means test; the second on a motion by the Opposition to raise the school-leaving age.

Of his departmental work there were two achievements of some importance. The first was a national survey of technical college buildings, and the allocation of £12,000,000 to be spent on modernizing and reconstructing them. The second was an attempt to improve the training of teachers in religious instruction with the object of inducing them to take it as one of their normal qualifications. Two important conferences were held in November 1933 and March 1935, and the results were published in a White Paper.

Apart from a Teachers' Superannuation Bill, and the Education (Necessity of Schools) Bill, a measure enabling uneconomic schools to be closed and the pupils accommodated in neighbouring schools of the appropriate denomination, there was no educational legislation during Irwin's second period of office. It had been permissible before to close schools of less than thirty pupils, and the Necessity of Schools Bill removed this qualification, and provided that any uneconomic school, of whatever numbers, was liable to closure.

Mr. Herwald Ramsbotham[1] had been Parliamentary Secretary under Sir Donald Maclean, and he continued in that office under Irwin. Being in the House of Commons, all the day to day Parliamentary work, Questions, Debates and Estimates, fell upon him as chief Government spokesman in that chamber, and he met with no interference from the President. Ramsbotham also made many speeches on education in the country.

Irwin, when accepting the office, had remarked to the Parliamentary Secretary: 'I shall be able to have my two days' hunting,' and Ramsbotham had noticed that his chief had very little work to do in his office, and that he took his duties lightly. He also observed, like Cunningham, that Irwin, when he was involved in the office work, was as quick as lightning at picking up a point, but that it was an affectation of his that he knew nothing, and required coaching, and was much given to the Socratic approach.

During this period of office Lord Irwin was an aloof figure at the Board of Education, arriving late in the morning, seeing few civil servants except his immediate staff, chiefly his Private Secretary Sir Griffith Williams, and leaving as early as possible for the week-end in Yorkshire and his congenial duties as M.F.H. In this second period at the Board he was so aloof that he became almost an object of awe in the office.

The respect of these civil servants was subject to some testing moments when Edward made remarks that seemed to emphasize the gulf between them. Williams sensed what seemed to him a strongly entrenched feudal

[1] Afterwards Lord Soulbury.

attitude of mind in Edward, as when he remarked casually on a visit to Hickleton: 'We need a new Church School here. Will the Board agree? We want a school to train them up for servants and butlers.'

Williams was sometimes invited to Garrowby, and it was perhaps his nervousness in these surroundings which led him to give the butler a tip of three pounds and to imagine that he received only a curt nod in return, while young Heathcoat Amory, who was also a guest, remarked to him: 'This staying away is very expensive. I have just had to give the butler five shillings,' and, according to Williams, received a deep bow. As he came to know him better Williams gradually formed a sincere affection for his Minister. He admired his simplicity and his irreproachable life. He was touched at the delight Edward felt in his own home where Williams found him a different being, relaxed in his oldest clothes, singing a part in 'London's Burning', sadly out of tune, for he had no ear for music.

He was indifferent to elaborate food or good wine, and luxury meant nothing to him. Williams and Edward regularly attended the Church of St. Mary's, Graham Terrace, a centre of Anglo-Catholic practice, and, like Father Langton, Williams observed the intensity with which he prayed. It was clear to him that Edward was never as polemical as his father, but that he shared his strong desire for the reunion of the Christian Churches. In spite of these bonds, and of a sincere admiration, Edward remained to Williams something of an enigma, and he found it difficult to measure the extent to which his affection was returned.

But when he bent his mind to the subject Edward did excellent work. He never became exasperated by the restrictions on his administration, and never gave way to discouragement. He must be given great credit for his efforts in religious education, and he was admirable in smoothing away difficulties with the Roman Catholic Church and the Free Churches.

But, as in the first period of office, his heart was not in it. To him education was a minor issue compared with India. Contrary to the general belief, Ramsbotham, Griffith Williams, and Maurice Holmes, at that time Deputy Secretary of the Board, were united in testifying to Edward's lack of any real interest in the subject. Domestic education in no way absorbed him; he had no reforming zeal, and no desire to talk shop about it, and it was inevitable that since this fascinating aspect of public work made little appeal to him, he should have regarded this office as a *pis aller*.

Depression and the ten per cent cut in teachers' salaries had made the Board of Education a place of gloom and frustration, and, his mind still teeming with the problems of India, he found himself in a Department over which he had already presided, again almost entirely debarred by economic circumstances from constructive work. Nor should it be forgotten that during this second period at the Board he had many other calls on his time, as he also answered in the House of Lords for Housing, and was much occupied with advising the Government on the India Bill. Perhaps the most notable incident of this period was the setting-up of the Committee under Mr. William Spens in 1933 to inquire into the organization of secondary schools, but their Report, *Secondary Education with Special Reference to Grammar Schools and Technical Education*, was not published until the end of 1938, by which time Irwin had long since left the Board of Education and was then Secretary of State for Foreign Affairs.

* * *

Whatever the thoughts of his departmental civil servants, Irwin was, during this period, constantly engaged with the problem of India. After the complete failure of the Second Round Table Conference to agree on the Communal issue, the Government was forced to impose a solution and to produce its own 'Award' on the issue of Communal representation, and the fairness and honesty of this attempt to compose an insoluble problem may be judged by the fact that it gave equal offence to all sections of Indian opinion. Three Committees were also sent to India: the Franchise Committee under Lord Lothian, the Federal Finance Committee under Lord Eustace Percy, and the Indian States Enquiry (Financial) under J. C. C. Davidson, and their reports were published in the summer of 1932.

Irwin was a Parliamentary delegate at the third and attenuated session of the Round Table Conference which took place at the end of 1932 and lasted only five weeks. The chair that Gandhi had occupied was empty, and his energies henceforth were to be used in resuming his plans for non-co-operation and abusing the efforts of the delegates in London. So irresponsible did he become at this moment that when the Bill eventually passed after four years of intense effort, he told the Viceroy that he had never read it.[1] The third session was brought to a close in order that the Secretary of State for India should be able to proceed to the next stage of a White Paper containing the Round Table proposals, and a Joint Select Committee of both Houses to consider them.

Irwin in the meantime had received disturbing news from the Commander-in-Chief Chetwode about the attitude of the Princes towards the proposed Federation. All-India could not become a reality until a sufficient number of them adhered to the principle, and in September 1932 Chetwode described their vacillations and lack of vision:

'I still think myself that the Princes will be the chief difficulty in producing a workable Federation. The majority of them are quite hopeless, and only a few have the foggiest idea of what it will really mean; they devote any time they have to spare to matters outside their own expenditure, to ridiculous demands for the enhancement of their dignities: more guns, flags to be lowered if any of them die, the right to go in before the Commander-in-Chief

[1] Hoare, *Nine Troubled Years*, p. 66.

and Governors, and above all the lessening of the power of the Foreign and Political Departments.

'The States that really count, Mysore, Travancore, Hyderabad, Baroda, Gwalior, Indore etc., take very little part in discussions on the future, and people in England do not understand that Bikanir, Bhopal, Alwar, and other talking folk, are of very little account in the real India.'[1]

The White Paper was circulated within three months of the ending of the Conference. In the words of the Secretary of State: 'It poured breath into the dry bones left by years of continuous discussion. The two hundred paragraphs contained in it represented the maximum of agreement it was possible to obtain between Indians and Indians and Indians and British.'[2] Less than three weeks after the publication of the White Paper Parliament approved the appointment of a Joint Select Committee of both Houses to consider the White Paper, and to make recommendations on which a Bill could be drafted. This was composed of sixteen members from each Chamber, representative of all parties; twenty representatives of British India and seven from the Indian States were appointed as assessors, as they could not constitutionally be full members of a British Parliamentary body. Once again Irwin's knowledge and experience were in demand, and he was one of the sixteen members from the House of Lords.

The Committee, under the Chairmanship of Lord Linlithgow, sat almost continuously from April 1933 until it reported to Parliament in November 1934, holding 154 meetings and examining 120 witnesses, its sessions being broken for two months in the spring of 1934 by an extraordinary charge by Churchill of breach of Parliamentary privilege against Lord Derby and the Secretary of State for India. Irwin's membership of this Committee and his attendance at many of its meetings during this period occupied a great deal of time that he would normally have devoted to the affairs of his own Department. The Report did not differ substantially from the White Paper, but it contained three changes. For direct election upon a limited franchise for the Central Assembly it substituted indirect election by the Provincial Chambers; it strengthened the provisions against terrorism, and simplified the restrictions on economic discrimination for political objects.

After a three-day debate the House of Commons accepted the Report by a 4–1 majority, and the way lay clear to the great India Bill. They were now nearing for good or ill the end of the momentous process which Irwin had set in motion. The second reading of the Bill embodying the Joint Select Committee's proposals was carried by 404 to 133 votes. The passage of this immense measure was an extraordinary *tour de force* on the part of Sir Samuel Hoare. When all was over and it had reached the Statute Book on 24 July 1935, he could boast that he personally had seen the 473 clauses and

[1] Hickleton Papers, Sir Philip Chetwode to Lord Irwin, 11 September 1932.
[2] Hoare. Op. cit., p. 69.

sixteen Schedules through all their critical stages, and had made the greater number of the 1951 speeches that, containing fifteen and a half million words, had filled four thousand pages of *Hansard*.

With passionate sincerity and almost singlehanded, Winston Churchill had fought the India Bill throughout all its stages, and had poured into the attack all the wonderful resources of his language, sustained by a dark apprehension of approaching doom. To him it was 'a gigantic quilt of jumbled crochet work, a monstrous monument of shame built by pigmies', whereas to Irwin it was a vindication at every stage of the democratic process.

It was not given to these men who had laboured so hard in the cause of India to read the future. They could not tell that the vital provision of the Act, the All-India Federation, would never be brought into operation, nor that the unity of India was destined to be destroyed. They had no foretaste of the agony that was to precede Partition. For the moment the battle seemed to be won, and they could reflect with some complacency, as did Sir Samuel Hoare, that 'never was there a better example of government by Parliamentary discussion. The full ritual of Parliamentary procedure was followed in every detail, the three sessions of the Round Table Conference, the expert inquiries in India, the White Paper, the Joint Select Committee, and finally the Bill, debated in every detail and passed without any closure of discussion. If the essence of democracy is government by debate, Parliament was never exhibited in a more truly democratic light.'[1]

Much of Irwin's time was also occupied during this period by his speeches on India in the House of Lords. He had made his Maiden Speech there on this subject on 8 December 1931, and he took part in thirteen Indian debates between 1931 and 1935. Throughout these speeches he stressed the danger of a representative Parliament with an Executive not responsible to it, and in the debate on the Resolution to appoint the Joint Select Committee, after quoting Lord Durham's celebrated words about Canada which he found apposite to India, he had continued:

'I confess that when I had been in India a short time I formed a definite view, a view supported by all my reading of Imperial constitutional history, that when you have conditions such as I have described, once political consciousness is aroused, any structure based on this foundation is bound to lack political stability and could not for long be expected to rest upon a basis of consent. If India had not reached the stage where such a constitution was unworkable, we were within sight of it.'[2]

It was not, he believed, because they suffered from a greater degree of original sin than others, that the Indian Parliamentarians were so prone to exhibitions of regrettable irresponsibility. Rather, he thought it was the

[1] Hoare. Op. cit., p. 101.
[2] *Hansard*, House of Lords, Vol. 87, 6 April 1933.

system which produced these wild outbursts, and speaking on 12 December 1934 about an All-India Federation on the basis of responsibility, he had said:

'The dominant consideration with the Committee [the Joint Select Committee], as on this matter with their critics, was the necessity of creating a strong Centre of Indian Government, and nothing, I think, was more remarkable in the devolution of the corporate mind of the Committee than the way in which as the examination proceeded they became impressed, looking at the present Centre, not with its strength but with its weakness, for reasons on which I need not dilate but which are familiar enough, for indeed they are of the essence of our constitutional history. As I read it, the whole of our British Imperial experience shouts at us the warning that representative government without responsibility, once political consciousness has been aroused, is apt to be the source of great weakness and, not impossibly, great danger. We had not learned that lesson, let me remind the House, in the eighteenth century, and we paid very dearly for it. We learned it some sixty years later and, by having learned it, we transformed the face and history of Canada. . . . Harmony between the Legislature and the Executive is a prerequisite. There are only two ways to get it. One is to abolish your representative but irresponsible Legislature, and the other is to invest it with some responsibility. . . . To do neither is to forego, in my judgment, all the advantages and incur all the disadvantages of both.'[1]

And on the second reading of the Government of India Bill on 20 June 1935 he was to set forth almost for the last time his unchanging belief in the future of India in tones whose sincerity made a profound impression on the House of Lords:

'May I say a word quite plainly to Your Lordships as to the reason for the assertion I originally made in 1929, when I was in India, and for the reassertion of that by the Secretary of State in another place. I do not believe that either I or anyone else who may ever be honoured by being called upon to represent the King in India can hope to justify to Indians the privilege and duty of remaining loyal to the Crown and the British Empire, of which the Crown is the head, unless he is able to assure them that we do at some time, when India has fitted herself for it, envisage for India a status not necessarily identic but most certainly equal to that of any of the self-governing Dominions.'[2]

With his work at the Board of Education, and his preoccupation with India, Edward was thus left little time during the week in London for his own affairs, but in the summer of 1933 he was invited to preside over a meeting of the Anglo-Catholic Congress held at the Albert Hall to celebrate the centenary of the Oxford Movement. In his speech he expounded his

[1] *Hansard*, House of Lords, Vol. 95, 12 December 1934.
[2] Ibid., Vol. 97, 20 June 1935.

religious belief in the strength of corporate life being maintained through the Sacramental system, and deprecated attempts to contrast the Evangelical Revival with the Oxford Movement, believing rather that they should be regarded as complementary.[1] His father, now ninety-four, in the following year made his last contribution to the cause of Church unity by effecting the amalgamation of Maurice Child's Anglo-Catholic Congress with the English Church Union, the two bodies becoming one society on 1 January 1934.[2]

Edward's career as an Oxonian received its crown in October 1933 when the Conservative Members of Convocation nominated him as candidate for the Chancellorship of Oxford University in succession to the late Lord Grey of Fallodon. On 7 December he was formally elected in the absence of any other candidates and installed as Chancellor at a special Convocation held in the Sheldonian Theatre. His biographer, Alan Campbell Johnson, described the scene:

'He was installed as Chancellor at a special Convocation held in the Sheldonian Theatre. The ceremony was conducted throughout in Latin with all the solemn pomp and circumstance of antique procedure which springs direct from the scholastic custom of the Middle Ages. The procession of the Vice-Chancellor, Proctors, Heads of Houses, and Doctors duly met the new Chancellor at the Great Gate of the Schools and escorted him to the Divinity School, where he remained behind while they proceeded to the Theatre. Then with traditional Latin ritual, the Vice-Chancellor, Dr. F. J. Lys, Provost of Worcester, after formally opening Convocation, directed the Bedells in these words: "Ite, bedelli, petite Dominum Cancellarium." They returned, ushering in Irwin dressed in his black robes of ceremony embroidered with gold, the train of which was carried by his son and heir Charles, who was then an undergraduate at Christ Church. When he was seated on the right of the Vice-Chancellor the Registrar was instructed to read the Instrument of Election, whereupon the insignia of office were brought forward and laid before the Chancellor. These were the Book of Statutes, the Common Seal of the University, the Sign Manual of the Chancellor brought by the Proctors, together with maces and staves of the Bedells, the Instrument of Election, and the Diploma of the Doctor of Civil Law. There then followed two Latin orations in which the Public Orator, Cyril Bailey, eulogized Irwin, distinguished "et mentis eruditione et morum suavitate", and Irwin eulogized Grey and referred to their common descent from Grey of the Reform Bill. Only through Lord Grey's illustrious example could we escape that headlong and unbridled licence usurping the name of liberty herself in danger of perishing beneath the feet of the dictator or at the hand of the revolutionary. At the end of his oration Irwin returned the insignia to the Vice-Chancellor and directed him to dissolve the Convocation.

[1] Campbell Johnson. Op. cit., p. 352.   [2] J. G. Lockhart. Op. cit., p. 368.

The procession left the Theatre and the historic ceremony was at an end.'[1] Shortly after this he became President of the Oxford Society, again succeeding Lord Grey.

In 1934 Edward was active in his new office. He opened part of the extensions to the Ashmolean Museum, and presided over the annual meeting of the Oxford Preservation Trust where he praised the efforts of those who were fighting the squalid encroachment on Oxford of the jerry-builder, saving part of Shotover Hill, and the meadows on the banks of the Cherwell and the northern and southern slopes of Boars Hill. Living in the country silence of Garrowby he was shocked by the interruption of Oxford's cloistral calm, and his strong support would always be forthcoming for any measures to arrest it. He opened the East Quadrangle of Somerville, and presided at a meeting of the Oxford Society at the Foreign Office, and on 7 June delivered a broadcast speech on University life. In this he sought to express some of the spell that Oxford had cast upon him:

'For myself I have only to close my eyes to see once again the sweep of the High Street from Magdalen Bridge to Carfax; with St. Mary's Church and the great dome of the Radcliffe; or Tom Quad and Tom Tower in Christ Church standing up against the moonlight, and recapture something of the reference and love that seemed to grow from looking on the work that nature and the hand of man had wrought together.'[2]

In the same year he held his first Encaenia making a splendid entrance with his son again carrying his train, and the event coincided almost to a day with that of the Duke of Wellington a century earlier.[3]

The Chancellorship was the last triumph in his son's career which the father was to witness. In January 1934, within a few months of the age of ninety-five, it was clear that he was coming at last to the end of the road. Still as intellectually vigorous as ever, he had carried on almost to the end a large daily correspondence. At ninety-three he had managed to attend a meet at Garrowby, riding a pony and in full hunting dress, and a picture was painted by Lionel Edwards of the scene on Garrowby Hill in the country father and son loved so dearly showing three generations, Halifax, Edward and his eldest son Charles, riding behind hounds towards a covert, with the old man's pony led by a groom: 'I would not have missed yesterday for anything,' Halifax wrote to Edward; 'a day ever to be commemorated and remembered. I thought I should certainly have to cut open my boots to get them off, but that disgrace was just avoided. I hope you were not too much ashamed of my appearance, but I think it was a triumph getting into my clothes at all. ... I am not really stiff this morning but my back aches a little.'[4]

After this his letters to Edward had become infrequent, and in the New Year of 1934 at Hickleton he began to fail swiftly. He had aberrations that

---

[1] Campbell Johnson. Op. cit., pp. 353–4.   [2] Ibid., pp. 370–1.
[3] Ibid.   [4] Hickleton Papers, November 1932.

troubled him, but from which he rallied and described to Edward the strange world of illusion; how he had insisted on being taken out of doors in a chair 'to see the sea', for he had wandered back through the years and believed that he was at The Moult, his old home in Devonshire. After taking his last Communion he had whispered to his daughter Agnes: 'I am worried about my sins,' and the end of that long and dedicated life came peacefully on the evening of Friday, 19 January.[1] Although he had long anticipated it, his father's death brought to Edward a sense of loneliness, and another sudden consciousness of the passing of the years. It was the end of a chapter:

'For my sisters and myself,' he said, 'his death was a very large element withdrawn from what had been our life. As had been the case when my mother died, it seemed almost instantly to add to one's years as one moved up, so to speak into an older generation. And such had been his influence on us from our youngest days that it was hard to think of normal life in which he would no longer be there to be considered or to take visible part. From the time that I first went to Oxford companionship had steadily grown between us into which, when I married, Dorothy had immediately been admitted with full rights. Nothing could have been happier than our relations.'

And in tender retrospect Edward could now remember that only two little altercations had disturbed the long harmony; how his father had been hurt when as a boy at Oxford Edward had refused to make a speech in favour of the damnatory clauses of the Athanasian Creed, and when he had converted one of the best bedrooms at Garrowby into a nursery.

Lord Halifax was buried at Hickleton, 'after a sung Requiem in the little church, which was so crowded that the only way we could get people in was by taking out all the chairs. The church had remained his sheet anchor to the end; every day he had worshipped in it, and every year now, on or about the anniversary of his death, a Requiem is sung for him there'. At the east end of the chancel Edward set a slab with the inscription:

PRAY FOR THE SOUL OF CHARLES 2ND VISCOUNT HALIFAX
BORN JUNE 7 1839. DIED JANUARY 19 1934.
THIS STONE IN GOD'S HOUSE
WHICH HE MADE BEAUTIFUL
IN WHICH HE WORSHIPPED AND HIS BODY RESTS
COMMEMORATES HIS WORK FOR THE CATHOLIC CHURCH
AND THE REUNION OF CHRISTENDOM

*   *   *

The Prime Minister, Ramsay MacDonald, had been for some time ailing. He had been much afflicted by his eyes, and could only with difficulty read

[1] J. G. Lockhart. Op. cit., p. 373.

the State Papers, and his resignation on 7 June 1935 had been long anticipated. Stanley Baldwin had always been accepted as his successor and his
arrival at No. 10 Downing Street meant yet another change for Edward who,
after his father's death, had become the third Viscount Halifax, as he must
henceforth be called.

He now became for the brief period of five months Secretary of State for
War, being appointed on 7 June 1935. In such a short period of office it was
impossible to make a deep impression on his Department. He began to
perform the routine work and in June, with the C.I.G.S. Field Marshal
Montgomery-Massingberd, accompanied a War Office Staff tour of the
Marne Battlefield. For the rest of that month he was much occupied with
Oxford affairs. In July he presided for the first time over a meeting of the
Army Council, and in September attended Army manœuvres in Southern
Command.

Edward had become Commanding Officer of the Yorkshire Dragoons in
1925 but had resigned his command in 1926 on being appointed Viceroy of
India. Now in 1935 he was made Honorary Colonel of the Regiment and his
tenure of that position was to be extended over the years until he resigned
in 1956, retaining the rank of Honorary Colonel.

The only significance of Edward Halifax's period as Secretary of State for
War was the insight it gave him into the deplorable state of the nation's
defences. It will be necessary in coming chapters to describe in some detail
the background of events; here it is only necessary to give his own impression
of the situation at the time he assumed office.

This, as he saw it, was that after the First World War had ended with the
complete overthrow and disarmament of Germany, the Cabinet had established, for the guidance of Service Departments in framing policy and
estimates, a conventional condition that there would be no major war for
ten years. At the time this was not unreasonable, and economy was still not
incompatible with security. But when Churchill was Chancellor of the
Exchequer during Baldwin's first Government, a much wider and more
dangerous extension of this rule was made. He was responsible for the
instruction issued to the Defence Departments that they should continue to
base their estimates on the assumption of a ten-year period of peace, withdrawing the time limit that had previously restricted the formula to a single
ten-year period.[1]

'This interpretation of the rule,' said Halifax, 'coincided with the mood
into which the British people always lapse after a war, of thinking that there
will never be any more war, and that therefore they can safely cut down their
armaments. The advent of Hitler to power in 1933 had coincided with a high-
tide of wholly irrational pacifist sentiment in Britain, which caused profound

[1] Sir Winston Churchill's explanation of this policy will be found in *The Second World War*,
Vol. I, *The Gathering Storm*, p. 40.

WITH HIS
FATHER, 1932

ANCELLOR
OXFORD,
H QUEEN
RY

damage both at home and abroad. At home it immensely aggravated the difficulty, great in any case as it was bound to be, of bringing the British people to appreciate and face up to the new situation which Hitler was creating: abroad it doubtless served to tempt him and others to suppose that in shaping their policies this country need not be too seriously regarded. I do not think, when I went to the War Office, that anyone outside the official world realized how great had been the damage wrought by the double operation of interpretation and mood upon our armament industry and our consequent capacity for war.'[1]

In November 1935 a General Election was held at which the National Conservatives were returned to office with Stanley Baldwin as Prime Minister. After the election Edward was moved from the War Office, and became Lord Privy Seal and Leader of the House of Lords. From that position he watched the unhappy events of the winter. He saw the fall of the Foreign Secretary Hoare, which followed his pact with the French Foreign Minister Laval when it was felt in the Cabinet, as Neville Chamberlain recorded in his diary, 'that we must own up to a mistake and Halifax carried most weight when he said that unless Sam went, the whole moral force of the Government would be gone';[2] he saw the abdication of the new King, and he remained in his office until Baldwin handed over the Prime Ministership to Neville Chamberlain in May 1937. As Lord Privy Seal he was a free-lance Minister with a seat in the Cabinet, and his friendship with Stanley Baldwin was of much comfort to the latter as he groped his way through the shoals and quicksands of the Abdication Crisis; and it was at this period, as we shall see, that he began his association with the Foreign Office, working closely with Anthony Eden who had become Secretary of State. From this moment his energies were to be increasingly devoted to foreign affairs, and when, after Baldwin's resignation, he became Lord President of the Council in Chamberlain's administration, he continued both his leadership of the House of Lords and his work at the Foreign Office until Eden's resignation in 1938, when he became Secretary of State for Foreign Affairs, and the most controversial period of his public life began.

[1] Halifax. Op. cit., pp. 181–2.
[2] Macleod. Op. cit., p. 189.

Part Three

FOREIGN AFFAIRS

CHAPTER XVIII

PRELUDE

AFTER the election of November 1935 it was necessary for Edward to make up his mind what his future was to be, and whether he should continue in public life. There were rumours, without foundation, that he would become Provost of Eton and that the rest of his days would be passed in that elegant backwater, but he had not yet done with politics, and when Baldwin offered him the position of Lord Privy Seal and the Leadership of the House of Lords, he accepted the offer. The implication was that without definite office commitments he would be useful in dealing with any problem, domestic or foreign, on which the Government required experienced advice. The Prime Minister had always felt Halifax to be a man after his own heart, and the idea of having him available for consultation and employment strongly appealed to him. As matters developed Halifax gravitated more and more towards the Foreign Office, and, from November 1935, became so closely associated with it that on Eden's resignation he was the obvious choice as his successor.

We should glance back a little distance over the years that had recently passed to understand the situation in which he found himself in February 1938, and the reasons why he thought it necessary to adopt the course he followed. No political event has ever made a more violent impact on the country than the so-called Settlement of Munich. As on Ulster before, and on Suez afterwards, families were bitterly divided, and sometimes old friends could not bring themselves to speak to one another. Nor has that bitterness altogether dissolved; the mention of the event can even now resuscitate old rancours, and the arena is still full of smoke. It is therefore necessary to trace briefly the events that led up to this humiliating event. We know much now that was hidden or obscure in the nineteen-thirties, and we should beware of hindsight, but when all considerations are made, the story of those locust years seen from a distance is like 'a tale told by an idiot', a strange and sorry record of national aberration and political ineptitude for which no section of the community can escape some measure of blame, during which we first ignored, then aggravated the menace, before drifting finally, and dangerously unprepared, into war.

Today it seems clear, as Winston Churchill has pointed out, that the key to the European situation lay in the continued strength of Germany. In spite of the loss of Alsace-Lorraine and the Polish Corridor she remained by far the most formidable Continental power. Russia, enervated by civil war and mutilated by the Treaty of Brest Litovsk, was licking her wounds, a pariah in Europe, her intentions sinister in the eyes of civilized nations, but her strength too consumed to make her a balancing factor in any foreseeable future. The disruption of the Austro-Hungarian Empire had left no counterpoise to eventual German domination in Central Europe, and to the realization of the old Teutonic dream of Mitteleuropa. For the thwarting of this ambition the great nations had long relied on the Balance of Power, and when this was removed there appeared no reason why this poisonous mushroom should not in the course of time be planted in their midst, and the ambitions of Germany, for a while furtive and concealed, be brought out again into the glare of noon.

For France, after all her sufferings, the victory of 1918 was a hollow one. She had lost a million and a half of her soldiers, and was never to recover from this sacrifice of the flower of her youth. Much of her northern territory had been reduced to an obscene lunar bleakness by the invader. She had felt the full severity of war on her own soil. For her the hour of victory was darkened by the shadow of a resurgent Germany, and from that moment security against that danger was not only her constant and supreme preoccupation, but almost, and with every reason, an obsession of the mind.

Nor did the danger to world peace come only from the losers of the First World War. Italy under a vain irresponsible dictator viewed with growing discontent her share of the spoils of a victory to which she had contributed little. Japan was nursing vast imperialist ambitions in the direction of China and South-East Asia.

Pacificism, muddled thinking, apathy and drift had by the early 1930s brought Britain's defences to a dangerously low level. No protest at this state of affairs was to be expected from the Labour opposition, and even the advent of Hitler as Chancellor at the beginning of 1933 did nothing to shake their hostility to rearmament. The only voice of sanity was that of Winston Churchill but his warnings uttered with growing desperation continued to receive the same dusty answer. He was still tainted with the reputation of alarmism and ill-judgment, and the English people went about their business and pleasure indifferent to those notes of approaching doom.

Although Japan had already successfully defied the League over Manchuria, international anarchy had not yet triumphed completely by 1933. By far the most important challenge which the British Government had to face from then onwards was that of Hitler's Germany. The Cabinet was deplorably slow in recognizing the gravity of the new situation in Europe, and the need for action. Those who from this distance criticize the National Government can be acquitted of the use of hindsight, for the writing on the wall was already clear for the political leaders to read. It is embalmed in the despatches of Sir Horace Rumbold, the British Ambassador in Berlin, who had not from the beginning entertained the slightest doubt as to the character of the German Chancellor, or the road he intended to pursue.

But those at the head of the British Government did not wish to be disturbed by such comfortless reflections. Baldwin was so bored by foreign affairs, and so ignorant of them that he was liable to yawn and fidget when the irksome subject was forced on his attention, while MacDonald, lost in a dream of universal disarmament and pacifist to the core, was hardly the man to inspire a *risorgimento* in the national spirit.

But certain basic tendencies in the Government's policy were clearly evident. In the face of the challenge of the unsatisfied States it was a policy of retreat in as good order as possible. There was a determination not to go to war for anything but a vital interest. They were concerned therefore to do nothing to provoke a war, and were prepared to pay a price to avoid one.

They were aware that for different reasons the United States and Russia could not be brought into the balance, and that it was therefore impossible to build up a diplomatic and military combination. Left alone with France they considered themselves outweighted, and prepared themselves to use the machinery of the League, ineffective as it was, to settle whatever disputes arose. When Baldwin made that famous speech three years later *à propos* of the East Fulham election, saying that if he had put forward a programme of rearmament it would have led to his electoral defeat, he was expressing a real dilemma, for however futile the Government's efforts at rearmament were during these fatal years, they were infinitely superior to anything that could have been expected from the Labour Party.

But although the Opposition and indeed a great part of the country contributed by their attitude to its defencelessness and had much with which to reproach themselves, the responsibility rested upon the Governments in power during these years, and their failure which was the direct cause of Munich cannot be excused, although it can be explained. In Strang's words:

'Going further back, it has been urged, fairly enough, that we ought to have rearmed earlier and halted Hitler at the very outset of his career of expansion. But this begs an important question. Given the prevailing non-interventionist climate of public opinion in the 1930s . . . was it certain that any Government with any hope of retaining office could have carried a really intensive rearmament or a resolute policy of armed intervention in Europe? Be that as it may, the Baldwin and Chamberlain Governments . . . were themselves also infected with an almost Cobdenite non-interventionism, and made no serious attempt to meet the challenge. They preferred peace at almost any price.'[1]

With the public relying blindly on a League of Nations from which America, Germany and Japan were now absent, the mere known facts about

[1] Strang, *Britain in World Affairs*, p. 321.

the state of the country's armaments, particularly in the air, should have conveyed an urgent warning. Russia came first on the list of operational aircraft with 1,890, and France second with 1,665. Britain was in sixth place with 884 planes, considerably less than Italy, and equal to the combined forces of Poland and Yugoslavia. The R.A.F. was ten squadrons short of the 1923 Air Force programme. Air Estimates for 1933–34 were actually down on the year before, and no new squadrons were in contemplation. Year after year since Locarno the estimates of the other fighting services had been reduced. The Navy was lower in personnel than it had been for forty years; nine cavalry regiments, sixty-one batteries, and twenty-one battalions of infantry had been scrapped, and the Territorial Army was 40,000 below strength. The Singapore dock would not be complete until 1938. The only suggestion of realism in this deplorable situation was that the original assumption that there would be no major war for ten years, which had so disturbed Edward at the War Office, was at last abandoned after having been repeatedly extended beyond the safety limit to the detriment of productive capacity and technical personnel.

The fall in the Air Estimates was justified as 'a further earnest of the whole-hearted desire of his Majesty's Government to promote disarmament'. Even these evidences of fatalism and helplessness did not restrain the Labour Party from denouncing what little armament there was, and in an election pamphlet of the time they told the voters: 'The Unionist Party wants war. Your husbands and sons will be cannon-fodder. More poison gas will mean dearer food. Register your distrust of the war-mongers by voting Labour.'[1] Thus while the Government were making no effort to rearm in a manner which bore any relation to the danger, Labour and Liberal encouragement of an hysterical pacifism paralysed all efforts to rearm when a supreme effort could still have limited the scope of disaster.

Another extraordinary speech by Baldwin in November 1933, in answer to Conservative attempts to get the Air Force programme of 1923 implemented, baffled friend and foe alike. He told a bemused House of Commons that he could not speak of what he knew of this matter, and that if he were to speak of the difficulties, and who were raising them, 'it would be perfectly impossible to advance one inch with regard to disarmament. My lips are sealed'.

Winston Churchill was meanwhile devoting his matchless eloquence to laying bare the weakness of the British Air Force, and the vulnerability of our cities to enemy attack. In pressing for massive increases in the R.A.F. and for measures of defence against enemy bombers he was reinforced by much accurate information about the German strength, carefully gathered by friends and experts who shared his own apprehensions. We read in his *The Gathering Storm* how in March 1934 he obtained an assurance from Baldwin

[1] William McElwee, *Britain's Locust Years*, p. 228.

that failing a general agreement the Government would 'see to it that in air strength and air power this country shall no longer be in a position inferior to any country within striking distance of its shores', which led in July to a meagre proposal to increase the Royal Air Force by forty-one squadrons to be added in the next five years. In no way appeased by this promise, Churchill pointed out that Germany had already, in violation of the Treaty, created an Air Force which, by the end of the next year, would be almost equal in strength to our own even after the promised increase had taken effect.

Proceeding on almost incredible misinformation, Baldwin assured Churchill in November that if the German Air Force continued at its present rate without increased production, we should, over the next two years, have a superiority over it of nearly fifty per cent. This claim was also challenged by Churchill in March 1935, and the first of many unpleasant shocks was administered by Hitler a few days later when he told Simon and Eden, who were visiting Germany, that the German Air Force had already reached parity with the British. It was a statement which probably contained some element of bluff, but it sufficed to stir the Government out of its torpor, and a new Secretary of State at the Air Ministry, Cunliffe-Lister,[1] was able to institute the measures by which Great Britain was to snatch a precarious victory in 1940.

And how were the other nations in Europe directing their affairs in the light of the new régime beyond the Rhine? After the French Prime Minister Barthou had been murdered by Croat irredentists in Marseilles in October 1934, he was succeeded by Pierre Laval, an able but unprincipled Auvergnat whose adaptability to events was suggested by the fact this his name could be spelled backwards or forwards. It was now at all costs necessary to build up a combination of Powers to keep Hitler in check. Barthou had been engaged in this task at the time of his death, and with the same object in view Laval, in January 1935, made a bargain with Mussolini which gave Italy some concessions for her citizens in Tunis, an enlargement of her Libyan territory, and a share in the Jibuti railway. He also, by recognizing Italy's 'economic' interests in that country, appeared to Mussolini to underwrite the plans of conquest which the Italian dictator had for some time been maturing, and to provide him with a *carte blanche* for the invasion of Abyssinia. No doubt this arrangement seemed to Laval a cheap price to pay for ensuring the friendship of Italy, and the possible transfer of eighteen French divisions from the Italian to the German frontier, and he may have hoped by this additional show of force on the Rhine to deter Hitler from interference in the west and set his steps upon a *Drang nach Osten*.

To most of the world Mussolini's invasion of Abyssinia was a shameless example of that unprovoked aggression which the League of Nations was designed to inhibit and restrain. The dictator naturally approached his

[1] Afterwards the Earl of Swinton.

adventure with very different feelings. He would remember how fifty years before Great Britain had encouraged Italy to occupy Marsowa to relieve the pressure of the Mahdi on her pocket of troops in the Eastern Sudan, and that it was with British approval that the Italians had made a treaty with the Emperor Menelek which gave Italy a protectorate over the country. And he would certainly not forget how Menelek had torn up that treaty and inflicted an appalling defeat and massacre on the Italians at Adowa, one of the greatest disasters in history for European civilization.

And if arraigned for aggression on a weak country, he would recall how the triumphant Amharas had carved out an empire based on the enslavement or serfdom of their weaker neighbours, and containing scarcely the rudiments of a modern State.[1] To avenge that shameful defeat when Italian soldiers in their thousands had lain mutilated on the field would have appeared as natural to Mussolini as the British plans to reconquer the Sudan. But above all he was driven by the lust for glory, and that incurable disease the paranoia of power was already eating into him like a cancer. It was inconceivable to him that the League would make a serious effort to stop him, or that England, who was as anxious as France for his support against Germany, would be the spearhead in the attempt. He therefore awaited the Stresa Conference, which was to begin on 11 April, in a mood of sunny confidence in spite of the warnings of his ambassador in London, Count Dino Grandi, that he might encounter opposition.

Nor did the proceedings of Stresa do anything to disturb his serenity. The Stresa 'front' now appears, in the words of Keith Feiling, 'not so much a "front" as a retreat *en échelon*, a scene not of action but of that "consultation" which, on the day of its assembly, Mussolini described as the last resort of indecision in the face of reality'.[2] No questions were asked about his intentions in Abyssinia, and a declaration was issued, characteristic of the day in sanguine vagueness, that 'the three powers, the object of whose policy is the collective maintenance of peace within the framework of the League of Nations, find themselves in complete agreement in opposing, by all practicable means, any unilateral repudiation of treaties which may endanger the peace of Europe, and will act in close and cordial collaboration for this purpose'.

The British delegates, Simon and MacDonald, were presumably under Cabinet instructions to undertake no new commitment, but at least they succeeded in having the need to preserve Austrian independence confirmed, in continuing negotiations for the security of Eastern Europe, and fortifying Locarno by the creation of aerial pacts. But the aggression envisaged at Stresa was aggression in Europe, and Abyssinia was not in Europe. This

[1] After the invasion of Abyssinia had begun Churchill remarked: 'No one can keep up the pretence that Abyssinia is a fit, worthy and equal member of a league of civilized nations.'
[2] Keith Feiling, *Neville Chamberlain*, p. 256.

distinction, made at the Duce's own request, confirmed him in his belief that he had nothing to fear, and that only the green light lay ahead.

From this distance the failure of MacDonald and Simon to utter a word of warning at Stresa about the danger of the Abyssinian adventure seems both weak and culpable. Simon had decided that it would be unwise to allow the discussion on Europe to be clouded by the inclusion of this bristly topic, and preferred to postpone its debate until the question was raised at Geneva on the appeal of the Emperor of Abyssinia.

Little did he imagine that his successor at the Foreign Office Sir Samuel Hoare would in a short time deliver such a clarion call at Geneva that it would echo over Europe, and stand forth for a brief moment of glory against the aggressor as the champion of an embattled League. There had been no mention of Abyssinia in the Commons debate that had followed Stresa, and Mussolini, although he had been incensed by strong language used by Eden at the end of May, had no conception of the change of British opinion which was to be given expression by a reconstructed Government under a new Prime Minister, and with a new Foreign Secretary.

On 7 June Baldwin became Prime Minister, and appointed Samuel Hoare Foreign Secretary with Anthony Eden as his assistant for League of Nations Affairs. The alternatives facing the new Government presented an unenviable choice. On 27 June Lord Robert Cecil announced the results of the Peace Ballot in the Albert Hall, and this enormous manifestation of ill-informed public opinion had been brought to an angry boil by Mussolini's clear intention of waging war with modern weapons upon a primitive and defenceless people.

The Government had made no attempt to contravert the pacifist argument, and found themselves in a serious dilemma. It appeared essential to European peace that Mussolini should be kept out of the hands of Hitler, and that the Stresa front should be preserved with the Italian dictator still on the side of the righteous, but a strong line on Abyssinia would, it seemed, infallibly disrupt the fragile unity of Stresa and drive Mussolini into the other camp. Yet such a course was now being urged from all sides in accents ever more shrill, and now the voices were not only those of pacifists, Liberals and Socialists. Conservatives had also been roused by the contrast between the brutality of the dictator and the sober dignity of the little Emperor.

Hoare and the Foreign Office were acutely conscious in this crisis of the danger of throwing Mussolini into Hitler's hands, and the Foreign Secretary embarked upon what he described as a 'double line of approach', continuing negotiations with Mussolini, and at the same time making 'a revivalist appeal' at Geneva. It was this utterance in which, speaking with great earnestness, he said that his country stood for 'steady and collective resistance to all acts of unprovoked aggression', which echoed round Europe. To Churchill on holiday in the Riviera sunshine it seemed that England had at last found her greatness again, but others realized that she was still inhibited by all the old frustrations.

Mussolini invaded Abyssinia on 3 October 1935, and the attitude of the British Government although as fundamentally dishonest as that of the Opposition, was, from an electioneering point of view, extremely adroit. Although Baldwin, on the eve of the General Election which came in November, had assured the Peace Society 'that there would be no great armaments', a promise he certainly kept—he was able to claim that the League was still the cornerstone of his foreign policy, and that there would be no weakening over Abyssinia. Three hundred and eighty-five Conservatives were returned to Parliament, and the new Government was dominated by that party. In spite of Hoare's stirring words at Geneva there had never been the slightest intention of applying military sanctions. They were ruled out, he said, because 'the precondition for the enforcement of such sanctions, namely collective agreement at Geneva, has never existed.'

Instead, by the end of October a derisory scheme of economic sanctions had been worked out which caused Mussolini little concern, but he made it clear that sanctions on the supply of oil which might have brought his operations to a halt, would mean war. This was not a prospect which Baldwin was prepared to face.

So they turned instead to France, whither the Foreign Secretary with the full approval of the Cabinet set forth to find some means of extrication from the impasse into which his country had drifted. Sir Samuel Hoare was in no condition to measure wits with the tortuous Laval. Exhausted by his incredible labours over the India Bill, he was a sick man subject to sudden fainting fits and in sore need of a long rest. The result of his journey was the Hoare-Laval pact of evil memory to be submitted subsequently, with the joint recommendation of Britain and France, to Geneva, and to the parties in the dispute. It was not in itself an unreasonable proposal, and might have been accepted had it emerged earlier. But its contents were prematurely revealed to the Press before any official statement had been made. British opinion was enraged at the sight of maps which appeared to give Italy sovereignty over two-thirds of Abyssinia. The storm that followed took the Government by surprise, and also the Foreign Secretary, who had placidly continued his skating holiday during which he fell on the ice in a fit of giddiness and broke his nose, yet another casualty on this disastrous foreign excursion. Baldwin deemed it prudent to submit to public anger and with many protestations of friendship sacrificed Sir Samuel Hoare as the victim of policies carried out with the full approval of the Prime Minister and his colleagues.

The Cabinet had succeeded with remarkable thoroughness in securing the worst of all worlds. Oil sanctions were tacitly dropped. Other economic sanctions, cautiously applied, and abandoned in June 1936 served to in-

furiate without in any way hindering Mussolini. Abyssinia was soon conquered, and the episode was yet another nail in the coffin of collective
security and the principles of the League. At the same time the Stresa front
had been destroyed; Hitler's aggressive policies had received the maximum
encouragement from Mussolini's success, and the Italian dictator had moved
decisively in the direction of a German alliance.

CHAPTER XIX

EARLY EXPERIENCE

SUCH in the broadest terms was the melancholy condition in Europe during the early months of Halifax's novitiate in foreign affairs. He was appointed Lord Privy Seal on 22 November 1935, and one of his earliest and least appetizing tasks in this capacity was to explain in the House of Lords the Government's conduct over the Hoare-Laval Pact. Here his speech was in refreshing contrast to the lame performance of the Prime Minister in the House of Commons. Baldwin had claimed previously that he had an unanswerable case, and that when it was presented he would 'guarantee that not a member would go into the Lobby against the Government'. But when the moment came to justify it he could only say that when he was confronted by something that appealed to the deepest feelings of his fellow-countrymen, he had realized that what he had done was neither wise nor right, and he had therefore bowed to the storm. The proposed Pact which had won the approval of the Foreign Office was now dead.

Edward's task was also difficult and unpleasant for his friendship with Hoare was a valued one, and their unanimity over India in the long battle had bound them closely together. But in treading this dangerous ground he showed himself remarkably sure-footed. He was also frank:

'I have never been one of those,' he said, '. . . who have thought that it was any part of the League in this dispute to try to stop a war in Africa by starting a war in Europe.' He emphasized that the risks arising out of League Membership were only tolerable if they were collectively met and that this condition had not been present:

'If I know the people of this country at all, they would never stand for membership of a League of Nations that was liable to land them into a single-handed war.'

The burden of his argument was that the League of Nations had never pretended that the Italian case was entirely devoid of substance, and that this fact was the background against which those who were seeking conciliation had worked. He was, perhaps, stretching a point when he claimed that Hoare had not been sent to Paris to discuss conciliation, and was therefore without instructions, and that it was only Laval's importunity that caused him to linger and become involved in talks, for the Cabinet were seeking a settlement in the company of the French, and were kept in touch with the negotiations throughout, although they were perhaps startled that Hoare should have come to so definite a conclusion.

Before the details of the talks reached London, Halifax explained, the communiqué had already been published in Paris, and a full description of its terms issued to the French Press. He admitted that the Government had not liked these terms, although in his opinion they were, in some respects, more favourable from the League of Nations' view than the Report of the Committee of Five[1] which had been accepted by Abyssinia:

'It was quite clear,' he continued, 'that the Government could never refuse assent on that Friday night at the price of repudiating their Foreign Secretary, a colleague who was absent and who would have been unheard.' At the same time a decision of some kind was urgently demanded in view of the French leakage, and here he was forced to admit that the Government was in error:

'If we erred, as we did, in giving approval under such conditions to these proposals, I venture to think that we erred for motives that will be appreciated by all who know how close are the bonds of trust that bind colleagues, and how essentially these bonds of comradeship are the foundation of all that is best in the political life of a free nation. I am quite prepared to admit that we made a mistake—not the mistake that is commonly imputed to us, but the mistake of not appreciating the damage that, rightly or wrongly, these terms would be held by public opinion to inflict upon the cause that we were pledged to serve. Accordingly we share to the full the responsibility for the mistake that was made.'

The 'trust that binds colleagues' and the 'sharing in the responsibility' did not prevent Sir Samuel Hoare from paying the penalty for this collective error, while the Government remained securely in being, but his sojourn in the wilderness was brief, and it was not long before he was solaced once again by office, returning as First Lord of the Admiralty to lend the force of his persuasion to the policy of appeasement. A less stilted version of Edward's views on this lamentable muddle can be found in a letter from him to Neville Chamberlain on 26 December:

'The whole affair was a thoroughly bad business. Looking back it seems to me that the initial mistake was Sam's, in publishing his (and therefore, except at great price *our*) assent in the Paris communiqué. And what of course explains—but doesn't justify—what we did was the habit of immense confidence we had rightly developed in him.

'I am still puzzled, though, by the condemnation meted out to proposals that were not, as you said all along, so frightfully different from those put forward by the Committee of 5. But the latter were of respectable parentage; and the Paris ones were too much like the off-the-stage arrangements of 19th-century diplomacy.'[2]

[1] A League of Nations Committee which had put forward a scheme for the solution of the Abyssinian question.
[2] Feiling. Op cit., p. 275.

Another event in 1936 besides the Abyssinian tragedy made a deep erosion
in the forces of those who, however misguidedly, were trying to preserve the
peace. In France, as in England, the Hoare-Laval Pact had left a rancid taste
behind it and had strengthened all the Left-wing elements in the Chamber
of Deputies who disliked Laval's policy of Italian appeasement. A new
Government under Sarraut, with Flandin as Foreign Minister, at once sought
reassurance in the East, and ratified the Franco-Soviet agreement which had
been shelved by Laval in his efforts to win Italian friendship. Hitler had been
ominously quiet for a year since he had repudiated the armaments clause of
the Versailles Treaty in March 1935. He now took another, and profoundly
menacing step towards the domination of Europe, the true significance of
which was not appreciated by the general public. Taking the Franco-Soviet
Agreement as a pretext, and choosing the week-end of 7 March, when his
opponents were dispersed on holiday, as a suitable moment to strike, he
declared the Treaty of Locarno at an end, and invaded the demilitarized
Rhineland, the key to France's system of Eastern European alliances. This
was not the first indication that Hitler had given of predatory intentions, but
it was far the most serious, and allowing him to occupy and promptly to
fortify the Rhineland practically meant the abandonment of Austria and
Czechoslovakia, at least without a far greater effort to protect them than
would have been required in 1936.

Looking back on this decisive episode of history after thirty years it is
obvious that this was the moment when Germany's fatal course could have
been arrested, and the dictator, with the approval of the German generals,
driven from power before his grasp upon it became too strong, and the failure
of France and England to take the appropriate action, as they could easily
have done, appears from this distance a monumental example of blindness
and irresolution. But to yield to the temptation of so regarding it is to ignore
the conditions in which it took place, and to attribute to the French and
British people a far clearer perception of German motives than they in fact
possessed, and a willingness to oppose them by force that was entirely absent.

For the English, in particular, were not thinking of Germany at this
moment. Their emotions were exclusively engaged in watching as helpless
spectators the agony of Abyssinia and the advance of Mussolini's victorious
armies. It is always difficult for British public opinion to concentrate on two
issues at once, and it was slow to grasp that something else, infinitely more
menacing to the safety of England, was happening at the same time.

Compared with Mussolini's perfidy, and the eclipse of the League of
Nations, Hitler's action seemed of trivial significance, and Lord Lothian
undoubtedly represented the general opinion when he said that Germany
could hardly be blamed for 'walking into her own back-garden', for the
British people, hypnotized by German propaganda about the iniquity of
Versailles, and obsessed by feelings of unreasoning guilt, were only too will-

ing to shrug their shoulders at this gross violation of the Treaty. Indeed as a result of France's vacillations over the oil embargo the feeling in the House, and even more in the country, tended to be in favour of Germany. The Franco-Soviet Pact was not popular, and since in the public mind the obligations of Locarno were secondary to those of the League, the ethic of Rhineland resistance did not seem to be on the same plane as the defence of Abyssinia.[1]

After Hoare's resignation Anthony Eden became Foreign Secretary, and his post as Minister for League of Nations Affairs was left unfilled. He and Halifax were now to be closely associated in foreign affairs, and their intimate friendship, even when they radically disagreed, was never impaired. In Eden's words:

'Lord Halifax, who had then no departmental duties, was Lord Privy Seal, as I had previously been, and stood in for me at the Foreign Office from time to time. He did not have a room, nor a Private Secretary, or any official position, but he eased some of my burden, especially on my brief spells of leave. We had long been friends and I was grateful for an arrangement which never caused me any anxiety, even when we did not agree about the decisions to be taken, as happened later.'[2]

It was now decided, at Eden's own request, that Halifax should accompany him to Paris on 9 March for discussions on the steps to be taken in the face of Hitler's flagrant violation of the Locarno Treaty. 'I thought it essential,' said the Foreign Secretary, 'to have a senior colleague with me.' Sir Winston Churchill has given in *The Gathering Storm* M. Flandin's own account of how he urged the British Prime Minister to join with the French in ejecting Hitler from the Rhineland, and how Baldwin had replied that if there was one chance in a hundred of the proposed 'peace operation' against Germany leading to war he had no right to commit his country which was in no condition or mood for military operations. And the story is also known that at a lunch party at the House of Commons during the Rhineland negotiations of March 1936 Flandin had told his hosts that if he could have obtained the approval of the British he would have taken military action, and that he had every reason to believe that 'the Germans would have withdrawn without firing a shot'.[3] Such records as these have long left the impression that the French Foreign Minister could have secured his country's effective action, but that she could not intervene alone, and remained inert because she was denied any possibility of help by the British Government.

The publication of the Memoirs of Lord Avon who, as Anthony Eden, played the central part in these negotiations for his country has put a somewhat different complexion on the matter. A study of his careful description

[1] L. B. Namier, *Europe in Decay*, 1936–40, pp. 20–21.
[2] The Earl of Avon, *The Eden Memoirs. Facing the Dictators*, p. 319.
[3] L. B. Namier. Op. cit., p. 11.

of the March negotiations makes it clear that while there was not the slightest intention on the British side to participate in any military action against Germany, M. Flandin had greatly exaggerated the determination of the French Government to see the matter through to a conclusion. He had begun by saying that he wished to put at the League's disposal all the resources of France, including military force, and to put such pressure on Hitler that he would be compelled to withdraw his army from the Rhineland. It seemed to Eden extremely improbable that the League would feel any obligation to take a step that would involve it in military action, and that there was no commitment that bound it to do so. Flandin had replied that in that case he expected the Locarno Powers who were directly involved, to take military measures by themselves. It seemed to both Eden and Halifax that in making this suggestion he was greatly overrating the solidarity of the French Government, and the readiness of the French people to face war.

It afterwards transpired that their suspicions were well founded, and that there was, in Flandin's own words, 'pitiful confusion' in the French Cabinet, and that their extreme intention was to man the Maginot Line and move two divisions from the Rhône Valley to the Eastern frontier. The Belgian Prime Minister, Van Zeeland, then suggested that a way out of the difficulty might be to accept the disappearance of the demilitarized zone, but to find some additional guarantees to replace it. Could it not be said categorically that the British Government should make its own obligation under Locarno precise, and undertake that an encroachment of German troops upon French or Belgian soil would be automatically met by British counteraction? It was an idea that appealed to Eden, since, in his own words, 'we could not join with the French in military action'. 'What I now believe to be true,' he wrote more than thirty years later, 'is that the French and Belgian Governments did not at the time have sufficient support in their public opinions to allow them to use effective force and that, being democracies, they could not have acted without it, even if they had wished to do so.'[1] France was in fact in the agonizing position of a democratic country torn by pacifism and paralysed by inaction, whose leaders were aware of the danger but dared not take the steps to protect themselves, and were aware that if it came to fighting their closest friend would not lift a finger to help them.

Eden and Halifax had to cancel their flight to London through bad weather, and had time, on steamer and train, to compare their impressions of the meetings. 'We decided,' said Eden, 'that if a negotiation were later to take place, France and Belgium must, in addition, at least be assured of our support in any new treaty replacing Locarno.'[2] When the delegates met again Flandin appeared to have resigned himself to the recognition of the remilitarization of the Rhineland and its military occupation, in return for a new and binding Locarno Pact, sewn tightly together by Staff conversations between the

[1] Avon. Op. cit., p. 354.   [2] Ibid.

contracting Powers. He had no doubt been disheartened by the tepid response of the League, some of whose members clearly intended to retreat into neutralism, and by the hopeless division of his own Cabinet.

The League Council next met in London at St. James's Palace, and at the same time British, French and Belgian Ministers continued the discussions that had begun in Paris. Eden presided over these meetings, and Halifax was a frequent attendant. It was his first direct experience of a diplomatic crisis as a participant, and he had much to learn in this new world with a language of its own of suave jargon, and habits of procedure to which he was a stranger. Now Flandin spoke no longer of military measures, but of some vague economic sanction which confirmed the Foreign Secretary's belief that neither before nor during the dispute had the French Ministers any settled plan of action:

'Theirs,' he said, 'was the agony of an essentially pacific, democratic country, believing that in this instance pacificism was not enough and searching for stronger action that might be carried through with the support of their own people, but without the risk of war. There was no such course. . . .'[1]

On 29 March Locarno was solemnly confirmed in Eden's room at the Foreign Office, and the General Staffs of the Locarno Powers were instructed to hold conversations. The Council of the League had already condemned Germany's violation. By the time these events were over Halifax had been initiated into the arcana of foreign affairs. He had been a prominent figure at the conference, and in the words of Campbell Johnson:

'From all the prolonged Cabinet meetings which went on late into the night, the babel of Geneva at the Court of St. James's, the complexity of double-barrelled League and Locarno diplomacy, Halifax emerged triumphant. Not for nothing had he haggled with the Eastern mind. "When everyone else was exhausted," wrote a foreign observer, "he seemed still as fresh as at the outset of the negotiations. His advice was the product of good sense and complete self-command." Although this was essentially his début in European diplomacy, he seems to have made as deep an impression upon the galaxy of experienced foreign statesmen gathered in London during these critical days and weeks as upon his own colleagues. Not only was his prestige enhanced within the Government; he was from henceforth a figure of consequence in Europe.'[2]

The peaceful outcome of this dangerous episode was received in Britain with relief and satisfaction. As Lord Avon wrote: 'There was nowhere a suggestion that we should have been sharper with Hitler, still less that we should have joined in military sanctions in the Rhineland or the Saar. . . . Academically speaking, there is little dispute that Hitler should have been called to order, if need be forcibly at his first breach of an accepted international engagement. But nobody was prepared to do it, in this country

[1] Ibid., p. 360.   [2] Campbell Johnson. Op. cit., p. 400.

literally nobody. Even the most warlike proclaimed that the League Council must be called, which would not have endorsed the use of force.'[1]

Such was the climate of opinion at the time in the experience of one who could scarcely be charged with weakness, and it is essential to project ourselves into the past if we are to gain any understanding of why these apparent follies were committed. But a disaster had taken place none the less, which was a curtain-raiser for Munich, and which we now know could have been scotched by resolute action. The first bastion had fallen, and this bloodless triumph had left the dictator convinced of the superiority of his judgment over that of his generals, of the vacillation and futility of the Western Powers; convinced too that no further act of violence or duplicity would cause them to incur the risk of war.

*   *   *

Certainly Germany's immediate actions after the Rhineland coup offered little encouragement to those who still regarded her as a normal state that could be brought within the pale of civilized intercourse. After her condemnation by the Council of the League the Locarno Powers asked Germany if she would submit her doubts about the Franco-Soviet Treaty to the Hague Court. She was also asked if she was prepared to limit her forces and to refrain from fortifying the Rhineland during negotiations over any proposals she might make. After an unsatisfactory reply from Germany a questionnaire was sent to Berlin on 7 May, asking her what part of the Versailles Treaty she was prepared to observe, and whether she would recognize the existing 'political and territorial status of Europe', except as modified by free negotiations in the future. To these and other similar questions Hitler responded with an insolent silence.

We get some idea of Halifax's views at this juncture from his speeches on international affairs. While waiting for the German reply to these questions he said in a speech at Bristol while deputizing for Eden:

'We want no encirclement of Germany. We want to build a partnership in European society in which Germany can freely join with us and play the part of good Europeans for European welfare. I have never concealed from myself that in asking what we did from Germany we asked a hard thing. Indeed I would have been prepared to say that just because it was so hard a contribution, it placed it within the power of Germany to do something that more than anything else, would have restored European confidence and have placed her in the position of making the greatest contribution of us all to the future of European peace.'[2]

It was the language of the day, but these public-school appeals to Hitler's sense of honour and duty were precisely those which roused his most savage contempt for the men he was to describe as 'those worms' of the Munich

[1] Avon. Op. cit., pp. 361–7.   [2] Quoted by Campbell Johnson. Op. cit., p. 400.

settlement. On 8 April a somewhat harder note had entered Halifax's words in a speech delivered just before his departure to join Eden in Geneva. He had spoken of the world standing at the cross-roads, and continued:

'A hundred years hence, if the world survives, we shall all be judged by the direction we now take; for upon the choice that we make depends much more than the issue of our immediate difficulties, and the price of wrong judgment will be a very high one. Though the cross-roads have long been in sight, it is true to say that the world has been brought right up to them by the recent action of Germany and by the inevitable reactions from it.'[1]

He refused to commit himself as to what the attitude of Great Britain would be to German claims to hegemony in Eastern or Central Europe, and although his words could in no way be interpreted by her as an encouragement they certainly did not constitute a threat. It should not be supposed, he said, that:

'. . . because we have assumed more specific obligations in the West which we are not prepared to repeat for the East of Europe, therefore we disinterested ourselves from all events and issues arising outside what perhaps I may call the Locarno area. In my view such an attitude would be quite impossible, partly because peace is indivisible, and it is very hard for me to imagine that if the East of Europe were really aflame you could feel any confidence that the flames would not spread across to the West; but also because of our obligations under the Covenant, which are obligations by which we abide and which we intend to implement to the best of our power.'

Hitler, however, would not have failed to observe where our regard for these obligations had left Abyssinia, and in the meantime things were going from bad to worse. As had been anticipated by the more cynical observers it was soon considered that the unhappy Hoare had sufficiently worked his passage home to be reinstated at the end of May as First Lord of the Admiralty. This return of the prodigal pleased neither Eden nor Halifax, the former pointing out to Baldwin that there would now be three former Foreign Secretaries in the Cabinet, and that this *embarras de richesse* would not make his own difficult position in any way easier. 'Lord Halifax, however,' wrote Eden, 'was much more outspoken when we met the next day. He criticized Baldwin sharply for yielding to Hoare's importunity. A few weeks earlier Sir Samuel had made a speech in Parliament about Baldwin so adulatory as to be embarrassing to all who heard it.'[2]

In the same month the elections in France brought in the Popular Front by a large majority, a Left Wing combination underpinned by Communist support, and the new Prime Minister, M. Blum, had to face a flight from the franc which was the result of strikes and public disorder which for a time seemed almost to threaten a civil war. In Spain civil war had in fact begun in

[1] Ibid.   [2] Avon. Op. cit., p. 383.

July, and continued to be waged with implacable ferocity in which there was little distinction between either side.

In England sympathies were divided, but to the Left it was a Holy war, a Jehad in which the Spanish Government stood embattled against the forces of evil. Spain became an obsession with them which has lasted to the present day; some of the more hardy, but usually least vocal of their number fought in the International Brigade, and Picasso's mural of Guernica was to become the image of a martyrology. Those with the responsibility for affairs looked at the struggle through eyes less starry. Even Blum, the majority of whose countrymen were in favour of the Spanish Government, had no wish to see the conflict extended, and it was he who devised the solution of non-intervention, which was accepted by most of those concerned with the intention of flouting it at every turn.

In welcome contrast to the anxieties of this unhappy year were two events in Edward's family which brought him the greatest pleasure. His daughter Anne married Lord Feversham on 9 May in York Minster. He was the son of Edward's old friend and fagmaster, Charlie Helmsley, and a great York-shire landowner, and Anne's choice was thought by her father to be perfect. A fortnight earlier, in St. Paul's Cathedral, his eldest son Charles was mar-ried to the daughter of another old friend, Lord Rosebery's son Neil Prim-rose who had slept so shamelessly while Edward discoursed at those bygone tutorials at All Souls, and had fallen in the First World War. In Feversham and Ruth Primrose Edward gained a son and daughter-in-law more delight-ful than he could have dared to hope, and with whom his relations were to remain those of deep affection.

                    *   *   *

In October 1936 the ability of Great Britain to exert an influence in Central Europe was further reduced by the declaration of the Belgian King Leopold that his country had ceased to adhere to the Locarno Treaty which in his opinion no longer afforded her adequate protection, and would remain neutral in all circumstances. This was another victory for Hitler who could rely with certainty on British and French squeamishness about infringing Belgian neutrality, while he was unlikely to be restrained by similar feelings of delicacy. It was clear that the greatest danger that could confront England was now no matter of academic consideration, and that this was a possible German threat to the heart of the British Empire coinciding with a Japanese attack on the Commonwealth east of Suez, with a hostile Italy disputing the free passage of the Mediterranean and endangering the Suez Canal. It was a prospect that seemed to many to have advanced a step when at the end of the year the German-Japanese Anti-Communist Agreement was signed.

By the end of 1936 the highly-charged international situation had con-vinced the Government that more serious military preparations should be

made. During the years that followed ministers would invariably excuse
weakness and surrender by the argument that forceful diplomacy could not
be practised unless it was based on physical force. Yet there was no real
urgency in the measures that were now taken nor any irresistible public
demand for a realistic programme which would inevitably dislocate the
normal life of the country. Baldwin's first action after the reoccupation of the
Rhineland had been one of almost comical inadequacy. He had appointed
the Attorney-General, Sir Thomas Inskip, a somewhat ponderous lawyer of
Evangelical persuasion as Minister for the Co-ordination of Defence, an
action which caused Churchill to echo the words of Gladstone in reflecting
that no stranger appointment had taken place since Caligula made his horse a
consul. Nor did the Estimates that followed this appointment, and the new
White Paper on Defence in any way correspond to the needs of the hour.
They increased the Defence expenditure by a mere £34,000,000, and brought
the total figure up to £186,000,000, less than a fifth of German military
expenditure that year. It is worth noting that even this paltry figure was
denounced by the Labour Opposition as being inconsistent with the policy
of Collective Security, to which, after all that had happened, they still firmly
clung.

A further White Paper appeared at the beginning of 1937 which made a
more resolute effort to meet the deficiencies, and was framed by Neville
Chamberlain who had begun to take a more serious view of the need for
Defence than some of his colleagues. But although it was an improvement it
still bore no relation to the danger. In February 1937 the Government took
powers to borrow £400 million for Defence, with a warning that this figure
might rise to £1,500 million spread over five years. Chamberlain's 1937
Budget increased defence estimates up to only £198 million which was less
than half of the sum Hitler was spending for the same purpose.

Winston Churchill was the most eminent of those who continued to draw
attention to the national weakness in a series of powerful but disregarded
speeches, and he was certain that by the end of 1936 the moment was long
overdue for the establishment of a Ministry of Supply. Halifax's response to
this suggestion in one of his speeches in the House of Lords made it plain
that he did not yet regard the European situation as sufficiently grave to
warrant the placing of the nation on a war-footing, and its transformation
into an armed camp which realistic competition in armaments with regi-
mented Germany would demand. He was not, he said, ready to adopt 'such
heroic remedies'.

'What is quite certain is that in the process you would gravely dislocate
trade, Budgets, general finance, and the general credit of the country. Are
we in fact to judge the question so serious that everything has to give way
to the military reconditioning of our Defence Forces? Such a conclusion,
in fact, appears to me to rest on premises, not only of the inevitability, but

of a degree of certainty as to the early imminence of war, which I am not prepared to accept.'

At the beginning of 1937 the Government could thus look back over a bad year, although Baldwin's masterly handling of the Abdication crisis had refreshed his jaded prestige like a watered flower, and unfortunately done much to divert public opinion from the ugly reminders of foreign danger. Those who preferred not to be so seduced could contemplate the debit side of this dispiriting balance-sheet—that the Italo-German *rapprochement* was now fully fledged, that the Rhineland had been occupied without bloodshed, the League of Nations mortally stricken, and, like Dolfuss, allowed to bleed to death.

*   *   *

As a member of the Cabinet without a department Edward had more time than some of his colleagues to contemplate what was happening round him, but it is improbable that he noticed with particular concern the recall of Sir Eric Phipps, the British Ambassador in Berlin, and his replacement by Sir Nevile Henderson. Phipps, like his predecessor Rumbold, had early recognized the criminal nature of the German Government, and he also had issued many warnings. He was transferred to Paris where his former robustness succumbed during the Czech crisis to the atmosphere of defeatism that surrounded him. No worse choice in the circumstances could have been made of his successor than Sir Nevile Henderson and we shall see him playing a prominent part in the events that followed. He was appointed by Eden, who had never met him, on the strong recommendation of Sir Robert Vansittart and the Foreign Office as an Ambassador who had coped successfully with King Alexander, the strong man of Yugoslavia, and might be expected to do the same thing in Germany. In fact he conceived himself as endowed with a mission to come to terms with the Nazis, and there were few actions on their part, however monstrous, for which he was not prepared to find some measure of justification. When the Nazis were engineering the destruction of the Czechoslovak State his despatches revealed an almost malicious resentment that the Czechs should betray even the briefest hesitation in hastening the moment of their own enslavement, and Eden himself freely admitted that his appointment was a most unhappy mistake.[1]

Meanwhile in the speeches that he made at this time on foreign subjects Edward continued to emphasize the fidelity of the Government to the principle of Collective Security, and its determination not to return to a system of exclusive alliances:

'We seek,' he said, 'to build our foreign policy on a plan more comprehensive than exclusive alliances or precarious balance of power, a plan which

[1] Lord Avon to author.

invites the co-operation of all nations who are willing to co-operate with us, without any line of exclusion anywhere, in the cause of a better understanding between the nations.' This was to be accomplished on so massive a scale that 'no country however powerful or well-equipped will venture to try to disturb or break the peace. I would not remain a member of any Government that had a policy smaller or less broad than that'. Two days later, however, in the House of Lords, he remarked, perhaps for conventional diplomatic reasons but a trifle unhappily, that Hitler's statement that the 'era of surprises was over' could be regarded as 'a reassuring element in the present situation'. He realized that there was serious danger to the West of Europe from possible complications in the East, but was cautious in anticipating preventive action in hypothetical cases:

'Unless you are prepared on the one hand to say: "I will fight in any case on behalf of peace which is one and indivisible," or on the other hand to say: "I will only fight when I am myself the victim of attack," there is an inevitable no-man's-land of uncertainty lying between which is quite incapable of antecedent definition.'

In the light of this belief he laid down the attitude of the Government in a manner that was afterwards to become familiar to those who sought to goad it into more positive action. In words carefully designed to exclude any unwelcome commitment, and containing several trap-doors of escape he continued:

'If we are unable to define beforehand what might be our attitude to a hypothetical complication in Central or Eastern Europe, this is not to say that we disinterest ourselves in the fate of these parts of Europe. We have repeatedly maintained our determination to carry out to the best of our ability our obligations under the Covenant, and if these obligations are not capable of achievement with precise exactitude, that is a feature, and I venture to think not an accidental feature—of the Covenant itself.'

It is obvious that this temporizing policy of keeping their opponents guessing as to their real intentions contained grave dangers of its own, although it was difficult to find an alternative. The deplorable slogan of 'keeping Germany guessing' was to gain a certain currency in the Foreign Office in the months to come, but the guessing was all done in fact by the British Government, and was directed to wondering which country Hitler would invade next. Meanwhile throughout the spring and summer the public mind was much occupied with the Spanish Civil War while the Non-Intervention Committee pursued its futile course. Halifax was under no illusions as to the farcical character of this body, but with a detachment rare at the time which enabled him to regard both sides with equal distaste, concluded that on the whole it had been worth while:

'I doubt whether a single man or gun less reached either side in the war as a result of its activities,' he said. 'What however it did do was to keep such

intervention as there was entirely unofficial, to be denied or at least deprecated by the responsible spokesmen of the nation concerned, so that there was
neither need nor occasion for any official action by Governments to support
their nationals. After making every allowance for the unreality, make-believe,
and discredit that came to attach to the Non-Intervention Committee, I
think this device for lowering the temperature caused by the Spanish fever
justified itself.'

Yet the war continued, savage and heart-rending, and to many victory for
the Spanish Government transcended all other issues. As in the religious
wars of old its defeat would be to them more terrible than the outcome of
any other struggle, and became invested with a mystical significance. But
there were others, no less transported by emotion, who longed for the victory
of the insurgents with an equal fervour, and saw in its achievement the conquest of anarchy and godlessness, and the triumphant reassertion of the
principles of Christian life. Both parties ignored or excused the barbarities
that were inflicted by their own champions, and few paused to wonder
whether the conflict might at bottom represent the collision of two rival
forms of tyranny.

Perhaps Edward's most notable performance at this time was an address
delivered at a Service of Prayer for Peace at St. Martin-in-the-Fields, and
broadcast to the nation in the summer of 1937. It was from the pulpit of this
church that there had long issued the disastrous but well-intentioned eloquence of Dick Sheppard[1] bringing to packed congregations of the faithful
in ghostly form the message of peace at any price. The spiritual earnestness
of this gifted man, and the sincerity of his beliefs lent a particular persuasiveness to his message of absolute surrender, and audiences who desired their
yearning for deliverance from war to be buttressed by spiritual authority sat
eagerly at his feet. The eloquence of this priest, so noble, yet so misguided,
was thus an endorsement for more elevated reasons, of the doctrines of the
League of Nations Union, and the other bodies whose propaganda had
wrought such havoc among the people.

In this temple of pacifism Halifax stood up to refute the arguments which
had so often issued from the same pulpit. As deeply religious as Sheppard he
yet had a realistic contempt for the pacifist attitude. He could not, as they did,
regard war as the ultimate evil, for he knew that there were others far worse.
Boldly, but in accents suitable to the place, he told the packed congregation—
as many people as ever assembled to hear Sheppard—that there was nothing
inherently evil in force:

'It is a question of degree and not of principle, and I do not think that we
can deny that cases may arise in which the use of force in the extreme form
of war may be both unavoidable and right. What matters always is the motive
on which resort to the use of force is had. I am therefore led to conclude that

[1] The Very Reverend H. R. L. Sheppard, Vicar of St. Martin-in-the-Fields, 1914–37.

the pursuit of peace under all conceivable conditions might mean the acceptance of greater evils even than war, conducted with all the devilish resources
of the twentieth century, and might therefore in itself be more reprehensible
than war seriously and solemnly undertaken in defence of vital principles
that would be denied and betrayed by a refusal to break the peace.'

*   *   *

Stanley Baldwin's retirement on 25 May 1937 brought to an end Halifax's
longest and most intimate political friendship. They had worked in harmony
for fifteen years, and there was much in Baldwin's character to appeal to a
man of Edward's temperament, his humanism, his love of the countryside,
his yearning for peace. There was in both these men indeed a feeling for the
pastoral scene in all its moods that contained an element of mysticism, and
the contemplation of a particular landscape filled them with a deep inner
contentment. It was impossible to meet Baldwin without succumbing to his
simple and modest charm. When war at last came he was the victim of many
spiteful letters by which he was deeply wounded, which claimed that the
disaster was due to his own lethargy and indifference during his years of
power. Unhappily these accusations were largely true, for although hampered
in every way, he had never made the attempt to break through the crust of
pacifism that lay heavy upon the country, and tell the people the truth.

He was a man of many virtues charged with supreme responsibility in
the wrong age, whose true fulfilment would have been in a period of more
stable values, and of realities less blatant. He was remarkably ignorant of
foreign politics, to him a *terra incognita* which he regarded as the domain of
experts, and he avoided them whenever possible, as a man avoids tampering
with the electricity in his house, preferring to rely on an electrician. He
confessed that one of the things that comforted him after leaving office was
that he would never again have to meet any French statesmen. He was far
more interested in personality and character than in policies, and it was
noticed that when he was sitting in the House indulging in his strange facial
contortions or sucking a pencil, 'the first thing he would do when a speaker
got up was to turn to Dod to look up his career, probably to wonder why on
earth he had wanted to get into Parliament or what he was like at home'.
In Cabinet it seemed to one of his colleagues that he was always much more
intent on studying them as interesting specimens of humanity than on listening to what they said. Something of his feeling for Edward, and of his own
character appear in his letter of farewell after leaving office with the triumph
that his handling of the Abdication crisis had brought him:

'I shall value your letter as long I live. Our friendship has been a very
real thing to me and a real influence which I treasure.

'The last ten days have been a strange time; a time that comes only once
and cannot recur.

'All hearts seem open for the moment; most will close again, some perhaps be kept ajar, but it is very wonderful. I feel tired, happy, and at peace; and mighty humble. I wish my dear Dickens hadn't destroyed what is really a very beautiful word; but you will know all I mean by it.

'I still have that sense of wonder that the Blessed Damozel showed in her face as she leaned over the gold bar of Heaven. It wore off; so will mine. But it leaves something good, I hope, behind.'

In the Cabinet changes Halifax became Lord President of the Council. It was an office like that of Lord Privy Seal which involved its occupant in no departmental duties, and allowed freedom to undertake any task that was allotted to him. It was certain that his relations with the new Prime Minister Neville Chamberlain would be as harmonious as those with Baldwin, although his character was in many respects exactly opposite. For while Baldwin's tendency was to dream and drift in the hope that matters would somehow sort themselves out, with a habit of taking a sudden, unexpected step that brought his colleagues up with a jerk, Neville Chamberlain was in every respect a man of action. But, like Baldwin, his remarkable gifts were not those demanded by this particular moment of history. He was an administrator of a high order, and a debater of uncompromising skill and severity. At the Ministry of Health he had shown himself one of the ablest Ministers who had ever occupied that post, and had made a magnificent and enduring contribution to the social and industrial problems which had been one of the main interests of his life. But, as was well said of him, 'the world he understood was a world of businessmen, where contracts were sacred and enforceable without violence, and difficulties could be ironed out round the conference table; and where the keenest rivals could by hard bargaining reach mutually profitable agreements'.[1]

While Baldwin was prepared to remain in placid suspense about the activities of his colleagues, Chamberlain quickly made it clear that he intended to be the master in his own Cabinet. A man of intense shyness and inner reserve who could not even unburden his thoughts and fears to his own colleagues, but only to his sister and wife and to the secrecy of his diary, there was to appear in him when crossed, a streak of ruthlessness which reminded many of his father, Joseph Chamberlain, and an autocratic tendency which led him to exercise an iron control over his Cabinet.

'He was a first rate debater,' wrote Amery, 'and enjoyed making mincemeat of his opponents' arguments. While himself deeply sincere in his concern for social reform he could not always conceal his contempt for the sentimental "sob-stuff" in which Labour members tended to indulge. They felt that he sneered at them as both fools and humbugs, an impression accentuated by his corvine features. They soon came to hate him both personally, and as a renegade over collective security and an appeaser of dictators.' Only those

[1] McElwee. Op. cit., p. 257.

like Edward, who had penetrated a little the reserve of this repressed man, were aware that there were deep passions behind it, and much that was agreeable and touching, a love of Shakespeare and music, birds and trees and flowers, and the peace of fishing.

Chamberlain had noticed his predecessor's refusal to interest himself in foreign affairs with strong disapproval. This was a view also taken at first by Eden who had sometimes despaired of Baldwin's indifference to his Department, and welcomed with relief a Prime Minister who from the first showed a strong interest in the affairs of Europe. Chamberlain's misfortune, and that of the country, was that his knowledge of the world was narrow, and that his political and business training had ill-equipped him at sixty-eight to comprehend the larger issues of foreign policy, while his obstinacy and self-confidence made it impossible for him to realize that their proper understanding demanded a life-time of study, and a knowledge of the world in which he was entirely lacking. From the first his approach to these matters had been pragmatic, and typical of the belief of a businessman in the advantage of personal contact with the man with whom he wishes to make a deal. He had a deep mistrust of the Foreign Office, and a belief that its cumbrous machinery was hopelessly outmoded in a day of swift air travel.

The policy of appeasement on which he now embarked and in which Halifax was to join, was based on the fallacious belief that such personal contacts must inevitably produce better understanding, and that when the dictators met the English statesmen they would discover that they were reasonable men who appreciated their problems, and were prepared to make various suggestions of how they could be met, usually at the expense of someone else's territory or of colonies which would not be consulted.

It was a policy that rested on the supposition that Hitler and Mussolini were normal statesmen who would have enough sense to recognize a favourable deal, and could be dissuaded from further acts of violence, and it showed a fundamental misunderstanding of the character of men already degraded by the narcotic of absolute power. It was not a policy of peace at any price, for there was a limit beyond which Chamberlain was not prepared to go, but it was an extreme limit indeed. Always in his mind also was the need to play for time while re-arming in order to reinforce his diplomacy, but not in a manner so drastic as to cause alarm at home or abroad.

The word 'appeasement' had always carried noble connotations, for there can be nothing finer than to appease a troubled world. Briand had used it to distinguish his policy towards Germany from that of Poincaré; Eden had used it with general approval in the debates on the German occupation of the Rhineland, but later it would come to have a sinister ring when associated with the coercion of a small people, and become a term of opprobrium and contempt.

It is easier now than at the time to realize that this policy would harden rather than mollify the dictators, and convince them of the decadence of the Western Powers, but it was then not entirely naïve to hope that Hitler would content himself with bringing back into the embrace of the Reich the Germans that were still outside it. Halifax was wholly in agreement with the Prime Minister. He was later to become unhappy and alarmed, but his loyalty to Chamberlain, and his belief in his policy, were never in question.

CHAPTER XX

HALIFAX AND HITLER

IT was Chamberlain's belief in personal contacts that made him encourage Halifax to visit Hitler in November 1937, in the hope that he might discover the real nature of his demands. Edward had received an invitation, sponsored by Goering, which asked him, in his capacity as Master of the Middleton Hounds, to attend a hunting exhibition in Berlin, and to shoot foxes in East Prussia, Mecklenburg or Saxony. It was suggested at the time in the Press that Chamberlain's object was for Halifax to make some arrangement which would give Hitler a free hand in Central Europe, and that he had behaved in a shabby manner to Eden in packing him off to Brussels in order to leave the way open. Edward was clear in his conscience that he had in no way acted behind the Foreign Secretary's back, and that he had his approval for his German visit. He recorded that he put his invitation card in an envelope and sent it to Eden saying that he thought he would accept, subject to Eden's approval. A few days later Halifax, Eden and Churchill met at a dinner at the Foreign Office, and in Edward's memory, after some banter about his fox-shooting, Eden suggested that it might be of some advantage for him to go to Germany under this cover, and that he would mention the matter to Chamberlain, after which they could all discuss it.

'This in due course we did, and it was in consequence of that talk that I ultimately went to Berlin and Berchtesgaden. The facts thus differed from the story that tends to become established of the decision being made by a Prime Minister, bent on appeasement, against the wishes and advice of a robust Foreign Secretary.'[1]

We learn, however, from the Eden Memoirs that the Foreign Secretary was far from happy about this expedition to which he had agreed with reluctance on the basis of the original arrangement that Halifax would meet Hitler in Berlin. When it became known that Hitler was not prepared to come to Berlin, and that Halifax, if he wished to see him would have to make a special visit to his mountain retreat at Berchtesgaden, Eden became disturbed. It seemed to him that the Germans were trying to pretend that the whole initiative in this visit came from the English, and he thought it most undesirable that the British Government should appear so eager for a meeting as to give the impression of running after the dictator. When he returned from Brussels he found that some newspapers had printed exaggerated

[1] Halifax. Op. cit., p. 184.

accounts of the scope of the talks which further disturbed both him and Halifax. Crossing over from the Foreign Office to No. 10 Downing Street, Eden then had an interview with Chamberlain which boded ill for the future, and which ended, after an acrimonious exchange about the slowness of re-armament, by the Prime Minister advising his Foreign Secretary to go home and take an aspirin.[1]

Foremost in Eden's thoughts at this moment, was the anxiety lest incautious words might be uttered to Hitler about Austria and Czechoslovakia which could be interpreted by that opportunist mind as encouragement, and he was determined that Halifax should be left in no doubt about his policy towards Central Europe. Hearing that Sir Nevile Henderson had submitted a memorandum to the Lord President on British policy towards Germany couched in terms too limp and permissive, he also sent him a paper prepared by William Strang of the Central Department of the Foreign Office which analysed and corrected Henderson's opinions, and stiffened his conclusions. Eden, after an interview with Halifax and Henderson when the visit was first proposed, had minuted:

'I have spoken to Lord Halifax and Sir Nevile Henderson together. The former will listen and confine himself to warning comments on Austria and Czechoslovakia. I have impressed on Sir Nevile Henderson the need for doing all we can to discourage German intervention in these two states. We must keep Germany guessing as to our attitude. It is all we can do until we are strong enough to talk to Germany.'[2]

This was a far from unnecessary warning for on 4 November Sir Nevile wrote to Halifax that it was essential that his visit should not be a disappointment to the Germans, and expressing the hope 'that the Prime Minister will go as far as he possibly can':

'I believe that, if we are not too niggardly, Germany will keep her word, at any rate for a foreseeable period. One cannot legislate for more. And particularly so, if we take it for granted that she *will* keep her word. The surest way of getting her to break it is to doubt. That is elementary.'

The Ambassador continued in accents that were to become depressingly familiar: 'Morally even we cannot deny the right of Germans living in large blocks on the German frontier to decide their own fate. If they were Hungarians or Croats everyone in England would be clamouring for it. We should, even if we don't like it, sympathize with German aspirations for unity, provided all change be based on the clearly established principle of self-determination.'[3]

Halifax replied on 9 November:

'As to the main business, I entirely recognize the force of all you say in your letter as to the necessity of this country going as far as we possibly can to secure a general all-round settlement.'

[1] Avon. Op. cit., p. 512.   [2] Ibid.   [3] Hickleton Papers.

A few days later Henderson, as if to reinforce his previous advice wrote again:

'We must drop all fears and suspicions (the worst of counsellors) and look facts in the face. The main point is that we are an *island* people and Germany a *continental* one. On that basis we can be friends and both go along the road to its own destiny without the clash of vital interests.'[1]

*   *   *

With this conflicting advice in his ears Halifax set out on his adventure with a sense of lively curiosity. He arrived in Berlin on 17 November where he was met by Sir Nevile Henderson who offered him some further advice on the line he should adopt with Hitler. Then he was taken to lunch with the Foreign Minister von Neurath who was held by many of the English to be a diplomat of the old school, a gentleman among gutter-snipes, and a moderating influence upon his master. Here everything was friendly and *gemütlich* 'with two little brown dachshunds just like Jemma', and von Neurath expatiated on the artistic, romantic and sensitive aspects of the Führer's character. It was perhaps as well that as he sat in this homely atmosphere Edward was not gifted with the power of clairvoyance. It would have distressed him had he known that at no distant date his suave and courteous host, this member of the Herrenklub who represented the grace of the old order, would be presiding as the Protector of Bohemia and Moravia over the enslavement of the Czechoslovak State, the suppression of its language, the obliteration of its history, the closing of its University, and the murder of its intellectuals.

He paid two visits to the Hunting Exhibition of which the most memorable exhibits were a gramophone record which reproduced the bark of a stag, and a large map which with Teutonic delicacy bore silent witness to the loss of the German Colonies. It was thought afterwards that the Germans had been careful during Halifax's visit to under-emphasize, as far as possible, the military character of the régime, but he was given ample evidence that the country was a vast military camp when he was taken by Ivone Kirkpatrick of the Embassy to Döberitz to see the new barracks and training grounds, where large areas were closed to the public, and barrack building was proceeding with great speed and upon a huge scale. Kirkpatrick assured him that the same thing was happening in every corner of Germany, expressing the sanguine opinion that it did not necessarily mean 'the gloomy conclusion of planning for war, but self-defence, and self-respect'.[2] Edward also recorded without comment in his diary Kirkpatrick's account of the persecution of the Christian Churches, and the murderous zeal of Goering in the massacre of 1934.

[1] Ibid.   [2] Hickleton Papers. German Diary. November 1937.

On 19 November the great moment had arrived, and he was taken to Berchtesgaden which he reached after a night in a special train. He was driven by storm-troopers directly to Hitler's chalet. Snow lay on the winding mountain road up which many pilgrims were later to journey to their cost to this unlovely shrine. A path had been swept clear up the steep steps to the house. At this moment Edward was in alarming danger of beginning his mission by mistaking Hitler for a footman. As he looked out of the car window at eye level he saw in the middle of the path a pair of legs clad in black evening trousers culminating in silk socks and patent-leather shoes. He was about to leave the car in a leisurely manner, perhaps passing his hat to this convenient retainer, when an urgent muttering from von Neurath of 'Der Führer, Der Führer', spared him a *bêtise* of classical proportions. Hitler greeted his guest in that quiet and seemly manner which he could assume at will, and led him into an over-heated study commanding a magnificent view of the mountains. In spite of the great heat Hitler appeared to be cold, and afterwards told the interpreter Schmidt that he had been feeling ill during the interview. He invited Halifax to begin the discussion.

Edward began the meeting by thanking the Chancellor for giving him this opportunity for discussion which he hoped would be completely frank, and create that better understanding between the two countries upon which the future of civilization might well depend:

'Although there was much in the Nazi system that offended British opinion (treatment of the Church; to perhaps a less extent, the treatment of Jews; treatment of Trade Unions), I was not blind to what he had done for Germany and to the achievement from his point of view of keeping Communism out of his country and, as he would feel, of blocking its passage West. And taking England as a whole, there was a much greater degree of understanding of all his work on that side than there had been some time ago. If and when we could achieve any success in this development of understanding, we should both, no doubt, feel it right to associate with any conversations we might have those with whom we had special contacts, Italy and France—and if we four could ever agree between ourselves we should have laid a very solid foundation for peace.'[1]

Hitler did not challenge these remarks, but said that formal agreement between the four Powers might not be very difficult to achieve, but would not be worth much unless it took account of the realities even if they were unpleasant. Germany had had to recognize such a reality in the shape of Poland. We all had to recognize such a reality in acknowledging Germany to be a Great Power. We had got to get away from the Versailles mentality and recognize that the world could never remain '*in statu quo*'. To this Halifax replied that nobody wished to treat Germany as anything but a Great

---

[1] This account of the interview is based on Halifax's diary and other documents among the Hickleton Papers.

Power, and that nobody in their senses supposed the world would stay as it was for ever. The whole point was how changes were to be brought about. This led Hitler to say that there were only two alternatives; the free play of forces, that meant war, and settlement by reason. The world had had experience of the first. Was it able to prefer the second?

At this point Hitler launched forth into a dreary tirade about the difficulties in dealing with democratic countries. All his offers of disarmament and political improvement had foundered on this rock. The party system of democracy was complicating the Colonial question, and Parliament and Press made any real progress impossible. Halifax responded to this outburst with commendable firmness.

'I replied by saying that if we were to wait for any advance until Great Britain had ceased to maintain a democratic system, then clearly I had wasted my time coming to Berchtesgaden, and, what was more important, made him waste his, by asking to see him, for I hoped that Great Britain would never be the least likely to change her method of Government. But with all respect to him the point was not very relevant. His disarmament and other offers had not failed on account of party, democracy or the like, but because for good reasons or bad other nations did not feel satisfied as to the measure of security that they in fact afforded. For reasons that seemed to him adequate he had ignored treaty obligations. I was not concerned to argue whether the reasons were good or bad, but it was not surprising that people remembered it when he offered new undertakings.'

Hitler had perhaps been coasting along a little too easily, and was somewhat taken aback by this unexpected vigour. To Halifax he appeared, for a moment, almost apologetic, and he explained rather lamely that in speaking of the evils of democracy he had principally France in mind. He then asked what other problems there were between the two countries apart from Colonies. Halifax replied that he thought English opinion would be interested to know his attitude to the League of Nations and to Disarmament, and Hitler expressed his bewilderment why Great Britain attached so much importance to Germany being in the League when she did not mind the United States being outside it. He could give no answer to the question of whether Germany would ever return. Disarmament was much more complicated than it was a few years ago. Now we were making up arrears; so was Germany, and experience suggested that the respect paid to nations varied with the weight of their armaments.

'Who is going to tackle this question and how he is going to tackle it, I don't know. Is there anything else?'

Halifax now came to the most delicate and dangerous moment of his mission. He had been instructed by Eden to 'confine himself to warning comments on Austria and Czechoslovakia', and he now approached the subject in a manner of which the Foreign Secretary could scarcely have approved: he spoke of 'possible alterations in the European order which might be destined to come about with the passage of time'.

'I said that there were no doubt other questions arising out of the Versailles settlement which seemed to us capable of causing trouble if they were unwisely handled, e.g. Danzig, Austria, Czechoslovakia. On all these matters we were not necessarily concerned to stand for the *status quo* as today, but we were concerned to avoid such treatment of them as would be likely to cause trouble. If reasonable settlements could be reached with the free assent and the goodwill of those primarily concerned we certainly had no desire to block them.' Hitler in reply said nothing about Danzig, but said that he had his agreements with Austria that were being respected, and that he hoped 'reasonable elements' in Czechoslovakia would make it possible for the Sudeten Deutschen[1] to 'enjoy a status which would safeguard their position'. We now know from the Hossbach Memorandum that a fortnight before this interview Hitler had secretly disclosed to his Foreign Minister, War Minister and Chiefs of Staff his plans for the subjugation of Austria and Czechoslovakia.

When later the Foreign Secretary saw the records of this part of the conversations, he was not pleased.

'I wished that Halifax had warned Hitler more strongly against intervention in Central Europe. "Alterations through the course of peaceful evolution" meant one thing to Halifax and probably something quite different to the Führer. Hitler was capable of taking this as giving him freedom to increase subversive Nazi activity in Austria, or to stir up the grievances of the Sudeten Germans.'[2]

The Colonial question arose in two or three forms in the course of the discussion, and Hitler's attitude to this was, 'that if the question could be settled between them, good. If not, he must note and regret. But he hoped that France and Britain would examine the question together, and arrive at some proposal. If there were countries which for strategic reasons we might not wish to give up, it was up to us to offer something in substitution.'

On this Halifax made it plain that it was out of the question for this or any other Government to touch the Colonial question except in the context of a general settlement which would afford a relief from the present tension, but that they were willing to discuss this, or any other question, and that it would be a good moment to decide what the next step should be.

Hitler showed no inclination to hasten. He said that conferences always needed careful preparation, and he did not believe in a conference every three months that achieved nothing. It was better to proceed through the diplomatic channels. At this moment he expressed the hope that 'we might get away from the atmosphere of imminent catastrophe'. The situation at present was not dangerous. 'If you believe the Press,' the Führer added with

_____

[1] The German minority in Czechoslovakia.   [2] Avon. Op. cit., p. 515.

AT BERCHTESGADEN WITH HITLER, 1938

virtuous indignation, 'you could of course expect to wake up one day to see German armed forces in Vienna and Prague.' The surest way was to go slowly. No one who had seen what war meant, as he had, could be so stupid as to want another, when we had all learned in war that even the victors lost.

The discussion, which Eden was to describe as 'aimless and therefore rather hazardous', had lasted for more than three hours. Hitler had been throughout in a quiet mood, only occasionally showing signs of vivacity at the mention of Russia or the British Press. Edward was not a perceptive observer of human beings; he was lacking in psychological insight, and his impressions were only those of the external Hitler—'very much alive, eyes which I was surprised to see were blue, moving about all the time, and points being reinforced by sharp gestures of the hands. The play of emotion—sardonic humour, scorn, something almost wistful—is rapid.' But he was vaguely conscious that he had made no real approach to the man, and that interposed between them was an intense reserve which was the barrier behind which Hitler shielded his grotesque personality, but which Edward attributed to fatigue, or to the fact that they had an entirely different sense of values, and were not speaking the same language. And it was surely a sign of a lack of knowledge and reflection on Hitler's record that made him conclude:

'He struck me as very sincere, and as believing everything he said.' But most of all Edward was struck by the gulf that seemed to yawn between them:

'It was not only the difference of outlook between a totalitarian and a democratic state. He gave me the impression of feeling that, whilst he had attained power only after a hard struggle with present-day realities, the British Government was still living comfortably in a world of its own making, a make-believe land of strange, if respectable illusions. It had lost touch with realities and clung to shibboleths—"collective security", "general settlement", "disarmament", "non-aggression pacts", which offered no practical prospect of a solution of Europe's difficulties.

'He regards the whole conception of equal States as unreal, based on no foundation of fact; and consequently does not believe that discussions between large numbers of nations, with varying interests and of quite unequal value can lead anywhere. Hence his preference for dealing with particular problems in isolation. With this goes the distrust of democratic method, to him inefficient, blundering, and unsuited to the hard world, constantly changing, in which we have to live.

'The League system moreover means the perpetuation of the *status quo*. It is useless to evade the issue by saying that Article 19 of the Covenant provides for peaceful revision. Such an argument is another symptom of self-illusion. It is impossible to imagine peaceful revision with the consent of all, since each member of the League will require the contribution to be made by others. . . . It is a fact, perhaps an inconvenient fact, that Germany is now a

13

great and powerful nation, pulsating with energy and determined to realize what she believes to be her legitimate aspirations.'

Later in this record, Halifax wrote of the alternative solutions which had been passing through his head, and were certainly a long way from the approach contemplated by the Foreign Secretary:

'It seems to boil down to whether or not we should feel it possible or desirable to explore a colonial settlement *on broad lines* with the idea . . . of using it as a lever upon which to pursue a policy of real reassurance in Europe. In other words, instead of trying to do a bargain on the line of getting him to drop colonies as a return for a free hand in Europe, to try for the more difficult but possibly sounder bargain of a colonial settlement at the price of being a good European.'

Above all, he was struck by the profound difference between Hitler's and his own background of thought:

'An explorer who has overcome countless perils in a savage land returns home to find his family unaware of his own achievements and still immersed in local politics and problems. Their meeting is friendly, but he feels that they are living in a different world and do not speak the same language. The analogy is not perfect, but it illustrates Hitler's attitude towards a meeting with a representative of the British Government.'

On this note he left the Führer, and proceeded to meet two of his most unsavoury colleagues, lunching first on 20 November with Goering in the vulgar splendour of Karinhall amid looted treasures. The host wore a green leather jerkin on which hung a dagger in a red leather sheath. They were waited on by footmen in eighteenth-century liveries, green and white plush, breeches, and gaiter spats. There was something symbolical of Goering's character in the fact that the meat was practically raw. His face, bloated by indulgence, still retained traces of the sinister beauty of his youth. His hands resembled the digging paws of a badger. This was the man who had established the Concentration Camps, and in 1934 had presided over the butchery at the rifle range at Lichtefelde, but although Edward wondered idly how many people he had been responsible for killing, the man's innate depravity seemed to escape him. To Edward he appeared to have a personality that apart from that episode was 'frankly attractive: like a great schoolboy, full of life and pride in what he was doing, showing it all off, and talking high politics out of the setting of green jerkin and red dagger. A modern Robin Hood: producing on me a composite impression of film-star, gangster, great landowner interested in his property, Prime Minister, party-manager, head gamekeeper at Chatsworth.'

Nothing in Edward's upbringing had equipped him with the instinct to fathom the true wickedness of these men. To him they were clearly bad, but at the same time slightly comical figures, and when Goebbels came to tea at the Embassy next day he noted:

'I had expected to dislike him intensely—but didn't. I suppose it must be some moral defect in me, but the fact remains.'

Goebbels complained of the unfriendly despatches of some of the English journalists in Berlin, who were performing a vital duty in trying to make the British public aware of the true character of the Nazi régime and the man who led it. He was more than Leader, said Goebbels; he was the national symbol of Germany, and as Head of the State every German bitterly resented attacks upon him. Halifax, after explaining that the British Press, unlike the German, was free, promised that his Government would do everything in its power to induce the London Press to avoid unnecessary offence.

In the train to Calais on 21 November on his way home he made some notes in an attempt to summarize the impressions of the last five days. He concluded that the view of most of the German leaders was that the Colonial issue was the only vital question between the two countries, although von Blomberg, far more accurately, had described it as secondary to other European issues. Halifax did not think that the Colonial question would lead to war. Hitler and Goering had both told him that it was the only one arising directly between the two countries, 'in the sense that it is only there that we have anything of value to Germany to give'. The territories in question were Togoland, the Cameroons and, as the cession of Tanganyika would present certain difficulties to Great Britain, an undefined area carved out of the Congo and Angola, although what the views of the Belgians and Portuguese would be on this matter was not elucidated.

When discussing the possible rendition of these colonies as though it were a game of chess in which a pawn might have to be sacrificed, it did not appear to have occurred to the British Government to question whether the Nazis were the ideal people to exercise a colonial mandate, although Hitler's suggestion to Halifax at the talks that unrest in India could easily be solved by shooting Gandhi and his main henchmen might have indicated that they held unorthodox views about trusteeship.

'As regards Austria and Czechoslovakia,' he wrote, 'I formed the impression that Germany believes time to be on her side, in the sense that the strong magnet will sooner or later attract the steel filings lying about within reach of its attraction, and intends to assist this process as far as possible. . . . I am sure Hitler was sincere when he said he did not want war: Goering too.

'But equally I have no doubt that they all feel that strong armaments are very valuable in making other people a good deal more reluctant to interfere with what they deem primarily their business. If we could get in some form a reassertion of respectable intention from Germany—as expressed in the present Austrian Treaty—and made applicable also to Czechoslovakia if the German minority was properly treated, that is probably as far as we can hope to get Germany to go. The whole thing comes back to this. However much

we may dislike the idea of Nazi beaver-like propaganda etc., in Central
Europe, neither we nor the French are going to be able to stop it, and it
would therefore seem short sighted to forgo the chance of a German settlement by holding out for something we are almost certainly going to find ourselves powerless to secure.'[1]

---

[1] Memorandum of 21 November. Hickleton Papers.

CHAPTER XXI

HALIFAX AND EDEN

WHEN Halifax returned to London, and reported to Chamberlain the results of the discussions, Chamberlain arranged a meeting with the French Prime Minister M. Chautemps and his Foreign Minister M. Yves Delbos to discuss a general settlement with Germany in the interests of appeasement. His idea of 'a fair basis of discussion' was that the Germans should be told that we would not forcibly oppose them in obtaining their objects in Austria and Czechoslovakia, provided they did so by peaceful means, and that the British and French would make a colonial offer of Togoland and the Cameroons, and a territory taken from the Belgian Congo and Angola. Hitler showed no interest in these suggestions.

Chamberlain turned instead to Italy, and it was over this subject that the relations between Prime Minister and Foreign Secretary, already taut as a result of fundamentally different views on foreign affairs, were finally ruptured. Mussolini had taken the initiative by approaching the Prime Minister through his Ambassador in London, Count Dino Grandi, and Chamberlain engaging in the first of a series of questionable manoeuvres had responded with a personal letter to Mussolini which he deliberately refrained from showing to his Foreign Secretary, offering the excuse that:

'I had a feeling he would object to it.'[1]

In this belief he was fully justified. It was Eden's opinion that any approach to the Italian dictator at this moment with the object of making an agreement would be an act of weakness which would do great harm to this country. The Bari Radio Station was pouring out streams of anti-British propaganda; the Italian Press was hostile; anti-British intrigue was in progress in Egypt, Palestine, and Arabia, and 70,000 Italian troops were still fighting in Spain in spite of the fact that Italy was a member of the Non-Intervention Committee. In November, while Halifax was visiting Hitler, Italy signed the Tripartite Pact with Germany and Japan, and in December she abandoned the League of Nations. Chamberlain became impatient as he saw the prospects of an agreement with either Hitler or Mussolini receding, and repeated his demand to Eden that the long-postponed conversations with Mussolini should at last begin. But the Foreign Secretary was still reluctant to make any friendly overtures until the hostile propaganda had been ended, and an honest beginning made to withdraw Italian troops from Spain.

[1] Feiling. Op. cit., p. 330, quoting Chamberlain's diary for 19 February 1938.

The Prime Minister held that these objects could only be attained by the opening of conversations. Halifax was in substantial agreement with Chamberlain that the talks ought to begin, and like him argued that when they did the propaganda matter would solve itself.[1]

Chamberlain was not yet ready to dispense with his Foreign Secretary, and he was aware that this could not easily be done with Parliament and public still incensed by Mussolini's behaviour over Abyssinia, and his shameless intervention in Spain. But he did not wish his personal relations with Mussolini to languish, and in order to assure him of his continuing interest he began the process of by-passing the Foreign Office by the use of a personal go-between, his sister-in-law, Austen Chamberlain's widow, a warm but naïve admirer of the Italian cause. At the same time Grandi established a contact with Sir Horace Wilson, and thus with the Prime Minister, through Sir Joseph Ball, the Director of the Conservative Research Department. The use of these emissaries, although less sinister than they have since been represented, was a lapse on the part of the Prime Minister hard for a Foreign Secretary to bear, and a violation of the principle that the Foreign Office was the proper channel for diplomatic communications.

A significant incident at this moment was the 'kicking upstairs' during Eden's tenure of the Foreign Office of the Permanent Under-Secretary, Sir Robert Vansittart, who had long discerned the German menace. Promoted to the new post of Chief Diplomatic Adviser, he found himself trapped in a gilded cage, and ceased to exert any effective influence on foreign affairs. Chamberlain now turned for advice on these matters, as far as he required advice, to Sir Horace Wilson, chief industrial adviser to the Government, and now seconded to the Treasury for service with the Prime Minister, a Civil Servant of great ability in financial and industrial matters, but wholly unversed in foreign questions.

By far the most bitter cause of complaint by the Foreign Secretary against the Prime Minister was Chamberlain's behaviour when President Roosevelt sent him a secret message on 13 January 1938, in which he proposed to call the whole Diplomatic Corps of Washington to the White House, and lay before all Governments the suggestion that they should agree on the essential principles to be observed in the conduct of international relations. If the response was favourable, the United States would ask a small number of the lesser Governments to join them in working out proposals which could be submitted to the other nations.[2] When this message arrived Eden was away on holiday in the South of France. Chamberlain did not like the suggestion contained in it, which appeared likely to jeopardize the negotiations he was so anxious to begin with Italy, and mean the abandonment of the whole policy of direct approach upon which he had set his heart. He also thought the message vague and non-committal, and was convinced that in the present

[1] Ibid., p. 335.   [2] Avon. Op. cit., p. 549.

temper of the American people, the President had not the slightest prospect of bringing effective influence to bear on harassed Europe. On his own initiative, and without consulting Eden whom he claimed it was impossible to reach, he sent a discouraging answer to Sumner Welles[1] who had transmitted the message, suggesting postponement of the President's proposal.

The extent of Eden's indignation at this rebuff, inflicted without consulting him, is evident in the long passage he devotes to it in his Memoirs.[2] To him it seemed that all the efforts he had made to bring America, by gentle degrees, to a realization of the need for her interest in the problems of Europe, had been obliterated by this clumsy stroke. Of all the points at issue between him and the Prime Minister this was the one by which he was most deeply affronted.

*   *   *

It was not, however, the last moment of friction. Hitler's appointment on 4 February 1938 of von Ribbentrop as his Foreign Minister was a warning that could not be mistaken by any who had been brought into contact with that public menace when he held the post of German Ambassador in London. Austria's hour was now approaching, and Mussolini instructed Grandi to ask for an early start to the conversations in view of 'possible future happenings', while the obliging Lady Chamberlain was the bearer of a message from the Duce saying that he desired an early agreement.

On 12 February disgraceful pressure put upon the Austrian Chancellor Schuschnigg by Hitler, to admit a Nazi to his Cabinet as Minister of the Interior and amnesty all political opponents, left no doubt as to what the 'possible future happenings' would be. If the seizure of Austria by Hitler anticipated an Italian agreement with Great Britain, there would be little left for Mussolini except to take refuge with Hitler, and assume a permanent hostility towards the Western Powers. Chamberlain now finally lost patience with Eden who insisted on a positive withdrawal of some Italian volunteers from Spain before conversations began. On the 18 February he asked Grandi to meet him at an interview at which Eden was also present, when the Italian denied that any agreement concerning Austria had been made between Hitler and Mussolini, but asked: 'How could he move troops to the Brenner as he did before, if he felt that Great Britain was a potential enemy?' A stormy interview followed at which the antagonism between Eden and Chamberlain reached its highest point, and even allowing for the desire of Grandi to represent himself in a dramatic light in his despatch, it must have been an unusual scene:

'Chamberlain and Eden were not a Prime Minister and a Foreign Minister discussing with the Ambassador of a Foreign Power a delicate situation of an international character. They were—and revealed themselves as such to me

---

[1] American Under-Secretary of State, 1937–1943.
[2] Avon. Op. cit., pp. 552–68.

in defiance of all established convention—two enemies confronting each other, like two cocks in true fighting posture.'[1]

At the adjourned meeting after luncheon Chamberlain told Grandi clearly that he intended to override Eden's objections, and, subject to Cabinet approval, immediately open conversations in Rome. His only request was that Mussolini would agree to a formula that after a certain number of volunteers from both sides had left Spain the two parties there should be accorded limited belligerent rights. Although Mussolini agreed to this, Eden had already said that his acceptance of the formula would not alter his own position. Chamberlain made it plain to the Cabinet that their choice lay between him and Eden, and although much shaken by Eden's intention to resign, they were unanimous in support of the Prime Minister.

Edward was one of those who tried, most strongly, to dissuade Eden from taking this final step, but it was clear to Eden that he did not fully appreciate the differences between the Foreign Secretary and the Prime Minister, and thought that Eden ought to accommodate himself to the situation, and that the Foreign Secretary and his friends were exaggerating the danger.[2] But it was now too late for an understanding with Italy to save Austria. With one of his lightning strokes Hitler invaded that country on 14 March, and after the entry of his troops, the gay and sophisticated capital was handed over to Himmler's murderous cohorts, and in view of what had passed, the Anglo-Italian agreement which was signed in April excited only cynical derision in the Italian leaders.

Halifax left an account of these proceedings which shows clearly his own impressions of his colleague's resignation, and of the 'two very disagreeable days' which it occupied. He played a central part in the efforts to find a way out of the dilemma, and, as we shall see, in doing so, did not forfeit Eden's friendship and goodwill. The Prime Minister had told the Cabinet that he thought that it would be in the highest degree wrong to miss this opportunity of accommodation with Italy, but that there was unhappily a sharp difference between the Foreign Secretary and himself on this point, and that he left the Cabinet 'to decide as it were, between them'. After Eden had explained his position, his colleagues, with some variation of emphasis, or qualification, agreed with the Prime Minister. Their main difficulty in understanding the Foreign Secretary's position was that no difference of principle seemed to be involved, since he himself had been freely discussing the proposal of conversations with Count Grandi, and that it was surely impossible for him to resign at this moment on a question of method or procedure. The meeting was adjourned until Sunday with no conclusion reached. After the Cabinet, Halifax recorded:

'Oliver Stanley[3] and I went over to the Foreign Office to see Anthony.

---

[1] *Ciano's Diplomatic Papers.* Ed. Malcolm Muggeridge, pp. 160–85.
[2] Lord Avon to author.   [3] The Rt. Hon. Oliver Stanley, President of the Board of Trade.

There we found with him Bobbety Cranborne,[1] his Parliamentary Private Secretary, Harvey, his Foreign Office Secretary, and there may have been somebody else, I forget. I felt at once that the atmosphere, emanating I thought mainly from Bobbety, was very much pro-resignation. It produced on me somewhat of the effect I should have expected from the corner of a boxing ring when the seconds received back the pugilist and restored his vitality by congratulations and encouragement. I could almost hear them saying, I thought, "You have done very well. You have won the first round. Hold firm, and all will be well!" We talked for some time in a rather restless atmosphere of whiskies and sodas, and cigarettes, but without I felt, making any impression, and when we came away Oliver Stanley said to me: "He has been through Hell to make up his mind, and he's damned well not going to unmake it." '[2]

It appeared from Chamberlain's opening statement on Sunday that the situation went deeper than a mere question of procedure, and that there was a fundamental difference between him and Eden on foreign policy which would make further collaboration extremely difficult. It was then that Edward, in the rôle of conciliator which he filled to perfection, made his effort to harmonize the two points of view, but even he was unable to bridge the gulf. He thought that the situation which had been created was both unfair to the Cabinet and unreal. It was unfair because they had until that moment had no intimation of this alleged fundamental difference, and unreal because it was precisely the difference of view-point of the Prime Minister and the Foreign Secretary that was of value to the Cabinet, as giving them the best of both minds. Edward recognized that this difference of temperament had been aggravated by the Prime Minister's tactlessness in writing to Mussolini without Eden's knowledge, and he should promise not to do that sort of thing again, but let there be further efforts at agreement.

At Edward's instigation these attempts, in which he played the leading part, were made, but for once his powers of persuasion failed. Eden was not prepared to change his mind, and the Cabinet, after some expressions of alarm and doubt eventually reached unanimity. The Foreign Secretary resigned on 20 February 1938. The conclusions at which Edward arrived suggest that he had given much thought to the reasons for his friend's perturbation of mind without fully grasping its true underlying cause:

'My impressions are still somewhat blurred as to the way things worked in Anthony's mind. I cannot help thinking that the difference on the actual timetable of conversations was not, and never has been, the principal difference. I suspect it has been the cumulative result of a good many different things: partly sub-conscious irritation at Neville's closer control of foreign policy;

---

[1] Under-Secretary of State for Foreign Affairs and afterwards Marquess of Salisbury.
[2] Hickleton Papers.

partly irritation at his amateur incursions into the field through Lady Chamberlain, Horace Wilson, and his own letter to Mussolini; partly Anthony's natural revulsion from Dictators, which I have always told him was too strong inasmuch as you have got to live with the devils whether you like them, or not; and particularly, as I have also often told him, his excessive sensitiveness to the criticism of the Left. I think myself, though I should never say this in public, that Anthony's judgment was not at its best; he was overstrained and tired; the thing had got out of proportion, and he was no longer seeing it straight. And once anybody begins to feel that they are being a martyr for high principle it becomes very difficult to avoid this conviction having melodramatic issue.'[1]

And how did these events affect the relations of Halifax and Eden? This question is best answered in the words of a letter from Eden when Edward had congratulated him on the speech he had made to his constituents at Leamington after his resignation:

'The main purpose of this letter is to try to thank you for your innumerable acts of kindness to me during the last two years. You were always so patient and so understanding of my difficulties and shortcomings, so ready to help however disagreeable the occasion, or untimely the appeal. Our friendship meant, and means, very much to me. I hated the parting in itself, and because it meant that I differed from you. Differing from some others was almost refreshing!'[2]

[1] Hickleton Papers.
[2] Ibid.

CHAPTER XXII

CZECHOSLOVAKIA

HITLER'S unchallenged success in forcing the Anschluss with Austria made it obvious to all intelligent observers that Czechoslovakia's turn was about to come. With the prospect of unlimited dangers ahead, Halifax alone had the prestige and experience to succeed Eden, and he did so on 21 February.

From Chamberlain's point of view it was in every way an advantage to have Halifax at the Foreign Office, for his ability was obvious and his character one that appealed to Chamberlain as it had to Baldwin, so that Edward was able to make a closer approach than others to intimacy with that reticent man. His appointment met with an unusually favourable reception by Press and Parliament, although the Labour Party challenged an arrangement which placed the Foreign Secretary in the sanctuary of the House of Lords. Churchill greeted the news with words of sober optimism:

'Lord Halifax must not be dismissed as a pious devotee of "peace at any price". Hitherto he has wielded undue influence in the Cabinet as a vague sincere advocate of making friends with everybody. Now in the collar of a great Department he will be brought face to face with grim duties arising from the movement of events, and I for one shall not assume he will be found unworthy of them.'[1]

*   *   *

The seizure of Austria had seriously weakened the strategical position of Czechoslovakia. The great natural mountain defences had been turned, and a vulnerable gap disclosed to a German entrance from the south-west. The Anschluss had also given Hitler a complete economic strangle-hold over her communications with the outside world. Czechoslovakia was an almost blameless victim of the disaster that was about to befall her, but there were certain peculiarities in her composition that Hitler was able to turn to good account for the purpose of subversive propaganda.

The new State had been erected on unstable foundations by the Peace Treaties. $7\frac{1}{2}$ million Czechs were given authority over $3\frac{1}{4}$ million Germans, $2\frac{1}{2}$ million Slovaks, half a million Hungarians, and another half million Ruthenes, besides 80,000 Poles. The Germans were refused self-determination, and the Slovaks' claim that they had been promised a state of equal nationalities was not accepted, while the economic bonds of the Ruthenes with Hungary were ruptured.

[1] Campbell Johnson. Op. cit., p. 452.

The first President of Czechoslovakia, Thomas Masaryk, and his lieutenant and successor Edvard Beneš had shown remarkable statesmanship in creating a democratic state out of this medley of races, and their minorities were treated with greater tolerance than any others in Europe. But they did so by establishing a centralized State in which the grievances of minorities about the proportion of officials, allotment of schools, census statistics—all those grievances inevitable in a land of antagonistic races—could be used when convenient, to foment disturbance from outside. No one was better aware than Dr. Beneš that there were imperfections in the structure of the Czechoslovak State, and that it fell short of the cantonal organization which exists in Switzerland, and which he and Thomas Masaryk had assured the Peace Conference in Paris that it would be their endeavour to attain. There was a further argument that Hitler found of great potency for his propaganda—that Czechoslovakia was a mere tool in the hands of Russia, and a consequent danger to the rest of Europe, and particularly to his own country where the lizard-shaped Czechoslovakian re-entrant was like a dagger thrust into the side of Germany.

None of these facts were of course the true cause of Hitler's rabid antagonism to the Czech state. Nor was he influenced by any affection for the Sudeten Germans whom his compatriots regarded with the same disdain felt by the metropolitan Greeks for the Greek Cypriots. The real crime of Czechoslovakia was her geographical position which barred the road to the conquests of Poland and Rumania, and above all to the rich black earth of the Ukraine. Halifax was naturally alive to the danger that had sprung from the Anschluss, and had told Ribbentrop that 'we were witnessing an exhibition of naked force', and that public opinion would inevitably ask:

'What there was to prevent the German Government from seeking to apply in similar fashion naked force for the solution of their problems in Czechoslovakia. . . . The conclusion must be that the German leaders were people who had no use for negotiation, but relied solely on the strong hand.'

The Western Powers were not alone in their concern about the immediate future of Czechoslovakia. To the Russians it was a vital stronghold of Slavdom, and an integral feature of the strategical situation in Central Europe. Soon after the Anschluss Russia had approached France with a view to mutual action, but the French had been distracted by strikes and internal dissension, and when the Blum Government fell, it had been succeeded by that of Daladier which represented a reaction against Russian influence, and was as yet not anxious to commit itself to a policy of containment of Germany. This was also the view of Chamberlain, who did not wish to form a binding alliance with France, and was extremely sceptical of either the intention or the ability of Russia to play a decisive rôle in Europe. His position was defined in a speech in the House of Commons on 24 March 1938 and it was one from which he was not until much later to be lured away. The furthest he was prepared to go was to say that while rejecting the idea of any automatic commitment to go to war on behalf of Czechoslovakia, if war came in Central Europe it would be unlikely to be confined to those who had assumed legal obligations. It was a limitation with which Halifax entirely agreed.[1] And here we should take note of the Government's policy towards Czechoslovakia as seen through the eyes of one of its leading members Sir Samuel Hoare. Weakness in armaments, he admitted, played a strong part in that policy but:

'The overriding consideration with Chamberlain and his colleagues was that the very complicated problem of Czechoslovakia ought not to lead to a world war and must at almost any price be settled by peaceful means.'[2] Chamberlain was convinced from the beginning that no action he could take would prevent the overrunning of Czechoslovakia, and would be simply a pretext for going to war with Germany, a war in which he saw no prospect of defeating her in a foreseeable time:

'I have therefore,' he said, 'abandoned any idea of giving guarantees to Czechoslovakia, or the French in connection with their obligations to that country.'[3]

Hitler's only response to Chamberlain's speech of 24 March was to bring to a head the growing agitation among the Sudeten Germans who were situated in Bohemia and on the western borders of Czechoslovakia, and were now to succeed the Austrian Nazis as the pawns in the *Drang nach Osten*. It was only a few weeks since Goering had lavished assurances 'on his honour', on the Czech Minister in Berlin that Germany had no hostile intentions towards his country, and now Hitler was taking the first steps towards disintegrating her by using the grievances of the German minority as a preliminary to her disruption. On 24 April their leader Konrad Henlein published at Carlsbad a programme which demanded far-reaching measures of autonomy for the German-speaking districts of Bohemia, treated as a single area within a Czechoslovak federation on the Swiss cantonal model. This would have involved the Nazification of the area, and the end of freedom not only for the Czech minority, but for the German Socialists, Liberals and Jews in the new province.

* * *

Three days after this demand the British Ambassador in Paris, Sir Eric Phipps, gave Halifax the alarming news that the French Foreign Minister thought that 'Germany meant to settle the question of Czechoslovakia this summer at the latest', and that he even feared that she might make her attack as early as May. This menacing situation brought the French Prime Minister Daladier, and his Foreign Minister Bonnet to London on 27 April. For two days the French Ministers tried to persuade Chamberlain and Halifax that Hitler's policy was aimed at the destruction of Czechoslovakia, and that

---

[1] Feiling. Op. cit., p. 348. [2] Hoare. Op. cit., p. 289. [3] Feiling. Op. cit., p. 348.

England should now say clearly that she would stand by France in the fulfilment of her obligations. Daladier spoke with great force in elegant and well-chosen language. Later he was to weaken through the protracted refusal of Britain to commit herself, but now his attitude was resolute and courageous. Even Bonnet, who was later to acquire a reputation for cowardice and intrigue, associated himself with his leader's demands.

But Chamberlain had made up his mind, and refused to budge from his statement of 24 March, and when it came to Halifax's moment to speak he associated himself fully with his leader. In his mind, perhaps even more than in that of Chamberlain, was a consciousness of the weakness of the two countries to face a major war:

'His Majesty's Government,' he said, 'regarded the military situation, viewed specifically from the military angle, with considerable disquiet. Not only was the military situation of Czechoslovakia exceedingly weak; His Majesty's Government could not regard the position of France and Great Britain as very encouraging in the event of a German attack upon Czechoslovakia, in consequence of which France might feel it her duty to take the offensive against Germany, and as a further consequence of which Great Britain might find herself involved in the ensuing war. For their part His Majesty's Government were ready, and indeed anxious to lend the fullest support in their power to whatever might make for European peace. They were not, however, able, as the Prime Minister had explained in the House of Commons, to assume fresh military commitments.'[1]

Daladier had emphasized the fact that the Czech army was efficient and well equipped, and that Russia, in spite of recent purges possessed the strongest air force in the world, if she could be brought within the alliance of peaceful countries, but Halifax expressed an opposite opinion:

'As regards Russia, recent events, such as the execution of many members of the Higher Command of the army, and the general state of internal unrest in that country, made it extremely doubtful whether Russia could be counted upon to make any great contribution, if indeed she could make any contribution at all, to the protection of Czechoslovakia if that country were attacked by Germany.'[2]

Chamberlain left the French Ministers in no doubt of his views. He argued that for the British and French Governments to threaten Germany would be to indulge in a game of bluff by which Hitler would not be deterred, and that if there was one chance in a hundred of that bluff being called, there was need for caution. He thought that Daladier had painted too dark a picture, and he doubted very much if it was Hitler's desire to destroy the Czechoslovak State. He made it clear that only dire necessity would persuade him to wage a preventive war.[3] This statement was echoed by Halifax in whose view:

[1] *Documents on British Foreign Policy, 1919–1939*, Third Series, Vol. I, p. 213.
[2] Ibid.   [3] Ibid.

'It would not be safe to rely on the use of force as Mr. Chamberlain had explained. It would represent a gamble, and he thought Mr. Chamberlain had been abundantly right when he said that this was a course which he thought this country would find itself unable to adopt. . . . He thought it would certainly be desirable and, indeed in his view essential, for the two Governments to join in making the strongest possible representations to the Czechoslovak Government.'[1]

When the French Ministers realized that they could expect no help from Great Britain they were not slow in following Chamberlain's line, and although Daladier was to return later to suggestions of a bolder nature, they never really stood up to the Prime Minister again. They could scarcely be blamed for refusing to confront Germany alone.

Two days after this refusal of the British Government to bind itself to stand by France, Halifax summoned the German Chargé d'Affaires, Herr Kordt, to assure him that no new and dangerous commitment had emerged from the meetings between the English and French Ministers:

'He attached value to assuring the Reich Foreign Minister that he remembered with peculiar satisfaction his close collaboration with him, and that he cherished the wish to continue in the future this co-operation which had been so fruitful. It was, therefore, especially necessary for him to inform Herr von Ribbentrop, immediately the negotiations with the French were concluded, that no fresh military commitments or obligations had been entered into by Great Britain during the negotiations. The Press had concocted much nonsense this morning about the alleged tenor of the military agreement, and he was anxious to prevent misunderstanding arising from this irresponsible scribbling.'[2]

When the Prime Minister and his Foreign Secretary had once decided that they would avoid, 'at almost any cost', a war over Czechoslovakia, it was inevitable that they would be forced to bring growing pressure to bear on that country to meet the German demands in the hope that it might be avoided. And the pressure began from that moment. It was to increase in force and meaning with every apparent Czech hesitation, until it almost seemed as though Czechoslovakia was herself a predatory state rather than a passive victim, who, since the Succession States had been established, had maintained the most exemplary democratic system of them all. The French from now on joined in exercising this pressure, Bonnet with avidity, Daladier with greater reluctance.

Halifax addressed himself with uneasiness to this odious task. On 2 May he received the Czechoslovak Minister in London, Jan Masaryk, son of the founder of the State, in whose warm and endearing character an intense

[1] Ibid.
[2] *Documents on German Foreign Policy 1918–1945*. Series D, 1937–45, Volume II. Germany and Czechoslovakia, 1937–1938.

joie de vivre was secretly in conflict with a profound Slav melancholy. This last element in his nature must have been uppermost when the Foreign Secretary told him clearly 'that the Czechoslovak Government would have to be prepared to go a very long way', and that 'it was a physical impossibility for any of Czechoslovakia's friends to prevent the country being overrun by Germany', and that even after a successful war, 'it was, I supposed doubtful whether, in fact, the Czechoslovak State would be re-created in its present form'.[1]

The pressure was sustained and intensive. On 7 May Newton, the British representative in Prague, was instructed to tell the Czech Foreign Minister Krofta that British public opinion would not tolerate a gamble in which a losing bluff might lead to war, and that Mr. Chamberlain's carefully chosen words in his speech in the Commons on 24 March 'meant nothing more than they actually said and that it would be unwise and dangerous to give too broad an interpretation to his statement'.[2]

*   *   *

By 16 May Halifax felt able to tell Newton that he was encouraged by a recent visit of Henlein to London, where by some miracle of deception he had left an impression of sincerity on such vigilant minds as those of Churchill and Vansittart, and that Beneš should now be able to make an offer to the Sudeten Germans based on the proposals that Henlein had made at Carlsbad. Three days later Henderson conveyed a soothing message that Hitler welcomed the good offices of the British Government 'because he shrank from the risks of war'.

Full freedom of municipal activity was already enjoyed by the Sudetens, and the approach of municipal elections in May and June offered Henlein a convenient pretext for working up excitement to the highest pitch, while Hitler stoked up the flames by concentrating troops on the frontier, a fact which was afterwards virtuously denied. It seemed that the crisis Bonnet had feared had come, and the Czechs responded by calling up one year's class of reservists. This ugly situation prompted Halifax to send a firm despatch to Sir Nevile Henderson, in which, after instructing the Ambassador to beg the German Government to exercise patience he concluded:

'You should add that if, in spite of His Majesty's Government's efforts a conflict arises, the German Government must be well aware of the dangers which such a development would involve. France has obligations to Czechoslovakia and will be compelled to intervene in virtue of her obligations if there is a German aggression on Czechoslovakia. Indeed French Ministers have repeatedly stated to His Majesty's Government that France would certainly so act. In such circumstances His Majesty's Government could not

---

[1] *Documents on British Foreign Policy 1919–1939*, Third Series, Vol. I, pp. 236–7.
[2] Ibid.

guarantee that they would not be forced by circumstances to become involved also.'[1]

This was the strongest language yet used, and it was followed, on 22 May, by further instructions to Henderson to inform von Ribbentrop that:

'If resort is had to forcible measures, it is quite impossible for me or for him to foretell results that may follow, and I would beg him not to count upon this country being able to stand aside if from any precipitate action there should start European conflagration.'

But this healthy warning was accompanied by a telegram from Halifax to Sir Eric Phipps which would have dispelled any optimism, which the Czechs, had they seen them, would have derived from these communications:

'It is of utmost importance that French Government should not be under any illusions as to attitude of His Majesty's Government, so far as it can be forecast at the moment, in the event of failure to bring about peaceful settlement in Czechoslovak question. His Majesty's Government have given the most serious warnings to Berlin, and these should have prospects of success in deterring German Government from extreme courses. But it might be highly dangerous if the French Government were to read into these warnings more than is justified by their terms. . . . If, however, the French Government were to assume that His Majesty's Government would at once take joint military action with them to preserve Czechoslovakia against German aggression, it is only fair to warn them that our statements do not warrant any such assumption.'[2]

Sir Eric Phipps, on whom the air of Paris seemed to have produced a debilitating effect, replied that M. Bonnet would willingly put any pressure on the Czechoslovak Government that might be thought desirable by the Foreign Secretary, and that he had told Bonnet that the alternative for the Czechs would be total annihilation, to which 'His Excellency heartily agreed'. It was at this point that Bonnet made his first reference to the ignoble suggestion that if Czechoslovakia proved really intransigent, France might well repudiate the treaty which bound the two countries together.

For the moment, the British warning, coupled with representations from the French, at least had the effect of causing Hitler to pause, and, after a week's brooding, to postpone until October his resolve 'to wipe Czechoslovakia off the map'. 'The crisis of 20–22 May,' wrote Sir Lewis Namier, 'coupled with a shooting incident in the Sudetenland, produced a new sense of anxious urgency in the British Government: threats and promptings with which she (Czechoslovakia) was hustled along were hedged in with reservations disowning all responsibility of His Majesty's Government; and France, lest she dragged in Britain, was gently encouraged to disembarrass herself of her treaty obligations.'[3]

By 24 May Beneš had become the villain of the piece, and Phipps expressed

[1] Ibid., p. 332. [2] Ibid., p. 347. [3] L. B. Namier, *Europe in Decay, 1936–1940*, p. 195.

the hope to the co-operative Bonnet that 'very firm and persistent pressure would be brought to bear on M. Beneš by the French Government, for it would be intolerable if he were allowed to wreck the now brighter chances of a peaceful settlement'. Henderson's mind at this moment was occupied by one of the strangest of his illusions, that of the extremists or 'wild men', as he called them, who surrounded Hitler and might at any moment drive him into some disastrous action. It was incredible, after the time that he had spent in Germany, that his psychological insight could still have been so shallow that he could imagine that that daemonic will could have been influenced by any outside agency, but he clung blindly to his belief in the power of extreme elements:

'As I see the position here today a struggle is going on between them and the moderates (of whom I believe Hitler himself in his saner moments to be one) as to whether the whole nettle should not be grasped immediately.'

On 25 May Halifax again saw Jan Masaryk, and told him that autonomy on the Swiss model was the smallest price that Czechoslovakia could expect to pay, but that externally she could scarcely be expected to jettison her French and Russian alliances at naked German dictation, but might do worse than to consider adopting a position of neutrality. An even more drastic plan was canvassed towards the end of the month when William Strang was sent to Prague, and investigated the possibility of holding a plebiscite. Both these proposals were abortive.

On 31 May Halifax sent a telegram to Phipps which indicated more clearly than any mere pressure the lengths to which the Government was prepared to go to force compliance on Czechoslovakia:

'I earnestly hope that the French Government will feel not less urgently than do His Majesty's Government the importance of putting the greatest possible pressure upon Dr. Beneš in person without delay. . . . You will recollect that . . . M. Bonnet told you that if Czechoslovakia were really unreasonable the French Government might well declare that France considered herself released from her bond. My feeling is that the moment has now come for a warning to be given to the Czechoslovak Government on these lines.'[1]

From these dire words the impression might be received that the Czechoslovak Government was adopting a position of mulish intransigence, but Newton in Prague, who although a friend of the Czechs was also an obedient servant of the Foreign Office and seldom questioned his instructions, was compelled to submit on 2 June in a manner almost indicating a feeling of guilt:

'I think it very desirable that we should continue to show sympathetic appreciation of the fact that Czechoslovak Government have hitherto accepted very far-reaching and doubtless unpalatable advice and appear to

---

[1] *Documents on British Foreign Policy, 1919–1939*, Third Series, Vol. I, p. 419.

have been doing their utmost of late at any rate to cope with the problems which might well baffle the wisest statesmanship.'[1] But the Foreign Secretary was shortly to return to the subject of the Franco-Czech Treaty, and to point out to Bonnet that a memorandum of warning sent by the latter to Beneš, 'does not contain any specific warning that France would have to reconsider her treaty position if the Czechoslovak Government were unreasonable on the Sudeten question'.[2]

* * *

By 8 July Henlein was sharpening up the tempo of the game. He informed his friends in London that the Czechs were deliberately dilatory, and that their latest proposals were entirely unacceptable, and that Beneš 'did not take the pressure from London and Paris at all seriously and thought he could fool them'. In view of this Halifax told Newton on 14 July that he was contemplating a most pressing *démarche* if the situation bore any resemblance to Henlein's description. If deadlock seemed likely to occur, he would warn the Czechs that Henlein might demand a plebiscite, and that British public opinion would not consider it an unreasonable request. Four days later an emissary from Hitler, Captain Wiedemann, came to England, and was received by Halifax at his private house with the permission of the Prime Minister. He bore a general message of German goodwill and peaceful intentions, but his visit had little effect beyond producing garbled accounts in the Press, and irritating some members of the Foreign Office who thought that their own premises were the proper setting for such an encounter.

Chamberlain next cast round in his mind for some further means of lowering the rising tension. He now pressed the Czechoslovak Government to accept Lord Runciman as 'investigator and mediator' between themselves and the Sudetens, and the introduction of this mild and conventional Liberal into the European snake pit was a striking example of the Prime Minister's lack of insight into the realities of foreign affairs. Beneš was dismayed by the suggestion. In the meanwhile the Sudetens must be assured that the Czechoslovak Government would not present its own scheme to its Parliament: Henlein was about to see Hitler, and had to be encouraged 'to persevere in his policy of moderation, which', wrote the Foreign Secretary, 'he is at present inclined to abandon in disgust', while Nevile Henderson on 22 July made his own extraordinary contribution to the discussion:

'Certainly those of my colleagues who know Beneš best are those who trust him least and extremists are not confined to one side of the frontier—or of any frontier, *vide* Cot and Mandel in France and the Jews and Communists everywhere.'[3]

The unworthy reference to the ill-starred Mandel, that resolute Jew, the disciple of Clemenceau, and the most indomitable champion of France

[1] Ibid., p. 439.   [2] Ibid., p. 545.   [3] Namier. Op. cit., p. 204.

against her mighty neighbour was, unhappily, characteristic of its author. On 23 July the Czechoslovak Government reluctantly accepted Lord Runciman, and the Prime Minister announced his appointment to Parliament in a manner which made a grave departure from the truth in saying that it had been made 'in response to a request from the Government of Czechoslovakia'.[1] And what was the Foreign Secretary's estimate at this moment of Germany's intentions? As late as 5 August Lord Halifax was writing to Sir Nevile Henderson that he did not believe that Germany wanted a general war, especially over Czechoslovakia, and that a large part of German policy might be bluff or fear.[2]

By mid-August Lord Runciman had made little, if any, progress except to make the acquaintance of such noble families as the Kinskys whose estates were guarded by Henlein's storm-troopers, and to learn with ingenuous wonder that the Sudetendeutsche Partei was not the only German political party in the Sudetenland, but that there were in fact four others who in no way shared the extreme views of Henlein's supporters. On 15 August had begun that series of rejections by Henlein of all plans put forward by the Czechoslovak Government, irrespective of any possible merit. The Prime Minister and the Foreign Secretary now understood that the affair was being so stage-managed by Hitler as to bring it to a crisis during the Nuremberg Party Rally in September where it was his intention to speak on the 12th. They realized that the moment might soon be at hand when they would be called upon to clarify the Prime Minister's inconclusive formula of 24 March defining his Government's position in the event of German aggression, and to decide clearly where they stood if their worst fears were realized.

While Runciman and Newton were invited to continue the process of badgering the Czechs into further acts of concession, the British Inner Cabinet which was now directing foreign policy, and consisted of Chamberlain, Halifax, Simon and Hoare, met on 24 August and decided that Sir John Simon should repeat Chamberlain's unspecific warnings of 24 March in a speech he was shortly to deliver in Lanark.

Meanwhile 'Plan II' and 'Plan III' which had been put forward by the Czechoslovak Government had shared the fate of 'Plan I', and been contemptuously rejected. It was now clear to all that Henlein was a puppet without volition of its own, being made to execute a carefully-timed and macabre dance at the bidding of its master's dexterous fingers. Dr. Beneš had no desire to remain a passive spectator until this sinister game was played to the end, and he decided on a move of extraordinary boldness by which he hoped to capture the sympathy of the civilized world. On 4 September he summoned the Sudeten leaders to the Hradschin Palace, the

---

[1] For a full description of the circumstances surrounding the appointment of Lord Runciman see John W. Wheeler-Bennett, *Munich*, pp. 71–5.

[2] *Documents on British Foreign Policy, 1919–1939*, Third Series, Vol. II, pp. 54–6.

great castle of the Bohemian Kings, standing proudly on its eminence, with its old Election and Diet Halls, and its Spanish Hall magnificent in white and gold. Calm among these splendours the President told his visitors that he was ready to give them everything they asked. He would make no conditions; they could write it down themselves. He offered them his own pen, but as they were too demoralized to use it he wrote in his own hand to their dictation what afterwards became known as the 'Fourth Plan', and which contained practically everything that had been demanded in the Carlsbad proposals.[1]

The Sudeten leaders were appalled by this brilliant stratagem. A generous offer and ready agreement were the last things they wanted: 'My God, they have given us everything!' was the agonized bleat of one of the most unsavoury of their number, Karl Frank, who was to be executed after the war for wholesale murder, and frontier incidents were hastily engineered to provide an excuse for breaking off the negotiations. One further insidious thrust was administered to Beneš at this moment, and his feelings may be conjectured when he read in *The Times* of 7 September the leading article from the pen of Geoffrey Dawson who carried his desire to smooth the German path to lengths not even approached by the Sudeten leaders, or Hitler himself, by suggesting that the German-speaking areas of Czechoslovakia should be separated from that country and ceded to Germany. Halifax from the Foreign Office immediately repudiated this subversive proposal from his old friend, but it was later to bear an evil fruit.

On 9 September a stiffer representation was prepared in the Foreign Office and sent to Sir Nevile Henderson on the authority of the Permanent Under-Secretary. The Ambassador was instructed to tell Ribbentrop that his Government was 'so greatly disturbed' at the deterioration of the negotiations at Prague that they were forced to tell the German Government that they were convinced that their French friends would discharge their Treaty obligations to Czechoslovakia and that this would result in a general conflict from which Great Britain could not stand aside.[2] There is probably no significance in the fact that this telegram lacked the authorizing signature of Lord Halifax himself, whereas the telegram of the following day which accepted Henderson's advice that this representation should not be made was initialled by him.[3] There is perhaps more significance in the fact that Sir Nevile Henderson's advice was communicated by telegraph from Berlin in the form of extracts from a letter addressed by Henderson to Sir Horace Wilson.[4]

At the Nuremberg Rally the *furor teutonicus* appeared in its full exultance and ugliness. On 10 September Goering, unrecognizable as Edward's

[1] Wheeler-Bennett. Op. cit., p. 91.
[2] *Documents on British Foreign Policy, 1919–1939.* Third Series, Vol. II, pp. 277–8.
[3] Ibid., p. 285.   [4] Ibid., p. 280.

genial host at Karinhall, raved like a maniac about 'those pigmies in Prague', and two days later Hitler, in accents of hatred so intense as to bring a shiver even to those of his listeners who did not understand German, spoke with concentrated venom about 'Tschechoslovakei'; the word was almost spat out. With simulated anguish he spoke of the sufferings of his oppressed fellow-countrymen, and of his iron resolve to come to the succour of 'those tortured creatures'. But blood-chilling as it was, the speech did not precipitate an immediate crisis or start a war.

While these grave events were proceeding, Chamberlain conferred with Churchill and Eden before making a statement on 11 September which seemed to show that he had come a long way in the meantime:

'Germany cannot with impunity carry out a rapid and successful military campaign against Czechoslovakia without fear of interference by France and by Great Britain.'[1] This statement to British journalists was made with the full support of Winston Churchill and Anthony Eden. Yet in spite of these firm words Chamberlain and his colleagues could not bring themselves to give the French Government the hard assurances for which they had so often asked. On 10 September Bonnet had requested a plain answer to the question whether Great Britain would march with France or not, and had received from the Foreign Secretary a message which must have caused the French to despair of ever getting a firm response from an ally who fluttered away like a moth at every positive approach, and was as difficult to impale. Halifax refused to commit himself in a question which:

'though plain in form, cannot be dissociated from the circumstances in which it might be posed, which are necessarily at this stage completely hypothetical.' He explained that the decision was not entirely their own, but that they would also be committing the Dominions:

'So far, therefore, as I am in a position to give any answer at this stage to M. Bonnet's question, it would have to be that while His Majesty's Government would never allow the security of France to be threatened, they are unable to make precise statements of the character of their future action, or the time at which it would be taken, in circumstances that they cannot at present foresee.'[2]

On the day after Hitler's speech Henlein broke off all negotiations and, the Czechs having declared martial law, fled to Germany on 15 September. Encircled by that strong arm he openly demanded the solution so obligingly planted in his mind by the brain-wave of Dawson—the cession to Hitler of the German-speaking districts of Czechoslovakia. After Beneš had deprived him of any conceivable grievance by the offer of the Fourth Plan he had been puzzled as to what to ask for next. The Editor of *The Times* had supplied him with the answer.

[1] Wheeler-Bennett. Op. cit., p. 97.
[2] *Documents on British Foreign Policy, 1919–1939*, Third Series, Vol. II, p. 303.

CHAPTER XXIII

MUNICH

THE Foreign Secretary's oracular reply to Bonnet's question no doubt contributed to the growing defeatism of the French Foreign Minister. This was increased by a frightening report from Colonel Lindbergh about the overwhelming might of the German Air Force, and by his own knowledge of the total inadequacy of that of the French as described to him by the Under-Secretary for Air, M. Guy La Chambre. According to this Minister, Germany was producing between 500–800 war planes a month compared to the French output of 45–50, and the British of 70. It later transpired that in August 1938 the French production fell to an incredible 13 when the aircraft workers were on holiday, and that her total Air Force in September consisted of only 700 machines, mainly obsolete, and none up to date, and containing not one modern bomber.[1] Bonnet's nerve was badly shaken, and although he was assured by Litvinov, the Russian Foreign Commissar, on 11 September that Russia would honour her pledges in the Czech-Soviet Pact, he side-tracked this suggestion by misrepresenting his words to the French Cabinet.

At this crucial moment on 13 September there were men in that Cabinet still bent on resistance, such men as Mandel, contemptuously dismissed by Nevile Henderson, Reynaud, Campinchi, the staunch Corsican Minister of Marine, and others. But the party of accommodation led by Bonnet was also strong in the Cabinet, and better organized outside it. It was left to the Prime Minister, Daladier, to lead the way, and if at this moment he weakened, it should be remembered that it was he who at that first meeting in April had urged resolute courses on the British Ministers, and received a dusty answer. Now, after Halifax's reply to Bonnet, he was still without any hard assurances of their support. A majority of his Cabinet by the evening of 13 September was against resistance. A victim of these circumstances, Daladier decided to throw the responsibility upon his allies, and to ask the Prime Minister to make the best bargain he could with the German Chancellor.

For some time Chamberlain, convinced of his mission to save world peace, had been nourishing an idea 'so unconventional and daring that it rather took Halifax's breath away'. This was to go himself to Germany and to talk with Hitler in order 'to find out in personal conversation whether there was any chance of saving the peace'. The first colleague to whom Chamberlain had mentioned this bold intention was Samuel Hoare, who had visited him in

[1] Wheeler-Bennett. Op. cit., p. 105.

393

the Cabinet Room of No. 10 Downing Street on the morning of 10 September. They were later joined by Halifax and Simon, and Chamberlain held an impromptu conference of the four men. 'This,' said Hoare, 'was the typically English beginning of what has since been known as the Big Four.'[1] It developed into a small committee to deal with the crisis, with Sir Alexander Cadogan, Sir Horace Wilson and Sir Robert Vansittart as its official advisers. On this occasion the Prime Minister raised the question of his personal visit, and the Ministers present agreed that it should be made, and that the approval of the Cabinet should be sought.

It was recognized that for a man in his seventieth year, who had never flown before, to go forth thus boldly to confront the monster in its mountain lair was an act of considerable courage. It was also fully justified by the fact that the French Government, for whatever reason, had abandoned the control of the crisis to the British, and at a moment of such extreme gravity he was entitled to take any step, however extraordinary, to retrieve the situation. He intended to do so alone, once the responsibility was his, and an effort by Daladier to accompany him was dexterously evaded. It was reported to the Prime Minister that Hitler had shown concern that a man of his age should have to make so long a journey, and had even contemplated coming to London to spare him, and Chamberlain's comment on this considerate thought shows how remote he was from any conception of the true nature of the German Chancellor:

'It shows a side of Hitler,' he said, 'that would surprise many people in this country.'[2]

Chamberlain's visits to Berchtesgaden, to Godesberg, and to Munich are a part of history. They have been described by many hands, and in minute detail, and we need not follow him on these journeys again. They are a part of the life of Chamberlain rather than of Halifax for the Foreign Secretary did not accompany his chief on any of them. This exclusion which might have disturbed many men holding his office was a matter of no consequence to Edward. He had agreed that Chamberlain should go to Germany, and he approved of what he was trying to do. If the Prime Minister wished to carry out his mission alone that was sufficient for him.

When Chamberlain had climbed the mountain road to Berchtesgaden he found an unpleasant shock awaiting him. He found that the dictator was prepared to make war unless the Sudeten areas were immediately transferred to Germany, and so taken aback was he that he does not seem to have made even the most perfunctory defence of the far-reaching concessions already made by the Czechs, but accepted without argument the position that the only question at issue was whether Hitler could be placated by the cession of the German-speaking areas. On this point, he told Hitler, he must consult his colleagues, but he would return, and report their decision. His personal

---

[1] Hoare. Op. cit., p. 301.   [2] Feiling. Op. cit., p. 364.

opinion was 'that on principle I didn't care two hoots whether the Sudetens were in the Reich, or out of it, according to their wishes, but I saw immense practical difficulties in a plebiscite. . . . In spite of the hardness and ruthlessness I thought I saw in his face, I got the impression that here was a man who could be relied upon when he had given his word.'[1] It is also clear that Hitler left Chamberlain under no illusion of the necessity of meeting the Polish and Hungarian claims on Czechoslovakia.

To Chamberlain's colleagues the idea of surrendering the Sudetenland came as a complete surprise, after the strong *démenti* from the Foreign Office of the week before. But at the Cabinet held on 16 September they had before them not only Chamberlain with his personal account of Hitler's demands, but also the report of Runciman's Mission, recommending sweeping Czech concessions of districts where Germans were in 'a substantial majority'. Daladier and Bonnet came to England on 18 September to be told what had taken place in Germany, and to be asked whether they accepted the principle of self-determination as the only way of avoiding war.

Again at this meeting Daladier made a brilliant and lucid analysis of the danger of yielding to Hitler. France was in a terrible position when confronted with such a proposal concerning a country to which she was united by ties of friendship and alliance. 'It was always,' he said, 'a most delicate matter to suggest to a friend and ally that he should submit to the amputation of one leg, or indeed possibly of both legs.' The French Prime Minister was labouring under an almost intolerable strain, and afflicted by the agony of his position: 'In front of me,' wrote Hoare, 'sat Daladier, square and squat, his face flushed redder than ever, the man who, as an artilleryman, had stubbornly fought through the First World War, and as a Minister had faced the Paris mob. By his side was Bonnet, as white as Daladier was red, sensitive and apparently on the verge of a *crise de nerfs*, with a mind that moved like quicksilver, made especially sensitive since he discovered that there were no gas-masks in France.'

When Halifax came to speak he said that although he shared Daladier's misgivings of the recognition of the general principle of the right of self-determination which Hitler might invoke in other countries besides Czechoslovakia as a prelude to annexation, they should keep clearly in their minds that it was the only basis upon which Hitler had insisted that a peaceful solution could be founded.

'The . . . important problem was to find a way to establish and keep these negotiations going. . . . Herr Hitler might well have in mind projects for the future aggrandisement of Germany. . . . The British Government and the French Government had to face hard facts.'[2]

In the end, Daladier against his better judgment and all his convictions

[1] Ibid., p. 367.
[2] *Documents on British Foreign Policy, 1919–1939*, Third Series, Vol. II, p. 385.

gave way, only salving his conscience and having something to show his more robust colleagues by asking for an international guarantee of the rump of Czechoslovakia. The agreement reached at this conference accepted self-determination, excluded a plebiscite as leading to dangerous claims from the other minorities, and provided for the transfer of all areas in Czechoslovakia containing over fifty per cent of Germans. It suggested that an international body, with Czech representation, should adjust frontiers and exchange of populations, and that the new frontiers would be confirmed by a general international guarantee in which the British Government was willing to join. These terms deprived Czechoslovakia of any possibility of defending herself, involved the complete disruption of her economy, and spelled the end of her existence as an independent State.

*   *   *

President Beneš had been placed in a hideous predicament. He had been asked to surrender the glacis of his mountain defences, and to accept a mutilation of his country which would leave nearly a million Czechs as a persecuted minority in Nazi Germany, and he had been told that refusal would result in a European war for which the responsibility would be held to be exclusively his own. Never, surely, was a Head of State confronted by his friends with a choice so agonizing. It was obvious that Beneš would not agree to such Draconian terms without desperate efforts at evasion, and that further pressure of the most remorseless kind would be necessary to bring submission.

The British and French Governments were now badly pressed for time. Chamberlain was to meet Hitler on 21 September, and it was in their view a matter of vital importance that he should be able to report to the Führer that the Czechs had accepted the terms. These were only submitted to them at midday on 19 September, and there was no time to waste. The British Government had now reached a position which left no alternative to the further application of pressure to Czechoslovakia, which in the eyes of the leaders of that country was to invite her to acquiesce in the act of suicide. It fell to Halifax, as Foreign Secretary, to apply the final turn of the screw, and the tragic story of how he did so can be read in the diplomatic documents which are the very bones of history.

When the terms were presented to him by Newton, Beneš had been 'greatly moved and agitated'. His Government, he said, had not been consulted when questions of such deep concern to it had been discussed:

'Speaking with self-control but with bitterness he showed that he felt that, after all the efforts which he and his Government had made, they were being abandoned.[1] . . . He said that he did not believe proposed solutions would prove final, or anything more than be a stage towards eventual domination by

[1] *Documents on British Foreign Policy, 1919–1939*, Third Series, Vol. II, p. 416.

Germany, and develop further German ambitions.'[1] Desperately casting round for a way out of this nightmare, Beneš and his Cabinet, which was now in permanent session, thought that a faint prospect of survival, or at least a stay of execution, might be found by appealing to arbitration under the Czech-German arbitration Treaty of 1925, and declaring their willingness to accept an arbitral award. In the face of this prevarication, Newton, on instructions from the Foreign Secretary, was without mercy at an interview with the unhappy Czech Foreign Minister, Dr. Krofta:

'I replied refusal or evasion at this last moment meant the destruction of his beautiful country.'

The formal Czech note of refusal was received in London on the evening of 20 September. It was a document moving and indeed pathetic in its dignity considering the haste and agitation with which it had been assembled. It pointed out that acceptance of the proposals meant acquiescence in the mutilation of the State in every respect. It would sooner or later fall under the absolute influence of Germany. Czechoslovakia had always been faithful to treaties, and now she was willing to accept any arbitral award. The Note concluded in sombre warning:

'It is not only the fate of Czechoslovakia that is in the balance, but also that of other countries and particularly of France.' The anger which this note, and particularly its reference to arbitration and delay produced in London, suggested that their eagerness to bring this crisis to an end had largely blinded the English leaders to the reality of what they were doing, and that their sympathy for the martyrdom of Czechoslovakia had become completely submerged in their frantic sense of urgency. There were moments when she, rather than Germany, seems to have become the delinquent in their eyes.

The Inner Cabinet met in London and sat until ten-thirty on the evening of 20 September, and after consultations with the French Ministers instructions were sent to the Legations in Prague. It was two-fifteen in the morning when Dr. Beneš, having been roused from a troubled sleep, confronted the two envoys, a grisly hour for such a message. The instructions which Halifax had given to Newton were bleak and final:

'You should at once join with your French colleague in pointing out to Czech Government that their reply in no way meets the critical situation. . . . You should urge the Czech Government to withdraw this reply and urgently consider an alternative which takes account of realities.'[2]

The 'realities' which they were invited to consider were that Britain and France were determined to prevent a war, for which Czechoslovakia, by a refusal of the terms, would be held directly responsible, and in which, if it came, she would fight alone. This was the *coup de grâce*. Beneš knew that he had done all he could, and that he must now capitulate. But it was with a

[1] Ibid., p. 417.   [2] Ibid., p. 438.

heavy heart and a sense of impending doom that at five o'clock on 21 September, Dr. Krofta handed the French and British Ministers the final note:

'Under pressure of urgent insistence culminating in the British communication of 21 September Czecho-Slovak Government sadly accept French and British proposals.'

Armed with this *carte blanche*, Chamberlain flew on 21 September to meet Hitler at Godesberg on the Rhine. The two men were lodged in hotels on opposite sides of the stream, and it was perhaps ominous that that of Hitler was the Hotel Dreesen from which he had issued to lead the massacres of 1934. As before, and to the surprise of some, Chamberlain did not take his Foreign Secretary with him, being supported by William Strang and Sir Horace Wilson who was later to be the startled recipient of one of Hitler's most maniacal outbursts of rage. This visit was essentially Chamberlain's ordeal and it is not necessary here to describe it in detail. Little though he realized it the Prime Minister had got ahead of Hitler's time-table. For the Führer had not imagined that Britain and France would accept his outrageous terms, still less that they would be prepared to force them on Czechoslovakia. Much as he despised the Western leaders he had not bargained for such an immediate execution of his orders. He had been savouring in his bloodthirsty mind the delightful prospect of a dramatic humiliation of the Czechs, in which he was convinced that Britain and France would not intervene, and of watching his forces grinding their army into the dust. Now, owing to the over-eagerness of the French and British, it seemed for a horrible moment that he was to be baulked of his war.

Chamberlain had come to Godesberg in buoyant spirits to discuss an orderly transfer of territory, but Hitler was not to be fobbed off by such a drab proceeding, and the outraged Prime Minister found himself confronted by a Führer far more menacing than on the first occasion at Berchtesgaden, who told him curtly that the suggested procedure was too slow and no longer applicable, and that he must now demand the immediate occupation by his troops of the German-speaking areas from which the Czechs were not to be allowed to move even a cow. After three hours of bitter argument the meeting was adjourned, and Chamberlain crossed the swiftly-flowing river to his hotel in a mood of deep anxiety. From there he sent a personal message to Halifax which might be considered the understatement of the century: 'First meeting unsatisfactory.'

In London, Halifax, Simon and Hoare debated whether they could any longer in the circumstances maintain the Anglo-French embargo on Czech mobilization, and decided that as the country appeared in imminent danger of invasion, it must now be lifted. It also seemed to Halifax that the moment had come to give the British Delegation at Godesberg a firm warning that public opinion in Britain would tolerate no further exactions of flesh from the mangled body of Czechoslovakia. He telegraphed to the Prime Minister:

'It may help you if we give you some indication of what seems predominant public opinion as expressed in Press and elsewhere. While mistrustful of our plan but prepared perhaps to accept it with reluctance as alternative to war, great mass of public opinion seems to be hardening in sense of feeling that we have gone to the limit of concession and that it is up to the Chancellor to make some contribution. We of course can imagine immense difficulties with which you are confronted but from point of view of your own position, that of Government, and of the country, it seems to your colleagues of vital importance that you should not leave without making it plain to Chancellor by special interview that, after great concessions made by Czechoslovak Government, for him to reject opportunity of peaceful solution in favour of one that must involve war would be an unpardonable crime against humanity.'[1]

But Chamberlain could make little impression upon the implacable Chancellor. He told Hitler that he did not think there was any likelihood of the Czechs accepting the terms, but the most Hitler would concede was that the time limit for occupation should be extended to 1 October, an empty gesture since it was the date on which his attack on Czechoslovakia, Operation Green, was in any case scheduled to begin. With a fervent assurance that this was Hitler's last ambition in Europe, and that the Colonies were not a matter for war, the Prime Minister returned to England.

At this critical moment Halifax had an extraordinary but fleeting moment of weakness. The Godesberg memorandum had already reached London, and the Permanent Under-Secretary, Sir Alexander Cadogan, head of the Foreign Office, was appalled by its terms. He wrote in his diary:

'It's awful. . . . *Now* Hitler says he must march into the whole area at *once*, and the safeguards—and plebiscites—can come *after*! This is throwing away every last safeguard that we had. P.M. is transmitting this "proposal" to Prague. Thank God he hasn't yet recommended it for acceptance. P.M. returned by lunch time. Meeting of "Inner Cabinet" at 3.30 and P.M. made his report to us. I was completely horrified—he was quite calmly for total surrender. More horrified still to find that Hitler has evidently hypnotized him to a point. Still more horrified to find that P.M. has hypnotized Halifax who capitulates totally. P.M. took nearly an hour to make his report, and there was practically no discussion. John Simon—seeing which way the cat was jumping—said that after all it was a question of "modalities" whether the Germans went in now or later! Ye Gods! . . . I gave Halifax a note of what I thought, but it had no effect.'[2]

A full Cabinet meeting was held at 5.30 p.m., from which Lord Winterton

---

[1] *Documents on British Foreign Policy, 1919–1939*, Third Series, Vol. II, p. 490.
[2] Sir Alexander Cadogan. Unpublished Diary.

hastened to call on his friend Leo Amery and to tell him that Chamberlain 'had come back prepared not only to transmit the Hitler ultimatum but to recommend its acceptance to the Czechs, and a great many of the Cabinet were prepared to endorse that'; four or five others, and in particular Duff Cooper, the First Lord of the Admiralty, were contemplating resignation if that was the decision.[1] The Cabinet was adjourned with no conclusion reached.

Halifax returned to the Foreign Office at 8 p.m., with his mind as yet unchanged, and later Sir Alexander Cadogan drove him home:

'Drove him home and gave him a bit of my mind, but didn't shake him. I've never before known him make up his mind so quickly and firmly on anything. I wish he hadn't chosen this occasion! . . . I've never had such a shattering day, or been so depressed and dispirited. I can only hope for a revolt in Cabinet or Parliament.'[2]

It was an extraordinary moment of weakness, from which Edward was soon to rally strongly. On the following day, 25 September, there was a Cabinet meeting in the morning, and another in the afternoon which ended at about 6 p.m. Edward returned to the Foreign Office and sent for Sir Alexander Cadogan who had been so deeply disturbed by his attitude. Something of great significance had happened to him on the previous night. He now said to Sir Alexander: 'I'm very angry with you. You gave me a sleepless night. I woke at one and never got to sleep again. But I came to the conclusion you were right, and at the Cabinet, when the P.M. asked me to lead off, I plumped for refusal of Hitler's terms.'

Edward arrived at his decision after a night of torturing reflection, and Chamberlain was badly shaken to find him an entirely different man from that of the day before. We gain a vivid impression of the shock which this change gave the Prime Minister, from an exchange of notes between the two men on 25 September. The first was from Chamberlain:

'Your complete change of view since I saw you last night is a horrible blow to me, but of course you must form your opinions for yourself. It remains to see what the French say.

'If they say they will go in, thereby dragging us in I do not think I could accept responsibility for the decision.

'But I don't want to anticipate what has not yet arisen.

N.C.'

And Edward had replied:

'I feel a brute—but I lay awake most of the night, tormenting myself and did not feel I could reach any other conclusion at this moment, on the point of co-ercing CZ.

E.'

[1] Amery. Op. cit., pp. 268-9.   [2] Sir Alexander Cadogan. Unpublished Diary.

The Prime Minister replied:

'Night conclusions are seldom taken in the right perspective.
N.C.'

To this Edward said:

'I should like the Czechs to agree on the facts—but I do not feel entitled to coerce them into it.'

The Prime Minister appeared not to realize that Edward's mind was now made up, and made a further effort to change it:

'I can't help feeling that there is some confusion. What pressure *can* we put on the Czechs except the negative one of saying that we are not coming in unless the French are in it? What we should do is to discuss frankly with the French the position. If in the end they do go in we must still be in the Mar. 24 position.

'What D.C.[1] and O.S.[2] want us to do is to encourage French and Czechs to resist and promise them our help. That I will not myself consent to.'[3]

But in spite of these arguments Halifax insisted that not only must the Godesberg terms be rejected, but, as will be seen in a moment, that a public assurance must be given to France that if she honoured her obligations to Czechoslovakia, Great Britain would be at her side.

*   *   *

Once more Daladier and Bonnet crossed the Channel, and sat with the British Ministers in the Cabinet Room at No. 10 Downing Street on 25 September. The meetings, wrote William Strang, who was present, 'were among the most painful which it has ever been my misfortune to attend'.[4] Daladier had by now recovered much of his earlier resolution, and had, the day before, ordered a partial mobilization of the French Army. The Czechs, who, with Allied consent, had already mobilized on the 22 September, had said that they would fight rather than accept such terms, and Jan Masaryk had immortalized the spirit of his people in the memorable phrase: 'The nation of St. Wenceslas, John Hus and Thomas Masaryk will not be a nation of slaves.'

The confidence of Chamberlain and his colleagues in their French ally cannot have been strengthened by a telegram from Phipps in Paris which had reached them on the eve of this conference:

'Unless German aggression were so brutal, bloody and prolonged (through gallantry of Czechoslovak resistance) as to infuriate French public opinion to the extent of making it lose its reason, war would be most unpopular in France.

---

[1] Duff Cooper.   [2] Oliver Stanley.   [3] Hickleton Papers.
[4] Strang. *Home and Abroad*, p. 140.

'I think therefore that His Majesty's Government should realize extreme danger of even appearing to encourage small, noisy and corrupt war group here. All that is best in France is against war, *almost* at any price. . . . To embark upon what will presumably be the biggest conflict in history with our ally who will fight, if fight she must, without eyes (Air Force) and without real heart must surely give us furiously to think.'[1]

It was a lamentable telegram and a more accurate description of the condition of France at this moment would have been that besides the weaker brethren there were also a number of patriotic men in her Cabinet strongly opposing further surrender, and that the country at large was awaiting the worst in a mood of dull resignation rather than of ardour.

The Prime Minister bluntly inquired of M. Daladier what his Government intended to do in the event of a German invasion of Czechoslovakia. Once again he answered that they 'would do their duty'. Chamberlain, his precise mind as always impatient of generalities then subjected Daladier to a meticulous cross-examination of what he meant by 'his duty', and Sir John Simon added his unrivalled forensic powers to the inquisition. Did it mean that they only intended to man the Maginot Line, or were they prepared to invade German territory, and bomb her from the air? Was the French public morally prepared for the devastation of German air-bombardment? Was it true that their Air Force was almost non-existent?

Daladier had listened to these pertinent but embarrassing questions with growing resentment. He could only reply that a million men who had cheerfully joined the colours were the best evidence of France's national spirit, and speak in unconvincing terms of the ability of the Air Force to attack German targets, and the Army to undertake offensive operations. It was a galling experience for Daladier to be thus harried by English Ministers who had not yet uttered a word of assurance about their intention to help France, and at one moment he demanded angrily:

'Do you suggest that France should remain aloof if Germany attacks Czechoslovakia?'

And Chamberlain had given him the cold answer:

'It is not for the British Government to express an opinion as to what France should do; that is a matter for the Government of France to decide.'

When the meeting was resumed next day, the arrival of General Gamelin with a more optimistic message about the state of the French Army encouraged Daladier to repeat with greater confidence the decision of France to support Czechoslovakia by force of arms. Chamberlain then made the announcement that had been urged upon him by Halifax. He would make a last appeal to Hitler to settle the affair by negotiation, together with a warning that if France fulfilled her treaty obligations, Great Britain would come to her assistance. This assurance was, thanks to Halifax, expressed in stronger

[1] *Documents on British Foreign Policy, 1919-1939*, Third Series, Vol. II, p. 510.

CHAMBERLAIN'S RETURN FROM MUNICH, 1938

terms in a Foreign Office statement on the evening of 26 September and made public next day:

'The German claim to the transfer of the Sudeten areas has already been conceded by the French, British and Czechoslovak Governments, but if in spite of all efforts made by the British Prime Minister a German attack is made upon Czechoslovakia the immediate result must be that France will be bound to come to her assistance, and Great Britain and Russia will certainly stand by France.'

This communiqué was issued without consulting Russia, presumably on the strength of an assurance by Litvinov at Geneva on 23 September that if France fought, Russia would also intervene, but it was a strange omission in view of the consistent attitude of Russia towards her obligations that the French and British Ministers took no steps to reach a closer military relationship with the Soviet Government in the event of war, or establish a common basis of action.

The tenacious mind of the Prime Minister had not yet abandoned all hope of a peaceful settlement. He had sent Sir Horace Wilson on 26 September on a doleful pilgrimage to try to persuade Hitler to indulge in further negotiations before presenting him with the warning, and we are reminded of some missionary of more than usual guilelessness in the heart of a primeval jungle. He had found the Führer in one of those emotional steam-baths in which it was his practice to work up a lather of rage on the eve of a great pronouncement. He was savouring in advance with ferocious relish the speech he was to deliver at the Sportspalast that night. Sir Horace judged that the moment was ill-chosen to deliver his message, but he had no alternative. Hitler was clearly enraged by this interruption of his sanguinary reverie. He behaved like a maniac, threatening to leave the room, refusing to listen, shouting that the German-speaking areas must be 'free of Czechs' by 1 October: 'If England and France decided to strike, let them strike. He did not care a farthing.' Sir Horace and the British Ambassador withdrew, with the distasteful prospect of another interview on the following day, and Hitler resumed the preparation of his speech.

To one who listened to that speech on the wireless: 'It was the most horrible thing I have ever heard, more like the snarling of a wild animal than the utterance of a human being, and the venom and vulgarity of his personal vilifications of "Beneš the liar" almost made me feel sick. There was something terrifyingly and obscenely sinister in this outpouring of sheer hatred, in the tumultuous roar that followed each point and the culminating almost endless "Sieg Heil!" that followed his outburst.'[1]

It was like some jungle incantation screamed to the fury of tom-toms, but this act of mental self-debauchery merely caused the imperturbable Sir Horace to murmur his felicitations next day to his terrible host:

[1] Amery. Op. cit.

14

'He had listened on the wireless to Herr Hitler's speech, and he desired to congratulate him on the reception he had received: it must be a wonderful experience for any man to receive such a reception.'[1]

Hitler showed no signs of being mollified by this piece of sycophancy, and told his visitors that if the Czechs refused the Godesberg terms, "Ich werde die Tschechen zerschlagen'—'I will smash Czechoslovakia.' This was the Chancellor's response to a message sent him by Chamberlain after hearing the contents of Hitler's speech. Even if Hitler had no faith in the promises of the Czech Government, the message had said, he could surely trust the British Government to see that they were carried out 'fairly and fully' and with no unreasonable delay, provided that the transfer was not accomplished by force.

Even this sample of Hitler's negotiating manner did not deter the Prime Minister, or cause him to abandon hope. On the night of the 27th Halifax despatched two messages to Prague on his behalf. The first warned Dr. Beneš that the British information was that the German Forces would have orders to cross the Czechoslovak frontier almost immediately unless by 2 p.m. on the following day the Czechoslovak Government had accepted the German terms, and added:

'His Majesty's Government cannot take responsibility of advising you what you should do but they consider that this information should be in your hands at once.'[2]

A second telegram which was sent by the Foreign Secretary on the same evening showed the lengths to which the Government was still prepared to go to clutch at the last straws. In effect it advised the Czechs to accept the Godesberg Memorandum, but under a modified time-table which the British Government would undertake to supervise.

But after Hitler's speech almost all hopes for peace had disappeared. By Tuesday night trenches had been dug in the London parks, and the apparatus of Civil Defence set in train, and in the evening the Inner Cabinet declared a State of Emergency by Order in Council, and Chamberlain agreed at last to the mobilization of the Fleet which the First Lord of the Admiralty, Duff Cooper had long been urging. By night time the English people had braced themselves to the fact that they might awake to a world at war. There was a ring of failure in Chamberlain's thin and exhausted voice when he addressed the nation on the wireless, and spoke of 'a quarrel in a far-away country between people of whom we know nothing'.

Yet that evening, before he retired, Chamberlain received an answer from Hitler to the message he had entrusted to Sir Horace which must have seemed like a benison. He was asked to continue to use his good offices, and bring the Czechs to reason. At once it occurred to Chamberlain that this was the

---

[1] *Documents on British Foreign Policy, 1919–1939.* Third Series, Vol. II, p. 565.
[2] Ibid., p. 510.

moment to put into operation the idea of a four-Power Conference which he had suggested to Jan Masaryk on 25 September, and having secured the agreement of the French Ministers, and sent an urgent message to Mussolini to underwrite the proposal, the Prime Minister, like a man reprieved on the scaffold's edge, telegraphed his reply:

'After reading your letter I feel certain that you can get all essentials without war, and without delay. I am ready to come to Berlin myself at once to discuss arrangements for transfer with you and representative of the Czech Government, together with representatives of France and Italy if you desire. I feel convinced that we could reach agreement in a week.'[1]

Making all allowance for the tension of the moment there was an ugly ring in this telegram, something almost effusive in the eagerness to continue the process of surrender:

'This was the nadir of diplomacy,' thought one historian; 'a personal deal between two men at the expense of a third party: I can give you all you want without war and without delay.'[2]

*   *   *

There is no need to linger over the last preliminaries to the Munich Settlement, but it should be clearly remembered that whatever happened later, the Prime Minister had the strong and indeed passionate support of the vast majority of the English people in this hour of trial. Edward had sat in the Peers Gallery in the House of Commons with the Archbishops of York and Canterbury on that unforgettable afternoon of Wednesday, 28 September. And when he had sent Hitler's message of acceptance to Chamberlain on the floor of the House, and it had been read to the Members, he had looked down upon such a spectacle of emotional relief as had never been seen in the House of Commons before, upon wildly cheering men, some weeping and many who would later be anxious to forget their participation. In the country outside men and women felt that they had awoken from some appalling nightmare, and the gratitude for the Prime Minister's courage and persistence was so profound, that in the prevailing atmosphere it seemed to many neither blasphemy, nor wild exaggeration when he was compared by a journalist to God.

Nor is there any need to linger over the Munich Settlement itself, for Chamberlain was the real architect of this unstable structure, and the Foreign Secretary was absent from this last scene, as he had been from Berchtesgaden and Godesberg. But Halifax, although any illusions he may have had had long since been replaced by intense anxiety, was still firmly behind the Prime Minister, and shared his responsibility for the Munich Settlement although to a minor degree, and with a far more acute perception of the danger. The atmosphere of the Conference was one of anti-climax,

[1] Feiling. Op. cit., p. 372.   [2] Mowat. Op. cit., p. 615.

almost of bathos. It was the dictators' hour, and although they masked with reasonable decorum both a sense of indecent triumph, and a contempt for the representatives of Western democracy, no such restraint was observed when the German leaders were alone, when Hitler derided the Prime Minister in obscene gutter language, and was said to have given a devastating imitation of his mannerisms and appearance.

The terms of the settlement were little different from those of Godesberg which the Prime Minister and his colleagues had rejected only a few days before. The main difference on which both Chamberlain and Halifax were to lay great stress, was that unlike Godesberg, the Munich Settlement was technically an 'agreement' which preserved the principle of peaceful negotiation, and provided for the occupation of the Sudeten territory in five stages between 1 October and the 10th, as opposed to the Godesberg demand that the German occupation should be completed in one operation by 1 October. An international Commission of which there was to be a Czech member was to delimit further areas for German occupation with or without plebiscites in a manner less peremptory than that laid down at Godesberg. A guarantee was provided which proved to be a meaningless gesture, of what was left of Czechoslovakia, by Britain and France, and after the other minority claims had been decided, by Germany and Italy. This general guarantee replaced Czechoslovakia's foreign alliances with France and Russia of which she was now deprived.

Her fortified frontier defences were lost, and most of her industrial resources, and her railway communications cut. Always in Chamberlain's mind in his stubborn search for peace had been the sufferings which war would bring to the ordinary people of the world, and obsessed by this fear he ignored the anguish worse than any war, which his settlement would inflict upon ordinary people in Czechoslovakia. For in the ceded territory were 800,000 Czechs, and many democratic Germans opposed to Henlein's party who would be left to his vindictive revenge when his efforts were rewarded by his appointment as Reichskommissar for the Sudetenland, and would be handed over to the storm-troopers and the Gestapo hangmen. He would imprison all political opponents, he said, 'until they turn black', and those who had tried to fly the country would meet the same fate.[1]

Hitler had boasted that his army would enter Czechoslovakia on 1 October, and the Munich Agreement had enabled him to honour this pledge without firing a shot, and having done so stand poised for the next, and long-determined step, the complete destruction of Czechoslovakia. But he had already inflicted a crushing defeat on Britain in the eyes of the world, and an even greater one on France whose system of European alliances had been shattered, her prestige tarnished, and her *dégringolade* begun. Russia had been repelled from the camp of the Western Nations where she might have

[1] Wheeler-Bennett. Op. cit., p. 198.

been, and turned from a possible ally into a vigilant and hostile neutral, and Poland had been laid bare to the next onslaught of the triumphant Nazi Power. And as Churchill was to warn the House of Commons: 'The road down the Danube Valley to the Black Sea, the resources of corn and oil, the road which leads as far as Turkey has been opened.'

After the Conference was over, and the two men met in Hitler's Munich flat, the Prime Minister had told his host how pleased he was by the course it had taken: 'He hoped that Herr Hitler was equally happy.'[1]

But the Czechoslovak delegates who had been summoned to Munich, not indeed to take part in the proceedings, but to listen passively to their fate, did not share this happiness. It was as though, as had been said of an earlier occasion, they had been invited to expire with tact, and even if possible with gaiety, in order not to cloud a day of national rejoicing which happened to coincide with their funeral. They were told plainly, finally, and brutally that they could either accept the terms or face the Germans alone. Mr. Chamberlain had sat yawning through these proceedings. He was feeling the strain, but although tired, he was, he said later, *pleasantly* tired.[2]

It was during the conversation in Hitler's flat that Chamberlain had produced a document which he invited Hitler to sign declaring the resolve of the two leaders to repudiate force in international affairs in favour of reason and negotiation, which became known as the Munich Declaration. We may conjecture the feelings of cynicism and contempt with which Hitler appended his signature.

'A horrible and wretched business,' Halifax was to call it, 'but the lesser of two evils.' With the other Ministers he was waiting at Heston Airport for the hero's return, and as they drove home together the crowds threw flowers into the car, and jumped on to the running board to touch the Prime Minister and try to clasp his hand. Halifax did not share Chamberlain's glow of accomplishment, and intruded with two important subjects upon him as the car passed through waving crowds to London. He told him that he must reject all efforts to make him capitalize his position by calling a snap election, and that he should reconstruct the Cabinet when he met Parliament in three days' time:

'He ought to have reconstituted his Government, bringing in Labour if they would join, and Churchill and Eden. He seemed surprised, but said he would think it over. Nothing however happened, and I have often wondered whether or how the course of history might have been changed if he had acted in the sense I suggested.'[3]

*   *   *

On 29 September it was Edward's duty to justify the Munich Agreement

[1] *Documents on British Foreign Policy, 1919–1939*, Third Series, Vol. II, p. 635.
[2] Wheeler-Bennett. Op. cit., p. 174.   [3] Halifax. Op. cit., p. 200.

in the House of Lords. The Chamber was crowded, and his speech delivered in that deep voice and in tones of great sincerity, was more impressive to hear than to read. After explaining the difference between the Godesberg and the Munich terms he tried to give some answer to the question which was on so many lips, the reasons why Russia had been excluded from the Munich Conference, and this answer, stripped of adornment, was that the Germans had not wanted her. It had seemed vital to the Government to get 'matters to a basis of negotiation', but when they faced the facts:

'We were obliged to recognize that in present circumstances the heads of the German and Italian Governments would almost certainly—at least without much preliminary discussion for which there was no time—be reluctant to sit in conference with a Soviet representative. Accordingly, if our principal purpose was to secure negotiation, we were bound to have regard to the practical conditions with which alone this purpose could be secured.'

When he came to speak of the guarantee to Czechoslovakia, he reminded the House that for months it had been pressed on him that if only Great Britain would say unmistakably that she would resist any unprovoked aggression against Czechoslovakia, no such aggression would be made. The Government had not felt able to use such language, but now:

'The deterrent value of such a settlement will be in full force in such a guarantee as we have expressed our willingness to give. . . . To guarantee a Czechoslovakia including within her frontier restless and dissatisfied minorities was one thing: to guarantee Czechoslovakia when its explosive minority questions have been adjusted is quite another.'

He also claimed that the guarantee was buttressed by other vital elements, among which was the fact that:

'Germany and Italy have expressed their willingness to guarantee Czecho-slovakia when the other minority questions have been settled.'

Like Chamberlain in the Commons he paid a tribute to Dr. Beneš for his courage and statesmanship, adding:

'I am very conscious of all that has to be entered on the debit side, but if the whole matter be fairly weighed I cannot doubt in my mind, for Czecho-slovakia herself as for the world where the balance rests. . . . I have never been able to take the view of the inevitability of war, which is perhaps more easily taken by those who are fortunate enough to have no final responsibility, and he is a rash man who would try to write history before the time.'

He believed that Munich was a victory for reason over force, for confer-ence over machine-gun, and therefore he would be troubled by no pangs of conscience, for the peoples of the world thought that they had been brought back from the brink of ruin:

'Herr Hitler has had a great triumph, and I for one would grudge him nothing of a triumph which he knows to be accorded, not only for what he has gained, but also for the contribution which he made to a settlement through agreement in preference to the arbitrament and catastrophe of war. I see in Munich not only a conference at which hard terms were imposed on the Czechs, but also an occasion on which it was found possible by discussion to effect a real abatement in claims, and at which all the nations taking part contributed to win a real victory for reason and understanding over the forces of unreason, hatred and distrust.' Such were the reasons which he gave for the fact that his conscience was clear and his mind at rest, and that he was able to tell their Lordships:

'I am not greatly moved, therefore, for myself or for His Majesty's Government by the reproaches that may be levelled against us. . . . The only reproaches that can wound are the reproaches of a man's own conscience, and he alone can know in what language conscience speaks. As I look back on these anxious weeks I readily confess that I may have had my share in decisions that can be held by some to be ill-judged. In a time of crisis, with grave questions demanding urgent answer at every moment, no body of men would dare claim to be judged infallible. There was indeed no clear way, but almost always a hideous choice of evils. I can only know for myself, that my mind will be at rest for having taken no decision inconsistent with what on all the facts I felt right.'

CHAPTER XXIV

POST-MORTEM

TIME would show that the vaunted 'guarantee' in reliance on which Czechoslovakia was deprived of her foreign alliances would never be ratified, and that it would be forgotten while Poland seized Teschen, and Germany and Italy decided how much of Czechoslovakia should be annexed by Hungary. When in March Hitler completed the process of rape, and, having occupied Prague was able to stand in ecstasy at the windows of the Hradschin Palace and survey the ancient city beneath, the guarantee was abandoned altogether on the grounds that as Czechoslovakia had disintegrated the obligation was no longer valid.

It was not long before the mighty thanksgiving that had greeted the Munich Settlement began to give way to a more sober examination of the price at which peace had been bought. It was then that there began that bitter controversy when families and old friends were divided by a rancour which was nourished by a deep sense of shame, and the word 'Munich' became a gage of battle. Powerful arguments, both at the time, and for years afterwards, were levelled against the Munich Settlement. They were led by Winston Churchill, the one man whose record was entirely clean, who had predicted this moment with the prescience of genius, and for years seen his warnings disregarded. Mr. Harold Macmillan found that in the group critical of Munich, of which he was a member, the opprobrium was reserved entirely for Neville Chamberlain as the *fons et origo* of the Settlement, and that Halifax, although he had played so great a part in appeasement, was exempt.[1]

Today there can be little dispute that Munich was a shameful chapter in the history of France and England, a disaster so great as to deprive France, for a time, of the dignity of a Great Power and set her feet upon that road of servility and panic concession that led to Vichy. England was scarcely less heavily involved, and it was her Prime Minister who by the force of his personality and his generous horror of war had so dominated the French Ministers that he had dictated the common policy, and assumed the function of leadership.

Yet, when all this is said, the question in the end resolves itself into a simple issue, and every path of exploration leads us back to the same point. Would it have been better to fight in 1938? On neither side of this question were the arguments free from dishonesty and special pleading, and when

[1] The Rt. Hon. Harold Macmillan to author.

passions were so strongly engaged it was hardly possible that they should be. And today, those who still seek to defend Munich often ignore facts inconvenient to their case, while those who attack it sometimes adduce circumstances which were not known at the time, and cannot fairly be used against the British Government. When the enormity of the betrayal of Czechoslovakia began to penetrate men's minds, those who revolted against it found themselves in the grip of such a sense of moral outrage that they were unable to achieve the detachment necessary to place themselves in the position of the Government and ask themselves with complete honesty, what they would have done if the responsibility had been theirs.

Churchill was of the opinion that if it could be proved that the year which Munich gained had saved England and France from defeat, the Settlement could be justified, but he denied that this was the case. Many shots were fired at the time at the Munich Settlement; the fusillade has not yet ceased, and the body is riddled with bullets. Nor did those who took an adverse view have any lack of ammunition. They could argue that Czechoslovakia had been stripped of her defensive position, that she was placed in complete economic vassalage, and that her mighty armament works passed into German hands. It would be claimed, and this was one of the less honest arguments, that the turning of Czechoslovakia's flank after the Anschluss had not made her defence impossible, that the German General Staff did not appear to place much reliance on such an exposed turning movement, and that most of their force was concentrated against the main Czech bastion.

A further argument in the light of later discoveries was that the leaders of the Germany Army were convinced that they could not have faced a war in September 1938, and that the West Wall would not last more than three weeks against an attack by the French Army which might have been in occupation of the Rhineland, and even of the Ruhr before Czechoslovakia had been disposed of. For the critics of Munich were unanimous in emphasizing the strength of the well-equipped Czech Army of 24–25 divisions, to which ten could have been added, and which they thought capable of a far more prolonged resistance behind their mountain barrier than the Poles could offer later on the open plains. It has been claimed also that the Wehrmacht was still lacking in trained officers, non-commissioned officers, and reserves, that its three Panzer Divisions were armed only with Mark I and II tanks. With Czechoslovakia strongly resisting, Russia in the war against Germany, and France making a determined assault on the West Wall, it was argued that the prospects of success were far brighter in 1938 than a year later. It was claimed that another later historical discovery had revealed that if Hitler had been resisted he would have been arrested, and overthrown by a military plot.

The critics of Munich also gave a natural emphasis to the fact that Russian advances had met with such a tepid response. They were confident that with proper encouragement she would have declared war in 1938; that the repeated declarations of Potemkin and Litvinov would have made evasion almost impossible, and that the adverse reports of British and French diplomatists throwing doubt upon her intentions did not carry conviction. They pointed out that the British calculations of weakness in the air which played so large a part in their policy ignored the Czech Air Force and the Russian reinforcements that would almost certainly have been sent, and which, they claimed, would have absorbed most of Germany's strength in the air while the main military decision was taking place in the West.

And to the argument of the defenders of Munich that our appalling vulnerability from the air made a policy of delay essential to survival, those who opposed the settlement argued that Germany had neither the intention nor the ability to make a strategic air attack on Great Britain in 1938, that she could only attack her at 300 miles range, and that the danger in 1938 was nothing like that of 1939 which this country successfully weathered. In any case, in their view, nothing that France or Great Britain did to strengthen their armed forces in the next twelve months was comparable to the increase in armed power achieved during the same period by Germany, and this was apart from the gain to her of 30–40 divisions by the elimination of the Czech Army, and the added production of Skoda and Witkovitz.

Such, apart from the strategic disaster suffered by France through the loss of Czechoslovakia, were some of the main arguments, stated in general terms, that have been made against the Munich Settlement. Many are valid, some wishful-thinking, some uttered à l'esprit de l'escalier. Even apart from the moral aspects involved they provide a powerful strategical indictment, and Halifax himself was to make the admission in January 1940:

'The Munich Settlement gave Germany all she immediately wanted. In applying the Agreement every contentious point was settled in Germany's favour.'

                      *   *   *

We should now take ourselves for a journey into the past, and, attempting to shed all prejudice, place ourselves in the position of the men who held responsibility in 1938 and were faced by this grave decision, and try to understand the considerations that were uppermost in their minds. Not the least of these was the report of the Chiefs of Staff to the Committee of Imperial Defence in the later summer of 1938 on the overriding need to gain time for the completion of the defence programme. Their conclusions were set out in a series of propositions, of which the first was that Great Britain was not ready for war, and the second that she could not fight a war on three fronts, German, Italian and Japanese without powerful allies. They had also pointed out that the Czech frontier of 2,500 miles could not be protected

from a German attack, that the French Army was neither willing nor able to undertake an offensive against Germany, and would remain on the Maginot Line, and that if the Government was not prepared to face a war of attrition on the Czech issue they must play for time.

It is essential to remember that statesmen of the day were influenced in their minds when they contemplated war by the fact that the conditions of the last were vividly in their memories while they had but dim conceptions of what the next would bring. The carnage of the trench warfare of the First World War had left in the minds of all responsible men in England and France a shrinking aversion from the mere thought of its repetition, and to this was now added an almost superstitious horror of the still untested power of that aerial bombardment which had all the terror of the unknown, upon great cities and upon the women and children in them. And since there could be no certainty about the nature of this ordeal until it had been experienced, their minds were filled with the darkest forebodings, and it was no conscious extravagance of expression when statesmen like Baldwin and Neville Chamberlain spoke of another world war as meaning the end of civilization. The fear of the unknown was, as always, more terrible than the actuality. We have since become familiar with air bombardment using high explosive which is now accepted as a part of conventional warfare, but the shrinking of the world at the prospect of nuclear warfare provides a fair parallel to the forebodings of the statesmen of 1938.[1]

In addition to these fears the men in power were continually oppressed by the knowledge of their own weakness in the weapons of war which they could fairly attribute to the lethargy of MacDonald and Baldwin. As Winston Churchill was later to observe, four years were required before armaments came in full measure, and 1934 was the latest at which a start could have been made to achieve this result by 1938. To arrive at a condition of complete readiness it would have been necessary in 1934 to place the country on a full war footing, with everything that involved, at a time when the vast majority of the people thought only of disarmament and were blissfully ignorant of the frightful dangers that were approaching. At a moment when a large part of Britain was pacifist to the core it is scarcely conceivable that such a step could have been taken. British Governments from 1931 onwards had been restrained from making such an attempt partly by the pacificism of the nation, and partly by their own irresolution. Chamberlain had indeed recognized the danger in 1937, but the programme then initiated, although a considerable advance, bore no relation to the dangers that were developing in Europe, and was in any case too late. Now the Conservative leaders felt that they had been left naked and unprotected, and that it was impossible for them to conduct a forceful diplomacy until it was underwritten by authentic military force. They were acutely conscious that it was they alone who were

[1] Amery. Op. cit.

responsible for deciding whether the war which they regarded with such
dread should take place. With all the information available to them from
their Intelligence Services and Military Advisers they believed that to make
war in 1938 would be a gamble of criminal recklessness, and it was one they
were not prepared to take. It would be idle to deny that there was much in
their position to justify this reluctance.

If the British Government was thus hag-ridden by the consciousness of its
own weakness, it had even less confidence in the moral vigour of France, or
in her capacity to wage a major war. Their meetings with Daladier and Bonnet,
and particularly that of 25 September when Chamberlain and Simon had so
mercilessly laid bare the French Ministers' inner uncertainty, had confirmed
their suspicions of the strong aversion of the French people from the thought
of war, and the defensive strategy of their military leaders.

They had taken note, as a prime consideration, of the pathetic weakness of
the French Air Force. It was impossible for them to accept the sanguine belief
of some that the French Army would open the war with an offensive in great
force, and delivered with irresistible *élan*, rolling back the Germans while the
Czech Army resisted strongly behind its mountain defences. They could see
the situation in no such rosy glow. It was contrary to all the expert advice
they had received which predicted that Czech resistance would be brief, and
that the French Army was incapable of major offensive operations. In
Cassandra-like despatches from the British Ambassador in Paris, more
portentous even than the situation demanded, they had been warned of the
moral weakness of the nation behind the French leaders, and its apathy of
spirit, a nation whose vigour had been sapped by internal conflict and a growing awareness of its impotence to play the dominating part in Europe which
had been the underlying assumption of the Versailles Settlement.[1]

The Government were much blamed for the cold shoulder they presented
to the Russian pledges of support to Czechoslovakia that were given during
the Czech crisis. Chamberlain and Halifax trusted neither Russian intentions,
nor her ability to make any serious contribution to a war. Chamberlain indeed
believed that nothing would please her better than to see the capitalist states
fighting one another, while Halifax felt that the recent purges in the Russian
High Command must have so disorganized and enfeebled the Red Army as to
prevent it for a long time from becoming an effective military force. Russia's
real intentions, when she made these pledges of help, remain a matter for
speculation, but there was nothing in her actions during the crisis of 1938
to suggest that she was not serious in offering them, and that she would not
have honoured her bond.

There was considerable excuse, however, for the doubts of the Prime
Minister and Foreign Secretary of the amount of help that might be expected
from Russia. Rumania and Poland having flatly refused to allow Russian

[1] Amery. Op. cit.

troops to pass through their territories, the only contribution that Russia could have made would have been in the air, and the amount of this contribution was uncertain, but it was of the utmost importance to have this vast if imponderable Power a declared ally, if only in a token capacity, and it must be counted a glaring error that more realistic efforts were not made to secure this end.

If Czechoslovakia had quickly collapsed, and France had offered no more resistance to a German offensive than in 1940, and the enemy had reached the Channel Ports, the position of England would undoubtedly have been critical. But even if they did not contemplate so extreme a disaster the Cabinet felt acute apprehension of air bombardment lamentably justified by the deficiencies in Civil Defence which the crisis so nakedly revealed. There had been only ten per cent of the full requirement of A.A. guns, and those of an obsolete pattern; only 1,428 searchlights out of a programme which provided for 4,128, only 140 barrage balloons out of 450, and, incredible fact, only 60 fire pumps in the whole of London.

The Government, whatever its own responsibility for them, could claim to have corrected these deficiencies in the year that followed Munich. Under Sir John Anderson's direction a strong grip was taken on all aspects of Civil Defence, and estimates of expenditure on Air Raid Precautions rose from £9¼ million in the current year to £42 million in the year 1939–40, while schemes for the evacuation of children were completed. And of overriding importance to the defence of Britain, the Government could claim that by the outbreak of war the chain of radar stations built under the direction of Sir Robert Watson-Watt, without which it was extremely improbable that the Battle of Britain could have been won, stretched from the Orkneys to the Isle of Wight, whereas at the time of Munich there had been only one installation in the Thames Estuary.

But from the Government's point of view the most powerful argument of all for gaining time was the need to produce an Air Force which could challenge that of Germany.

This vital object was achieved, and in doing so the Government were reaping the harvest of Lord Swinton's brilliant tenure of the Air Ministry. The programme Schedule L which had been approved in April 1938, and had only just begun to operate, provided for 12,000 planes in two years, ordered off the drawing-board, a figure which was raised to 17,000 on the eve of war. The expansion of aircraft factories and the construction of shadow-factories was vigorously advanced, and sub-contracting developed. As a result of Swinton's foresight, whereas in 1938 the R.A.F. had only one operational squadron equipped with Spitfires, and five in the process of being equipped with Hurricanes, by the summer of 1939 it had 26 squadrons of modern eight-gun fighters, and a year later, when the hour of trial came, it was to have, on an average, 47. The expansion of the German Air Force was nearly complete in 1938, that of the R.A.F. beginning, so that the disparity between the two in the year that followed, although it was increased in the comparative size of the two forces, was decreased in their quality, and the Government could claim that it was the superior quality of the new aircraft, together with the devotion and skill of their pilots, and the finished radar detection system that enabled the R.A.F. to snatch a precarious victory in 1940.

Besides these glaring defects in the defence system four other important elements disturbed the minds of Halifax and Chamberlain. They were much concerned by the aftermath of the economic crisis of 1931; they were apprehensive of the situation in the Far East, and of what action Japan might take there if Great Britain became involved in a war with Germany in the West; and they were at all times uneasily conscious of America's neutrality, and of the unpalatable fact that no help could be looked for from that quarter in case of trouble. The British Government was also alarmed about the attitude of the Dominions to involvement in war. South Africa had decided to remain neutral, should it come; the Australian Labour Party were against intervention, and there was grave doubt whether Mackenzie King could bring the Canadian people into war.

After these general reflections we are driven back once again to that original question: Would it have been better to have fought in 1938? Was the Government responsible not only for the enslavement of Czechoslovakia, but for a military miscalculation as well? No final answer can be given, for the question upon which it rests is hypothetical, and we have no means of judging what would have been the issue of an earlier conflict. It is unlikely that history will give a more convincing verdict than that of one who wrote a classical account of these debasing events, and, a friend of the Czechs, witnessed in that expiring country their agony of spirit:

'Let us say of the Munich Settlement,' wrote John Wheeler-Bennett, 'that it was inescapable; that, faced with the lack of preparedness in Britain's armaments and defences, with the lack of unity at home and in the Commonwealth, with the collapse of French morale, and with the uncertainty of Russia to fight, Mr. Chamberlain had no alternative to do other than he did; let us pay tribute to his persistence in carrying out a policy which he honestly believed to be right. Let us accept and admit all these things, but in so doing let us not omit the shame and humiliation that were ours; let us not forget that, in order to save our own skins—that because we were too weak to protect ourselves—we were forced to sacrifice a small Power to slavery.'[1]

---

[1] Wheeler-Bennett. Op. cit., p. 433.

CHAPTER XXV

IN THE FOREIGN OFFICE

MUNICH marked the end of the first crisis in the relationship with Germany during Halifax's Foreign Secretaryship, and it is a convenient place to pause and glance at his outlook on foreign affairs, and the impression he made upon his colleagues at the Foreign Office. By a happy chance, one of his later Private Secretaries, Valentine Lawford, was a born writer, and after observing Halifax for a while was able to describe him with an artist's eye:

'When Halifax moved, he could be graceful and grave and shy simultaneously, like a tall water-bird wading in the shallows. . . . Architecturally, the upper half of Halifax's head resembled a dome which, since it rested on rather more than usually jutting ears, appeared illusively to taper towards the apex. It was a fine head though. When he walked it fell very slightly forwards; and as he sat reading at his desk he would cup the weight of it in the palm of his right hand. But the loftiness of the face as a whole could not cause one quite to forget an ever-present, questioning look in his eyes; and beneath a long upper lip the line of the mouth itself was expressive less of wit or irony than of a controlled and philosophical melancholy, innate and instinctive rather than acquired. Yet his was by no means the neglected body of a dreamer. His back and legs were magnificently straight and he looked his best astride a horse . . .

'Halifax's clothes were well cut, well cared for (it is tempting to say well preserved, for his black office coat in war-time, with its long vent up the back, had a greenish tinge in sunlight) and even when they were new they were slightly dated, as for some reason befits an Englishman who is fond of horses. . . . And there were the recognizable marks of the squire and the Colonel of Yeomanry in the forward tilt of the bowler hat and the way he carried his umbrella, less frequently in the crook of his elbow than horizontally in the hand, as it might have been a riding-crop or a woodsman's tool. . . . He walked each day through the parks to the Foreign Office, arriving one particularly wet November morning in a pair of rubber boots a yard high, inside which, in the words of the half-admiring, half-scandalized office-keeper whom he had summoned to help him pull them off, "there was only his Lordship's bare feet".'[1]

We have already seen that Halifax was extremely reluctant to accept the Foreign Office; that he thought at the time that Eden had resigned on a

[1] *The Cornhill*. Winter 1956–57, pp. 73–5.

technicality, and that he should have accommodated himself to the situation, and had done his utmost to dissuade the Foreign Secretary from resignation. And one of the first impressions his subordinates received was that he was ill at ease in this office, that he had assumed it with perhaps too little thought for his own suitability for it, and without knowing much of its problems or where they would lead him.

It was at once evident that he did not, like Austen Chamberlain, find the study of foreign affairs a matter of absorbing interest, and it sometimes seemed to others that he was doing his work at the Foreign Office as an unpleasant duty, that he had no strong convictions about it, and few pre-conceived views about European problems. His attitude towards them was pragmatic; he liked to settle each question from day to day as it arose. This method was inevitable since his interests had never particularly inclined towards European politics, and he had therefore never given them sustained thought, or arrived at a long view or hard conclusions. Much of his later life had been spent out of Europe, and he had for long devoted all his thoughts to Eastern problems. It is scarcely surprising that he was one of the many who had failed to grasp the implications of Sir Horace Rumbold's warnings about Nazi Germany, and while Foreign Secretary he admitted to his friend Dr. Don, the Dean of Westminster, that he had never read *Mein Kampf*.[1]

He was thus in no sense a specialist in foreign affairs like Eden, and his aloofness prevented him picking up diplomatic gossip. There have been Foreign Secretaries to whom an intimate knowledge of Europe was as the breath of life, and such a man would have the gossip of the European capitals at his fingertips and a host of foreign acquaintances. He would know what Dr. Beneš was saying to his friends in Prague, and Mr. Gafencu in Bucharest, and the private lives of French Ministers would be an open book to him. Such a man would speak French fluently, and perhaps other languages; he would read European newspapers, and realize that there was sometimes much to be learned from foreign journalists, and, discarding some things he was told, and accepting others, remain continually abreast of events. He would have sympathy with the countries that came within his view, and an easy familiarity with their customs, and their study would be more than a duty; it would be an absorbing interest in his life, an ever-fascinating supplement to the red despatch boxes of the Foreign Office. He would, in fact, be a European.

Halifax was not qualified either by knowledge or inclination for such a rôle. He accepted the position of Foreign Secretary in the same manner as he had that of President of the Board of Education, without enthusiasm, but because he had been invited to do so by Chamberlain, and thought it his duty to accept. Although he was perhaps only dimly aware of it, there was an unhappy atmosphere in the Foreign Office at that time, a feeling of strain and

[1] Dr. Don to author.

tension on the part of many officials who disapproved of the policy they were asked to carry out. Halifax, in fact, made no disturbing innovations, and officials who disagreed with the policy remained in their posts, although their advice was not taken. He gave considerable latitude to his Under-Secretary, R. A. Butler, who appreciated the fact that his chief was always fair in allowing him his head,[1] and was diligent in reading his papers, but his knowledge of Europe was clearly limited. It was noticed by his subordinates that although he took a long time to make a decision, once it was reached his mind hardened like cement. It was noticed too that he was a man of high moral courage who did not shirk unpleasant duties. The cypher department of the Foreign Office when he arrived there was a relic of the First World War, staffed partly by a strange medley of old clubmen, one of whom proved to be a traitor, and was sentenced to a long term of imprisonment. The Permanent Under-Secretary, Sir Alexander Cadogan, decided that he must send the lot of them packing, and make a fresh start. It was an odious task to expel innocent men, but Edward at once said to Cadogan: 'Would it help you if I did it?' And at the beginning of his office in February 1938 he summoned the cypher department *en masse* and explained to them with great kindness the reasons for their dismissal. They were replaced by civil servants. No more unpleasant way to begin his office could be imagined, and it was a task he could easily have avoided.

When he became Foreign Secretary he believed it to be his duty, like Chamberlain, to make every effort short of over-stepping the frontiers of honour to avert a war which he was convinced at the time Great Britain was certain to lose. He was impressed by the necessity for a Foreign Secretary to make this attempt to preserve peace if it was reasonably possible, and, if not, at least to delay a war for which in his opinion the country was hopelessly unprepared. But his belief in the inevitability of war was slow in coming. On the eve of his Foreign Secretaryship he thought that Eden and his friends were exaggerating the danger, and in spite of his visit to Berchtesgaden had still not fully grasped Hitler's true character and intentions. When he reached the Foreign Office his judgment was quickly influenced by the strong opinions he found prevailing there, and his eyes were opened. But he continued to carry out the Prime Minister's policy because he did not believe that there was any alternative. He remained on friendly terms with Eden, and they met often in London or Yorkshire. Eden sometimes found the Foreign Secretary a prey to acute anxiety about what was happening but always believing that the hand could not be played in any other way.

Halifax had from the beginning accepted the Prime Minister's policy. He admired and liked Chamberlain, and assumed office as Foreign Secretary in the knowledge that the Prime Minister would take a far livelier interest

---

[1] R. A. Butler to author.

than his predecessor in the control of foreign policy. He was also fully aware of what that policy would be, and was willing to associate himself with it. He was, however, as we have seen, sufficiently disturbed by the time of Munich to urge Chamberlain vainly to reconstitute his Government, and it has sometimes been wondered whether he ever felt the situation sufficiently grave to consider the threat of resignation with which he could have undoubtedly brought a powerful lever to bear on the Prime Minister. He never did so, and it would have been in every way contrary to his character if he had. It is impossible to doubt the truth of the words of Lord Salisbury who knew him well, and admired him:

'He was by no means, by nature, a man for a lonely fight. On the contrary, I suspect that his instinct was, where conceivably possible, always to accept the views of the majority of his friends and colleagues. . . . I have always imagined that it was this feeling—a feeling which I suppose might be described, partly at any rate, as one of loyalty—that made it possible for him to continue as a member of Neville Chamberlain's Government.' And so, in Salisbury's opinion, however fragile the hopes of appeasement with such a person as Hitler—'To separate himself from his colleagues and to bring the Government down, as he must have known he probably would have done—and that at a moment of great international tension—was something which would, I believe, have been quite impossible for him; and so he stayed on. It was a great pity.'[1]

And apart from this reluctance he might have reflected, if he had ever contemplated resignation, that there was no alternative Government which could be relied upon to take more vigorous action. The Foreign Secretary could not be unaware that there was a strong opposition to the policy of appeasement from a minority in Parliament and the Press. The great Daily of his own county, the *Yorkshire Post*, had for some time been demanding a stronger line with the dictators, and although Halifax had never been in any way identified with that newspaper, he had known its Editor, Mr. Arthur Mann, for many years, and remained on friendly terms with him. In August 1938 Mann sent Halifax a memorandum setting out the case against appeasement on the lines expounded in his newspaper's leading articles during recent months, and a few days later called by arrangement on the Secretary of State at the Foreign Office. His memorandum lay on the table and was the subject of their discussion. Halifax was as always courteous and charming, but the interview brought little comfort to the Editor. 'Lord Halifax,' he said, 'whatever doubts he may have had, gave no expression to them. Then and always he was loyal to his chief.'[2]

Halifax was undoubtedly strongly influenced by his loyalty to the Prime Minister, but some saw in him also a willingness to shut his eyes to what he did not want to see, and in the opinion of Eden he was capable to a remark-

[1] Lord Salisbury to author.   [2] Mr. Arthur Mann to author.

able degree of persuading himself that it was his duty to take a given course of action.

We can trace the development of Halifax's views immediately after Munich in a letter of 1 November 1938 to Sir Eric Phipps in Paris. While he was prepared to accept that 'henceforward we must count with German predominance in Central Europe', he deleted from the draft a following phrase recognizing that it would be a mistake ever to try to prevent such predominance. In these present conditions it now seemed to the Foreign Secretary that 'Great Britain and France have to uphold *their* dominant position in Western Europe with adequate armed strength, and maintain their hold on the Mediterranean, the Near East and their colonial empires.

'The greatest lesson of the crisis has been the unwisdom of basing a foreign policy on insufficient armed strength.'

There was also the problem of Poland and the Ukraine, and here Halifax expressed the hope that France would 'protect herself—and us—from being entangled in war with Germany, though he did not advise the denunciation of the Franco-Soviet pact'.[1]

This letter indicates that Halifax had reached a half-way point. He no longer thought that Hitler could be appeased by a colonial offer, and he saw that the threat to Britain and France themselves must be countered by strong defence, but he did not in this letter formulate the proposition that any further German expansion would in itself form part of a developing threat to British security.

*   *   *

William Strang, head of the Central Department of the Foreign Office' thought Edward inscrutable. He used words with extreme care, and it was almost impossible to fathom his thoughts. The Foreign Secretary would extract information by intensive and prolonged questioning, which made Strang feel that he had been drained dry. 'You poured a great deal in, but got very little out.' Sir Alexander Cadogan also found that Halifax had a curious, hesitating way of talking round a subject, and that he felt that every aspect of a problem should be minutely examined. This habit grew upon him, and later, under Churchill, began to depress and disturb the Cabinet to whom it appeared to indicate that he was growing very tired.[2] To Strang it seemed that, put in simple words, Halifax's attitude was: 'Here is the Prime Minister. He has got his own policy, and he knows his own mind. Let us go along with him.'[3] And Hitler must be recognized as a fact. Whether they liked it or not, he was there, at the head of a mighty nation, and his presence must be accepted, and foreign policy realistically adapted to it. He was encouraged in this belief by the failure of Churchill's long campaign for

[1] *Documents on British Foreign Policy, 1919–1939*, Third Series, Vol. III, pp. 251–3.
[2] Sir Alexander Cadogan to author.   [3] Lord Strang to author.

military preparedness which had struck no echo from the people, causing many to turn away from him in boredom, and even charge him with being a war-monger. It was Chamberlain's remarkable strength of character and single-minded determination that kept Halifax and others at his side, and Sir Orme Sargent[1] was astonished by his iron hold on the Cabinet.

The Prime Minister and Foreign Secretary can have been in no doubt of the repulsive cruelties that were practised by Nazi Germany as a matter of common policy, and of her flagrant breaches of faith, and it is strange that these did not produce a more positive reaction on their minds. It was, no doubt, unfortunate that the most forceful exponent of anti-German opinion in the Foreign Office was Sir Robert Vansittart, who, although almost invariably right in his predictions, was given to violent over-statement which deprived his warnings of the greater part of their force. This great public servant used an unfortunate style in his minutes to the Cabinet, violent, facetious, fizzing with bad epigrams, and they were read with growing boredom and indifference by Chamberlain and Halifax, a tragic failure which could be blamed almost as much on Vansittart's own temperament and methods as on those who ignored his warnings.

But Edward's old friend Lord Brand, who was devoted to him, thought that the reasons for his failure to grasp the full debasement of Hitler's mind was to be found in his own character and upbringing, and that such a degree of evil lay beyond his comprehension:

'Baldwin, Dawson and Halifax all had this in common. They were all English country gentlemen, all good public school men, and all good churchmen. They seldom visited Europe, or knew what Europeans were like. None of them could have the slightest conception of the enormity of Hitler. Their whole upbringing conspired against understanding that such people could exist, and that the Nazi State was a lunatic State.'

In Brand's eyes Edward had none of the awareness of a man like Leo Amery who had been engrossed in European politics since boyhood, spoke many languages, and always had his ear to the ground. He could not have failed to think Hitler a bad man, but had no yardstick by which to measure his pathological wickedness:

'Although Edward was very clever the world was an innocent world to him. To live in it during Hitler's epoch with the ideas his father had planted in him was extremely difficult. He was so bound by tradition that he never wavered in the principles he was taught when he was young. No new view of the world or violent change dinted his orthodoxy.'[2]

But with all the sources of information at his disposal at the Foreign Office he was a worried and unhappy man at the time of the Munich crisis. He was

---

[1] Sir Orme Sargent was Deputy Under-Secretary at the Foreign Office in 1939, and later Permanent Under-Secretary.

[2] Lord Brand to author.

often unable to sleep at night, a most unusual condition for him, and although outwardly calm the burden of office was pressing upon him more heavily than at any other time in his life. He was haunted by the knowledge that he shared the responsibility for finding a solution. There had been that extraordinary moment of weakness after Godesberg which had so disturbed Sir Alexander Cadogan but after a troubled night he had woken with a new resolution. And when Munich came, he had no further doubts about Hitler's intentions, but saw the matter as 'a horrible and wretched business', a choice between 'two hideous alternatives'; he had no hesitation in deciding which to choose. He allowed himself to take refuge in the argument that Czechoslovakia could not be protected from invasion, and that even after a victorious war could not be reconstituted in her present form with the boundaries drawn again along the old frontiers.

It would be wrong, when considering the springs of Halifax's actions at this time, to ignore that detachment from mundane affairs which was part of the spiritual side of his nature. The belief in a Divine control over the affairs of the world led him to think that human beings could only move the course of events a little in certain directions, so that while prepared to do this, he was not ready to step in and stem the flood; and his profound belief in a future life made the disasters of this world seem by contrast transient and insubstantial. Thus armoured he could envisage human afflictions with an almost unearthly calm, and face war, when it came, with complete inner tranquillity, regarding the deaths of those he loved not as 'utter desolation', but as softened by a sure knowledge of the immortality of their souls. We can gain some understanding of this state of detachment from a letter he wrote to a bereaved friend a year before Munich:

'If, as I believe and as surely all human nature impels us to believe, there is something in man which is higher than, and independent of, his physical state, then do not these events fall into a different scale? Is there is in man's nature that which is eternal, then at once everything that happens to him here becomes or may become a beginning of something greater than we know, rather than the end. And then natural as it is for us to sorrow over what we meet in this life, it is constantly redeemed in our thought by the certainty that the true life goes on, even though unseen by us during our present state.'[1]

*   *   *

Halifax was also criticized for too ready acquiescence in the use by the Prime Minister of personal advisers, particularly Sir Horace Wilson, in a manner which frequently encroached upon the sphere of the trained officials of the Foreign Office. Chamberlain was a man of unusual shyness with few friends in whom he was willing to confide, and he was influenced by a strong

[1] This letter was written on 7 January 1937 to Mrs. Wigram, later Lady Waverley, after the death of her husband Ralph Wigram.

distrust of the Foreign Office which he believed to be hostile to his policy and reluctant to advance it, and too cumbrous in its machinery for the air age, when the heads of Governments could fly to meet one another in a matter of hours. It was for this reason that he chose Sir Horace Wilson, whom he knew well and trusted, to advise him on foreign affairs, and installed him in a room in No. 10 Downing Street, settling many questions of policy at the highest level in consultation with him.

The baleful influence of Wilson as an *éminence grise* has no doubt been exaggerated, for the Prime Minister's personality was so strong, and his conviction of the rightness of his policy so unassailable, that he was unlikely to be influenced by anyone else. Sir Horace Wilson was a hard-working civil servant and a future head of the Treasury, eminent in many fields but with no qualifications or training for offering advice on foreign affairs. He was in agreement with the policy of appeasement, or at least prepared to pursue it to the furthest limits. There was nothing new in a Prime Minister relying upon advisers on foreign policy outside the Foreign Office, but it is, in general, a practice to be condemned, and in the past Lloyd George, by using Philip Kerr and others for this purpose, enfeebled the position of the Foreign Secretary Lord Curzon, making it equivocal and indeed humiliating.

In this case the Permanent Under-Secretary Sir Alexander Cadogan found that Sir Horace Wilson worked loyally with him,[1] frequently visiting the Foreign Office for consultation, but there were other members of the Office who, while not denying this, resented his influence on foreign affairs, and his interference in their transaction, William Strang holding, as he has since said, that neither Grey nor Eden would have tolerated it. Nor could they understand the reasons for the Foreign Secretary's acquiescence in these encroachments on his authority since he was in a strong position after Eden's resignation to assert himself, as the Prime Minister could scarcely have discarded another Foreign Secretary. And there could be no doubt that even if Wilson was not in a position to influence Chamberlain's policy he was invested with unusual power which he did not always use with discretion in his dealings with the Foreign Office.

When J. P. L. Thomas was Parliamentary Private Secretary to Eden he had been expected to act as a sort of reporting agent in the Office for Wilson who sent for him in order to make this suggestion, and during Halifax's régime, Reginald Leeper, the head of the Press Department in the Foreign Office, who although scrupulously correct in his behaviour was not in sympathy with Chamberlain's policy, was summoned by Wilson who informed him: 'Some members of the Foreign Office say that you are not loyal to the Government'; adding: 'If that is the impression you create you are not suitable for work in the Foreign Office in London.' Leeper protested that if he

[1] Sir Alexander Cadogan to author.

had done wrong he would no doubt hear about it from his diplomatic superiors, but Wilson answered: 'Be that as it may, you have no future in the Foreign Office. You must seek that future abroad,' and a few days later Leeper was posted to Bucharest without Halifax being consulted about his transfer.[1]

Why then did the Foreign Secretary tolerate this situation? To Strang it seemed that the Foreign Office had never had the same meaning for Halifax as for Eden, and since he was in any case in full agreement with the Prime Minister's policy, and unswerving in his loyalty to him, he had no objection if Chamberlain preferred to conduct affairs in this way. But Edward's Under-Secretary R. A. Butler thought that he was frequently irritated by Wilson's interference. Sometimes indeed, but seldom, he uttered a mild protest, but only if the provocation was too great to be ignored.[2] But the truth is that Halifax was simply not concerned with minor characters, and the fact that a civil servant unversed in foreign affairs was often used to carry out decisions of high policy which were the normal function of the Foreign Office, however tiresome, appeared to him neither scandalous, nor a just cause of resentment.

*   *   *

Looking back then from this stopping place of the Munich Settlement, we see that Halifax's somewhat nebulous outlook on Europe had been brutally clarified by the realities of office. He realized now that Hitler could not be appeased by a colonial offer, and that the threat to France and England must be met by strong defence, but he had not yet expressed the belief that any further aggression by Germany would constitute a direct threat to British security. His later thinking before Munich was influenced by the belief that the Prime Minister and he had received a fatal heritage; that owing to the lethargy of their predecessors the country was naked and vulnerable to attack, and that to resort to war in 1938 would be a desperate gamble against odds which could not be entertained by men responsible for making the decision. It is likely too that he agreed with Chamberlain that war would be in itself a disastrous admission of failure which would disrupt the Empire, ruin the country and end civilization. He thought that by exercising his powers as he could he might influence events, and so he stayed.

Although Halifax described Munich as a 'horrible business', he believed to the end of his days that the decision was right. He was not at the time nor afterwards oppressed by a sense of guilt, and could he have retraced his steps would not have acted differently. In his considered opinion:

'When all has been said, one fact remains dominant and unchallengeable. When war did come a year later it found a country and Commonwealth

[1] Sir Reginald Leeper to author.
[2] R. A. Butler to author.

wholly united within itself, convinced to the foundations of soul and conscience that every conceivable effort had been made to find the way of sparing
Europe the ordeal of war, and that no alternative remained. And that was the
big thing that Chamberlain did.'[1]

[1] Haljfax. Op. cit., p. 198.

CHAPTER XXVI

THE TWILIGHT PERIOD

NEITHER shame nor anger, nor the criticism that followed the relief of Munich weakened the faith of the Prime Minister in the policy of appeasement, and his determination to continue applying it. It endured through the winter of 1938–39, sustained by infusions of spurious optimism from the Prime Minister's Office frequently over the protests of Lord Halifax. For the Foreign Secretary had by now few illusions about what was in store, and was urging a more intensive rearmament upon the Prime Minister, although not with the vigour which the situation demanded, and certainly not to the point of threatening resignation.

In this twilight period between the Agreement at Munich and the occupation of Prague Chamberlain and Halifax had hardly concluded their defence of the Settlement when Hitler made a speech at Saarbrücken in which with incredible effrontery he threatened that if the present administration in England were to be replaced by such men as Churchill, Eden or Duff Cooper, it would be impossible to maintain friendly relations between the two countries. On 1 November the Prime Minister told the House of Commons that to criticize Munich was to 'foul their own nest'; and on the following day the German and Italian Foreign Ministers Ribbentrop and Ciano met at the Belvedere Palace in Vienna, and settled the Hungarian claims on Czechoslovakia without any reference to Chamberlain or Daladier.

Now it was seen of what value to the Czechs was that 'guarantee' which had been extolled in Parliament as a shield and buckler to the prostrate state. The 'Vienna Award' was a flagrant breach of the Munich Agreement, but far from protesting the Government expressed relief at a possible danger averted, and denied that they had ever guaranteed the frontiers of Czechoslovakia, but had only given a general guarantee against 'unprovoked aggression'. So indifferent indeed was Chamberlain to this further mutilation of Czechoslovakia that on the day on which it occurred he told the House of Commons that 'the time was ripe to take a further step forward in the policy of appeasement', and to bring into force the Anglo-Italian Agreement concluded in the previous April, the issue over which Eden had resigned.

On 7 November the Government were given yet another sickening glimpse of the true character of the men opposed to them, when the Jewish *pogroms*

which followed the murder of a German diplomat by a half-mad Jewish boy
sent a shiver of horror round the civilized world. But the Prime Minister
still refused to be discouraged or turned from his path. His inflexible mind
had determined its policy. He had negotiated Munich, and was convinced
that he alone had prevented war; he still believed in Hitler's word, and
was blinkered against criticism. With the same disastrous *naïveté* that
would later cause President Roosevelt to 'have a hunch that I can make a
deal with Uncle Joe', Chamberlain believed that there was an affinity between himself and the German Chancellor denied to other men, and when
reminded of that trail of violated pledges had said: 'Ah, but this time he has
given his promise to me.' 'Europe is settling down to a more peaceful state,'
he said at the Guildhall on the day before the *pogroms* began.

If England was bewildered by the sunny pronouncements of her leaders,
and the stark events in Europe which appeared so sharply to belie them,
France, where Bonnet was beginning a process of wholesale appeasement
with Hitler more yielding even than Munich, was in a state of moral collapse.[1] The depression of the French was increased by the assurance given
by Chamberlain to Parliament that in spite of the deficiencies revealed by the
Munich crisis, there was no intention of applying industrial or military conscription. It was not therefore surprising that when Chamberlain and
Halifax visited Paris on 23 November, they were not only greeted with cries
of 'Vive Eden', and 'A bas Munich', but also by a sullen French Cabinet
anxious about the tenuous nature of the potential British military contribution to a war, and demanding an increase in the size of the Expeditionary
Force that would be sent overseas in case of emergency. Chamberlain was not
in a position to answer these questions to the satisfaction of the French
since he was not yet able or willing to impose conscription, and contented
himself with a request that France should address herself at once to rectifying
her deplorable weakness in the air.[2]

Three days after their return from Paris the Foreign Office announced
that Chamberlain and Halifax would pay a visit to Rome in the first half of
January. The Duce had declared that he would welcome the visit 'in principle', and two days after he had done so a demonstration was clumsily stage-
managed in the Italian Chamber with transparent official backing, for the
claims of Italy on French territory in the Mediterranean. Shouts of 'Tunisia!
Corsica! Nice! and Savoy!' were raised by members of the Fascist Party,
and the session ended in pandemonium. It was a ridiculous scene, but it had
its effect in France where Daladier, on 5 December, announced his intention
'to ensure respect by any means for the absolute integrity of all territories
flying the national flag'.

It was in these unpromising circumstances that Chamberlain and Halifax
made their journey to Rome on 11 January 1939. The Foreign Secretary

[1] Wheeler-Bennett. Op. cit., pp. 300–1.   [2] Ibid.

IN ROME, 1939, WITH NEVILLE CHAMBERLAIN, MUSSOLINI AND CIANO

thought that on the whole this visit had done good, and he was much struck by the obvious goodwill of the Italian crowds who disliked Mussolini's association with Hitler, and desired to show their feelings in no uncertain manner. Edward endured the social demands that were made upon him with his usual patience. At an official banquet they were received by the Duce wearing the Order of the Bath. He was accompanied by his daughter Edda.

'I reminded the latter,' Edward said, 'of the time that she had dined with us in India, though I did not remind her of the report of her having kicked a young subaltern in the stomach who had tried to kiss her at some moonlight entertainment at Humayun's Tomb.' His abiding memory of the visits to Mussolini was of passing through ranks of Blackshirts standing to attention with drawn daggers into which he felt in constant danger of running his throat. The talks were desultory, and the host civil but evasive, and Edward's description of Mussolini in a subsequent note on the talks, suggested that little suspicion of his duplicity had entered the Foreign Secretary's mind.

'The atmosphere was most friendly and easy. My impressions of what I expected to find were quite at fault. Mussolini spoke quite quietly, very reasonably, and so far as I could judge, with sincerity.'

But the conversations made little progress. After the usual preliminaries, the Prime Minister asked Mussolini if he could give him any reassurance about the menacing German activities which seemed to presage an attack at no distant date, on the Ukraine, Poland, or Russia, and were keeping the whole of Europe in a state of nervous anticipation, and driving every country into increased programmes of rearmament. Mussolini appeared to consider his answer carefully, as well he might, and replied slowly and with pauses between the sentences[1] that Hitler's armaments were for purely defensive purposes, and that he desired a long period of peace to 'fuse together the component parts of the expanded Reich, and develop its productive forces'. The situation between Germany and Poland had been greatly improved, and the stories of a German move eastward were in his view without foundation, and had been probably started by propagandists. Mussolini did not believe that Hitler had any intention of setting up a separate Ukraine or of disrupting Russia:

'As to any idea of a German attack in the West, such a thing was absolutely out of the question. Hitler would never send the youth of Germany to fall on the frontier which he regards as already decided.'[2]

The Prime Minister and Halifax were not satisfied by this fatuous explanation, and Chamberlain pointed out that Germany could not conceivably want further armaments for defensive purposes. 'What then did she want them for?'

[1] Hickleton Papers, Rome Visit, 1939.   [2] Ibid.

Mussolini replied that the Germans had to take into account the possibility that there might be another anti-German coalition like that which had crushed her in 1918. And with that they had to be content, although as to the rest, Edward thought:

'Mussolini's attitude towards the French questions was much more restrained than I had expected, and I am left with a pretty clear feeling that so far as Mussolini is concerned, he does not want to embark on any policy of adventures endangering peace, but I also felt that he was not nearly so sure of his big brother in Germany and his apologia for German rearmament was frankly unconvincing.'

Apart from these frustrating encounters the British Ministers spent much time at banquets and receptions, and on conducted tours. For formal occasions they wore morning coats, and this dull plumage was in striking contrast to the peacock glitter of the uniforms of the Dictator's Fascist entourage, causing one observer to say that they resembled a pair of undertakers' mutes. Their two days of general conversation were described by Count Ciano to Ribbentrop on the telephone as 'an innocuous farce'. Such was the degree of contempt now felt for His Majesty's Government by this upstart little voluptuary and his perfidious father-in-law.

The visit, in Mussolini's eyes, in fact marked the quiet interment of the attempt to win him over to which Chamberlain had devoted the last two years. Although the fruits of Munich were already turning sour in the mouths of the general public, the Prime Minister still appeared to cling to the belief that Germany had reached the point of satiation, and was contemplating a long digestive period. It is clear from the Italian conversations that Chamberlain, when affairs had reached this stage, was not as naïve as his public utterances would suggest, and was now acutely anxious as to what Germany's next aggressive step might be, but he found it impossible to admit to the people that his whole policy had been based on a vast misconception, and must soon be radically refashioned. Therefore, in the face of the most strident warnings, he refused to admit alarm. On 30 January 1939, Hitler told the Reichstag:

'In the future, we shall not tolerate the Western Powers attempting to interfere in certain matters which concern nobody except ourselves in order to hinder natural and reasonable solutions by their intervention.'

Nothing could have been clearer than that, but the Prime Minister refused to place a sinister construction upon the words:

'I very definitely got the impression,' he said, 'that it was not the speech of a man who was preparing to throw Europe into another crisis. It seemed to me that there were many passages in the speech which indicated the necessity of peace for Germany. . . .'[1]

He continued this lullaby when on 10 March he told Press corres-

[1] *Hansard*, House of Commons, 31 January 1939, Col. 81.

pondents that 'Europe was settling down to a period of tranquillity', and on the same day Sir Samuel Hoare denounced the 'jitterbugs' who were predicting war, and offered to an audience of his constituents in Chelsea, the glowing vision of a Golden Age. A complacency so suicidal reminds us almost of the death-wish of the lemmings, and it was strengthened by infusions of optimism in the Press inspired by the Prime Minister's office at No. 10 Downing Street over which Sir Horace Wilson presided with iron control and all the resources of the State. It was from here, and not from the Foreign Office, as some thought, that there bubbled up this refreshing spring. Halifax did not lend himself to this seductive process:

'The inspiration,' wrote John Wheeler-Bennett, 'was alleged to come from the Foreign Office and there was much talk among the less well-informed, though well-intentioned, critics of the Government of this broad-shouldered whipping-boy of Whitehall being continually "taken by surprise". But the Foreign Office was not sleeping. From each of its European outposts there came "ancestral voices prophesying war", and soon Lord Halifax was sharing the view held far earlier by a number of his officials that a new outbreak of the *furor teutonicus* was upon them.'[1]

*   *   *

Hitler was furious at having been baulked at Munich of a sensational war, and the savage elation of an entry into Prague and the palace of the Bohemian Kings. That blood-lust predominant in all the raging energies of his being had been frustrated; the 'devil had been caged, and it came out roaring'. He was contemptuous of any response by the Allied Powers, for had he not 'experienced those worms at Munich'? Profiting from internal divisions in Czechoslovakia, Hitler delivered the *coup de grâce* on 15 March. We need not linger over the manner in which he encouraged Slovakia and Ruthenia to proclaim their independence under German tutelage, nor of how the aged President Hácha was summoned to Berlin to a reception ranging from a bouquet of flowers at the railway-station to a hypodermic syringe in the small hours of the next morning. This miserable old man, grey with fatigue, and under the threat that Prague would be laid in ashes, signed a treaty at 4.30 a.m. which placed his country under German 'protection'. The German Army at once moved into Czechoslovakia; Prague was occupied by nine that morning, and 'Bohemia-Moravia' declared a German Protectorate. And when the Gestapo with its ghastly apparatus of torture followed in the wake of the army it would have been far better for Czechoslovakia if Hitler had been able to carry out his threat to wipe her off the map.

Hitler had never intended, as he later admitted to his generals, to abide by

[1] Wheeler-Bennett. Op. cit., p. 329.

his word at Munich, since the complete occupation of Czechoslovakia was an essential preliminary to further conquests in Poland, Russia or Rumania. The Czech Army was now disbanded, and all its arsenals and military equipment seized. Warned by the fate of her neighbour Rumania hastened to conclude a trade agreement which gave Germany effective control over her economic life.

This blinding revelation of Hitler's villainy had the remarkable effect of causing the scales to fall simultaneously from the eyes of the Prime Minister, Sir Nevile Henderson and the Editor of *The Times*. Yet in Parliament Chamberlain did not at first seem to be greatly disturbed, and treated angry questions both from the Opposition and from his own side in a manner approaching levity, and on the afternoon of 15 March when Hitler was making his triumphal entry into Prague refused to admit that Britain's previous guarantee to Czechoslovakia could be held applicable to something that had ceased to exist.

It was at this point that Halifax asserted himself, and imposed his will on the Prime Minister. He had supported Chamberlain without reservations in the policy that led to Munich, but already, by the time that settlement was concluded, his earlier hopes had vanished. It was then that he had told the Prime Minister that he must strengthen his Government by the inclusion of such men as Churchill and Eden, and the leaders of the other parties; he had pressed upon him a measure of conscription. In both these appeals he had failed:

'He had gone along as far as loyalty demanded—and some thought farther —in his approval of the Prime Minister's attitude, but he was not prepared to see the Conservative Party founder on the rock of personal obstinacy. He had been ready to serve as the chief mate in the barque of appeasement but he had never nailed his colours to the mast.'[1]

He put the issue before Chamberlain with all the force at his command. By nature prone to over-caution, he now told the Prime Minister that the moment had come when Britain's attitude to further German aggression must be forcefully proclaimed, and that the Party, the House of Commons, and above all the British people demanded that this should be done with no further delay. The Prime Minister was to make a speech at Birmingham on 17 March on the eve of his seventieth birthday, said Halifax; he must seize the opportunity of this much-advertised occasion to make the policy of the Government plain. If he failed to do so he must expect insurrection both in the Conservative Party and the House of Commons. Chamberlain was not an easy man to dissuade from his convictions, and it says much for Halifax's vigour that his advice was accepted, and the Prime Minister's speech amended before his departure for Birmingham.

Halifax's own speech on the crisis in the House of Lords on 15 March

[1] Wheeler-Bennett. Op. cit., pp. 354-5.

had given little indication of this hardening of outlook. He had recited the course of events without comment, describing how the Slovak Diet had declared the independence of Slovakia, and how a new Government had been formed under Dr. Tiso. When he came to the famous guarantee he gave the Government's decision, having first explained how the British Government had tried in vain to achieve an agreement with the other Governments represented at Munich about its scope and terms:

'In our opinion the situation was radically altered as soon as the Slovak Diet declared the independence of Slovakia. The effect of this declaration was to put to an end by internal disruption to the State whose frontiers we had proposed to guarantee, and accordingly the state of affairs described by Sir Thomas Inskip, which was always regarded by us as being only of a transitory nature, has now ceased to exist, and His Majesty's Government cannot accordingly hold themselves any longer bound by this obligation.'

The only positive step he announced was the decision to postpone the visit of the President of the Board of Trade to Germany, and his general references to this shameless breach of the Munich Agreement were mild and non-committal:

'I do not want to make any specific charges as to breach of faith, but I cannot admit that anything of the kind that has now taken place was in our minds at the time of Munich or was in any way contemplated. . . . They [the Germans] have now, without so far as I know any communication with the other three signatories of the Munich Agreement, sent their troops beyond the frontier there laid down. Even though it may now be claimed that what has taken place has occurred with the acquiescence of the Czech Government, I cannot but regard it as inconsistent with the spirit of the Munich Agreement. . . . These events cannot fail to be a cause of disturbance to the international situation. They are bound to administer a shock to confidence, all the more regrettable since confidence was beginning to revive and offer the prospect of concrete measures which would be of general benefit. Unless there is some material change in the situation as it now appears, there must inevitably be a postponement of these measures.'[1]

This was the old language of appeasement, and it can be explained only on the grounds that Halifax did not think that any action could now be taken to stop Hitler occupying Czechoslovakia and had therefore written off that country, and proposed to concentrate his new-found vigour in opposing Hitler's next aggressive move. But if he spoke weakly in the House of Lords, he used very different language when the German Ambassador called on him in the Foreign Office the same day. Herr von Dirksen was not one of the more appealing members of his race, and the Foreign Secretary treated him with an icy severity. Had the Ambassador not been a man destitute of

[1] *Hansard*, House of Lords, 15 March 1939, Vol. 12, Col. 214–18.

humour he must have found something inexpressibly droll in his own opening remarks in which he hoped that the Foreign Secretary would agree that
the recent German action had been a contribution to the re-establishment of
peace and order.

Having listened to his dreary justification of events Halifax addressed the
Ambassador in measured and cutting terms. What had taken place, he said,
was in flat contradiction of the Munich Agreement which had contemplated
that if such measures affecting the whole structure of European confidence
were to arise they would be settled by consultation and not by this method of
the naked application of force. Hitler had publicly stated the day after
Munich that he had no more territorial ambitions and on the morrow of that
declaration the world saw action of an exactly different kind. The immediate
result was that everyone felt the assurances of the German Government to be
worthless, and asked themselves where and when the next blow was going to
fall:

'I could well understand Herr Hitler's taste for bloodless victories, but
one of these days he would find himself up against something that would not
be bloodless; and recent events would certainly have made opinion in many
parts of the world feel that this kind of thing was a good deal more probable
than they had previously hoped, and they would make their plans accordingly. The German Government must have weighed all these consequences,
and the conclusion that everyone in this country and far outside it would
draw must be that they had no great desire to establish good relations with
this country, that they were prepared to disregard world opinion, and were
seeking to establish a position in which they could by force dominate Europe,
and if possible, the world.'

Twelve days after the German Army had entered Czechoslovakia he
attended a meeting of the Foreign Policy Committee of the Cabinet where he
expressed the view that it was unlikely that Great Britain and France could
prevent Poland and Rumania from being overwhelmed. The Government,
he argued, was therefore faced with the alternatives of remaining inactive or
embarking on a devastating war. If they remained inactive they would be up
against greatly increased German power, while sympathy and support for
Britain in America, South Eastern Europe and elsewhere would be greatly
reduced. In these circumstances, concluded the Foreign Secretary, if it came
to a choice between two evils, his choice would be war.

*   *   *

Although Chamberlain's speech at Birmingham on 17 March marked the
beginning of a new chapter in British foreign policy, it did so in a somewhat
peculiar manner. It was of course galling to his self-esteem to discover that
for two years he had been so indecorously led by the nose by the German

Chancellor, and there was in his speech a note of petulance, as of some alderman on whom a shabby trick had been played by a colleague he was inclined to trust. There was no searching of the heart over past actions, no suggestion that the policy of appeasement had failed, no contrition, no recantation. But with all its limitations the speech was a landmark and many who listened to it felt happiness at the thought that a supine policy had at last come to an end.

It was now necessary to make preparations of a hurried character in time to meet the next challenge. An opening seemed to have been provided by a speech of Stalin's on 10 March, in which he suggested in sarcastic language that nothing would please England and France more than to see Russia involved in a war with Germany, and accused them of having betrayed the principle of Collective Security in favour of a policy of cowardly neutralism.

The references to Collective Security encouraged the Government to think that in spite of the astringency of the speech it might still not be too late to bring Russia within the fold. It was Halifax who again took the initiative in trying to bring this happy reconciliation into being. It was he who authorized Sir Robert Vansittart to consult with the Russian Ambassador Maisky on the obvious threat that was now disclosed to Poland, and he who instituted inquiries in Moscow about the attitude the Soviet Government intended to adopt towards the strategic dangers now facing Eastern Europe.[1]

In response to these advances, the Russian Government proposed on 18 March a conference of the British, French, Russian, Polish, Rumanian and Turkish Governments to discuss the organization of resistance of aggression against any one of their countries. Lord Halifax is believed to have welcomed this proposal which seemed to him to show a willingness on the part of Russia to play her part in a combination against Hitler, but other members of the Cabinet believed that it might lead them into those 'unspecified commitments' they had always shunned, and the proposal was overruled as 'premature'. Premature. It was growing very late in the day for the use of that ominous word.

Instead Chamberlain proposed on 21 March that a declaration should be made by Britain, France, Russia and Poland that they would act together if there were symptoms of new aggressions by Germany. But Poland and Russia were alienated from one another by the memories of historical strife and the bitterness of disputed territory. Each could produce compelling arguments against the other, but the hard fact remained that Poland, thrice partitioned, feared Russia far more than Germany, and this mistrust blinded her to her own mortal danger from another quarter. The Poles refused this suggestion because they knew that to reach the theatre of war the Russian Army must march through Poland, and they believed that once in the country it would never leave it.

[1] Wheeler-Bennett. Op. cit., p. 367.

15

The next few days brought alarming indications of Hitler's designs on Poland, and it was clear that she was the next object of the dictator's aggressive purpose. On 21 March the Polish Ambassador in Berlin was summoned by Ribbentrop, and confronted by a set of grievances and demands, as familiar in language as those that had preceded them. The Free City of Danzig must be ceded to Germany and a settlement must be reached over the Polish Corridor. Troop movements were already reported. On 22 March Memel was ceded by Lithuania to Germany on the threat of immediate occupation, and Poland appealed for help.

This time the Prime Minister moved with astonishing speed. Even before the Polish Foreign Minister Colonel Beck arrived in London for consultations Chamberlain startled the House of Commons and the world outside by announcing that pending wider negotiations with other Powers he had given Poland an assurance of the full support of Great Britain in the event of any attack on her independence. This was later converted, during Beck's visit, into a bilateral agreement in which the support of Great Britain extended even to German attempts to undermine Poland's independence by economic penetration. Similar guarantees were later to be given to Rumania and Greece, in a last-minute attempt to shore up two other threatened countries. Meanwhile Mussolini's dictator's paranoia had been fretted beyond endurance by the Napoleonic progress of a man whom he regarded as his disciple, but who had sadly outgrown his tutelage. On 7 April he invaded Albania, tastefully choosing Good Friday as a suitable day for this paltry triumph. In May an Anglo-Turkish Declaration proclaimed that the two countries would take joint action against any aggression in the Mediterranean.

These actions gave the Prime Minister's opponents an ample field for comment, of which they were not slow to avail themselves. They pointed out that six months before Chamberlain had rejected every plea for standing by Czechoslovakia on the grounds that nothing we could do could save that state from destruction, and that even after a victorious European war the old frontiers would not be redrawn. They argued that we were now in every way in an inferior position to help Poland who was far worse situated to defend herself than Czechoslovakia; that in 1938 the Government had been willing to coerce that country into surrendering to a claim that dismembered and destroyed her. This time no concessions were demanded of the Polish Government which was presented with a *carte blanche* which left no room for diplomatic manœuvre.

The Government had now come round full circle. From appeasement they had passed to challenge, and to those foreign commitments they had been so anxious to avoid. Both Halifax and Chamberlain had come to feel that it was unendurable to go on waiting for the next blow, and the agonizing search which ensued, too late, for a way to parry it. They wanted to set up a signpost, or danger warning, so that if that was ignored the decision would be out of their hands, and the suspense over. The decision was hastened by news from Germany brought by Mr. Ian Colvin[1] who had been in touch with German Generals hostile to Hitler, and wished to propose some positive action to the Foreign Secretary. He was taken to see him by Sir Alexander Cadogan, and by Sir Reginald Leeper, who found Halifax 'most impressed, and itching to do something'. Colvin was taken on at once to see Chamberlain, and in Cadogan's opinion his story 'provided the last straw, and the guarantee to Poland followed very shortly after'.[2]

It is interesting to see the manner in which Halifax justified the new departure. His views are contained in an unpublished memorandum in which he defended the policy for which he had been so largely responsible against the attacks which have been enumerated above.

In this document Halifax argued that if war had come in 1938: 'South Africa had decided to remain neutral; a powerful opposition in Australia had declared against participation, and the attitude of Canada was uncertain. So the British Commonwealth, which was unanimously behind war in September 1939, would certainly not have been united for war in 1938.' He described how the change of policy had come about as the consequence of Hitler's rape of Czechoslovakia which exposed his purpose of dominating Europe and convinced the Dominions that he must be resisted.

It might still be possible to deter him from its execution if, as she had failed to do in 1914, Great Britain made it unmistakably clear that the particular acts of aggression he was believed to have in mind would result in a general war. And if the event showed that Hitler was not to be restrained, it was better that the nations under threat should stand and fight together than that they should await German attack one by one. With regard to the practical worth of such guarantees, Halifax emphasized that neither the Polish nor the Rumanian Government was under any illusion as to the measure of concrete help that they might expect from Great Britain in the event of Hitler choosing war. For them, he argued, as for us, the guarantees were the best chance, and indeed the only chance, of warning him off that decision.

'Why then, granted the guarantees, was it not possible to associate Russia with them, and so give them greater operative power? For months through 1939, the British and French Governments laboured to get Moscow, Warsaw and Bucharest to reach accord in this sense. Their efforts failed, and for a variety of reasons on the side of the Polish and Rumanian Governments, neither was prepared to accept the relationship with the Soviet Government that such policy involved. An inherited, and not unnatural suspicion of Russia dominated their thought, in which the acceptance of Soviet protection seemed only too likely to supply the excuse for Soviet penetration. Their

[1] The distinguished journalist later on the staff of the *Daily Telegraph*.
[2] Sir Alexander Cadogan to author.

fear of the Soviet was at least as great, and probably greater, than their fear of Germany. An intelligent rabbit would hardly be expected to welcome the protection of an animal ten times its own size, whom it credited with the habits of a boa-constrictor.'

Halifax went on to say that he had never agreed with those who argued that by refusing to yield to the Soviet on points arising in the negotiations concerning the Baltic States, Poland or Rumania, the Government had confirmed the Russian leaders in their mistrust of British policy and driven them to make an accommodation with Hitler:

'I never believed in 1939 that this was a correct diagnosis, nor has anything that has happened since given me cause to change my view. I thought that Russian policy then, as now, was entirely inspired by what Stalin judged to be in Russia's interest, and that the largest element in the mind of the Kremlin was the imperative necessity of buying time. This, to complete the Soviet five-year plan, restore the army, develop industry, and so on, against the evil day which was probably bound to come.

'And every argument that is used against Mr. Chamberlain in regard to British and French unpreparedness and consequent incapacity to give fighting reality to the Polish guarantee was surely in Soviet thought, and from the Soviet point of view, there must have seemed singularly little to set against the very real danger of exposing themselves at that moment to German attack. For these reasons I gravely doubt whether anything that we or the French could have said or done would have had the smallest effect in leading Russia to accept a position calculated to invite sharp and early reaction from the German side.'[1]

*   *   *

Even at this extreme moment the Prime Minister remained reluctant to sanction the obvious measures of preparation which the situation demanded. He had, perhaps, not grasped the full scale of Hitler's armaments and was satisfied that the British programme was as thorough as could be expected. And so, in normal conditions it would certainly have been held, for the increase in armaments judged by past standards was substantial. The defence estimates of March were nearly £600,000,000, and it was announced that the proposed metropolitan Air Establishment of 2,370 first-line aircraft would be reached during the year. By the end of 1939 it had risen to 9,000. The Navy had been greatly strengthened, while the Secretary of State for War claimed on 8 March that his plans envisaged six Regular divisions, of which two were to be armoured, and thirteen Territorial divisions. Three weeks after Prague he announced that the establishment of the Territorial Army was to be doubled.

[1] Hickleton Papers.

So far, in view of the danger, all this had been merely toying with the situation. The Prime Minister refused to appoint a Minister of Munitions, as he had before refused a Ministry of Supply. But on 26 April he made the startling announcement that the Government would introduce a measure for conscription. Since this proposal involved no more than the calling up for six months' military training of all men of the ages of 20–21, it could have no immediate effect upon the armed strength of Great Britain, but to impose conscription in peacetime was an extraordinary departure from the traditions of the past, and a clear sign that the Government realized that they would face war at no distant date. It was bitterly opposed by the Labour Party.

In Germany everything was now ready for an attack on Poland, and Hitler was not to be deterred by this or any other gesture of warning. His only problem was, if possible, to isolate Poland. On 28 April he demanded the return of Danzig, and denounced the German-Polish treaty he had concluded with Pilsudski in 1934 with devout promises of vistas of unending friendship, and on 6 May he embraced Mussolini in the so-called 'Pact of Steel'. Few now doubted that war was coming, and the spring and summer of that year were a time of waiting. To Halifax it was a far less trying period than 1938. In that nerve-racking year, although he never betrayed it to others, even his incredible composure had sometimes been badly shaken. Now that he was certain that war was coming he awaited it with calmness, and indeed with relief.

The summer was occupied with protracted and fruitless efforts to bring Russia into the alliance. Chamberlain having rejected the Russian proposals of 18 March turned again on 14 April to resume his courtship of this evasive creature. The British request was that a declaration should be made that if Britain and France were 'involved in hostilities' following their guarantees of Poland and Rumania, the Soviet Government would come to their assistance.

The Russians had responded to this suggestion with a proposal of a pact of mutual assistance between Britain, France and Russia, and a guarantee to all the border states from the Baltic to the Black Sea. But in the face of the violent objections of the smaller powers, and their terror of Russian 'protection', the Government, unless they were prepared to repeat the ruthless pressure they had applied to Czechoslovakia, had no option but to reject the Russian terms on 1 May, and return to their original proposals. The result of this action was the replacement of Litvinov by Molotov, a man far more suspicious and implacable, who reminded Halifax of 'smiling granite', and the cautious beginnings of an approach by Germany to Russia by way of a trade agreement.

In spite of these reverses the British and French Governments opened discussions with Russia on 27 May through their ambassadors in Moscow.

The British Government has been much criticized for the dilatory manner in which these negotiations were conducted, and the lack of urgency that marked their progress throughout. Halifax was invited by Molotov to go to Moscow, but refused, sending instead Strang to help the Ambassador Sir William Seeds who was in charge of the negotiations, and it was thought that the despatch of an official, however distinguished, on such a critical occasion was no substitute for the Foreign Secretary. Nor did it escape attention that Chamberlain, who had flown three times to see Hitler, betrayed no eagerness to establish contact with Stalin. And when on Molotov's insistence it was agreed on 27 July to send a military mission to Russia, on the pretext that a military agreement should precede a political one, the mission did not leave London until 5 August, and after an unhurried cruise in the Baltic reached Moscow on 11 August.

We cannot tell with certainty why Halifax refused to go to Moscow, and it may well have been, as Wheeler-Bennett suggests 'that the risk of failure was too great; that if the British Foreign Secretary went to Moscow and failed to reach agreement it would prove too great a source of satisfaction to Hitler'. However this may be, Halifax was to record his regret two years later that he had not made a warmer response to Russian overtures when it was still possible. When Ambassador in Washington in 1941, he wrote in his diary:

'I am just reading a book by Joseph Davies who was American Ambassador to Moscow in 1936–39. I am pretty clear that if circumstances had permitted us to make a firm alliance with Russia, ignoring all considerations that made this difficult, they would not improbably have come down on that side. It was a mistake; we mustn't make it again.' But this, and the other signs of a lack of serious purpose, could easily be construed as diplomatic errors, and have been used against the Government to explain the failure of these negotiations.

Yet however tactless and clumsy the behaviour of the Government may have been, it is ridiculous to suppose that it produced the slightest effect upon the outcome of the discussions. Indeed the appearance in Moscow of the Prime Minister, the Foreign Secretary, and the Imperial General Staff in a body would not have caused the Soviet Government to be deflected by an inch from a policy which was solely, and naturally, concerned with the forwarding of their own interests, and the preservation of their state.

The roots of their profound suspicion were deeply embedded in the past; they had found lodgment in those days after the last war when Bolshevik Russia had been the leper of Europe against whom a *cordon sanitaire* had been drawn. For twenty years mutual dislike and distrust had persisted between the ruling classes of Great Britain and Russia, and each attributed sinister motives to the other, the Soviet leaders doubting the will of the Western Powers to wage war, and wondering if it was their intention to direct Hitler against the East, and allow his armies to exhaust themselves in the bogs of the Ukraine.

New barriers had been raised between the two countries by the events of 1938, when England and France had made humiliating terms with the capitalist aggressor, and excluded Russia from Munich. Was there not a likelihood of this process being repeated? Above all the Russians, like the British, were painfully conscious of their unreadiness for war, and the necessity for gaining time. If they became involved in war now, and had pledged themselves to join England and France, the prospect, in their eyes, cannot have been an inviting one. They were in grave doubt of the serious intentions of the allies to fight Germany, and even if they did, in Sir Lewis Namier's words:

'The assurance, repeatedly given, that they [the Russians] would not be expected to enter the war till after the Western Powers had done so, was hardly sufficient. Were the Germans to attack in the East, patrol activities in the Saar would have been to the Russians of as little comfort as, in effect, they were to the Poles. If the French meant to remain behind the Maginot Line, and the British to operate mainly at sea, in the absence of an active Second Front the brunt of resistance would fall on Russia—and she, for one, must have had a fair idea of the material unpreparedness of the Polish Army. Suspicion, justified and unjustified, whispered caution into Russian ears.'[1]

The negotiations[2] dragged on from 27 May to the outbreak of war. At the end of June Halifax made a speech at the annual dinner of the Royal Institute of International Affairs at Chatham House which defined British policy in broad terms and which met with general approval.

'British policy,' he said, 'rests on twin foundations of purpose. One is determination to resist force. The other is our recognition of the world's desire to get on with the constructive work of building peace. If we could once be satisfied that the intention of others were the same as our own and that we all really wanted peaceful solutions—then I say here definitely, we could discuss the problems that are today causing the world anxiety. In such a new atmosphere we could examine the Colonial problem, the problem of raw materials, trade barriers, the issue of *Lebensraum*, the limitation of armaments, and any other issue that affects the lives of all European citizens.

'But this is not the position which we face today. The threat of military force is holding the world to ransom, and our immediate task is—and here I end as I began—to resist aggression.'

There were protracted wrangles in the negotiations with the Russians

[1] Sir Lewis Namier, *Diplomatic Prelude*, p. 150.
[2] For details of the Anglo-Soviet negotiations see *Documents on British Foreign Policy, 1919–1939*, Vol. VI. Also L. B. Namier, *Diplomatic Prelude*; J. W. Wheeler-Bennett, *Munich*, Part 4, Chapter 11. *The Russian Sphinx*, and Lord Strang, *Home and Abroad*, Chapter V.

about the definition of 'indirect aggression', about the circumstances in which the pact might be invoked, about which countries were to receive guarantees. The British and French, anxious to reach agreement, yielded on many of the points raised by the Soviet negotiators. From the 12 August the Germans were also in the bidding, and from that moment the negotiations began to resemble a four-handed game of poker, for by that date the Russians had given the German Government to understand that they were now ready to respond to those overtures for political talks that had first been made by Germany in mid-July.

A fatal obstacle to a military agreement between Russia and the Allies, even if the former had intended it, was the categorical refusal of Poland and Rumania to allow the passage of Russian troops over their territory, although it is possible that the British Government might have been prepared to apply greater pressure to those countries had their intelligence services provided them with a more realistic appraisal of Russian strength. Now it was the Germans who were desperate for an accommodation with Russia in order to neutralize that formidable power in time for the operation against Poland. The Russians, in the words of a historian of this period:

'were ready, but not too ready to reciprocate. Too early a breach with Britain and France would put them at Hitler's mercy; too early an agreement with Hitler might lead the Western Powers to give Hitler another bloodless conquest and reopen the possibility of a coalition against Russia. For Russia's safety both sets of negotiations must be kept going until as near as possible to the time when Hitler must, if at all, start his attack on Poland: the classic time for beginning war, around 1 September, between the gathering of the harvest and the coming of autumn rains.'[1]

There is no need and little temptation to linger in any detail over the glutinous knavery that surrounded the German-Soviet Non-Aggression Pact. The writing was on the wall when a Russo-German trade agreement was signed on 19 August. This had been preceded by a message from Hitler the day before requesting in urgent terms that Stalin should invite Ribbentrop without delay to Moscow for political conversations. After the logistics necessary to their safety had been calculated by the Russian leaders, they invited Ribbentrop to visit them on 26 August, but this was too late for the Führer's time-table, and a frantic telegram was sent on the 21st asking for the date to be advanced.

Eventually it was agreed that Ribbentrop should come on the 23rd, and the negotiations were concluded on the same day. There was indeed little to prolong them for Hitler had ordered Ribbentrop to give the Russians everything they asked for, and they had not been sparing in their demands. From this rogues' kitchen emerged immediate and even breathless assurances from the German Foreign Minister that Finland, Latvia, Estonia and Bessarabia

[1] Mowat. Op. cit., p. 643.

were for Russia to shape and refashion to her heart's desire, and the preliminary steps were taken to the fourth Partition of Poland. And on the 25 August the military conversations between the Allies and the Russians died like a decapitated snake.

CHAPTER XXVII

THE LAST ACT

WE pass now to the last act of the tragedy. War was certain, for the German-Soviet Non-Aggression Pact besides inflicting a stinging slap in the face to Franco-British diplomacy, had neutralized Russia and isolated Poland. It was Hitler's masterpiece, and it was received with horror and incredulity throughout the civilized world. It was in the second week in August, when all the news coming into the Foreign Office, official and secret, was pointing the same way that M. Birgar Dahlerus,[1] a Swedish business-man, and friend of Goering became active in efforts of mediation. He met Halifax on a number of occasions at his house in Eaton Square, seeking to convince him that his messages carried a promise of hope, from which further progress might follow. The Foreign Secretary could only repeat with almost wearisome monotony that Great Britain certainly had no wish for war if it could be avoided, but that she intended to honour her obligations to Poland, and that it was therefore for Hitler to convince the Poles of his willingness to have honest negotiations with them of an entirely different character to those with Czechoslovakia.

On 21 August a message was received from Germany suggesting that Goering should come over to London if he could be assured that he would meet the Prime Minister:

'Arrangements were accordingly set in hand for Goering to come over secretly on Wednesday the 23rd. The idea is that he should land at some deserted aerodrome, be picked up in a car and taken direct to Chequers. There the regular household is to be given *congé* and the telephone is to be disconnected. It looks as if it is going to be a dramatic interlude, and having laid the plans we await confirmation from Germany.'[2]

But no answer came until Thursday, 24 August, when a message was received that Hitler did not think that the visit would be immediately helpful. We can pass over the abortive negotiations and the false dawns of the next five days as they crept heavily on to the 1 September.

1 *September*. 'Alex [Sir Alexander Cadogan] called for me at Eaton Square about 9 and told me he had heard at 7 that Danzig had declared its incorpora-tion in the Reich, and a little later that the Germans had crossed the Polish

---

[1] For details of the activities of M. Dahlerus, see L. B. Namier, *Diplomatic Prelude*, 'An interloper in Diplomacy'.

[2] Hickleton Papers. Halifax. A record of events before the war, 1939.

frontier. On hearing this I asked the German Chargé d'Affaires and the Polish Ambassador to call upon me at No. 10. I told the German Chargé d'Affaires that we had had this news and said that if confirmed it would create a most serious situation between his Government and mine. He evinced ignorance but said he would make inquiries. The Polish Ambassador gave me further information concerning the German invasion, and asked me whether our pledge to Poland would operate. I told him that if the facts were as stated, I had no doubt that we should have no difficulty in deciding that our guarantee must at once come into force.'

Statements were made in both Houses, that in the House of Lords by Halifax, and Sir Nevile Henderson was instructed to call on Ribbentrop that evening and to issue a warning, but not an ultimatum, in which the German Government were called upon to withdraw their troops from Poland:

'He did not in fact say this to the German Government but I said it to Ciano the following day.'[1]

But all next day, the 2 September, it seemed to the tense and expectant nation that while the German armies were advancing in Poland their own Government was in a state of suspended action, and there was a long and ominous silence heavy with suspicion and conjecture. We can trace the happenings of that day as they appeared to Halifax, in his private papers. There was no answer from Berlin, and the morning was occupied in making preparations for the war that now seemed inevitable. A statement was drafted for Parliament which was to meet at the usual time:

'The great difficulty was the French, who did not want to present any ultimatum until noon tomorrow, with a 48 hour time limit. At 2.30 p.m. Ciano rang me up again at the office to tell me that Mussolini wished to propose a Five-Power Conference—Germany, France, Russia, Italy and ourselves.

'I managed to rush over to the House of Commons to stop John Simon making the statement that had been prepared for 2.45 in order to give time to get in touch with the French about the Conference proposal and to synchronize with them any action we may decide to take with Germany. I never remember spending such a miserable afternoon and evening. From 3 to 5.30 we were telephoning to Bonnet who I suspect had committed himself rather further than he was willing to admit to the Conference, and to Ciano to say that we could not accept the Conference idea unless German troops were withdrawn. Ciano said it was quite useless to press that on Germany.'[2]

The Cabinet met at 4.30 p.m., and it was soon clear from their angry demeanour that they were in no mood for further delay and that they were 'pretty unanimous' in the view that the statement for which both Houses of

[1] Ibid.   [2] Ibid.

Parliament were anxiously waiting should contain a short time-limit within which the Germans should be asked to halt their invasion and withdraw their troops. It should be plainly stated that failure to do so would mean war.

'It was explained to the Cabinet,' wrote the Foreign Secretary, 'that what we were able to say must depend upon the French, who were certain to be difficult, but the Cabinet itself was in an extremely difficult mood.'

It was indeed. It was working up into a state of extreme tension and emotional anxiety at the delay, which was to be even more forcefully displayed at its later meeting that night. As soon as the first Cabinet was over, Halifax again made contact with the French Ministers, and eventually Daladier agreed to a statement being made in both Houses at seven-thirty in which the British would restate their position, but in deference to the French include no time-limit, saying only that the two Governments were in consultation on that point. The anxiety of the French to avoid a premature declaration of war was mainly due to their failure to take timely measures for the evacuation of children from Paris, and to the conviction that their capital would be bombed immediately after a declaration.

'This statement was accordingly made in both Houses, and in the House of Lords went quite well. I went back to Eaton Square and was just going out to dinner with Dorothy at 8.30 when I was rung up by the Prime Minister to ask me to go down to Downing Street at once. The statement had gone very badly, he said, in the House of Commons, people misinterpreting the inability to give a time-limit to be the result of half-heartedness and hesitation on our part, with the result that there had been a very unpleasant scene in which much feeling had been shown. I had never heard the Prime Minister so disturbed. I accordingly went straight off to No. 10 where he gave me dinner. He told me that the statement infuriated the House, and that he did not believe, unless we could clear the position, that the Government would be able to maintain itself when it met Parliament next day.'[1]

It was strange that either Chamberlain or Halifax should have been startled by the anger of the House of Commons or the bewilderment of the people who had seen Germany making war on Poland for thirty-eight hours without the slightest overt response from their Government, and Members were enraged by the Prime Minister's statement. When Arthur Greenwood, the deputy-leader of the Labour Party rose to speak, Leo Amery had cried: 'Speak for England!' in the same tones in which he was later to echo Cromwell's terrible words to the Long Parliament.

Sir Alexander Cadogan was bidden to join the dinner at No. 10, and Sir Horace Wilson was also co-opted, and afterwards, having summoned the French Ambassador M. Corbin, Halifax and Chamberlain telephoned to

[1] Ibid.

Phipps, Daladier and Bonnet in turn, exhorting the Frenchmen to agree to imposing a time-limit on Germany as short as possible.

In the meantime, after the angry protests in the House of Commons, a dejected and unofficial meeting of deeply anxious Cabinet Ministers took place in the Chancellor's room in the House—Sir John Anderson, the Lord Privy Seal, Hore-Belisha, W. S. Morrison, Malcolm MacDonald, and the Minister for Agriculture Sir Reginald Dorman-Smith who vividly described the scene. On hearing that a meeting was taking place:

'I hurried to find Sir John Anderson in the chair beside a phone directly linked to Number 10. My colleagues already there, had decided that they would not leave that room until such time as war had been declared. As we sat there and waited by the phone and nothing happened, I felt like a disembodied spirit. It didn't seem real. We were on strike.'

There were no words of recrimination:

'But there was a feeling of great emotion. All of us were getting back to our natural selves. I became more Irish, and Hore-Belisha more Jewish—talking of rights and indignities and so on. . . . As we waited we got scruffier and sweatier. I don't remember we had any food brought in.'

Eventually the call came for them to go to Downing Street:

'We got to No. 10 by now all of us really scruffy and smelly and it rather shook us to find Halifax who had been dining with the P.M. and Cadogan in evening clothes. The P.M. had evidently not changed for dinner. In we went to the Cabinet Room. Again reports are quite wrong about stormy scenes. This was a plain *diktat* from the Cabinet. . . . I remember that the P.M. was calm, even icy cold, all the time we were there. . . . I am quite certain that he was holding back now only because of the French. He was terribly worried that Paris might indeed be attacked from the air.

'But now—facing a Cabinet on a "sit-down strike" he had no alternative. The climax came most dramatically. The P.M. said quietly: "Right, gentlemen, this means war." Hardly had he said it when there was the most enormous clap of thunder, and the whole Cabinet Room was lit up by a blinding flash of lightning.'[1]

In Halifax's less colourful description of these events:

'The Cabinet met at about 11.30, and agreement was finally reached in the sense that we should instruct Henderson to deliver an ultimatum at 9 o'clock next morning, which should expire at 11 a.m. The French said they must act rather later.'[2]

At eleven-fifteen on Sunday morning, the 3 September, the Prime Minister at last declared war, but to those who listened this was no tocsin ringing to arms. There was pathos in the voice of a tired old man whose world had crashed in ruins about him, but as before there was a note of

[1] Sir Reginald Dorman-Smith, *Sunday Times*, 6 September 1964.
[2] Hickleton Papers. A record of Events before the War, 1939.

petulance, of personal betrayal: 'Everything that I have worked for, every-thing that I have hoped for, everything that I have believed in during my public life'—it all lay in ashes before his eyes. And in this manner the greatest war in the history of the world began—'not with a bang but a whimper'.

CHAPTER XXVIII

THE BEGINNINGS OF WAR

WHEN war came Edward and Dorothy were still living in Eaton Square, but soon moved to the Dorchester Hotel which for him had the advantage that it was close to a place of worship of which he was to become fond, the Grosvenor Chapel in South Audley Street, which reminded him of the chapel at Garrowby, and the notes of its bell of that of Kirby Underdale.

Chamberlain at once reorganized his Government, and on 3 September Churchill was at last admitted to the Cabinet from which he had so long been excluded, and returned to the same post he had held in 1914, that of First Lord of the Admiralty. In making this appointment Chamberlain could be certain that the magnanimity of this great man would wipe out all rancour of the past, and the bitter memories of disregarded warnings, and that he would from now look only to the future. Mr. Anthony Eden was also brought into the Government as Dominions Secretary, but the Labour and Liberal leaders refused to serve under Chamberlain so that the Government was far from national, or representative of the nation as a whole.

Edward remained at the Foreign Office where the nature of his work was completely altered. There was now little to be done by that office in the way of direct contact with enemy Governments, beyond the routine transactions which followed the rupture of relations. The necessary exchanges with Allied Powers outside the scope of the Service departments were still conducted by the Foreign Office, but its principal business henceforth was to be done with powers that were still neutral. And with many of these, he found, it was greatly increased, for at almost every point it was inevitable that war should disturb the normal life of any nation whose conduct, through commercial activity, or by reason of its geographical position, affected any of the belligerent powers:

'Agreements have to be made,' said Edward, 'conventions established; the right blend of persuasion and threat has to be found, for every case differs from every other; efforts must be made to win support, or at least stave off active alignment with the enemy; all of which takes much time, so that the Foreign Secretary is seldom idle.'

One of Edward's first important diplomatic duties was to reject the peace offensive launched by Hitler after the defeat of Poland, and in doing so he said in a broadcast to the world:

'When the challenge in the sphere of international relations is sharpened, as today in Germany by the denial to man and woman of elementary human rights, the challenge is at once extended to something instinctive and profound in the universal conscience of mankind. We are therefore fighting to maintain the rule of law and the quality of mercy in dealings between man and man and in the great society of civilized States.'[1]

Edward made many speeches during this early period, in the House of Lords, and elsewhere. For a debate in the House he would use the brief prepared for him in the Foreign Office, filling it out as he might require with suave but effective extempore replies to points made by previous speakers. Over-qualification, that worm in the apple that had enfeebled so many of his public speeches, had by no means left him. He was still capable of such a sentence as:

'I should have thought that one might say that it could reasonably be held that . . .'

His Private Secretary Valentine Lawford, who observed all his masters so closely, wrote of his occasional deviations from the Foreign Office brief:

'But when Halifax had to prepare a speech that was near to his heart— his broadcast on the purpose of war, on 7 November, 1939, and the address which he delivered as Chancellor of the University at the Sheldonian Theatre on 27 February, of the following year—he worked for long hours in solitude. Thoughts and words were largely his own; for it was almost inconceivable that a professional bureaucrat should have presumed, even if he had been trained, to frame such an un-contemporary, unbureaucratic sentence as: "For in this matter, as indeed in all life, it is finally the spiritual side that counts." '

In his speech at Oxford he tried to resolve the conflict of thought which surrounded the question of the justification of force, and to answer the views of those who held it to be both futile and negative in character. It was a question which had often exercised a mind always reflective upon moral subjects:

'Nor can I doubt,' he said, 'that if under what I hold to be a one-sided and mistaken interpretation of Our Lord's teaching we refrain on principle from replying in kind to the use of force, we may be surrendering to extinction the most sacred causes for which we stand to posterity as guardians and trustees. Thus force, by resisting the destructive power of evil and guarding the field in which good can work, can render positive service which can be given in no other way. As I see this problem which is today so tragically forced upon our thought, it is the spiritual motive, alike in national as in individual action, on which judgment has to be passed. Always it is the spirit behind the application of force which makes or mars its value.'[2]

One of the few major diplomatic successes which could be accomplished

[1] Campbell Johnson. Op. cit., p. 551.
[2] *The Challenge to Liberty*, by Viscount Halifax. Clarendon Press, Oxford, p. 12.

in this early and stagnant phase of the war was the Tripartite Treaty with France and Turkey, which was the result of careful preparation by Halifax and the Foreign Office during the summer of 1939. Italy was still neutral, but Mussolini was possessed by a consuming jealousy of his rival's progress, and by the shame of his own inactivity. Bitterly conscious of declining prestige, and eluded by the glory that was now as necessary to him as heroin to a drug addict, he was drawing ever closer to Hitler, and must soon cross his fatal Rubicon.

Edward's two eldest sons, Charles and Peter, had left in the early months of 1940 with their regiments for Palestine, where Charles was shortly joined by his wife by methods into which his father thought it better not to inquire.

Peter, a handsome young man of strong personality and intellectual promise, had just finished his time at Oxford, and in the tradition of his family had already become Master of the Exmoor Hounds. Richard left Eton in December 1939, and, still too young to serve in the army, became an attaché in the British Embassy in Rome, remaining there until Italy entered the war. After this he worked on the farm at Garrowby until he was called up in 1940. He went overseas in September 1941.

In London it soon became the practice for Ministers in the Cabinet to take three or four days off every few weeks by turn, and Edward would often spend these moments of freedom at Garrowby. There were various incidents in the war before the fall of France which affected him. The Russo-Finnish war was to bring the Foreign Office many vexing problems of neutral rights and obligations. Halifax regarded this attack as a direct consequence of German policy and refused to join the violent anti-Soviet chorus of abuse which greeted this latest outrage at the expense of a small power. The fact that Allied aid to Finland had been inadequate for her needs was due to the fact that Sweden and Norway had refused to allow British and French troops to pass through their territories. Halifax was fully justified in his warning to neutrals in December 1939 when he told them:

'We do our best to apply the policy with restraint and consideration. We try to alleviate hardships to neutral trade, and nothing that we have done on the sea has brought into peril a single life of any neutral citizen.'[1]

In February 1940 he was concerned with the naval action in boarding the German ship *Altmark* and releasing the British prisoners confined in her hold. He was not given much time for a decision which raised many thorny diplomatic problems, and his own action was admirably prompt: '16 *Feb*. In the evening Winston rang me up to ask whether I agreed to his destroyers going into a Norwegian fjord to fetch the prisoners off the *Altmark*. I asked him how long he could give me for reflection, to which he replied that they were facing one another now, and at any moment there might be trouble. I therefore agreed to give him my view in 10 minutes,

[1] Campbell Johnson. Op. cit., p. 553.

within which time I rang him up again to make one or two suggestions about his orders which he accepted, and so the thing went ahead.'[1]

On 4 April the Prime Minister ventured the injudicious opinion that 'Hitler had missed the bus', and two days later Edward showed that his own confidence was also far greater than the situation warranted:

'6 *April*. Whether we shall succeed in getting Musso into a better temper remains to be seen. I still adhere to my view that he is going to bark more than bite. It is all part of dictator technique to keep poor timid democracies jittering. What they cannot as yet succeed in understanding is that we are much less frightened of them jumping out on us now than we were at the time of Munich. It really looks as if the Air position is at last showing real improvement.'[2]

How premature such views were was shown by the disastrous outcome of the Norwegian campaign which started with the German invasion of Norway on 9 April. The news of the evacuation of British troops on 1 May from Andalsnes and Namsos had a shattering effect on public confidence, particularly after the optimistic terms in which Churchill and Chamberlain had spoken in mid-April. The Government yielded to demands for a debate on the failure of the expedition, which took place on 7 and 8 May and was one of the most momentous in the history of the House of Commons. It was on this occasion that Amery used with terrible effect the words of Cromwell dismissing the Long Parliament:

'You have sat too long here for any good you have been doing. Depart, I say, and let us have done with you. In the name of God, go.'

And Lloyd George too had spoken with a last flicker of destructive genius:

'He has appealed for sacrifice. The nation is prepared for every sacrifice so long as it has leadership. . . . I say solemnly that the Prime Minister should give an example of sacrifice, because there is nothing that can contribute more to victory in this war than that he should sacrifice the seals of office.'

The Government spokesman in the House of Lords, Lord Hankey, left the impression of one trying under heavy pressure to discharge a necessary, but impossible duty, and of an administration that was approaching the end of its tether. It was Edward's task to wind up the debate, and he knew that the Government's days might well be numbered, but unlike the intense Hoare and the exhausted Hankey he spoke with a strange and almost unearthly detachment:

'We have all one purpose,' he said. 'If it was at any time thought to be the case that other men could do the job better, certainly no member of the Government, so far as I am aware, would be unwilling to be relieved of responsibility that can bring no personal satisfaction, but only a burden that at times must be well-nigh insupportable.'

The Government's majority in the House of Commons had fallen to 81,

[1] Hickleton Papers. Diary.   [2] Ibid.

some 40 Conservatives voting against it, and more than 80 abstaining. Chamberlain at once considered resignation so that a National Government might be formed including Labour and Liberals, but before doing so he decided to see whether there was any possibility of forming such a Government himself. With this object in view he sent for Attlee and Greenwood, the Leader and Deputy-Leader of the Labour Party, to meet Halifax, Churchill and himself at No. 10 Downing Street. We shall follow these events through Edward's eyes as he saw them at the time, and recorded them in his diary, but there is an important question that must first be answered. What were Halifax's own thoughts and desires when the prospect that he might become Prime Minister seemed to loom before him?

The question can be simply answered. Although it would have been inhuman not to feel pride and gratification at the thought that his political career might be crowned by this great reward, Halifax was so disturbed by the prospect, and so strongly averse from the thought of acceptance that he experienced a feeling of physical sickness in the pit of his stomach when the question was under discussion. He had no illusions whatever as to his suitability for the rôle which a Prime Minister would have to play at this desperate moment in history. He was acutely conscious that his great gifts were in many ways the exact opposite of those required in the fighting leader of a forlorn cause, and that he was lacking in the drive and ruthlessness which the situation demanded. He knew that Churchill was pre-eminent in both, and to Halifax it seemed that the whole of that turbulent life might almost have been a preparation for this moment of destiny.

On 9 May he received a letter from the Under-Secretary at the Foreign Office, R. A. Butler:

'Dalton called to see me at dinner time yesterday evening and told me that his party would come into the Government under you but not under the P.M. or in the company of Simon. . . . This was the view which he and his friends hoped I would pass on to you.

'I cross-questioned him as to whether the Labour Leaders would serve under the present P.M. if he pruned his team first. Dalton said—no. The Labour Party had too many grudges against Neville.

'After the debate I saw Herbert Morrison who said that the idea of Labour joining the Govt. was "coming along well". But he made it clear that the conditions were the same as those which Dalton had outlined. . . .

'Dalton said there was no other choice but you. Churchill must "stick to the war" and Anderson had not been sufficiently "built up". He saw no objection in the Lords difficulty. I confine myself to passing this on. . . .'[1]

Later on that same day Edward wrote in his diary:

'*Thursday*, 9 *May*. Anne's wedding day. The P.M. asked me to go and see him at 10 o'clock, when he told me he thought the position could not be left

[1] Hickleton Papers.

as it was by the House of Commons Division, and that it was essential to restore confidence in the Government. This he thought could only be done by having all Parties in, and asked my view. I told him I thought this was essential. He told me that Winston had been doubtful about it when he had spoken to him immediately after the Division last night.

'We then discussed the chances of Labour serving under him, and agreed that they were negligible. He thought that it was clearly Winston, or myself, and appeared to suggest that if it were myself he might continue to serve in the Government. I put all the arguments I could think of against myself, laying considerable emphasis on the difficult position of a Prime Minister unable to make contact with the centre of gravity in the House of Commons. The P.M. did not think so much of this, arguing that *ex hypothesi* in the new situation there would be comparatively little opposition in the House of Commons. The conversation and the evident drift of his mind left me with a bad stomach ache. I told him again, as I had told him the day before, that if the Labour people said they would only serve under me I should tell them that I was not prepared to do it, and see whether a definite attitude would make them budge. If it failed we should all, no doubt, have to boil our broth again. He said he would like to have a talk to Winston and me together in the afternoon, and then went off to the House of Commons where we had a Cabinet at 12 o'clock.'

After luncheon Edward crossed the street to No. 10 Downing Street to keep his historic appointment at 4.30 p.m.:

'The P.M., Winston, David Margesson[1] and I sat down to it. The P.M. recapitulated the position, and said that he had made up his mind that he must go, and that it must either be Winston or me. He would serve under either. It would, therefore, be necessary to see the Labour people before they went to Bournemouth,[2] and ask them whether they would, on principle, be prepared to join the Government (a) under the present Prime Minister, or (b) under other leadership. David Margesson said that unity was essential, and he thought it impossible to attain under the P.M. He did not at that moment pronounce very definitely between Winston and myself, and my stomach ache continued.

'I then said that I thought for the reasons given the P.M. must probably go, but that I had no doubt at all in my own mind that for me to take it would create a quite impossible position. Quite apart from Winston's qualities as compared with my own at this particular juncture, what would in fact be my position? Winston would be running Defence, and in this connection one could not but remember how rapidly the position had become impossible between Asquith and Lloyd George, and I should have no access to the House of Commons. The inevitable result would be that being outside both these vital points of contact I should speedily become a more or less honorary

[1] The Chief Conservative Party Whip.   [2] For the Labour Party Conference.

Prime Minister, living in a kind of twilight just outside the things that really mattered. Winston, with suitable expressions of regard and humility, said he could not but feel the force of what I had said, and the P.M. reluctantly, and Winston evidently with much less reluctance, finished by accepting my view.

'So there we left it for the moment, Winston and I having a cup of tea in the garden while the P.M. kept some other appointment before we all saw Attlee and Greenwood together at six-fifteen.

'The P.M. put the position to them and they were a bit evasive, but eventually said that they did not think they could get their Party to agree to serve under the P.M. It was finally left that they should consult their Executive tomorrow on the two points; would the Labour Party join in principle (a) under Neville, (b) under someone else. They were to telephone tomorrow afternoon "yes" or "no" to both.'[1]

On Friday, 10 May, Edward was awakened at six o'clock in the morning by a message from the Foreign Office that the Germans had invaded Holland, and the Dutch Minister followed quickly in the wake of this news. Soon afterwards the Belgian Ambassador called on a similar mission, and Edward gave them both the assurance of immediate British help. At a Cabinet meeting later in the morning Chamberlain told Ministers of his discussions with the Labour leaders, but that he did not think that further steps could be taken until the war situation had been clarified.

'The P.M.,' Edward wrote, 'told me that he had a feeling that Winston did not approve of the delay, and left me guessing as to what he meant to do.'

At four-thirty another Cabinet meeting was held:

'The P.M. then told us that he had decided not to wait, and was seeing the King this evening to advise that Winston should take over. This he accordingly did, and broadcast a short message to the country at 9. He has acted with great public spirit. The Labour people having said they would join a Coalition Government, but not under him, he did not think delay was possible.'

When this important matter had been disposed of to the satisfaction of both Churchill and Halifax, the new Prime Minister sent a note to Edward inviting him to continue his work at the Foreign Office. Again devoid of rancour, Churchill had put behind him all causes of bitterness. He had forgotten India and Munich and was now thinking only of the immediate future. There was both generosity and resolution in his letter:

Admiralty, Whitehall.

10.5.40.

'My dear Edward,

Now that I have taken up this task, I write to thank you for the chivalry and kindness with which you have treated me. The task I have assumed is

[1] Hickleton Papers. Diary.

one of sombre and dire consequence. No one knows better than I what weaknesses lie undisclosed, and we both have a full realization of the dangers which crowd in upon us, and their problems, from every side. However, with your help and Neville's I do not shrink from the ordeal.

It gives me so much pleasure to feel that we shall be fighting this business through together to the end. I feel sure your conduct of Foreign Affairs is an essential element in our war strength. I am so grateful to you for being willing to continue your work in this great office of which you are at once the slave and the master: and that you will of course lead the House of Lords.

I am assuming that I may count on this, and that no formal invitation is required from

Your sincere friend,
WINSTON S. CHURCHILL.'

Edward was touched by this letter, but he was irritated by its easy assumption that he would lead the House of Lords as well as continue as Foreign Secretary, and wrote in his diary:

'*Saturday*, 11 *May*. I got a note from Winston early asking me to go on with the F.O., and throwing in casually "and you will of course lead the House of Lords". I hastily told him this was quite impossible, and he must think again. I have seldom met anybody with stranger gaps of knowledge, or whose mind worked in greater jerks. Will it be possible to make it work in orderly fashion? On this much depends.'

Edward thus continued at the Foreign Office and as Member of the War Cabinet, but he was successful in persuading the Prime Minister to relieve him of the leadership of the House of Lords which he had given up when he first went to the Foreign Office early in 1938. Later in the autumn he resumed it and continued to lead the House until he was appointed Ambassador to the United States at the end of 1940. Churchill had proposed a small War Cabinet, in which Attlee and Greenwood would take the place of Simon, Hoare and Kingsley Wood, and in Edward's opinion: 'We shall not have gained on intellect.' At the Foreign Office therefore and in the War Cabinet: 'I shared responsibility under the Prime Minister through the days that preceded, witnessed and followed the collapse of France, Belgium, and the miracle of Dunkirk, the main burden of all of which necessarily fell upon Churchill and inspired him to give leadership to the British people, matchless and unforgettable.'

But two days later Edward was given some indication of the sort of hours the new Prime Minister was likely to keep. His own preference was for a regular routine and early bed, and he was of the firm belief that late night sessions impaired the efficiency of Ministers, and even more of staff officers, and that exhausted men could not arrive at sound judgments. This was a matter on which Halifax felt strongly since irregular hours disorganized his own system, and we shall see how later in America this habit of the Prime Minister jarred his normal serenity to an unusual extent. Now on 12 May he noted:

'The meeting Winston called for 6.30 was put off till 10.30; quite intolerable, but one must acquiesce during these two or three days. After that I shall tell him that if he wants midnight meetings he can have them without me.

'10.30. Meeting in the Admiralty Board Room, at which the new Service Ministers appeared. Archie Sinclair[1] at the Air Ministry seems to me a major disaster. A long and rather discursive discussion which left me uneasy as to Winston's methods. Got to bed at 1. These hours are bad enough for anybody; worst of all for the Chiefs of Staff. I am seeking to organize a rebellion with Neville on the subject.'[2]

Edward's relations with Neville Chamberlain were those of two men who had shared both adulation and abuse, and he was as we have seen, able to achieve a closer approach to intimacy with this shy man than any of his colleagues, and to penetrate deeper into his profound reserve. He found him unhappy about the course of events, but relieved that he no longer bore the responsibility for them:

'He is a good deal shaken by political events, but very good. He told me that he had always thought that he could not face the job of being Prime Minister in war, but when it came he did; and yet now that the war was becoming intense he could not but feel relieved that the final responsibility was off him. He said, what is quite true, that in the last resort the Prime Minister can nearly always impose his will on the Cabinet; hence the responsibility.'[3]

To Edward, like all his colleagues, the collapse of France in May 1940 was a staggering blow. The one firm rock on which all had been willing to build for the last two years was the French Army, and the Germans had walked through it as easily as they had through the Poles. Edward had the same sick feeling at the pit of his stomach at this moment that had come upon him when the new Prime Minister was being chosen. He and Dorothy had spent a perfect summer evening walked over the wolds soon after they had heard the news, and on their way home sat in the sun and looked down upon the Vale of York:

'All the landscape of the nearer foreground was familiar—its sights, its sounds, its smells; hardly a field that did not call up some half-forgotten bit of association; the red-roofed village and nearby hamlets, gathered as it were for company round the old greystone church, where men and women like ourselves, now long dead and gone, had once knelt in worship and prayer.

[1] Sir Archibald Sinclair, the Liberal Leader, became Secretary of State for Air in Churchill's Coalition Government.
[2] Hickleton Papers. Diary. [3] Ibid.

Here in Yorkshire was a true fragment of the undying England, like the white cliffs of Dover, or any other part of our land that Englishmen have loved. Then the question came, is it possible that the Prussian jackboot will force its way into this countryside to tread and trample over it at will? The very thought seemed an insult and an outrage; much as if anyone were to be condemned to watch his mother, wife or daughter being raped.'

Before it was all over in France it had been thought by the French that a last approach might be made to Mussolini, and a Cabinet was held on 27 May. Halifax had observed the Prime Minister's magnificent courage and defiance at this black moment with admiration and wonder, but Churchill's temperament was so radically different from his own that even at this crisis Halifax could feel exasperated by his methods. We shall study the difference between these two men more closely when describing Halifax's life as Ambassador in Washington, and the reservations which existed between them, but for the moment should notice his comments on this Cabinet:

'At the 4.30 Cabinet we had a long and rather confused discussion about, nominally, the approach to Italy, but also largely about general policy in the event of things going really badly in France. I thought Winston talked the most frightful rot, also Greenwood, and after bearing it for some time I said exactly what I thought of them, adding that if that was really their view, and if it came to the point, our ways must separate. Winston, surprised and mellowed, and, when I repeated the same thing in the garden, was full of apologies and affection. But it does drive me to despair when he works himself up into a passion of emotion when he ought to make his brain think and reason.'[1]

But although Edward was to be frequently irritated by the Prime Minister's habits, and methods of transacting business, his heart was warmed again and again by his magnanimity. The British Expeditionary Force was evacuated from Dunkirk between 26 May and 4 June, but even at such a moment of strain Churchill found time on 6 June to detain the War Cabinet after its meeting in order to exhort Sinclair and the Labour Ministers to suspend the heresy hunt against members of the previous Government, particularly Neville Chamberlain and Kingsley Wood. To him the past was forgotten, and need only be resurrected as a warning for the future:

'The truth is,' said Edward, 'that Winston is about the only person who has an absolutely clean sheet. Both Labour and Liberals have to share with Conservatives the responsibility for being late with rearmament by reason of the great part they took in creating an atmosphere in which Stanley Baldwin, though I think wrongly, not unnaturally thought a large bill for rearmament was not politically practical.'

It was at this Cabinet meeting that Churchill told Ministers that he thought it would be well to invite Lloyd George to join the Government, a

[1] Ibid.

matter about which he had already consulted Edward and Neville Chamberlain:

'The latter [Lloyd George] had felt it would be pretty difficult, but had not raised final objections. We shall see whether he accepts. Winston told me that he meant to put him through an inquisition first, as to whether he had the root of the matter in him. By this he means, so he explained to me, adopting a formula I suggested to him, that any peace terms now, as hereafter, offered must not be destructive of our independence.'[1]

On 13 June, five days before Marshal Pétain sued for an armistice and while Paul Reynaud was still in office, the Prime Minister took Edward with him to France. With an escort of eight Spitfires they flew out over Portland Bill and the Channel Islands, and entering France over St. Malo, landed at Tours. The atmosphere that greeted them suggested a state of complete disorganization. The deserted aerodrome was pitted with bomb craters, and there was no one to meet them, and at the Préfecture they could not even tell them where the British Embassy was. At last they were able to make contact with the French Prime Minister, and arrange a meeting with Reynaud at three-fifteen. A heavy rain poured down on streets and roads choked with refugees, and motor cars with mattresses on the roofs, and miserable huddles of people sitting forlornly on the pavement:

'Reynaud, when we met, asked us the flat question whether, if it became necessary, we would consent to France making a separate peace. We told him, while we had every sympathy with all their suffering, we could not discuss this until we could see what Roosevelt would say to the further appeal Reynaud had said he meant to address to him.'[2]

The next day Edward heard from the Prime Minister that he had just had a message from France that the French Army was in process of dissipation, and on the 17th came the news that Reynaud had resigned, and that Pétain had formed a Cabinet. Edward found some strange reassurance in the fact that Admiral Darlan had been appointed Minister of Marine, while Churchill, he thought, already believed that 'we should do better without the French than with them', and was in a mood of robust optimism.

'*Wednesday*, 19 *June*. A very discursive Cabinet, all the worse because we really had some practical things to do, and only an hour to do them in. It is the most extraordinary brain, Winston's, to watch functioning that I have ever seen, a most curious mixture of a child's emotion and a man's reason. Neville rather concerned about some intrigues that are going on in the House of Commons with the object of getting him out. I told him that there was nothing that applied to him that did not also apply to me, and that it all left me comparatively unmoved.'

On the following day Edward's old friend George Lloyd, who had returned that evening from France, came to visit him with a graphic account of how

[1] Ibid.   [2] Ibid.

'he had taken hold of Pétain morally and shaken him', and how Jeanneney, President of the French Senate, and Herriot, President of the Chamber, were standing firm, and how Mandel had asked if he could come to England with him, saying that he had also *"des bagages"*, which had been interpreted to Lloyd as his mistress, and at which he had drawn the line, little realizing that Mandel would soon be murdered.

After the fall of France, and shortly after Hitler had made his expected peace offer, it fell to Edward to give the answer of the Government in a broadcast to the nation. He asked the Prime Minister if he might submit it to him before delivery, and Churchill invited Edward and Dorothy to spend the week-end at Chequers so that he might read to him what he intended to say. His speech was, of course, a flat rejection of the offer, and Edward tried to emphasize the point that whatever successes Hitler might achieve in Europe and elsewhere, he could not win the war until he had made an end of the British Army, Navy and Air Force. He told Churchill that he found it difficult to mention the three Services by name in a manner which would not sound cumbrous, but that he supposed that it was unavoidable.

'He thought for a moment or two, walking up and down the long room, and then said: "Why not say unless that man can sap the might of Britain?" As of course I did. But what an example of how to use the language—and nearly all monosyllables.'

At the end of July the Prime Minister told Edward that he wished all Ministers to be at their posts when the bombardment of London began, and that he should leave the Dorchester Hotel and live in a flat that was being prepared at the Foreign Office. The flat was still unfinished when he left for Washington, and he never occupied it, although occasionally sleeping on a camp bed in the Office during a particularly heavy raid. But for a while he and Dorothy were busy with preparations for the move, and a fortunate visitor to Messrs. Bolding, the sanitary engineers, on Tuesday, 30 July, would have seen the Foreign Secretary, to whom the affair seemed in no way peculiar, climbing into one bath after another and stretching his length in them.

The first great night attack on London came on 7 September, and Edward and Dorothy watched it beginning on the operations board at the Head-quarters of Fighter Command, and later that night gazed from the roof of their hotel upon a burning city, pin-pointed with fires, and flushed to an angry red. When the air attacks on London were in progress the shelter of the hotel would be thronged by a motley assortment of residents. Dr. Chaim Weizmann was sometimes to be seen there placidly reading the Old Testament amid the bombardment, and foreign ambassadors clad in dressing gowns would formally present junior members of their staffs to the similarly attired wife of the Foreign Secretary. Later, when the attacks became more intense, they were encouraged by the management to sleep in the Turkish

Bath underground where the din of the bombs scarcely penetrated. Here, as in other deep recesses of the hotel, a sleeping colony was established consisting of the Halifaxes, the Duff Coopers and Sir George Clerk, and sometimes their friend Lady Alexandra Metcalfe. Edward was conscious of a warm *camaraderie* in these unusual conditions:

'We all had beds behind screens; by polite fiction we ignored each other's existence, and quickly became acclimatized to each other's snores. My only trouble was that Churchill would occasionally through the hotel porter call me to the telephone, waking me out of my beauty sleep, to ask some question which I felt I should have answered with greater wisdom and certainly with better temper in the morning. As we woke, we clad ourselves in dressing gowns, picked up the bag of personal effects which always accompanied us in case we were bombed in the night, made our way to the lift, and so back to civilization.'

He had little recreation that summer while the country waited for a German invasion, and longed for the onset of the equinoctial gales which would put a term to their anxiety. He found that the best restoratives of this time were the Saturday nights or week-ends he was occasionally able to steal to visit friends within easy reach of London, watching from Victor Cazalet's[1] garden in Kent one of the summer battles in the air, and forgetting the war as he gazed at Mereworth, and at Leeds Castle standing in its great sheet of water.

Edward and Dorothy liked to spend their free moments whenever possible in the company of people whom they knew so well that their relaxation could be complete. Such a friend was Lady Alexandra Metcalfe, Lord Curzon's youngest daughter, and now, during his last phase at the Foreign Office, and later when on leave as Ambassador in Washington, it was to her beautiful house, Little Compton in the heart of the Cotswolds, that Edward went with the greatest pleasure to snatch a few moments from the anxieties of his daily work. In her they had an intimate friend whose company was always delightful to them, and whose able mind always stimulating. Edward would put on his oldest clothes at Little Compton, and, resting in the garden, or helping in the haymaking he loved, for a brief spell put care behind him.

Sometimes he would ride Lord Barnby's polo ponies with Valentine Lawford before breakfast on Wimbledon Common, leaving his hotel in the early morning. He had not ridden there for thirty years, and now all the open spaces were covered with trenches, but otherwise he found it little changed. Lawford thought his superior a delightful companion on these excursions before the cares of the day had begun to descend on him. They rode past Leslie Hore-Belisha's house on the Common, and Edward reflected on the way in which Belisha used to send for 'poor Gort there when the latter was C.I.G.S., in order to harangue him from his bed'.

[1] Captain Victor Cazalet, M.P. for Chippenham.

In September he had a depressed letter from his friend Neville Chamberlain, who was now seriously ailing:

'Alas! I have proved to be a broken reed, as doubtless you will have heard. If only I were physically fit, I could stand that constant "banshee howling" and even the noisy nights. But the conditions were getting worse and worse because this confounded ulcer from which I suffer and which will, I suppose, eventually carry me off developed symptoms which required attention every hour or so and in between gave me sensations which though not painful were so intensely disturbing as to prevent my attending to anything else. . . . Every morning I feel so sick that I can hardly touch anything till lunch.'[1]

Churchill treated Chamberlain with the greatest kindness and delicacy, sending him away to the country to recuperate, but knew that he would never work again, and spoke to Edward about the political changes that would be necessary:

'Winston was divided in his mind between putting Anthony, or John Anderson, into the War Cabinet: certain political advantages about the first though it was a bore to move Anthony from the War Office: on the other hand John Anderson likely to be better at tying up endless cross problems that arise on the Home Front, and of which Winston wants to disembarrass himself. I was, on the whole, for the first solution. On further reflection through luncheon I came to feel that John Anderson would, in fact, give him more help, and wrote him a note to tell him so. At an afternoon Cabinet Anthony told me that Winston had offered him the choice, and asked my advice. I told him on the whole I should think it better for him to stop where he was. I think this was very much his view. It is a melancholy business for poor Neville, and I tried to write to him. He has had a rough time from politics and fate.'[2]

As in the First World War, he was convinced that no overtures for peace must be entertained from the enemy until they had suffered an exemplary defeat, and when the Dutch Ambassador showed him some papers containing exploratory efforts that Dutchmen had been making as to the possibility of a negotiated peace, he wrote:

'A negotiated peace with Hitler would be a poor deal for Holland and Company, and would almost certainly mean that our number would be up later. The more I ponder it, the more convinced I feel that the Germans have got to be more knocked about before they will be in any mood to learn any lesson. If we can persuade them to get rid of Hitler, all the better, but at least we want them to learn that war does not pay them.'[3]

On 1 October Edward expounded to the Cabinet his views on how the Vichy Government, which had been formed by Pétain in France, could best be treated:

'I want to get to the point of having it clearly out with them what we want

[1] Hickleton Papers. Diary.   [2] Ibid.   [3] Ibid.

from them, what we will tolerate, and what we won't. And, in spite of the croakers, I still think that, if we play our cards well, French opinion is likely to turn more and more our way, with satisfactory issues in the Colonial Empire. The ultimate alternative is something like hostilities with Vichy. We had a long discussion in the Cabinet which went fairly well, and Winston was not unhelpful, much as it goes against his natural instinct for bellicosity. By dint of constant reminder that our purpose is to beat Germany and not to make new enemies I think we shall get along.'[1]

Edward was saddened, in November, by the news that the days of Neville Chamberlain were numbered, and by the pathetic condition to which this man was reduced, who knew that his policy had failed, and that by many of those he had tried so hard to preserve from war he was regarded with derision and contempt. Edward and he had passed through much together in the last few years, shared the brief triumph of Munich and its bitter aftermath, and during that time they had known the stench as well as the gardenias of public life. It was Chamberlain's tragedy that he could reveal himself only to a few, and to the Labour Members of Parliament he had been an odious figure, mirthless and brutal in debate, finding a grim relish in demolishing them from the despatch box, a man without warmth or the spark of human kinship. But to Edward he seemed as one shabbily treated by his contemporaries, whose verdicts upon his actions would be calmly revised by history, a man enriched by many hidden graces, in whose reticent heart was a deep affinity with the countryside; who, like Grey, would listen to the dawn chorus of the birds and could distinguish their song. He knew that the public image of Chamberlain was false, but to pierce his reserve a man must first win his confidence and friendship. He had given both to Edward.

On 7 November he went down to the house Chamberlain had been lent in Hampshire to see his friend for the last time. Mrs. Chamberlain spoke frankly about him, saying that it was now only a question of a very few days; that he could eat nothing on account of the nausea that continually overcame him, and that he was growing steadily weaker:

'I was taken up to his room before luncheon to find him propped up in bed, with a little bed-table, on which he had a bowl of blue gentians that someone had sent. I began by saying something about what a rotten time he must have had with his sickness, to which he replied that he had been a bit better the last day or two. "Approaching dissolution, I suppose, brings relief," he said with a half laugh. Then he spoke of our work together, and what it had meant to him in a way that moved me much. And then he was plainly tired, and Anne[2] looked in, and I said good-bye. He took my hand in both his, and held it, and so with no more said but with the full understanding of friends who go to different duties, we parted.

'It was all quite natural, and no shadow of constraint. He was brave and

[1] Ibid.　　　[2] Mrs. Neville Chamberlain.

quite resigned. He had wondered, he said at one point, how best to satisfy himself that Anne knew about how bad he was, but he was happy now that she knew everything, though he feared she would be lonely. I left him with her.'[1]

Chamberlain's political reputation had sunk low in the months before his death, and Edward shared much of the abuse that was showered upon his former chief. Many still believed that they had taken the right course at Munich, and that the deficiencies revealed at Dunkirk proved how disastrous would have been a recourse to war in 1938. But there were others who could not forget the fate of Czechoslovakia, and sneered at them as the 'Men of Munich', and the book *Guilty Men*, in which Edward was one of the principal victims, was widely circulated. He was in no way disturbed by twinges of conscience over the Munich episode: 'My withers,' he told John Wheeler-Bennett, with that old difficulty in pronouncing his r's, 'are completely unwung.'[2]

There were other signs of diminished popularity. He was criticized when it was announced that elaborate preparations were being made to convert and redecorate rooms at the Foreign Office to provide him with a flat. The fact that it was on Churchill's orders and against his own wishes that this was being done, was not taken into consideration. There was much criticism also of the failure of British diplomacy to make an accommodation with Russia, and the bulk of this fell on Halifax as one whose aristocratic birth was thought to make him a natural opponent of a proletarian State. And when in October Churchill decided that for military and diplomatic reasons the Burma Road, China's life-line, must be closed, although Halifax had opposed this step, it was widely assumed that the policy was his, and that he was now pressing upon Japan the appeasement that had failed with Germany. In November there were rumours of drastic Cabinet changes, and it was even predicted that Halifax would retire into private life, although this was at once publicly denied. On the contrary, he was about to assume duties for which he was far better fitted than for those of the Foreign Office, and to enter the last and perhaps the most satisfying phase of his public life.

[1] Hickleton Papers. Diary.
[2] Sir John Wheeler-Bennett to author.

Part Four

WASHINGTON

CHAPTER XXIX

'THIS HIGH AND PERILOUS CHARGE'

WE notice for the first time in Halifax's papers a reference to the vacancy in the ambassadorship in Washington on 12 December 1940:

'When I got back from luncheon I found the stunning news of Philip Lothian's[1] death. As far as I know, no one had any suspicion he was seriously ill. Another victim for Christian Science. He will be very difficult to replace. Looking back I wonder whether his being constantly very sleepy when he was over here was a sign of this poisoning. A talk to Winston in the afternoon about possible successors. We agreed to think over the week-end.'[2]

By 17 December no decision had been made, and Edward noted in his diary: 'This business of choosing a successor to Philip Lothian is the devil. The truth is there is nobody with all the things one is looking for. In the afternoon Max Beaverbrook came to see me to say that he thought I ought to go. Whether his feeling was due to genuine conviction about Washington or a desire to get me out of the F.O. I am not quite sure.'

Two days later, on the morning of the 19 December, he received a letter from Winston Churchill on the subject of the vacant ambassadorship:

'My dear Edward,

Before proceeding further about the American vacancy I should like to know whether you yourself would care to undertake this high and perilous charge. I feel I ought to put this question to you before considering lesser alternatives. In doing so let me assure you that I am in close personal and political accord and sympathy with you, that I value and admire your work at the Foreign Office and wish for its continuance, and that only the vital issues now open between us and the United States, on which our whole future depends, induce me even to contemplate the loss and disturbance which a change in your sphere of action would cause to the Cabinet.

Yours as ever
WINSTON S. CHURCHILL.'

On the afternoon of the same day the two men discussed the proposition. Edward had no desire to leave the Foreign Office and England at such a moment of history. He was a creature of habit, and he did not relish the thought of establishing a new position in a strange country among people

---

[1] Philip Kerr. Afterwards Lord Lothian, and British Ambassador in Washington.
[2] Hickleton Papers.

whose ways were unknown to him, and the idea of being three thousand miles away from the centre of great events disturbed him. He went round to the War Office and sought to persuade Mr. Anthony Eden to undertake the ambassadorship, saying: 'Either you must go or I must,' but Eden answered that he did not want the position.[1] The proposal also involved a step downwards from Secretary of State to Ambassador, but the vital importance of the post in Washington at that moment eclipsed a mere technical demotion, and it was not in any case a consideration which would have carried the slightest weight with a man so tepid in political ambition.

Perhaps with slender hope he sought to dissuade Churchill:

'I told him all the things that seemed to me to weigh against this but said that in the last resort I thought he should decide. It is an odious thought if he decides for me.'

Next day he recorded in his diary that: 'I thought that I had shaken Winston off the Washington idea as regards myself in my talk last night. But when I got to the Office I found this letter from him':

'My dear Edward,

Your public spirit has prompted you to leave yourself in my hands in the matter of this great appointment.

I have no doubt whatever that the national interest will be best served at this juncture by your becoming our Ambassador to the United States. If you thought well to have Sir Gerald Campbell made Minister, you would be relieved of some of the pressure, and it would be possible for you to come back here for periodic visits. On such occasions I should wish you immediately to resume your position as a Member of the War Cabinet and sit with us for all purposes.

The business we now have with the United States can only be handled by one who knows the whole policy of the Government, and is in constant direct relation with us. If New York and Washington were as near as Paris used to be, all important affairs would be transacted by personal meetings between Prime Ministers and Foreign Secretaries on both sides. The Atlantic requires that this intimacy should be achieved by other processes, and you are, I am sure, the one person best qualified for this paramount duty.

Yours ever

WINSTON S. CHURCHILL.'

Edward had already written to the Prime Minister, but when he received this letter, held up his own. In it he had put forward arguments against his appointment in which even he can have reposed little confidence. He reported that there was a section of opinion which believed that the United States would welcome a Liberal Ambassador which might indicate Sir Archibald

[1] Lord Avon to author.

Sinclair. He repeated the argument he had already used with Churchill that they were in danger of exaggerating the influence any particular emissary might have on American policy which would evolve quickly under the pressure of their own appreciation of facts, 'provided whoever we sent was discreet and adequate'. In his anxiety to extricate himself he had even suggested that Lord Woolton possessed many of the qualities desirable for the post. 'But it is in your hands,' he had concluded with gloomy resignation.

He told Dorothy of Churchill's last communication as they drove to Lothian's Memorial Service at Westminster Abbey. She was convinced that the Prime Minister was making a serious error, and so impressed by her arguments was Edward that he took her to 10 Downing Street after the service to give her views to him in person.

'I have not often assisted at a more interesting interview. Dorothy began, with suitable apologies, by saying that she thought he was making a profound mistake, as it would appear to be pressing the Americans too hard. Secondly, although at the present moment Winston was at the height of his popularity and could do no wrong, he might later on strike a bad patch and there was nobody else at such a time who would be more loyal and perhaps able to help him with certain sections of opinion than I should. It was well done and Winston listened with the utmost attention.

'When she had finished he developed the case on the other side. He said two things that were revealing: in the course of laying stress on what an opportunity it was for me to do a piece of work that would reflect great credit on me personally, he said that he was conscious of certain currents of opposition against my being at the Foreign Office, and that from my own point of view I should gain from taking the other work.

'It would seem quite unintelligible to him that anybody should not consider personal advantages or disadvantages, and Dorothy was left perhaps a little unjustly, with the conviction that there was something a little sinister in the way in which the appointment had been pressed by Beaverbrook and commended by Winston. Nothing could have been kinder than he was, but he and Dorothy were certainly talking a different language, and she said that she felt there to be an abyss between his thought and hers. Anyhow, there we are. One clearly could say no more when he put it on the grounds he did.'[1]

There was an atmosphere of depression in the family when the decision had been taken, and when they broke the news of Washington to their son Richard he did not like it any better than they, and 'we all walked down to the Office feeling rather shattered'. On the 22 December Churchill told him of the consequential changes; that Eden was to succeed him at the Foreign Office, and Margesson to go to the War Office, and that Roosevelt had answered the Prime Minister in a genial welcoming telegram about Edward

[1] Hickleton Papers. Diary.

by which Churchill had been greatly reassured. On the evening of that same day he heard again from 10 Downing Street about the details of his journey:

'I have asked the First Sea Lord to make proposals about a battleship or a battle cruiser not sooner than ten days and not later than twenty.... I agree with you that the change should be speedily effected, I suppose some time in the Christmas week. You will of course be a Member of the War Cabinet until you actually sail, and although you will no doubt have many things to settle, I hope you will be able to attend our meetings.

'I am most grateful to you for undertaking this heavy task, and setting out upon a spirited adventure. I do not think you will regret it. If they do not help us wholeheartedly, there will only be miseries to share in this Island. If they give us the aid we deserve you will have brought us inestimable blessings.'[1]

Edward, at this moment, felt not only despondency but also a little chill of apprehension at the thought of the long separation from home that now confronted him: 'I felt as if my roots had been suddenly pulled up,' he said, 'or much as a fish must feel when suddenly pulled out on to a bank.' He spent the afternoon of 23 December at the Foreign Office making his farewells which did nothing to dispel his gloom. It still seemed to him that Churchill had made a mistake, and had exaggerated the significance of this particular appointment however highly he estimated the importance of American action. 'How far,' he asked the Prime Minister, 'should we change our policy here because the United States sent us Cordell Hull?' Later he answered letters 'to all the kind people congratulating (spare the word) us on Washington'.

Not for the first time some found hypocrisy in these professions of distaste for high political office, but they were genuine. In that side of his character which concerned itself with external duty Halifax was not wanting in ambition but such instincts were far less deep than his roots in religion or country life. Nevertheless they existed, and were prompted by a sense of the duties of his position, and a natural desire to play a part in the drama of the world. To some who knew him well it seemed that he had another world of his own which was separated from that of his colleagues, that this personal world was partly the result of his religion, and partly of his position as a landed aristocrat, and that the whole of his public life was a duty external to his real interests and desires.

*   *   *

They left London on Tuesday, 14 January, by special train from King's Cross to Thurso to join the newly commissioned battleship *King George V* in Scapa Flow, their last impressions of the battered city those of rime glittering on the rubble of the bomb-sites. The Prime Minister was with them

[1] Hickleton Papers, 22 December 1940.

ON BOARD *KING GEORGE V*, GOING TO WASHINGTON, 1940

to speed his ambassador on the way, and to combine with this gesture a visit to the Fleet to which he had invited Mr. Harry Hopkins who had recently arrived in England as the President's personal representative, and whom Edward had met for the first time five days before, little realizing how indispensable and how intimate his relations with this strange man were to become.

They woke to a white world next morning, and found that they had stopped on a snow-covered moor outside Thurso where they were delayed for three hours by a derailed truck. The tedium of waiting was beguiled by the Prime Minister. It was found that Mr. Churchill had a sore throat, and his wife and doctor tried in vain to dissuade him from continuing the journey to Scapa Flow. Charles Peake, Edward's friend and Private Secretary at the Foreign Office who was accompanying him to America, embalmed the scene in his diary:

'He came beaming into the breakfast car where he consumed a large glass of brandy and then said hoarsely: "I'll go and get my Morthersills." After a bit the P.M. began to talk about a new anti-aircraft device we were going to see, and which he said he was going to fire: "It costs about £100 a minute to fire it," the Captain of the Fleet said rather drily. The smile faded from the P.M.'s lips and the corners of his mouth turned down like a baby. "What, not fire it?" "Yes, darling," Mrs. Churchill added quickly, "you may fire it just once." "Yes, that's right, I'll fire it just once. Only once. That couldn't be bad." Nobody had the heart to say that it would be bad, and he was soon beaming again.'[1] Mrs. Churchill described to Edward her husband's habit when ill of consulting a succession of doctors and continuing the process until he had obtained from one of them the opinion he wanted. According to her, one of his favourite minor economies was using up the remains of old medicine bottles not always with strict reference to the immediate disease.

They found an invigorating morning when they left the train, the sun just risen above the horizon, sky and landscape like pale steel, the sea black in the sun and laced with white horses, and the bitterest north-easter blowing that Edward could remember. It was a hazardous business reaching the *King George V*, involving a double transfer from minesweeper to destroyer, and from destroyer to battleship, the little vessels rising and falling in the swell, and the decks treacherous with powdered snow above a coat of ice. But it was accomplished without accident, and they passed the gates into the vast landlocked bay of Scapa, and, rounding a headland, came suddenly upon the Fleet. The Prime Minister, who had made the transfer from minesweeper to destroyer with astonishing agility, leaned upon the rails smoking a cigar and watched the agonized efforts of Hopkins to follow him with a radiant smile.

Edward had been told that there had been much speculation among the

[1] Charles Peake. Diary.

ship's company about the identity of the travellers. Some expected to see the
dusky features of the Emperor of Ethiopia surmounting the companionway;
others anticipated the haughty figure of de Gaulle, and the belief that the
Princesses were being evacuated from England to the haven of the New
World also had its adherents. The battleship was under the command of
Captain W. R. Patterson whom they were to meet again in Washington as
Chief of Staff to Admiral of the Fleet Lord Cunningham, then head of the
British Admiralty Delegation.

Edward found his fellow passengers on this voyage easy and agreeable.
There was his friend and fellow Anglo-Catholic, Charles Peake, who was to
act as his adviser during the early period of the ambassadorship, the Canadian
Minister of Munitions, Mr. Howe, and Admiral Ghormley of the United
States Navy. Another American officer of whom he was to see much in
Washington was General Raymond Lee, late Military Attaché in London.
Beside these was a group of British officers on their way to discussions with
the American services, the nucleus of the future Combined Staffs organiza-
tion.

The great vessel seethed across the Atlantic on evasive zig-zag courses,
and all the way they hoped in vain for some diversionary signal that might
put them on to the track of an armed raider. Edward's devouring curiosity
led him into many corners of the ship. In the gun-room he drank beer with
the midshipmen, and they hung upon his words as he spoke to them, as
was his charming habit, as though they were his contemporaries, or even
fellow members of the Cabinet, about his visit to Goering's hunting lodge.
His great height was a disadvantage in cramped quarters, but undeterred by
cracking his head on a ventilator shaft he penetrated the shell and cordite
magazine, a greasy place of intolerable heat, and the after gun turret which
was manned by marines.

The Captain of Marines had told Peake that it was difficult to get into the
turret, and that he feared that for a man with one hand it would be next to
impossible, but when it came to the point Edward was quicker and neater
about the business than the Captain of Marines or any of his crew. Peake
noticed the grace and dexterity with which he made the climb: 'I could not
but admire,' he said, 'the beautiful judgment and economy of movement
with which he went up a vertical ladder using only his right hand without
haste or hesitation.'[1] The chaplain of the *King George V*, Mr. J. C. Waters,
was impressed by Edward's habits of devotion: 'I reckoned to be in chapel
in good time before the morning celebration of Holy Communion, but always
Lord Halifax was there before me, on his knees.'[2]

On the morning of 24 January the battleship steamed up Chesapeake Bay
in a dense fog which prevented any sight of their surroundings, and at two
o'clock dropped anchor. For some time nothing happened, and they waited

[1] Ibid.   [2] Rev. J. C. Waters to author.

while a heavy rain poured down upon the vessel. Two days before, they had been staggered by the news that the President intended to come down the bay and meet Edward in person, and there had been much anxious talk of the means by which their august but disabled visitor could be brought on board.

'We were all agreed,' said Peake, 'that by hook or by crook this must be done. We decided to have a hoist made for the jib crane so that he could be raised from his destroyer to the quarter deck. Then we thought that we could send him a personal telegram from Edward saying what an honour it would be if he would visit the ship. Found the Captain a bit shaky on ceremonial. I thought that I might organize this. We shall clearly receive the President with all the honours due to a Sovereign. This is agreed. I came down to the quarter deck and began to step it out on the ground.'

Their first encounter with America had been the arrival of a deputation of American Admirals in the morning, who had come to visit the ship, and the Ambassador's flag, designed by the ever-ready Peake, was broken at the fore and saluted. Peake had already begun one of the many functions of his office, that of writing the Ambassador's speeches, and he was performing this duty with tremendous gusto:

'Letters from the Embassy came aboard at 7 a.m. And I found that H.E. is to see Mr. Cordell Hull at 11.30 on Saturday and is to take with him the speech he is to make when presenting his letters—Sat down and wrote it in ten minutes. Wrote another for him to make to the Press and he liked this too. Wrote a little one for Lady H., and another short one for him to do to the movie-tone people.' Edward saw some inkling of the life ahead in these ominous preparations, but it must be admitted that although he accepted Peake's drafts for his speeches, he did not always do so without comment: 'I admit you have written the speech,' he said on a later occasion, 'and I have agreed to deliver it. You assure me that it will be a success, but can I believe it? As I wade through this succession of painful platitudes, the words of my father come back to me: "After all, Edward, if the worst comes to the worst, it may still have all the advantage of a moral humiliation." '

A quarter of a mile away through the sea-wrack the President's yacht *Potomac* lay at anchor, and in the afternoon she made a circuit of the battleship, receiving the appropriate compliments. Then a barge put out bringing Nevile Butler and Frederick Hoyer Millar of the Embassy with a message from the President that he was sending his launch to bring the Ambassador and Dorothy off to the *Potomac* for tea, and that they would afterwards sail in her to Annapolis. When the barge came they were piped over the side, and disappeared into the mist.

They were welcomed at the companionway of the *Potomac* by Frank Knox the Secretary of the Navy, and by a man who was to be almost as invaluable in liaison with Roosevelt as Hopkins, the President's personal aide General

Watson. Halifax had looked forward with some curiosity to this first meeting. They were taken into a little dining saloon where the President was seated at the table, and he was conscious that events of incalculable importance might depend on the relationship he could establish with this man. His first impression was one of a compelling charm and a refreshing absence of formality:

'In one moment he had put us completely at our ease, and we were chattering away as if we had known each other all our lives. Nothing could have been more friendly, and he said that he regarded this as dispensing with any formal business of presentation of credentials. Much talk over tea—quite easy and intimate, and at times pleasantly indiscreet.' After tea they 'discussed everything under the sun, and I liked him very much. He spoke a great deal about his experiences in Europe at the end of the last war and about various common friends. Finally he told me that he hoped I should find myself free to ring up the White House at any time and ask to see him, and be prepared myself to be called by him at any time.

'I hope and believe that thanks to his natural qualities and the relations on which he has been with the P.M., I have been placed pretty quickly on easy terms with him.'[1]

To a friend in England he wrote of this first encounter: 'The President coming to meet us was generally taken to be, as indeed it was, a very significant gesture. I liked him awfully—very easy, jolly and genuine. A bit optimistic I should guess about political difficulties, and curiously like Winston in some ways with his brushing aside things which he did not wish to recognize as difficult, and the broad brush with which he touched matters he discussed. But a very likeable fellow.'[2]

There was considerable meaning in this gesture of the President. With that sense of timing which he could at moments so brilliantly exhibit he intended to certify to the world in a manner at once dramatic and unmistakable his sympathy with the cause of embattled Britain, and he completed this welcome by himself driving the Ambassador to the door of the British Embassy. The President's touch might sometimes falter in the years that lay ahead, but Halifax would never forget this moment of kinship and welcome. He would have echoed the words of the President's American friend who, stirred by the gesture, had cabled: 'Meeting Halifax was a stroke of genius, for in your action you personified the nation. The gesture was more than a welcome. It was a symbol of brotherhood.'[3]

*   *   *

When he stepped into the Embassy on Massachusetts Avenue for the first time he was conscious of something familiar out of the past. It had been

---

[1] Hickleton Papers, Washington Diary.   [2] Halifax. Private correspondence.
[3] Herbert Bayard Swope to President Roosevelt. National Archives, Franklin D. Roosevelt Library, Hyde Park, N.Y.

built by Sir Edwyn Lutyens in the intervals of constructing his great palace in New Delhi, and Edward remembered how he would come out to them there in the cold weather before returning to his labours in Washington. Now, as he entered the house, he remarked: 'This seems very familiar,' and next morning, after passing a night which was a sharp reminder of the short-comings of Lutyens as a domestic architect, he added: 'It *is* very familiar,' for it was designed in a manner characteristic of its author, and was at once noble and inconvenient.

Fresh from the rubble and squalor of London under enemy fire, with its monotonous days and darkened nights, its depression and irksome privations, he found it difficult at first to accommodate himself to the conditions in an America still at peace and lapped in abundance. The contrast had struck him with extraordinary force when he drove with the President from Annapolis to Washington with its brilliantly lit streets which made him uneasy after London where the darkness was almost palpable, and it was strange that here the scream of sirens from the motor-cycle police carried no more sinister message than a warning to traffic. But he reflected that although the scene now before his eyes seemed like the awakening from some evil dream, and the war merely a distant horror, the Congress of the United States was at that moment being invited by the President to take a step conceived in a moment of genius, and to pass the statute of Lend-Lease which, in Edward's words, 'gave his measure of the extent to which an unprecedented act of generosity to a foreign nation could serve the enlightened self-interest of his own'.

When Halifax arrived in Washington in January 1941 the Lend-Lease proposals were before Congress and were passed into law in March of that year. Under the Lend-Lease Act Great Britain obtained from the United States materials for the prosecution of the war. In the course of the war the United States supplied without charge some $30 billion of Lend-Lease to the British Commonwealth, of which nearly $27 billion went to Great Britain, and received some $6 billion of reverse Lend-Lease articles in return.

Discussions lasting for eight months took place between the British and Americans on the proposed Mutual Aid Agreement which laid down the principles governing the supplies of Lend-Lease. Article VII dealt with the eventual terms of Lend-Lease settlement and post-war economic planning. Trade discrimination was a practice obnoxious to Americans and to none more so than Mr. Hull and the State Department, and the Ottawa Agreements of 1932 had been offensive to them.

The question of repayment of Lend-Lease articles was left deliberately vague in the Lend-Lease Act because the Administration feared that its discussion would jeopardize the bill's enactment by Congress. Most Americans, to whom in 1941 neutrality was still a practical possibility, thought that

Lend-Lease should be repaid either in cash or by some territorial or raw materials concessions. Accordingly the Act laid down that the settlement should contain some 'benefit to the United States'. The 'benefit' which the President and his advisers decided to obtain in 'consideration' of Lend-Lease was a promise by Britain and other aid recipients to co-operate in the post-war reconstruction of multilateral trade.

The 'consideration' clause of Article VII proved extremely controversial. It included within its scope discrimination, trade barriers, bilateral and barter arrangements and all so-called 'Schachtian' devices, but the British were left in no doubt that they were being asked to abandon Imperial Preference in return for being absolved from repayment of Lend-Lease goods. Keynes,[1] who visited Washington in May 1941, searched for a formula which would make abandonment of discrimination dependent upon joint Anglo-American effort having created conditions in which discrimination would no longer be necessary. In August Lord Halifax and Mr. Opie, his economic adviser, with the State Department drafted a new form of words on the lines of the final version. The matter was still unresolved at the time of Pearl Harbour, and was not finally settled until the New Year after interchanges between the President and the Prime Minister. The Mutual Aid Agreement, including Article VII, binding the signatories to the objective of multilateral trade and non-discrimination to be attained 'in the light of governing economic conditions', was signed on 23 February 1942.

But when Edward arrived in Washington the Lend-Lease Act had yet to be passed, and was by no means out of danger, and friendly hints from Members of Congress suggested that it would be advisable to postpone the speech which is conventionally made by the incoming Ambassador to the American Pilgrims, and which was one of the many that had been composed for him on the battleship by the resourceful Charles Peake. These warnings were clear indications that there were sections of American opinion which would observe the Ambassador's behaviour with an appraising and some-times censorious eye. They were danger signals which in this early period of his ambassadorship he had neither the experience nor the insight to recognize. They suggested that there were many hostile and vigilant people ready to seize upon any action of the British Ambassador, however innocent, which might be interpreted as an interference in their affairs, or a manœuvre to inveigle them into the war. It was some satisfaction to him that although the speech was postponed, it was eventually delivered, and that he was then able to renew an old friendship with Thomas Lamont who was to be their host on many occasions in New York, and who was to endear himself particularly to Edward by a gift of 500,000 dollars to Canterbury Cathedral.

When Edward pondered the President's reception of him, and the easy

[1] J. M. Keynes, the Cambridge economist, later leader of the British negotiators in the American Loan discussions.

relations which he insisted should be observed, it seemed to him that Roosevelt was anxious to leave no doubt in any quarter where his administration stood with regard to the war:

'It was indeed to Roosevelt's lasting honour,' he said, 'that he had grasped the nature of the Nazi challenge to the world as long ago as October 1937 when he made his famous "Quarantine" speech in Chicago: and though administrative action might still be hampered by Neutrality Acts and the like, he was steadily leading his public opinion to understand what this struggle, in which the British Commonwealth stood alone from June 1940 to June 1941, involved for free men everywhere.'

In spite of this appreciation, Edward came early to the conclusion that there were many anomalies in the American system of government. To him it seemed at first like some ponderous machine in which many of the component parts were in conflict with one another, and which worked only with much groaning and crepitation. In March 1941 he wrote to Churchill describing what he considered to be the peculiarities of the Administration:

'The President seems to me all out to be helpful whenever I see him. But every day that I am here makes me see more and more how terribly disjointed is the whole machine of government. I don't think the President ties up awfully well; I am quite sure Harry Hopkins doesn't, and as for the Government Departments they might almost as well be the administration of different countries. The result is, I suspect, that individuals like Hopkins try to do too much, and we have no means of following up their activities, and that a great deal of what we try to do from the outside seems like hitting wads of cotton wool. But when all this is said and done, the fact does remain that when you think of where these people are now compared to where they were eighteen or twelve months ago, it seems almost a miracle.'[1]

In fairness to the American Constitution it must be stated that the Ambassador, never then nor by the end of his term, succeeded in mastering all its ramifications. The apparent contradictions, the intricate checks and counter-balances, the divorcement of the Executive from the Legislature—all these seemed to him to conspire against efficient administration. At first all these matters were to him almost *terra incognita*, but he knew that it was his duty to become familiar with them, and he gave the matter serious study although with less fruitful results than those of Bryce. It seemed to him that in general terms the American Constitution rested on statute, and the British on convention, and that for reasons familiar to students of history, the American Constitution was far more diffuse than the British in its distribution of power.

'If an American comes to London,' he wrote, 'and says he would like to see the British Government, his British guide will assure him that nothing is

[1] Hickleton Papers, March 1941.

simpler. At a crowded question-time in the House of Commons he will show him most of the Government, sitting on the Front Bench, and can then take him across the lobby to the House of Lords. . . . There may be one or two absentees, but he will have seen His Majesty's Government in whose hands, so long as they enjoy the support of the House of Commons, effective power resides.'[1]

But if the position were reversed, and a British visitor to Washington asked to see the United States Government, a different scene would unfold. He would probably be told first of the President in the White House, and it would be explained to him how great in some respects was his personal power, but how in others he was dependent on Congress. He would be shown the Majority leaders in either House, and the Chairmen of important Committees, and the duties and rights of the Supreme Court as interpreter and protector of the Constitution would be expounded to him. He would be told how unless the Constitution was formally amended, the powers of Congress were rigidly confined within it, unlike Parliament which was sovereign in its power and, in the words of Dicey, able, at least in theory, to decree the death of every blue-eyed baby in the land.

The English visitor would also, thought Edward, not fail to observe that the President was in effect chosen by direct vote of all qualified citizens, but that once he had been elected and installed he was in office for four years, and liable to no popular power of dismissal, whereas the Prime Minister of England could be ejected at any moment by an adverse vote of the House of Commons. He would also learn that while the President enjoyed wide authority to act in emergencies, for the carrying out of his ordinary policies he must look to Congress which might well have a majority not of his own party.

Another most significant difference between the two countries which at once occurred to him was that while in England a man may become Prime Minister only after a long period of political experience and public appraisal, an American President need never have held executive or elective office of any sort before being chosen to fill his exalted post, and that 'to one who looks on, the American people take an appalling risk in this latitude of choice they now hold in their hands, for one would suppose that circumstances might easily bring to the White House a Presidential candidate whose only qualifications were the gifts of demagogic appeal'.[2]

Perhaps most striking of all to his mind was the fact that in America the heads of the administrative departments did not sit in Congress, and that there was a complete separation of function between the Executive and the Legislature, which nourished the activities of political columnists syndicated all over the United States who flourished like green bay trees, and whose words were invested with oracular awe by millions, and made the Press

[1] Halifax. Op. cit., p. 243.   [2] Ibid.

conference the instrument for questioning the Government. He regarded it as a poor substitute for the regular cross-examination of Ministers at question time in the House of Commons.

* * *

But if he grasped the broad principles of American politics, he was constantly bemused by their details: 'One funny thing about him,' said his friend Walter Lippmann, 'was that he could never understand the complicated American political system, and every time an election took place he had to have the whole thing explained to him all over again.'[1]

He was particularly baffled on arrival by the attitude of many Americans to the President. In his innocence and unfamiliarity with American life there had been a vague picture in his mind, as in those of many Englishmen, of an august figure combining the rôles of Sovereign and Prime Minister, and secure in the reverence of his countrymen. By March 1941, to be sure, he had written: 'I like the President, but he's a very discursive talker and nearly as difficult to keep to the point as Winston. And I have a feeling that he doesn't tie up very well,' but he had envisaged him being, in the eyes of Americans, the occupant of an almost celestial sphere, 'the acknowledged and respected standard bearer, opposed indeed by the Republican party in domestic policy, but truly the champion of the whole country in the international sphere.'

This rosy vision was swiftly erased at a dinner party to which he was invited soon after reaching Washington by a group of Republican Congressmen. After the Ambassador had by custom made a short speech, he listened with stupefaction when one of them remarked: 'Mr. Ambassador, before I ask my question, I would like you to know that every one of us in this room thinks President Roosevelt as dangerous a dictator as Hitler and Mussolini, and that he is taking this country to hell just as fast as he can.' Thus he first became aware of the ferocity of the emotions which the President inspired in large sections of the American people. The image of a father figure dissolved from that moment, and as the weeks passed it was borne in upon him ever more strongly how corrosive was the hatred in some quarters for the Head of the Administration, and for the policies he had adopted. After the dinner party he had written:

'I dined with a lot of Republicans last night—Senators and Congressmen. My word—they do all hate F.D.R. They regard him almost exactly as we used to regard Lloyd George at his worst; stirring up class feeling; no responsibility or knowledge of serious things; pure vote-catching, etc., etc. And I can see something of what they mean. It must be infuriating to big business people to think that Harry Hopkins, who knows less than nothing about all that sort of thing, is having a big hand in industrial and financial

[1] Walter Lippmann to author.

policy. But our idea in England that F.D.R. is a great national hero like Abraham Lincoln over here is just miles away from the truth.'

Apart from his efforts to understand the new political system confronting him, it was necessary for the Ambassador to gather up the threads of Embassy life, and to meet the members of his staff who were unknown to him. This was no easy task because the wartime British Embassy in Washington had already been greatly expanded. When the United States entered the war it was indeed to become a body of almost fabulous distinction in American eyes, a centre of political life, rich in intellectual talent which at one time included six Fellows of All Souls, and comprising with the Military Mission, twelve hundred members. Americans like Senator Vandenberg in search of information would find that it was often more fruitful to consult the British Embassy than their own State Department.[1] The various purchasing missions brought the figure of the staff up to between four and five thousand, and at the apex of this enormous body of men and women the Ambassador was to preside. To Dean Acheson 'The British Embassy under him became a very large, but most efficiently organized unit, and over this the policy and orders of Halifax were perfectly understood and always prevailed'.[2]

Already he found the staff experienced and efficient, and recorded that he was admirably served by Angus Malcolm as Private Secretary, and by many others who afterwards filled posts of high responsibility. Nevile Butler was his second in command when he arrived in America. Gerald Campbell came to him from Ottawa, and Ronald Campbell from Belgrade. Frederick Hoyer Millar also served him in Washington, and among his other subordinates were Michael Wright, John Balfour, Roger Makins and John Russell, while later arrivals included William Hayter and Isaiah Berlin. An industrious Donald Maclean also laboured in the Embassy with exemplary devotion and none of the eccentric moments which were later to distinguish his career in Cairo.

The size to which the British Missions became inflated during the war caused the President, in jocular vein, to remark to Edward that there were more English in Washington in 1942 than there had been when they had burned the White House in 1814. Beside the provision of tanks, guns and aircraft, and other military requirements the work of supply came to embrace almost every activity of the modern industrial state:

'Food, headed for some time by our old friend Bob Brand, raw materials by Clive Baillieu, shipping in the able hands of Arthur Salter, finance under the eye of Frederick Phillips, the untiring watchdog of the Treasury—these and many other subjects of greater or less importance were attended to by the special British missions working in co-operation with their American counterparts. Of this many sided activity the nucleus was the British Supply

[1] *The Private Papers of Senator Vandenberg*, p. 21.   [2] Dean Acheson to author.

Council presided over during my first months in Washington by Mr. Arthur Purvis.'[1]

Thinking it important that the members of these different missions should be aware of what their colleagues were doing, Edward instituted a fortnightly meeting of the heads over which he presided, when each would give a brief account of anything of interest that was happening. He found these meetings tedious, but believed that they served a useful purpose. After one of them he wrote in his diary: 'I had a meeting of the heads of missions and Embassy people in the morning, which I have once a fortnight to keep them in touch with one another. It is rather waste of time, but the kind of waste of time that is worth it, and I don't let it last for more than an hour and a quarter.'

It was not to be expected that presiding over so large a body he could achieve in it the family atmosphere of an ordinary Embassy, and he was prevented in any case from doing so by the demanding nature of his duties, for he had never worked harder in his life than in Washington. We shall see him submitting meekly to the tyranny of social engagements he detested, and which consumed a disproportionate amount of his time and the greater part of his leisure. Much of his work lay outside the Embassy, in seeking the acquaintance of Congressmen and Senators, in cultivating the President through the medium of Hopkins and Roosevelt's personal aide General Watson, in his relations with all Americans of influence who could enlarge his knowledge, and in the tours which were to lead him into every State of the Union.

All these activities left him little time for the daily Embassy routine. Nor did he show much inclination for it, spending most of his time when at home in his own study and seldom entering the Chancery. Often he would walk in the garden which was overlooked by the Chancery windows, and could be seen from them pacing the lawn, a tall figure, a little bent, followed by his dachshund Frankie.

Thus he failed to achieve the close relationship with his immediate subordinates customary in a smaller Embassy. Ronald Campbell found him 'an aloof character'; to William Hayter he was 'too detached and aloof to be popular with the Embassy staff'. But others thought this talk of aloofness somewhat unjust, causing Angus Malcolm to ask:

'What did they expect, and who did they think they were to him? He wasn't "one of them" like a career Ambassador would have been: and to him they (we) were just another set of officials whose names and jobs he had to try and remember as he'd been doing for years in one high office after another, but experts at a kind of mumbo-jumbo that was new to him and didn't make much appeal to him at 60-plus.'[2]

Isaiah Berlin, perhaps the most coruscating of the Fellows of All Souls who graced the Washington scene, was to see the Embassy in his day as

[1] Halifax, Op. cit., p. 262.   [2] Angus Malcolm to author.

'a Public School with Halifax as Provost rather than Head Master', and to attribute his lack of intimacy with the staff to the fact that in his rare moments of leisure he sought the company of old friends with whom he need make no effort. He thought that it was an essential part of Edward's nature that he liked to be amused by those who spoke the same language as himself, and welcomed familiars like Victor Cazalet and Malcolm MacDonald with whom he could relax and be entertained by the gossip he so much enjoyed.

Among such special friends were John Wheeler-Bennett and Isaiah Berlin himself, and both noticed that in spite of his monk-like appearance Edward, in an innocent manner, enjoyed the company of pretty women, indulging in flirtatious but safe conversations, and sometimes seeking to dissuade them from divorcing their husbands. Berlin also observed that Edward developed a tendency to surround himself with non-diplomatic young men, at one time having two Private Secretaries who were not members of the Foreign Office, and that some of the staff did not take kindly to this viceregal atmosphere.

But if Edward was a trifle remote from the senior diplomatists on his staff, he was regarded in an altogether different light by its junior members. To Miss Hudson who took some of the dictation of his diary the Ambassador was a far from awe-inspiring figure, while Dorothy endeared herself to the servants and made herself personally responsible for all the staff of two hundred, persuading the Foreign Office to contribute money for a canteen. Chester Barksdale, the charming coloured doorman who had been in the Embassy for forty years, remembered how much Edward appreciated everything he had done for him, and how he used to invite the staff into the ballroom for cocktails at parties that are still talked about in the Embassy, and how when the tiny Negro and the Ambassador were walking side by side the others used to say: 'There go the long and the short of it.'[1]

Edward was also devoted to another coloured servant at the Embassy, Charlie Brown, who was even smaller than Chester, and far older. He was at his delightful best with these Embassy servants, and, as with the workers on his estates, liked to think of them not only as his personal friends, but almost as members of his family. To Tom Keep, his chauffeur, who was later to have the doubtful privilege of teaching him to drive, 'he was one of the nicest men I have ever met', infallibly considerate, and Keep was to notice the boyish zest which Edward showed in driving the big Buick that was used for official occasions, to picnics at Mount Vernon. He opened the Embassy garden to the staff so that any of them could go in there to relax or eat their lunch, and in Keep's eyes he was 'more like one of you than like an Ambassador'.[2]

[1] Chester Barksdale to author.   [2] Tom Keep to author.

CHAPTER XXX

A NEW WORLD

ONE of Edward's first requirements in Washington was a congenial place of worship, and this need was satisfied, like so many others, by his fellow Anglican Charles Peake who had discovered the Mission Church of St. Agnes, twenty minutes by road from the Embassy, and escorted him there on their first Sunday. They went at nine-thirty to what proved to be the patronal festival. Both men found the homely and unsophisticated atmosphere much to their taste. 'It was just what we both liked,' said Peake, 'with incense and little boys in scarlet cassocks, and nice children with hymns.'

Peake had already saluted the incumbent Dubois with the hearty inquiry, 'Have you thrown your biretta into the ring?' and the priest had looked forward eagerly to Edward's arrival, for apart from the fact that he was the British Ambassador the news of his devoutness had preceded him. A throng of Press-men accompanied Edward even on this deeply personal occasion, and after the service expressed a desire to photograph him shaking hands with the priest, who refused the request. It was one of Edward's earliest intimations that no occasion was too private to be sacrificed to the insatiable hunger of the American public for information.

Edward told Dubois that he would like as little publicity as possible, and that he wished to be treated like an ordinary layman. Charles Peake had warned the priest that the Ambassador was unlikely to become a parishioner as St. Agnes was too far from the Embassy, but the following Sunday he was there again, and after that, until Dubois left to become a chaplain in the army, he seldom failed in attendance.

Edward always came for the same service, the nine-thirty Mass, and the priest vividly recalled the tall figure worshipping among small children and helping them with their hymnals. When in church he seemed to Dubois to be almost an inhabitant of another world, and on one Good Friday, in spite of a diplomatic crisis, remained for the whole three hours of the service. Dubois was much struck by the simplicity and friendliness of so eminent a man for a young priest. When Edward wished to speak to him on the telephone he invariably put through the call himself instead of through a secretary, ringing up full of apologies when he wished to confess out of normal hours at moments of crisis. It was an almost entirely family congregation, and it seemed to the priest that it was this that appealed to the Ambassador, and that it was a relief to him to be treated exactly as though he were one of them, and that this was the reason why, although on formal occasions he often attended the Cathedral, he found his true fulfilment at St. Agnes.

Edward and Dorothy soon found that their life would afford little time for relaxation. In the summers ahead they would play tennis in the Embassy garden and bathe in the swimming pool, but they were to find that Washington was most beautiful in the spring when the city was like a teeming garden with the Japanese flowering cherry trees in bloom, so that when their blossoms fell it seemed to Edward as though he was sitting in a pink snow storm, and when the dogwood was white and dull red in the parks; lovely too in the fall when the splendour of autumn was almost as breath-taking as in New England.

They had always been fond of walking, and began in all weathers to explore the paths among the rocks and woods of Rock Creek Park, or wander down the bank of the Chesapeake and Ohio Canal which reaches George-town above the left bank of the Potomac river. Once surveyed by George Washington, it was a waterway long disused and a restful place to walk, shaded by trees and full of birds and wild flowers with sometimes a patient angler intent on his float. They would often walk in the grounds of the Naval Observatory, round which Massachusetts Avenue throws an encircling arm to the right above the British Embassy. There were few open spaces round Washington offering promise of exercise which they neglected to explore, and when pressed for time they would take their exercise by the Dalecarlin Reservoir on the banks of a solitary lake, which lay deserted in a wooded hollow with an irregular natural shore line that reminded them of Virginia Water. When he had more leisure Edward would sometimes go riding from a livery stable on the River Road.

Apart from these explorations round Washington they had already in February found a haven for their free week-ends almost as soothing as The Retreat at Mashobra after the tumult of the capital. This was the Gibson house 'Mirador' in Virginia, where Lady Astor had lived as a girl, and which had been put at their disposal by its owner Mrs. Ronald Tree. The house was built in about 1810, proclaiming in its grace the classical manner in its expiring elegance, the rooms grouped round a circular hall from which a slender staircase climbed to the first floor. The atmosphere of the place was that of England in the 1860s. Stewart, the coloured butler, addressed Dorothy as 'Miss', and he and the English housekeeper Helen looked after them 'as if we had belonged to each other all our lives'. The Halifaxes had always been fortunate in their gardens, and that of Mirador was exquisite, and redolent of the Southern past with its slave quarters and white pavilions, its judas trees and dogwood, its hedges covered with honeysuckle in May, filling the garden with scent, and in September orchards bright red with apples and smelling of cider. On one of his early visits as they stood looking at the garden on a perfect morning of April sunshine Edward's eye had fallen upon the slave quarters:

'I regret that there are no slaves,' he said; 'this would be my hour for visiting my slaves. I should talk affably with them. I should visit the sick and aged and read the Bible to them, and when gross impropriety or misconduct demanded it, I should correct them, and every now and then I should bend to pat a little head. Finally I should make them all sing Spirituals to me.'

As to things of the spirit, a church lay nearby built by the Langhorne sisters, Mrs. Dana Gibson, Mrs. Robert Brand and Lady Astor, in memory of their mother, with two storeys of sash-windows and a brick cloister leading to the parsonage, and inside everything, even the box-pews, painted a dazzling white. The service was by no means to Edward's taste as it was distinctly 'low' and appeared to him more a pretext round which a social gathering was built than an occasion for the practice of religion as he understood it. He found that all the activities of the place seemed to belong to some bygone age, and were grouped round the church, and that the village hinged upon it, as in England in the last century, but now for social rather than devotional purposes, although he and Charles Peake were prepared to concede that there was a certain amount of 'easy piety' as well. Later they had inspected the Home Farm where 'Edward prodded shorthorns and decided that he would spend every spare moment in Virginia'.[1]

*   *   *

At first there was much that was strange about America to the Ambassador. He had only visited her once before for a few weeks as a young man and he knew little about the American character and institutions. He had, as we have seen, a curious lack of interest in foreign countries until he was actually brought into contact with them, and it was only when new people and scenes were before his eyes that his curiosity was aroused and the differences of life and custom presented themselves to him with a delightful novelty. In America he discovered a new and often perplexing world, and he was continually noticing that although its inhabitants spoke the same language as himself they were in some ways more foreign to him than the races of Europe. 'They really are the most extraordinary people,' he would note in his diary in naïve bewilderment after some particularly baffling event, and perhaps the most remarkable feature of his ambassadorship was the swiftness with which his character adapted itself to the new surroundings.

The greater part of his previous life had been spent in sheltered places and within a limited circle of friends. He had been born an aristocrat and had inherited great possessions. As Viceroy of India his word had swayed the destinies of three hundred million human beings, and he had lived with all the majesty and adornments of a king. At the Foreign Office he had presided

[1] Charles Peake. Diary.

over the most stophisticated department in Whitehall where, in spite of divisions on policy and rising tension the transaction of affairs had been invariably civilized and suave. He knew little of ordinary people except as the squire on his estates. In America, the calm, selective life came to an abrupt end, and he was now brought into continuous and direct contact with the most uninhibited population in the world.

In the tours which Edward undertook and which were to lead him into every State in the Union, the first Ambassador to achieve this feat, he was the centre of enormous crowds who wrung his hand and clapped him on the back. He debated with hard-headed business men and Labour representatives, and submitted himself with steady nerve to hours of gruelling and sometimes hostile questions. He was known to have made ten speeches in a single day.

In this post his patience and slow-kindling temper were an asset rather than a liability, and an ample strain was placed on both. It did not take him long to discover that there were sections of the population with conceptions of his own country which seemed to him both ill-informed and perverse. Throughout his ambassadorship hard words about colonialism and oppression in India were thrown in his face, and he was staggered by the ignorance of many of his questioners—astonished that they should hold such views without even having read an elementary textbook on India, and that the Mayor of St. Louis should be under the impression that the Indian 'Congress' was a legislative body like their own Congress whose yearning for freedom was being stifled by the same colonial oppressors who had burned the White House.

To counteract such misconceptions Edward gave patient explanations of the truth, but his patience did not extend to criticisms of his country's efforts in the war. On one of his early tours in 1941 a C.I.O.[1] leader accused the British of cowardice for not advancing in the west.

'This spurred me to reply by telling him that many people in England wondered by what earthly right it was that they presumed to criticize what we were doing, when all our people were liable to be killed any night by bombing, and when we were fighting on three fronts, and they were not fighting at all. This went very well with his colleagues, and he remained quiet for the rest of the meeting. I don't think it will have done any harm to have a snap.'

A great deal of Edward's character was revealed by the manner in which he adjusted himself to these strange surroundings, and to a breezy familiarity and an assumption of equality he had never before encountered. But those who believed that he felt miserable throughout, that he winced under the back-slapping of Senators and the exuberance of crowds, and that he only won the affection of Americans by playing a part and indulging in a huge deception, were wholly mistaken. Beneath his shrewdness and the gravity of

[1] Congress of Industrial Organization.

his bearing his character remained simple and flexible, accommodating itself to the new conditions by a change of colour as natural as that of a chameleon.

Completely lacking in affectation it never occurred to him that his dignity had suffered from the sometimes boisterous approaches of the American people. Rather was his ever-curious mind entranced by the discovery of their difference from his own countrymen, so that far from resenting American directness, he enjoyed it, and shirked no public invitation, however alarming, to speak for his country and silence her detractors. We shall follow him later on some of these tours. It was on them that he came to discern and to love what he believed to be the true America, generous, buoyant, avid for information, winning his heart and filling him with warmth, and wiping from his mind any recollection of resentment or slight.

But this new life demanded an exhausting effort, and brought many fugitive moments of irritation. The American habit of forthright speech caused many things to be said to him which might have been construed as offensive without in any way being intended to give that impression. Edward was, as ever, impeccably polite, but always firm when the credit of England was questioned. When Mrs. Eugene Meyer, the wife of the proprietor of the *Washington Post*, spoke of American mistrust of Britain as an aristocratic rather than a democratic country split into two class structures by the Public Schools and State Education, he told her that he did not think that the English had anything to learn from America about democracy, and that the main difference was that 'they were more sensible about it, and did not drive it to insanity by wanting to elect their judges'.

Sometimes, after some particularly ill-informed heckling about India, he would make caustic entries in his diary about the position of the Negro in American society. As he came to know the Americans better it seemed to him that this readiness to criticize from a basis of complete ignorance was the principal weakness of the national character, and when the Governor of Richmond told him that an audience of two thousand, strongly hostile to British rule in India, had been completely won round by a speech from the Indian Agent-General, and had left the hall converts, he observed:

'It never seemed to occur to him that this was quite a sharp indictment of the intelligence of the two thousand, and in particular of their presumption in having an opinion at all that could be so completely and promptly changed!

'I feel more and more that what is lacking in these people is that essential element in judgment of knowing what they don't know. They are self-assured, warm-hearted, emotional, enthusiastic, but by reason of that lacking essential, are temperamentally volatile and insecure. But, as Dorothy points out, there are compensations in that they are more ready to be idealistic and less disposed to be cynical perhaps than we are.'

The hungry publicity machine used Halifax without mercy, and he submitted cheerfully to its embrace. 'He may not have been much in the rough

and tumble before,' said Walter Lippmann, 'but he was not in the slightest
disconcerted by it,'[1] and to John McCloy, then in a leading position in the
War Department and afterwards Chairman of the Ford Foundation, it
seemed that Edward 'spared himself no indignity at the hands of the people',[2]
a fact that was soon to turn their sympathy strongly toward him. There were
indeed to be many undignified moments rare in his former life, but far from
disconcerting him they were a source of rich amusement to Edward and
Dorothy, and the subject of many droll entries in his diary. His first and most
unhappy interview with the photographic Press alone caused him serious
offence, and after it Edward gave Peake some moments he did not quickly
forget:

'I thought when Edward came in I was in for trouble,' said Peake. 'There
were 30 photographers who had already photographed Lady H. They asked
him to sit down, and then to my horror one of them having twitched his coat
tried to get hold of his *left* hand and "arrange" it. I could have murdered
him. I looked at his face which remained impassive, but I knew that he had
been touched on the raw.' After a time Edward said coldly: "I have had
enough," and went into the small drawing-room to the tea table where he sat
glowering at Peake until it was time to go to the press conference.

'So we went,' said Peake, 'and he faced about 150 Press-hounds. I have
never known him more charming or more skilful. I could see that the incident
of the hand had touched him on the raw and he was still quivering inside like
a nerve. The three of us dined, and after dinner we went into the library and
worked. Every now and then he would look up and regard me gravely and
make some remark. We went upstairs, and as we parted he said: "Brek
tomorrow?" I said: "Yes, brek at a quarter to nine." "Good night, dear
Charles." "Good night, Edward." "Brek" was meant, I think, to be a peace-
offering, and was rather like offering a child a visit to the Zoo. His charm is
formidable, but he is very exacting and makes more severe demands on one
than anyone I have ever known. It is partly my own fault because I let him,
but I can see he means to keep his staff at arm's length. If greatness means
anything he probably has it, but I wish he needn't be so sensitive.'

This was one of the few occasions in America when Halifax, even for a
moment, felt his composure shaken. All the other curious episodes in which
he was involved were subjects for hilarity recounted eagerly in his inner
circle, and growing in the hands of accomplished bards. 'Look soulful,
Lord,' said the Press-men to the scowling Ambassador in the ferry-boat that
was taking him to the Statue of Liberty. 'Are you Mr. Halifax?' asked the
lift-boy in a New York hotel, putting him at his ease by adding a reminder
of kinship: 'I'm Welsh myself.' It was necessary to reconcile himself to the
most peculiar activities—broadcasting *à deux* with an American seaman,
being photographed with the Mayor of Des Moines clutching a huge Iowa

[1] Walter Lippmann to author.   [2] John McCloy to author.

turnip, wincing under the Kleig lights of Movietone News, and in Florida the photographers swarming over him at 8 a.m. to record 'a typical English family breakfast'.

And there was the G.I. to whom he had given a lift, and who, when told that he was the British Ambassador, said with a puzzled look but with the pleasure of a new discovery: 'Then your name will be Joe Kennedy.' 'I told him that he had got the idea, but not quite right.' He who had jealously guarded his Christian name had to submit to its frequent and sometimes incorrect employment, Joseph Davies, the former American Ambassador in Moscow, seeking to strike an informal note by beginning a letter to him 'Dear Arthur'. The Mayor of Milwaukee, after proposing a vote of thanks to the Ambassador, told his audience: 'Up to now there have always been some of us here who would have expected when we met the British Ambassador that we should find him too smart for us. After meeting Lord Halifax we don't think so any longer.' At a party for the Congressman for Hawaii he was decked with lilac and azaleas like a sacrificial bull.

Always a man disposed to quiet evenings and early bed, he was obliged to attend such dinner parties as that given in honour of Senator George Norris which seemed to him to illustrate more clearly than any other experience the difference between the English and American character:

'The Senator who was our host began by reading laudatory letters which took some time. Then, according to the custom here, he handed over the business to a judge, who also produced a lot of letters from young men all saying how much they had profited by the example of the elder statesman Senator. To this the judge added about a quarter of an hour of his own and then called in succession upon four others, who made speeches ranging from fifteen to twenty-five minutes. The most flowery crude stuff to which I have ever listened; one sentence remains with me—

' "There are from time to time in the world minds that can apprehend at once all the great mysteries of nature from the tiniest grain of sand (pointing to the floor) to the most mighty constellation (pointing to the roof). One of these minds is that of our dear friend George Norris"—(the last words in a dramatic whisper). Thomas Jefferson, Fox, Daniel Webster, Lincoln, Woodrow Wilson, all came into it and meanwhile the chairs got harder.

'All this went on until 11.15 when the old Senator rose to reply to this torrent of praise. He spoke till 11.50 and the burden of the speech was a violent attack on the Republican party or those elements in it that were supposed to be out for big business and high tariffs as opposed to the better world that all right minded people must want to build. He quoted the Beveridge Report as if it were already an accepted and accomplished policy, to show how far ahead we were: "The British people, whom many Americans had not liked and did not like today, had yet found wonderful unity under the reign of death from the sky. The Duke and the labourer between whom there had been so deep a gulf had found their innermost thoughts to be the same as they crouched deep below the ground from this hail of bombs," and much more of the same sort. I thought I should really have expired, if it had not been a most amazing object lesson in the differences between the American and the British mind. No British audience could possibly have stood it, and I am constantly wondering what the explanation is.'

*   *   *

Thus an entirely new form of social intercourse confronted the Ambassador as his daily duty. He who abhorred cocktail parties and most enjoyed relaxing in patched shooting clothes with a few cronies was assiduous in his attendance at this tedious ritual. He hated noise and packed crowds of people, and bellowed conversations with strangers he might never see again and with whom it was an effort to grope for a topic of mutual interest. He went partly out of politeness but mainly because he always hoped that he might find some Senator or Congressman he had not met before, or a member of the Administration he did not know well, and thus enlarge his acquaintance and improve his position.

It was all part of the job he had undertaken, and he performed it gracefully and with no appearance of boredom, a tall figure balancing on one leg, an unwanted glass in his right hand, captivating the ladies by that charm he knew so well how to exert. It was inevitable that he should become a darling of the Washington hostesses, the delightful Mrs. Bliss with her home at Dumbarton Oaks, the brilliant but sharp-tongued Mrs. Longworth disposed to isolationism and mistrustful of England, and Mrs. McLean whose parties swelled to incredible proportions.

Edward observed with wonder the practice of some hostesses of turning a dinner party into a political forum at which guests were invited to stand up and give their opinions on current affairs. He noticed too, the tendency of Americans to regard mealtimes not as a period of relaxation, but as an extension of office hours. Accustomed to English apathy in the face of other people's eloquence he was baffled by the passion of Americans for listening to speeches. It was an ordeal which he felt to be almost as tedious as that of making them which was already his duty on every conceivable occasion.

'Oh these speeches!' he wrote to a friend after four months in America; 'they exhaust me in preparation and bore me in delivering! But it's very difficult to keep out of it, and I conceive one of my principal duties to be to "get around" and show oneself and if possible hearten them all up.' Here he was guilty of exaggeration for it would have been physically impossible for him to find time to compose his own speeches, which was done by Charles Peake and afterwards by his Secretaries, Angus Malcolm and Jack Lockhart, his father's biographer, although Edward made many alterations and improvements in their drafts.

And how did the Americans regard the new Ambassador? When the 'phoney war' was in progress America was not particularly alarmed, and from three thousand miles observed its course sometimes with disparaging comment, but from the time the war passed from that passive phase until the attack on Pearl Harbour she was deeply divided, and Halifax's position correspondingly delicate. Against him were the Isolationists, led by such men as Wheeler and Borah, and the whole Mid-Western group, the *Chicago Tribune* and Colonel McCormick. The Pacific Coast was believed to be largely isolationist, and many Americans clung to non-engagement. To offset these facts the Selective Service Act had been passed in September 1940 bringing compulsory military service, and the Destroyer deal was transacted in August 1941 and associated with Lend-Lease, and these events seemed to indicate the belief that American interests were linked with those of Britain.

Before leaving England Edward had felt considerable doubt whether he was the kind of man who would be congenial to Americans, but when it became obvious that he must accept the post, had given much thought to what his attitude to the country should be. It was Dorothy who had found the right answer saying that the only way to behave was 'to be ourselves', and whenever Edward followed this counsel of sanity he pleased the Americans, while on the few occasions when either by accident or through inept advice, he departed from it, a false note was struck which was immediately detected.

Nearly all the Americans who were brought into contact with Halifax liked him because he was the sort of Englishman they expected him to be, and it seemed to many that in appearance he resembled a Victorian statesman or that there was a suggestion of Lincoln in his gaunt figure and austere features. His aristocratic birth was not, as he had feared, a disadvantage in the eyes of most of them. 'It was soon realized by Americans,' said Lippmann, 'that Halifax was a great gentleman, and such a man is never a snob or patronizing,' and it was the view of Christian Herter that 'Americans at heart liked an aristocrat provided he did not put on side'. Arthur Krock, the able political analyst of the *New York Times*, also noticed that Halifax's distinguished exterior was impressive to Americans, and that when they found that beneath that surface he was simple and unaffected, and further that there was much gaiety in his nature, they warmed to him instantly. Krock believed that his historic name, if anything, lent *cachet* to him as an ambassador, while in the opinion of Senator Saltonstall he was regarded by most Americans as 'an Englishman at his best'.

But all were united in saying that one of the main reasons for their admiration was that Edward was so essentially and obviously himself, and their senses were alert for any symptoms of spurious *bonhomie*. During the first few months when he was trying to absorb the atmosphere he was not always well advised. When he played his natural part he did so supremely well, and his past high office and engaging simplicity produced a warm response, but there were, as we shall see, occasional early lapses, and it was somehow wrong in the eyes of Americans, as his friend Averell Harriman said, when he was photographed eating a hot dog at a baseball match, 'for that was not Halifax'. Yet if he was at first sometimes badly advised on what would jar the American mind, it was also a deficiency in his own character that he had neither the instinct nor the knowledge of the world to realize that the advice was wrong.

There could be no question that Churchill had chosen the most distinguished man available to him to be his ambassador and that he continued throughout the war to rate very highly Halifax's efforts in America. But although he had a high opinion of his abilities he did not wish to keep him in the Foreign Office, and it was, in the opinion of Sir Alexander Cadogan,[1] a brilliant solution on the part of Churchill to send him to Washington. The Prime Minister was at that time at the height of his glory in American eyes, and any emissary he sent would have been certain of a warm welcome, but Halifax was never regarded by Americans as the discard of a Prime Minister anxious to banish the priests of appeasement from his shores. Well aware that Churchill believed the assistance of America, in whatever form, and preferably as a participant in the war, to be his country's main, if not only hope of victory, they were convinced that he would never send them, at such a crisis of history, a man of whom he merely wished to dispose. On the contrary they felt it a compliment that the Ambassador should be a statesman who had already held such high offices.

But if it was an advantage to Halifax that he had been sent by a Prime Minister whose resolution and glowing eloquence had so stirred American hearts, it was a severe handicap that it was his fate to follow Lord Lothian who in a period of the greatest difficulty had proved himself the most successful ambassador ever sent from England to Washington. It is a curious reflection that although Halifax incurred a passing odium in America for his association with Munich, his predecessor, whose record had been far more blameworthy and assessment of Germany infinitely more deluded, had never been tainted with the smear of appeasement. The reason for this immunity, which puzzled many familiar with Lothian's past, was that in American eyes he had not been publicly identified with the policy, and had not, like Halifax, occupied a prominent position such as Foreign Secretary. He was also a man apt in personal contact, a great Ambassador with an intimate knowledge of American life and custom, with the advantage of having visited every university in America as Chairman of the Rhodes Trust before assuming his office.

As we pause a little longer on the threshold of Edward's ambassadorship we may note some further characteristics that were observed both by the

[1] Sir Alexander Cadogan to author.

Americans and by his own colleagues. He was to develop an absorbing interest in the American people. From the beginning, aware of his ignorance, he was determined to understand their character, and to fathom all the motives that governed their lives. That insatiable curiosity that Walter Durnford had noticed at Eton stimulated him on this voyage of discovery. As avid for knowledge as Rudyard Kipling he questioned his American friends remorselessly until both they and the subject were exhausted. He showed more curiosity than anyone Lewis Douglas[1] had ever met: 'He wanted to know *everything.*' 'He had,' thought McCloy, 'an amazing instinct for gathering information. He was a really *inquiring* Ambassador.' He had never, he said, met a man so inquisitive and so voracious to ascertain facts, and he was surprised how simple, and even naïve was his approach to problems, how he asked with unsophisticated directness 'what sort of man Hopkins was', without the slightest circumlocution. 'Winston said I ought to know about the Civil War,' he told McCloy; 'how could I find out about it?'

McCloy at first found it difficult to believe that this man who had occupied such great positions could really be as simple and straightforward as he seemed, or as diffident and self-effacing, but afterwards realized that this was indeed the case. As time passed this interest in the lives and customs of Americans grew as his knowledge of them increased, and, as the effect of his unassuming personality bore fruit, he imposed himself upon them as a figure whom they admired both as man and ambassador, and who, by his masterful projection of Britain at war, was to give them the best impression of her that they had ever received.

The effect on his own character of the contact he was to make with Americans in every State from Maine to California was wholly good. Almost for the first time he was brought into the dust of the arena and, his natural aloofness neutralized by hearty encounters on equal terms with every sort of man and woman, he became far more human and, after a while, relaxed and at his ease. It was a process of natural acclimatization by which he worked his way into the affections of the American people, stopping to talk to them on the street, and looking down upon them with a gentle smile from his great height, or giving them lifts in his Rolls-Royce, and it was a new Edward, humanized by experience, who was to invite two ordinary seamen he had casually met in the street to dine at the Embassy with himself and Lord Brand.

Another factor in his success was to be the moral courage he had always possessed in a high degree. Charles Peake may have rightly discerned in him a tendency to keep his official staff at arm's length, but in moments of trouble, whether right or wrong, they could depend on his robust support. And here his formidable independence and complete indifference to rebuke from above made his position impregnable, so that he did not hesitate to disregard later a

[1] American Ambassador in London, 1947-50.

peremptory order by Churchill to dismiss a subordinate for an act of indiscretion, appointing him instead after a suitable pause to a more desirable position.

Moral courage too was already evident in the way he would never shrink from submitting himself to the most intimidating encounters with his opponents because he regarded the correction of false impressions as one of the main duties of his office. He first entered the lion's den at the Wednesday Evening Club in May 1941 as the guest of Mr. Winthrop Kean. The majority of its members came from the Middle West, and many were strongly isolationist. An account of the meeting suggests that some of the audience were bristling with hostility, and that there was many a rod in pickle awaiting the Ambassador at question time. Edward made a short speech, 'and then', said Kean, 'came the vital question and answer period. I remember that I thought one question was very unfair, and tried to rule it out, but Lord Halifax—smart politician that he was—quickly interrupted me to say how pleased he was to have the question asked as that was just the one he wanted to answer'.

A searching inquisition followed, and Edward's mind had to leap from topic to topic, but he had been trained in a hard school and was able to parry the questions with good temper. It was, however, a lonely and frightening ordeal. To one member of the audience 'his general appearance was that of a church mouse or a poor country cousin—but he seemed very fair and frank in his replies; actually told as much as he wanted to tell—no more; very crafty, keen and smooth as a silkworm'. Edward was enchanted by this description when informed of it, but it was clear that the temper of some members of the club was such that no words of his, however persuasive, could have convinced them of anything, as the angry notes on the meeting by Senator Bradley of Michigan clearly indicate:

General Impressions.

1. England is extremely selfish.
2. She will use anybody to help herself, and having gained her ends will dump them overboard.
3. Their statesmen are very smart and have too much experience in power politics for our statesmen to deal with for our own best interests.
4. England looks out for herself first, last and all the time.
5. England has no intention of repayment of any past, present or future war debts.
6. England would like us to help police the world—she to establish the policies—we to pay the bills.
7. More than ever before I am convinced that we should stay out of this war.

8. I had little respect for England before. I have much less now.[1]

Edward was not put out by these churlish reflections, and he was encouraged in the practice of meeting Senators and Congressmen and answering their questions by such friends as Francis Biddle the Attorney-General, and Senator Fulbright.[2] The Senator began arranging parties of half a dozen Congressmen who would meet without formality in the rooms of Edward's Secretary Jack Lockhart for two hours' conversation after dinner, and were designed for him to meet Congressmen, understand how they were thinking, and answer all the questions they raised. It proved a good way of ironing out differences, and to Fulbright the memory of those evenings was of Edward lying back at ease, his long legs stretched out before him, and a haze of tobacco smoke over the room. Biddle remembered an evening of challenge when he invited the Ambassador to meet 'the insiders, the Chairmen of the Committees that ran the country, the Isolationists, and the Irish, apt to be suspicious of a British gentleman'.

'There were fifty or sixty Congressmen who, after bourbon whisky, fried chicken, sweet potatoes and apple pie, relaxing on a Saturday night, formed a circle round the Ambassador who talked to them of England and the war for twenty minutes, and then for an hour answered every conceivable question. He came out of it very well, never saying that anything was off the record, and not evasive, so that they went out murmuring that he was not such a bad guy. An abstemious man and modest, but now all shyness gone, mopping his brow in relief he asked for a whisky and soda. "It wasn't really bad, Biddle," he said. "I had rather dreaded it you know. But I really enjoyed it. Nice chaps, your Congressmen. . . . Don't forget to send me a list, or perhaps a little note on each." '[3]

---

[1] Mr. Winthrop Kean to author.

[2] Democratic Senator of Arkansas since 1945. Associated with the Fulbright Act of 1948; at his suggestion a Commission was set up for travel scholarships for university graduates to be financed from funds derived from the sale of surplus U.S. war stocks in countries which had received Lend-Lease aid. Chairman of Senate Foreign Relations Committee, 1959.

[3] Francis Biddle, *In Brief Authority*, pp. 144-5.

CHAPTER XXXI

RELATIONS WITH THE ADMINISTRATION

Two matters of interest among both English and Americans in official positions were how Halifax would acquit himself in the constant negotiations which would come his way, and whether he would succeed in adapting himself to the demands of a Press far more intrusive in its methods than that of his own country. American officials had anticipated a machiavellian subtlety on the part of the Ambassador, and it is interesting to note the later opinions of some of those who sat in conference with him. Christian Herter strongly approved of his methods because Halifax always put his cards on the table: 'Americans very much liked this method,' he said, 'because they are suspicious of devious and cunning people, being rather clumsy negotiators themselves.'[1]

Lewis Douglas, remembering a shipping negotiation with Edward, was struck most by the equable manner in which he conducted the discussion. Unlike most men, he was never in the least disturbed by an argument with which he did not agree and which seemed to threaten his position. Nor was he lacking in guile: 'He had the negotiating trick of asking questions,' said Douglas. 'It produced the impression that this man was really trying to find out what the truth was, and it was this that made him so effective. He was extremely shrewd and his questions often blew up the person with whom he was conferring.'

'Halifax,' said John McCloy, 'did not resent plain, or even rough speaking in negotiation and was always equable. As a result of this he usually walked away with the argument. If he saw that some point was a tender one he would drop it, so that afterwards you felt that you would like to accommodate him on it.'[2] When the negotiations concerned abstruse economic questions Edward admitted that he was an amateur in these matters, and that he felt a little stifled at such rarified heights, but he was far too experienced and shrewd in business to give any impression of inadequacy, and we shall see that some of his most successful negotiation was accomplished in this field. Robert Lovett, then working in the War Department, thus described his methods:

'In negotiation Halifax went by the book. That is to say he worked from an *aide-memoire*. He was good and well-primed, and was capable of dealing

[1] Christian Herter, Republican diplomatist and politician, Secretary of State 1959–61, to author.
[2] John McCloy to author.

496

adequately with an economic problem. The routine was for the Ambassador to state his country's position, and enumerate her needs, and then he handed over to the experts and they moved in. In fact Halifax acted as a sort of traffic controller and mastered his brief perfectly, and the British Missions and staff were first class.'

But it is unlikely that Edward had felt any serious doubts about his ability in this direction for he was a born negotiator, self-confident, quick-witted and calm, always ready for a tactical concession without losing sight of his main objective. The triumph in his marathon with Gandhi had further strengthened his self-assurance and he must have felt that anything awaiting him in America would be child's play after that experience.

The question of his relations with the Press was a different matter, and it seemed to many that he was unlikely to achieve that blend of *camaraderie* and indiscretion that had so endeared his predecessor to American journalists. It was feared that his manner would seem to them feudal and remote, his method of speech patronizing, and his resentment of intrusions on his privacy unfriendly. It was a new form of inquisition and a critical body, and even his warmest admirers could not have anticipated that he would gain an outstanding success in such an improbable field. Yet three of the leading figures in American journalism, Walter Lippmann, James Reston and Arthur Krock, were unanimous in the view that Halifax won not only the acceptance but the admiration of the Press, and there was no more remarkable example of the levelling effect of American society on his character than this particular achievement.

He was always ready to address their institutions, and the National Press Club and the Women's Press Club were no beds of roses for the foreign visitor. The ladies in particular could be alarming when roused, and he could expect many penetrating questions, some of them of a hostile and provocative character. But with his political experience they presented no difficulties to him. His adroitness in answering questions was extraordinary, but in doing so, said Lippmann, 'he gave an impression of great sincerity. He did not try to be subtle and devious, but answered simply and seriously, leaving the impression that he was an honest and good man'.[1] Edward was pleased when a woman journalist told him how much she had appreciated the fact that he had not talked down to the audience.

But James Reston was to find, in the years ahead, that the Ambassador was not entirely compounded of milk and honey in his relations with the Press, and that if an indiscretion took place likely to impair his credit with the United States Government he could be ruthless and hard. Reston remembered how papers had been circulated by the Allies before the Dumbarton Oaks Conference giving their views about the coming World Organization, and how he had gained access to these documents and begun publishing

[1] Walter Lippmann to author.

them in the *New York Times* with the approval of his Editor. The Administration had tried to stop their publication, thinking that it would produce an
unfortunate effect on the Russians. They believed that the information had
leaked from the British Embassy, but Reston had assured the Ambassador
that he had not received it from that source. Halifax had answered that he
was also satisfied that this was so, and that he believed Reston, but that he
would never receive him again as he was not prepared to have further relations with a man who had been in any way involved in the affair. He adhered
to this decision even when Reston showed him a letter he had sent to the
State Department saying that he had not received his facts from the British
Embassy.[1]

Edward was thus in due course to be accepted by his American friends
and many of his English colleagues as straightforward, modest, and able and
in essence a simple man, but there would be some who believed that this
was far too facile an analysis of his character, and that, however friendly,
there was something impenetrable in him which seemed to indicate that
there was much that was withheld from others. Sir Arthur Salter of the
British Shipping Mission thought that although the Americans' sense of the
integrity of Edward's character helped him to establish a great position, he
had a strong reserve which shut his colleagues off from wide areas of his
thought; and Francis Biddle was struck by the combination of the spiritual
side of his nature with a shrewd political sense, and believed that Edward
was unaware that one side of his character was contradicted by the other:

'Yet he was not innocent, and below the faith one suspected a layer of
shrewd worldliness sometimes found in dedicated Anglicans. . . . Lady
Halifax was always at his slightly bewildered right hand, suddenly gay and
quick to laugh, altogether courageous, outgoing, and warm beside his more
reticent good manners.'[2]

The lines on which he intended to work had soon become clear to the
officials at the Embassy. They found that although the Ambassador would
insist upon London being told the whole unvarnished truth, however ugly,
and that no distortion was ever practised, he was sometimes prepared to
suppress facts which he did not wish to be revealed. 'It is always a matter of
emphasis,' he explained to Isaiah Berlin on occasions when he thought such
a step desirable, and Berlin came to the conclusion that the Ambassador was
a realist who believed that there were moments when moral principles must
yield to expediency.

His staff would also notice that Halifax showed an almost 18th century tendency to behave as though his office entitled him to personal privileges denied
to others, and that he saw nothing wrong in reserving seats on aircraft for
friends and henchmen at a time when space was short and badly needed for
official purposes. 'I send you Ashley Sparks's letter,' he told one of those he

[1] James Reston to author.   [2] Francis Biddle. Op. cit., p. 144.

EDWARD AND DOROTHY AT GARROWBY WITH THEIR GRANDCHILDREN, 1942

was thus obliging; 'on second reading I see he says something about "public or semi-public errand"—which doesn't quite fit you. So I am returning it to him and telling him to talk about "urgent private affairs", and I understand he wishes to be completely co-operative!' Edward himself made no bones about this propensity, and he was later to write in his diary: 'I am all for useful ramps if they can be kept out of sight.'

But all this lay in the future when America had entered the war, and the British Embassy under Halifax became a centre of the diplomatic life of Washington and its Ambassador an accepted part of the American hierarchy and Establishment. Then the Embassy on Massachusetts Avenue would seem to many to resemble a little Downing Street, and the Ambassador an *alter ego* of Churchill.

In the meantime he had begun meeting and often winning the friendship of the members of the Administration and the staffs. To the British Ambassador, the Secretary of State Cordell Hull was the most important of these, and it was with him that Halifax was to be principally concerned. From the moment of his first visit to the State Department Halifax was convinced that in Hull he had a man with whom he could work in complete harmony, although his moods would demand study, and his obstinacy patience. In these early days the Ambassador had much in mind the relative positions of the two countries. The Lend-Lease proposals were still before Congress, and the outcome of the discussions uncertain. He was conscious of the fact that American opinion was still groping, and that large sections of it were continuing to hope that their country might be spared a war, but were uncertain of the direction in which their duty lay. No such doubts harassed the Secretary of State: 'For anyone holding his convictions,' said Edward, 'and holding them with such passionate loyalty as they aroused in Mr. Hull, it was scarcely possible to think or feel neutrally, and he made no pretence at concealment of his detestation of Hitler and of all his works, or of his admiration for the bearing of the British people under Churchill's leadership.'[1]

The Ambassador made constant visits to Hull in a room heated to the temperature of a greenhouse to discuss the many matters of concern to their two countries. 'The first impression on meeting him,' he thought, 'was apt to be misleading. His eyes seemed often to be looking out upon the middle or far distance whether past or future one could not tell; the features of his face, distinguished and sharply cut, were those of someone who had seen many sides of life and had learned the need and the power of patience. But let a word or some train of thought strike the spark, and the whole man would, as it were, spring to arms in support or condemnation.'[2]

Fond as he became of the Secretary of State, Halifax found that the full exercise of his own patience was demanded in his more difficult moments,

[1] Halifax. Op. cit., p. 255.   [2] Ibid.

and every vein in his head felt like bursting in the hot-house air whenever the discussion approached the subject of Argentina on which Hull seemed to him to hold almost obsessive views. But he recognized in the Secretary of State a true ally, whose sympathy with England's predicament was real, and he soon became aware that he had also found a personal friend. 'I like the old boy very much,' he wrote in August 1941, 'and he talks freely to me,' and he was conscious of something reassuring even in his moments of silence: 'It is what seeps out of the pores,' he thought, 'rather than what is actually said.'

And it is pleasant to feel that Hull had for the Ambassador a regard equally warm. 'While I keenly regretted Lothian's death,' he wrote, 'I saw at once that I could work on the same effective, cordial terms with his tall, thin, ascetic-looking successor. Halifax, who possessed unusual ability, engaged in prodigious, fruitful labours while serving in Washington, and the extent and importance of his accomplishments were unexcelled by any other foreign representative during my tenure of office.'[1]

He came gradually to know the other able men Roosevelt had collected round him, the Republican Stimson, who was to become one of his closest friends, and Knox, in charge of the War and Navy Departments respectively, the elegant Dean Acheson whose outstanding brain and brilliant conversation delighted him; Morgenthau at the Treasury, Stettinius at the Office of Lease-Lend, and Finletter at that of Economic Warfare. In Forrestal, the Under-Secretary to the Navy, Edward thought that he saw a man of infinite promise, and found attractive in him a shy manner and a hint of melancholy. At the War Department he found two men who were to become valued friends, John McCloy and Robert Lovett. It was with these departments that most of his work was concerned, and with the chiefs of which he was most closely associated. Besides these, he was brought into frequent contact with the Chiefs of Staff, Generals Marshall and Arnold, Admiral Stark, and later Admiral King.

Of all the American military leaders Marshall was to rouse the Ambassador's greatest admiration, and he was convinced that in the area of the Services the common cause was advanced by the relationship between General Marshall and his English opposite, Sir John Dill, hardly less than that between Churchill and Roosevelt. 'Marshall,' he wrote, 'had to create an American army from an even more complete state of unpreparedness, and no praise can be too great for what he achieved. Both men were entirely devoid of any thought of self-seeking and were heart and soul devoted to the achievement of Allied victory. With complete confidence in each other's motives, they could examine every case without risk of the conclusion being affected by any consideration smaller than the merits of it.'

When these new friends entered his life, many of them forthright and

[1] Cordell Hull, *Memoirs*. Vol. II p. 926.

informal men, Edward was forced to make some painful adjustments in his practice with regard to the use of Christian names. By long habit and natural reserve he was reluctant to make too swift an approach to this stage of intimacy. When unwilling to address Lord Beaverbrook as 'Max' in a letter, and yet feeling that their relations suggested it, he took refuge in sending him a telegram instead. Charles Peake noted in his diary a discussion on the subject in the privacy of the Embassy:

'Edward said: "Not a bit. I always make Ruth my daughter-in-law address me as 'Lord Halifax'. I am certainly not going to become 'Popsy' or anything like that, and as I have often to speak to her for her own good it would be highly inconvenient to let her call me Edward." My anger was about to blaze forth at him for this icy and inhuman attitude, but swallowed it down and am reserving it for the next time we are alone when I am going to talk to him for *his* good.'[1]

Edward was told that this frigid practice could not be continued in a country so given to fraternal heartiness and so vigilant for airs of superiority and condescension. 'I find your Ambassador so cold after Lothian,' General Watson confided in Sir John Balfour,[2] and Edward was told that the moment for decision had come. He must ring up the General and call him by his nickname 'Pa'—Americans expected it. Edward picked up the telephone as though it was a rattlesnake, and, with a reluctance palpable to those who observed the scene, inquired in a husky voice: 'Is that you, P-P-P*a*?' The effect was instantaneous: a flood of *bonhomie* rippled back over the wires, the General turning to his wife and exclaiming warmly: 'He is a good fellow.'[3] The Ambassador also long procrastinated in thus breaking the ice with Harry Hopkins, although he could not have been unaware that Hopkins had for some time been addressing him with gruesome incongruity as 'Ed'.

The Ambassador did his utmost to win the confidence of these men and continually to enlarge the circle of his acquaintance, and he realized from the earliest days that many in important positions, such as Marshall, Dean Acheson, Forrestal, Lovett and Frankfurter, had fully grasped the fact that this was an American war, and that the survival of America depended on entering it.[4] Edward thought that Felix Frankfurter, then Associate Justice of the Supreme Court, had one of the most penetrating minds he had ever encountered, and he became devoted to this stalwart figure, five feet five inches in height, with his cleft chin and fine bluish-grey eyes, who lived in Spartan simplicity, whose loyalty to his friends was proverbial, and whose ruling passion was a devotion to democracy, and a determination that social problems should be solved within its framework. But he never forgot that his paramount duty was to establish, and to keep, an easy and confidential relationship with the President.

[1] Charles Peake. Diary. [2] Sir John Balfour to author.
[3] Mrs. Watson to author. [4] Joseph Allsop to author.

Their birth inevitably created a bond between the two men, and Halifax's Eton-Oxford, Yorkshire background could be expected to blend naturally with that of Groton, Harvard and the Hudson Valley. On the other hand, many believed that Roosevelt with his record of progressive legislation and deep-rooted mistrust of British Imperialism might well take Halifax to be a natural enemy of the first and a living symbol of the second. He might in fact be torn between his inclination towards a British aristocrat and his hatred of colonialism. And there was at least one member of the British Embassy who was under the erroneous impression that Halifax regarded Roosevelt as a traitor to his class, and believed that his New Deal policies smacked dangerously of Socialism.

Such fears proved to be unjustified. Halifax, who once boasted that 'he was a bit of a Socialist himself', felt nothing but admiration for the President's efforts to cure unemployment and, like others, was lost in admiration of the courage with which he had conquered his physical affliction. And Roosevelt, although he had confided in a friend that he was not looking forward to his first meeting with the British Ambassador, had set himself out from the beginning to be helpful.

From that moment an excellent working relationship was established between the two men, and although Halifax's regard for the President was not free from reservations, their friendship lasted unbroken until his death. The Ambassador was told that he could make direct contact by telephone with the President through General Watson whenever he wished, an arrangement which lapsed after Halifax's departure, and that he could enter the White House through a private side door, and thus escape the attentions of the ubiquitous American Press.

He had quickly got on confidential terms with Roosevelt, having a two-hour session with him within a fortnight of their first meeting, and it was not long before he was eating those uncomfortable lunches off a corner of his desk in the White House when the President, relaxed in his own study, held forth on every subject under the sun. Edward did not much enjoy these haphazard repasts, but he realized that they were a heaven-sent opportunity for cornering a man at once so occupied and so discursive. They contained their golden moments too, and he listened spellbound when Roosevelt spoke of bygone Presidents, of Lincoln's fondness for dubious stories, and how Coolidge used to put a mark on the cheese when they had finished with it at luncheon, and go down to the kitchen in the evening alone to see whether the servants had eaten any more of it.[1]

They also gave him exceptional opportunities for observing his host. After a little he was no longer affected by the exuberant charm which became to him faintly synthetic, and seemed to interpose a screen between him and the man who used it. It seemed to him that there was a faint aroma of hypocrisy,

[1] Hickleton Papers.

a whiff of the *faux bonhomme* about the President, something which prevented him putting all his cards on the table, and made Edward feel that it was always necessary to keep his wits about him in their discussions. But these doubts were accompanied by an admiration for his flashes of imaginative genius, his sure instinct for balancing the forces of internal politics, and his astonishing vitality. Although he felt such reservations they were buried in the silence of the grave, and it was only to those closest to him that he admitted that he did not always trust the President, and that 'he was never within streets of Winston's quality'.[1] Sometimes too, there were hints in their conversations of that intense suspicion of British motives in foreign policy which was later to pervade Roosevelt's mind.

But to Halifax these failings were more than offset by his many virtues, and he felt that he could detect beneath the agile politician a warm love of the human race:

'He was genuinely interested in human beings *as* human beings; problems stood before his mind's eye always as human situations; the treatment of them spelt greater happiness or greater unhappiness for men or women; and all the time it was on the relations of men with men that the whole of the world turned.'

It was not enough to have made the President's acquaintance, and to have been given a friendly welcome. The Ambassador had also to understand his character, and to learn to avoid those sensitive points, a pressure upon which might have blighted their relations. He must learn when the President was approachable, and when not, study the best ways of winning and holding his attention, become aware of the right and wrong way of putting a case to him, and the means of forestalling those fits of boredom to which Roosevelt was so easily prone. For these reasons his relations with Harry Hopkins were scarcely less important than those with the President himself, for it was one of Hopkins's many useful functions to act as intermediary between the two men.

This remarkable man, a former social worker who went far to kill himself by his exertions in the war, enjoyed by old association the entire confidence of the President. He was one of those strange figures who, by an American practice rare in other countries, are suddenly snatched from obscurity by the confidence of the Head of the State and placed upon the ramparts of power. He, like the President, had nourished many prejudices about British colonial history stemming from a similar ignorance, but in his case slowly eroded by contact. He was in some ways a rather disreputable figure, *farouche* in appearance, fond of the bottle, and magnificently indifferent to the great. Winston Churchill had paused in a midnight harangue at Chequers to find Hopkins fast asleep on a sofa; to Mrs. Watson he was 'a completely direct person with no circumlocution and extremely crude. He had no manners at

[1] Halifax. Private correspondence.

all, and Pa used to get very angry with his slipshod ways in the house. But he dripped with charm'.[1] Miserably ill during the whole of his service, having had cancer of the stomach and a liver deficiency which made it difficult for his body to dispose of food and caused great expansion of the stomach, his labours were performed against a background of constant suffering.[2]

On every ground such a man might have been expected to regard Halifax as distant and snobbish, and the lordly Ambassador to look askance upon this raffish figure, but by some freak of human relationship there ripened between the incongruous pair a warm and enduring friendship. Perhaps there was in it some strange application of the theory of the attraction of opposites, but to Dean Acheson it was based on the fact that neither man made the slightest attempt to adapt his personality or alter his normal mode of behaviour to harmonize with the other. 'Hopkins remained raffish and tough-talking; Halifax remained exactly as he was, pleasant, friendly and non-censorious.' And it did not take Edward long to realize that this battered man was performing inestimable services and that he was working himself to death in the cause, a heroic and doomed figure.

Part of his great strength to the Ambassador lay in his uncanny sense of judgment. Sometimes when totally ignorant of the subject, said Dean Acheson, he would say: 'I think that man is right,' leaning back in his chair, sick and often weak after a night's excesses. He was seldom wrong. His direct mind had the power of stripping away, as it were, the outer petals of a subject and penetrating at once to its heart, and it was no idle tribute that Churchill paid him when he called Hopkins 'Lord Root-of-the-Matter'.

Hopkins's first impressions of the Ambassador, whom he had met in London before his departure, indicate at once his fairness and prejudice:

'A tall stoop-shouldered aristocrat greeted me in an old office taken over by the ministers of Churchill's Government. I did the talking—or most of it—telling him the people I thought were important for him to see and know in Washington. When I got beyond the President and Hull I was in deep water and quit. I liked him. I think and hope the President will like him. He has no side—has been about—I presume is a hopeless Tory—that isn't too important now if we can get on with our business of licking Hitler. I would not like to see him have much to say about a later peace.'

In spite of these typical reservations their acquaintance flourished, and Hopkins's half-formed doubts succumbed to Dorothy's gaiety and the Ambassador's simplicity and charm. Although there were some who thought the friendship so unnatural that it must be a *mariage de convenance*, Hopkins's second wife Louise insisted that her husband and Edward 'hit it off wonderfully', and that even before Hopkins first met him and before he came to know him well he 'never had the slightest impression of him as a "stuffed shirt" ', and when Hopkins and she were living at the White House Edward

---

[1] Mrs. Watson to author.   [2] Mrs. Louise Gates, formerly Mrs. Hopkins, to author.

would call there three or four times a week to see him. It was a regard that was strongly reciprocated, and Averell Harriman noticed the obvious respect felt by Hopkins for the Ambassador, and how he would frequently say: 'I'll go and see Halifax.' To some, however, it seemed that Edward stood a little in awe of Hopkins's sharp tongue, and John Wheeler-Bennett remembered him saying on one occasion: 'I don't want to see Harry. I don't want to risk a rebuff.'

We shall see that the greatest value of Hopkins to Edward was to reveal itself in the near future at those meetings which were to take place between Churchill and Roosevelt from which the Ambassador was sometimes excluded, and at which Hopkins would represent his interests, and keep him in the game. Invaluable too would be his advice in the innumerable delicate questions for the President with which Edward was bombarded by the Foreign Office but which did not justify asking for a personal interview, and in which he always sought the advice of his friend. Edward had learned quickly. He had fathomed a new type of man, about whom he was to write after his death: 'There were few people I genuinely admired more, and whose good opinion I thought more flattering to have.'

*   *   *

Halifax was to become immensely popular with all classes of Americans with whom he was brought into contact, but success was not immediately reached, and it would be idle to pretend that his early months in the country were easy. His initial failure in Washington was due partly to the difficulty of following Lothian, to that lack of worldliness we have already noticed, and partly to the fact that he took advice from people who, although expert on other parts of the world, were unfamiliar with the American character.

His position on arrival was delicate in the extreme. The Isolationists were poised ready to interpret minor indiscretion as interference in domestic affairs and underhand manœuvres to entice them into the war, and he was regarded by such hostile groups with considerable suspicion. A position so vulnerable demanded both insight and vigilance, and at the beginning he failed to display either. We are in fact struck by the frequent artlessness of his behaviour, and by how he allowed situations to arise, innocuous and trivial in themselves, but in the circumstances damaging to his position and reputation. Each of them could have been avoided by a man of greater sophistication, or by advisers more attuned to the American scene, and for the first six months in Washington it was Dorothy rather than he who kept the flag flying.

The suggestion that the Ambassador should stay with Walter Lippmann,[1] whose pro-British sympathies were widely known, showed a curious lack of understanding of the American suspicion of interference. Then, in February

[1] Walter Lippmann to author.

1941, having been told that it would be better if he did not attend the Lend-Lease debate he was allowed by his advisers to call on Mr. Sol Bloom the Chairman of the Foreign Affairs Committee in the House of Representatives, giving his enemies the opportunity to accuse him of trying to influence the Legislative side of the Government, a blunder which caused attacks to be made upon him lasting for weeks. Edward was not wholly to blame for this particular mistake, for a leading American journalist had advised him to make the call as part of his initial visits to high officers of Congress, saying that while the Isolationists would doubtless try to exploit it, the call itself was normal protocol, and that its omission would be cowardly.

The clamour had scarcely died away when in the next month the Ambassador accepted an invitation to hunt at Wilmington in Virginia with Mr. Plunket Stewart, in spite of being urged to refuse it by John Wheeler-Bennett who had anticipated the reaction with depressing accuracy. Edward had not hunted for fifteen months, and the temptation was too much for him. In any case, he saw nothing wrong in the suggestion. He was, according to a reporter, ill-clad:

'Lord Halifax was attired in what a fox-hunt expert assured reporters was "mufti". To reporters the Master of Fox-Hounds of Middleton Hunt looked a trifle bedraggled compared to some of the less aristocratic participants. The "mufti" in fact looked like a pair of khaki riding pants, a grey pull-over sweater and a brown tweed coat topped by a white but slightly soiled rain-coat.'

At least Edward enjoyed this unfortunate day's hunting, particularly the afternoon when: 'hounds streaked away, and we had a real good burst of 30 minutes. Really great fun—very light country to ride over, rolling hills, nothing to jump except three split railed timber, not too high to be alarming, and a real gallop. Eventually the fox took us into a lot of rough hills and woods where, as it was obviously petering out, I came home.'

This day of simple amusement provoked another onslaught on the Ambassador, the climax of which was a vicious attack on him by the American writer Carl Sandberg, rebuking him for indulging in such effete pleasures when his countrymen were dying in action. He was shaken by this assault, but at the same time baffled and angry. He asked why he should not be allowed to relax in his own way when no word of protest was raised at the President big-game fishing from his yacht in Florida. It was the old lack of *savoir-faire* which prevented him from realizing that foxhunting was regarded in America as a privileged and aristocratic sport, and that no objection would have been taken to a day's duck-shooting which was held to be a democratic recreation.

Later, said Isaiah Berlin, Edward made another *faux pas* when he attended a baseball match, 'leaving in the middle for tea with the British Consul, and saying that it reminded him of cricket except that we did not question the umpire's decisions so often in England'.[1] Partly as a result of such trifling incidents as these and his own inexperience, but mainly through the hostility that was bred by fear of involvement in the war, the Ambassador reached his nadir in 1941 when it was said of him that his popularity had risen from zero to freezing point, but the ground was quickly recovered as his character asserted itself, and he was never to relapse in a career which was henceforth to be roses all the way. By October 1941 he had felt his feet on firm ground at last, and could write to a friend: 'I feel strangely more at ease with these people than I could have imagined possible six months ago.'

Perhaps it was inevitable that Halifax should have an uneasy novitiate, for he had much to learn, but some of the incidents which contributed to it could undoubtedly have been circumvented by a more worldly man. The diaries which he kept at this time are rich in examples of this appealing simplicity of one part of his mind. He was surprised to learn that Jews were not welcomed in the more exclusive New York clubs; when Maynard Keynes brought his wife, the renowned ballerina Lopokova, to America in May 1941, he wrote in his diary: 'I believe she used to be in Russian Ballet,' and when one of the most famous columnists in the world, Walter Winchell, called on him he noted that he had been visited by 'a man named Winchell'. Later he wrote: 'I have fixed an appointment to see Senator Bankhead, who Dorothy says is the uncle of Tallulah Bankhead whom everybody seems to know all about except me.'

Another sign of this unworldliness was that although Edward was a good judge of the political situation, he found it hard to grasp the influence exercised by Big Business on the Administration. He did not understand how much the political system was subject to commercial pressure. Forces like the Rubber Lobby might have great political influence, and a Minister of Supply to be appointed might have to stand well with General Motors, but Edward could not understand this, and his innocence in these matters was one of his great attractions in American eyes.[2]

The Ambassador's subordinates were sometimes concerned about this naïvety. His Private Secretary Angus Malcolm recalled that: 'Sometimes it used to worry us a little. Quite early we had to stop him telling the following story at things like Chamber of Commerce lunches:

'In World War I a battalion captured a barrel of German beer. The officers tried it and found it undrinkable, and the mess-sergeant asked if the men could have it. Later the officers asked what the men had said about it. "They said it was just right," replied the sergeant. "They said that if it had been any better they wouldn't have got it and if it had been any worse they couldn't have drunk it."

'Now Lord H. was too innocent, or too little conscious of rank to see that the story rested upon class distinctions—things which Americans officially

---

[1] Sir Isaiah Berlin to author.   [2] Lord Chandos to author.

abhor—and therefore came all the worse from the lips of a Lord. He was puzzled, but he took our advice.'[1]

One of the turning points in his popularity was an incident in Detroit when he was touring the Middle West. On his way to call on the Roman Catholic Archbishop Mooney, whom he had known in Bangalore, he was waylaid by a party of women pickets bearing placards abusing Great Britain in general and her Ambassador in particular. It was an organized rather than a spontaneous act. These militant elderly ladies had made a rendezvous outside the Archbishop's door, and when Edward appeared uttered shrill reproaches against his country for her supposed desire to lure their sons into the firing line beside her own. They supported these accusations by booing and lobbing tomatoes and eggs at him, one of which, to his annoyance, exploded on the bottom of his trousers.

This kind of demonstration was, of course, a mere bagatelle to one accustomed to fighting elections in England but there was something in the atmosphere which made him feel that there might be more serious trouble: 'The police seemed to me quite incredibly inert and intimidated. I told the ladies I should hear better what they said if they did not all talk at once, which reduced them temporarily to complete silence. Quite a little crowd collected, and I thought we were going to have a scrap, and I accordingly stepped back into the Archbishop's house.'[2]

Here the maid washed the débris from his clothes while he talked to the Archbishop. One who watched this ridiculous scene thought that Edward behaved with the melancholy composure of a French aristocrat on his way to the guillotine, and his alleged remark that he was happy to think that they had eggs to throw away was widely circulated. The episode, in fact, did him nothing but good, and after it there was a strong revulsion of feeling to his side and in favour of giving him a fair chance.

In a few days he realized that the incident had been a boomerang, and told Churchill: 'The egg business has been quite useful in the odd way these things work.' The attack meant nothing to him, but he noticed that many Americans had been touched on the raw by this gross breach of hospitality:

'The Americans are a very courteous people, and that a visiting Ambassador should be treated in this ill-mannered fashion was in their view indefensible. The natural effect, arising on the rebound from resentment at the bad manners, was larger sympathy with the country whose representative had been thus insulted. This effect was greatly strengthened as it was widely reported that the Ambassador's only comment had been that the United States was a very lucky country to have eggs and tomatoes to throw around, when in England we got only one egg a month.'[3]

[1] Angus Malcolm to author.
[2] Hickleton Papers. Washington Diary.
[3] Halifax did not, in fact, make this remark. It was contained in the first news flash of the Ministry

Although Edward's own character had much to do with the unbroken popularity which was to follow these first bleak months, he owed an immense debt to his cousin Angus McDonnell who began to act as his bear-leader in the early summer of 1941, explaining the Ambassador's Anglo-Saxon reserve to Americans, establishing his personality, and planning his tours. No better choice could have been made. His father was Lord Antrim, and his mother the grand-daughter of Grey of the Reform Bill. He was a jolly middle-aged man of Falstaffian appearance, and Wheeler-Bennett had been amused when Edward told him unsmilingly that 'Antrim's boy' was to join him as adviser.

Angus had an encyclopaedic knowledge of the country and the people. He had spent much of his life in America and had once built railways in the American South and the Far West. They were a strange pair. Edward's formal courtesy was offset by his cousin's ribald joviality. He seemed to have friends who welcomed him with open arms in every corner of the United States, and the whole atmosphere of the tours was to be transformed by his Rabelaisian presence. Casting himself in the rôle of clown he was inevitably the comic relief on any Halifax tour; he fell asleep and snored while Edward was being awarded honorary degrees; put the police up to arresting the Ambassador's industrial adviser for jay-walking; and when Edward asked him for help in addressing sixty Mayors in Minnesota, said: 'If I were you I'd whinny.'

Behind this buffoonery was a shrewd organizing mind, and a brilliant flair for presenting the Ambassador to the Americans in a desirable light, and on the tours he was often to be seen talking to Edward in a low but urgent voice. Before the arrival of this masterly go-between those relations had often been stilted. McDonnell revealed Edward to them as an ordinary man like themselves, so that it seemed to them that if one as human and forthcoming as Angus was so devoted to him he must possess those qualities himself.

One of McDonnell's many advantages was a small house in Washington which Edward called his 'pitch', where he had arranged sandbags over the door so that the Ambassador should not bang his head, and where he did the cooking himself, frying sausages and bacon, his enormous figure clad in workman's overalls with the label of the maker on the back. His wide acquaintance ensured that every type of American visited the 'pitch', and there was an atmosphere of informality and banter in the little room that was much to Edward's taste.

His cousin's complete indifference to his exalted position was also a tonic to the Ambassador who had been seldom crossed in recent years. When he told McDonnell that he had found the Americans at first a rather odd people, he had replied: 'No! On the contrary. It is you who are odd! You have led a

_____

of Information, and was attributed to him next morning in the American Press. He realized its value, and made no attempt to deny its authorship.

very sheltered life, and always kept yourself to a small circle of friends you have picked. You know nothing about people.' He not only planned the tours but went on ahead to prepare the ground and explain his cousin's peculiarities, sometimes putting forward his claims like a racehorse. When doubts were raised as to Halifax's ability to stand tough questioning and one man threatened: 'We will pepper him when he comes,' he said: 'I'll back my horse against yours. He's a good horse, and he's been in the House of Commons a long time.' Sometimes, when telling Americans how much they were going to like the Ambassador, he would add: 'He's a curiosity, but a very good curiosity.'[1]

Edward was probably only dimly aware that all was not well in the early months, and his life in the British Embassy was pleasantly informal. Mrs. Watson, a frequent visitor, thought that Edward always treated himself as a guest in his own house, and never as the host, and that Dorothy carried everything, and that although she knew him well he never remembered her face, so that she always had to murmur: 'Frances Watson,' when Edward would say: 'Oh, of course,' with a charming smile. The presence of Charles Peake was a great boon to Edward and Dorothy. His Washington Diary reflects the light-hearted relations between the three, and the easy companionship which can only exist between old friends, and reminds us of Edward's lifelong difficulty in pronouncing his 'r's:

'The three of us went to church on Palm Sunday where we were provided with the largest palms (about 3 feet long) that I have ever seen.

'We return to the Embassy. He and I go to his study, and Dorothy upstairs. After a time we go to collect her for breakfast. As we approach her door we hear "swish, swish, swish", and a protesting squeal. We open the door and there we behold Dorothy beating Frankie the dachshund with a palm.

'E. (Horrorstricken): "Dowothea! That is a blest palm. And you are beating Frankie with it. Dowothea, how often have I told you?"

'D.: "Yes, darling, but he's wee-wee'd on the bath mat again." (Looking at his face): "Oh Edward, it's very wrong of me. I always forget. I'm very bad. I ought to remember. You've told me so often. I'm sure I shall remember the next time."

'E. (majestically): "Dowothea, give me the palm. Charles and I will nail it above your bed. And Dowothea, you will remember to burn it next Shrove Tuesday." '

---

[1] Angus McDonnell to author.

CHAPTER XXXII

TOURING IN AMERICA

THE Ambassador had soon realized that one of his most important duties was to leave Washington as often as he could and travel the land, projecting an image of England at once stirring and unprovocative in as many States as it was physically possible to visit. He may have been guilty of early misjudgments but he never made the cardinal error of overselling his country. He grasped at once the essential fact that of all methods to adopt when projecting the image of England the most fatal was propaganda, and in any case his direct and undevious mind would have been ill-fitted for such a purpose. But there was an insatiable demand for information, and this he was ready to supply.

'Nothing,' he said, 'has done more to poison relations between the two countries than the widely accepted myth of an unscrupulous and powerful British propaganda machine in the last war. If, however, we can succeed in impressing on Americans some idea of Britain as it is today, they will begin to see it in a new light, and many old misunderstandings will be gradually eradicated. Every day makes me more convinced that the simple policy of trusting them and going forward to discuss all our sore points is a much safer way to what we want.'

This was the task he set himself. He knew that the British case was going by default in enormous areas of the American continent, and he was to discover on his tours distant regions where an Englishman had never been seen before, and where the ignorance of England was as complete as the curiosity to learn was touching. Even in the most sophisticated States he would find Americans who knew little more about his country than the average Englishman would know about the Corn Belt, or the blue-grass country of Kentucky. But everywhere he went the demand for information and facts was the same, and an even greater need was the correction of false impressions and the dispersal of prejudice. The British Information Services under H. B. Butler were working well but they could not cover the whole area. As Edward told Brendan Bracken, the responsible Minister:

'There are still vast stretches of this country, particularly in the Middle West and mountain country, untended by your faithful shepherds.

"The hungry sheep look up and are not fed,
But swoln with wind and the dank mist they draw,
Rot inwardly and foul contagion spread."
511

Thus when the winds of isolation blow from the mountains and the contagion of ignorance spreads from the great plains, the only antiseptic is more and more information.'

And how impressive was the manner in which he set out on this gigantic task. For success in presenting a true image of his country, in gently prising out deeply embedded prejudice against her, he relied partly on his own charm and unruffled coolness in the face of hostility, but also on those who accompanied him. There was Angus McDonnell who planned the tours and never allowed Edward to make a mistake, greeting his old friends in every State with elephantine banter, and making new ones within the first five minutes of acquaintance, but keeping a vigilant eye on the Ambassador in the midst of the harlequinade.

There was Edward's Secretary, Jack Lockhart, whose dry humour was a godsend in difficult moments, and whose well-stored mind was always at his disposal; and Archie Gordon who had been seconded from the Ministry of Labour to advise him on industrial questions, and who arranged the meetings with leaders of American Labour.

But most important of all, as in every moment of his life, was Dorothy who exerted on all she met a fascination even greater than his own. No day was too long or hard for her. She was prepared to address large public meetings without notice and with steady nerve. She took press conferences and women's clubs in her stride. Gordon was of the opinion that 51 per cent of the success of the ambassadorship was due to her enchanting personality, and 49 per cent to Edward, while Angus McDonnell described her as 'like someone gaily running a cricket XI, and saying: "I hope our side wins." She was always waiting at second-slip to retrieve any possible *faux pas* by Edward'.

Edward had understood that the Middle West was the centre of Isolationism, and he went there several times to beard it in its lair, and his memory of those tours was of immense distances, of sleeping on the train, of royal welcomes, and learned societies with precious relics, of lunches at Rotary Clubs, Mayors in City Halls, of Press conferences and the shaking of innumerable hands. 'What an actor one becomes,' he reflected. And above all, there were memories of speeches—speeches on every occasion and to every kind of audience, and the answering of interminable questions at which he excelled—speeches from gun-carriages, speeches from farm wagons, speeches in shipyards and aircraft factories, impromptu speeches in schools and universities—until he was staggered by the avidity for facts of his listeners. Pittsburgh, Minneapolis, Kansas City, Chicago—it was a hard road, but he had great staying-power, and even discovered to his surprise that he was enjoying himself: 'It is rather like a General Election,' he told one of his friends.

Sometimes, in a lull between official engagements, that youthful zest for life made him behave like a schoolboy in an amusement park who is restrained by an adult from trying the more dangerous machines. To satisfy this puerile yearning he was on one occasion allowed to drive the train between cities:

'It was a Diesel engine,' said Charles Peake, 'so one sat in front as in a car. The engineer showed him where the "dead man's handle" was, and E. installed himself in the engineer's seat. The train, I noticed, was travelling about 60. "Hasn't this train got a whistle?" he asked after a few minutes. The engineer indicated a cord. Edward pulled it and a hideous blast awoke the valley. Finally the engineer asked him to desist. "I can if I like," said E., his mouth set in an obstinate line. After a minute he said: "I thought all American trains had a bell." "Yes," said the engineer, "but we only use it for shunting or when we are pulling out of cities." "Show me," said Edward. The engineer silently pointed. Edward yanked at the handle. The bell began to toll mournfully. Soon bell and whistle entered into hideous competition. The train entered a large defile where the line ran straight as far as the eye could see. "How do you make it go faster?" queried Edward. "We don't want to go faster," said the engineer, "since we are on time. But if we do, all one needs do is push the handle of the governor forward." Forward at that moment went the handle of the governor to the limit of its capacity. The great monster seemed to gather itself in hand, and a pulse began to beat throughout its length. The speed crept forward to 85 miles an hour. I cocked an inquiring eye at Dorothy. "Let him," she said, "if it makes him happy. And after all," she added, "mercifully the passengers don't know what's happening." The engineer thought differently. "I will now drive," he said, and E. got down reluctantly.'

He was receptive to suggestions. On Gordon's advice whenever possible he met the Trade Union and Labour leaders, and it seemed to Gordon that the Ambassador found a particular relish in matching himself against those tough men, and gaining an insight into their views on the war. After his first three tours his meetings with the Labour leaders became a routine, and they plied him with questions. Usually he won the confidence of those who represented Labour, and when the introduction had been made, no one could handle them better. Gordon soon discovered that in spite of his modesty the Ambassador was shrewd and hard-headed, and that he had a first-class brain. His conclusion from watching him on these tours was that he was the greatest public servant he had ever met, and that his only fault was an unthinking selfishness which consisted in taking advantage of other people's services without realizing his indebtedness.

Gordon was lost in admiration of the bland resourcefulness with which the Ambassador answered questions and demolished hecklers. His mind seemed to have formulated the answer almost before the interrupter had finished his question. At a meeting of hard-boiled shipbuilders at Portland, Oregon, after he had answered questions for two hours, a man rose and asked in an offensive manner, 'Isn't all your talk about liberty bunk?' Edward replied with a charming smile:

'We certainly value liberty highly, although we often slang each other, but when we sense danger we close our ranks quicker than most. In 1926 we had a General Strike. I was standing at Hyde Park Corner and a truck came by with soldiers with bayonets, and on it a caption: "This truck is working by orders of His Majesty's Government." Then a second truck passed with the caption: "This truck is working by the orders of the Trade Union Council." Then came a little man wheeling a little barrow and on this was written: "Working to the orders of my own bloody self." We certainly value liberty'; and this sally, as Gordon remembered, 'had brought the house down'.

On these tours the Ambassador was brought into contact with thousands of people in every State in a manner never equalled by any British Ambassador before or after. He discovered with exhilaration the vast distances, and the wonderful variety of the continent never ceased to delight him, from the marismas of Florida and the cactus forests of Arizona to the industrial might of the Middle West and the white clap-boarded villages of New England, so prim and orderly, and her countryside with the maples in glorious insurrection in the fall. In these travels, far from the hot-house atmosphere of Washington, he felt that he was meeting the real America face to face, lapped in her fantastic warmth, and exposing himself without fear to her moments of censure.

He was particularly touched by the welcome he was given on all his visits to the Middle West, and he believed that the fear of involvement there had been greatly exaggerated:

'My reading of the broad divisions of opinion,' he said in 1941, 'as given to me by most of those with whom I have talked is that the section that wishes to be strictly isolationist is much smaller than its spokesmen, who are spokesmen of a small vociferous minority, suggest. The Mayor of Chicago said that he thought 70–75 per cent of Chicago were in favour of giving us all help, whatever the consequence. Other people say much the same thing, that there may be 15 or 20 per cent who want to go into the war at once—another 15 or 20 per cent who want to stay out of it at whatever cost, and the great middle group who want to give us all help, and who would do so quite happily regardless of consequences if they got what they thought a clear lead from the President.

'One thing that cuts across the picture is the firm distrust of domestic policy that many of his opponents feel for the President. One meets this everywhere, and I would say that that feeling and the dislike that those who disagree with this policy in Chicago have for the President were the two factors which occurred most frequently in many talks.'[1]

[1] Hickleton Papers. Washington Diary.

As in India when certain moments detached themselves from his general experience, and remained pictorially established in his mind—walking in the dusk in the Shalimar Gardens, or pitching camp under the Himalayan stars, so too in America, out of the kaleidoscopic memory of his tours, a few episodes, sometimes trivial, remained sharply defined. One of these was the recollection of a place near Boise in Idaho:

'It was in summer, and for that reason as well as for that of numbers it was decided to have the meeting in the open air. Imagine a most perfect evening, a farm wagon doing duty as platform, a lovely country of grassy hillsides with blue mountains in the distance, a really big crowd of all ages and callings on the slopes, the majority straight from farm work in shirt sleeves, the colour of the shirts and dresses and scarves making everything look gay in the slanting sunlight; it remains in my mind's eye as if it were only yesterday.'

Memorable too were those tours which were to lead him to exotic places— to New Mexico where Santa Fé slumbered in the heat scarcely changed for three hundred years, like some drowsy provincial town in Spain, where Indian villages with mud houses clustered round it and the Angelus sounded from the Cathedral at dawn. Nor could he ever forget coming to Arizona, flying over a desert of indescribable bleakness like the crater of some burned-out moon, over grotesque rings and humps of mountains, and rocks of flamboyant colours where the air was crystal-clear and the distances blue and immense, and Tucson where the dust was laid by a tropical thunderstorm and the parched oleanders on the street freshened by rain.

Here he was taken to a giant cactus forest, one of the strangest things he had ever seen, the stems rising from the scrub like blasted tree trunks, and dominating the desert plain. He who had seen so many strange places was at once captivated by the sights and sounds of Arizona, by the ranches and the Mexican cowboys with their big spurs, by his drives down the desert tracks where he saw jack rabbits and wild boar and coyotes and badgers rolling in the sun, and watched the flight of doves while the hills grew purple, and blue, and red and black.

Unforgettable too was his first sight of the Grand Canyon. They went there from Prescott where Dorothy was made a deputy sheriff, pausing on the way at a little bungalow where the trunk of a vine grew inside the house which reminded him of an old-fashioned inn by a trout stream in Westmorland, and on across the Painted Desert, a great plain where the rocks were pink and red and there was snow on the peaks of distant mountains. They traversed this strange country passing through forests of pine and juniper, and past deserts and rocks until they came to their first sight of the Grand Canyon, and as he looked at this awful spectacle Edward was conscious of a sense of littleness and humility.

'Lord Curzon, I think, once said that some touch of sadness was inseparable from perfect beauty. This is true of the Taj, about which, I believe, he said it; but I did not feel it with the Canyon. The Grand Canyon is the most fantastic place I have ever seen or imagined—5,000 feet deep, 17 miles broad, and the Colorado River that is 150 yards wide looking like a stream at the bottom. Masses of every coloured rock tossed and tumbled in every conceivable shape, and everything on the scale of vast and gigantic planning that made you feel what an atom man was! You just gaped. The sun was just setting when we got there, and the reds looked all on fire, and the purples and blacks setting them off. One could have stood there for ever.'

His travels often took him to simple places and unsophisticated people, but with Dorothy beside him his touch seldom faltered. He was neither put out by failure of organization nor jarred by strange behaviour, and he recorded the more trying occasions with humour and good temper. At Winslow in Arizona:

'We were guided on arrival into a large gravel patch of ground, destined to be a recreation centre, in which were gathered a few citizens in knots, and at one end of which was a platform with an Indian band below it. After a little hand-shaking, we were led to the platform, and a little hunchback took charge through a loud speaker, the Mayor sitting silent. The hunchback announced to the citizens that it was the first time Winslow had ever had 'a bit of Royalty', and therefore was giving a warm welcome and spontaneous.

'This was only mildly true for owing to a breakdown of communications, they had not known, or had not let others know, what time we were arriving. However, before the citizens who appeared a little bored but also a little curious, the band played, and the Mayor spoke; but owing to a breakdown in the microphone could not be heard except by those on the platform whom he addressed with his back to the citizens. I then had to speak and the hunchback thrust the microphone, whose base had collapsed, into my hand to hold as I got up.

'The main Santa Fé railway and shunting yard was near our gravel patch, so my speech was made to the accompaniment of discordant screams from engines, and other interruptions, and was not therefore an effort of which I was at all proud.'

Edward encountered on these tours a strange mixture of deference and familiarity. Having his hand wrung, and being slapped on the back pleased him because he felt that these gestures of equality meant that he was accepted by ordinary Americans as one of themselves. When placed in ridiculous positions he learned to carry them off with an air of enjoyment. All trace of grandeur and remoteness had now been wiped away. At Fort Worth in Texas he was photographed on a small pony, wearing a cowboy hat and his feet nearly touching the ground, and taken to what he described as 'disgusting stockyards', where he was forced to watch the mass slaughter of beasts with an expression of simulated interest; it was here too that Dorothy was kissed by the Mayor and given a box of chocolates by him with the words: 'Now, honey, I think you're lovely. If you're a bit sick on the aeroplane you can open it and eat some.' It was a long cry from the Investitures in the Durbar Hall at New Delhi, but such incidents were now a source of delight to both of them.

As a result of his early tours, before the United States entered the war, he thought that he could detect the gradual evolution of a common conviction about it, and about the direction in which her duty lay. At times, he admitted, the feeling of impatience at the slowness with which that opinion moved was almost overwhelming, but during 1941 he was conscious of a conviction insensibly growing that here was a great human challenge from which the United States could hardly stand aloof. President Conant of Harvard University seemed to him to be speaking for many others when in June he had asked at the academic celebrations: 'How long will the people of the United States think it right to let the British do all the fighting for them?'

Edward's tours were a grinding effort, and contained some uneasy moments, but they were a triumph in the propagation of understanding. When he came to look back on them his recollections were mellow and contented, and he was conscious of a strong desire to return to the scenes of his wandering:

'So one may see again the charm of Charleston and New Orleans, and the spring glory of the dogwood in Atlanta; the foothills against the blue distance of larger mountains in Wyoming and Montana; the skyline of New York City at sunset; the limitless expanse of the great central prairie plain; Chicago on its great lake, the trim countryside of New England; the bluegrass country of Kentucky; the romantic appeal of Santa Fé; the war-time memories of Stonewall Jackson; the Indian settlements of Oklahoma; the desert grandeur of Arizona and Utah; the Grand Canyon and the wonders of the West; the fragrance of the grace of early Colonial life that still clings round the houses on the James River and in the Deep South; but the line of vision and memory recedes all the time; there is always another ridge to climb, and at the end of the day one would still not have the full measure of the spell that the United States and its people cast round us during those war years.'

CHAPTER XXXIII

WASHINGTON *V.* TOKYO

FROM the moment of his arrival in the United States in January 1941 until the collapse of the Japanese Empire Halifax was directly involved with almost every great issue, and to describe his diplomatic activities in detail would be to write the history of the Second World War. Here it is only possible to give a general picture of his life as Ambassador, but we should be conscious that all the time behind it was an unceasing application to the diplomatic problems of each day, only a few of which can be examined. From the point of view of Winston Churchill, and also of his Ambassador, the attack on Pearl Harbour and the entry of the United States into the war was the most important of these events, for it brought an end to the awful isolation of Great Britain, and provided her with a mighty ally.

It fell to Halifax, in his diplomatic relations to the problem of Japan, to continue the policy which had devolved upon Lord Lothian. By September 1939 the war between China and Japan had subsided into a struggle of attrition which both sides believed they could eventually win. Similarities in temperament and policies alike disposed the Japanese leaders to sympathy towards the Axis Powers, and it was their resentful belief that the support given by Great Britain and the United States had alone enabled China to survive up to that moment in a manner that would have been otherwise impossible. Alert for some method of breaking the deadlock they saw, in the outbreak of war in Europe, a heaven-sent opportunity of consolidating their influence in China so strongly that it could not in future be disputed by whichever Power was victorious in the European war.

The Japanese Government at first affected an attitude of compromise in the accomplishment of this end, but with the collapse of France, which they anticipated would be followed at no distant date by that of Britain, their demands became more pressing, and their attitude more insolent. It did not escape the attention of either side that if Japan did not quickly establish her claim, the Germans, if they won the war, would show scant consideration for her interests when disposing of the Asiatic possessions of her conquered enemies. The Japanese, who admitted openly that if they did not seize the opportunity presented by the fall of France they 'would earn the obloquy of their descendants', therefore demanded the closing of the Burma Road and the frontier of Hong Kong, and the withdrawal of British troops from Shanghai. The British Government felt that America should respond to demands so far-reaching by some gesture equally emphatic. Could they not now enforce a full economic embargo on Japan, or make their position equally clear by sending warships to Singapore? Or, if they preferred a less dangerous policy, could they not offer to be the honest brokers in negotiating peace with China on the basis of the restoration of Chinese independence and of her annexed territories?

To these suggestions a negative answer had been returned by the American Secretary of State, Cordell Hull. His Government, he said, was not yet ready to risk a war with Japan, and the British Government was forced to close the Burma Road for three months from 18 July 1940 in the rainy season on the sanguine condition that during that time renewed efforts should be made by both Japanese and Chinese to accomplish a just and lasting peace in the Far East. The situation had further deteriorated with a change of Government in Japan in which Prince Konoye, whose admiration for the Axis was unconcealed, became Prime Minister; nor were his tendencies likely to be restrained by the new Foreign Minister Matsuoka, who had not hesitated, shortly after assuming office, to tell the British Ambassador in Tokyo, Sir Robert Craigie, that Japan 'was determined, and in fact compelled by circumstances, to set up a new order in the Far East', and that Great Britain 'was resisting these tendencies with every means at her command. It was therefore difficult to see how a fundamental clash of interests and purpose could be avoided'.

This sombre prediction seemed to be underlined by the events that followed it. The Japanese made it clear that they had not the slightest intention of making any accommodation over China; on 5 September they concluded an agreement with the French Vichy Government which allowed Japanese troops to pass through Indo-China, thus opening the way for a further assault on the Chinese; and on 27 September came the announcement of a tripartite pact between Germany, Italy and Japan for the creation of a 'New Order' in Europe and Asia, which, by its phrasing, was clearly directed against the United States. There could be no question now of renewing the agreement for the closing of the Burma Road, and this decision was conveyed to the Japanese in October 1940, and justified by the fact that they had not only made no attempt at a settlement in the Far East, but had actually increased existing tensions by entering Indo-China, and had crowned their misdemeanours by signing a pact with the Axis Powers.

Cordell Hull had not thought it expedient to try to restrain the Japanese from penetrating Indo-China. He had also made it clear that he could not give a pledge of American support if the reopening of the Burma Road led to a Japanese attack on British possessions. Thus Britain was left to take this step alone, and face the risks it might involve, and it is probable that the Japanese failure to take strong action at this point was prompted by the defeat of the Luftwaffe in the Battle of Britain and the failure of the German

Army to carry out an invasion. They may also have noted, with an apprehension only temporary, the economic measures taken by the United States in September forbidding the export of all iron and steel scrap except under licence.

By the beginning of Halifax's ambassadorship in January 1941 the rhythm of Japanese policy was therefore abundantly clear. It required little insight to realize that the immediate situation was one of great danger for Britain, and that her most prudent policy in 1941 would be directed towards deterring Japan as long as possible from entering the war, and making her situation as difficult as possible if she did.

When Halifax came to look back on this first year in America he wrote: '1941 is probably the most important date in American history since 1776. In 1941 America, for the first time since the Revolution, became involved in a foreign war in which the very existence of the Union was at stake.' But, he reflected, 1941 was not a war year; it was a year of preparation, physical and moral, for a development which the great majority knew was inevitable. To those who, like himself, lived through it, it was also the year of Lend-Lease, of America First, of the Office of Production Management, of proclamations on America as the Arsenal of Democracy while factories poured forth millions of motor cars and refrigerators instead of tanks and aeroplanes.

It seemed to him that the political division was no longer between Republicans and Democrats but between Isolationists and Interventionists. Particularly he noticed that Japan was more strongly disliked and distrusted by Americans than any other nation in the world. In February 1941 Congress agreed to the fortification of Guam, which they had refused to consider before on the grounds that it would be a provocation to Japan. A credit of $4,700,000 was secured by the Naval Staff for this purpose, and Sumner Welles, commenting on one of the many Japanese assertions of their peaceful intentions, remarked sourly that 'in every critical world situation the United States Government were far more interested in the deeds of other nations than the statements of some of their spokesmen'. Halifax observed that public opinion had remained solidly unfavourable to Japan, and in February it seemed to him that the Administration underrated the popular willingness to stand up to her. The fact that the new Japanese Ambassador in Washington had been received on arrival by the German and Italian Embassies did not diminish this mistrust, and in the last six months Halifax felt that in spite of the predictions of the Gallup Poll a resigned expectation that her entry into the war might become necessary had begun to grow upon America.

British policy towards Japan required close collaboration with the United States, and there had been indications towards the end of January 1941 that Japan was about to renew her southward move and might be contemplating action against British or Dutch territory. It was in this belief that on 7 February the British Foreign Secretary Anthony Eden plainly informed the

Japanese Ambassador in London that his Government would resist further Japanese aggression in the Far East, but on the following day the President warned Halifax that American public opinion would be unlikely to endorse a declaration of war on Japan unless she first attacked American territory, and that he himself would consider dangerous a diversion of forces from the main theatre of operations in the west.

He told the Ambassador that he was contemplating other means of deterring Japan from her disastrous course. On 11 February the Foreign Secretary instructed Halifax to return to the charge. He was to point out to the President that if we were forced into war with Japan it might be necessary to move the fleet for a time from the Mediterranean into the Indian Ocean, and that such a step would make ultimate victory impossible without full American participation. He was instructed, therefore, to suggest that a joint Anglo-American declaration that an attack on British or Dutch territory would result in the United States as well as Great Britain being at war with Japan, would be the best deterrent, but that since the United States Government was not yet prepared for so positive a step the President might, as Hopkins had suggested, make plain America's interest in the Far East 'in words of one syllable'.

Cordell Hull next summoned the Japanese Ambassador Nomura on 12 February, and the President received him two days later. Hull gave the envoy credit then and afterwards for being sincere in his desire to avoid war. He found him 'tall, robust, in fine health, with an open face, differing considerably in physique from the average Japanese. . . . His outstanding characteristic was solemnity, but he was much given to a mirthless chuckle and to bowing'.[1]

The President also exercised the full force of his personality on this forbidding figure, inviting him with his infectious charm to sit down with himself and State Department officials, and in a calm atmosphere smooth out the questions at issue between them. But the President and Cordell Hull were soon to find that Nomura was already a broken reed. He was clearly not empowered to offer any concrete suggestions, and he was unable to clarify his country's position *vis-à-vis* America in the Tripartite Pact.

At the solitary meetings in Hull's apartment, on which he insisted, he repeated feebly that Japan was not committed to courses of conquest. On this question his host left him in no possible doubt:

'As long as Japanese forces are all over China,' he said, 'and Japanese troops, planes and warships are as far south as Thailand and Indo-China, accompanied by such threatening declarations as Japanese statesmen are making week after week, there can only be increasing concern by nations vitally interested in halting world conquest by force and barbaric methods of Government.'[2] The Japanese Ambassador could only retort that if the

[1] *The Memoirs of Cordell Hull*, Vol. II, p. 987. [2] Ibid. p. 989.

embargoes were continued the military group in control of Japan might 'be forced to proceed further in a naval or military way'.

The next step in this grimy drama was the visit to Europe of the Japanese Foreign Minister, Mr. Matsuoka. To the British Foreign Office he was a bird of ill-omen. He had come, on his own admission, to see what sort of 'New Order' his unsavoury allies were proposing to establish in Europe, and it was reasonable to suppose that he had also come with the object of reinforcing the Tripartite Pact. In May he was able to conclude a neutrality agreement with Russia which left Japan free, as far as she was prepared to regard the tainted Soviet word as binding, to continue her aggressive explorations southwards. Disturbing reports of troop movements suggested that she was already contemplating such a move and that its objective might well be Singapore. Such a possibility prompted the British Government to make another attempt to obtain a joint declaration by the United States, Great Britain and the Netherlands, but the proposal was again declined on the grounds that it was too provocative.

*   *   *

On 17 May Halifax reported to the Foreign Office that he had heard from Cordell Hull of a *démarche* by the Japanese Ambassador in Washington, made on 12 May, which at first caused some alarm in Whitehall. Nomura put forward formal proposals for a settlement with China which, in Hull's words, called 'for a species of joint overlordship of the Pacific area by Japan and the United States, with Japan the baron of that part that embraced nine-tenths of the population and the wealth, and with very little consideration for the rights and interests of other nations'.

Other parts of the document were couched in terms equally arrogant, and some of them were clearly intended to intimidate the United States. Nomura claimed that the proposals had the support of all members of the Cabinet, with the exception of Matsuoka, and of the military leaders. Neither Hull nor the President thought that the document offered any serious basis for an agreement, but Hull took the view that it was a formal and detailed proposal from Japan, and that to reject it outright would be to squander their first real chance of entering with Japan into a fundamental discussion of the questions that lay between them. It was their hope that by treating with the Japanese the harsher aspects of the proposals might be softened, and some of its more offensive suggestions eliminated, but in fact, the mere acceptance of the document as a basis of negotiation was to lead the Japanese into further and more exorbitant demands.

Halifax, on 21 May, was instructed to convey the views of the Foreign Office to the American Secretary of State. He explained that it was their belief that Matsuoka himself had inspired these proposals with the object of splitting the policy of the United States from that of Britain, of retaining Manchukuo and the commanding position in Indo-China, and of extricating Japan from her embroilment in China with the least possible public discredit. Cordell Hull had resented what he had described as this 'lecture' from the British Government which he perhaps thought was an unfair reflection on his own gullibility, and persisted with the conversations, but they had arrived at no conclusion before the Japanese Army advanced into southern Indo-China.

The exiled Netherlands Government had also been awaiting the outcome of these events with great anxiety. From moment to moment they anticipated the invasion of their own soil, and now asked for the assurance of British support in the event of a Japanese attack on the Dutch East Indies. This was not a commitment that the Foreign Office was anxious to undertake without the certainty of American aid, but the British Government felt that they could not refuse the request. Halifax told Hull on 23 May that his Government was contemplating a declaration that Great Britain would regard Japanese action against the Dutch East Indies as a threat to British interests, and the Secretary of State asked that the pronouncement should be couched in unprovocative terms, but feared that the Japanese would discover intimidation in it however mildly it was expressed.

The Dominions Governments were also doubtful about any guarantees which were not underwritten by the United States, and eventually the British Foreign Secretary told the Netherlands Government on 1 August that Great Britain would do her utmost to support the Dutch East Indies in the event of aggression, but must remain 'sole judge' of what military action might be practicable.

The next item of villainy in this lamentable catalogue, the German invasion of Russia on 22 June, brought a new twist to the Japanese situation. 'In America,' Halifax noted, 'it provoked some commentators to urge an amicable settlement with Japan, but in the Administration it was felt that this must not be pursued by a policy of appeasement with Mr. Matsuoka on whom pressure must be maintained.'

Public opinion was confused by the attack on Russia because of the strong anti-Communist feeling throughout America, but the Prime Minister's speech had a steadying effect. The Communists and other left-wing organizations who had hitherto strongly supported the Isolationists, now swung in behind the Interventionists. It seemed to both Foreign Office and State Department that although the Japanese might remain neutral for a time, they were unlikely to resist this opportunity of turning their faces south.

Sinister reports of Japanese military preparations for a major war appeared to confirm this belief. Under cover of a glittering Imperial Conference at Tokyo on 2 July between one and two million men were called to the armed forces; Japanese merchant ships were suddenly recalled from the Atlantic, and travel restrictions and strict censorship of mails and communications were imposed in Japan. Sumner Welles told Halifax that his Government did not yet intend to make any communications to the Japanese of a 'mandatory kind' until they had committed what he described as some 'overt act'. In this event they contemplated the freezing of Japanese assets and the consequent rupture of all trade between the United States and Japan except under special licence. The 'overt act' was not long in coming.

On 21 July 1941 the Japanese obtained from the Vichy Government permission to establish eight air and two naval bases, and the right of complete freedom of movement for Japanese troops, in southern Indo-China. Thus, in Hull's words: 'They occupied the southern portions of Indo-China and were now in possession of the whole of France's strategic province pointing like a pudgy thumb towards the Philippines, Malaya and the Dutch East Indies.' The freezing order was brought into effect by the United States and by Great Britain who had decided to follow her. Halifax saw a particular significance in this event:

'For the first time since Japan started on her expansionist career,' he reported, 'an aggressive movement on her part was met by immediate measures taken in concert by America and Great Britain. Measures taken include freezing of Japanese funds, restrictions on trade with Japan, and defence measures in the Philippines. They have received practically unanimous support in the country, even Senator Wheeler giving them his approval. There has been a refreshing absence of accusations that England was inveigling America into the war by the Japanese back door.' In fact the reception of the measures showed, in his opinion, that most Americans were Isolationists only in regard to Europe.

The British decision to join in the freezing of Japanese assets might well have served as a pretext for an immediate attack on her East Indian possessions, and she was still without any effective guarantee of American help in such an emergency. To Halifax's inquiries as to the amount of American aid that Great Britain might expect in the case of an attack on Singapore, Hull replied in general terms that his Government was 'visualizing these broad conditions, and the problem of resistance they present'.[1] American activities would be affected by Britain's defensive position in Europe, and hence the amount of American aid that might be necessary. The British War Cabinet was prepared to take on trust that such help would be forthcoming in case of need, but the Australian Government, in uncomfortable proximity to the danger, demanded more binding assurances.

On this occasion Churchill himself submitted a memorandum to the President. The Japanese were now taking up positions threatening Singapore and the Dutch East Indies, and he felt justified in asking Roosevelt to commit himself to the statement that if any third Power was attacked by Japan as a result of the freezing of Japanese assets he would seek authority from Congress to provide aid to such Power. The President, on 11 August, made

[1] Hull. Op. cit. Vol. II pp. 10–17.

it plain that he could give no such assurance, explaining to Churchill that the Japanese were showing signs of wishing to resume the negotiations which were suspended after the Japanese action in Indo-China.

The new Japanese proposals submitted to Hull on 6 August seemed to the President to be 'fundamentally unacceptable', but he told Churchill that he would entertain them for a few weeks in order to gain time for the strengthening of the position at Singapore. An analysis of the new Japanese proposition convinced Hull that they had moved even further from a basis of possible negotiations. Acceptance of it would have meant that the United States would have had to lift her trade restrictions, abandon defensive preparations in the Philippines, and aid to Great Britain and the Netherlands, and agree to Japan's special military position and preferential political and economic status in Indo-China. There was no mention of the President's suggestion of neutralizing this area.

The President had told Nomura that any further move by Japan 'would produce a situation in which the United States Government would be compelled to take counter-measures even though these might lead to war between the United States and Japan'. Churchill was agreeable, after this *démarche*, to the continuance of negotiations, but the Foreign Office thought that the situation was unfavourable to Great Britain in the sense that the President's warning was not in itself a guarantee of American help in the event of a Japanese attack on British or Dutch territory in the Far East. Later they found that the President had not, in fact, delivered the warning in the terms accepted by Churchill, and that he had omitted any reference to Great Britain. A different form of 'parallel' warning on the part of the British was therefore necessary, and on 24 August Churchill, in a broadcast speech, stated plainly that Great Britain would be at the side of America if the latter were involved in war with Japan.

While these events were proceeding Halifax tried to measure the reaction to them of the American people. He had noticed the consensus of opinion when retaliatory action had been taken, but now he seemed to detect a certain lethargy in the public about the whole issue. He reported that the tone of a recent debate in the Senate on oil 'furnished more proof of the country's apathy and refusal to believe in a real crisis threatening to change the day to day life of the American people. The President is clearly conscious of this'. He felt that at this period Roosevelt was carrying his gifts of political dexterity too far and, after hearing his speech on Labour Day, remarked: 'Its terms may represent a balancing between the desirability of spurring on the public, and of giving no obvious handle to the Isolationists. It is an example of the fatal gift of manipulation bestowed by a bad fairy which disposes him to manœuvre.' But Halifax could find no sign of any appeasement movement in public opinion in respect of Japan.

In September it was reported to the British Ambassador in Tokyo by a member of the Konoye Government that the military extremists, now hell-bent on war, were, with German connivance, attempting to wreck Konoye's efforts towards a settlement. Whether these efforts had in fact been inspired by the slightest sincerity might well have been doubted, but it was obvious that any change in the Japanese Government must be for the worse. This change was brought about on 16 October when the Konoye administration fell on the issue of the Washington negotiations, and he was replaced by General Tojo, the first serving officer ever to occupy the position of Prime Minister of Japan, a man of unbridled chauvinism whose armies left a trail of havoc and torture in the Far East, and who was eventually executed by the Allies as a major war criminal.

The Russian Government had been forced, under heavy German pres-sure, to abandon Moscow for the temporary retreat of Kuibishev, and it seemed to the British Foreign Office that an assault on Russia in her hour of agony was an act of treachery from which the Japanese Government was unlikely to refrain. But Halifax's inquiries of Cordell Hull of what the attitude of the United States would be in that event made it clear that they had not yet come to a decision.

Meanwhile the Japanese negotiators were reinforced by the arrival of a special envoy, Mr. Kurusu, a former Ambassador in Berlin, and from this point the negotiations assumed an even more ominous guise.

We are conscious, in America, of a people slowly awakening to the necessity of positive action, and in Japan, of a nation without the luxury of choice, whose destinies were being shaped for their own insane ends by a junta of evil and ambitious men. Cordell Hull indeed tried to find some explanation for their conduct by reminding himself that for years Japanese leaders and writers had been preaching the doctrine of territorial aggrandisement in the quest for military and economic independence. Now the jaded ghost of 'Encirclement' had been revived by Japan and used to justify the rape of vast territories as a *cordon sanitaire* for her protection.

Halifax noted on 19 November that the country was calm and determined not to make any further concessions which would enable Japan to gain time while continuing to pursue her aggressive policies: 'Mr. Roosevelt,' he reported, 'made it clear in a Press conference that he regarded war with Japan as a possibility. Kurusu, the special Japanese envoy, arrived in Wash-ington on 15 November for the final negotiations with the United States Government, but there was no general expectation that he would offer any new proposals that would be acceptable to the United States or that any satisfactory agreement would be reached.'

Indeed, the object of this emissary, on whose features Hull saw deceit clearly marked, was to stiffen his colleagues in forcing the Americans to accept their terms, and, failing that, to detain them in distracting *pourparlers* while the Japanese forces matured their monstrous act of treachery.

Kurusu began his mission by warning Hull that Japan was in such a state of ferment that an explosion might be expected at any moment. He therefore suggested a proposal that the Japanese might withdraw from Indo-China in return for a moderate relaxation of the embargo, and Hull explained the proposal on 22 November to the representatives of Australia, the Netherlands, China and Great Britain. Kurusu had made a previous suggestion which, when submitted to his own Government, had been amended, and the result that emerged was even less satisfactory than the original proposition. Cordell Hull, although noting that it would leave Japan free to attack China and Russia and to obtain oil from the Dutch, still considered it unwise to reject it out of hand. He put forward proposals on the lines of Kurusu's original document, which came to be known as the *modus vivendi*.

Before this step was taken Halifax had told Cordell Hull that his Government had every confidence in the American handling of the negotiations, but thought that complete withdrawal from Indo-China of *all* Japanese military, naval and air personnel, and the suspension of advances on China should be emphatically demanded. In return for this there might be an offer of a limited export of those goods which were needed by the Japanese civilian population with the exception of oil.

On 25 November Halifax telegraphed an account to the Foreign Office of his interview with Hull at which the latter had explained his *modus vivendi* to the three Ambassadors concerned. It suggested an agreement of a three-months' period by which Japan would withdraw all but 25,000 of her forces in Indo-China in return for substantial economic concessions, and was, said Hull, intended to cover the contingency of an attack both on Soviet territory and on the Burma Road. Placed in this position, Halifax said that he hoped that the proposal could await the opinion of the British Government, but he took the responsibility of promising that if Hull felt forced to act at once they would trust his discretion and he would receive their full support.

Cordell Hull, now intent on spinning out the negotiations, did not feel in a position to insist on a total withdrawal from Indo-China, or on a suspension of hostilities with China herself, and it was now constantly in his mind that the whole defensive situation of the United States in the Pacific depended on winning time. His *modus vivendi* was received with consternation by his protégés the Chinese. Their reaction to it was violently hostile, and the indignation of Chiang Kai-shek was inflamed by a message from his ambassador and brother-in-law, Mr. Soong, who was in Washington and who believed that if the terms of the *modus vivendi* were followed there would be a complete collapse of morale throughout Asia. Faced by such vehemence Hull was forced to abandon the suggestion. He handed to the Japanese, instead of the *modus vivendi*, a statement said to be, in general terms, the lines on which the United States Government thought a Pacific settlement might be reached.

This statement had not been previously seen by Halifax, and it had no chance of acceptance by the Chinese. Halifax believed that the violence of Mr. Soong's protests, and perhaps the intervention of the President himself, had caused the substitution of this plan for the *modus vivendi*, but he could not help feeling that Hull had, for once, acted improperly in failing to show the British Government so important a document. But he believed that no harm would have been done, and was not seriously concerned. He was, however, stung when Hull, who at the time was under noticeable strain, blamed the British Government for the failure of the *modus vivendi* proposal, and Halifax thought it necessary to remind him that the British had made comments and suggestions in response to an invitation to do so, and that on his own authority, before the British Government had seen the document, he had guaranteed its acceptance.

*   *   *

Twilight had now descended on the negotiations. They were soon to end, but not without a few dying convulsions. On 28 November the President held an abortive conference with the Japanese representatives, before leaving Washington for Palm Springs where he proposed to stay until 4 December. He had told his visitors that the United States was not prepared to make economic concessions to Japan until she had given positive evidence of her peaceful intentions, and on 29 November Hull told Halifax that the situation was unchanged, and that he anticipated early Japanese action. Throughout these proceedings the British Government had been unable from that distance to gauge the danger of the situation, but had gladly relied on the judgment of the President, and of Cordell Hull whom they now invited to take them fully into his confidence about any further proposals which the United States intended to place before the Japanese.

When Halifax spoke in this sense to Cordell Hull, he replied that he did not believe there was now any hope of reviving the *modus vivendi*, and he referred bitterly to the 'unbalanced' conduct of Mr. Soong and its deplorable effect on Chiang Kai-shek. He gave a description of the document he had recently presented to the Japanese, but when Halifax asked for a copy of it Hull could not find one on his table, and it was not produced until 2 December. By 30 November it was clear that Churchill had come to the conclusion that these futile exchanges had lasted long enough, and he sent instructions to Halifax to request from the United States a plain declaration, in which Great Britain would join, that any further act of aggression by the Japanese would lead to the gravest consequences. The Ambassador was also to report that we expected a Japanese attack on Thailand which might include the seizure of strategic points on the Kra Isthmus, and to ask for the assurance of American support in such action.

On the afternoon of 1 December the President, who had returned that day to Washington, received Halifax and Hopkins at a long interview at the White House. He explained that he also had been considering a parallel statement to the Japanese by the two Governments, but thought it advisable first to put to them a series of questions about the movements and destinations of their troops, and the purpose of their deployment.

This did not seem to Halifax a fruitful proposal, and he asked what the President had next in mind since the answers to both these questions would be either mendacious or evasive. The President's answer was sufficiently encouraging to enable Halifax to report that in his opinion the United States would support whatever action we might take in any of the contingencies outlined by the President. We could, in any case, count on American support of any operations in the Kra Isthmus. Roosevelt also suggested that the Government of Thailand would be stiffened by a promise from Great Britain of their future sovereignty and independence if they resisted a Japanese attack. The President had by now little belief in the possibility of an accommodation, but as a last hope was contemplating a letter to the Japanese Emperor which, while cordial, would leave no doubt that persistence in the present Japanese policy could lead only to war. He asked Halifax to find out the intentions of the British Government in certain contingencies.

The British Foreign Secretary replied on 3 December to the President's questions, saying that he knew that Japanese reinforcements were arriving in Indo-China, and that we should warn Japan that any use of that country as a base for further aggression would be at her own risk. He also explained British plans in the event of an attack on Thailand in the Kra Isthmus. He wished to be assured categorically of American support in such a move, but he did not like the suggestion of a guarantee to the Thais as we could hardly ask them 'to accept the virtual certainty of partial extinction in order to secure their ultimate independence'.

On the evening of 3 December the President assured Halifax that he approved of the operation plans for the Kra Isthmus, and that the British could count on 'armed support', but that his own belief was that the next Japanese assault would be made on the Dutch East Indies. The following day, on the night of 4 December, Halifax, after suitable thanks to the President, told him that his Government thought that the warning to Japan should apply to attacks on Thailand, Malaya, the Dutch East Indies and the Burma Road, and again the President agreed to these terms with reservations about the Burma Road.

But he had still not, even at this late hour, abandoned all hope of a temporary agreement with the Japanese. He was still contemplating an approach to the Emperor which Kurusu had intimated might lead to a truce. But Halifax pressed on him the dangers of postponing the warning message, and suggested that the appeal to the Emperor might in itself serve as a positive warning, and the President had agreed, and said that he would decide on

6 December, after receiving the Japanese reply to his inquiries, whether to approach the Emperor or not.

Halifax, while they were still fresh in his mind, sent the Foreign Secretary a despatch describing the events of 7 December and 8 December as seen from His Majesty's Embassy in Washington. The negotiations between the United States and Japan proceeded normally but with a sharply increasing tempo up to the moment of the disaster. On 6 December the President sent his message to the Emperor of Japan which remained unanswered. The intention was that warning notes to the Japanese Government should be addressed by all the Powers concerned if no reply, or some worthless prevarication, was received by the evening of Monday, 8 December.

On Sunday morning Halifax sent to the White House the text of the note which the Government proposed to send to the Japanese Government. At this tense moment, while remaining at the Embassy awaiting the President's comments on this draft, he was rung up by Roosevelt shortly after two o'clock that afternoon with the staggering news of the Japanese bombing of Hawaii. He immediately put a call through to the Foreign Office, and while he was awaiting it the news of the attack on Manila was announced on the wireless.

During that afternoon there were two considerations foremost in Halifax's mind. First there was the recollection of the Prime Minister's declaration that if the United States were attacked by Japan, Great Britain would be at war within the hour; and secondly the reflection that it was essential to avoid any action which might suggest that she was manœuvring America into war with Japan. He remained, therefore, in close contact with the State Department in order to hear at once any formal pronouncement that a state of war with Japan existed, but refrained from approaching any member of the Administration, or issuing any public statement. There were many pitfalls in his way, but he avoided all of them. At about 6.30 p.m. he learned from Cordell Hull that Winston Churchill had spoken to the President on the telephone, and assumed from this that the British and American declarations of war had been decided, a view which was confirmed by the news that Japan had declared war on the United States and Great Britain.

He described to Eden how, at the very moment when the President was telephoning to him the news of the attack on Pearl Harbour, the Japanese Ambassador and Mr. Kurusu were sitting in conference with Cordell Hull to give the answer to the last American memorandum of 26 November. This reply, when delivered, struck Hull as so preposterous in its insolence and dishonesty that he threw diplomatic protocol to the winds.

For months he had engaged in hollow negotiations with these men. They had lavished upon him meaningless Oriental assurances and fulsome protestations of good faith. There had been in the manner in which they advanced their claims a stale and sickening whiff of the German technique, and a

WITH WINSTON CHURCHILL IN WASHINGTON, 1943

similar flavour of hypocrisy and cant. Cordell Hull must have felt that he had received the kiss of death. Throughout these futile parleys his conduct had been irreproachable in patience, and he had held language that had been invariably honourable and constructive. Perhaps he had even gone too far in the pursuit of peace, realizing that it was impossible for the Japanese to reverse overnight a trend of conquest that had begun in 1931. Often in bad health he had confronted with his own blunt decency forces at once tortuous and evil. Little wonder that his anger exploded, that he betrayed 'the greatest indignation', and that he turned with ferocity upon his smiling and hissing visitors.

'I must say,' he told them, 'that in all my conversations to you in the last nine months I have never said one word of untruth. This is borne out absolutely by the record. In all my fifty years of public service I have never seen a document that was more crowded with infamous falsehoods and distortions— infamous falsehoods and distortions on a scale so huge that I never imagined until today that any Government on this planet was capable of uttering them.'

And when Halifax saw Hull on the afternoon of the following day, he said that 'those two fellows had looked like a pair of sheep-killing dogs'.

Halifax reported that the news of the Japanese action was received by the public in Washington with 'stupefaction', but calm, and that a curious but orderly crowd gathered outside the Japanese Embassy to watch the unconcealed destruction of secret archives. Congress was summoned at twelve noon on 8 December and invited to declare that since the 'unprovoked and dastardly' attack by Japan a state of war existed between the United States and the Japanese Empire. Less than one hour later both Houses of Congress had agreed to the necessary declaration. No vote was cast against it in the Senate, and in the House of Representatives only an elderly and eccentric lady, who had voted against the entry of the United States in the First World War, stoutly recorded her disapproval of the Second. And if Halifax had sometimes thought that the President and Hull had reposed too much hope on even a temporary agreement with the Japanese, he was assured by the Secretary of State after the event that he believed their main decision had been made in July, and had never felt that there was more than a slender chance of extremist policy being deflected by moderate opposition.

Thus ended one of Halifax's first and most important diplomatic experiences in America which was perhaps of greater consequence than any other, closing, as it did, with her entry into the war. In spite of an element of unreality in these negotiations, conducted by the Japanese with a cynical disregard of every principle of international honour, his own part in them established beyond question his skill in diplomacy and his delicacy in human contacts by the end of the first year of his ambassadorship. Although his main duty was to transmit the instructions of the Foreign Office, and in turn to keep them informed of the views of the President and the State Department, there was ample scope for personal influence. In the absence of instructions it was necessary to act on his own initiative; he must study the moods of a temperamental President and tranquillize a Secretary of State whose feathers were easily ruffled.

He reported that 'the manner in which America was precipitated into the war left no room for the Isolationists' previous charges that the Administration was manœuvring the country into hostilities, and produced immediate harmony. The America First Committee was dissolved (ostensibly at any rate) and all the former Isolationists draped themselves in the flag. Nevertheless the first few weeks of the war were passed in an atmosphere of confusion and uncertainty; the extent of the damage done at Pearl Harbour was concealed, and consequently exaggerated by rumour, and there were false alarms of air raids on the Pacific coasts. But the nation soon began to settle down to work; very extensive powers were accorded the President by unanimous votes in Congress, and the arrival of the Prime Minister in Washington had a tonic effect'.

It was while still in the grip of excitement and indignation that he wrote to a friend in England: 'Isn't this Japanese business astonishing? I had been betting against their throwing their hats over the fence just yet, but no doubt the Germans have convinced them that it was a good thing to do, and I expect the Japanese military are a pretty *tête montée* set. Certainly if war was to come to this country it could not have come in a fashion that would more completely unite and infuriate American opinion. It is going to have one good result in getting them to work harder. The President told me today that they were going to get on to a 7-day week and a 24-hour day, and showed me a graph of what they think this will do to their production. I have no doubt that in the end the Japs will see that they have made a big mistake, but I fancy they will break a good deal of china first, and we are in, I would guess, for a disagreeable six months or year. The little swine—I hope they will get it thoroughly in the neck.'

CHAPTER XXXIV

AFTER PEARL HARBOUR

WITH America in the war the nature of the British Ambassador's task altered. On his arrival in America his problem had been different from that of Lothian when, with fear of involvement and isolationism rampant, it had been mainly a question of cautious propaganda and personal influence. Halifax had faced easier conditions, but he also had had to contend with Isolationism, and to try to represent to America those aspects of England that Americans liked. When the United States and Great Britain became allies it was still necessary for Halifax to give a projection of a country fighting for her life, but his main task henceforth was to be on good terms with the President and the executive part of the Government, to be accepted by them as a confidant, and to have access to them at all times. He succeded in this object so well that his standing in official circles was, and remained, as high as Churchill could have hoped in his most optimistic moments.

It was then that Edward realized how great was the benefit the President had conferred on him by the confidence he had shown him, and how kindly a chance it was that a man capricious in personal relations should have bestowed his friendship upon him, and given him unlimited opportunities of friendly contact. And from the moment of America's entry into the war he became more conscious every day that without the shrewd guidance of Hopkins that relationship could easily have been imperilled. So as the months passed he became increasingly grateful to him, and aware of a warm and reciprocated affection. It was in his approach to the President that this relationship was of particular benefit to Halifax, and it was to Hopkins now that he was increasingly to turn.

It was not only in the Ambassador's transactions with Roosevelt that Hopkins played so useful a part. He was equally indispensable on those occasions when Churchill visited America after her entry into the war to concert matters of mutual importance with the President. Winston Churchill crossed the Atlantic to meet Mr. Roosevelt six times during the war, from that first meeting on board ship in Placentia Bay, Newfoundland, in August 1941 to the Second Quebec Conference of September 1944. It was also during Halifax's embassy in Washington, when no longer Prime Minister, that he paid a further visit to the United States in 1946, and delivered the Fulton speech.

After a few days at the White House Churchill would generally move on to be Edward's guest at the Embassy. The Ambassador was fully aware of the advantages which the Prime Minister's extraordinary prestige in America lent to these informal meetings, and of the electric effect of his eloquence and personality on the American people and on Congress:

'On several occasions,' he said, 'he was invited to address a joint session of both Houses, where the range of thought, the easy humour, courage and dynamic force of the speaker, and the language, all had a profound effect on his audience. That by birth he was half an American gave him an especial entry to the sympathy of his hearers, and both in speaking to the Houses and to the smaller numbers such as the Foreign Relations Committee of the Senate, the atmosphere was always very much that of a friendly family party. . . .

'But great as was the esteem and affection in which Churchill was held in every quarter of the United States and by all parties in it, this completely genuine and almost unique admiration was in curious fashion blended with quite another set of emotions. When these obtained he was acclaimed not only as a war leader, but as a brilliant survivor of a past age. Part of his greatness indeed was that he brought alive to the world of today the outlook and temper of the world of yesterday, making these singularly vivid and attractive. But the general effect of this was not free from disadvantage. The evident influence on his thought of great persons and great events of times long past helped to make easy the transition through the enjoyment of this resurrection of the past to a belief that his own outlook too belonged to those earlier days. The consequence was that by many Americans, and by many in high places, he was expected, if not assumed, to cherish sentiments which the American mind, priding itself on its progressive vigour and virtue, must inevitably judge reactionary. From such thoughts were born doubts and a lack of trust, of which we have not everywhere seen the end.'

Thus although Halifax realized the stimulation which the Prime Minister's golden oratory brought to the American people, and how much they were heartened by his combative presence, he believed that there was a reverse side to the coin, and this impression was not diminished by the embarrassment which these visits sometimes caused to his own official position.

When Churchill visited Washington his practice of holding private conferences with the President, sometimes late at night, when matters of high policy were decided, was liable to make the Ambassador's position an unenviable one. As Roosevelt did not want the informality of these meetings to be impaired by the presence of members of the State Department, the Ambassador was also often excluded from them. From the point of view of the Prime Minister and his advisers there was much to be said for these private sessions. In their relaxed atmosphere the President and he were able to achieve an intimacy which would have been impossible in the presence of others, and which was of the greatest consequence in the prosecution of the war.

But it was Edward's misfortune that this necessity should weaken his own position as the local representative. This exclusion was in itself a matter of small concern to him as he greatly disliked late nights, but he was sometimes mortified by the fact that major decisions were made about which he had not been consulted, and the nature of which he only later discovered. It was perhaps an added irritation that the Ambassador was conscious that his American friends were aware of his exclusion from many of these conversations, and sympathized with his predicament. Mrs. Watson, the wife of Roosevelt's confidential aide, remembered how sorry she had felt for the Ambassador as he sat neglected in his Embassy, and how General Watson had sometimes to insist on Roosevelt sending for him, saying that he was, after all, the Ambassador.[1] Dean Acheson too noticed how difficult the Ambassador's position was rendered by these private meetings, and how once again it was Hopkins who saved the situation by attending many of the late night sessions for the endurance of which he was far better fitted than Edward, representing his views and reporting the decisions to him without delay.[2]

To Dean Acheson it seemed that Edward accepted his position with exemplary patience and restraint, and he did not believe that the Ambassador was often tempted to send telegrams of protest to the Foreign Office. This indeed he seldom did, but he could not refrain from strong private comment on the difficult position in which he was placed, and it is clear from his papers that this treatment contributed to the ambivalence of his attitude towards the Prime Minister.

It was an unusual relationship. There existed between them an undoubted affection, and up to a point a mutual respect. Long ago they had been colleagues, but since then they had followed different paths. There were polar extremes of difference in the temperaments of the two men, Halifax with a mind as flexible as the bamboos of Japanese legend bending in a tempest, a tendency to see both sides of every question, an instinct to secure his ends by accommodation, an innate caution: 'I am like an elephant,' he had told William Hayter. 'I test the ground first before venturing on it'— and the other possessing all the canine virtues, supreme courage, tenacity, love of the chase, a man of strongly held convictions which had never been enfeebled by public indifference, and a sombre and prescient interpretation of history.

On two of the greatest issues of the time they had been bitter opponents. Churchill could not have forgotten how Halifax had smoothed the hackles of what he had held to be the forces of subversion in India, and beckoned the 'half-naked fakir' into the viceregal sanctuary. Nor could he have forgotten

[1] Mrs. Frances Watson to author.   [2] Dean Acheson to author.

that his Ambassador, like so many others, had failed to recognize the menace of a resurgent Germany, and when she could no longer be stifled had joined in appeasing her.

It was not the habit of this great man to nourish bitterness, or, by recalling his disregarded warnings, feel anger at the lethargy and ignorance of others, but these reflections must sometimes have been at the back of his mind. In spite of such difficulties he rated Halifax's abilities highly, but their relationship was complicated by the fact that he could exercise no influence over him except an appeal to duty, for Halifax was one of those rare politicians who did not care whether they were in office or not, and when he expressed a desire to leave it Churchill could be certain that he meant exactly what he said.

On his side Edward believed that Churchill was a man with the authentic stamp of genius. He thought that his whole life had been a preparation for that moment of destiny in 1940. His personal affection for his leader was considerable but entirely devoid of sycophancy. He was charmed by his humour and envious of his powers of expression and the rich accumulation of his mind. But he was never dazzled by him. Slow to catch fire, when others were lost in hero-worship he remained cool and appraising. He was by no means blind to the Prime Minister's faults. Their habits of life, their political philosophy, and their approach to religion were alike poles apart. It sometimes seemed to Halifax that Churchill was so obsessed by his own thoughts that he had no inkling of what was passing in the minds of others or of what gave them offence. He was aware of a vast disparity of thought.

'Part of my feeling here,' he wrote to a friend at the beginning of 1942, 'is affected by my awareness of how remote my mind and thoughts are from Winston's and Max's.[1] When they were here the other day I was profoundly conscious of how differently their minds worked to my own, and how impossible it would be for me to establish any real community of sympathy in thought with them. I don't quite know what it is. Partly intellectual, partly moral! Incidentally, I was terribly shocked by Winston's growth in the egotistic habit of thought. *I* can do this: *I* won't do that etc. etc. Humility is an attractive gift but all too rare. But perhaps it would never naturally go with the qualities that are necessary to lead in wartime!'[2]

In spite of such radical differences of temperament and frequent moments of exasperation, Edward succumbed as of old to the sorcerer's spell. He was fascinated, on Churchill's first visit, by the *dégagé* atmosphere that prevailed at the White House:

'After seeing Hull in the morning I went across to the White House, where I hoped to have seen Winston, but when I got there found the President talking to him in his bedroom! Max Beaverbrook and I sat on a box in the passage for a few minutes and exchanged views, Harry Hopkins floating past in pyjamas and dressing gown. Quite the oddest *ménage* anybody has ever

[1] Lord Beaverbrook.   [2] Halifax. Private correspondence.

seen. When I was fixing up with him last night what would be a good time to come and see him in the morning, I said what about 12 o'clock. He thought this was a bit late as that was about the time the President was apt to blow into his bedroom. He had, two or three days before, and found Winston with nothing on at all, and he had quickly to drape himself in a towel! "He is the only head of State I have ever received in the nude." '

And of Churchill's third visit to America in May 1943 when trouble arose between the State Department and the Foreign Office over General de Gaulle, Edward wrote:

'I have never seen him in better heart or form, an amazing contrast to the very tired and nerve-strained P.M. I saw last August in England. He chuckled a lot over a story he said was a chestnut but which I did not remember hearing, which was designed to point out the extremely mechanical development of American civilization. Two Americans in England, and one said to the other: "I think we ought to see Coventry. They tell me that a naked woman rides through the streets on a horse"—"Yes, let's go, I haven't seen a horse in years."

'He was completely off de Gaulle and said that when he saw Hull, he would bet that he, Winston, would slang de Gaulle more than Hull would. When he had refused de Gaulle an aeroplane to go to Africa, de Gaulle had apparently said: "Enfin je suis prisonnier. Bientôt vous m'enverrez a l'Iloman." Winston had made him repeat this three times until he discovered that l'Iloman stood for the Isle of Man, whereupon Winston had said in his best French: "Non, mon Général, pour vous, très distingué, toujours la Tower of London." '

On this visit Churchill had arranged to address the Senate Foreign Relations Committee and the Foreign Affairs Committee of the House of Representatives, and Edward warned him that he might be asked questions about Lend-Lease and whether Great Britain could repay it:

'Oh, I shall like that one. I shall say, yes by all means let us have an account if we can get it reasonably accurate, but I shall have my account to put in too, and my account is for holding the baby alone for eighteen months, and it was a very rough brutal baby I had to hold. I don't quite know what I shall have to charge for it.'[1]

Edward observed the almost hypnotic effect that Churchill's monologues had on his guests at the Embassy:

'I managed to get him talking over dinner and afterwards. In some chat about the colonies he developed the argument that what was wrong with us was not our purpose, but being poor, and that "all these funny little West Indian colonies are therefore loyal but lousy". He let himself go a bit about de Gaulle, saying that he had brought him up from a pup, but had never got him properly trained to the house!'[2]

[1] Hickleton Papers. Washington Diary.   [2] Ibid.

As Ambassador Edward was delighted with the Prime Minister's success, and invigorated by the atmosphere of robust defiance that spread round him, but he had found this visit a considerable strain and was not sorry when it was over:

'Winston came to dine last night, having proposed himself with a party of Averells, Hopkinses and sisters etc., and sat drinking whiskeys and sodas and jawing, sometimes quite well, but at the end not at all, till 1.30 a.m. Isn't that pretty criminal? And what makes it worse is that as the President is away for the week-end we have got to put him up here, and have got dinners for people to meet him each night. I shall be utterly exhausted and unbalanced mentally by the time we get to Monday. How can you live like that? It is bewildering to me to see how utterly intoxicated and bemused he is with his own large words. Surely it is impossible for a judgment to be steady and sure under such conditions. I am sure his being here is immensely valuable for the war and for his getting to know the President so well, and all that. And I am fond of him: but I shall be glad when the visit comes to an end and we can settle down to work again!'[1]

And when this third visit was at last over he wrote a letter which reveals clearly that blend of emotions which always followed sustained contact with his illustrious guest:

'He was in good shape here, and with all his faults of egocentricity—and total lack of the right sort of humility—and utter inconsiderateness for anybody but himself, I do take off my hat to the sheer confidence, vitality and vision of the man. It's that that gives him his strength, and that has really impressed people here. The force of it just wells up. There is nothing artificial about it, and the stream seems quite inexhaustible. He was very mellow on the whole, and had a lot of nice things to say about my position and prestige here which he thought were all right. I must be prepared to come back and join the Government: "If the Labour people pull out, I shall have to form a Conservative administration, and I shall count on your help." To all this I said that when my job was done here, I retired to Garrowby, but he wouldn't have this! A funny man.'

*   *   *

To the Ambassador watching the American scene, the year 1942 following Pearl Harbour was one of many vicissitudes in public opinion, and his interpretation of them was contained in his despatches to the Foreign Office. Its opening days were honeymoon days in the relationship of the two peoples and Governments. He had seen the American people give Churchill a reception which recalled the triumphant visits of Lafayette, and the harmony was still untouched by a breath of hostile criticism. Britain was a gallant ally with a peerless leader. A unified Anglo-American strategy and command was

[1] Halifax. Private correspondence, 21 May 1943.

widely expected, and many looked forward to a joint condominium which would preserve the peace for ever.

That such enthusiasm could not last was ensured by the normal operation of human frailty, but few, he admitted, foresaw the steep decline in British prestige and the impoverishment of Anglo-American goodwill that took place during the first two months after Pearl Harbour even before the fall of Singapore. The Ambassador reported that the full extent of the havoc at Pearl Harbour had been kept from the public until December 1942, and that those responsible for reporting the progress of the war showed a natural tendency to pass as lightly as possible over American reverses. It appeared to him that as a result of this much of the nation's disappointment at the steady retreat of the Allies before the onslaught of Japan was directed towards the British. He explained that the shifting of attention from the European war to the Pacific was itself one of the largest causes in the sudden and alarming decline in British popularity. No longer could it be maintained that she was America's first line of defence because that was now held to have moved to the Pacific.

From a European war in which Britain's single-handed fight against Germany had won her an admiration which even the most Anglophobe propagandist could not check, public attention shifted to Asia where Britain's colonial and Indian operations were already suspect, and where 'heroic China', the only country which had been able to stem the Japanese advance, took pride of place.

He noticed also that the tendency of the moment was to criticize defensive strategy. The capacity 'to take it' was of little recommendation when the most popular slogan was that 'defence could not win the war'. Even Churchill began to be identified with the defensive strategy of keeping armies locked up in Britain for the defence of the British Isles.

He observed with distaste that the Isolationists, who had kept silent during the honeymoon period, had begun to 'crawl out of the woodwork' as the opportunity for fomenting trouble occurred: they began to call it America's war—America should fight for America first, for Pacific rather than Atlantic objectives. He had not expected these incorrigible people to restrain themselves for long, and he was far more disturbed to find that even outside Isolationist circles there was now powerful support for the view that the war should henceforth be largely American led and American managed, and that a new conception of the post-war world tended to relegate Britain to a junior position in what was still, but with diminished confidence, thought of as an Anglo-American condominium.

This sharp decline of British prestige took place before the fall of Singapore, and the capitulation of that fortress, when it came, coincided unhappily with the news of the escape of the German warships *Scharnhorst* and *Gneisenau* through the English Channel.

The effect of these disasters dealt another violent blow to the already shaken British prestige. Edward sometimes found the contemptuous disparagement of his country difficult to bear. He was struck, once again, by the fickleness of American public opinion. The desperate eighteen months when England held that 'rough brutal baby' alone might have happened in some distant and forgotten epoch: 'It makes me boil at times,' he said, 'to feel the atmosphere, but the people who know, and are responsible at the top, don't feel like that.'[1]

He reported that the hostile messages of American press and broadcasters in the South-West Pacific daily repeated allegations of the incompetence of British Commanders and colonial administrators at a time when Britain was loyally abstaining from criticism of American blunders at Pearl Harbour and the Philippines. The impression was given, reported the Ambassador, that the British were no longer capable of protecting and ruling their colonial possessions. This suggestion was seized upon and expanded by American liberals and American imperialists, who with the able assistance of Axis sympathizers developed the themes that the British Empire was 'finished', that the English looked upon Asiatic peoples, including their Chinese allies, as inferiors, that the Prime Minister did not intend the Atlantic Charter to apply to the Pacific area, and that therefore in future the United States must take the lead as guide, philosopher, friend and universal provider.

The President and Halifax in broadcasts, and spokesmen of the Administration in speeches, issued solemn warnings against this internecine folly, and in the second quarter of the year, after a full interchange of visits by high officials and experts, including Churchill, the wave of criticism of British conduct of the war became less extreme. The Cripps Mission to India did much to dispel the American illusion of British intransigence to that country, and the landing in Madagascar was enthusiastically acclaimed. Halifax reported all these reactions, but he knew by now that the next reversal of fortune would send the weathercock wildly spinning in the opposite direction. He had not long to wait. The fall of Tobruk in June caused another wave of anti-British criticism in Congress and in political circles almost as venomous as that which arose in the earlier part of the year.

Believing that when two great nations were in alliance they should regard one another's reverses with sympathy rather than condemnation, he felt depression in having to report that this hostile feeling was inflamed by American despatches from London emphasizing the lack of aggressive spirit in British troops, and the incurable 'Singapore' attitude of British military leaders. Cries arose for a unified command, of course under American leadership as American troops would not serve under British command.

The weathercock spun again with the battle of El Alamein and the pursuit of Rommel by the Eighth Army, and this victory did much to efface the

[1] Halifax. Private correspondence, 16 February 1942.

defeats of the first half of the year and restore American faith in the British as allies, and the criticism of British officers and Generals was silenced. The Ambassador reported with cautious optimism that this more favourable atmosphere was enhanced by the British share in the landings and operations in French North Africa, which out-balanced the harm done to Anglo-American relations by the controversy over Darlan.

In press and official circles, however, the impression grew that the British were backing de Gaulle's Free French movement as opposed to the American support of Darlan with a view to the ultimate control of France after her liberation. As 1943 approached the Ambassador reported that something like an international controversy was beginning between the Press of the two nations. American officials blamed the Foreign Office for inspiring, or at least not restraining, British Press attacks on American foreign policy, and this continued to be a cause of growing irritation to Mr. Hull.

CHAPTER XXXV

IN ADVERSITY

WHILE the Ambassador was immersed in such matters he was always conscious of the fact that his three sons Charles, Peter and Richard were all on active service in combative rôles. He was sometimes oppressed by the great distance which separated him from them, and seized eagerly on any news of them that reached him from the theatres of war in which they were serving. It was during the *détente* that eased Anglo-American relations at the end of 1942 that he heard on Sunday, 1 November, that Peter had been killed. It was heartrending that so much promise should have been so brutally curtailed, and that this vivid and attractive young man should have been denied the fulfilment of his considerable natural gifts.

'The day finished sadly. After I had gone to bed Jack Lockhart brought me a telegram saying that Peter had been killed on 26 October. I went to St. Agnes at seven, and when I got back told Dorothy about Peter. After breakfast we went for half an hour's walk in the sun round the Observatory Garden before I had to go in to see the Polish Ambassador. I rather hope Dorothy may get something in the way of helping collect money for what they call the Community Chest which will fill up her time. One doesn't want too much spare time to think in these days.'

Six months before he had written to a friend analysing the justification for prayer. He had said then:

'I am always asking myself just what is the basis of one's prayers for those one is fond of and who are in danger. Clearly it can't be "Protect *my* son, because I should be so unhappy etc."—nor "Protect my son for it would be so sad if *his* life was cut short"—because both of these are comparisons with other people, and essentially selfish. Nor can we tell whether it is really better for anyone to live or die. And at the end of it all you come back to "Thy will be done" and "Thy will is best". But it's difficult for human nature with its bounded horizons, and its natural desire for what it thinks to be happiness to standardize that feeling, isn't it? I really don't know, dim as one's hold is on the Christian faith, how people with no faith get along at all.'[1]

And now that his second son, as Peter himself had foretold on the eve of Alamein, had died, he was deeply stricken. Like his father, he was sustained at moments of dereliction by the mysterious solace of religion, and his

[1] Halifax. Private correspondence, 16 February 1942.

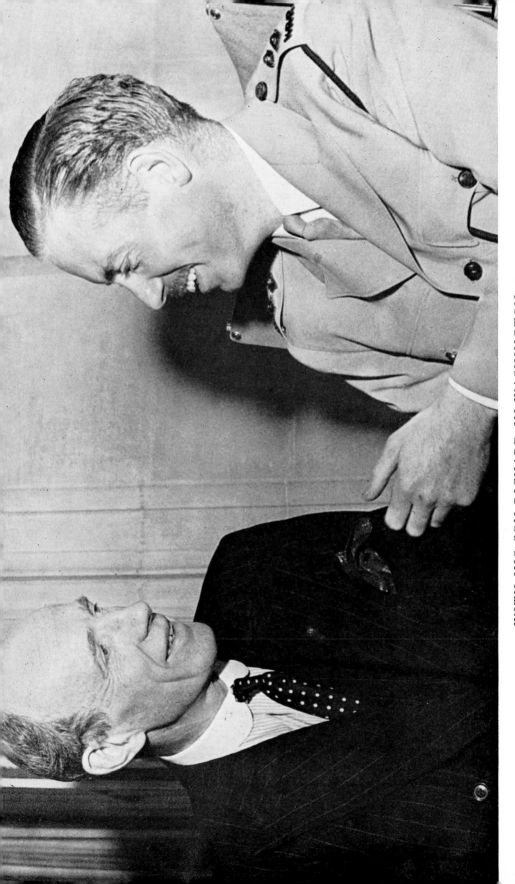

WITH HIS SON RICHARD IN WASHINGTON, 1943

reflections were not altogether sad although he was desolated by the thought of Dorothy's sorrow.

'Dorothy has been as you would guess wonderful, brave, carrying on, never a word of self-pity or anything of the sort. And that just wrings one's heart, for I know how she feels and it hurts me to see how much it hurts her. It makes me happy to think that we have been able to get very close to Peter by letters all this time he has been away. He wrote a lot. I would like to show you some one day which I think have explained him to me quite a lot. I had not always known him well, if you know what I mean, and sometimes found him difficult. But these two years have changed all that, which is and will be enduring happiness.'

Self-pity—Edward was always vigilant lest it should take possession of him in the guise of sorrow, and he began to muse on the anatomy of grief:

'I am constantly feeling myself reflecting as this war proceeds upon the character and quality of human sorrow. I am afraid I think in the main it is *self* pity, for one cannot be presumptuous enough to pity the person who dies if one has a belief in the future life, and indeed I always think it strange the emphasis the Church has placed upon praying for the dead. Humility would suggest that it was much more important they should pray for us!'[1]

After this blow the Halifaxes immediately began to transact their ordinary business, Edward resuming his duties the day after the news reached him. Their dignity and self-control were extraordinary, and they had need of both qualities, for on 6 January 1943 Casey, the Australian representative in Washington, received a telegram in the evening which was shown to Edward after dinner and which said that Richard had been wounded: 'The telegram said severely,' he noted, 'which Casey said was not too bad: the Army apparently have three categories, lightly, severely, dangerously, and the Matron, so Mrs. Casey said, reported encouragingly. We shall no doubt hear more soon.'

The following day they were in New York. 'When we got to the Waldorf Hotel we had a message that was very tormenting about Richard having lost both legs, and it took us some time to get hold of the exact telegram. The sub-manager came and gave me a garbled message he had had from Washington in a most funeral manner to which by way of being comforting he added: "I don't think he is dead." '

Early in the morning a further message came to say that Richard had been wounded on 30 December, and that his general condition was good. This was confirmed a week later by Edward's old friend and Military Secretary in India, C. O. Harvey, who was now in Washington, and had seen Richard in Cairo: 'He told us all about Richard, whose presence in Cairo he had discovered by chance, but whom he had found in good heart and quite determined to get into a position to walk and do everything else as soon as he

[1] Ibid.

could. His general account was most encouraging, and made us all feel much better.' And on 21 January Richard's first letter after his wounding reached them: 'His first four or five days being brought back over desert roads must have been absolute hell, but he makes very little of it, and wrote cheerfully enough.'[1]

When the President had heard the news he had offered his private plane to fly Dorothy and Edward to Cairo, but Edward had replied that Richard would be in hospital with many men whose fathers were not Ambassadors, and could not have their parents flown to them in Presidential aeroplanes. He therefore refused even though he knew that Richard might die.

The extraordinary fortitude with which Dorothy and Edward supported the death of Peter and the grave wounding of Richard made a profound impression upon their American friends and on all who were brought into contact with them. Edward was perhaps quieter, and looked a little older, but their busy life continued without interruption, and Americans, perhaps more emotional than the English about personal bereavement, were amazed by their self-control. The admiration and affection felt for them in the country had reached its highest point and was never to be lost. They were now firmly established in the hearts of Americans as people of the highest integrity and character.

They were much heartened by a visit from their eldest son Charles, who arrived in Washington on 1 February bringing good news of Richard: 'He said that you could not see him for a moment without feeling completely cheered about him. He said that the only thing that annoyed him was when kind people wrote and commiserated too much with him as he had himself made up his mind that he was not going to let events so shape themselves as to require too much commiseration. All this is perfect and does one immense good to hear.' Edward took Charles to the White House to see the President who treated them both with sympathy and understanding:

'He began by asking much after Richard, about whom Charlie was able to tell him everything, saying that the only thing Richard disliked was excessive sympathy, or the idea that he was the victim of a great tragedy which had completely wrecked his life. The President at once said: "He is quite right; that is fine. I have no legs, but I get around very well." '[2]

This admiration for the Ambassador was vicariously increased by Richard's wonderful courage when he joined them in America for convalescence. Edward and Dorothy had been as solid as rocks at the first sight of him at the airport. From the beginning he expressed the view that 'I was damned lucky to get away with it', and as soon as he realized the extent of his wounds, was determined to prove that a legless man could have a normal career.

Their American friends were lost in admiration of the way he made light of his great misfortune; he was dissolved in mirth by a huge Irish policeman

[1] Hickleton Papers.   [2] Hickleton Papers. Washington Diary.

crying over him at the Reservoir; he visited American amputees in the hospitals and showed them how a man could cheerfully face the world without legs. Canon Dubois remembered that when Edward brought Richard to St. Agnes there was never a servant with him to help, and how the laymen carried Richard up the steps and how Edward himself wheeled his son up to receive Communion. And later, when artificial legs had been fitted, Richard arranged to go to the Walter Reed Hospital in Washington to talk to amputees when the roads were covered with snow and ice. The car could not get up the hill, so he left it and walked, an effort of courage and determination which profoundly impressed its American witnesses.

*   *   *

When the Foreign Secretary came to America in March 1943 for conversations with Cordell Hull, Halifax opened his heart to him for the first time on the question of returning home. He told Eden that in his opinion the work of the Ambassador had to a certain extent declined in importance since the United States had been in the war, and since Churchill had established direct personal relations with the President.

This was perhaps a modest way of expressing the opinion that he had so consolidated the position of Ambassador that his personal direction there was no longer essential. He added that he welcomed the Prime Minister's visits, but that they reduced the responsibility and function of the Ambassador. There were also private reasons for not wishing to remain indefinitely in his post. He had long been out of contact with his affairs in England, and with the administration of his estates, and he thought that Dorothy would wish to be as much as possible with Richard during the next year.

He was in fact to remain until May 1946, but in the meantime, although he was often distracted by thoughts of home, the Ambassador did not in any way reduce his efforts in America. In April 1943 he set out on a tour of the South where he visited the Negro college Tuskegee in Alabama. Here he addressed an enormous assemblage with a fluency that came from incessant practice—'my platitudes are coming more easily to mind now'. He was strangely moved, as he spoke, by the rows of eager faces, reflecting how great were the hopes of these people, and how meagre their realization.

'They are asking for bread,' he said, 'and getting a stone. The whole Negro problem looms very large to whomever you talk—once you get near it. It's the one general subject in which people are interested. They all condemn Mrs. Roosevelt for her well-meant but clumsy gestures on the Negro side, and all say how nice the Negroes are if you manage them right and keep them in their place etc. etc. All of which the South only understands.

'Yet few people seem to me to be clear where their present policies lead. The Governor of Alabama gave me a speech to read that he had made at Tuskegee last week. Lots of economic opportunity, equal rights of citizenship and all the rest, as they became fit for it; but everything in a rigid mould of race segregation. Is this maintainable? The Negro President of Tuskegee doesn't believe it is, yet he could give me no clear picture of what he wanted for his people. One has the impression of a great human problem building up, not being tackled by very wide-seeing people, and a good many of the things that are being followed being pretty hollow or will-o'-the-wisps.'[1]

Although he believed that he had broken the back of his task he did not in any way relax his control over each diplomatic issue that arose. He took a prominent part in 1944 in the conference at Dumbarton Oaks, the home of his friend Mrs. Robert Bliss, which decided the preliminary details of what afterwards became the Charter of the United Nations, and at this conference he was made forcibly aware of the nature of Russian diplomacy. At an early stage the meeting encountered difficulties connected with voting. How many votes were different powers to have? On what questions was voting to be accepted, and how far was it allowed to be decisive?

It was to Halifax's credit that he realized at once that these wrangles were merely playing with words, and that it was futile to rely on voting to preserve peace. He penetrated to the heart of the matter when he said that no machinery conceivable by man could force concord upon the three Great Powers, and that unless the United States, Russia and the British Commonwealth could agree, no system could be worked. It was the language of common sense. To Halifax it seemed that in spite of recurring phases of Russian obstruction the debates at Dumbarton Oaks had been pursued with a substantial solidarity of purpose, but he could not pretend that the attitude of the Soviet Government offered any smooth assurance on much that was likely to concern the future comfort of the world.

One incident in particular which occurred in March 1945 on the eve of the San Francisco Conference was an unmistakable danger signal. It was obvious that the Russians had no intention of allowing Poland, after all her ghastly sufferings, the independence in defence of which she had taken up arms. Every step in that direction had been mulishly blocked, and there was something like consternation when it was discovered that sixteen representative Polish leaders, to whom the Soviet Government had given a safe conduct, had disappeared. This was another lurid flash of the red light, and later explanation that they had been conspiring against the Red Army was unlikely to satisfy the most naïve intelligence.

It was the same story at San Francisco in April 1945, the conference at which the Charter of the United Nations was painfully evolved with many damaging concessions. Here again the Ambassador had ample opportunities of studying the alien character of Soviet thought. He tried in vain to penetrate the icy reserve of Molotov whom he described as looking like 'smiling granite'; he was reduced almost to despair by the Soviet representative

[1] Hickleton Papers. Washington Diary.

Gromyko, who had been given no freedom of manœuvre, and whose answer to all questions was an unadorned repetition of the formula: 'The Soviet Government does not agree.'

Edward took an active part in this conference, attending regularly, intervening on many occasions and sometimes losing his temper, an occurrence so rare that it produced an astonishing effect. The shadow of the Russian veto hung darkly over the proceedings, and the conference seemed at one point likely to founder over the Russian interpretation of the Yalta formula, a view which would have made it possible for any one Great Power to block even discussion on the Security Council of any matter to which that Power was not strictly a party. It was a suggestion wholly unacceptable to the Western delegates, and the parrot-like insistence of Gromyko was too much even for Edward's patience to bear:

'I told him that I could hardly have believed that any Government could have given its representative instructions to behave in a fashion so unreasoning, unreasonable and intolerable as those on which he had evidently been acting all morning.'

Halifax's skill in negotiation was greatly admired at San Francisco, and the American Press acknowledged the part he played in convincing the smaller powers that the whole settlement depended on their voluntary concessions on the veto question. When this matter had been settled, the final result of the conference and the outlook for the future did not appear too bleak to the Ambassador:

'Smuts expressed the view to me that he thought the whole world could reasonably look forward to an era of security from war, inasmuch as the three Great Powers were all, speaking broadly, satisfied Powers. No doubt we should have plenty of rough spots and untidiness but no more. I think this is a reasonably true judgment.'[1]

Although he realized that all hopes of a tolerable world would rest in future on harmony between the Great Powers, he was slow to realize how swiftly and with what brutality Russia would shatter that dream. In fairness it should be remembered that the prevailing mood with regard to the Soviet Union was one of optimism. She was an ally who had made a prodigious contribution to the war, and on her soil had been fought some of the most terrible battles in the history of the world. Hundreds of thousands of her civilians had been murdered. The mere thought of her defection from the alliance after victory disclosed vistas so disturbing that few chose to contemplate it, and most were prepared to remain in hopeful suspense. The general view, said Edward, was that it would be churlish and suspicious to think otherwise:

'I feel much the same way as you do about our 3rd great ally,' he wrote to a friend. 'But I doubt whether we need be too gloomy about the future of

[1] Ibid.

her world plans; for I think she genuinely does want to co-operate for world peace and order, though her methods of doing so leave a great deal to be desired.'[1]

There were, he discovered, a few who held different opinions which he was inclined to regard as alarmist. Some time before, William Bullitt and Edward had walked for half an hour in the Observatory Garden discussing the enigma of Russia's secret intentions:

'I found Bullitt in a great state of excitement about the Soviet and very anti-Russian. He thinks we and his own Government are completely blind to the kind of thing he anticipates Stalin will want to do. As he sees it he will seek to dominate and control all Central and South-Eastern European Governments . . . and one of these days we shall all wake up to find Russia a great menace to our free democracies. I told him that this was not the impression gathered by those who had had to do with Stalin, but this naturally made no impression on him. He is a strange fellow, and I don't think judgment is his strongest quality.'[2] And after a luncheon party at the Embassy at which Mrs. Cairns of the National Gallery of Art was a guest, Edward recorded:

'She talked to me with, as I thought, complete lack of balance about what a danger Russia was to the world. After some time I told her that the only conclusion to her argument was that we should reconstruct Germany to fight Russia. She said that was what she thought. I had never met anything quite so wrong-headed, or so brutally blatant of its kind before.'[3]

It is not hindsight to say that Edward showed a certain obtuseness and lack of vision in the views he held at the time on this all-important issue. The history of Bolshevik Russia, and all her recent conduct had screamed their warnings. To fail to grasp the true nature of the régime was to ignore the chasm that separated the Soviets in character and habit from their Western allies; to forget the suspicions cold as the arctic snows that obsessed their minds, and their oriental disregard for human life. When the uncertain unity produced by common danger was weakened, the alien Marxist creed would resume its full and self-centred operation, and opposite extremes of political morality would again be revealed to a world yearning for the end of conflict. The danger signals had not been wanting from the beginning. The German-Soviet non-aggression pact, the inhuman treatment of the Poles, and the base ingratitude for the freezing arctic convoys, among many other portents, had certainly afforded little foothold for optimism.

But if Edward was lacking in vision in his estimate of Russian intentions, there was no confusion of mind in the fate he wished to see meted out to the Germans. He had lost one son in this war, and another had been severely mutilated, and thus bereaved he had no time for Christian forbearance. As

---

[1] Halifax. Private correspondence.   [2] Hickleton Papers. Washington Diary.
[3] Ibid.

in the First War, his feelings for the nation that had wrought such havoc in the world were devoid of mercy, and his desire for revenge grew as blood-chilling reports of German atrocities reached his desk:

'More and more I find myself wishing that lots and lots of Germans may be killed before the job is over—from top to bottom, for I believe justice would best be served by them feeling something of what either directly or by acquiescence they have done to other people.'

*   *   *

The belief that the British position in America had so improved that his own presence there was no longer essential persisted in 1944. He was sometimes told that he grossly exaggerated the American goodwill to England, and that the situation had in fact deteriorated. Being aware of the capricious nature of American favour he knew that there would always be criticism of his country varying in intensity, as well as friendship, and was not disturbed. One of the messengers of gloom who tried to shake the Ambassador's equanimity was Lord Beaverbrook, and in September 1944 Edward gave him his own assessment of the British position at the moment as fairly and objectively as he could. He admitted that 'you are quite right in thinking that there is plenty here to cause us anxiety', but argued that the general situation was far from unfavourable:

'You put considerable emphasis on the rise or fall of pro-British feeling in the U.S. This is of course important. But our relations with the U.S. ought not in my view to be judged or conducted solely on the basis of emotion. Practical results must be considered too. The fact is that in the last year the Administration with the support of public opinion has gone immeasurably further than ever before, and further than appeared likely in 1943, along the road of co-operation with ourselves and other countries. They have come a long way with us in the Food Conference, over U.N.R.R.A., in the discussions on the future financial policy, in the negotiations for a future World Organization, in their thinking on Russia, France and Germany, and in many other matters of policy large and small. In fact we have made progress towards a working partnership with the U.S. such as we have never made before and beyond most people's expectations.'[1]

Meanwhile apart from his daily diplomatic problems the Ambassador seldom had an idle moment. He visited shipyards and aircraft factories and ordnance works, and recognized the song of victory in the clatter of great arsenals where, as he told the crowd, 'the might of America was hammering out the doom of the Germans and Japanese'. He went to Lexington and the blue-grass country of Kentucky and saw the great American racehorse Man o' War, an occasion after his own heart, the smell of the stable, the

[1] Ibid. September 1944.

stamping of horses' feet on straw, sounds and scents so familiar and dear to him, and the tremendous patriarch within:

'One of the best things of the morning was his coloured attendant whose life had entirely revolved round Man o' War for the past seventeen years. No lover has ever been so devoted to his loved as this coloured Will to Man o' War. He made us a long speech on all his virtues and achievements, standing in the box, and it was quite one of the most touching things I have ever heard. He says the horse understands all he says; they almost live together. The owner had been offered, and refused $1,000,000! He was a beautiful horse, back, shoulders and quarters all perfect.'

He went to Charleston where he was taken through little brick alleys, past eighteenth-century houses in leafy seclusion, through gardens with open glades of oaks, and pines covered in hanging moss, full of camellias and azaleas. He visited the battlefield of Gettysburg with McCloy, and was shown the ground where Pickett's Division made its final attack on the third day against the Union's centre; he was taken over the terrain where Robert E. Lee once fought by the historian Douglas Freeman.

He saw much of General Marshall, perhaps of all Americans the one he most revered: 'I don't know,' he said, 'that there are many people in the world I respect more, or who seem more solid right through.' But his relationship with the other American leaders too had remained stable and affectionate. Even in the privacy of his diary or in his personal correspondence he seldom made a spiteful comment about these men. Occasionally he expressed surprise at the eminence some improbable figure had attained, and when received by the former Governor of New York State, Al Smith, he had remarked:

'He was exactly like a rather elderly and demoralized bookie—brown billy-cock—and it is rather terrifying to think that he should have aspired to be President of the United States a few years ago,' and a chance meeting with Joseph Kennedy brought back some of the sour rancour of the past when Kennedy had foretold the downfall of England.

On 23 May 1944 a message reached Halifax from the Prime Minister offering him an earldom, and he wrote to a friend in England:

'I was astonished two days ago to get a telegram from Winston expressing a desire to submit my name to the King for an Earldom!! Don't laugh too much. Confidence, good work, gesture to Americans etc. My first reaction was definitely adverse. Incongruous in wartime: and likely to be equally incongruous when we are all living in a bankrupt new world afterwards. And moreover one felt that one was contributing comparatively little in effort and sacrifice by the side of thousands of others. So it seemed to me slightly discordant and ridiculous.

Dorothy however took the view that while one was still doing the job (assuming no sinister trick about it!) it was rather a compliment to me and to

Photo Karsh, Ottawa

AT HIS DESK IN WASHINGTON

the U.S. which it would not have been if it had been offered when one was pushed out or retired; and that the world at large would take it as a recognition of the importance of the job etc. Also, which I felt too, that there was something to be said for the resuscitation of the Irwin name (though Charles won't like it much, I expect) which would otherwise remain buried. So after much debate, and not without some doubt I have telegraphed to W. assenting. I'm sorry to let go Viscount which I think is a nice title; and which my father and grandfather had made very respectable: but I think the main point is that the name itself remains.'[1]

He was saddened by the death of friends. In November 1944 John Dill had gone, and his loss was followed by the news of Lord Moyne's murder in Cairo and the death of Geoffrey Dawson.

On 12 April 1945 the President himself departed. The news of his death did not come as a surprise to Edward who had for some time noticed his ghastly appearance with alarm and pity. He reflected on the rough road that lay ahead for his successor:

'I think Truman will be a pretty good President. But he hasn't got the stature yet, and won't have for some time. And that will be a real and dangerous loss just now. Terrible to be pitch-forked into that job at such a time. But I think he'll be honest, painstaking, sensible, fair, friendly to us all with the right international ideas. Maybe he'll turn out very good.'

The invasion of Europe took place on 6 June 1944 and the day of victory came at last on 8 May 1945 while the San Francisco Conference was still pursuing its contentious way. Towards the end of July the Ambassador went on leave to England, and he was at sea when he heard the news of the Labour landslide in the General Election. He had often been irritated by the Prime Minister in the past but now he was only conscious of a profound sympathy for him at the moment of his fall:

'I think it must be a cruel and bitter blow for him, and quite apart from every public consideration I feel more sorry for him than I can say. For one would suppose that this must be the effective end of his political life, and of his power, which has been food and drink to him for the last four years. It remains a terrible act of ingratitude.'

And later, when the ship was still bearing him across the Atlantic, the fallen Titan came into his thoughts again and he expressed them in a homely and typical analogy:

'The more I think about Winston's downfall the more I personally commiserate with him. It is rather like being carried by your best hunter over very stiff country without a fall, and when you get home instead of taking him into a nice stable with a good mash and making him comfortable, giving him a clip on the backside and turning him into a field full of thistles.'

On his first day in England he lost no time in visiting Churchill:

[1] Halifax. Private correspondence.

'He didn't disguise that it was a bitter blow to him but was large minded about it all. He said that it was almost impossible to believe that a week ago he had been at Potsdam; the measurement of time seemed to have no relevance. He had for five years had everything through his hands day and night, and it was hard to realize that this had suddenly evaporated.' Churchill asked Edward what his intentions now were, and he told him that subject to his new Labour masters he would carry on with the plan he had arranged with him of returning to America for six months, and on 7 August he met Ernest Bevin the new Foreign Secretary, who asked him to continue his work in Washington until 1 May 1946:

'To see Bevin at the Foreign Office who was very nice and impressed me very favourably. I should be surprised if he doesn't do very well at the Foreign Office. I got in a word about not frightening the Americans with rough language of what might be in mind to do here. He seemed to take the point very readily.'

CHAPTER XXXVI

END OF A MISSION

WHILE Edward was at Garrowby after the Japanese surrender on 10 August 1945, he heard on the 22 that the United States Government had suddenly brought Lend-Lease to an end:

'Bob Dixon rang up from the Foreign Office to say that Bevin and other Ministers were in a flap about the Americans having cut off Lend-Lease, which looked like precipitating us into almost immediate conversations about Stage III. This meant that Keynes and Co. would have to go Washington almost at once, and Bevin wanted me to what he called "lead the delegation", and accordingly get there as soon as possible.'

Stage II of Lend-Lease covered the period after the defeat of Germany and during the war with Japan. The British Government had hoped that Stage III would be an extension of Lend-Lease after the defeat of Japan and during the transition period, and it had been a bombshell for them when on 22 August President Truman, without prior notice or consultation, gave instructions that all Lend-Lease operations should cease. By 8 September Edward was back in Washington, and a delegation from England headed by John Maynard Keynes arrived there at the same time to seek a settlement of the British Lend-Lease account, and some new measure of American aid to tide over the transition period. Keynes hoped for a grant-in-aid, or at least an interest-free loan, of $6 billion, and Edward thought that he seemed reasonably happy about the prospects of obtaining it.

On 13 September economic talks were opened with the Americans by the Ambassador and Keynes which were to last for three months. The American delegation consisted of the Secretary of the Treasury Vinson, Clayton, Wallace, Crowley, Marriner Eccles and McCabe; the English of Maynard Keynes, Robert Brand, Henry Self and Hall Patch. Sir Roy Harrod has told us that Keynes found the atmosphere in the United States less favourable than he had hoped:

'There was still much kindly concern for Britain. But the war was now over. The Americans had suffered heavy loss of life; there was anxiety for the future. The dangers of inflation were vividly present to their minds.'[1] There was also a feeling that the nations whose freedom had been saved in the war must now fend for themselves, and settle down to the task of repairing their own homes. To President Truman's advisers it also seemed that the

[1] Harrod, *John Maynard Keynes*, pp. 547–8.

553

British had overstated the gravity of their position, but the true financial status of the United Kingdom was never determined although it was obviously serious.[1] It was agreed that the United States must provide substantial aid to Great Britain to enable her to base her foreign economic policy on a multilateral basis rather than on a sterling bloc arrangement.

Keynes explained his country's plight in a memorable speech in the Board Room of the Federal Reserve Building, describing her staggering load of foreign debt and her present inability to pay her way from day to day, but he found that the Administration was more interested in future policies than in past performances. The Ambassador played an indispensable rôle in these negotiations, and the Americans, in Harrod's words, 'came to have the highest regard for him [Keynes] and for Lord Halifax. If at moments they were nervous when Keynes let his imagination take wing, there was always Lord Halifax at his side, with his feet firmly planted on the earth, whose very lack of financial detail gave his support the weight of common sense. The Americans could not conceive that the British could have been better represented than they had been by Keynes and Lord Halifax.'[2]

It was a period of anxiety for the Ambassador, and apart from the full sessions there were also small meetings at which Halifax, Keynes, Clayton and Vinson threshed out all the points at issue between them. On 25 September Halifax wrote in his diary:

'When I thought it had been going pretty well we ran into trouble. The Americans made it plain that they could not contemplate any Interest-Free Loan, and we said we could not contemplate paying interest because we should not see our way to it. And so there we were. Whether there is any way round these head-on collisions I am not sure.'

It was during these anxious days he was taught to drive a car by the Embassy chauffeur Tom Keep, who noticed that Edward enjoyed driving the powerful Buick and 'got a kick out of it'. 'How all the mysteries you have to cope with ever become second nature,' he said, 'I can't imagine. I regard the car as a natural enemy, much as one thinks of a horse that would run away if you let it gallop,' and the fact that he was successful in passing his driving test may have been due to the bottle of whisky which was handed to the instructor when their affair was concluded. Edward was not the cautious type of beginner, and a few weeks later skidded across a frozen road on his way to church: 'Dorothy was craven hearted and suggested we should come back but I resisted this and we made the rest of our journey very successfully.'

It was soon evident that there was no way round 'the head-on collisions' over the Loan, but the Ambassador did not lose hope, and on 9 October he remarked:

'They continue to harp upon the difficulty of getting anything through

[1] Harry Truman, *Years of Decision*, p. 413.   [2] Harrod. Op. cit.

Congress except a low-interest loan, and I cannot but think they exaggerate the difficulties. My feeling has always been that if the Administration went flat out for any scheme they would, in fact, get it through.' On 16 October he wrote:

'When we all gathered we plunged very deeply into figures. The point of the argument was whether we really did want about 5 billion to balance ourselves, or whether we were pitching our estimate too high. But meanwhile we rather go round and round.'

The talks did not go easily. On 18 October Keynes spoke of breaking off negotiations and returning to London, and Edward realized they were getting into deep water. By 15 November matters had become even worse. Speaking of the situation arising out of the last American proposals Halifax wrote:

'These we found in some respects quite unacceptable, and I had to tell them so in language of rather melancholy menace, pointing out how near they had brought us to the precipice of failure. My feeling still remains fairly firm that they do intend in the end to settle.'

But ten days later he felt that there had been a further deterioration in the atmosphere:

'It is much less favourable than it was six weeks ago. Russia is much more of a question mark than it was; anxieties over the labour situation are rightly much sharper and the general result has been to make American opinion less buoyant and confident and sure of itself. If only the Administration had been wider or bigger, they would have seen the advantage of treating the British case as a special case, and handling it with great decision and swiftness on large lines. But unhappily they are not made that way.' By 30 November he was in a state of deep anxiety:

'Our finance talks are in a dreadful bog on our latest, much too rigid as we think, instructions from London. Keynes is talking freely of resigning and I have had quite a business calming him. Bridges[1] is coming over hot foot and supposed to arrive tomorrow, and we are to have what will be a pretty difficult and perhaps explosive meeting with the Americans on Sunday.'

We read in Harrod's pages that the American negotiators regarded the arrival of Sir Edward Bridges as a slight on Halifax and Keynes, and were determined to make no concessions to him. At the meeting on Sunday, 2 December, at the Treasury, papers were exchanged between the two sides, and the exhausting process of reconciling them continued until 7.30 p.m.

'We all felt by the time we had finished that we knew pretty well what they would give and what they wouldn't. In the light of this telegrams were drafted to London which the party brought up to discuss with me at 11.45 p.m. We got through them by about 1 o'clock in the morning, and now we sit back to see whether London will accept or break. Bridges says they will grumble but accept.'

[1] Sir Edward Bridges, Permanent Secretary to the Treasury.

On 5 December a telegram came from London that they would agree with certain stipulations to the American draft. Halifax and Keynes had had ample cause for the anxiety they had felt during this dour negotiation. The result they achieved fell far below their intentions. Instead of a free gift or an interest-free loan of $6 billion they had got a loan of $3.75 billion, carrying interest at 2 per cent per annum. They could not have got more. American generosity had been stretched to what at the moment was its limit, and their only alternative was to break off negotiations and return home. Edward was a little sanguine in his interpretation of the result:

'I am thankful we have got through, though in getting there each side had had to give way to the other, and therefore the settlement is certainly not what we had originally hoped to get. I do not think it is an unfair one and it is vastly better than what would have been the alternative of failure. I hope those concerned will defend it well in Congress and in Parliament. I would not think it was too difficult to do. Anyway we are over what we used to call this "big fence" of Stage III discussions, and in the jumping of it have made the Americans realize much better than they ever did before what are the essentials of our position both as it affects us and as it affects our capacity to reconstruct the world.'

The Ambassador and Maynard Keynes had been drawn closely together during these negotiations, and a friendship had grown between them of men associated in a great purpose, and it is significant that Edward should have been so highly regarded by a man of such outstanding intellect and low opinion of that of others. When it was all over Keynes sent to the Ambassador a poem written in praise of a Lord Halifax from an earlier period of history, which seemed to him to fit perfectly a later bearer of the name who had stood by his side during the recent storms:

> *Of those Rich Lights Great Halifax shined there;*
> *In Pow'rs whole Constellation, None more Fair;*
> *In Calms or Storms, in every varying Gale,*
> *The Furl'd, the Hoysted, or the Slackened Sail;*
> *The Helm to manage, or the Mates to Cheer;*
> *No Pilot-Hand could ever Worthier Steer,*
> *TRUST the Magnetic Load-Star of his Soul;*
> *And FAITH and ZEAL, his Needles to the Pole.*

*   *   *

The Ambassador was more angry than he had been for a long time when he read in the newspapers that the Conservative Party had decided to abstain on the vote in the House of Commons on the American Loan, and in his disgust convinced himself of the operation of sinister influences which had no existence in fact:

'This seems to me to be a final confession of impotence and futility. To say that you have no opinion or take no responsibility in an immense decision by Parliament scarcely seems calculated to restore the fortunes of a great Party. I picture to myself this being another example of Max Beaverbrook's evil influence. I can imagine him and Brendan and Rob Hudson arguing with passion in the Conservative Shadow Cabinet that support of the proposals would be regarded as disloyalty to the ideals of Imperial Preference, and that it would split the Conservative Party and that the only possible way of avoiding this disaster was not to vote. I can understand Winston being taken in with this kind of thing because I have always thought that after changing his party twice he was much less sure of himself in domestic policies than those of us who remained where we began, and he has therefore all along exaggerated the strength of the Conservative Right Wing. But I cannot understand John Anderson, Anthony Eden and Rab Butler being taken in by it. All this may be badly off the mark and indeed I hope it is.'[1]

As in India a feeling approaching contempt for his own Party overcame him. In a private letter he spoke of 'this supreme act of ineptitude and folly', and his belief in the party system, never robust, sank to its lowest ebb:

'I have never felt more humiliated by the Party to which I am supposed to belong,' he added, 'and which I should find it very difficult today to support.'

While this feeling of exasperation was still upon him he wrote to Eden asking for an explanation: 'Enlighten me,' he begged, 'for as I write I am feeling gravely wounded in my loyalty to the Conservative Party as at present led, and should not find it easy to whip myself into a great desire, as long as it is so led, to serve it.'[2]

He was not mollified by Eden's reply, reasonable as it was and dispelling his wilder illusions:

'I am sorry that we distressed you so much, but we did not have at all an easy time ourselves. The Loan was extremely unpopular here, and the object of our inaction was to try to prevent the Tory Party collectively voting against it. In this we were not so successful as we hoped, and Winston and I were naturally considerably annoyed to find so large a section of the Party ignoring our advice. If left to ourselves he and I would probably have voted for the Bill, with probably a small number of followers, while the great majority of the Party would have voted against. There was a further complication in respect of the Lords. If we had had a "free-for-all" vote for the Opposition in the Commons the Lords would have demanded the same, and Bobbety[3] felt confident that the majority would have voted against the Bill. We felt that this would be a disaster, and since Bobbety felt that he could only hold his peers if we abstained in the Commons we did abstain, despite taunts and jeers.

[1] Hickleton Papers.   [2] Ibid.
[3] The Marquess of Salisbury, Leader of the Conservative Opposition in the House of Lords.

'You can be sure of one thing: that it was not Max's influence which caused us to take our action. Indeed he had nothing to do with it, and was not present at our gatherings. It is so difficult to explain the problems of one side of the Atlantic to the other, and the Tory Party in opposition is not a bed of roses, as I shall no doubt discover in the next two months!'

On 29 January he learned of another death in his circle of friends. Hopkins, indomitable to the last, had gone, worn out by sickness and incessant labour. In the course of their friendship Edward had come to realize the true quality of this extraordinary man. He thought of that unerring judgment in all the things that mattered, and of his powers of affection: 'He was a very fascinating friend; stimulating, direct, full of vigour in judgment and with a very powerful blend of courage and wisdom that must have meant a great deal to Roosevelt.' These thoughts were passing through his mind at Hopkins's funeral on 1 February, at which the Rector had remarked with breezy satisfaction: 'Well anyhow, I think we have given him a good send-off!' 'I think Harry would have chuckled no end at that,' he said, 'and I laugh every time I think of it.'[1]

Meanwhile the ill-fated loan had met with little approval on either side of the Atlantic, and was now being buffeted in America. Edward remained calm about its prospects, but watched the scene closely:

'Things are in an increasingly confused state. The Administration is at loggerheads with Congress (our poor loan). The President is generally judged inefficient and pretty lost with it all, and there are even whispers, and not too ill-founded either, that he is at times contemplating the extreme remedy of resignation. I find it hard to believe this last, but it is not without significance that the idea even should be floating round. I still think our loan will go through. After an interminable quantity of talk, a great deal malevolent, and nearly all ignorant. But Congress is in a bad temper and we can certainly assume much more delay than we had bargained for. Isn't it funny how wrong we have all been in our feeling when F.D.R. died: "Well at least Truman will get on well with the Congress!!" '[2]

In February he was visited for the last time by Winston Churchill who had come to deliver the Fulton speech in which he developed the idea of Fraternal Association he had foreshadowed at Harvard two years before, and which was designed to emphasize the supreme importance of Anglo-American co-operation in the face of Russian estrangement. It was in this speech that Churchill introduced that phrase which was soon to be used by the entire Western world: 'From Stettin in the Baltic to Trieste in the Adriatic an iron curtain has descended across the continent.' This time there was no hint of friction between the two men, and Edward's heart warmed to his illustrious guest. He observed his preparations for the speech with fascination:

[1] Hickleton Papers. Washington Diary.   [2] Halifax. Private correspondence.

'He rehearsed to me a great deal of the speech that he has in mind to deliver, with tears almost rolling down his cheeks as he thought of the great strategical concept of the future which was the happy cottage home of happy, humble people, and quoted *Childe Harold* to reinforce his eloquence. He really is a most astonishing creature, but Dorothy and I agreed that we had never seen him so benign'—and they talked nostalgically of those distant days at the Colonial Office, and what a surly reception he had given his Under-Secretary. Later he regaled Edward, by then on a sickbed, with an account of the trip he had made with President Truman to Missouri:

'Winston came in and sat with me after tea, which was quite amusing but left the room stinking like a third class smoking carriage. He had enjoyed his trip to Missouri with the President. They had played poker each night from a quarter past eight till 2 a.m. The first night he had lost $100 and had won 25 of them back the following night. But he thought it had all been well worth it! The President had asked him to call him Harry, which he said he would do if the President would call him Winston. He really is the most engagingly naïve creature I know. Apparently at dinner they talked about their respective powers of sleeping. Winston said that he got into bed and said "To hell with everybody", and was asleep in two minutes. He had only missed one night's sleep in the last ten years. Everybody supposed that this would be during Dunkirk. But he said it was the night of Anthony's resignation from Neville Chamberlain's Government.'

Halifax did not altogether approve of the Fulton speech. He thought that Churchill's condemnation of the Soviet, giving the impression that he accepted the division of the world into two blocs, had been the cause of its mixed reception in America. He had a shrewd suspicion that an enormous majority of Americans accepted Churchill's diagnosis of the Russian situation, but were embarrassed by the thing being so nakedly said, and reluctant to accept its full implications. He thought that the average American did not wish to think that this was the only answer, because in some vague way it appeared to him the abandonment of the United Nations and an acceptance of the inevitability of war with Russia.

When Stalin responded to the Fulton speech in a vitriolic interview attacking Churchill, Edward took a step which showed more clearly than any long analysis the fundamental difference between the characters of the two men. He sent Churchill a message suggesting the attitude he might adopt in the speech he was to deliver in New York the following evening. This was the course he would himself have taken and it was characteristic of its author—a manœuvre bland and emollient involving patience after insult, a contempt for retaliation, and an assumption that his opponent, even if like Stalin he was as amoral as Peter the Great, could be brought to a reasonable mood by the onset of a sense of guilt:

'Uncle Joe's speech is pretty insolent but any public argument between you will get the world nowhere except in a worse temper. I would like to see you say publicly tomorrow something on these lines:

(a) U.J. has completely misunderstood what you said at Fulton;

(b) U.J. does not appear to appreciate any of the causes that are responsible for the present anxiety about Russian policy;

(c) You attach too much importance to your war comradeship with U.J. to be willing to allow it to be frosted over if this can be avoided; and therefore,

(d) With the permission of His Majesty's Government you have sent a message to U.J. suggesting that after your return to England you should pay a visit to him for the purpose of full and frank discussion.

'I believe that something of this sort would have a profound effect both in the U.S. and at home and that it might do something that neither Attlee nor Truman could do.'[1]

But to Churchill such a proposal could have only one meaning. It must have seemed like some resurrection from the past, another indication of that incapacity for righteous anger in the face of evil that had been the brand of appeasement. When he received the message he rang up Dorothy and said that he could not possibly do it—it would be 'the whipped cur coming to heel', and like 'going to see Hitler just before the war'.[2] It was an unintentional though deadly thrust, but Edward had a thick skin on this subject, and he was in no way mortified: 'I thought at the time,' he said, 'as I have thought since, that he was wrong.' He felt no resentment either, and when Churchill returned to England, it was to his letters describing the progress of the Labour Government, and rich as some rare old wine, that he turned with the greatest expectation. He felt a strong curiosity about how the other party was faring in office, and was amused when Churchill wrote to him on 12 April:

'The Government seem to me to be learning a good deal from responsibility and contact with events. The Chancellor who has inherited the mighty revenue gained by the Coalition Government on the impulse of the struggle for life, proposes to lead a lush life upon it and finds little small change in his pocket for local charities designed to give him a good name in the neighbourhood.'

*   *   *

They had now come almost to the end of their Washington life, and from now on it was a period of farewell. It began with an immense dinner party given for them by Mrs. McLean with:

'the Hope Diamond and every other diamond in the world in full prominence. Crowds of people, including plenty of Senators which gave me a

[1] Ibid.   [2] Ibid.

chance of having a talk with Burt Wheeler, Taft, La Follette, and in fact every person under the sun.'

They took their last walks in the woods round Washington where the dogwood was still in bloom, and down the Canal bank fragrant with honeysuckle. On 6 May he addressed the Overseas Writers Club, and spoke of the influences that caused the two countries to approach their problems in a different manner:

'Among these, I said, was geography, that always made it easy for Americans to say that we ought to call somebody's bluff, whether it was Hitler, Mussolini or the Arabs, because it would not be on their heads that the stick would fall if the bluff-calling business turned out badly. I told them that I could suppose it was much easier for someone standing behind the elbow of a friend playing poker to tell him to see the other fellow's hand, because the counsellor would not have to fork out the dollars if his advice was wrong.'

We gain some impression of the position Halifax had won in America from the farewell letters of some of her leading men: 'Edward,' wrote Stettinius, 'I admire you as much as any man I have ever known, and mingled with the admiration is a deep affection which will remain always in my heart. We must not allow our wartime friendship to drift away';[1] and he was moved by the words of Henry Stimson, who later wrote to him:

'In my comparative seclusion in Washington you were the one friend from the outside diplomatic world with whom I always felt on intimate terms, and with whom I could discuss freely and fully all problems. I cannot bear to think that such relations should now be entirely ended.'[2]

Arthur Krock reflected the feelings of most of those who had met Edward in America when he wrote:

'Now at the end of the years the detractors are silent, or join the overwhelming tributes to Halifax. The contrast with Lothian which at the time was mentioned unfavourably by many has been forgotten. It would not be responsibly questioned in Washington that the retiring Ambassador will leave the United States with the respect and admiration of all in Government here, and with the record of a hard task brilliantly performed for his own people.'

Perhaps the most remarkable tribute of all to the departing Ambassador was a spontaneous message from the Press Corps of Washington. Signed by the leading correspondents of the capital, it is a convincing proof of the admiration in which Edward was held by the American Press:

'We, the undersigned Washington correspondents, would like to tell you of the great enjoyment and value we have derived from association with you during your service here as British Ambassador.

'It seems to us that the whole Embassy staff has reflected the spirit of candor and helpfulness with which you yourself have worked with the Press.

[1] Ibid.   [2] Ibid.

And we would like you to know that we look upon your return to London with a sense of personal loss.'

When the time came to leave he was conscious of the same sadness as in India, the same ending of a chapter in his life. They said good-bye to the household staff in the ballroom, and he hated every minute of it. Afterwards they walked from the front door of the house past the Chancery buildings to the street through ranks of the Embassy staff who had come to see them leave. Edward felt so moved that he was glad to get into the car that was following and put a term to his emotion. At the station there were more farewells, and again in New York before they boarded the ship.

'We left New York,' he said, 'on 14 May and I got up at 6 a.m. to see the last of the wonderful skyline and to salute the Statue of Liberty, and as the ship moved eastwards one was conscious both of the keen pleasure with which one looked forward to returning home and of the real sorrow with which one bade farewell to the United States.'

*   *   *

So Edward left Washington, full of warm memories, and the sense of a great achievement. He had at first been clasped in a wintry embrace, but by the steadfastness of his character and his dignity in bereavement had passed serenely into the sunshine. His particular qualities, modesty, sincerity, consummate tact, and perfect equanimity in all circumstances were those most demanded in an ambassador at such a moment, and his agile mind and diplomatic suppleness of particular value in misunderstandings which might appear ominous over three thousand miles of salt water. He left behind not only the image of a great Ambassador, but also memories of enduring affection. He could never be quite the same man as before. His somewhat narrow horizon had been enlarged, and his knowledge of men enriched by human contact. Every corner of a teeming continent with inhabitants differing so widely in opinion and custom had been brought before his eyes, and whereas in India he had seen the people on his travels only from the dizzy heights of his viceregal splendour, in America he had met them in field and factory, or on the street, and had mingled with them on terms of salutary equality.

Taking every advantage of his wonderful opportunities for exploration he had become absorbed in his study of the American people which had before been an entirely virgin field, and he had grown to love them. Even the faults which he so frequently noted became to him the symbols, sometimes enraging, of a fundamental idealism. But his service in America had not only enlarged the Ambassador's knowledge of the human condition. As after the reading of some novel and engrossing book his vision of the future was born anew. He had had better opportunities than any other Englishman to appreciate the growing might of America. He saw her like a giant stretching, and had no doubt of the part she would henceforth play in the world, and to him, fresh from his intimate experience, the problem, transcending all others, would be how the ligatures that bound the United States and the British Commonwealth of Nations, relaxing as the common danger passed, could be tightened and maintained.

Part Five

THE LAST YEARS

CHAPTER XXXVII

BACK TO GARROWBY

EDWARD was now sixty-five. The pattern of his remaining years would soon take shape. There was much to be done on the estate at Garrowby from which its master had long been absent. The thought of bringing order and neatness into farms which had languished during the war, of becoming absorbed again in the pastoral life of the village, had sustained him in America as in India, and after long confinement in one country he was also filled with a desire to travel. Although he had sometimes dreamed of leaving politics altogether to enjoy these pleasures, he must have realized that since his later life had been spent at the summit of great events and in the company of the leaders of nations, such a position could not be suddenly surrendered without a feeling of emptiness and deprivation. So he would become an elder states-man. The House of Lords would be his forum, and in his last years he would exercise there a greater influence than at any time of his life before, emerging from Yorkshire on particular occasions, one of those rare beings who could win a hostile House to his side by the authority of his presence. He would also be saved from a sense of exclusion from the world by his work on the Governing Body of Eton and as Chancellor of Oxford University.

But it was Garrowby on which his thoughts had been wistfully fixed during those years of war, and on the ship he had been conscious of a great lifting of the spirit at his first sight of the English coast, and the knowledge that he was coming home:

'Such a lovely day to approach England after five years. The sun shone and made the sea blue, and the blue sea made the cliffs of the Isle of Wight more white, and the land more green. There can surely be no place that smiles more sweetly upon its visitors than England. One could hardly believe it all to be real.'

He was surprised how quickly the sense of strangeness disappeared, and how easy it was to slip back into his old life. On the day after his arrival he walked down to the House of Lords across the bed of the lake in St. James's Park which had been drained to dispose of a bomb, and he soon began to meet his friends. He wrote in his diary of the political situation:

'There seems to be a lot of unrest in the Party, and most people seem to say that the predominant desire is that W. should give up the leadership. Irregular attendance, too much of a one-man show; and too much interested in trying to score off the Socialists, which, incidentally, he mostly fails to do.

And the result in the country is to appear factious. I don't know, of course, what truth there is in all this, but I have a hunch there is a growing atmosphere of *malaise*. I am told that both Smuts and Clemmie C. have been trying to persuade Winston to give up the leadership—but so far without result! . . . Anthony [Eden] told me that when Winston got back from the States he told him that he wished to give up the leadership in the House of Commons, while possibly keeping the titular leadership outside. Anthony had liked this, but in a week or two, under pressure as it was presumed from Max;[1] he had changed his mind. So everybody was back where they started.'[2]

Edward was now able to regard such affairs with a certain detachment. While he was still in Washington Churchill had asked him to join the Conservative Shadow Cabinet on his return, but for the moment he had declined, feeling that having served for several months under a Labour Government and been privy to some of their secrets it would be improper for him to make an immediate return to party politics. Nor had he any desire to do so, although had a Conservative Government been returned he might have been prepared to join it. He was busy picking up the threads of his old life, and lost little time in resuming it. Within a few days of his return he had lunched at Buckingham Palace, held an Encaenia at Oxford, and attended a Governing Body meeting at Eton.

But above all, after nearly five and a half years abroad, he felt the need to return to Yorkshire to put his affairs at Garrowby and Hickleton in order, and to see Richard completely rehabilitated. He had come to the sad conclusion that both from motives of post-war economy and the encroachment of Doncaster he could no longer live at Hickleton, and he thought that it might be used by a youth organization or an institution. It was a heavy blow to part from this haunt of childhood. Most of the memories of early youth were bound up in this grey house which had once stood proudly in such lovely country, memories of bygone Christmases, of stables full of horses, and of the sound of a corncrake on misty mornings when he sat at work in the schoolroom, and over all the benign ghost of his father. Now its past glories had long departed. During the war it had been requisitioned by the Army immediately after Dunkirk, and later the garden where they had played prisoners' base in the snow had provided a camp for German prisoners, and the bare house and the deserted garden seemed to convey an air of cold reproach.

Edward began to make inquiries about the uses to which it might be put. Always more sensitive to criticism of his religious practices than of any other aspect of his life he was enraged when the Bishop of Pontefract said that he thought that the type of Hickleton churchmanship might militate against the use of the house for any general purpose. He then approached the Sisters of the Paraclete, a teaching order at Whitby, who were looking for a house which could be used as a school and, beguiled by the church and chapel,

---

[1] Lord Beaverbrook.   [2] Hickleton Papers. Washington Diary.

agreed to take Hickleton. The sisters remained there until the house became a Ryder Home, and during their tenancy the tradesmen and estate workers, unfamiliar with the theological import of the Sisterhood's title, would casually refer to 'having trouble with the Paraclete', or 'settling up with the Paraclete', in a manner that would have sent old Halifax into paroxysms of mirth. The property remained in Edward's hands, and rather than sever all connection with this abode of his youth he converted part of the stables into a small cottage which he used on his visits there, and where hangs today an original letter written by the highwayman Dick Turpin, which had been found at Cantley near Doncaster, and which Edward prized as one of his greatest treasures:

'I William Turpin Highwayman was drove in here by stress of weather and fear of being discovered but I desire you dear friend you who belongs this Barn not to make any discovery of anybody being here for I am forced to stay in the neighbourhood for a considerable time and shall not do much more mischief than I have done you this night to anybody hereabout. You perhaps have heard that there is a great reward offered for taking me but let not that make you endeavour to seek my ruin who means you no harm perhaps I may be forced to lye another night.'

William Turpin, commonly known as Dick Turpin, was hanged in York in 1739, and Edward never knew how this curiosity came into the possession of his family, but he refused to believe that the highwayman's exploits were not genuine: 'No wonder,' he said, 'that we rebelled then, as I rebel now, against attempts to relegate Black Bess and Dick Turpin's ride from London to York to the shadowy limbo of unsupported legend.'

*   *   *

It is doubtful whether any statesman enjoyed retirement more than Edward. All his life he had longed to live at home in Yorkshire and have time for his farms and tenants, his children and grandchildren, and the transaction of his affairs. When he had thought of Garrowby in those long years in America when his mind was constantly occupied by great issues, his spirit had been that of the exile who had once sighed for home in an alien land:

From the lone shieling on the misty island
Mountains divide us and the breadth of sea,

and amid all his preoccupations, and across three thousand miles he had often longed for the simple rhythm of the Yorkshire countryside. It was with a profound relief that he came at last to the familiar scene and knew that he need never leave it again, and that the rest of his life would be lapped in its repose. Now he could walk again from the house to the top of Garrowby Hill, and see the Vale of York spread out beneath him, and sometimes a glitter in the sunshine from the windows of the distant Minster, and wander back down the paths through Kingtop Wood; or ride again over Cheesecake Wold and look down upon the valley of Megdale encircled by the wolds, a sweep of fields and woods and rolling country, and in a dip of the hills the little village of Kirby Underdale tranquil beside its stream.

From Garrowby Hill he could see Givendale and Wayrham dale on either side. This country was in his blood, the wide clean spaces where the wolds stretch to the horizon in vast and gentle undulations, in sudden upward curves of ploughland beyond the slabs of pasture, caused by some ancient upheaval, enfolding the dales between them. The fields on the wolds are larger than those in the south, and it is good barley country. Here and there rises a shelter belt of trees to protect the farms from the piercing wind of winter. The immense expanse of wold and dale runs from Garrowby to the sea, and it has an abiding fascination through the changing seasons, even when the wold lies under snow in winter, and icy winds rake the hilltops, and the remote farms are severed from the world outside. In summer with its yellow cornfields and green expanses of roots curving against the sky it has an extraordinary beauty, and now Edward could turn his horse again to Burdale, and ride between its high ridges, and through Thixendale, like a narrow sword cut through the hills, its sharp flanks towering over him on either side, dotted with sallow thorn.

Like everyone else, they found living a grimmer business than before the war. Dorothy, who had returned tired after her exertions in America, would speak on the train to Yorkshire of 'going back to my chores', and with her usual adaptability performed much of the household work. They were more fortunate than many in that their children's nurse Miss Gaywood, and Harry Salkeld, who had driven Edward's first car in those bygone elections, were still with them, and they were able to keep the house on something of its old footing.

His happiness was now complete. His heart was in the village church and in the land, and we can see a charming aspect of his character in his relations with the men who worked on it, and with others who were his dependents on the estate. It was often said of him that he knew little of those beneath him, but he embraced these people in his own clan. Jimmy Barker, who had first come to Garrowby in 1931 as second horseman, remembered 'that he had butterflies in his stomach' when he first met Edward, but he had shaken hands with him and at once put him at his ease, and told him that he would be treated as one of the family.

And Barker had quickly noticed how fiercely his master clung to the old ways, and how stoutly he barred the road to change. He observed his obstinate devotion to disreputable old clothes, and his particular loyalty to an ancient and much-patched coat made from the wool of his own Jacob flock of brown and white sheep, a garment which Dorothy had long been anxious to destroy.

After his pony had thrown him over its head into a barbed wire fence, causing further ravages to the coat, Edward's first thought was for yet another patch to be put upon it, and Dorothy had to wait for years until it had almost disintegrated, and could be burned without further protest on a Guy Fawkes. After being in formal dress he would change at the first opportunity into his old clothes with the relief of some creature assuming a new skin, but he was illogically angry when dubbin was used on his shooting boots to make them waterproof, because he wanted them highly polished, and he gave Barker a week to get all the dubbin out and induce a perfect sheen.[1]

He was on the same friendly terms with his gamekeeper Charles Harrison. After wartime neglect the park at Garrowby was teeming with rabbits, whose numbers Edward was anxious to reduce, and the two men often went after them with the gun. The keeper remembered Edward asking him on one of these expeditions: 'Do you think rabbits know each other? Do they call each other by their names? Do they say: "Has Mary come home yet?"' He still liked what he called 'the poaching days' better than the formal covert shoots, when he would walk up the hedgerows with a keeper and a dog, but this method of shooting made little impression on the rabbits which continued to multiply. At last he asked Harrison if he could find a long-net man, and the keeper unearthed one in Goldthorpe, a mining village near Hickleton, who brought four miners with him, and went to work on the rabbits at midnight at Martinholm. Edward watched them at work with his usual curiosity and admired their adroitness: 'I derived much gratification from looking on as our visitors set about their business—no buttons on the coats to catch in the nets; a sureness of touch that was as much at home in the dark as in the broad light of day.' He thought it would be amusing if this dubious party encountered the police, and was delighted to hear that they had indeed been stopped near Doncaster, and that the long-net man had produced a letter of permission from Lord Halifax which had greatly enraged the constable; for these men were all expert poachers of the old-fashioned breed who worked only with the long-net and were as quick as lightning in spreading and pegging it. By these methods the rabbits were much reduced, and the poachers allowed to keep what they had caught, until myxomatosis wiped out what they had left.[2]

Harrison noticed, too, how Edward liked to talk to anyone he met on the road, particularly old tramps whom he was fond of questioning about their vagrant lives. 'Good morning,' he would say, and ask them where they were going and where they had slept the night before, and, if they looked tired, would give them a lift in his car. 'Old mad Harry' was one of these tramps who had done service in the army, and sometimes helped with the threshing on the wold, and was one with whom Edward was on terms of particular cordiality.

[1] James Barker to author. [2] Charles Harrison to author.

19*

All the most delightful aspects of his character were shown in his relations with his dependents. If there was something feudal and obsolete in his outlook on the world it was amply redeemed by this affectionate confederacy, and those who worked for him were treated as members of the family and as personal friends. There was no trace of patronage or condescension in the easy comradeship which existed between him and his bailiff Charles Cook, who had been close to Edward's regiment in France, but in a different branch of the service. 'I want you to stay with me as long as I live,' Edward had said, and in all Cook's years at Garrowby he only once spoke sharply him to about gates that were out of order on the estate about which he was very particular, always riding round the farms to examine them in September, but had at once apologized, saying: 'I'm afraid I upset you, Charlie.'

They went for long walks together over the estate. Cook found it hard to keep up with his long stride, and trotted after him like a dog. On heavy plough Edward envied his gumboots, and said: 'I will have a pair,' adding with Yorkshire caution, 'Yes, seventeen and six reconditioned.' Cook found that Edward knew to the smallest detail everything that was happening on the estate, how many ewes there were, and how many lambs on each farm, and every morning had to send him a note setting forth his plans for the day. In the evening he was required to tell Edward every detail of the day's happenings; how many lambs he had lost, the condition of the cattle, the work of repair on gates and roofs, and all the miscellaneous items of a farming day. He liked to work himself during the harvest, and when he did too much haymaking and harvesting was inclined to become stiff in the evening. He would take his tea with Cook, the two men sitting with their backs to a stook. There was an atmosphere of easy friendship between them: 'I always felt comfortable with him,' said Cook, 'and when there was a fire at the Home Farm he did not put the blame on to me but shared it fifty-fifty.'

Cook was always conscious of Edward's profound love of the land. He talked to everyone about his farms and tried to glean their secrets of husbandry from others. He had the farm prices at his fingertips, and often questioned the profits his sales were earning, and would tell Cook to mix with other farmers and pick their brains. It was here, in the soil at Garrowby, that his roots lay: 'After all the travelling I have done,' he told Cook, 'Garrowby Hill is the finest view I have ever seen.' He loved the sounds and smells of the farm, and liked to watch the pigs being weighed, and the sheep-penning, and to go down to the lambing, although he never lambed a sheep himself, calling the place where it happened 'the maternity shed'. When Cook looked back on this long period of mellow association he said that he had sometimes felt that he and his employer were more like brothers than master and man.[1]

                              *   *   *

[1] Charles Cook to author.

Edward noticed that there were certain changes at Garrowby which did not displease him. Steel grates and coal had given way to open brick hearths and wood, and he preferred their warmth and comfort. Edward spent much time at this period of his life in the room in the tower. A steep flight of stairs led up to this sanctuary which looked over the stable yard and the garden, and he liked the room for its remoteness. It became a centre of his Yorkshire life, and there he transacted his affairs, and was visited by the workers on his estate and the grandchildren who were now a constant delight to him. In such a remote place it was difficult to obtain staff, so that he and Dorothy entertained infrequently, and this was his only regret. Most of his time, as he had always wished, was now spent among country people, and he felt a warm contentment in their society:

'Moving as he does so much with nature, and of necessity at her pace, the countryman may seem slow and over-cautious. But this is a natural outcome of his circumstances and life. He is accustomed to disappointment from the weather, and obliged always to wait upon its vagaries; he is therefore patient, tolerant and unhurried. Living on the inherited learning and accumulated experience of long years, he is often suspicious of gifts which find their natural level in the crowded competitive bustle of great cities. . . . He may not indeed know, or be able in words to tell the secret of true happiness; but a wise instinct tells him enough to know that it is not something to be made to order or by mass production. On the material side every year that passes teaches us more of what there is to know about the secret of the soil, and also how much there is on which we are still feeling our way. The best farmers are still in many ways pioneers, proving or disproving some theory by the hard process of trial and error.'[1]

Edward therefore found much to occupy him farming and looking after his estate. It was soon evident that this required more attention than he had expected. The expenses of administration and maintenance had steadily risen, outstripping agricultural rents. New farming methods brought to the landowner repeated demands for capital improvements. Living standards were continually rising, and even he observed that the rising generation was no longer satisfied with what had seemed tolerable to their parents forty years before. He devoted to all these problems the commercial shrewdness and accumulated knowledge of a lifetime, and the whole of the Garrowby estate was electrified and put into the hands of a full-time land-agent.

He gave much time and thought to such institutions as the Meynell Church Trust established in 1889 by his aunt Mrs. Meynell Ingram to maintain the Catholic tradition in England. The Trustees, of whom Edward was one of the most active, were responsible for the stipend of the vicar of Hoar Cross, the Fabric Fund of the Church of the Holy Angels in that village, and the Orphanage Fund, and they also held the patronage of nine

[1] Halifax. Op. cit. pp. 302–3.

other livings included in the Trust. Edward was mainly responsible for interviewing and selecting incumbents for the churches in the north, and his old friend Fra Meynell, and after him his son Hugo, for the livings of Hoar Cross, Laughton, Fleetwood and Ashley.

All these churches were dear to Edward, particularly the Church of the Holy Angels which had been built by Mrs. Meynell Ingram as a memorial to her husband, a superb example of Bodley's art. Its style is his interpretation of fourteenth-century English Gothic and represents the mediaeval ideal as understood by architects and artists of the later Victorian period. Mrs. Meynell Ingram had spared neither money nor time in the creation of this church, and it remains one of the most beautiful monuments of the Catholic revival.

Edward had been appointed a Trustee in 1902, and during these last years was assiduous in his duties. It was at his suggestion that the incumbents of all the livings foregathered each year at Hoar Cross for services in the church, consultations and discussions and meeting one another; when the income received by the Trustees was no longer sufficient after the war to maintain the Orphanage, the Home of the Good Shepherd, he was the moving spirit in the decision to co-operate with the Church of England's Children's Society for a home for boys and girls to be called St. Michael's House, with the use of the income originally earmarked for the Orphanage; and when there was a suggestion in 1954 by the Church Commissioners for uniting St. Edward's, Holbeck, Bodley's masterpiece, with another church in the district and eventually demolishing one of them, it was Edward who, supported by Canon Hood, priest for the Meynell Trustees and a former Head of Pusey House, fought the proposal tooth and nail, and forced it to be dropped.

*   *   *

The land and the spiritual life—these were the two solaces of the evening of his days, and in the chapel at Garrowby and the parish churches of Kirby Underdale and Bugthorpe the placid routine of the services continued. The little church at Kirby, dear to father and son, lies half-way up the western escarpment of the wolds. Some time, earlier in the century, Edward's father had managed to exchange another living for the advowson of Kirby Underdale, perhaps so that the Woods might be able to present men doctrinally acceptable to themselves, but the incumbent Canon Shepherd had for long gently frustrated their intention by remaining *in situ* for forty-six years. He had been succeeded at last by Canon Hurst, a man after Edward's own heart who shared his religious observances, and unlike his predecessor approved of the services held in Garrowby chapel, and was always prepared to officiate at them.

At Christmas and Easter when there were many communicants and the services tended to be drawn out because the priest was single-handed, it was an advantage that the chapel at Garrowby should be served over the week-end by one of the Mirfield Community whose duty it became to preach the sermon at the morning Eucharist in Kirby. Notices of services were always posted at Garrowby outside the chapel, and usually present in the congregation on Sundays and on week-days were members of the household staff and estate employees living near. Canon Hurst made himself responsible for most of the services in the chapel which fell on week-days, and they gave him some of the happiest mornings of his life. 'This is my chapel, Hurst,' Edward would say, 'and if you don't mind, this is what I should like to do,' and the Order was set out. As it happened to coincide with Hurst's own wishes they were able to proceed in harmony, although the priest sometimes became somewhat snarled up in the Garrowby Missal—'it was something of a nightmare,' he said, 'as it had bound up in it half a dozen variant Liturgies and no little skill was needed to ensure remaining in the same Liturgy one had started out on if the marking-ribbons went askew.' Frontals were changed, and the vestments put out by Edward himself, and he served the priest at the altar.

On those mornings at Garrowby the Canon was always fetched from Kirby by Edward or Dorothy, and returned, but sometimes he stayed overnight, and Edward would read them some story from his father's collection in his deep voice. The Canon noticed that he read beautifully. He would rise at six-thirty and enter the chapel for his prayers, and then he would finish reading *The Times*, *Guardian* and *Yorkshire Post* from the day before, go upstairs to shave, wake up Hurst, and prepare the chapel for the Celebration. Father Langton of St. Mary's, Bourne Street, had found that 'it was an awe-inspiring experience to feel Edward's concentration in prayer, kneeling motionless and upright', and Hurst, too, became accustomed to finding that tall figure on his knees completely immersed in his devotions long after all other worshippers had left the chapel. After breakfast there would be interviews with the staff and the two men would stroll round the garden, and Edward would question Hurst about the affairs of the parish and the people in it, with comments on the world at large. Sometimes he would pause with a friendly salutation for the gardener:

'I've been useful. I've pulled up all those weeds for you.'

'Thank you, my Lord. I planted them only yesterday.'

Pocklington Rural Deanery was scattered and it was not easy in times of petrol restriction for the clergy to meet. It occurred to the Canon that Garrowby chapel would be a perfect setting for Quiet Days so invaluable for country clergy afflicted by loneliness. He made this suggestion to Edward who said at once: 'Anything that will help the chapel to earn its keep,' his only condition being that he should be allowed to intrude and join the brethren.

How natural the devotions of this family were, and how much a part of their daily life! There is no effort here, no consciousness of virtue. We feel that it was as natural for them to worship as to breathe. On Sundays after the early service in Garrowby the family and its guests would attend the morning service at Kirby Underdale three Sundays out of four, and on the fourth go to Bugthorpe where the Canon suspected that the ritual was more in accordance with the Halifax taste. Edward would perhaps have welcomed some alteration in this direction in the services at Kirby Underdale, but Hurst thought that the moment was not ripe for change, and Edward did not try to alter his mind. 'You are the parson,' he said, 'and are the best judge.'

He would go to the early morning services at Kirby in the week, and so much a part of his life were they that he would sometimes tie up his horse at the churchyard gate and join the service on his way back from cubhunting in the autumn. Then the tall figure in riding breeches, with no thought of incongruity, would take his place often in the midst of the village children, and the Canon could tell if he was present, even with his own eyes closed, by the sounds that proceeded from him during the hymns.

The Canon's ingenuity was severely taxed in trying to find a theme for his sermons which would be of equal interest to the Chancellor of Oxford University, the American judges and Oxford dons and other eminent men who might be his guests, and the Yorkshire village children who composed a large part of the congregation. But he found that Edward showed infinite patience with his difficulties, and it meant much to him when he would say diffidently: 'You won't think me uppish if I say Thank you for that?' After service he would linger behind and talk to people outside the church, and he enjoyed walking up the steps into the village surrounded by the church-wardens, particularly Jack Sykes who had worked on the estate from time immemorial.

The Canon had always thought Hickleton Church the most miserably illuminated he had ever seen, and his desire for light led him to the opposite extreme at Kirby Underdale. When Edward came to inspect the result he blinked in the sudden incandescence:

'Hurst,' he said reproachfully, 'you've lit it as if it were a pub.'

'I'm sorry, my Lord, but I haven't your experience.' Edward was delighted by this reply and consented to what had been done, as he usually did when given a reasonable or humorous explanation. He who was often thought to be close with money, gave it ungrudgingly in any matter that concerned the Church. When he found that the value of the living was twenty-five per cent less than when he had first offered it to Hurst, owing to the reduction of tithe that had occurred after Canon Shepherd's death, and that Hurst was having difficulty in keeping his daughter at a Medical School, he at once offered to help with the fees, saying: 'You can think of it as a sort of scholarship.' He modernized and divided into two at his own expense the sprawling rectory which in the tenancy of a fecund Victorian parson had thrust out odd rooms and alcoves in a quest for living space with each annual addition to the family.

He was as absorbed in the well-being of his village church as in the august affairs of York Minster, hovering about it for weeks like its attendant spirit when experiments were made with the painting of the chancel roof as part of the village memorial to those fallen in the Second World War, and it was he who found the artists to design its memorial windows and Communion rails, and execute its delightful carvings. 'They must think of it as *their* church, as it is, and not as mine, which it isn't,' he said. 'I will gladly do my share'; and this he did, and much more, often arriving at church with some unexpected gift from the seemingly inexhaustible treasure-houses of Garrowby and Hickleton—new altar furnishings, an exquisite crystal crucifix, or a fresh vestment. He took, perhaps, the greatest pains of all over the new altar itself, designed by Esmond Burton in remembrance of the fallen soldiers of the village.[1]

*   *   *

Edward did not allow himself to be chained completely by this rural contentment where the rhythm of life was regular and gentle and each day more absorbing than the last. From the sanctuary of Garrowby he made frequent excursions to further those outside interests to which he could at last give full attention, the Eton Governing Body, the Oxford Chancellorship and the affairs of his college, All Souls. He had been admitted a Fellow of the Eton Governing Body on 25 February 1936, and, after his Fellowship had twice lapsed owing to absence, was readmitted again on 25 May 1946 on his return from Washington. He resigned at the end of the summer half 1951.

He attended a reasonable number of Governors' meetings and was always available when wanted. Although he had not much enjoyed himself there as a boy he was strangely knowledgeable about Eton. The Headmaster Mr. Claude Elliott found him a trifle aloof at these meetings, and had the impression that his mind was always attuned to more important matters. He did not talk a great deal unless he had something definite to say, but if he felt deeply he would suddenly assert himself with surprising force, as when he refused to admit a prematurely developed candidate for College where he would have to sleep in a dormitory with other new boys. The thought of potential immorality had greatly disturbed him and the unlucky youth was not admitted to the school, a victim of his own untimely virility. The humility of one side of Edward's character did not escape the Headmaster. He remembered how he listened in the billiard room with the greatest courtesy and respect to a long dissertation on the Dutch political situation by an Eton boy who was the son of the British Ambassador at The Hague, even going to the

---

[1] Canon Frank Hurst to author.

length afterwards of quoting from the boy's harangue in the House of Lords.[1]

Elliott noticed, too, that Edward showed little interest in the arts or in the pictures that hung in the Provost's Lodgings. As might have been expected, his deepest interest at Eton lay in the Chapel Services, and he was responsible for the appointment as Provost of another as zealous as himself in ecclesiastical matters, his old friend Lord Hugh Cecil. His early years on this body had been brightened by the eccentric behaviour of Lord Hugh, who in 1939 had angrily opposed the Headmaster's plan to build air raid shelters for the boys on the grounds that the duties of the Governing Body were to educate their minds, and did not extend to their physical protection, a position which he defended with a fusillade of wayward logic.

Edward, on the grounds of old friendship, was on such occasions expected to soothe and convert his colleague, but the Provost had been fertile in complaints about the Headmaster's organization of A.R.P. Such fuss was ridiculous, he said, arguing that 'the only occupation for a gentleman was controversy', but the Headmaster, his feet more firmly on the ground, had answered that the boys could not engage in controversy if they were dead. Cecil had retaliated with a long letter to Edward full of angry ridicule of the scheme, threatening to descend on the Foreign Office and place his arguments before him, but they were considered void of reason, and the shelters were built. Edward was invigorated all his life by those shafts of rich humour that pierced his friend's theological discourse like flashes of sunshine. He could never forget Lord Hugh's instructions for his own funeral:

'Due reverence ought to be shown to my body at my funeral having regard to the fact that during its life it was the Temple of the Holy Ghost. At the same time, this reverence ought not to be overdone, any more than one would overdo respect for a telephone into which a very distinguished person had spoken.'[2]

When Cecil had been Provost of Eton the two men earnestly disputed the religious aspect of the services. They had many discussions, some acrimonious, on points of doctrine, and a long correspondence about the Provost's projects for their reform. It is diverting to speculate how many of the boys for whose spiritual quickening they imagined themselves to be toiling could have followed these two Churchmen through the labyrinth of their liturgical squabbles. It was perhaps a healthy experience for Edward that Cecil was his intellectual equal, and that his grasp on the principles of his beliefs was as tenacious as that of Edward himself. When their views differed he was an agile and dangerous antagonist. The Provost's ideas for the reform of the services were not altogether in harmony with Edward's own views or those of the other Fellows, but one of his objects was to encourage the boys to more than mere compulsory attendance at chapel, and to communicate more regularly. To this end he wanted to have a late Celebration of Holy

---

[1] Sir Claude Elliott, Headmaster and later Provost of Eton, to author.
[2] Halifax to Sir Charles Peake, 8 February 1957.

Communion in order to attract what he called 'lazy communicants', since he attached more importance to frequent Communion than to the observance of the rule of fasting.

For most of his life Edward had had his own way in matters of religion, and was unaccustomed to opposition, but here he had an opponent worthy of his steel whose views were strongly held and trenchantly expressed:

'When you told me,' Edward had written, 'that you had it in mind to make a change which would, if I understood you *rightly*, have the effect of making the ordinary service consist of somewhat shortened Mattins, followed by the Ante-Communion Service, I confess I was greatly shocked and disturbed.' He begged the Provost to make no final decision until he had reconsidered the matter in the light of reflections which had emerged from talks he had had with Ted Talbot. He then set out at length his reasons for disapproving of the changes advocated by Lord Hugh and suggested that it might be found possible to have a plain sung Eucharist, which boys might attend instead of Mattins. The Provost did not take kindly to this suggestion, and a lofty and almost dictatorial note crept into his answer:

'I aim at bringing Eton to my type of churchmanship rather than yours. Mine is more strictly Tractarian—with one important omission, that is austerity—than yours; and it accepts the tradition of the Reformed Church as being, though very faulty, yet in a degree authoritative, to be improved and adapted but not to be cast aside and trampled on. My aim is first to make Eton College Chapel a seemly place of open prayer according to the tradition, Catholic and Protestant, of the Church of England.

'Your plan of a Sung Eucharist is quite impossible. If there are to be communicants at it on your principles it would have to be before breakfast. If there are no communicants I could not permit it on principle; and if there are only a few it would excite grave and mischievous suspicion of the "Roman Mass" among Protestant parents. You see I value immensely what you don't like, and that is the respectful treatment of the Protestant tradition. I want to maintain and develop that tradition, greatly Catholicizing it, but never alarming opinion by a clear break from it. Moreover there would be immense disciplinary difficulties in substituting attendance at the Eucharist for attendance at Morning Prayer. This coupled with the suspicion of Romanism would be altogether fatal to the plan.

'In short Pharaoh's heart was butter compared with mine. I am sure I see a way through to what I call a Catholic conclusion and I am going to pursue my way thither.'

*   *   *

Long after these controversies had died down Edward continued his duties as Fellow until 1951 when he resigned. But if he had returned to the Eton scene with relative indifference, his first visit to All Souls after the war was that of a wanderer who sees the beckoning lights of home. It was this great foundation which had given him his first assurance of intellectual power. In his mind were memories of festal evenings and the comradeship of gifted men. Always happiest in his own house he had yet found solace and intimacy in the traditions of this place, in the library and ancient grey buildings, in the Mallard Song[1] and the green quadrangle where the Fellows played bowls.

We get a glimpse of his contentment there in the evening of his life through the eyes of the Warden Mr. John Sparrow, with whom he often stayed on his visits to the College. Sparrow had known little of him before and, rather to his surprise, found him gay and easy company. He invariably attended Early Service at St. Mary Magdalene, but was not in the least priggish about it and never made the Warden feel a pagan when he did not accompany him. The night before Early Service he would say: 'I'll call myself, and clean my own shoes.' During these visits to the Warden's Lodgings Sparrow came to the conclusion that Edward was 'both truly humble and truly aristocratic', that he enjoyed a certain amount of gossip, and listening to informed comments on other people, and that he appreciated free criticism. Particularly he found in Edward a man of great tranquillity of soul with whom it was comforting to associate, and on whom, when acutely anxious or perplexed, he could unburden his troubles, and on the two occasions on which he did so the Warden was relieved to discover no trace of the 'holier-than-thou' in Edward's attitude.

Like others before him the Warden was intrigued by the amusement which frivolous matters held for the Chancellor. Edward was seldom up-to-date in the argot of the modern world, but he was intrigued on hearing for the first time of the cult of 'U' and 'Non-U', and gloomily concluded from the fact that he called the stationery at Garrowby 'note-paper' that he must be classified as 'Non-U'. The Warden also found that it was not in his guest's nature to harbour a grudge. Sparrow had been irritated while Edward was staying at All Souls by an article in a Sunday newspaper about the Bolshoi Ballet which inquired lyrically if those splendid young dancers were the Commissars of the future. He had written to the proprietor of the paper to say how nauseating he had found these outpourings, and how strongly they reminded him of the way certain people before the war had eulogized the Aryan Hitler Youth. 'Appeasement,' he had added, 'is no more attractive now than it was then.' Forgetting he had written this, he showed the letter to Edward who read it carefully, and arriving at the fatal word had remarked:

'Appeasement covers a great many things. What is Anthony Eden trying to do now?' but had borne no grudge then or afterwards, and this, thought the Warden, was typical of the man.[2]

---

[1] Sung at an ancient College ritual when the Fellows of All Souls make a ceremonious search for an imaginary mallard.

[2] Mr. John Sparrow to author.

Sometimes it fell to Edward to deliver memorial addresses on Fellows who had died. His method of oratory and deep resonant voice were particularly suited to defunctive occasions, and of none did he speak more effectively than his old friends Leo Amery and Dougal Malcolm who had been his first fag-master at Eton and his examiner at All Souls.[1] His words on Amery show a distinction of language he rarely achieved, and deserve quotation. Speaking of Amery's ruthless patriotism he said:

'Once conclusions had been clearly apprehended and established, their consequences must override all other considerations. The right to be asserted, the truth to be proclaimed, the dominant end to be secured; these were what mattered, and to these everything else must yield. Private friendships and the ordinary conventions of human relations counted for nothing if some great cause called. The supreme example of this ruthless courage was seen in the speech that Amery made in the House of Commons which was instrumental in bringing Chamberlain's Government to an end. For years he had been one of the most devoted adherents of the Chamberlain family. From the father he had first drawn the milk of the economic gospel of which he himself was thereafter to be one of the most indefatigable of champions; he revered his memory as of one who had breathed upon the dry bones of the larger British family; he had been intimate with, and had worked with both the sons; for years he had shared in all their efforts to strengthen the Unionist position in Birmingham. All those ties, however, snapped as easily as Samson snapped the green thongs of Delilah, once Amery came to think that the leadership of the last of the Chamberlains was endangering the prosecution of the issue of the war.'

---

[1] The Address on Amery and Malcolm was delivered on 6 November 1955.

CHAPTER XXXVIII

'HIS HONOURS THICK UPON HIM'

OXFORD had been the great formative influence of his life, and he was under so heavy a debt to her, and loved her so much, that his appointment as Chancellor of the University had given him a more genuine pleasure than any of the other great offices he had held. The Vice-Chancellors, who in succession carry out the day-to-day administration of the University, found him a perfect occupant of his position. He had all the necessary qualifications, a background of high political office, academic distinction, and an impressive appearance. When Vice-Chancellor, Sir Maurice Bowra, that brilliant man who for fifty years has enriched the Oxford scene, both as undergraduate and don, testified to Halifax's success and popularity as Chancellor. And in the eyes of a later Vice-Chancellor, Sir John Masterman, Provost of Worcester College, with whom his relations were particularly harmonious, 'he was an absolutely ideal Chancellor of Oxford University, extremely easy to work with, always ready to adapt himself and to take any trouble that was needed'.[1]

Masterman noticed that besides being considerate the Chancellor was capable of great courage and endurance. At his last Encaenia a long walk in heavy robes was necessary starting from Worcester College. Masterman knew that Edward had been having serious trouble with his breathing, and suggested that the procession should form up at the Bodleian Library to spare him a long walk and that he should go there by car, but Edward had refused flatly, saying: 'That would be a great confession of weakness.' The most he would agree to was a pause at the Martyrs' Memorial.

Although he had been acting Vice-Chancellor for part of his predecessor's term Masterman formally took office in January 1957. At his suggestion the Vice-Chancellorship was reformed. The Chancellor traditionally invited the senior Head of a House to hold office as Vice-Chancellor for three years. The reform laid down that the Chancellor should pass over any Head of a House who would not have concluded his period of office before reaching the age of sixty-five, and that the three-year period should be reduced to two. The main reason for the reform was the number of casualties among Vice-Chancellors who were often unable to carry out their duties owing to illness or old age.

During Edward's period of office Regius Professors of History and

---

[1] Sir John Masterman to author.

Divinity were appointed, and he was well qualified to express an expert opinion on both subjects. Masterman believed that it was of fundamental importance that the new Regius Professor of History should be a man who would inspire Oxford historians and give life to the School, and that he should also be capable of assisting men working on later periods, particularly the nineteenth century. Of the names considered in this light, it was thought that either H. R. Trevor-Roper of Christ Church or A. J. P. Taylor of Magdalen would be the best choice. It was Edward's duty as Chancellor to inform the Prime Minister, in whose hands the appointment lay, of the advice of the relevant Oxford authorities, and Trevor-Roper, one of the most inspiring of the younger school of historians, was appointed in May 1957.

Much of his time as Chancellor was occupied in the later years with the Oxford Historic Buildings Appeal, and in his devotion to this object Edward showed, as he had so frequently in America, that no trouble or boredom was too great to be tolerated if it could in any way advance the duty he had undertaken. The American *Life* Magazine had promised to publish articles in support of the appeal, and had suggested that the Chancellor should hold a meeting of the Heads of Houses at a luncheon party which the magazine would provide. This could not be accepted, but Masterman said that he as Vice-Chancellor would give a luncheon for the Chancellor to meet Heads of Houses, and that *Life* could arrange for photographs to be taken of them afterwards at All Souls. It was the sort of occasion that Edward particularly disliked, but he submitted cheerfully to it, and Masterman thought that few other Chancellors would have done so.

Further honours now descended upon him. He had already received the Order of Merit in 1946 for his services in America, and become Chancellor of the Most Noble Order of the Garter in 1943, and was a member of the Committee formed to help St. George's Chapel, Windsor Castle, the foundation with which the Knights Companions have been closely associated since the reign of King Edward III.

Soon after his return from America he was invited to succeed Lord Harewood as Chancellor of Sheffield University, which like all provincial universities was to grow quickly in numbers, and celebrated its jubilee in 1955. He became Governor of Pusey House, the centre of Anglo-Catholic practice in Oxford, and of Liddon House, its larger counterpart in London. One of his last honours was conferred upon him when he was appointed Grand Master of the Order of St. Michael and St. George in July 1957.

Of all the resounding titles which had fallen on him as the reward of public service the High Stewardship of Westminster probably gave him the greatest satisfaction after the Chancellorship of Oxford. He was invited by the Dean of Westminster to succeed Lord Salisbury in that office after his death in 1947. Before the Mayor and Council were established the Dean was the Chairman of the Court of Burgesses who ruled Westminster, and the High

Steward his principal lay officer and right-hand man. The office had long since become a sinecure, but Edward treasured it because it was redolent of the past, and brought him close to the Abbey, to him the cradle of English history, and the 'parish church of the Empire'. When it was threatened by decay and ruin, his words were not the hackneyed ones common in appeals on such occasions, but came from a deep love and a true sincerity:

'The Abbey is a peculiarly British institution. From the time of that saintly king, Edward the Confessor, this has been our Coronation Church, loved, honoured and cared for as a sacred shrine by a long succession of British Sovereigns. There we and those who went before us have been accustomed to assemble for the making of our Solemn Acts of Intercession or thanksgiving to Almighty God. . . . This last earthly resting place of saints and kings; of statesmen and men of genius; and of the Unknown Warrior; with the Chapel commemorating the Few of the R.A.F. to whom many have owed so much; this place of glory and loveliness is part of the very life and soul and story of our race.'[1]

*   *   *

After a long spell at Garrowby in 1946–7 Edward and Dorothy began their travels, and he found in the changing scenes a source of mental and physical renewal. It had sometimes been said of him that he had little knowledge of Europe, but much of the British Empire, and that this had been a source of weakness at the Foreign Office. Now he became absorbed in travel and seemed anxious to visit and study as many European countries as his remaining years allowed in a succession of leisurely wanderings. But first, in 1947, he made what he called 'a purely personal visit' to the United States, visiting his friends and some of his former haunts, and renewing old memories. His years in America had convinced him that the only hope for the future lay in the maintenance of the bonds which had held the two countries together in war, and the resolution not to drift into indifference and separatism, and the following year, on the death of Lord Greenwood, he was appointed to a post which enabled him to strengthen these links when he became President of the Pilgrims of Great Britain.[2]

He was to pay his last visit to America in 1951 to tour American universities on the invitation of the Commonwealth Fund, and the most agreeable part of this tour was the time he spent on the Pantana ranch in Arizona as the guest of his old friends Lewis and Peggy Douglas. It was invigorating to breathe again that pellucid air, and to ride among cattle with the Mexican foreman Frederico Leon through a country of scrub oaks and thorns which reminded him of Rajputana or Dholpur, and of the dales at Garrowby, and in the evening to talk under brilliant stars in a velvet sky. No one could find a

[1] *Yorkshire Post and Leeds Mercury*, 14 November 1953.
[2] The main object of the Pilgrims Society is to entertain and provide a platform for distinguished Americans visiting England.

long enough pair of jeans for him to ride in. Those he borrowed came half-way down his legs, and his appearance was rendered even more peculiar by a ridiculous straw hat.

Meanwhile, in 1948, he had gone with great curiosity to Germany, and had left the vanquished country with uneasy feelings:

'I didn't like Adenauer too much—he struck me as rather twisty. He had a lot to say about our stupidity in not having from the first kept a land approach to Berlin. I am perpetually speculating about what the Germans are think-ing. Though they don't show it, and though obedience and acceptance of orders from authority come to them much more naturally than to us, they must be resentful—and even if they blame Hitler (and I fancy many are rather sorry for the failure than the attempt!), they must be moved by national feeling to dislike the instrument of his downfall. But it must remain such a complete change of approach for the Germans to like our methods or our-selves, that I fancy most wise people would reserve their judgment on how things would go over the next 10, 20, 50 years. I think I come back with no very high hopes of German re-education in the democratic way!'[1]

*　　　*　　　*

In April 1952 he visited Athens for the first time, as the representative of the United Kingdom at the unveiling of the Commonwealth War Memorial to the soldiers who fell in Greece. Charles Peake had left Belgrade and was now Ambassador in Athens, and the Halifaxes were accompanied by Lady Worsley and 'the fat old one', as Edward called the evergreen Angus Mc-Donnell. Here Edward fell in love with the country, with the harsh mountains and ruined temples and violet sunsets, and the peasants stately and courteous in their villages, and the aroma of the past. As in America, certain pictures were clearly formed in his memory. Somewhere beyond Thebes 'we found ourselves among tall trees in a garden brilliant with flowers; roses in full bloom, green grass, masses of honeysuckle and nightingales singing—a veri-table land of dreams'. And there were other moments that lingered in the mind—when they went up the slopes of Hymettos and reached a little church dedicated to St. John the Hunter, and burnt a candle in his honour, and descended down slopes alight with wild flowers, gladioli and ground honey-suckle, cistus and wild chrysanthemums, the whole place aromatic in the sun. Nor would he forget Crete to which they flew over a string of islands in a sea just darker than turquoise, and plodded on donkeys up a mountain track to the place where Venizelos was born. Of Crete his memories were of Minoan splendour, of dark mountains, and dust on silvery olive groves, and meals in little restaurants on the sea, roofed over with bamboos to keep out the sun, of Cretan food and wine, of roast sucking-pig and goats' milk cheese, of cobbled streets and the sound of bells.

[1] Hickleton Papers.

They went to Rhodes, and to Patmos where they entered the grotto where St. John is held by legend to have written the Revelation:

'It was to me a strangely moving sensation to find myself on the spot where that history had been made. Originally the back half of the cave must have been, as indeed it is now, a cave formed by the overhanging rock, with a rock floor and looking straight on to the blue sea 500 feet below. You are shown the place where St. John's head is supposed to have rested, and an irregularity in the stone by which he is supposed to have pulled himself up from a recumbent position to write at a desk-like ledge above. The legend also is that when he had the Revelation, the roof of the cave opened, and subsequently came back again. One can quite easily imagine him sitting there and seeing the glassy sea before him, and transferring the imagery of it to his writing.'

They spent an unforgettable day at Delphi where the past lived more for him than anywhere else in Greece:

'A delightful little hotel, very clean, perched on the very edge of the hill with the valley of rocks and scrub down to thick olive groves and a drying river-bed right below; and further away the violet waters of the Gulf of Corinth, with the mountains of the Peloponnese beyond. They were blurred in that haze and one could not see their snow tops, but one could get the outline clearly enough.

'Then on to what I really wanted to see, which was the Temple of the Oracle—and the way up to it—which is really exactly as it was, so that one could imagine the whole approach. One can see where the Priestess used to appear in the sulphur spring fumes and give her cryptic utterances which puzzled kings: and the sheer rocks stretching hundreds of feet above you from which those who insulted the god Apollo, like Aesop, were thrown. I must find out more about what poor Aesop did. From the Oracle Temple we climbed up to the Theatre and the Stadium; the tiers of seats and the "Royal Box" still in perfect preservation, and the starting marks for the racing chariots. And finally up to a bit of high ground to get the full view, and so scrambling down home through the end of a very primitive Greek village. It's a curious feeling being on the exact site of a dead cult which meant everything to the world that the Delphi Oracle did.'

Back in Athens at the beginning of May he found it already uncomfortably hot. He made a speech at the University, and was given a doctorate, and returned to the Embassy to find that Field-Marshal Montgomery was one of his fellow guests. After dinner Edward was somewhat put out by the Field-Marshal's self-esteem:

'An argument developed between Charles Peake and him on the subject of the Lessons that he should read in church on Sunday. Monty thought he would read his own choice; Charles pressed for the choice laid down. Monty thought the Church wanted 'binging up', and much more to the same effect.

I got caught into the conversation and asked Monty why he should feel presumptuous enough to suppose that the lesson he liked would be one that I and his congregation would like. To this he said that he looked at his congregation and decided accordingly. I thought I had never met a little man who was so devoid of any slightest admixture of humility. An entertaining character, but not to me a very attractive one.'

After they had gone Charles Peake found that 'an awful vacuum descended, what the theologians call accidia. Your visit was an enormous encouragement to us, and you worked for me like a black and never complained. I can hardly bear to go into the garden, and I never do so without hoping that I shall see you in your chair. You must try to come to us again next year. It will be something for us to look forward to'.

With memories of Greece so fragrant Edward had no hesitation in accepting this offer the following year, but the itch for travel was now strongly upon him, and in 1953 he also visited Egypt, India, Yugoslavia and Turkey, where his daughter Anne and his granddaughter Clarissa met them at Istanbul. In Ceylon he was taken ill with broncho-pneumonia and placed in a nursing home, and his devoted friend the Maharana of Dholpur, who had fed his tigers with chilled milk and frozen cheeses in the hot weather in those days that now seemed so distant, flew down from India to visit him. Edward was delighted to see him, but it was in some ways a melancholy reunion. He found the Maharana listless and depressed, and was glad to be able to pay a short visit to him as they returned through India:

'The new order in India,' he thought, 'that was strange, and built upon the destruction of the old India that he had loved, had left him depressed and sad. And whatever may have been the cause of his premature death in 1954, I can hardly doubt that in great measure it was accelerated by a broken heart.'

* * *

Perhaps the most deeply satisfying of all these wanderings was a sentimental journey to Madeira in 1954. He had not returned to the island since that visit sixty-four years ago when his parents had taken his brother Charlie there in the vain hope that the gentle climate would save his life, and Edward had risen early as the ship dropped anchor, and seen the island purple in the dawn, and the lights still twinkling on its volcanic slopes.

He found it little changed. There, beside a dry ravine, still stood the old Quinta Bianchi where they had lived, and he saw the same paths down which they had ridden on ponies. Now there were motor-cars on the island, but there were still the same old bullock carts, and the posadas with their wine barrels, the muleteers with their melancholy cries, the banana trees with ragged leaves, and the pink and white houses looking as though they had been cut from cardboard, and the bougainvillaea, purple and brick-red, sprawling over the walls.

He recognized the little Fort that his father had sketched, and retraced the walks the old man had taken with the Abbé Portal when they had spoken of the reunion of the Churches and the glory of God. Books were now one of Edward's greatest pleasures, and at last he had ample leisure to fill the wide gaps in his reading. He would sit in the grey stone arbours of Reid's Hotel with the Atlantic far beneath, reading Trollope and Dickens, with the poinsettias and hibiscus all round him, and little green lizards darting from the crevices and basking on the wall.

There was another echo from the past when he was taken by 'the elder Blandy', head of the leading island family, to his house for luncheon, for it was the same house in the mountains they had visited as children as a great expedition that took all day, riding and in bullock carts. Now they reached it in twenty minutes by car by roads flanked by precipices as terrifying as those in the Himalayas, and in the house which he vaguely remembered from childhood, they drank Madeira wine which had been made in the year when the Terror of the French Revolution began, and ate peacock that tasted like turkey, and afterwards walked in one of the loveliest gardens in the world, as rich in exotic trees and shrubs as any in India, with the camellias and mimosa in bloom.

He and Dorothy were now able to visit places that had been inaccessible in 1890. They could drive over the highest mountain across the middle of the island to Riberia Frio, the Cold River, through woods of pine and eucalyptus, and clouds of mimosa in the mountains. When they got near the top and over the watershed they found themselves in a world of cloud and fog, and they walked along the Levada to the look-out place in a fine rain:

'It is a built-out platform in a great rock, standing up with a deep abyss on every side of you. It gave Dorothy and me dreadful jitters in our toes. I don't think I have ever seen a more frightening place.'

He loved these expeditions into the interior of the island where there was snow on the higher peaks, and the mist and clouds dissolved slowly under a hot sun. He liked to pass the terraced slopes where the Portuguese labourers sang over their work, and stop in fishing villages like Riberio Bravo where he got out and stretched his legs, and sat on the little quay and watched the children cluster round him, chattering and laughing at him, and looking, he thought, 'like little puppies or little pigs'.

*   *   *

Each year they made some new excursion, to Spain in May 1954 to stay with Jock Balfour, his old colleague of Washington days, at the Embassy in Madrid, and in 1955 to France, and in the following year to Cairo, Luxor and Athens. In 1954 Edward had also begun to search his mind for recollections of those childhood Christmases at Hickleton for an article which he hoped to incorporate in his autobiography, 'if I ever get to that'. He found memories of those arcadian days floating back readily across the years, standing out in nostalgic detail when much that had gone between had vanished. He called it 'Christmas at Hickleton', and it was the seed of his autobiography *Fulness of Days*. Charles Peake persuaded him that it should be published in the Christmas number of *Time and Tide*, and the review was anxious to have it, but insisted on cuts to which Edward would not agree, and it did not appear.

In 1955 he began to write the autobiography. The ever-resourceful Peake was ready with a synopsis in June, and he was advised throughout its writing by the experienced Jack Lockhart. But unlike certain other compilations which had appeared in the past above his signature, this work was entirely his own. The earlier chapters in which the author describes his childhood are delightful and evocative, and there is a leisurely charm in the book, and an aroma of spacious days, but, like Kipling's autobiography *Something of Myself*, it reveals little of its subject except by implication, and is often tantalizing in its reticence.

The manner in which Edward and Charles Peake set about trying to arrange for suitable writers, favourable to Edward's interest, to review the book was a diverting example of his lordly approach to such affairs. He appeared to think that these matters were settled entirely by the author and publisher, an arrangement which would certainly contribute to the peace of mind of both. We find Peake writing to him in February 1957 enclosing a list of suggested reviewers—C. V. Wedgwood for *Time and Tide*, G. M. Young for *The Sunday Times*, and someone suitable for *The Observer* which Peake thought important. Edward thanked him for these suggestions and said that he would place them before the publishers in due course. Later Peake proposed that Christopher Hollis should be added to the names of possible reviewers, and we find Edward, a few days later, writing to Collins the publishers 'to find out what they have in mind about reviewers'.

We are always conscious in these years of the religious background to all Edward's thoughts, and in 1956 an event took place of deep personal significance to him, the dedication by the Archbishop of York on 1 July of a Memorial which Edward had erected to King George VI on Garrowby Hill. The Memorial took the form of a figure of Christ on a cross twenty feet high with a concrete base bearing the inscription:

TO THE GLORY OF GOD, AND IN MEMORY OF GEORGE, KING,
SERVANT OF HIS PEOPLE.
1895–1952.

Set on the roadside on the fringe of a wood, the crucifix has a narrow roof which suggests some wayside shrine in the Swiss Alps, and the cross and part of the base were made in the workshops of Garrowby Estate. The inscription, so simple, so exactly true, moved the bereaved Queen to write a letter of gratitude:

'Most Memorials are either dull or ugly or unsuitable, but this sounds exactly what one would wish and like most, and I felt that I must write to you a line to say how touched I feel.

'The inscription too is perfect for the King did dedicate his life completely to his country and people. When I read about it this morning, I felt so glad that the King's name would be commemorated in this way, and especially by such old and dear friends as you and Dorothy.'

CHAPTER XXXIX

THE HOUSE OF LORDS

POLITICS still played a major part in Edward's life, and when great issues arose on which he held strong opinions, he would travel from Yorkshire to London to take part in the debates in the House of Lords. Soon after he had returned to England from America he had made his own contribution to the last stages of the drama of India in which he had played so great a part, and to the hasty act of emancipation to which he had given so strong an impetus. On 26 February 1947 a motion by Lord Templewood[1] sounded a sombre warning of the dangers that lurked in the Labour Cabinet's decision to hand over India to an Indian Government in June 1948 'without any provision for the protection of minorities or the discharge of their obligations. . . .'

The most ghastly massacres that have ever defiled even Indian history, and which resembled some canto in the Inferno, were not far distant, but although Halifax was aware of the dangers he did not feel that in the circumstances he could oppose the action of the Government in thus throwing the responsibility directly and finally on Indian shoulders. He saw great peril in delaying any longer in the state of near-anarchy into which India was drifting, and felt that the Government was in an impossible position where its responsibility exceeded its power. None the less, as he made clear in his speech, he was a prey to many forebodings which were shared to the full by Winston Churchill who read Edward's words with anger and resentment:[2]

'It is plain,' said Halifax, 'as has been pointed out with great force today and yesterday, that there is a very great risk of leaving an Indian situation confused, if not chaotic, and the noble Marquess Lord Salisbury dwelt . . . with great passion upon the abandonment of our obligations and on the betrayal of our duties in that regard to India. . . . The balance sheet to my mind is not a very good one, and the debit side is very dark. I have no doubt that the entry on the debit side which gives just cause for misgiving is that to which one noble Lord drew forcible attention yesterday—the so-called betrayal of less powerful interests who hitherto have looked to the British Crown and Parliament for their justice and their protection.

'But if we are to face realities in this matter, surely we must realize that whatever we may seek to write into the agreement on behalf of Dr. Ambedkar,[3] or any of the other millions of people for whom we seek justice and decent opportunity, the execution of anything written into the agreement

---

[1] Formerly Sir Samuel Hoare. [2] Halifax to Peake, 4 June 1947.
[3] The leader of the Depressed Classes.

will, and must, always depend upon the goodwill of those to whom we will have delegated the effective power. There is no way of getting away from that except by saying that we will go back from our purpose, and change our minds about trying to establish Indians in the effective seat of power.'[1]

Halifax's misgivings about this dilemma are apparent in every word of this speech, but he could suggest no way out of it—:

'I have the gravest doubt,' he went on, 'about this early fixing of the date in June 1948. Indeed, I am sure that no one who has ever worked in India can think of these problems . . . without a feeling in his heart very much more poignant and painful than mere anxiety. But while it is easy to say: "This is wrong", it is not easy to say what is right. With such knowledge as I have I am not prepared to say that, whatever else may be right or wrong, this step must on all counts certainly be judged to be wrong. I am not prepared to say that, for the truth is that for India today there is no solution that is not fraught with the gravest danger. And the conclusion that I reach . . . is that I am not prepared to condemn what His Majesty's Government are doing unless I can honestly and confidently recommend a better solution.'[2]

Read today it appears to have been a weak speech, but it was so delivered as to make a profound impression on the House, swinging many wavering or hostile Peers to the support of the Government. Edward seems to have been oppressed by the suspicion that something terrible was about to happen, but he could offer no constructive advice. He had no reason to look far for the cause of Churchill's anger.

By July 1947 events in India had moved even more swiftly than had been the Prime Minister's intention. The unhappy Lord Wavell had been recalled from India in February, and been replaced by Lord Mountbatten, and by 3 June a new plan for Indian independence involving partition had been accepted by Congress and the Muslim League. Mountbatten, the new and last Viceroy of India, announced at a press conference in New Delhi that the transfer of power would actually take place on 15 August, now only nine weeks ahead, and ten months earlier than had been announced on his appointment. It was therefore necessary to rush the Indian Independence Bill through Parliament in July. This measure, hastily conceived, conferred on India full independence; it provided in principle for partition, subject to local ratification; it ended the relationship between the Crown and the Indian States. India and Pakistan were born. They were invested with Dominion Status, with freedom, if they wished, to leave the Commonwealth.

Halifax spoke on 15 July 1947 on the Second Reading of this Bill. One painful aspect of it, to which he referred, was the fate of the Indian Princes, and he did so with less generosity than their predicament deserved. It could scarcely be denied that many of the Princes had behaved with a

[1] *Hansard*, House of Lords, 26 February 1947.   [2] Ibid.

suicidal lack of prudence in their attitude to joining the All-India Federation, and to the approach of the independence of British India, but the fact remained that, unlike Congress, they had been constant, in two wars, in their loyalty to the British Crown, and that they were bound to it by ancient and solemn Treaties, some perpetual, which were now to be unilaterally abrogated.

Left to the tender mercies of the new Indian Government, the days of these colourful feudatories were numbered. Some had governed well, some badly, but if it is true that the Princes had shown little political intelligence, or even sense of self-preservation, it is a travesty of history to ignore the ruthless and characteristic part played in this matter by Congress. It had begun in 1937 a policy of undisguised hostility to the States Governments, and had openly encouraged agitation against the Princes through agents both inside and outside the States. This process of subversion had naturally produced a hardening in the attitude of the Princes who were alarmed at the thought of inclusion in a federation of which Congress, their inveterate enemy, would be the predominant factor. Congress, on its side, feared that an *entente* in the federation between the Moslems and the Indian States might provide a combination too strong for them to withstand.

It would be wrong, too, while emphasizing the narrow vision of the Princes to pass over in silence the record of the Congress Party in the greatest crisis in English history. When condemning the Princes it would be well to remember that it was the policy of Congress during the war to exploit the war situation, and to demand self-government at what they regarded as the moment of England's greatest weakness, and to abstain from all participation in the war effort. It would also be wrong to forget the Congress rebellion in 1942; how they abandoned the theory of non-violence and embarked on a violent revolution at a moment when British fortunes in the Far East were at their lowest ebb, and how, when that rebellion was put down, it left the Congress Party so crushed and impotent that if Great Britain had wished to cling to power after the war she could not have been prevented. Instead she pressed self-government on the people who had thus used her in her hour of need.

Halifax paid a tribute to the past loyalty of the Princes, but his conclusion was frigid and devoid of emotion:

'The conclusion, of course, is that as matters stand today, you are faced with what has been truly called a dilemma, from which no easy escape offers.'

*　　　*　　　*

Echoes of the experience he had gained in the United States could be often heard in his speeches on every subject concerned with the protection of Europe from encroachment from the East. On 11 May 1949 he spoke in the House of Lords on the conclusion of the N.A.T.O. Pact, and it was on the adherence of the United States to that agreement that he was moved to dwell with the greatest pleasure. It would, no doubt, have been possible to secure a pact without their inclusion, but it would have been an entirely different instrument, and one lacking in potency and virtue. He saw in the new attitude of America the symptoms of a mighty change:

'It is, perhaps, permissible and right for us, on an occasion such as this, to have in our minds how fundamental a change in the approach of the United States to these problems that fact represents. To anyone—and there are many here—who remembers how the bright hopes excited after the last war suffered eclipse when, under domestic stresses and strains, the United States withdrew from the international effort, the transformation of the scene is almost unbelievable.'[1]

The House of Lords always listened to Halifax with particular interest when he spoke about India or America, and now he told them that such a transformation would have been impossible had not both great parties in American politics substantially agreed upon the removal of foreign policy from the party political arena:

'Great nations made great mistakes after 1918, which reacted very unhappily upon one another. We certainly did, and the United States certainly did. But no nation—and this I think is one of the characteristics of the greatness of the United States—is more quick to learn than they are, and this pact seems to me to be a measure of the extent to which we have both learned a very bitter lesson.'[2]

Halifax spoke in the debate on the Parliament Bill in February 1948, and on the Schuman Plan in June 1950. In July 1951 he again drew on his American experience when supporting Lord Cherwell's motion to transfer the development of atomic energy from the Civil Service to a special and more flexible organization under the direct control of the Head of the Government. He adopted a bold and intelligent attitude on this important decision against which were ranged powerful vested interests, and claimed that the remarkable results achieved in America would never have been accomplished if the matter had been treated as an ordinary administrative problem. He goaded the Labour Government by recalling with gentle malice their disastrous experiment with groundnuts:

'In some special ventures into which this Government has gone, they have been prepared to relax the strict canons of Treasury administration with great liberality; and that has presumably been done in the interests of achievement. . . . There is no comparison whatever between the urgency of producing groundnuts, shall we say, in East Africa, and relaxing all the canons in order to get atomic bombs. If, therefore, the noble Lord [Lord Cherwell] is right in feeling that the Government have unconsciously—and I emphasize the word unconsciously—been placing the interests of Treasury security

[1] *Hansard*, House of Lords, 11 May 1949.   [2] Ibid.

before the interests of national security, he is abundantly right to bring the matter before your Lordships for the expression of your views.'[1]

Halifax continued to express his opinions in the House of Lords under a Conservative Government after the election of October 1951. Whenever a debate on international affairs permitted he continued to emphasize the belief he had long held that Anglo-American understanding was the sole hope of the civilized world. He returned to this theme on 21 November 1951 fresh from a recent visit to the United States:

'The whole fortune of the world ultimately depends on what is the broad opinion held in the British Commonwealth of Nations of the United States, and on the broad opinion held in the United States of the British Commonwealth of Nations.'[2]

It was his belief that the mould was now far more firmly set in America than it had been even two or three years before; that their responsibilities in the world were far more widely recognized by the great bulk of American citizens, and that any open advocacy of isolationist policy was now rare. It seemed to him that an immense revolution had taken place in American thought, which ten years before would have seemed a fantastic illusion. He had no patience with those who believed that England was being brought insidiously under American domination. She need not fear, he said lightly, that Britain would become the 49th State of the Union, and Colonel Mc-Cormick need not fear that the United States would become the latest and largest of the British Dominions. But he did not pretend that everything was perfect, nor that the relationship was not a difficult one which must be kept in continuous repair like a successful marriage:

'The attitude that American opinion will take towards this country and the British Commonwealth will, in the long run, depend on the judgment they form about the efforts that we are making, first to help ourselves, and secondly to help Western Europe to resolve in whatever may be the wisest manner, the real obstacles that exist in the way of closer and more effective unity.'[3]

*   *   *

One of Halifax's offices during these years was the Chairmanship of the General Advisory Council of the B.B.C., whose views he presented when necessary in the House of Lords, and on 30 June 1954 he opposed the Commercial Television Bill on the grounds that it would place too much power in the hands of the advertisers. This was a modern problem of a kind on which he was ill-qualified to offer an opinion in tune with contemporary thought. He believed that since the Bill had been amended in such a way as to enable advertisers to see in advance the type of programmes with which their advertisements would be associated, so that they might, if they wished,

---

[1] *Hansard*, House of Lords, 5 July 1951.   [2] Ibid., 21 November 1951.   [3] Ibid.

dissociate themselves from a company which would be unremunerative to them, too much power would fall into their hands.

'The door,' he said, 'is immediately thrown open to them to exercise irresistible pressure to secure that the programmes are planned according to their interests and requirements.'[1] He believed that effective control would be placed at the outset in the hands of the advertisers, and his real fear was that they would abuse their position. He saw vistas of lurid and probably salacious programmes being forced on Commercial Television in order to provide a desirable medium for the advertising interests. His object in taking this attitude was to uphold the level of public entertainment, and it is an ironical reflection that after Commercial Television was established, when the bounds of good taste and public decency were sometimes infringed, it was done as often by his own B.B.C. as by her commercial rival.

Almost the last interventions of his life in the House of Lords were to criticize the Government in their handling of the most controversial issue that had arisen since Munich, the Suez Crisis. Once again an extraordinary bitterness pervaded the country. As in the days of Munich, it was a subject on which men and women felt so strongly that they could hardly bear to hear the presentation of the opposite view, so that again families were divided and old friendships shaken. Sometimes such an occasion strikes a spark in the English people, and those who were old enough remembered that nerve-racking summer of 1911 when the tar melted in the streets and ladies cut each other at the opera when the future of Ulster was at stake.

Halifax gave his own views on the affair on 11 December 1956. On 3 December the Foreign Secretary Selwyn Lloyd had made a statement in the House of Commons that United Nations forces were arriving in Egypt, and that the Secretary General had accepted responsibility for the clearance of the Canal, and would promote negotiations as quickly as possible on the future régime of the Canal on the basis of the six requirements set out in the Security Council resolution of 13 October. Lord Salisbury invited the House to endorse this policy.

At this stage Halifax avoided expressing a direct opinion as to whether the Anglo-French action in Egypt was right or wrong, doubting whether anyone outside the Government had enough knowledge to draw the balance correctly. He preferred to speak of the injury that had been inflicted on Anglo-American relations, and the best means of repairing it. But even here his speech was so indefinite that it was difficult to discover from it which side he thought was in the wrong, the British for beginning the action, or the Americans for bringing it to an end. We may take two passages as showing this tendency to examine both sides of a question without pronouncing a clear verdict:

[1] *Hansard*, House of Lords, 30 June 1954.

'If things have been done or have not been done of a sort and in a way to cause deep resentment in the United States, responsible people in the United States would have made a great mistake if they had failed to realize the counter-feeling aroused in this country by some of the things said and done on the other side of the Atlantic.'[1]

Yet having said this, a few minutes later he recorded his surprise 'that at a moment when many of our people here—we have all heard them—were expressing the greatest indignation at the attitude . . . of the Americans who up to then they had judged to be our friends, it did not occur to them, these voluble indignant people here, to wonder whether it might not have been partly we ourselves who were responsible for this sudden and unwelcome change of temper among the Americans. That struck me as very odd.'[2]

He arrived at the poor conclusion that there had been faults on both sides.

On 23 May 1957 he spoke again on the subject of the Suez Canal. This debate had followed a statement from the new Prime Minister Harold Macmillan that he could no longer advise British ship-owners to refrain from using the Canal, a statement which caused Lord Salisbury to say that this decision looked like a cowardly capitulation to Nasser, and to give notice that he would raise the matter in the House of Lords. Halifax was in favour of accepting this course on a temporary basis, and he also advised making arrangements as independent as possible of the Canal, such as building tankers to go round the Cape, and of helping Israel to secure passage of her ships through the Canal. His criticism was directed not so much at the action against Egypt, for he could be ruthless on occasions, as at the manner in which it had been conducted. He expressed himself with perfect clarity on this question, and clearly felt no doubt or hesitation, his language being entirely free from those qualifying clauses and elaborate reinsurances that sometimes encumbered it:

'Since then,[3] it has, of course, been obvious that the Great Powers are not likely to agree, and therefore, as the noble Viscount, Lord Cherwell, has more than once pointed out to us in this House, that no plan of running the world by way of majority voting or abstract notions of equality was likely to be very convincing, continuous or successful. The shape in which the feeling of ordinary people has crystallized, as I see it, on this side of the business, is not therefore so much one of condemnation of disrespect shown to the United Nations—for this was obviously a very blunt and imperfect instrument—but rather that those who decided on military action, and abandoned it a few days later, could hardly . . . have thought out fully the conditions of a successful issue from the venture on which they had embarked.

Everyone can make his own guess at what was the cause of that sudden

---

[1] *Hansard*, House of Lords, 11 December 1956.   [2] Ibid.
[3] The San Francisco Conference 1945, at which the United Nations Charter was signed.

change of plan. The sharp Party division that existed here; the official reaction in the United States; the moral opprobrium that the world so hastily attached to the appearance of an insult to the United Nations; the pressure of finance—whatever the cause, it was to many of us the main ground of difference with Her Majesty's Government that those difficulties could not have been adequately measured and foreseen so that we might have avoided the discredit of a course of action which we could not, in fact, carry through.'[1]

[1] *Hansard*, House of Lords, 23 May 1957.

CHAPTER XL

REST ETERNAL

His perfect contentment during these last years was clouded by one ever-present anxiety—his health. The efforts of his doctors, and in particular of Dr. Rossdale, who was in almost continuous contact with him, were directed to trying to alleviate an alarming breathlessness which had become a severe handicap to him in every activity of life. The combination of emphysema, a disease producing a restriction of breathing, with asthma, put a strain on a heart otherwise sound, so that when it came, death was caused by a cerebral thrombosis consequent upon a failing heart.

The symptoms first appeared after his visit to Germany in 1948. In the beginning he suffered only phases of breathlessness usually caused by a cold or a bronchial condition, but by 1958 it had become continuous and was induced by any physical exertion. Warmer weather brought relief, and he found on his visit to Madeira that he was able to climb hills and to walk freely at his own pace in that gentle climate.

Difficulty in breathing is a frightening affliction familiar to all sufferers from asthma, of which there was a history in Edward's family. He had always been a vigorous man and this new condition was a sombre background to his daily life, restricting many of his physical activities. Dr. Rossdale noticed that he had the habit of detaching himself from corporal discomforts, and that his mind had an exceptional ascendancy over his body.

He was determined to overcome his ailments and was prepared to try anything, more than once asking his physician to investigate practitioners of whose miraculous cures he had been told by his friends. His search for a remedy for this terrible breathlessness thus ranged from the Respiratory Unit of the Hammersmith Post-Graduate Hospital to unqualified practitioners, the demand from one of whom for an advance fee of four hundred guineas made little appeal to his thrifty soul. He took a highly intelligent interest in his own condition, and it seemed to Dr. Rossdale that 'Lord Halifax's courtesy and unvarying consideration did not interfere with a keen critical appraisement of the remedies my colleagues and I put forward to him'.[1]

The doctor found that Edward was not above infantile devices to get his own way: 'During 1958, when his breathing had become troublesome, I advised him not to get up at eight o'clock to take Communion. He listened and assented, and said that he would not. Only subsequently was I to find

[1] Dr. Rossdale to author.

out that he had followed my advice implicitly and had got up at seven o'clock instead.'

He had his own views on medical subjects and once spoke to Dr. Rossdale of the lack of courage which so often prevented doctors informing patients that they were dying. But no thought of death was in Edward's mind in spite of his infirmity, although those who stayed at Garrowby during the last years saw that at times he had serious difficulty in breathing. He took great pleasure in driving the car which was like a new toy to him, and Lady Worsley was bold enough to go on a motoring tour of Scotland with Edward at the wheel. She remembered being driven very fast by him with Sir Francis Humphrys over hilly country round Garrowby, and that the chauffeur told her after this drive that the car had been harshly treated. His sons thought him an appalling driver, and he confessed to Richard that he kept 'hitting little things', and he had a tendency, these days, to fall asleep at the wheel. It was at one of these moments that he swerved across the road, narrowly missing a milestone, and had been outraged at being taken to court, and there convicted of careless driving and fined £10.

*   *   *

In July 1959 Edward broke his thigh tripping over a flower pot while watering the garden at Garrowby one evening during that hot summer. He was flown by ambulance plane to University College Hospital where it was found that he had fractured the neck of his left femur. The surgeon Mr. Cecil Flemming advised an operation to pin the fracture as offering the quickest way to recovery.

It was the first time Edward had been given an anaesthetic, and in view of the strain which breathing placed upon his heart, there was a certain risk involved. He realized this clearly, and on the morning of the operation made his Communion in his hospital room, and satisfied that his affairs were scrupulously in order, faced with serenity whatever might come. He made a good recovery from this operation, and regained all his vitality and interest in life, but the breathlessness, when he made any exertion, continued to increase.

Their Golden Wedding was celebrated by Edward and Dorothy on 21 September 1959, two months after his accident. It was a friendly informal occasion with their children and grandchildren, and seven hundred guests in the grounds of Garrowby, the tenants and workers from their estates, and to many of the older of these it recalled that party Edward had given for his bride fifty years before. It was a Yorkshire occasion of the kind he loved, where the guests sat down in a huge marquee to a high tea of ham and cold roast turkey, and his health was proposed jointly by representatives of the three estates.

Edward conducted his party from a wheel-chair, and Dorothy, who had a touch of arthritis in her right arm, shook hands with the seven hundred guests with her left hand, but it was evident that they were both full of happiness. Edward made a speech from his chair of extraordinary wit and vigour; he spoke of that other gathering of fifty years ago as though it had been yesterday, and his words were natural and without preparation for he was among his own people. He spoke of the happy days of the past, but made no apology for the present:

'A good many people,' he said, 'think this sort of party a hangover from earlier times, quite out of date, old-fashioned, quite useless, and of no importance at all. Lady Halifax and I take a slightly different view. We felt that so much of our happiness had been due to those who lived on these estates that we should like to share our happiness with them.' He spoke for a considerable time, and his pleasure in doing so was obvious to all. He understood his audience perfectly, and made the sort of jokes about marriage that he knew they liked, and would make them laugh:

'After fifty years I hope we are a good advertisement for matrimony. I won't tell you how we have done it, but someone told me that if you made the wife the boss on the wedding day you would have a happy married life. I think that is what I have done, but on one or two occasions I have asserted myself. We have had a lot of arguments. I think I have always been right and no doubt Lady Halifax thinks the same, but we have managed to get along. I would get my way on Monday, and Lady Halifax on Tuesday.'

Afterwards there were fireworks, and a set piece of Edward and Dorothy, and presents set out in a smaller marquee from the estate workers, a large drum table, and two decorated urns. Golden tulips and laburnum were planted for them in the garden by the tenants.

After this celebration he was present at his granddaughter's[1] wedding in October at York Minster, and during that month and November resumed his ordinary routine with visits to Hickleton and to London where he attended the House of Lords, and met his many friends. His interest in life was unabated, and, greatly intrigued by a car with an automatic gear change brought to Garrowby by a friend, he ordered a new Humber from Rootes after a trial in Hyde Park. During his last visit to London on 30 November, he attended in his capacity of High Steward of Westminster the installation of the new Dean Dr. Abbott, but found the long procession up the nave a severe tax on his breathing.

* * *

It was not until 16 December, exactly a week before his death, that there was any change in Edward's condition. Four days before at a meet of the Middleton he had walked among the hounds and talked to his son Charles and the villagers. He spent that week-end at Hickleton, and returned to

[1] Susan Wood, daughter of Lord Halifax's eldest son Charles.

Garrowby on Monday. On Wednesday, 16 December, he awoke feeling un-
well, and disinclined to rise. For the next two days he could do little and
spent much time sleeping, but eventually he was able to get up and sit in
another room in his dressing gown. On Saturday he did not go into the Chapel
when the vicar came to the house but asked him to bring Communion to him
in his bedroom.

When Richard saw his father again on Sunday evening after a week's
absence, Edward was sitting in his dressing gown in an armchair in the
drawing-room. He spoke of the coming Christmas party, and of the charades
which always took place after dinner. For the first time Richard noticed that
his father appeared to have difficulty in maintaining a train of thought, and it
seemed that time and place had become a little vague in his mind.

On Monday Edward rose again and put on his dressing gown. He inter-
viewed two callers about some church matters connected with the Meynell
Trust, but Dorothy noticed that he was confused and desperately tired, and
far from his true self. That night he went back to his own bedroom after
having occupied a ground-floor room for several weeks while a small lift
was being installed to the bedroom floor. On Tuesday he remained in bed,
but showed interest in planning with Dorothy how the pictures could best
be rehung in his bedroom which had been altered by the construction of the
lift. That night Charles brought his medical friend, Sir Horace Evans,[1] to see
his father. He took an extremely grave view of Edward's condition.

On Wednesday, the last day of his life, Edward talked little and passed
much time in sleep, and in the evening, his heart suddenly collapsed. We
may look at the final moments through the eyes of his son Richard, who was
summoned from London on Wednesday morning:

'I got to Garrowby at tea time, and went to my father's room with something I had fetched from London. He seemed not far from consciousness and
a flicker of a smile crossed his face as I talked to him for a few minutes. Even
then I did not realize how near he was to death. My mother went a little later
to have her evening drink with him, and Alice[2] said he seemed a little better.
Shortly afterwards, when my mother, Anne and I were sitting downstairs,
Alice hurried in to say that his heart seemed to have collapsed. We went to
his room where the nurses tried for some minutes to massage his heart.
Charles and Mr. Hardwick,[3] the Vicar, arrived about the time of his death.
We all knelt while Hardwick prayed for his soul.' It was the 23 of December
1959.

The coffin was moved to Garrowby Chapel on the evening of Christmas
Day and lay there until Sunday, 27 December, when towards dusk it was
lifted on to a farm cart in the courtyard and drawn along the old road where
he had so often ridden, past Cheesecake Farm to Kirby Underdale. Father

---

[1] Afterwards Lord Evans.   [2] Alice Fisher, Edward's New Zealand nurse.
[3] Mr. Hardwick had succeeded Canon Hurst in the living of Kirby Underdale.

Speight of Mirfield said the Vespers of the Dead as the coffin was carried into the church. It lay below the chancel step, covered by a black pall and surrounded by four great candles, until the burial next morning.

There could be no more profound atmosphere of tranquillity than in this little church he had loved, lying in the deep stillness of the countryside, and he could have been committed to no friendlier earth.

'28 December, the Feast of the Holy Innocents, was cold and clear and very beautiful,' said Richard. 'The Dean of Windsor, Bishop Eric Hamilton, said the Requiem in the little church which overflowed with people. The Archbishop of York, Dr. Ramsey, committed my father to his grave on the north-east side of the church. The great amphitheatre of hills round Kirby Underdale shone as the sun rose on the frosted fields.'

Later in the morning a service was held in the Minster in the form of a memorial and Requiem. Edward had himself prepared the service, and had chosen the hymns. He wished it to follow not the Order for Burial, but the more ancient and solemn Form of Requiem habitually rendered in this cathedral on All Souls Day. 'He desired no sermon but the prayer of the Christian family in the presence of its living Lord for one who all his days sought humbly and with unswerving faith to serve and love Him.' The Archbishop of York attended, and the celebrant was the Dean of York, Dr. Milner-White.

On 2 February 1960, the Feast of the Purification, a Requiem was held in Westminster Abbey. Again at Edward's wish there was no sermon nor panegyric, and the service was the same as that at York Minster, except that there the 'Communion Devotions' had been omitted. Edward had spoken to Dr. Don, the Dean of Westminster, about the form a memorial service might take if it was held at Westminster Abbey after his death, and the Dean, who had appointed him High Steward of Westminster a few years before, had told him that such a service would certainly be held. Together they had drawn up a provisional form for a Requiem which was filed for further consideration when the time came. Dr. Don had retired from the Deanery shortly before Edward's death, and the final decision as to the order of service rested with his successor, Dr. Eric Abbott.

At noon there was silence in the Abbey as hundreds waited in the transepts and nave. The high altar and the nave altar had frontals of purple, and candles were burning on them. Headed by Cross and lights the procession of clergy came to the Sanctuary, among them the Archbishop of York and the Bishop of London Dr. Montgomery Campbell, and the Dean and officiating clergy. The choir sang the Introit in plainsong: 'Rest eternal grant unto them O Lord'; and with immense dignity, and the majestic beauty of the English liturgy the service proceeded: Collects, Epistle, Gospel, Offertory, and on to the most solemn moments of the Requiem, the Salutation and the Sursum Corda sung by the Dean, and the Prayer of Humble Access which followed.

20*

But although the service was magnificent, it was also homely as Edward had wished, for there were the hymns he loved—'Let Saints on Earth', 'Rock of Ages', and 'The King of Love my Shepherd is', so that simplicity was blended with grandeur, and it seemed to many as though they had been assisting at a family occasion. For a time the candles remained lighted, and the bells of Westminster rang a half-muffled peal.

CHAPTER XLI

FULFILMENT

HALIFAX was one of those rare statesmen for whom politics was far from being the most engrossing part of existence, but the fact that from the beginning his ambition was secondary to his spiritual life and his deep love of the countryside should not blind us to the fact that he became absorbed in politics and a shrewd and adroit practitioner of the political art. Yet in a way he seemed to step out of the eighteenth century, or out of those early Victorian days when the squires, particularly on the Liberal side, exerted a major influence on the government of the country, and although Halifax was nominally a Conservative, he would be more accurately described as a Whig of the same school as Palmerston or Russell, or, if we look further back, of Charles James Fox who united the tradition of great birth with a warm instinct for popular liberties.

When we contemplate Halifax's life we are struck by the fact that his religion caused him to regard the problems of the world in a different manner from ordinary men, and in politics gave him an unusual detachment of mind. However menacing the course of events, it was but a part of this mortal coil, and seemed to have something impermanent and transient in his eyes. A conviction so profound of a future life could not fail to diminish the tribulations of the present. But this was no unworldly saint who had somehow wandered into politics. He was not without ambition and a natural desire to play his part in the drama of the world, and his shrewdness was not free from a vein of cynicism. He had early learned the lesson that politics was an inexact science demanding compromise; that principles must sometimes be sacrificed to expediency, and that, in his own words, men could not always 'reconcile what is ideally right with what is practically possible'. Indeed there were those who sometimes thought that Edward went too far in this interpretation of political life, and that he had to a great extent the power of persuading himself that a course of action which others might think wrong, was inevitable, and could be justified upon that ground.

One of his most notable characteristics in politics was an extreme caution, a source of both strength and weakness. Caution was indeed a part of his nature, and he himself had said that he liked to test the ground like an elephant before venturing on it.

Edward once admitted that by the composition of his mind his tendency was to see both sides of any question that presented itself to him, and this

HALIFAX

objectivity, admirable in itself, affected his attitude to world affairs. His instinct in an explosive situation was to conciliate. When nations or men became inflamed with passion, he did not catch fire. His first thought was to lower the temperature, and somehow to produce a *détente*, and some, more emotional than he, found something unnatural in the coolness which prevented him being easily moved by events which outraged others. His devoted friend Ted Talbot had not failed to observe how often and with what little difficulty Edward shut his eyes to unpleasant realities and obliterated them from his vision, nor the facility with which he could find a justification for a course of action which might be condemned by others. We feel that his mind, gentle and reflective, had not registered the full impact of the horrors through which he had lived; that a certain sluggishness of imagination prevented him ever receiving a blinding realization of terrible events, and that his emotions were but languidly engaged by secular disaster. Perhaps it was for this reason that he was never moved to censure or condemn except with tepid interest, or to show himself a violent protagonist of any particular cause. It required a moral or religious issue to infuse authentic passion into his beliefs and engage the absorbed and exclusive interest of his mind. Then only would there be glowing conviction, and even hardness.

This desire to compose, to pacify, to turn discord into harmony, if necessary by yielding, can be seen at its best in his attitude to Ireland. From that day when, on leave from France in 1916, after the Easter Rebellion, he had entreated the House of Commons to bestow self-government on Ireland as the only means of forestalling further tragic events, he had never abandoned that desire, and had persisted in it even at the darkest moments of the Troubles when the indignation of others demanded that violence must be met by violence, and murder by reprisal. Earlier than most he had recognized the limitations of power, and the irony of creating a desert and calling it peace.

In India he had found an even greater opportunity to use these gifts of conciliation and persuasiveness, and among the devout of all creeds, and enriched by his own experience, point to the universal guiding star of religion in his search for peace. In this it might be said of him as of Mazzini that 'his was the rarer and the greater part; to lift mankind out of the stale air of common life into the realms where thought is rarer and life runs richer, and the great verities are seen undimmed by self and sophistry'. The message can be read in all his Indian speeches. There was little rhetoric in them, no grace notes, but their idealism reached the hearts of even those who most hated the British raj, and left in their minds a grudging acceptance of the Viceroy's altruism. There was much scope, too, in India for another quality, a monumental patience which he showed there in full measure. This patience, a slowness to anger, and an obstinate refusal to be discouraged were priceless assets in enduring the sometimes intolerable contortions of Eastern politics, the shifty devices of Patel, and the grasshopper leaps of Gandhi's mind. In the last great office of his life in Washington the same qualities had enabled him to survive an unhappy beginning, and to win his way into the hearts of the American people, leaving behind him warm memories of reciprocated friendship.

But it is evident that these qualities depended for their virtue upon the circumstances in which they were engaged, and when confronted by an inhuman *realpolitik* and by minds of unlimited depravity were of little avail. To the European dictators of the 1930s patience was of merit only when maturing an act of treachery, and conciliation a contemptible recourse of weaklings and cowards. Edward was thus not fitted by nature to preside over the Foreign Office at such a moment of history. He found himself confronted by evil and ambitious men whose appetites were whetted by each successive conquest, and in whom attempts at appeasement produced not only derision but an incitement to further violence. We cannot resist the conclusion that he, like many others whose fingers had not been steady on the pulse of Europe, was slow to grasp the full enormity of Hitler's ambitions and the appalling debasement of his character. When these matters had become clear to him, it could fairly be said that partly from motives of loyalty he had failed to induce in the Prime Minister the sense of urgency demanded by the hour, and to exert on him a more powerful influence which he alone in the Cabinet could have commanded.

*   *   *

He had held three of the highest offices of the State, each at a time of crisis, but when we look back on this long and fruitful life it is not the great moments of achievement that linger most vividly in the memory. Our minds do not turn at once to India with her grey dust and implacable heat, her temple bells and glittering durbars, even in the mood in which he had loved her most when the parched earth had drunk its fill after the monsoon, and the land was green with rebirth. Nor do we think of America where he had learned so much of ordinary men, and undergone a subtle transformation of the mind; still less of that uneasy tenancy of the Foreign Office. We remember rather those last years in Yorkshire when he was occupied with things small, local and kindly, and at the end 'made his soul' and prepared himself for death with a tranquil mind. His days had not been free from sorrow, but at moments of grief he had been solaced by his unshakeable belief in the world to come. Here, with the grandchildren he loved, there was something patriarchal about him. We see him climbing, a little more slowly now, the steps that led from the church of Kirby Underdale to the village with the churchwardens beside him; serving at the altar and putting out the vestments in the little panelled chapel at Garrowby, and remaining on his knees long after others had left it. And the thought comes back to us of him sitting in his room in the tower transacting with quick mind the affairs of his estate, or reading, while there was still time, the books he had neglected in the busy years. We remember how he liked to ride his grey pony Dolly to the farms on the estate, and how he drove his car so badly but with such pleasure, and how much he liked harvesting with Charlie Cook, and watching the lambing and the pigs being weighed with the smell of the farm in his nostrils. It was here that he found his true fulfilment, and that we can best remember him and take leave of him, in the heart of the East Riding, and about him the wolds and the dales and the windy Yorkshire sky.

SOURCES AND SHORT BIBLIOGRAPHY

Documentary authorities
  Hickleton Papers.
  Archives, India Office Library.
  National Archives of India, New Delhi.
  National Library of India, Calcutta.
  Documents on British Foreign Policy, 1919–1939, Third Series.
  Documents on British Foreign Policy, 1918–1944, Series D.
  Documents on German Foreign Policy, 1918–1945, Series D, 1937–41.

Other Sources
  I would like to make a particular acknowledgement of my indebtedness to
Mr. Alan Campbell Johnson's biography *Viscount Halifax*. The author,
although without many of the papers available today, conducted extensive
and admirable personal researches which have led to many most interesting
discoveries. I have availed myself freely of the results of these researches, and
I am much indebted to this full and thorough biography which, in the
circumstances, was an exceptional achievement.

  I have also availed myself freely of Sir Llewellyn Woodward's invaluable
book *British Foreign Policy in the Second World War*, without which it
would be difficult to disentangle the diplomatic events leading up to Pearl
Harbour.

  I am deeply indebted to S. Gopal's *The Viceroyalty of Lord Irwin*, a
brilliant little work by an Indian with sympathy for the difficulties of the
British position, and in particular that of the Viceroy. I have drawn freely
upon this scholarly book.

  To one describing the childhood of Lord Halifax and the influences that
were brought to bear upon it, the biography of his father, *Viscount Halifax*
by J. G. Lockhart, loving and admirably documented, is an essential source,
as is also Lord Halifax's autobiography, *Fulness of Days*.

  The four lines from 'Sussex' by Rudyard Kipling quoted on page 3 are
reprinted by permission of Mrs. George Bambridge, Rudyard Kipling's
daughter and owner of his copyrights, Methuen & Co. Ltd., and the Macmillan Co. of Canada Ltd.

610

SHORT BIBLIOGRAPHY

The Rt. Hon. L. S. Amery, C.H.: *My Political Life*—Hutchinson.
The Earl of Avon: *The Eden Memoirs*—Cassell.
H. C. Barnard: *A History of English Education from 1760*—Oxford University Press.
Francis Biddle: *In Brief Authority*—Doubleday and Co.
Robert Blake: *The Unknown Prime Minister*—Eyre and Spottiswoode.
Sir Valentine Chirol: *India*—Ernest Benn.
Winston S. Churchill: *The Second World War*—Cassell.
J. Coatman: *Years of Destiny*—Jonathan Cape.
Duff Cooper: *Old Men Forget*—Hart-Davis.
S. J. Curtis: *History of Education in Great Britain*—Oxford Tutorial Press.
H. C. Dent: *Secondary Education for All. Origins and Development in England*—Routledge and Kegan Paul.
Keith Feiling: *The Life of Neville Chamberlain*—Macmillan.
Louis Fischer: *The Life of Mahatma Gandhi*—Jonathan Cape.
The Forrestal Diaries: The Inner History of the Cold War—Cassell.
S. Gopal: *The Viceroyalty of Lord Irwin, 1926-1931*—Clarendon Press, Oxford.
Richard Gott and Martin Gilbert: *The Appeasers*—Weidenfeld and Nicolson.
Percival Griffiths: *Modern India*—Ernest Benn.
The Earl of Halifax: *Fulness of Days*—Collins.
R. F. Harrod: *The Life of John Maynard Keynes*—Macmillan.
Stuart Hodgson: *Halifax*—Christophers.
The White House Papers of Harry Hopkins—Eyre and Spottiswoode.
The Memoirs of Cordell Hull—Hodder and Stoughton, London. The Macmillan Co., New York.
The Secret Diary of Harold L. Ickes, Vol. III, The Lowering Clouds—Weidenfeld and Nicolson.
Alan Campbell Johnson: *Viscount Halifax*—Robert Hale.
J. G. Lockhart: *Viscount Halifax*—Geoffrey Bles.
G. A. N. Lowndes: *The Silent and Social Revolution*—Oxford University Press.
Percy Lubbock: *Shades of Eton*—Jonathan Cape.
Iain Macleod: *Neville Chamberlain*—Muller.
William McElwee: *Britain's Locust Years, 1918-1940*—Faber.
Arthur Mee: *The King's England: Yorkshire*—Hodder and Stoughton.
C. L. Mowat: *Britain Between the Wars*—Methuen.
L. Namier: *Diplomatic Prelude, 1933-1939*—Macmillan.
B. R. Nanda: *Mahatma Gandhi*—George Allen and Unwin Ltd.
Sir Harold Nicolson: *King George V. His Life and Reign*—Constable.

Lord Eustace Percy: *Some Memories*—Eyre and Spottiswoode.

A. L. Rowse: *All Souls and Appeasement*—Macmillan.

Paul Schmidt: *Hitler's Interpreter*—Heinemann.

Sir Henry Sharp: *Delhi: Its Story and Buildings*—Oxford University Press.

Lord Simon: *Retrospect*—Hutchinson.

J. A. Spender: *Great Britain, Empire and Commonwealth, 1886-1935*—Cassell.

Lord Strang: *At Home and Abroad*—Deutsch.

Lord Strang: *Britain in World Affairs: Henry VIII to Elizabeth II*—Faber-Deutsch.

The Earl of Swinton: *I Remember*—Hutchinson.

Lord Templewood: *Nine Troubled Years*—Collins.

Harold S. Truman: *Truman Memoirs*—Doubleday and Co.

The Private Papers of Senator Vandenberg—Victor Gollancz.

Sir John Wheeler-Bennett: *Munich: Prologue to Tragedy*—Macmillan.

Sir John Wheeler-Bennett: *Life of King George VI*—Macmillan.

J. Wilkinson: *Worthies of Barnsley*, First Series—Bemrose and Sons.

Lord Winterton: *Orders of the Day*—Hutchinson.

Edward Wood: *John Keble*—A. R. Mowbray.

Philip Woodruff: *The Men Who Ruled India*—Jonathan Cape.

Sir Llewellyn Woodward: *British Foreign Policy in the Second World War*—H.M.S.O.

G. M. Young: *Stanley Baldwin*—Hart-Davis.

INDEX